SEX OFFENDERS
LAW, POLICY AND PRACTICE

Cathy Cobley
Cardiff Law School
Cardiff University

JORDANS
2000

Published by
Jordan Publishing Limited
21 St Thomas Street
Bristol BS1 6JS

British Library Cataloguing-in-Publication Data
A catalogue record for this book is available from the British Library.

ISBN 0 85308 622 2

Typeset by Mendip Communications Ltd, Frome, Somerset
Printed by MPG Books Ltd, Bodmin, Cornwall

PREFACE

There has been an unprecedented rise in the level of concern over sex offenders in recent years and this concern has resulted in a flurry of political and legislative activity. This book charts the process of the growing concern and examines the changes brought about by the resulting activity, thereby providing a comprehensive account of the law, policy and practice relating to sex offenders. Sexual offending may impact on the work of numerous professionals, not only those who have direct contact with the offenders through the criminal justice system but also those concerned with the protection of children and other potential victims, the allocation of housing and the treatment of offenders themselves. The book has been written with all such professionals in mind and I hope it will prove to be an invaluable source of reference. It includes relevant general information on the criminal justice system so that those who do not have a detailed knowledge of legal issues and procedures can understand the significance of the many recent developments which have taken place in relation to sex offenders.

For the sake of simplicity, the offender or defendant is referred to as 'he' and the victim or complainant as 'she' throughout this book. Although this may reflect the situation in many cases, it will, of course, not be true in every case and should be read accordingly.

My thanks to the publishing team at Jordans, in particular to Helen Cowan, who first encouraged me to write the book, and to Martin West and Mollie Dickenson, whose assistance and expertise have been invaluable. Finally, no preface would be complete without an acknowledgement to those who have suffered most during the writing of the book – in this case my family, who have had to live with me through the bad times as well as the good. My sincere thanks, therefore, to my daughters Rachel and Kate and to my husband Peter, whose constant support and encouragement (whether in the form of e-mails, lending a sympathetic ear or simply pouring a glass of wine) undoubtedly made the writing of this book that little bit easier.

The law is stated as at 1 March 2000.

CATHY COBLEY
Cardiff Law School
March 2000

CONTENTS

TABLE OF CASES

References are to paragraph number.

TABLE OF STATUTES

References are to paragraph number. References in bold are to appendix page numbers where statutory material is set out.

TABLE OF STATUTORY INSTRUMENTS AND CODES OF PRACTICE

References are to paragraph number.

TABLE OF EUROPEAN AND FOREIGN MATERIALS

References are to paragraph number.

Chapter 1

SEX OFFENDERS AND SEXUAL OFFENCES

SEX OFFENDERS – A MODERN PROBLEM?

1.1   The spotlight is firmly focused on sex offenders. In recent times, they have been accorded an increasingly high profile by the media[1] and it has been claimed that sex offenders have been built up into 'modern folk-devils' by the popular press.[2] Public concern over sex offenders has been matched by almost frantic political and legislative activity in recent years.[3] Yet, prima facie, there is nothing startlingly 'new' about sex offenders to justify this high profile – sex offenders are not a creation of the late 20th century. Laws prohibiting certain forms of sexual behaviour have existed since time immemorial. Bresler has traced the earliest sexual laws, enshrined in murals on the walls of tombs, to the ancient Egyptians in about 3000 BC, with the first written laws on sex emanating from the ancient civilisation of Babylon and dating from about 1750 BC.[4] In England and Wales, at common law, for many centuries only three specifically sexual offences were known: rape, sodomy and bestiality. Over the centuries, many more offences regulating sexual conduct were created and the law now recognises several hundred different offences of a sexual nature, the majority of which date from the reign of Queen Victoria or later. These offences are now almost entirely embodied in statute, principally the Sexual Offences Act 1956 which was designed to codify and consolidate the law as it then stood. Many of the statutory provisions in fact create more than one offence. For example, s 1(1) of the Protection of Children Act 1978 creates 16 different substantive criminal offences. In addition to each substantive offence, there will be the associated inchoate offences of inciting, conspiring or attempting to commit it, and liability for aiding, abetting, counselling or procuring its commission.

1.2   When all of these permutations are taken into account, the number of different sexual offences in our law must run to several hundred, the majority of which have been on the statute book for a considerable number of years. Sex offenders are not, therefore, a modern creation. Nor should they be seen as a modern problem. Admittedly, the criminal statistics do show a steady increase in the number of sexual offences notified to the police in recent years. However, the rise in recorded crime is not a recent phenomena. The average number of notifiable sexual offences recorded by the police in England and Wales immediately before the Second World War (1937 and 1938) was 4,448.[5] By 1954, this number had become 15,636, an increase of 252% over a period of

---

1   Soothill and Walby *Sex Crime in the News* (Routledge, London, 1991).
2   Sampson *Acts of Abuse: Sex Offenders and the Criminal Justice System* (Routledge, London, 1994).
3   Much of this political and legislative activity will form the basis of subsequent chapters.
4   Bresler *Sex and the Law* (Century Hutchinson Ltd, London, 1998).
5   Radzinowicz *Sexual Offences: A Report of the Cambridge Department of Criminal Science* (MacMillan & Co Ltd, London, 1957).

approximately 16 years.[1] Over the last 44 years, there has been a further increase of more than 100% and 37,492 notifiable sexual offences were recorded by the police in the 12-month period between October 1998 and September 1999.[2] But, even with the growth in notifiable sexual offences recorded by the police, sexual offences account for less than 1% of all notifiable offences recorded[3] and sex offenders still account for only a small proportion of those found guilty or cautioned.[4] Despite this fact, the public response to sex offenders during the past decade and the resulting political reaction has been remarkable and has far exceeded anything seen to date. It would appear that much of the public debate about sex offenders has been fuelled by growing concern over the activities of paedophiles, a concern which has arguably been exploited by the media. Rape and sexual molestation by strangers have always been reported sensationally in the media, especially when the victim is very young or very old. Following the events in Cleveland in 1987,[5] the issue of child sexual abuse, particularly intrafamilial abuse, was thrown to the fore, thereby adding to the panic over sexual offending in general. 'Paedophile' has become a household word. A computer search showed that during the first 4 months of 1998, the words 'paedophile' or 'paedophilia' appeared in 712 articles in six leading British newspapers, whereas the word had only appeared 1,312 times in total in the 4-year period between 1992 and 1995.[6]

1.3   Several reasons have been suggested for this growing concern over sex offenders.[7] Sexual offences are seen as being particularly disturbing and dangerous crimes which cause considerable public concern and it is generally agreed that the official statistics give a misleading indication of the extent of offending as far more sexual offences are thought to be committed than are ever reported to the police.[8] Furthermore, the costs of sexual offending are high, both in terms of the emotional and psychological damage done to victims, and in the risk that some victims become abusers themselves. Whatever the underlying reasons, sex offenders, particularly those who offend against children, are probably now accorded the highest profile of all offenders and are regarded by many as the most feared, hated and despised group of offenders. Even those convicted of other offences wish to distance themselves both symbolically and territorially from those identified as sex offenders, thereby adding to the tendency to adopt what has been referred to as 'criminal apartheid'.[9] Successive governments have indicated their commitment to implementing measures to improve protection of the public and enhance opportunities for the treatment

---

1   During the same period, the number of offences of violence against the person notified to the police rose from 2,722 to 7,506, an increase of 176%.

2   Home Office Statistical Bulletin 1/00 *Recorded Crime Statistics, England and Wales, October 1998 to September 1999* (Home Office, London, 2000).

3   Between October 1998 and September 1999, a total of 5,234,211 notifiable offences were recorded by the police in England and Wales.

4   See **2.87**.

5   Butler Sloss *Report of the Inquiry into Child Abuse in Cleveland 1987* Cmnd 412 (HMSO, 1988).

6   Soothill et al 'Paedophilia and Paedophiles' (1998) NLJ 148 (6844) 882.

7   Fisher and Mair 'A Review of Classification Systems for Sex Offenders' Home Office Research and Statistics Directorate Research Findings No 78.

8   See further **1.69**.

9   Soothill and Francis 'Sexual Reconvictions and the Sex Offenders Act 1997' (1997) NLJ 6806 at 1285.

of sex offenders. Some such reforms have already been implemented, but there remains an on-going debate as to the most effective response to sex offenders and further reform of the criminal justice system will inevitably follow. The spotlight will no doubt remain firmly focused on sex offenders for the foreseeable future.

DEFINITIONAL PROBLEMS – SEX OFFENDERS AND SEXUAL OFFENCES

1.4   As a matter of logic, perhaps the first question to be asked is: 'Who is a sex offender?' A simple answer would be that a sex offender is a person who commits a sexual offence. This then raises the question: 'What is a sexual offence?' At first sight, the term 'sexual offence' suggests that there is a clearly definable group of offences committed by offenders who thereby become categorised as sex offenders. Whilst it is true that a list of offences where the central prohibition relates to some form of sexual activity can be compiled relatively easily, to restrict consideration to such offences when referring to sex offenders would be seriously misleading. Almost any offence may be committed for a sexual motive. The theft of underwear from a washing line may be committed by a fetishist, burglary may be committed by a man who enters a building as a trespasser with the intention of raping any person therein,[1] assaults and more serious offences against the person may be committed during the course of a sado-masochist encounter,[2] and murder or manslaughter may be committed as a result of extreme sexual desire or jealousy. Yet, as a matter of practice and convenience, not all such offenders are labelled or treated as sex offenders. Indeed, there appears to be no universally accepted definition of what constitutes a sexual crime. Definitions have been bitterly fought over by experts from the fields of psychology, biology and sociology, whose divergent academic and political viewpoints have tended to vitiate the kind of balanced discussion that might produce informed consensus.[3] Even within the criminal justice system, there is no consensus as various classification systems of sexual offences can be found. For example, offences classified as notifiable offences for the purpose of recording crime differ from those classified as sexual offences for the purpose of recording the outcome of proceedings.[4] Different classifications are adopted for defining sexual offences for the purposes of sentencing, for the requirement that convicted offenders inform the police of their name and address and for the imposition of sex offender orders.[5] Furthermore, an examination of the substantive criminal law reveals that even those offences which are universally categorised as sexual offences are far from a homogenous group.

---

1   Theft Act 1968, s 9(1)(a).
2   For a much publicised example of this, see the decision of the House of Lords in *R v Brown* [1993] 2 WLR 556.
3   Colton and Vanstone *Betrayal of Trust* (Free Association Books, London, 1996).
4   See Appendices 3 and 4 Home Office *Criminal Statistics for England and Wales 1997* (HMSO, 1998).
5   Sex Offender Act 1997 and Crime and Disorder Act 1998. See **7.8** and **7.19**.

Distinctions between sexual offences – offences of sexual aggression and breaches of sexual taboo

1.5   Perhaps the most obvious group of sexual offences are those which involve the actual performance of a sexual act. Thus, for example, rape, indecent assault, unlawful sexual intercourse with a girl under 16, incest and buggery are clearly categorised as sex offences. Other offences, such as the taking or possession of indecent photographs of children, although involving a sexual motive, are not so obviously categorised as sexual offences as they involve no overtly sexual act. Nevertheless, those convicted of such offences are treated as sex offenders for many purposes.[1] Yet other offences, such as bigamy (which is categorised as a sexual offence for the purposes of criminal statistics), have even more questionable relevance to sex offences, and bigamy's inclusion in the category has been questioned.[2] However, even in cases where the offence involves the performance of a sexual act, important distinctions between the types of offences can be identified.

1.6   It has been suggested that it is possible to distinguish two different types of sexual offences: offences of sexual aggression; and breaches of sexual taboo.[3] Offences of sexual aggression involve non-consensual behaviour, where lack of consent is an essential element of the offence. Such offences can be viewed as a sub-group of offences of violence. For example, rape can be defined as a crime of violence where sex is merely the weapon used, although the use of the word 'violence' can be problematic as it suggests the use of physical force, which is not a pre-requisite of rape. There can be no doubt that those who commit offences of sexual aggression are universally regarded as sex offenders. Statistics show that the majority of those convicted or cautioned for indictable sex offences commit offences of sexual aggression, ie rape and indecent assault on a male or female. In 1998, of the 6,300 offenders found guilty at all courts or cautioned for an indictable sexual offence, over 4,500 committed offences of sexual aggression.

1.7   Yet not all sexual offences require an absence of consent. In contrast to offences of sexual aggression, breaches of sexual taboo are predominantly consensual acts which are nevertheless illegal, either because of the nature of the act involved (such as the offence of buggery), or because of some characteristic of the participants involved (such as the offence of incest). However, this distinction is not precise and this is particularly evident when the offence is committed against a person under the age of 16.[4]

Offences of sexual aggression

Absence of consent

1.8   The essence of offences of sexual aggression is an absence of consent. Yet consent is hard to define.[5] It is clear that the victim must be capable of giving

---

1   For example, those convicted of offences under the Protection of Children Act 1978 are deemed to be sex offenders for the purposes of the Sex Offender Act 1997.
2   Howard League *Unlawful Sex* (Waterlow, London, 1985).
3   Williams *Textbook of Criminal Law* (Stevens, London, 1983) p 227.
4   See further **1.32**.
5   Williams *Textbook of Criminal Law* (Stevens, London, 1983) p 550.

consent which the law will recognise. Thus, a person who is asleep or insensible through drink or drugs is not capable of giving consent.[1] In order to give valid consent, the victim of an offence must not be deceived about the nature and quality of the act or the identity of the actor. If a person is entirely innocent about sexual behaviour and is mistaken about the very nature of the act involved, the law will refuse to recognise any apparent consent. For example, in *R v Flattery*,[2] the defendant was convicted of rape after inducing a woman to have sexual intercourse by pretending to perform a surgical operation. For the same reason, a very young child would be deemed incapable of understanding the nature of the act and any sexual activity involving such a child would be classified as an offence of sexual aggression. As a matter of strict law, there is no age limit below which a child may not consent for these purposes, although it is argued that adequate alternative protection exists in the form of breaches of sexual taboo.[3] A deception as to the identity of the actor will also vitiate consent. Initially, it was thought that such a deception was restricted to impersonation of a victim's husband. The Criminal Law Amendment Act 1885 provided that a man committed rape if he induced a married woman to have sexual intercourse with him by impersonating her husband and this provision was later re-enacted in the Sexual Offences Act 1956. Not surprisingly, the supposed restriction to impersonating a husband has been questioned in recent times and in 1995 in the case of *R v Elbekkay*,[4] the defendant was convicted of rape after impersonating the victim's boyfriend. Following *Elbekkay*, in what has been described as a 'governmental and parliamentary blunder',[5] the statutory provision relating to impersonation of the husband was yet again re-enacted in the Crime and Public Order Act 1994. It is generally agreed that the existence of the statutory provision will not prevent the application of the common law rule as confirmed in *Elbekkay*.

1.9   An issue which the courts have found rather more problematic is the distinction between consent and submission through fear. In cases where a person submits to sexual activity because of violence or threats of violence, few problems arise. Any apparent consent is vitiated by the violence or threats. More problematic are the cases where the threat relates to something other than direct force. There exists a specific statutory offence of obtaining sexual intercourse by threats and, adopting a narrow view, it has been suggested that where the threat does not relate to the use of force, consent will not be vitiated for the purposes of rape.[6] Presumably, the same argument would also apply to indecent assault. However, in the case of *R v Olugboga*,[7] where the defendant was charged with rape, a far wider approach appears to have been adopted. The trial judge directed the jury to consider whether there were any 'constraints' operating on the victim's will. In upholding the conviction, the Court of Appeal noted that there was a difference between consent and submission, but failed to elaborate on the distinction. Instead, the Court preferred to leave the meaning of consent to the 'good sense' of the jury, having been directed to concentrate on:

---

1   *Larter v Castleton* [1995] Crim LR 75.
2   (1877) 2 QBD 410.
3   See **1.22** et seq for a discussion of offences involving sexual activity with children.
4   [1995] Crim LR 163.
5   Smith and Hogan *Criminal Law* (Butterworths, London, 1996) p 469.
6   Williams *Textbook on Criminal Law* (Stevens, London, 1983) p 552.
7   [1981] 3 All ER 443.

'... the state of mind of the victim immediately before the act of sexual intercourse, having regard to all the relevant circumstances, and in particular the events leading up to the act, her reaction to them, showing their impact on her mind.'[1]

The issue of consent is therefore one for the jury to determine and, in the absence of violence or threats of violence on the part of the accused, difficulties will inevitably be encountered in distinguishing between consent and submission.

Rape

1.10   Rape is generally regarded as the most serious sexual offence, although some cases of indecent assault may involve equal or worse degradation for the victim. For many years, rape was an offence at common law and was defined by the courts to mean unlawful sexual intercourse with a woman without her consent by fear, force or fraud. In 1956, s 1 of the Sexual Offences Act of that year merely stated that it was an offence for a man to rape a woman and so the common law definition remained until the enactment of the Sexual Offences (Amendment) Act in 1976. This legislation was passed as a result of the decision of the House of Lords in the case of *DPP v Morgan*.[2] The central issue in the case concerned the mens rea, or fault element, of the offence of rape and whether an honest but mistaken belief in consent negatived the required mens rea. The House of Lords, whilst upholding the defendants' convictions for rape by the application of the proviso to s 2 of the Criminal Appeal Act 1968 (as amended), held that an honest belief in consent could negative mens rea, even if it was an unreasonable belief. This decision was thought by many to amount to a 'rapists' charter' in that an alleged rapist need only claim that he honestly thought the woman was consenting in order to escape liability. In response to the evident concern, an advisory committee was appointed by the Home Secretary to consider the law relating to rape. The Heilbron Committee recommended the implementation of a statutory definition of rape.[3] This recommendation was accepted and enacted in the Sexual Offences (Amendment) Act 1976, which provided that a man commited rape if he had unlawful sexual intercourse with a woman who at the time did not consent to it and the man either knew that she did not consent to the intercourse or was reckless as to whether she consented to it. On the face of it, this provision did nothing to address the 'rapists' charter' concerns, as it effectively endorsed the decision of the House of Lords in *Morgan*. Section 1(2) of the 1976 Act provided that if, at a trial for a rape offence, the jury had to consider whether a man believed a woman was consenting, the presence or absence of reasonable grounds for such a belief was a matter to which the jury was to have regard, in conjunction with any other relevant matters, in considering whether he so believed. This has been described as no more than a 'public relations provision',[4] as it does no more than state a matter of common sense which was actually already permitted in law.

---

1   [1981] 3 All ER 443 at 448–49.
2   [1976] AC 182.
3   Cmnd 6352 (1975).
4   Smith and Hogan *Criminal Law* (Butterworths, London, 1996) p 468.

Extending the definition of rape

1.11 Despite the enactment of a statutory definition in 1976, the offence of rape remained controversial in two respects: the restriction of the offence to 'natural sexual intercourse'[1] and therefore to female victims; and the so-called 'marital immunity' to rape. In relation to the former issue, it was argued that the definition of rape contained in the 1976 Act was indicative of a male-dominated society, with its male-fixated view as being restricted to one form of intercourse.[2] Although non-consensual anal intercourse with a man or a woman constituted the offence of buggery and was punishable in some cases with life imprisonment,[3] it was thought by many that such conduct should be brought within the definition of rape. The issue of rape within marriage had been the subject of judicial attention for some time even before the enactment of the 1976 Act. At common law, dating back to the writings of Sir Matthew Hale in 1736, it had always been thought that a husband could not be convicted of raping his wife because a wife gave consent to intercourse on marriage and she was unable to retract that consent.[4] Doubts were cast over the precise ambit of this proposition during the second half of the 20th century,[5] but in drafting the statutory definition of rape in 1976, the draughtsman defined rape as '*unlawful* sexual intercourse'. The phrase 'unlawful sexual intercourse' appears in the definition of many offences contained in the Sexual Offences Act 1956 and had previously been defined by the courts to mean sexual intercourse outside the bonds of marriage.[6] However, subsequent case law continued to extend the circumstances in which a husband could be guilty of raping his wife, culminating in the case of *R v R*[7] when Lord Keith in the House of Lords effectively abolished the marital exemption, concluding that the word 'unlawful' had no meaning and was therefore surplusage. Lord Keith justified this conclusion by the fact that the status of women has changed out of all recognition since the days of Hale and they were now regarded as equals to their husbands. The decision in *R v R* has been criticised from a constitutional point of view[8] and the defendant took his case to the European Court of Human Rights alleging breach of art 7 of the Convention, in that he had been convicted in respect of conduct which at the relevant time did not constitute a criminal offence. However, the European Court of Human Rights decided that there had been no breach of art 7, as the removal of the marital immunity was consistent with the essence of the offence of

---

1   Defined to mean intercourse per vaginum.
2   Selfe and Burke *Perspectives on Sex, Crime and Society* (Cavendish Publishing Ltd, London, 1998).
3   Prior to 1994, non-consensual anal intercourse was punishable by life imprisonment if the victim was a woman or a boy under the age of 16. In all other cases the maximum sentence was 10 years' imprisonment.
4   *History of the Pleas of the Crown* (1 Hale PC (1763) 629).
5   See, for example, *R v Clarke* [1949] 2 All ER 448, where it was held that the wife could revoke her consent to intercourse by a further process of law, in this case by the making of a court order that she was no longer bound to cohabit with her husband, and *R v O'Brien* [1974] 3 All ER 663, where it was held that a decree nisi revoked the wife's implied consent.
6   *R v Chapman* [1959] 1 QB 100.
7   *R v R* [1992] AC 599.
8   See Giles 'Judicial Law-Making in the Criminal Courts: The Case of Marital Rape' [1992] Crim LR 407.

rape and the law had reached a stage where judicial recognition of absence of immunity was reasonably foreseeable.[1]

1.12 The two areas of controversy have now been addressed by the enactment of the Criminal Justice and Public Order Act 1994, which amends the statutory definition of rape by removing the reference to unlawful sexual intercourse and extending the offence to include anal intercourse and therefore male victims. A man now commits rape if he has sexual intercourse with a person (whether vaginal or anal) who at the time of the intercourse does not consent to it and at the time he knows that the person does not consent to the intercourse or is reckless as to whether that person consents to it.

Indecent assault

1.13 Sections 14 and 15 of the Sexual Offences Act 1956 provide that it is an offence for a person to make an indecent assault on a woman and a man respectively. Indecent assault is a form of aggravated assault, in that an assault (or battery) is a precondition for an indecent assault. To the majority of people, the word 'assault' is used to describe unwanted physical contact between two people. The legal definition of assault is, however, much wider than the common concept of assault. In 1952, Lord Goddard CJ explained that:

> '... an assault can be committed without touching a person. One always thinks of an assault as the giving of a blow to somebody, but that is not necessary. An assault may be constituted by a threat or a hostile act committed towards a person.' [2]

Later cases show that the act need not be hostile.[3] Therefore, an assault can be any act, committed intentionally or recklessly, which causes another to apprehend immediate or unlawful violence. The term 'assault' in statutes is used both in its strict sense (sometimes called 'psychic assault') and to include a battery, ie any act which intentionally or recklessly inflicts unlawful personal violence on another (sometimes called 'physical assault'). Indecent assault may be either a psychic assault or a physical assault, although in practice most indecent assaults will include a battery. Although assaults may be committed intentionally or recklessly, it appears that, for the purposes of indecent assault, the assault itself must be committed intentionally.[4] However, the intention need not necessarily extend to the circumstances of indecency which must accompany the assault. If the circumstances of the assault are objectively and unambiguously indecent, the offender need only be aware of those circumstances, he need not necessarily have an indecent intent. It is only when the circumstances of the assault are ambiguous that the offender must have an indecent purpose or intention before he is liable. If the circumstances of the assault include no element of indecency, the assault is not an indecent assault, however indecent the purpose or intention of the offender. So, for example, in the case of *R v George*[5] the defendant had a 'foot fetish' and attempted to remove a girl's shoe from her foot in order to gain sexual gratification. It was held that, as there were

1   *CR v The United Kingdom: SW v The United Kingdom* [1996] 1 FLR 434.
2   *R v Rolfe* (1952) 36 Cr App R 4.
3   *Faulkner v Talbot* [1981] 3 All ER 468.
4   *R v Court* [1988] 2 All ER 221, HL.
5   *R v George* [1956] Crim LR 52.

no circumstances of indecency, the act was not an indecent assault. If the assault takes the form of a battery, the victim need not be aware of the assault or of the circumstances of indecency. For example, it is possible to indecently assault a person whilst he or she is sleeping. But if the assault takes the form of a psychic assault, the victim must be shown to have been aware both of the assault and of the circumstances of indecency.[1]

Breaches of sexual taboo

Incest and incitement

1.14   Historically, incest was an ecclesiastical, not a criminal, offence. Prior to 1908, incest was not punishable as a crime, but was dealt with by the Ecclesiastical Courts. However, by the mid 19th century, these courts were moribund and few cases came to their attention. The second half of the 19th century saw an increased social awareness of the problem, yet official reluctance to include incest within the scope of the criminal law remained until the early 20th century. Incest was thought to be a taboo subject in the 19th century, and to have acknowledged its existence would have tarnished the reputation of the Victorian home and family as a repository of the highest Christian virtues. Additionally, it was felt that State interference in the home and in family relationships was incompatible with the 'laissez-faire' practice in the sphere of social policy. The National Vigilance Society, established in 1885, and the National Society for the Prevention of Cruelty to Children (NSPCC), established in 1889, both attempted to increase public awareness of what they considered to be the need to criminalise incest. In addition, the Home Office was aware that the absence of any law making incest a criminal offence frequently led to straining the offence of rape. If the female involved was over 16 and consented to the intercourse, the act of incest was not punishable at all. If the girl was under 16, the act of incest was the criminal act of unlawful sexual intercourse with a girl under 16 years,[2] yet any prosecution had to be made within 3 months of the commission of the offence. (This period was extended to 6 months in 1904[3] and is now 12 months.[4])

1.15   Unsuccessful attempts were made to pass Incest Bills in 1899–1900, 1903 and 1907, before the Punishment of Incest Act was implemented in 1908. The offence is now contained in ss 10 and 11 of the Sexual Offences Act 1956, which provide that it is an offence for a man to have sexual intercourse with a woman whom he knows to be his grand-daughter, daughter, sister or mother; and for a woman of the age of 16 or over to permit a man whom she knows to be her grandfather, father, brother or son to have sexual intercourse with her by her consent. The relationships within ss 10 and 11 are restricted to blood relationships, whether legitimate or illegitimate. Therefore, if a father has consensual sexual intercourse with his 14-year-old daughter, he commits incest and is liable to a maximum of 7 years' imprisonment. However, if a stepfather commits the same act with his stepdaughter, he is only liable under s 6 of the Sexual Offences

---

1   *R v Court* [1987] 1 All ER 120 at 122, CA.
2   Criminal Law Amendment Act 1885, ss 4 and 5.
3   Children Act 1904, s 27.
4   Sexual Offences Act 1956, Sch 2, para 10.

Act 1956 and may face a maximum of 2 years' imprisonment. It is irrelevant in the eyes of the law that the stepfather may have played a far more active role in the girl's upbringing. For example, the father may have deserted the mother before the daughter was born, but if he has intercourse with the daughter, presuming he knows she is his daughter, he is guilty of incest. Yet the stepfather may have brought the child up from infancy as his own. Nevertheless, he commits no offence in having consensual sexual intercourse with her once she reaches the age of 16 years, and if she is between 13 and 16 years, he is only liable to 2 years' imprisonment, as opposed to 7 years' for incest. In today's society, with a high divorce rate and stepfamilies becoming more common, it is difficult to see that such a distinction is logical.

1.16 The main justification for the intervention of the criminal law would appear to be genetic, ie that a child born of an incestuous relationship carries a high risk of suffering birth defects. It is notable that the prohibition does not extend to intercourse between a grandmother and grandson, presumably because there was thought to be no risk of conception.[1] Yet nowhere in the Home Office papers in relation to the Punishment of Incest Act 1908 is there any reference to the physical or mental consequences of incestuous relationships, except very occasionally in the evidence submitted by the NSPCC.[2] It seems that the genetic factor was by no means crucial to the criminalisation of incest. Additionally, as pointed out by the Policy Advisory Committee in its evidence to the Criminal Law Revision Committee:

> 'Society does not yet prohibit sexual intercourse in other circumstances in which there is a high genetic risk of abnormality in the offspring of the relationship, for example with hereditary diseases such as "Huntington's Chorea".'[3]

It is generally agreed that a further justification of incest is the protection of the young and vulnerable against sexual exploitation within the family. However, once incest is justified in these terms, the distinction between, for example, father and stepfather in today's society becomes illogical and irrelevant. Proposals have been made to modify the existing offences in several ways.[4] First, by extending the offence to adoptive as well as blood relationships between father and daughter and mother and son. Secondly, by providing that it should cease to be an offence for brother and sister to have intercourse where they have both reached the age of 21 years. Thirdly, by providing that daughters, grand-daughters and sons under the age of 21 should be exempted from liability; and, finally, by providing a defence for a person who believes his partner to be of such an age that the intercourse would be lawful. The creation of a new offence, analogous to that of incest, involving sexual intercourse with a stepchild under the age of 21 years has also been suggested.[5]

1.17 As a result of the restriction of the offence under s 11 to females over the age of 16, a girl under the age of 16 who permits incestuous intercourse

---

1 An assumption which is questionable in this day and age.
2 Bailey and Blackburn 'The Punishment of Incest Act 1908' [1979] Crim LR 708.
3 Criminal Law Revision Committee *Fifteenth Report: Sexual Offences* (1984) Cmnd 9213 (HMSO, London).
4 Law Commission 177, clauses 103 and 104.
5 Ibid, clause 105.

commits no offence. Consequently, inciting a girl under the age of 16 to have incestuous intercourse was no offence at common law.[1] In such circumstances, if the girl was under 14, an offence of inciting a child under the age of 14 to an act of gross indecency would be committed under s 1 of the Indecency with Children Act 1960, but there was thought to be an unacceptable gap between the ages of 14 and 16. Consequently, s 54 of the Criminal Law Act 1977 provides a specific offence for a man to incite to have sexual intercourse with him a girl under the age of 16 whom he knows to be his grand-daughter, daughter or sister. It is still no offence to incite a girl under the age of 16 to have incestuous sexual intercourse with a third party.

Buggery

1.18   Buggery has long been an offence at common law. Section 12 of the Sexual Offences Act 1956 now provides that it is an offence for a person to commit buggery with another person or with an animal, but no statutory definition of buggery is provided, and hence the essential elements of the offence remain governed by the common law. Buggery at common law consists of intercourse per anum by a man with a man,[2] or by a man with a woman,[3] and intercourse per anum or per vaginum by a man or a woman with an animal (bestiality).[4] However, statutory reform since 1956 has limited the extent of buggery in two ways; by decriminalising buggery between men and buggery of a woman by a man in certain circumstances and by restricting buggery to consensual acts.

1.19   Following the recommendations of the Wolfenden Committee Report,[5] in 1967 the Sexual Offences Act provided that a homosexual act in private between two consenting males over the age of 21 was no offence. In 1994, the age of consent was lowered to 18.[6] At the same time, consensual buggery in private of a woman by a man where both parties are aged 18 or over was decriminalised.[7] Thus, two consenting men, or a man and a woman, who are aged 18 or over commit no offence by having anal intercourse, as long as the act takes place in private. The act does not take place in private if more than two people take part or are present, or if the act takes place in a lavatory to which the public have or are permitted to have access, whether on payment or otherwise.[8] The government is committed to equalising the age of consent for heterosexual and homosexual activity and the age limit of 18 for buggery will inevitably be reduced to 16 in the near future.[9]

---

1   *R v Whitehouse* [1977] 3 All ER 737.
2   *R v Jacobs* (1817) Russ & Ry 331.
3   This includes husband and wife, *R v Wiseman* (1718) Fortes Rep 91.
4   *R v Bourne* (1952) 36 Cr App R 125.
5   Cmnd 247.
6   See **1.24**.
7   Criminal Justice and Public Order Act 1994, s 143.
8   Sexual Offences Act 1956, s 12(1A) and (1B).
9   See **1.28**.

BUGGERY AND CONSENT

1.20   Originally, consent was irrelevant to a charge of buggery[1] and, hence, the offence was hybrid in nature – it was an offence of sexual aggression if one party did not consent but became a breach of sexual taboo where there was *de facto* consent. The extended definition of rape contained in the Criminal Justice and Public Order Act 1994 now means that all non consensual buggery between men and between a man and woman constitutes the offence of rape. Therefore, buggery is limited to intercourse per anum or per vaginum by a man or a woman with an animal and consensual acts of intercourse per anum between a man and a woman and between men in certain circumstances. Buggery is now clearly a breach of sexual taboo.

INDECENCY BETWEEN MALES

1.21   Other forms of sexual activity between men is also subject to control by the criminal law. By virtue of s 13 of the Sexual Offences Act 1956, it is an offence for a man to commit an act of gross indecency with another man, whether in public or in private, or to be a party to the commission by a man of an act of gross indecency with another man, or to procure the commission by a man of an act of gross indecency with another man. As with buggery, the offence of gross indecency is not committed where both participants are aged 18 or over and the act takes place in private,[2] although it remains an offence to procure a man to commit an act of gross indecency with a third man, even though that act of gross indecency is not itself an offence by virtue of the restrictions.[3] Gross indecency is not defined in the statute and no definition has been forthcoming from the courts. The Wolfenden Committee Report suggested that gross indecency would usually take one of three forms: mutual masturbation, intercrural contact or oral-genital contact. However, as the Committee pointed out, techniques in heterosexual relations vary considerably, and the same is true of homosexual relations. It appears that there is no requirement of physical contact between the men as long as they are behaving in a grossly indecent manner viewed from an objective point of view.[4] The offence is clearly a breach of sexual taboo, as it requires the men to act in concert.[5] In the absence of consent, provided the requirement of an assault has been satisfied, the behaviour will amount to an indecent assault.

---

1   Although, following the Sexual Offences Act 1967, the maximum punishment for any particular act of buggery depended upon factual circumstances, including gender, age and consent.
2   See **1.19**.
3   Sexual Offences Act 1967, s 4.
4   *Hunt v Badsey* [1950] 2 All ER 291.
5   *R v Hornby and Peaple* [1946] 2 All ER 487.

Sexual activity involving children[1]

Children as victims

1.22   The vast majority of sexual offences, whether they be offences of sexual aggression or breaches of sexual taboo, are not age specific. For example, rape, indecent assault and incest can be committed against a child in exactly the same as way as they may be committed against an adult victim. Thus, a range of offences already exists to protect children against unwanted or inappropriate sexual behaviour. However, the law takes the view that such general protection is inadequate and, therefore, has enacted several offences for the specific purpose of protecting children against what is deemed to be inappropriate sexual behaviour.

THE AGE OF CONSENT

1.23   The law has regulated sexual activity with children from early times and one of the methods used has been to impose a statutory age of consent. The primary reason for imposing an age of consent is seen as being to protect the individual child, although it has been suggested that there are also concurring moral motives which aim to prevent certain forms of undesirable behaviour.[2] There has been a statutory age of consent to sexual intercourse for the purpose of the criminal law from at least 1275. Originally 10 years, it was raised to 13 years in 1875 and to 16 years in 1885. In 1880, an age of consent of 13 years was introduced for the offence of indecent assault. It was raised to 16 years in 1922, thus bringing it into line with the age of consent for sexual intercourse. However, more recent legislation has departed from the age of consent. Section 1 of the Indecency with Children Act 1960 provides for an offence of gross indecency with or towards a child under the age of 14 years. It is difficult to see why the age of 14 years was adopted in this legislation, as in practice it results in no protection in certain circumstances for a child of 14 or 15 years. The Government has recognised this as an unacceptable anomaly, which is now being addressed by a review of sexual offences.[3]

CONSENT AND HOMOSEXUAL ACTIVITY

1.24   The age of consent has been the subject of controversy in recent years. Much of this controversy has arisen in relation to the age of consent for homosexual activity. Most other countries have equal ages of consent for homosexual and heterosexual activity. But in England and Wales, although the age of consent for heterosexual activity has been 16 for many years, when male homosexual activity was first legalised in 1967 the age of consent was set at 21

---

1   There is no universal age limit at which a person ceases to become a child. For the purposes of criminal law, the law provides specific protection for children under the ages of 14, 16 and 18 (see **1.23** to **1.24**). For the purposes of criminal liability and procedure, a child is a person aged 10 years or more but under 14 years of age; a young person is aged 14 years or more but under 17 years of age; and a young offender is aged 14 years or more but under 21 years.

2   European Committee on Crime Problems *Sexual Behaviour and Attitudes and their Implications for Criminal Law* (Strasbourg, Council of Europe, 1984) p 147.

3   HC Deb vol 319, cols 49–50, 9 November 1998. See further **1.45**.

years,[1] which at that time was the age of majority. Following much debate, during the passage of the Criminal Justice and Public Order Act 1994 through Parliament, MPs were given a free vote on an amendment to bring the age of consent for homosexual activity into line with that for heterosexual activity (ie 16 years), or alternatively to lower the age of consent for homosexual activity to 18 years. This latter compromise was finally adopted[2] and s 145 of the 1994 Act reduced the age of consent for homosexual activity to 18 years. The remaining discrepancy between the ages of consent for homosexual and heterosexual activity was said to be justified by the argument that many young people experienced an ambivalence about their sexuality in their teenage years and that a reduction to the age of 18 would allow more time for this to be resolved while still protecting the vulnerable during the period of transition.[3]

1.25   Having lowered the age of consent for homosexual activity to 18, it was inevitable that the matter would not rest there. In 1994, Euan Sutherland, a young homosexual brought a complaint before the European Commission of Human Rights, arguing that, in applying the differing ages of consent for homosexual and heterosexual activity, the United Kingdom was in breach of arts 8 and 14 of the European Convention on Human Rights.[4] Article 8 grants everyone the right to respect for his private and family life, his home and his correspondence, and art 14 provides that the enjoyment of the rights and freedoms set out in the Convention shall be secured without discrimination on any ground such as, *inter alia*, sex. The Commission ruled that there had been a violation of the Convention and that the case was admissible.[5] In October 1997, the Government announced that it had agreed with Sutherland and Morris, an applicant in a parallel case, to ask the European Court of Human Rights for the cases to be deferred pending a vote in Parliament at the earliest opportunity.[6] Although the Government had earlier rejected the suggestion that a measure to lower the age of consent be included in the Crime and Disorder Bill when it was first introduced in the House of Lords,[7] various backbench amendments relating to homosexual offences were tabled in time for the report stage of the Bill in the House of Commons in June 1998.[8] Following a free vote, there was a 207 vote majority in favour of equalising the age of consent in the House of Commons, but the following month the House of Lords voted overwhelmingly against the reform,[9] triggering what has been described as 'one of the most serious constitutional clashes between the two Houses of Parliament in decades'.[10] Concerned that the dispute would delay the implementation of the entire Crime and Disorder Bill, the House of Commons reluctantly accepted the House of

---

1   Sexual Offences Act 1967.
2   The amendment to lower the age of consent to 18 was won by 427 votes to 162. The alternative amendment to lower the age of consent to 16 was defeated by 307 votes to 280.
3   See *Blackstone's Guide to the Criminal Justice and Public Order Act 1994* (Blackstone Press Ltd, London, 1995).
4   Application no 25186/94.
5   *Sutherland v UK* (1997) 24 EHRR CD 22.
6   Home Office Press Release 033/97, 7 October 1997.
7   HC Deb vol 298, col 347, 18 July 1997.
8   HC Deb vol 314, cols 754–811, 22 June 1998.
9   HL Deb vol 592, cols 936–976, 22 July 1998.
10   (1998) *The Times*, 23 July.

Lords' decision, but the Home Secretary announced that legislation dealing with the age of consent would be introduced in the 1998–99 session.[1]

1.26 The Sexual Offences (Amendment) Bill was presented to the House of Commons in December 1998. The Bill contained provisions on both the age of consent for homosexual activity and the creation of a new criminal offence of abuse of a position of trust.[2] Previous debates in Parliament had linked the equalisation of the age of consent with the need to provide protection for young people from abuse of trust, and the proposals for the creation of a new offence were reported in the press as being intended to allay fears that lowering the age of consent for homosexuals would leave teenagers vulnerable to exploitation. However, it has been made clear by the government that the two issues of age of consent and abuse of trust are to be treated as being entirely separate.[3]

1.27 Clause 1 of the Bill reduced the age of consent for homosexual activity in England and Wales from 18 to 16, thus bringing it into line with the age of consent for heterosexual activity.[4] Following a free vote, the Bill was endorsed overwhelmingly by the House of Commons and was introduced into the House of Lords on 2 March 1999. However, on 13 April 1999, following a free vote at the end of a 7-hour debate, the House of Lords once again rejected the provisions of the Bill by 222 votes to 146.[5]

1.28 Thus, on two occasions, the House of Lords has blocked attempts by the Government to equalise the age of consent for homosexual and heterosexual activity. Under the procedures of the Parliament Act 1911 and 1949, a Bill which has been passed by the House of Commons in two successive sessions but rejected by the House of Lords in each of those sessions can be presented for Royal Assent following its second rejection by the House of Lords. The fact that the first attempt to lower the age of consent was made as an amendment to the Crime and Disorder Bill, which was introduced in the House of Lords, means that the Government was previously unable to rely on the provisions of the Parliament Acts. However, the Bill was presented to the House of Commons in January 2000 and it has been made clear that, if necessary, the Parliament Acts will be used to secure its passage.[6] In the meantime, the Government has sought a further extension from the European Court of Human Rights in the stayed cases of *Sutherland* and *Morris* until July 2000, in the hope that the outcome of the Bill will be known by that time.

CONSENT AND HETEROSEXUAL ACTIVITY
1.29 Whilst controversy has raged around the age of consent for homosexual activity, the age of consent for heterosexual relations has also been called into question. It has been suggested that the arbitrary determination of an age level below which willing participants in a sexual act are deemed incapable of that act

---

1   HC Deb vol 317, cols 182–183.
2   See **1.49** to **1.58**.
3   See House of Commons Research Paper 99/4, 21 January 1999, p 29.
4   Clause 1 also reduces the age of consent for homosexual activity to 17 in Northern Ireland, thus bringing it into line with the age of consent of heterosexual activity.
5   HL Deb vol 599, cols 758–761, 13 April 1999.
6   Home Office Press Release 225/99, 23 July 1999.

is inconsistent with contemporary sociological and psychological thought.[1] One solution would be that the age of consent be abolished and the existing criminal law intervention be substituted by social intervention, using the provisions of the Children Act 1989. However, some would argue that the criminal law has an important role to play in the protection of children, particularly girls, and that a major part of this protection would be abandoned if the intervention could only be made where it could be proved that a child was suffering or was likely to suffer significant harm. Furthermore, such a move would also mean that there would be no provision to penalise anyone who did take advantage of a child.

1.30   If the age of consent is to be retained (as it undoubtedly will be), the question remains as to what the age should be. The present age of 16 years is said to be quite arbitrary, with no biological justification and to take no account of the willingness, not to say preparedness, both physiologically and emotionally, of many girls and boys under that age for sexual experience. However, medical evidence suggests that premature sexual experience may result in physical and psychological harm, and it has been argued that there has been no significant increase in recent times in the level of psychological maturity of girls under 16 years, even though they may be physically more mature at that age.[2] It seems that the age of consent for heterosexual activity will remain at 16 for the foreseeable future. Indeed, the Government has made this quite clear. On 25 August 1998 an article in the *Daily Mail* claimed that ministers were to examine the possibility of reducing the age of consent to 14. This brought an immediate response from Jack Straw, the Home Secretary, who issued a press release, referring to the suggestion as 'absolute nonsense' and having no basis in fact whatsoever. Mr Straw said that the Government had never considered lowering the heterosexual age of consent to 14 and had no plans to do so in the future. In this respect, English law is in line with several European countries, for example Belgium, the Netherlands and Germany, and most states of the USA, where the age of consent for heterosexual activity is also 16 years. However, there are exceptions to this age. In Ireland the age of consent is 17 years, but in Denmark and France it is 15 years. In Spain and in most of South America there is no statutory age of consent. In general, consensual sexual relations are not penalised from the age of 12, although a person over 16 who has sex with a person aged between 12 and 16 may be liable to prosecution.[3]

UNLAWFUL SEXUAL INTERCOURSE AND INDECENT ASSAULTS ON CHILDREN

1.31   Having taken the view that children below the age of 16 should not be indulging in any form of sexual activity, specific statutory offences have been enacted to achieve that aim, regardless of any apparent consent the child may give. On the face of it, this would seem to imply that offences enacted specifically to protect children are all breaches of sexual taboo. For example, ss 5 and 6 of the Sexual Offences Act 1956 provide that it is an offence to have unlawful sexual intercourse with a girl under the age of 13 and 16 respectively. The offences are

---

1   Grey 'Sexual Law Reform Society Working Party Report' [1975] Crim LR 323.
2   Policy Advisory Committee on Sexual Offences *Report on the Age of Consent in Relation to Sexual Offences* (1981) Cmnd 8216 (HMSO, London).
3   House of Commons Research Paper 99/4, 21 January 1999, p 19.

ones of strict liability, in that a mistaken belief, even if it is a reasonable belief, that the girl is over the prescribed age will not amount to a defence. The only exception to this is the so-called 'young man's defence' to an offence under s 6 of the Act. Section 6(3) provides that a man is not guilty of the offence 'if he is under the age of twenty four and has not previously been charged with a like offence, and he believes the girl to be of the age of sixteen or over and has reasonable cause for the belief'. The girl's consent is irrelevant, as the act of having unlawful sexual intercourse with a girl under the age of 13 or 16 is itself an offence – it is clearly a breach of sexual taboo.

1.32 However, ambiguity arises over the issue of consent when the offence of indecent assault is considered. Section 14(1) of the Sexual Offences Act 1956 provides that it is an offence for a person to make an indecent assault on a woman, and s 14(2) provides that a girl under the age of 16 years cannot in law give any consent which would prevent an act being an assault for the purposes of that section.[1] The effect of s 14(2) is to prevent a female under the age of 16 years from consenting in law to an indecent assault, unlike s 6 of the Act which provides for the offence of having unlawful sexual intercourse with a girl under the age of 16 years without referring to the issue of consent. Thus, any indecent assault on a female under 16 years becomes an offence of sexual aggression, as it is deemed in law to be non-consensual. Although the outcome of ss 6 and 14 is identical, ie it is an offence to indecently assault or have unlawful sexual intercourse with a female under the age of 16 years, the two sections define the offences in different ways: one being a breach of sexual taboo, the other being an offence of sexual aggression. As a general rule, offences of sexual aggression are viewed more seriously than breaches of sexual taboo and this is reflected in the maximum sentences available. An offence under s 14 of the 1956 Act carries a maximum sentence of 10 years' imprisonment, whereas an offence under s 6 of the Act carries a maximum sentence of only 2 years' imprisonment.[2] Obviously, problems would arise if s 6 adopted the same approach as s 14. For example, if s 6 provided that a female under 16 years could not in law consent to sexual intercourse, it would be difficult to distinguish this offence from the offence of rape. If a female under 16 years is not deemed capable of consenting to intercourse, then any sexual intercourse would be without her consent and, therefore, would amount to rape if the man knew or was reckless as to her age.

1.33 Yet further problems arise if s 14(2) is carried to its logical conclusion. If a female under the age of 16 years cannot consent to indecent assault, then surely she cannot consent to sexual intercourse, which itself must necessarily amount to an indecent assault. Therefore, any act of sexual intercourse must be without her consent, which again would amount to rape, provided the necessary fault element was established. These difficulties arise because of the fiction of legal consent contained in s 14(2) and the categorisation of indecent assault as an offence of sexual aggression. It is difficult to see any logical reason for this distinction and the fiction of non-consent has been criticised.[3] Although the problem is predominately a theoretical one, as the distinction is unlikely to give

1   Section 15 makes similar provision for male victims.
2   Although an offence under s 5 of the Act, where the girl is under 13 years of age, carries a maximum penalty of life imprisonment.
3   See, for example, the recommendations of the Criminal Law Revision Committee **1.36**.

rise to any serious difficulties in practice, it is argued that the justification and rationale for imposing criminal liability on individuals should be clear and consistent.

LACUNAE IN THE LAW

1.34   Given the wide-ranging definition of indecent assault and the provision in ss 14(2) and 15(2) that a child under the age of 16 is incapable of consenting to what would otherwise be an indecent assault, one may wonder why it has been thought necessary to enact further specific offences of indecent conduct involving children. The fact is that on several occasions in recent years, Parliament has found it necessary to legislate after blatant lacunae in the law were uncovered.

Acts of gross indecency

1.35   In 1951, the case of *Fairclough v Whip* came before the Divisional Court.[1] The respondent had exposed himself in the presence of a 9-year-old girl and invited her to touch his exposed person, which she did. He was charged with indecently assaulting the girl, but was acquitted because the requirement of an assault was not satisfied. Lord Goddard CJ commented:

> 'I cannot hold that an invitation to somebody to touch the invitor can amount to an assault on the invitee. It might be a very good thing if Parliament passed an Act providing that any indecent conduct in the presence of a child or in relation to a child – or any form of words the draftsman saw fit to use – should be punishable, but at present, the law has not gone beyond saying that an indecent assault on a child is punishable whether the child consents or not.'[2]

Similar cases followed and in 1959 the Criminal Law Revision Committee was established to review the law. In the words of Lord Justice Lawton:

> '... the Home Office decided that if there were these sorts of defects in the law, the sooner a committee was formed to have a look at the law and make recommendations for its reform, the better it would be for all.'[3]

1.36   Following the Criminal Law Revision Committee's first report, Parliament enacted the Indecency with Children Act 1960, which provides that an offence is committed when any person commits an act of gross indecency with or towards a child under the age of 14 years, or incites a child under that age to such an act with himself or another.

1.37   The offence obviously includes an indecent assault, but it is much wider than that. This is illustrated by the facts of the case of *R v Speck*[4] in which an 8-year-old girl, uninvited, placed her hand on a man's penis, outside his trousers and continued to keep her hand there for 5 minutes. In consequence, the man had an erection, but stayed passive and did nothing to encourage her. He was convicted under s 1 of the 1960 Act, the Court of Appeal holding that his conduct amounted to 'an invitation to the child to do the act'. The decision has been criticised as being 'an abuse of language because there was no invitation in the

---

1   [1951] 2 All ER 834.
2   Ibid.
3   Lawton 'Sexual Offences' (1982) *Medico-Legal Journal* 50 at 19.
4   [1977] 2 All ER 859.

ordinary sense of the word'.[1] Yet the Court of Appeal clearly felt that liability should arise in such circumstances and was prepared to stretch the wording of the Act in order to obtain a conviction. Had the draftsman extended the offence to include 'permitting an act of gross indecency to be performed', no such problems would have arisen. The problems regarding the requirement of assault continue when the child is older than 13 years.

Indecent photographs of children

1.38 In 1977, the case of *R v Sutton*[2] illustrated yet another defect in the law. In this case, the defendant photographed small boys (aged 11–13 years) in the nude for the purposes of selling the photographs to magazines. He did not touch the boys except to arrange their poses. He was charged with indecently assaulting the boys, but was acquitted. The touching was held not to be an indecent assault, as it was not indecent. (There was also held to be no common assault, as the boys had consented.) Once again, Parliament stepped in to remedy the defect in the form of the Protection of Children Act 1978, which provides that it is an offence to take indecent photographs of persons under 16 years, or to distribute or show or advertise such photographs. In 1988, this offence was extended by s 160 of the Criminal Justice Act 1988, which creates a summary offence of possession of an indecent photograph of a person under 16 years of age. Yet further reform followed in 1994, when the Criminal Justice and Public Order Act of that year amended the 1978 and 1988 Acts to include references to making pseudo photographs (images made or manipulated by computer which are not photographs in the technical sense) and also extended liability to data stored on a computer disc or by other electronic means which is capable of conversion into a photograph. These amendments were found to be necessary because advances in computer technology had led to a considerable increase in both the creation and distribution of digital images resembling photographs and concerns were mounting over the use and transmission of such material via the Internet, especially by organised paedophile rings and networks.

Children as offenders

THE AGE OF CRIMINAL RESPONSIBILITY

1.39 A child under the age of 10 is said to be *doli incapax*, ie incapable of crime, and therefore a child under the age of 10 cannot be convicted of a criminal offence.[3] Children below this age whose behaviour causes concern may be made the subject of a Care Order if they are suffering or are likely to suffer significant harm, and the harm, or likelihood of harm, is attributable to, inter alia, the child's being beyond parental control.[4] The Crime and Disorder Act 1998 also provides further powers to deal with children under the age of 10 who have committed acts which, in the case of those over 10, would have constituted

---

1   Williams *Textbook of Criminal Law* (Stevens, London, 1983) p 235.
2   [1977] 1 WLR 1086.
3   There is an irrebuttable presumption that a child under 10 years of age at the time an alleged offence was committed cannot be found guilty of that offence – s 50 of the Children and Young Persons Act 1933, as amended.
4   Children Act 1989, s 31. See further **8.106**.

criminal offences. The local authority may apply to the magistrates' family proceedings court for a Child Safety Order, which places the child under the supervision of a responsible officer[1] for a period of up to 3 months and subjects the child to certain restrictions of conditions.[2]

1.40   In the past, where a child was 10 years of age or over but under the age of 14 at the time of the alleged offence, there was a rebuttable presumption at common law that the child was *doli incapax*. The prosecution could rebut this presumption by calling evidence to show that a child had 'mischievous discretion', ie that the child knew that what he was doing was seriously wrong. In 1995, the Divisional Court expressed the view that the presumption did a serious disservice to the law and ruled that it was no longer part of the law of England and Wales.[3] However, the House of Lords took the view that any change in the law was a matter for Parliament, not the courts.[4] The issue has now been resolved by the Crime and Disorder Act 1998, which abolished the rebuttable presumption of *doli incapax* for children aged between 10 and 14 years.[5] As a result, all children over the age of 10 years are now treated equally, in that they are all assumed to have reached the same level of moral culpability as adults.

BOYS AND SEXUAL OFFENCES

1.41   In the past, there was an irrebuttable presumption that boys under the age of 14 were incapable of sexual intercourse. This meant that they could not be convicted as the perpetrator of a rape[6] or any offence involving sexual intercourse,[7] nor of buggery, whether as an agent or patient.[8] In recent years, the presumption has come under increasing attack as being outdated and, therefore, the presumption was abolished by the Sexual Offences Act 1993.[9] Thus, there is no longer any restriction on convicting boys over the age of 10 of offences involving sexual intercourse.

CHILDREN AS PARTIES TO CRIMES CREATED FOR THEIR OWN PROTECTION

1.42   When an indictable offence[10] is committed, criminal liability will generally be imposed not only on the principal offender, but also on accomplices who aid, abet, counsel or procure the commission of the offence.[11] However, where a statute is designed for protection of a certain class of persons, it may be construed as excluding by implication the liability of any member of that class who is the victim of the offence, even though that person does in fact aid, abet, counsel or procure the offence. There is clear authority for the application of this principle to sexual offences. In the case of *R v Tyrrell*,[12] it was

---

1   Namely, a social worker or a member of the youth offending team.
2   Crime and Disorder Act 1998, s 11.
3   *C v DPP* [1994] 3 All ER 190, DC.
4   *C v DPP* [1995] 2 ALL ER 43, HL.
5   Crime and Disorder Act 1998, s 34.
6   *R v Groombridge* (1836) 7 C & P 582.
7   *R v Waite* [1892] 2 QB 600.
8   *R v Tatam* (1921) 15 Cr App R 132.
9   Sexual Offences Act 1993, s 1.
10   See **3.88**.
11   Accessories and Abettors Act 1861, s 8.
12   [1894] 1 QB 710.

held that a girl between the age of 13 and 16 who encouraged a boy to have sexual intercourse with her could not be liable as an accomplice to the offence of having unlawful sexual intercourse with a girl under the age of 16 because the offence had been created for her own protection. Thus, if a sexual offence has been created specifically for the protection of a certain class of individuals, a member of that class will not incur criminal liability by aiding, abetting, counselling or procuring the offence when they are themselves the victim of the offence. Prima facie, this can have no application to offences of sexual aggression, such as rape, where absence of consent is an essential element of the offence. However, although indecent assault is generally classified as an offence of sexual aggression, the fiction of non-consent contained in s 14(2) of the 1956 Act arguably turns the offence into a breach of sexual taboo if the victim is under 16 years of age and in fact consents,[1] and thus the victim will presumably not be liable as an accomplice to the offence.

Reform

Codification of the criminal law

1.43   English criminal law is derived from a mixture of common law and statute, but the majority of crimes, including sexual offences, are now defined by statute. There have been numerous reforms in recent years, but these have occurred in a rather piecemeal fashion, as the above review of sexual offences shows, and it is generally agreed that further, more comprehensive, reform is necessary in all areas of criminal law. The most radical suggestion for change is the move towards codification of the entire criminal law, ie to produce a Criminal Code within which would be found a statement of general principles of liability and their application, the law relating to specific offences, and a Code of Criminal Procedure (including a comprehensive statement of the law of criminal evidence and possibly a section on punishment). The aim of codification is seen as being to make the criminal law more accessible, comprehensible, consistent and certain.[2] A Criminal Code would provide what the current mix of common law and statute never can – one fixed starting point for ascertaining what the law is. Codification is a different process from law reform, as codification may entail no more than a restatement of existing law and principles. However, where the existing law is inconsistent, or where lacunae have been identified, such deficiencies obviously should not be reproduced within the Code and, thus, codification inevitably entails substantial reform of the criminal law. The idea of codification is not new. Attempts to codify the criminal law of England and Wales have had a long but chequered history, dating back to the mid 19th century.[3] In more recent times, in 1968 the Law Commission set out in its Second Programme its objective of a comprehensive examination of the criminal law with a view to its codification.[4] Some progress

---

1   See **1.32**.
2   (1985) Law Com No 143 *Codification of the Criminal Law* paras 1.3–1.9.
3   (1968) Law Com Consultation Paper No 17 *Codification of the Criminal Law. General Principles – The Field of Enquiry.*
4   (1985) Law Com No 143 *Codification of the Criminal Law.*

was made in relation to substantive offences[1] and general principles of liability.[2] In 1981 a Code team, consisting of distinguished academics, was established to consider and make proposals to the Law Commission in relation to a Criminal Code. The Code team submitted its report, which included a draft Criminal Code Bill, to the Commission in 1984. The Report was published in 1985[3] and stimulated substantial support for the principle of codification. In 1989, with the assistance of the Code team, the Law Commission published a revised and expanded draft Criminal Code Bill and a commentary on it.[4]

Reform of sexual offences

1.44   The Law Commission acknowledged that the draft Criminal Code Bill, if enacted, would amount to substantial reform of the existing substantive law, particularly in the areas of offences against the person and sexual offences. The reforms in relation to sexual offences were based on the recommendations of the Criminal Law Revision Committee in their Fifteenth,[5] Sixteenth[6] and Seventeenth[7] Reports. Some of the recommendations have effectively been made redundant by subsequent events, for example the removal of the marital immunity to rape. However, further reforms are still awaited. Finding the necessary legislative time to introduce a Bill of the size of the draft Criminal Code was never going to be easy, and, since 1989, the Law Commission has published several other Reports dealing with discrete areas of law which are considered to be in urgent need of reform, most notably offences against the person.[8]

1.45   However, until 1998, reform of the substantive law of sexual offences had received very little attention, either from law reform bodies or from Parliament itself, which was somewhat surprising in view of the intense public and political attention focused on sex offenders themselves. There have been occasional calls for specific reforms, such as the enactment of an entirely new offence of child sexual abuse to cover all forms of inappropriate sexual activity with children,[9] but virtually no Parliamentary time has been taken to discuss possible reform. Indeed, it appears that that there has been no comprehensive debate on sexual offences law in Parliament in modern times. It has been pointed out that the Sexual Offences Act 1956 was a consolidating measure passed under the fast-track provisions of the Consolidation of Enactments (Procedure) Act 1949 and, as a result, it was debated in Parliament for only 3 minutes. The 1956 Act simply re-enacted in virtually identical language provisions of the Offences Against the Persons Act 1861, the Criminal Law Amendment Act 1885 and the Vagrancy Act 1898, which was itself amended by

---

1   For example, the Criminal Damage Act 1971 was enacted following the Law Commission Report on *Offences of Damage to Property* (1970) Law Com No 27.
2   For example, the Criminal Law Act 1977 was enacted following the Law Commission Report on *Conspiracy and Criminal Law Reform* (1976) Law Com No 76.
3   (1985) Law Com No 143 *Codification of the Criminal Law.*
4   (1989) Law Com No 177 *A Criminal Code for England and Wales.*
5   *Fifteenth Report: Sexual Offences* (1984) Cmnd 9213 (HMSO, London).
6   *Sixteenth Report: Prostitution in the Street* (1984) Cmnd 9329 (HMSO, London).
7   *Seventeenth Report: Prostitution: Off-Street Activities* (1985) Cmnd 9688 (HMSO, London).
8   (1993) Law Com No 218 *Legislating the Criminal Code.*
9   See, for example, Colledge 'The True Scale of the Problem' (1998) NLJ 148 (6846) 955.

the Criminal Law Amendment Act 1912, all of which had been enacted without detailed debate in either the House of Commons or the House of Lords.[1] However, in June 1998 attention was finally re-focused on the substantive criminal law when the government announced its intention to reform the law relating to sexual offences.[2] Home Office Minister Alan Michael acknowledged that this area of law was ripe for reform, but said that careful consideration was needed. Stressing that public protection from sex offenders was of the utmost importance, he announced a review of the law which would ensure that the framework of sexual offences and penalties is coherent and effective.

1.46   The terms of reference of the review, which were announced in January 1999, are to review the sex offences in the common and statute law in England and Wales, and make recommendations that will:

(1) provide coherent and clear sex offences which protect individuals, especially children and the more vulnerable, from abuse and exploitation;
(2) enable abusers to be appropriately punished; and
(3) be fair and non-discriminatory in accordance with the European Convention on Human Rights and the Human Rights Act.

The review is looking at the law on rape and sexual assault, at the homosexual offences, at offences of sexual exploitation and indecent exposure, but is not considering decriminalising prostitution or pornography, further revision to the age of consent or procedural or evidential issues.[3]

1.47   The initial canvassing of views took place between January and March 1999. The contributions received were then passed to a Steering Group of officials, lawyers and advisers for consideration of the whole framework of sexual offences. The Steering Group is advised by an external reference group, which includes individuals and organisations concerned with women's issues, the children's charities, gay and lesbian groups, medical, ethical, legal and religious interests, who have relevant information, experience and strong views about issues relating to sexual offences. In order to seek an even wider range of views, a number of conferences and seminars on particular topics were held at various regional centres (for example, rape and sexual assault formed the basis of a major seminar in Leeds in July 1999).[4] The Steering Group aims to develop proposals for a new framework, which will be published in a consultation document.[5]

'Date rape' and consent

1.48   Even before the publication of the consultation document, there can be little doubt that the offence of rape will receive a considerable amount of attention. Home Office research published in July 1999 demonstrated that there has been a sharp drop in conviction rates for rape in recent years, but that this

---

1   Martin Bowley QC 'A Sexual Scandal' (1998) *The Times*, 23 June.
2   Home Office Press Release 222/98, 15 June 1998.
3   Home Office Press Release 028/99, 25 January 1999.
4   Home Office Press Release 198/99, 1 July 1999.
5   The consultation document is expected to be published in May 2000 (personal communication with the Home Office).

has been matched by a corresponding rise in reported rapes by people known to the complainant.[1] This has led to speculation that juries are unwilling to convict 'date rapists' because the penalty is too high.[2] The suggestion that there should be a distinction between rape by a stranger and date rape has been acknowledged by those responsible for the review of sexual offences and one of the issues that is being considered as part of the review is whether a lesser offence of date rape or non-consensual sex might improve the conviction rate, an issue on which pressure groups are divided.[3] The other key reform under review is changing the law on consent and suggestions have been made that the burden of proof should be reversed so that the defendant would have to prove that the victim did consent.[4]

Abuse of trust

1.49   Whilst the Steering Group is considering proposals for reform of the whole framework of sexual offences – reform which will inevitably take some considerable time to reach the statute book – one particular part of this area of substantive law has been singled out for particular attention and proposals for the creation of a new criminal offence of abuse of a position of trust seem likely to be enacted well before any reforms brought about as a result of the review of sexual offences.

1.50   Closely linked with the efforts of the Government to equalise the age of consent for homosexual and heterosexual activity, proposals for the creation of a new criminal offence of abuse of trust have tended to focus on protecting boys from homosexual men.[5] Whereas the existing criminal law generally protects children under the age of 16 from inappropriate sexual activity (subject to the potential lacuna in protection for 14- and 15-year-old children created by the Indecency with Children Act 1960), concern has been expressed that the lowering of the age of consent for homosexual activity could lead to the exploitation of vulnerable young people over the age of 16 by older men, particularly by those in a position of trust or with authority over the young person.

1.51   Many jurisdictions have recognised the danger of exploitation and have adopted measures to protect vulnerable young people. For example, in Austria, it is illegal for a male over the age of 19 to commit homosexual acts with a male between 14 and 18 and in Portugal it is illegal for a person aged 18 or over to commit sexual acts with a person under the age of 18. In Canada, a specific offence has been created of sexual exploitation of a young person by one who is in a position of trust.[6]

---

1   *A Question of Evidence? Investigating and Prosecuting Rape in the 1990s* Home Office Research Study 196 (July 1999).
2   Guidance from the Court of Appeal suggests that the 'starting point' for a contested rape case is five years' imprisonment. See **4.143**.
3   (1999) *The Times*, 2 July.
4   See further **2.9**.
5   For a full review of the proposals for reform in this area, see House of Commons Research Paper 99/4, 21 January 1999, Part II, C.
6   Canadian Criminal Code, s 153.

1.52 When amendments were introduced to the Crime and Disorder Bill which would have had the effect of lowering the age of consent for homosexual activity to 16, amendments were also tabled which aimed to introduce protections similar to those which exist in other jurisdictions.[1] However, these amendments were rejected by the House of Commons before the Bill went to the House of Lords, and in June 1998 the Government announced the establishment of an interdepartmental working group of officials to consider how to prevent those who were unsuitable from working with children and to look at further possible measures to protect 16- and 17-year-olds who may be vulnerable to abuse by those in a position of trust, such as carers, teachers and leaders of organised residential activities.[2]

1.53 The working group was asked to prioritise work on the issue of abuse of trust because of the Government's commitment to give Parliament a second opportunity during the 1998–99 session to consider the equalisation of the age of consent, and so the group published an interim report in November 1998 dealing solely with this issue.[3] Although the large majority of organisations that responded to the consultation exercise carried out by the group in August and September 1998 believed that conduct amounting to abuse of a position of trust in relation to those over the age of consent was better regulated by professional codes than by a criminal offence, the group concluded that a new criminal offence would be justified in certain limited circumstances. The group also recommended a major initiative to strengthen codes of conduct generally to protect young people from those in a position of authority over them.[4] The recommendations of the group in relation to a new criminal offence of abuse of trust were incorporated into the Sexual Offences (Amendment) Bill, which was first introduced into the House of Commons on 16 December 1998.

THE PROPOSED OFFENCE OF ABUSE OF TRUST
1.54 The Bill created a new criminal offence of abuse of trust. A person aged 18 or over would commit the offence by having sexual intercourse or engaging in any other sexual activity with a person under that age where they are in a 'position of trust' in relation to the younger person. No reference is made to the lower age limit for the younger person below which only the existing criminal offences would apply and so there would be a number of circumstances in which several alternative charges would be possible. As the proposed maximum penalty for the new offence is 2 years' imprisonment following conviction on indictment, the existing criminal offences, the majority of which carry a higher maximum penalty, will presumably continue to be used where the younger person is below the age of consent. The new offence would be included in Sch 1 to the Sex Offenders Act 1997, so that anyone cautioned or convicted of the offence

---

1   HC Deb vol 314, cols 754–811, 22 June 1998.
2   HC Deb vol 313, cols 304–305, 4 June 1998. See further **8.150**.
3   *Working Group on Preventing Unsuitable People from Working with Children and Abuse of Trust. Interim Report: Abuse of Trust*, 25 November 1998.
4   Guidance has now been issued by the Home Office, Northern Ireland Office, National Assembly for Wales, Department of Health, and Departments for Education and Employment, setting out the main principles which should form the basis of Codes of Conduct for all organisations caring for young people or vulnerable adults. *Caring for Young and Vulnerable People?: Guidance on Preventing Abuse of Trust* (1999). See further **8.151**.

would be subject to the notification requirements of the 1997 Act.[1] The Government expects that the offence of abuse of trust would act more as a deterrent than result in a large number of actual prosecutions and has estimated that prosecutions would amount to around 10–15 a year.[2] The estimated number of prosecutions under the Protection from Harassment Act 1997 has subsequently proved to be a gross underestimate[3] and the accuracy of the predicted number of prosecutions for the offence of abuse of trust remains to be seen.

'Sexual intercourse and sexual activity'

1.55   Sexual intercourse includes both vaginal and anal intercourse and thus covers homosexual activity. Sexual activity is defined objectively, as activity which a reasonable person would regard as sexual in the circumstances, but behaviour which a reasonable person would only regard as sexual activity if he were aware of the parties' intentions, motives or feelings is specifically excluded.

'Position of trust'

1.56   A person aged 18 or over is said to be in a position of trust in relation to a younger person if he is regularly involved in caring for, training, supervising or being in sole charge of persons under 18 at the relevant institution and:

(1)   the younger person is detained in an institution under a court order and any other enactment;
(2)   the younger person is resident in and provided with accommodation (or accommodation and maintenance) by a local authority or a voluntary organisation in a home or other place;
(3)   the younger person is in any of the following:
    (a)   a hospital,
    (b)   a residential care home, nursing home, mental nursing home or private hospital,
    (c)   a community home, voluntary home, children's home or residential establishment, or
    (d)   a home provided under s 82(5) of the Children Act 1989; or
(4)   the younger person is in full-time education in an institution.[4]

Defences

1.57   It would be a defence for a person charged with the proposed offence if at the time of the intercourse or sexual activity he did not know or could not reasonably have been expected to know that the younger person was under 18 or that he was in a position of trust in relation to the younger person. It would also be a defence if the older person was married to the younger person. This latter defence was thought necessary in order to ensure compliance with the European Convention on Human Rights, although the working group was concerned that

---

1   See **7.1** to **7.15**.
2   *Explanatory Notes on the Sexual Offences (Amendment) Bill,* as introduced into the House of Commons on 16 December 1998, para 21.
3   See **7.47**.
4   These four conditions may be added to by an Order made by the Secretary of State and laid before and approved by both Houses of Parliament.

such a defence would provide a means to 'marry your way' out of an offence.[1] Transitional provisions would also apply to ensure that the offence would not apply where the older person was in a sexual relationship with the younger person at the time when he was in a position of trust in relation to the younger person immediately before the enactment of the legislation.

1.58   The Sexual Offences (Amendment) Bill was defeated in the House of Lords in April 1999, but was reintroduced in the House of Commons in January 2000.[2] The creation of the new offence of abuse of trust is inextricably linked with the equalisation of the age of consent for homosexual and heterosexual activity and the provisions of the Bill will no doubt stand or fall together.

But who is a sex offender?

1.59   Despite the absence of a definitive definition of a sexual offence, there is at least a central core of offences which clearly relate to sexual activity and which are categorised as sexual offences for all purposes. So, for example, rape and indecent assault are clearly sexual offences, but as one moves away from this central core, it becomes more difficult to decide if an offence can justifiably be classified as a sexual one. In practice, the response has not been to seek a definitive definition but to categorise sexual offences according to the purpose for which the definition is required. For example, the category of sexual offences defined for the purpose of notifiable offences recorded by the police[3] differs from the category of sexual offences defined for sentencing purposes,[4] which in turn differs from the category of sexual offences defined for the purposes of imposing notification requirements under the Sex Offenders Act 1997.[5] As a result, an offender may be classified as a sex offender for some purposes, but not for others. Although this may work well enough in practice, it does have implications for policy – how can policy decisions be taken in relation to sex offenders if there is no readily identifiable group of such offenders?

1.60   Yet, even if the problems of defining a sexual offence could be overcome, defining a sex offender as someone who commits a sexual offence tells us nothing about the offenders themselves, other than the fact they have committed what has been defined as a sexual offence for one or more particular purposes. Just as sexual offences are far from a homogenous group, sex offenders themselves are not a homogeneous group of individuals and it is not possible to identify a 'typical' sex offender. Numerous variables have been identified, but the most commonly referred to include offenders' choice of victim, their criminal backgrounds, their sexual arousal patterns, their social functioning and their risk of re-offending.[6]

---

1   *Working Group on Preventing Unsuitable People from Working with Children and Abuse of Trust. Interim Report: Abuse of Trust*, 25 November, 1998 para 23.
2   See **1.28**.
3   See **1.74**.
4   See **4.69**.
5   See **7.8**.
6   Grubin *Sex Offending Against Children: Understanding the Risk*, Police Research Series Paper 99 (Home Office, London, 1998).

'Sub-groups within the group' – classification systems for sex offenders

1.61   Putting to one side the problems associated with defining the terms 'sex offender' and 'sexual offences', on the assumption that a group of offenders can be categorised as sex offenders, attempts have been made to devise classification systems for offenders within that group, in effect classifying sub-groups within the heterogeneous group of sex offenders. The various professionals who have to deal with sex offenders in the course of their work have to make key decisions about appropriate measures, and not only do these professionals have differing immediate objectives, they also lack specialist knowledge about sex offenders. Although not confined to the criminal justice system, the problem is particularly acute in this area. The Home Office and Scottish Office felt that a classification system for sex offenders would be potentially useful in helping criminal justice professionals to make decisions about sex offenders, and so commissioned a review of the existing classification schemes, with a view to making recommendations about any scheme which might be suitable for testing in practice.[1] The review considered the following kinds of classification schemes:

(1) general classification schemes – single, comprehensive schemes applicable to all sex offenders, for example schemes based solely on the type of offence committed;

(2) psychometrically derived typologies – based on psychological tests, some of which had been designed specifically for use with sex offenders;

(3) psychiatric classification – broad systems which seek to bring uniformity to the debate over classifying abnormal behaviour, including deviant sexual behaviour;

(4) physiological/behavioural classification – for example, penile plethysmograph used for measuring sexual arousal; and

(5) specific classification schemes for child molesters and rapists.

1.62   After reviewing existing classification systems and seeking the views of various professionals working in the area of sex offending, the research concluded that none of the schemes reviewed was immediately useable in a criminal justice context, although it was thought that some of the classification systems could be developed further to test out their potential. It was also suggested that panels of criminal justice professionals might be set up in order to assess sex offenders and suggest the most appropriate methods of dealing with them and that a study might be commissioned to investigate the working classifications of sex offenders used on a daily basis by criminal justice professionals. The key objective of classifying offenders at present is to assess their risk of future offending and risk assessments of individual offenders are now undertaken as a matter of routine.[2] The review concluded that classification concerned with appropriate sentence and form of treatment could follow from this initial assessment. No doubt, further research in this area will follow, but a definitive answer to the question 'Who is a sex offender?' remains elusive.

---

1   *A Review of Classification Systems for Sex Offenders*, Home Office Research Findings No 78 (Home Office, London, 1998).

2   See, for example, **4.73**, **5.85** and **6.30**.

Sex offenders and other offences

1.63   Labelling an offender as a sex offender tends to suggest that the offender is solely that, ie that he commits only sex offences. However, this would be a misguided assumption. It is clear that many sex offenders also commit a variety of other offences, and one of the dangers of focusing the spotlight on sex offenders as categorised by the offences they commit is that other offending behaviour is effectively ignored. This has been referred to as criminal apartheid – that sex offending is set apart from other types of offending, with the implication that sex offenders are somehow distinct from the general run.[1]

1.64   The potential significance of the link between sexual offences and other offending behaviour has been highlighted by a recently completed major criminological follow-up of all those offenders convicted of an indictable sexual offence in England and Wales in 1973.[2] For each of these offenders, details of their criminal history for the previous 10 years and the subsequent 21 years were obtained from the Offenders Index at the Home Office. The series consisted of 7,401 males and 41 females who were convicted of 49,264 offences over the 32-year period of 1963–94 inclusive. The results of the study offer a fascinating insight into the criminal profiles of the offenders in question. For example, nearly half (46.8%) of the 346 men convicted of rape in 1973 had a conviction for a standard list violent offence – a much higher proportion of violence offences than expected, whereas only 5% of the 1,529 men convicted of indecency between males in 1973 had a conviction for violence – a far lower proportion of violence offences than expected. Furthermore, those convicted of rape in 1973 were twice as likely to be convicted of a violence offence (46.8%) over the 32-year period than to have a second conviction for a sexual offence (23.1%), which suggests that those convicted of rape may be much more prone to violence in general than sexual offending per se.

1.65   As interesting as these results may be, the researchers point out the difficulties with this conventional type of approach: that interpretation rests heavily on statistically significant differences and, perhaps more importantly, that it is difficult to summarise what is actually happening. In an effort to overcome this latter point, the researchers adopted a correspondence analysis technique which analyses tables of counts or percentages, and identifies differences in column profiles between rows and row profiles between columns. The results can be portrayed as 'maps', which can greatly enhance an understanding of the data collected. By superimposing profiles of sex offender groups onto profiles of other offences committed, the researchers were able to conclude that there are three main groups of offenders who are convicted of sexual offences at some point in their criminal career:

(1)   group 1: those offenders whose criminal life is essentially organised around violence – they rob, rape, damage property, procure, abduct and drive dangerously;

---

1   Soothill and Frances 'Reviewing the Pantheon of Sexual Offending' [1999] *Journal of the Society for Advanced Legal Studies* 17 at 4.

2   Ibid.

(2) group 2: those offenders who essentially tangle with the law simply on account of their illicit sexual behaviour, but are not generally involved in other kinds of criminal behaviour – they commit buggery and indecency with other males and may be convicted of gross indecency with children; and

(3) group 3: those offenders who are essentially deceptive – they perpetrate fraud and deception and pretend they are not married when they are, thereby committing bigamy.

1.66   An alternative way of looking at these finding is that those who commit offences of sexual aggression (group 1) are more likely to commit other offences involving violence, whereas those who commit breaches of sexual taboo (group 2) are less likely to commit other kinds of criminal offences. The third group offenders, which include bigamists, should arguably not be classified as sex offenders at all.

1.67   Taking into account the entire criminal profiles of those convicted of sexual offences avoids the danger of criminal apartheid. The researchers suggest that identifying among those committing sexual offences a patterning in the type of other kinds of offences may help to develop a new conceptualisation of sexual offending and guard against the rather narrow focus on sexual offending in isolation which current theory and practice seem to encourage.

1.68   Whilst the findings of the criminological study are extremely interesting and undoubtedly merit further consideration, the reality is that the sex offenders are currently identified solely on the basis of the offences they commit and will continue to be so identified for the foreseeable future. Therefore, for all practical purposes, a sex offender is someone who commits a sexual offence, albeit that the categories of sexual offences may differ according to the purpose for which the classification is made. Although this may lead to anomalies and perhaps even injustice for certain individuals, these will be few and far between.

THE EXTENT OF THE PROBLEM

The 'dark figure' – problems of unreported and unrecorded crime

1.69   The portrayal of sexual offending in the media would suggest that sex offenders pose a huge threat to the personal safety of all members of a community and that the level of sexual offending has grown rapidly in recent years. Although it is true to say that criminal statistics show a general increase in the number of notifiable sexual offences recorded by the police in recent years, criminal statistics are of limited use in assessing the true extent of sexual offending. It is generally accepted that the number of crimes officially recorded in statistics compiled by the Home Office does not reflect the true extent of offending. This is due to the so-called 'dark figure' of unrecorded crime. There are many reasons why offences are never reported to the police in the first instance. In some circumstances, those involved, either as participants or as witnesses, may simply fail to realise that an offence has been committed. Some victims may not realise the criminal nature of the behaviour. In many circumstances, there will be no identifiable 'victim' and, even if the participants know an offence has been committed, they may have been willing parties to the offence, or they may take the view that the offending behaviour causes no harm. In other circumstances, the offence may not been seen as sufficiently serious to merit reporting, or the view may be taken that the police would not be interested, or would not be able to do anything much about it. Some people would rather deal with the matter themselves, or would not want the inconvenience of having to report the matter. Finally, offences may not be reported because of fear of reprisals.

1.70   Even when offences are brought to the attention of the police, there is no guarantee that all such offences will be officially recorded. The police have a discretion whether or not to take action. Offences may not be officially recorded because they are not seen as serious enough or because they are subsequently defined as involving 'no crime'. There may be economic or political reasons for not recording the crime or the police may not accept victims' accounts of incidents or feel that there is simply insufficient evidence to justify recording the incident as a crime. Therefore, there is an acknowledged discrepancy between officially recorded crime and the actual number of offences committed for every kind of offending behaviour.[1]

The 'dark figure' of sexual offences

1.71   The discrepancy between officially recorded crime and the actual number of offences committed is thought to be particularly acute in relation to sexual offences. The vast majority of sexual offences take place in private, with only the offender and victim present. In cases involving the sexual abuse of children, the victim will often not understand the nature of what has taken place and, especially in cases of intrafamilial abuse, simply will not realise that there is anything wrong or unusual in the behaviour. Even if the child does realise that an offence has been committed, the abuser often uses threats as a means of keeping the child silent. The problem is thought to be particularly acute when a child is in institutional care. The physical and sexual abuse of children in care has become a source of grave concern and cases of alleged abuse in care dating back to the 1960s are now being investigated in some areas.[2] In many cases, a child in institutional care will have no-one in whom to confide, but if the child does confide in a non-abusing carer, the matter is by no means certain to be reported to the police. Even if the non-abusing carer is prepared to take the matter further, an internal review may be carried out to determine whether a criminal or disciplinary offence has occurred before reporting the matter to the police,

---

1   See **2.1** for a discussion of the process of attrition after an offence has been reported to the police.

2   For example, 'Operation Goldfinch' involving police forces in South Wales, Gwent and Avon and Somerset (*Western Mail*, 6 November 1998); and *Lost in Care – Report of the Tribunal of Inquiry into the Abuse of Children in Care in the Former County Council Areas of Gwynedd and Clwyd since 1974* (The Stationery Office, London, 2000).

thereby hindering the collection of vital evidence.[1] It has been suggested that a legal requirement should be imposed on professionals to report all alleged cases of sexual abuse on children, akin to the system of mandatory reporting that exists in the USA. However, enforcement of such a duty would be problematic and evidence from the USA suggests that a system of mandatory reporting does little to decrease the 'dark figure' of sexual crimes against children.[2]

1.72 In cases where the offence is reported to the police, witnesses and corroborating evidence are rarely available. When the victim is older, because of the intimate nature of the many kinds of sexual offending, they may be too embarrassed or ashamed to report the incident. Fear of what may be required of them in any investigation and subsequent court proceedings may also deter many victims from reporting. It is generally accepted that sexual offences are particularly affected by the process of attrition[3] and the media frequently portray rape trials as degenerating into a test of the victim's credibility. Where the offence committed is a breach of sexual taboo, rather than an offence of sexual aggression, there will be no 'victim' in the usual sense of the word. The consenting participants to breaches of sexual taboo are unlikely to report the matter themselves and, unless the offending behaviour comes to the attention of a third party who decides to take action (such as the aggrieved father of a pregnant 14-year-old girl), it is unlikely that such offences will ever come to light.

Officially recorded sexual offences

1.73 In view of the acknowledged 'dark figure' of unrecorded crime, the number of sexual offences reported to the police in reality may well be the 'tip of the iceberg' and it would be unwise to place too much reliance on such figures in estimating the true prevalence of sexual offending. Nevertheless, officially recorded figures, both of reported crime and those cases which result in a formal caution or conviction, are important as the vast majority of measures aimed at controlling sex offenders can only be applied to those who come to the attention of the criminal justice system in the first place.[4] All 43 police forces in England and Wales are obliged to provide monthly crime returns to the Home Office. Such returns include 'notifiable' offences reported to the police, which they are required to notify to the Home Office for statistical purposes. The resulting statistics have been published annually since 1857.[5] The list of notifiable offences broadly covers the more serious offences and most indictable and triable either way offences are included. From April 1998, the number of notifiable sexual offences was widened to include, inter alia, offences of soliciting or importuning by a man and indecent exposure.

1.74 Notifiable sexual offences recorded by the police are:

---

1   *Speaking up for Justice: Report of the Interdepartmental Working Group on the Treatment of Vulnerable or Intimidated Witnesses in the Criminal Justice System* (Home Office, London, 1998).
2   See further Cobley *Child Abuse and the Law* (Cavendish Publishing Ltd, London, 1995) chap 2.
3   Croall *Crime and Society in Britain* (Longman, Harlow, 1998).
4   See further chaps 5 and 6.
5   With a break during period of 1939–45 (but grouped figures for this period were published in 1947).

(1)   buggery (which includes offences under ss 12 and 16 of the Sexual Offences Act 1956 [buggery and assault with intent to commit buggery] and offences under s 128(1) of the Mental Health Act 1959 as applied by s 1(4) of the Sexual Offences Act 1967 [by a male member of staff of a hospital or mental nursing home committing buggery or an act of gross indecency with a male patient or by a man committing buggery or an act of gross indecency with a mentally disordered male patient who is subject to his care]);

(2)   indecent assault on a male (s 15 of the Sexual Offences Act 1956);

(3)   indecency between males (s 13 of the Sexual Offences Act 1956);

(4)   rape (which includes offences under ss 1 and 7 of the Sexual Offences Act 1956 [rape of a woman or a man and unlawful sexual intercourse with a woman who is a defective] and offences under s 128(1) of the Mental Health Act 1959 [by a male member of staff of a hospital or mental nursing home having unlawful sexual intercourse with a female patient or by a man having unlawful sexual intercourse with a mentally disordered female patient who is subject to his care]);

(5)   indecent assault on a female (s 14 of the Sexual Offences Act 1956);

(6)   unlawful sexual intercourse with a girl under the age of 13 (s 5 of the Sexual Offences Act 1956);

(7)   unlawful sexual intercourse with a girl under the age of 16 (s 6 of the Sexual Offences Act 1956);

(8)   incest (which includes offences under ss 10 and 11 of the Sexual Offences Act 1956 [incest by a man and by a woman] and s 54 of the Criminal Law Act 1977 [inciting a girl under the age of 16 to have incestuous sexual intercourse]);

(9)   procuration (which includes offences under ss 2, 3 and 4 of the Sexual Offences Act 1956 [procuring a woman by threats, false pretences or using drugs to obtain or facilitate sexual intercourse], ss 25 and 26 of the Sexual Offences Act 1956 [householder permitting unlawful sexual intercourse with a girl under the age of 13 and under the age of 16], s 24 of the Sexual Offences Act 1956 [detention of a female in a brothel or other premises], s 28 of the Sexual Offences Act 1956 [person responsible for a girl under the age of 16 causing or encouraging her prostitution], s 29 of the Sexual Offences Act 1956 [causing or encouraging the prostitution of a female defective], s 13 of the Sexual Offences Act 1956 [procuring or being party to the commission by a man of an act of gross indecency with another man] and s 4 of the Sexual Offences Act 1967 [man procuring an act of buggery between two other men which by reason of s 1(1) of the Sexual Offences Act 1967 is not an offence]);

(10) abduction (which includes offences under s 17 of the Sexual Offences Act 1956 [abduction of a woman by force or for the sake of her property], ss 19 and 20 of the Sexual Offences Act 1956 [abduction of an unmarried girl under the age of 18 or under the age of 16 from the parent or guardian] and s 21 of the Sexual Offences Act 1956 [abduction of a female defective]);

(11) bigamy (s 57 of the Offences Against the Persons Act 1861);
(12) soliciting or importuning by a man (s 32 of the Sexual Offences Act 1956);
(13) gross indecency with a child (s 1 of the Indecency with Children Act 1960); and
(14) indecent exposure (common law and s 4 of the Vagrancy Act 1824).

1.75   In total, 5,234,211 notifiable offences were recorded by the 43 police forces in England and Wales in the 12-month period between October 1998 and September 1999,[1] which represents an overall increase of 2.2% over the number of offences recorded in the previous 12 months. The vast majority (83%) of these offences were property offences. Violent crimes (which include violence against the person, robbery and sexual offences) accounted for only 13% of all offences recorded during this period and only 6% of violent crimes were sexual offences. In total, 37,492 sexual offences were recorded. Sexual offences, therefore, account for less than 1% of all recorded crime. The number of sexual offences notified between October 1998 and September 1999 increased by 2.2%, which is less than the average increase during the last 10 years. However, the number of recorded rapes has more than doubled in the last 10 years. The limitations of official crime statistics have already been noted, but in comparing the number of offences reported to the police over a period of years, it should also be noted that the propensity of the public to report offences to the police also changes over time and, therefore, statistics recorded by the police may not accurately reflect the underlying trend in certain areas of crime.[2]

Estimating the true extent of offending – British Crime Surveys

1.76   Given the acknowledged limitations of the criminal statistics, various attempts have been made to investigate the true extent of offending by asking potential victims about their experience of crime, regardless of whether or not the incidents were reported to the police.[3] The most comprehensive survey of this nature is the British Crime Survey (BCS), which has been conducted seven times by the Home Office since 1982.[4] The BCS measures crimes against people living in private households in England and Wales by asking individuals aged 16 and over about their experience of victimisation in the previous year. The main purposes of the BCS are to provide an alternative measure of crime to offences recorded by the police, provide information on crime risks, provide a picture of the nature of crime and take up other crime-related issues. The BCS and police-recorded figures are seen as being complementary series which together provide a better picture of crime than can be obtained from either series alone. Whereas the police figures provide a good measure of trends in well-reported crimes, are an important indicator of police workload and can be used for local crime pattern analysis, for the crime type it covers the BCS is said to give a better reflection of the true extent of crime because it includes crimes which have not

---

1   Home Office Statistical Bulletin 1/00 *Recorded Crime Statistics, England and Wales, October 1998 to September 1999.*
2   See **2.2** for a discussion on the change in the pattern of rape reporting.
3   See, for example, Hall *Ask any Woman: A London Inquiry into Rape and Sexual Assault* (Falling Wall Press, Bristol, 1985).
4   The most recent BCS was conducted in 1998: HOSB 21/98 'The 1998 British Crime Survey'.

been reported to the police. The BCS is also said to provide a better indication of trends in crime, because it is unaffected by changes in levels of reporting to the police, and in police recording practice. The BCS undoubtedly has some advantages over statistics of notifiable offences recorded by the police. However, the measure of crime it produces is based on estimates from a sample of the population and, therefore, the estimates are subject to sampling error and other methodological limitations. The general advantages are limited as far as sexual offending is concerned. In the most recent survey, the number of sexual offences (defined to include the offences of rape, attempted rape and indecent assault) was so small that the results were thought to be too unreliable to report. Woundings with a sexual motive were simply included in the estimates for offences of violence. An additional shortcoming of the BCS is that it does not include crimes against those under the age of 16; therefore, the activities of paedophiles are excluded from the survey.

1.77 Direct comparisons between the finding of the BCS and criminal statistics are difficult because only 62% of all BCS crimes fall into categories which can be compared with police recorded crime. To allow comparisons, various adjustments are made to the recorded-crime figures, mainly to exclude those against non-domestic targets and children. Overall, the findings of the BCS indicate that, of all comparable BCS crimes, only 44% were said by their victims to have been reported to or become known to the police, and only about half of those were actually recorded by the police. Therefore, in total, only 24% of crimes against private individuals and their households end up in the recorded-crime count. The remaining 76% make up the 'dark figure' of crime. Furthermore, it is likely that sexual offences make up a considerable proportion of that 'dark figure'. The BCS found that theft of a car was reported to the police in 97% of cases and burglaries where something was stolen were reported in 85% of cases. Thus, offences against property are far more likely to be reported than offences against the person, and within the latter category, sexual offences are far less likely to be reported than other forms of assault or wounding. This should come as no surprise when one considers the obstacles in the way of reporting a sexual offence when compared with reporting a stolen car. Most car owners are insured against theft. It has been suggested[1] that owners of stolen cars will automatically report the theft because they are confident that, even if the police cannot trace the car, compensation will be forthcoming from the insurance company. Furthermore, in reporting the crime, no physical danger, guilt or social stigma is involved. Car owners are not physically or emotionally damaged by the theft and they can be confident that, if they have to go to court, which is unlikely, their words will not be twisted, their credibility will not be attacked and they will not be accused of fabricating the whole affair. Overall, victims of car theft can be confident that they will be treated with due respect and be compensated. The same cannot be said for victims of sexual offences. Thus, there is every likelihood that sexual offences constitute a substantially higher proportion of the 76% of unrecorded crime than other offences, particularly offences against property.

---

1   See Colledge 'The True Scale of the Problem' (1998) NLJ 148 (6846) 955.

Estimating the true extent of sexual offending

1.78 The shortcomings of criminal statistics and the BCS in relation to sexual offences has led to alternative methods of estimating the true extent of sexual offending. For example, in 1982, in what it claims to be the first of its kind in England, and in many respects, the first in the world, Women Against Rape (WAR) carried out an inquiry into rape and sexual assault in London.[1] The inquiry took the form of a survey designed to find out about, inter alia, the incidence and effects of rape and sexual assault. There were 2,000 question-naires distributed to a broad cross-section of London women and 1,236 were returned, giving a response rate of 62%. Altogether, including marital rape (which was not at the time a criminal offence), the inquiry concluded that two women in every five had experienced rape, attempted rape or another kind of sexual assault at least once. Although a legal definition of rape was given to the respondents, no guidance was given on the meaning of sexual assault and, thus, it is difficult to assess the kind of incidents which were reported as sexual assaults. However, even adopting a cautious interpretation of results, the inquiry supports the view that sexual offences are drastically under-reported and a large proportion of sexual offences never come to light. The inquiry also provided a useful insight into reporting rates. Although, when asked whether, if they were raped, they *would* report to the police, 76% of the women said they would, in reality only 8% of the women who had been raped reported the incident to the police. A higher reporting rate of 18% was found amongst those who had been sexually assaulted. At first sight, this seems surprising as it suggests that women are more likely to report the (usually) less serious offence of indecent assault than the more serious offence of rape. However, this can be explained by the fact that just over half of the sexual assaults were by strangers, whereas under a quarter of the rapes were by strangers. The inquiry found that, where the rape or sexual assault had been committed by a stranger, the reporting rate was 31%, whereas in cases where the assailant was known to the woman, the reporting rate was only 5%. Thus, women are far more likely to report an attack by a stranger than an attack by someone they know. Overall, it can be stated with confidence that the reluctance of the victim of a sexual offence to report the incident to the police is clearly a major factor contributing to the 'dark figure' of sexual offending.

The problem of child sexual abuse

1.79 The problem of estimating the true extent of sexual offending is particularly acute when the victim of the offence is a child. Child sexual abuse has generated such public and professional interest in recent years that attempts have been made to establish the true extent of the problem. It is now acknowledged that children are far more likely to be the victims of a sexual offence than previously thought. In the inquiry carried out by WAR, of those who admitted to being the victims of rape or sexual assault, 27% said the offence had happened first when they were aged 12 or under, 42% when they were 15 or under and overall 63% had had their first (or only) such experience as children

---

1   Hall *Ask Any Woman: A London Inquiry into Rape and Sexual Assault* (Falling Wall Press, Bristol, 1985).

or teenagers. Criminal statistics are of little assistance in estimating the prevalence of child sexual abuse as, in addition to the general limitations associated with unreported crime, the statistics do not always reveal the age of the victim. Unlawful sexual intercourse with a girl under the age of 16 and under the age of 13, gross indecency with a child under the age of 14 and offences involving indecent photographs of children under the age of 16 are the only recorded sexual offences where the age of the victim is an essential component of the offence itself. Individual police forces do, however, record information about the age of sexual offence victims, although this is not analysed centrally, or even routinely collated, beyond force level. Research conducted for the Home Office concludes that official statistics not only underestimate greatly the number of sexual offences against children, they also have the potential to mislead in terms of patterns of sexual crime.[1]

1.80   Therefore, alternative means have been sought, usually by surveying a sample of the adult population and questioning them about any inappropriate sexual behaviour that occurred during their childhood. Such surveys have obvious limitations. As the subject matter is a sensitive, personal topic, the questions must be restricted to the adult population only, referring, as a general rule, to the adult's experience during childhood. It is inevitable that a person's perceptions of events in the past will change over a period of time, and many respondents will be unwilling to admit to a comparative stranger that such abuse has occurred. These limitations must be borne in mind when reviewing the results of such surveys.

1.81   One of the first attempts to establish the extent of child sexual abuse in the UK was made in 1981.[2] A postal survey of 1,599 GPs, paediatricians, child psychiatrists and police surgeons was carried out, requesting details of the number of sexually abused children seen during the target year, designated as 1 June 1977 to 31 May 1978. No one definition was used, but sexual abuse was defined in three ways: a battered child whose injuries were primarily in the genital area, a child who had experienced attempted or actual intercourse or other inappropriate genital contact with an adult and a child who had been inappropriately involved with an adult in sexual activities not covered by the first two categories. A child was defined as a person under 16 years of age, and only sexual abuse by adults was included in the study. The response rate, at 39%, was not high. Even so, the total number of cases seen in the target year was 1,072, the largest number (874) being seen by police surgeons. Based on these figures, the authors suggested an annual incidence of 1,500 cases, or 1 in 6,000 children affected. Subsequent studies show this to be a very conservative estimate, arguably because insufficient account was taken of the 'dark figure' of unreported cases. Further research was carried out in the UK during the period 1982–84.[3] Overall, 48% of respondents had experienced some degree of sexual contact with an adult during their childhood. However, the research definition of sexual abuse was very wide, including verbal suggestions, obscene phone calls and 'flashers', and in 19% of the cases reported there was only a single incident

---

1   Grubin *Sex Offending Against Children: Understanding the Risk*, Police Research Series Paper 99 (Home Office, London, 1998) p 5.

2   Mrazek et al *Sexually Abused Children and their Families* (Pergamon, Oxford, 1981) p 35.

3   West *Sexual Victimisation* (Gower, Aldershot, 1985).

of abuse. This would suggest that the figure of 48% is, perhaps, too high to reflect the true prevalence of the problem. The first attempt to establish a national prevalence rate was made in 1986.[1] The authors collaborated with Market and Opinion Research International (MORI) to produce a nationally representative sample of the population. Those interviewed were aged 15 years and over. The definition of child sexual abuse was given as:

> 'A child (anyone under 16 years) is sexually abused when another person, who is sexually mature, involves the child in activity which the other person expects to lead to their sexual arousal. This might involve intercourse, touching, exposure of the sexual organs, showing pornographic material or talking about sexual things in an erotic way.'

Of the 2,019 respondents, 206 (10%) reported sexual abuse as defined.

1.82   More extensive research has been carried out in the USA, but it has been suggested that until US studies have been repeated in the UK, it would be unwise to assume that they hold for the UK's society, which differs from that of the USA in many ways.[2] However, bearing this in mind, US research has consistently suggested higher rates of abuse than that reported in the UK. For example, one study found a prevalence rate of 38% amongst a random sample of 930 women aged 18 years and over in San Francisco.[3] Thus, it seems that a 10% prevalence of child sexual abuse in the UK is a conservative estimate. Using this figure of 10%, it has been estimated that over 4.5 million adults (15 years of age and over) in this country will have been sexually abused as children, and a potential 1,117,000 children will be sexually abused before they are 15 years of age. An estimated 143,000 of these will be abused within the family.[4]

1.83   Although there is nothing to suggest that the actual number of sexual offences being committed has risen dramatically in recent years, the statistics are certainly a cause for concern. Calculating the 'dark figure' of unreported sexual offences accurately may well be impossible, particularly in relation to offending against children. Indeed, it has been suggested that any attempt to arrive at a realistic estimate of the actual rate of child sexual abuse in England and Wales has to rely on assumptions, guesswork, and a bit of putting one's finger to the wind.[5]

1.84   Despite these difficulties, there is more than enough evidence to suggest that many sex offenders are living freely within our communities and can offend, perhaps time and time again, safe in the knowledge that they are unlikely to be brought to justice. They may form only a minority of offenders in general but, bearing in mind the potentially devastating effect of such crimes on the

---

1   Baker and Duncan 'Child Sexual Abuse: A Study of Prevalence in Great Britain' (1985) *Child Abuse and Neglect* vol 9 457.
2   La Fontaine *Child Sexual Abuse* ESRC Research Briefing (1988) p 2.
3   Baker and Duncan 'Child Sexual Abuse: A Study of Prevalence in Great Britain' (1985) *Child Abuse and Neglect* vol 9 457 at 462.
4   Baker and Duncan 'Child Sexual Abuse: A Study of Prevalence in Great Britain' (1985) *Child Abuse and Neglect* vol 9 457.
5   Grubin *Sex Offending Against Children: Understanding the Risk*, Police Research Series Paper 99 (Home Office, London, 1998) p 11.

victim, the current trend to focus the spotlight on sex offenders is under-standable. The danger is that, once the spotlight is focused and sex offenders increasingly become seen as modern folk devils, 'knee jerk' reactions follow, both in the form of the public's reaction to sex offenders in their midst and hastily passed, ill-thought-out legislation in response to the public reaction. The task society as a whole now faces is to ensure that its response to sex offenders balances the rights of offenders against the needs of victims, the demands for more effective measures to protect the public and the sometimes conflicting demands of punishment and rehabilitation.

Chapter 2

THE PRE-TRIAL PROCESS

REPORTING TO THE POLICE

The process of attrition

2.1   Although it is impossible to calculate the extent of sexual offending with
any precision due to the 'dark figure' of unreported and unrecorded crime, it is
generally acknowledged that only a small percentage of sexual offences are ever
reported to the police. Yet, even once an offence is reported, there are still often
many hurdles that have to be overcome before the perpetrator is convicted in a
criminal court. Research has identified four major points in the process from
reporting to conviction at which cases are excluded from the criminal justice
system.[1] First, the police may fail to record the reported incident as a crime. Even
if initially recorded as a crime, the police may subsequently 'no-crime' the case,
for example in a rape case, Home Office guidance advises that the police may
no-crime a case where the complainant 'retracts completely and admits to
fabrication'.[2] Secondly, the police investigation may fail to find enough evidence
to justify charging a suspect and passing the case to the Crown Prosecution
Service (CPS) and so no further action will be taken. Thirdly, the CPS may decide
not to proceed or to reduce the charge through plea bargaining. Finally, if the
case reaches court, the offender may be acquitted.[3] Many cases will fail at one of
these hurdles and the attrition rate for sexual offences recorded by the police
and those which result in a conviction or caution is high. For example, in recent
years the number of sexual offences recorded by the police over a 12-month
period has been approximately 37,000.[4] Yet in 1998 less than 6,400 offenders
were found guilty or cautioned for a sexual offence.[5] The process of attrition is
perhaps best illustrated by the statistics for rape cases. A Home Office research
study of 500 incidents originally recorded as rape by the police in 1996 found
that:[6]

(1) 25% were no-crimed by the police;
(2) no suspect was identified in 11%;

---

1   Lees and Gregory *Rape and Sexual Assault: A Study of Attrition – Multi-agency Investigation into
       The Problem of Rape and Sexual Assault in the Borough of Islington* (Islington Council, London,
       1993).
2   Home Office Circular 69/1986.
3   Lees *Carnal Knowledge: Rape on Trial* (Penguin, London, 1997) p 96.
4   In the period October 1997 to September 1998, 36,690 sexual offences were recorded by
       the police. In the period October 1998 to September 1999 this number had risen to 37,492.
       Home Office Statistical Bulletin 1/00 *Recorded Crime Statistics, England and Wales, October
       1998 to September 1999.*
5   Home Office Statistical Bulletin 21/99 *Cautions, Court Proceedings and Sentencing, England and
       Wales 1998.*
6   *A Question of Evidence? Investigating and Prosecuting Rape in the 1990s* Home Office Research
       Study 196 (Home Office, London, 1999).

(3)   the police took no further action against the suspects in 31%;
(4)   8% were discontinued by the CPS;
(5)   7% resulted in an acquittal or the case to lie on file;
(6)   7% resulted in a conviction for an offence other than rape;
(7)   6% resulted in a conviction for rape.[1]

Rape – a change in the pattern of reporting

2.2   Although the number of notifiable sexual offences recorded by the police has risen at a similar rate to recorded crime as whole (about 3% a year since 1986), the number of rapes recorded by the police has increased at a far higher rate. In 1986, a total of 2,288 rapes were recorded by the police. Between April 1998 and March 1999, the number had risen to 7,636, which included 504 male victims. Such an increase can be attributed in part to changes in the legal definition of rape, such as the removal of the marital immunity of rape and the extension of rape to include male victims.[2] However, the extended definition of rape is unlikely, in itself, to explain the increased levels of reporting. More likely explanations would appear to be the changes in public attitudes to rape and the increasingly sympathetic treatment now being accorded to rape complainants by the police.[3] In the 1970s, a rape victim reporting the offence at a police station was often treated with suspicion and subjected to interrogation by male police officers. Indeed, anecdotal evidence suggests that police officers tended to develop their own 'techniques' for determining the credibility of the complainant. These included such tactics as making the complainant of an alleged recent attack sit on a hard chair throughout the initial interview, then conclude that 'she couldn't possibly have been raped recently if she could sit on that hard chair without visible discomfort'. In 1982, the BBC television series 'Police' screened a live investigation of a woman reporting rape. The ordeal the woman was subjected to by the police caused public outrage which led to the Home Office issuing a circular calling for improved police training to deal with rape and sexual assault, the appointment of more women police surgeons and the provision of better facilities for the medical examination of women who had been attacked.[4] Overall, police treatment of victims of serious sexual offences has improved dramatically in recent years and this change in attitude has undoubtedly been a major factor contributing to the increase in the number of reported rapes.

The changing nature of rape cases

2.3   There has also been a significant change in the nature of rape cases recorded by the police in recent years. A Home Office research study examined nearly 500 incidents initially recorded as rape by the police in 1996 and followed

---

1   As recorded figures do not include no-crimes, the figure of 6% of the initial sample of cases reported to the police represents 9% of crimed rapes, which is a similar figure to that recorded in the National Statistics.
2   See **1.11**.
3   *Speaking up for Justice: Report of the Interdepartmental Working Group on the Treatment of Vulnerable or Intimidated Witnesses in the Criminal Justice System* (Home Office, London, 1998).
4   Home Office Circular 69/86 *Violence Against Women.*

their progress through the criminal justice system.[1] Some comparisons were possible with an earlier study of the Home Office, which drew on 1985 rape cases.[2] The 1996 study found that, whereas the number of recorded rapes had risen approximately three-fold between 1985 and 1996, the actual number of stranger rapes had not changed significantly. The increase in recorded rapes was found to be attributable to a substantial increase in the number of acquaintance[3] and intimate rapes.[4] The changing nature of rape cases goes some way towards explaining the change in conviction rates for rape, which have decreased sharply in recent years – from 24% in 1985 to 9% in 1996. The 1996 study found that cases involving acquaintances and intimates were most likely to be no-crimed, for no further action to be taken by the police, or to be discontinued by the CPS and that, in the minority of stranger rape cases where the suspect was identified, the case was more likely to proceed to court than in those cases where the complainant and suspect were previously acquainted.

PROBLEMS OF INVESTIGATING SEXUAL OFFENCES

2.4   Once a sexual offence has been reported to the police, there exist two main areas of difficulty which are said to be unique to the investigation of sexual offences: false reporting and withdrawal of complaints after report, and the question of consent.[5]

False reporting and the withdrawal of complaints

2.5   Given the acknowledged reluctance on the part of victims to report sexual offences to the police, the suggestion that some reports are false at first sight appears to be anomalous. However, for many years the evidence of a victim of a sexual offence was treated with suspicion, both by the police and the courts. In 1984, the Criminal Law Revision Committee noted that by no means every accusation of rape is true.[6] An analysis of reports of rape received by Scotland Yard in 1990 revealed that in 28% of the incidents listed as 'no crimes', the report was admitted to be false or withdrawn, in 13% the victim refused, was unwilling, or failed to substantiate the allegation and in another 13% the police believed that they had evidence that the allegation was false.[7] However, in the absence of a more detailed study into why the victim withdrew or in some way failed to

---

1   *A Question of Evidence? Investigating and Prosecuting Rape in the 1990s* Home Office Research Study 196 (Home Office, London, 1999).

2   *Rape: from Recording to Conviction* Research and Planning Unit Paper 71 (Home Office, London, 1992).

3   Acquaintance cases were those where the complainant and suspect were casually known to each other, for example the complainant had accepted a lift from the suspect, they had a prostitute and client relationship or they had met at a party.

4   Intimate rapes covered those where the suspect was having, or had had a relationship with the complainant, was a friend or was a member of her family – such cases often involved children.

5   Blair *Investigating Rape: A New Approach for the Police* (Croom Helm, London, in association with the Police Foundation, 1985).

6   *Fifteenth Report: Sexual Offences* (1984) Cmnd 9213 (HMSO, London) para 2.7.

7   (1991) *The Independent*, 14 February.

substantiate the allegation, it would be unwise to draw too many conclusions from these figures. Although it is commonly assumed that a victim who retracts a complaint was lying when the complaint was made, there may be other explanations. In cases where the perpetrator is known to the victim, a complaint may be withdrawn as a result of pressure from the perpetrator. Alternatively, if the victim's complaint is met with disbelief in the first instance, the victim may withdraw the complaint to avoid further challenge, or simply because of a realisation of what will be required from her as a witness if a prosecution proceeds.

2.6 Although complaints will usually be withdrawn at a comparatively early stage in the investigation, a complainant may decide not to co-operate with the criminal justice process at a late stage. A late withdrawal can have serious implications, not only because of the potential to cause considerable stress to the alleged offender, the alleged victim and any other witnesses, but also because of the question of financial costs. In December 1999 a man was acquitted of rape after his alleged victim refused to give evidence at his trial.[1] The alleged victim, who had gone back to her home in Florida and refused to return, had apparently been under the misapprehension that her written statement could be read to the court. The trial left the taxpayer with a bill of £100,000 for legal costs. No order for costs could be made against the alleged victim as she was not a party to the proceedings for these purposes, although the trial judge commented that he sometimes wished a judge did have power to make such an order. Limited information was available in this case as to why the complainant refused to proceed with the prosecution. If it could be established that the refusal was attributable to a genuine fear of giving evidence in court, a fear that is now acknowledged and is being addressed by changes to procedures in court,[2] it would be entirely inappropriate to consider the exercise of any such power.

2.7 Despite such explanations for withdrawn complaints, there is thought to be a widely held belief amongst the police that many reports of sexual crime are false and mendacious.[3] Suggestions have even been made that between 50% and 70% of all allegations of rape are false,[4] and police officers themselves have suggested that the majority of complaints of rape are unfounded,[5] although there appears to be no credible basis for such claims. Certainly, if an allegation of rape is later proved to be false, severe consequences can follow for all concerned, even if a complaint is not made to the police. In February 2000, following a successful High Court defamation action, Lynn Walker was ordered to pay damages of £400,000 to a former colleague against whom she had made an allegation of rape to their employer.[6] In November 1999, a 19-year-old girl who claimed that her former boyfriend raped her and later threatened her with a knife was sentenced to 6 months' imprisonment by Winchester Crown Court.[7] The couple had lived together for 2 years, but shortly after the relationship broke up, the girl told a friend that he had raped her and made a detailed statement to

1 (1999) *The Times*, 14 December.
2 See chap 3.
3 Sampson *Acts of Abuse* (Routledge, London, 1994) p 31.
4 Blair *Investigating Rape: A New Approach for the Police* (Croom Helm, London, in association with the Police Foundation, 1985) p 54.
5 Birch 'Corroboration in Criminal Trials' [1990] Crim LR 667 at 679.
6 Referred to in an article in *The Times*, 8 February 2000.
7 (1999) *The Times*, 3 November.

the police, as a result of which the alleged offender was arrested and held by police for 17 hours before being released on bail. The girl then complained that he had threatened her with a knife and he was rearrested, but the following month she admitted to police that both allegations were false and that she had made them up as revenge for the way she had been treated. Such malicious reporting of rape does little to encourage the police to believe genuine complainants, but instances of such deliberate false reporting are not thought to be common and criminal prosecutions for wasting police time or, more seriously, attempting to pervert the course of justice arising out of such reports are comparatively rare. The change in the pattern of reporting and the recording of rape offences by the police in recent years suggests a change in attitude and it is hoped that the 'culture of disbelief' that certainly operated amongst police officers in the past is now being replaced by a willingness to believe and support the victim of a sexual offence.

2.8 In the past, Parliament and the courts have also lent support to the view that the evidence of a victim of a sexual offence is to be treated with suspicion. In cases involving statutory procuration offences,[1] the Sexual Offences Act 1956 specifically provided that no person could be convicted of any such offence upon the evidence of one witness, unless the witness was corroborated in some material particular by evidence implicating the accused. Procuration offences were said to belong to a class of charges which were easy to make and difficult to rebut.[2] In the case of other sexual offences, for many years it was the practice of the court in a criminal trial to warn the jury of the danger of convicting the accused on the uncorroborated evidence of the victim.[3] Although the requirement to warn was equally applicable to male and female complainants, the majority of complainants were women and the justification was said to be that the complainant may have made a false allegation 'owing to neurosis, jealousy, fantasy, spite or a girl's refusal to admit that she consented to an act of which she is now ashamed'.[4] In more recent times, the corroboration requirements and the implied assertion that women tended to fabricate allegations of sexual offences have been seen as something of an insult to women and have been described as 'an unholy relic of the bygone days when it could be intellectually respectable to argue that women were less objective, accurate or honest witnesses than men'.[5] Following the recommendations of the Law Commission,[6] s 33 of the Criminal Justice and Public Order Act 1994 repealed the statutory requirement for corroboration in procuration offences and s 32 of the Act abrogated the requirement to give a corroboration warning for all other sexual offences. Thus, the tendency to disbelieve victims of sexual offences is diminishing. Sufficient hurdles remain within the criminal justice system to ensure that false allegations are filtered out at an early stage.

---

1   Sexual Offences Act 1956, ss 2–4, 22 and 23.
2   Tapper *Cross on Evidence* (Butterworths, London, sixth edition, 1985).
3   *R v Jones* (1925) 19 Cr App R 40, *R v Freebody* (1935) 25 Cr App R 69.
4   Criminal Law Revision Committee, *Eleventh Report: Evidence (General)* (1972) Cmnd 4991, para 186.
5   Wasik and Taylor *Blackstone's Guide to the Criminal Justice and Public Order Act 1994* (Blackstone Press Ltd, London, 1995) p 47.
6   (1991) Cmnd 1620, Law Com No 202.

Consent

2.9   The issue of consent is often one of the greatest problems in investigating sexual offences. If the offence reported is one of sexual aggression, the absence of consent by the victim will be an essential element of the offence. The definition of rape requires that the sexual intercourse takes place without the consent of the victim and it is clear that the prosecution must prove that the victim did not consent.[1] Indecent assault requires the application, or causing the victim to apprehend the immediate application, of 'unlawful' personal violence. The word 'unlawful' is generally taken to mean without the consent of the victim, thus making absence of consent an essential element of the offence itself.[2] An alternative view holds that consent is a defence to a charge of indecent assault,[3] which would mean that the defence would be obliged to introduce evidence of absence of consent. Although the distinction is fundamental to legal theory, the importance of its practical application is limited as, in either case, the ultimate burden of proving the absence of consent rests with the prosecution.

2.10   When a victim first reports an offence of sexual aggression to the police, the investigating police officers will be only too aware of the need to prove absence of consent. In cases involving violent assaults and rapes by strangers, the main evidential problems are likely to be identification of the perpetrator and proving that the alleged assault or intercourse actually took place. In such cases, the issue of consent is unlikely to be problematic. However, many incidents of rape and indecent assault do not present themselves with the outward signs which police officers expect to see before they are convinced that an assault has taken place.[4] In particular, in cases where the victim and perpetrator either knew each other before the time of the offence or spent some time in each other's company before its commission, either as acquaintances or intimates, consent is likely to be a contentious issue and it has been suggested that a claim of consent will be raised by the defendant in the majority of such cases.[5] The 1996 Home Office study of rape cases found that in more than half of the cases where information about the defence deployed by the suspect was available, the main defence relied upon was consent and in only 25% of cases did the suspect totally deny the offence.[6] However, this should not be taken to indicate that violence and injuries are more likely to be inflicted by strangers. In one study, 71% of stranger rapists used physical pressure against the victim, as against 67% of acquaintance rapists.[7] However, the same study found that acquaintance rapists were slightly more likely to injure their victims. Twenty-one per cent of

---

1   *Larter v Castleton* [1995] Crim LR 75. The issue of consent is being considered by the Sex Offences Review, set up by the Government to review the substantive criminal law in relation to sexual offences. See **1.45**.
2   Smith *Smith and Hogan on Criminal Law* 8th Edn (Butterworths, London, 1996) p 418.
3   See the views of Lord Jauncey in *R v Brown* [1993] 2 All ER 75.
4   Chambers and Miller *Investigating Sexual Assault* Scottish Office Social Research Study (HMSO, Edinburgh, 1983).
5   Blair *Investigating Rape: A New Approach for the Police* (Croom Helm, London, in association with the Police Foundation, 1985) p 62.
6   *A Question of Evidence? Investigating and Prosecuting Rape in the 1990s* Home Office Research Study 196 (Home Office, London, 1999).
7   Lees *Carnal Knowledge: Rape on Trial* (Penguin, London, 1996). For these purposes, no distinction is made between acquaintances and intimates. See **2.3**.

acquaintance rapists beat, punched or kicked the woman as against 9% for stranger rapists, 11% of acquaintance rapists harmed the victim with a weapon, as against 9% for stranger rapists and 11% of women raped by an acquaintance were left with serious cuts and wounds, as against 7% for stranger rapists. Many victims of offences of sexual aggression will not, therefore, present with the physical injuries which are generally seen as being indicative of a non-consensual attack. In the absence of such injuries, the police must look elsewhere for evidence to support the victim's side of the story.

2.11　Traditionally, the police have tended to focus solely on the complainant's behaviour, paying little or no attention to the behaviour of the defendant. This resulted in what has been described as a 'noticeable failure to formulate the issue of consent in bipartisan terms, that is as one which also imposed certain obligations on the [defendant] prior to intercourse'.[1] Research in the USA in the 1980s found that new police training techniques involved encouraging police officers to move the focus of their investigations from the rape itself to the surrounding circumstances and to divide those circumstances into five areas: initial contact; coercive efforts; intimidation; rape; and report.[2] Attention was also given to the movements of the complainant and accused before and after the rape, and the manner in which those movements may indicate coercion and intimidation. This enabled the police officers to concentrate on proving that the victim had not consented, and also on obtaining evidence about the behaviour of the perpetrator to determine whether or not consent had been sought. Such an approach not only tends to reduce the stress commonly felt by the complainant, who often feels as if she is being interrogated by the police as to her own conduct, but it also undoubtedly increases the prospect of a successful conviction. If a perpetrator alleges that the complainant consented, not only will the prosecution need to establish that she did not in fact consent, but also that the defendant either knew she was not consenting, or was reckless, in that he was aware of the risk that she was not consenting.[3]

GATHERING EVIDENCE FROM THE VICTIM

Medical examinations

2.12　The objective of a medical examination is to obtain evidence from the victim by noting any injuries sustained and by collecting evidence for forensic examination. A medical examination of the victim, carried out by a police surgeon, is therefore routine when the offence has been reported within sufficient time of its commission for some physical evidence to be collected for forensic examination or for injuries allegedly sustained as a result of the offence to still be apparent. However, one research study found that the police often take the view that it is necessary to conduct a medical examination of complainants

---

1　Chambers and Miller *Investigating Sexual Assault* Scottish Office Social Research Study (HMSO, Edinburgh, 1983) p 92.

2　Blair *Investigating Rape: A New Approach for the Police* (Croom Helm, London, in association with the Police Foundation, 1985) p 63.

3　*R v Satnam* (1983) 78 Cr App R 149, *R v Savage*; *DPP v Parmenter* [1991] 4 All ER 698.

who allege sexual offences in order the ascertain whether their allegations have sufficient merit to warrant further investigation. Thus, the police are using the medical examination to test whether allegations of sexual assault have any merit, without first interviewing the complainant, and this was said to be source of friction between the police and some police surgeons.[1]

2.13   An additional concern is that this allows the opinion of the police surgeon to influence the police perception of the case. It has been pointed out that, given the authority of the medical profession, the opinions of doctors may well carry considerable weight with police officers.[2] Whilst this may be justified if the opinion of the police surgeon is based solely on medical evidence, it seems that in some cases, the police surgeon will convey to the police his or her opinion of the victim's credibility. Research has found that, in at least one area of the country, police surgeons tended for the most part to be judgmental, not to say punitive, in their attitude to many women who reported rape and would convey their scepticism to the police officers involved in the investigation.[3] If a police surgeon tells the investigating police officer 'It's all a load of rubbish ...', as one police surgeon admitted she may do,[4] this will inevitably influence the officer's perception of the case and, thus, could change the whole tenor of the investigation.

2.14   Criticisms have also been made in the past that medical examinations have been carried out badly, losing vital evidence, and it has been suggested that this may be due partly to lack of collaboration between the investigating officers and police surgeons.[5] The medical examination will invariably be a traumatic event for the victim. In recent years, it has been recognised that efforts must be made to reduce the trauma experienced by the victim, whilst at the same time ensuring that forensic evidence, which may be vital to a successful prosecution, is not lost. Complaints about the conduct of medical examinations led to a number of responses in the 1980s. In 1983, the Home Office issued a circular[6] which emphasised the importance of allowing complainants to wash and change as soon as possible. The Metropolitan police set up a working party, which led to special arrangements for screening victims for sexually transmitted diseases, recruitment of more female doctors to conduct the examination and the creation of examination suites. Following this, the Home Office issued another circular in 1986, highlighting the need to recruit more female police surgeons,

---

1   Roberts and Willmore *The Role of Forensic Science Evidence in Criminal Proceedings* Research
     Study No 11, Royal Commission on Criminal Justice (HMSO, London, 1993).
2   Temkin 'Medical Evidence in Rape Cases: A Continuing Problem for Criminal Justice'
     [1998] 61 *Modern Law Review* 821 at 843.
3   Temkin 'Medical Evidence in Rape Cases: A Continuing Problem for Criminal Justice'
     [1998] 61 *Modern Law Review* 821. The research study was based on in-depth interviews with
     10 police surgeons in the Metropolitan Police area and Sussex. The doctors in Sussex were
     found to be judgmental in their views, but most London doctors had diametrically opposite
     views to their Sussex counterparts.
4   Temkin 'Medical Evidence in Rape Cases: A Continuing Problem for Criminal Justice'
     [1998] 61 *Modern Law Review* 821 at 843.
5   *Speaking up for Justice: Report of the Interdepartmental Working Group on the Treatment of
     Vulnerable or Intimidated Witnesses in the Criminal Justice System* (Home Office, London, 1998)
     p 170.
6   Home Office Circular 1983/23.

the value of special victim examination suites and the need to provide complainants with more information.[1] Most police forces now have rape examination suites, although they may not necessarily be available in isolated rural areas. Whilst the availability of such suites is a positive improvement, in practice, concerns have been raised about the housekeeping and facilities provided by the suites.[2] In addition, it seems that some police surgeons avoid using these suites, preferring to use their own surgeries.[3]

2.15 Improvements have been made in the past decade, although there is still room for further improvement. In particular, the following recommendations have been made.[4]

(1) More female doctors should be recruited. Female doctors may not always handle a medical sensitively, but victims should have a choice about who conducts the medical. The suitability of doctors for this type of work needs to be vetted carefully. Ensuring the availability of suitable doctors may require reconsidering the way such work is funded. At present, in most police forces, fees are only paid for each examination conducted: paying an additional fee for doctors to be exclusively available over a set period might improve the availability of doctors.

(2) Doctors' training should cover rape trauma syndrome and counselling techniques. Such training should also challenge prejudicial and stereotypical assumptions about rape and the women who complain of it. Questioning by doctors should also be minimised by greater collaboration with the investigating officer. This will help to avoid the victim being upset by having to retell her story, and also avoid possible problems at trial by having too many accounts of the same events.

(3) The ethical dimension of the issue of consent of the victim to the examination should be emphasised in training, together with the victim's right to make her own informed choice as to the information she discloses. Research has found that some doctors obtain a great deal of information from victims, which may ultimately be disclosed, providing the defence with authoritative and otherwise mostly unavailable information which, although irrelevant in most cases to the legal issues, provides strong ammunition with which to discredit the victim. This issue should be addressed in guidelines or a code of practice.

(4) Some procedures should be eliminated. For example routine plucking of pubic hair for DNA tests is unnecessary and upsetting for victims (DNA can be obtained from blood and if a hair sample is needed it could be taken at a later date).

---

1   Home Office Circular 1986/69.
2   Temkin 'Medical Evidence in Rape Cases: A Continuing Problem for Criminal Justice' [1998] 61 *Modern Law Review* 821 at 829.
3   Temkin 'Medical Evidence in Rape Cases: A Continuing Problem for Criminal Justice' [1998] 61 *Modern Law Review* 821 at 828.
4   See the recommendations contained in *Speaking up for Justice: Report of the Interdepartmental Working Group on the Treatment of Vulnerable or Intimidated Witnesses in the Criminal Justice System* (Home Office, London, 1998) p 171 and Temkin 'Medical Evidence in Rape Cases: A Continuing Problem for Criminal Justice' [1998] 61 *Modern Law Review* 821.

2.16   The evidence obtained from a medical examination can be crucial to a successful prosecution, not only in that samples taken for forensic analysis may ultimately identify an offender, but also for the recording of any injuries sustained by the victim. Although advances have undoubtedly been made in recent years, there is still room for improvement. It has been suggested that in practice, due to budgetary constraints, many of the samples taken during the medical examination are not sent for forensic examination until the police know whether a prosecution is to proceed and that this delay results in samples being lost or destroyed.[1] The Home Office study of rape cases reported to the police in 1996 found that cases in which there was evidence of violence were often dropped and concluded that there appeared to be scope for better evidence gathering, for example, through photographs and medical reports, and for ensuring that such evidence is given due weight in later discussions.[2] Clearly, these are issues that need to be addressed.

The unknown offender

2.17   Statistics indicate that approximately 25,000 of the notifiable sexual offences recorded by the police each year do not result in a conviction or formal caution.[3] Given this high attrition rate, it may be thought that many of these cases do not proceed because the offender cannot be identified. However, between April 1998 and March 1999 68% of the notifiable sexual offences recorded were 'cleared up'.[4] An offence is categorised as being 'cleared up' if a person has been charged, summonsed or cautioned for the offence, or if the offence is admitted by the offender and taken into consideration by the court in other proceedings. An offence will also be categorised as being 'cleared up' in certain circumstances where no further action is taken, for example if the offence is admitted during a prison interview where the offender is already serving a long custodial sentence for other offences or in other circumstances, such as the offender being below the age of criminal responsibility or the victim being unable to give evidence. Thus, an offence will only be 'cleared up' where the offender has been identified, which leads to the conclusion that no offender is identified or there is insufficient evidence to justify charging a suspected offender in 32% of sex offences notified to the police (approximately 10,000 cases each year). Whilst the clear-up rate for sexual offences compares favourably with the overall clear-up rate for notified offences (which was 29.2% in 1998–99), the clear-up rate for rape offences is low in comparison with other serious offences. For example, in 1998–99 the clear up rate for homicide was 94.7% and the rate for

---

1   Temkin 'Medical Evidence in Rape Cases: A Continuing Problem for Criminal Justice' [1998] 61 *Modern Law Review* 821 at 835.

2   *A Question of Evidence? Investigating and Prosecuting Rape in the 1990s* Home Office Research Study 196 (Home Office, London, 1999).

3   Precise calculation is difficult, as many of the actual cases which are recorded as resulting in a conviction or formal caution in each year will actually have been recorded as notifiable offences in the previous year.

4   Home Office Statistical Bulletin 18/99. Statistics on the offences cleared up are not provided in Statistical Bulletin 1/00, which covers the period October 1998 to September 1999.

violence against the person (excluding sexual offences) was 71.2%. However, over the same period the clear-up rate for rape was 64% – the lowest since 1986.[1]

Identification of the unknown offender[2]

DNA AND FINGERPRINTS

2.18   In recent years, the most significant advance in identifying an unknown sexual offender has been the development of DNA profiling.[3] However, a DNA profile of the offender must be available to the police in order for an identification to be made in this way. Although the DNA database is increasing in size annually, if an offender has never previously been the subject of a police investigation, DNA cannot be used to identify an unknown offender. Similar considerations apply to fingerprints as a means of identification. A sex offender may leave fingerprint evidence at the scene of the crime, but if the police have no record of the offender's fingerprints, this evidence alone will not result in the identification of an unknown offender.

'INFORMAL' IDENTIFICATION

2.19   In all cases where the identity of the offender is not known, one of the first pieces of information that will be sought from the victim of the offence and any witness who may be able to identify the perpetrator will be a description of the perpetrator. A record must be made of this description as first given by a potential witness,[4] a copy of which must be provided to the suspect or his solicitor before any formal identification procedures are carried out at a later stage in the investigation.[5] If an offence is reported to the police soon after its commission and there is reason to believe that the offender may still be in the immediate vicinity, the victim or any potential witness may be taken by a police officer to the area in which the crime was committed to see whether an identification can be made.[6] Although this does not amount to a formal identification, the safeguards against contaminated evidence should be borne in mind.[7]

IDENTIKIT PICTURES

2.20   In the early stages of an investigation, a police artist may work with the victim and any witnesses to construct an identikit picture of the perpetrator. This picture may then be circulated, possibly nationally, in an effort to identify the perpetrator.

---

1   Home Office Statistical Bulletin 18/99 table 6.
2   The notes for guidance in Code D define references to a suspect being 'known' as meaning that there is sufficient information known to the police to justify the arrest of a particular person for suspected involvement in the offence.
3   See further **2.50**.
4   Code D para 2.0. The obligation to keep a record of the description of the suspect as first given by a potential witness was introduced for the first time by the latest revision of Code D (SI 1995/450).
5   See further **2.68** to **2.73**.
6   Code D Appendix C para 2.17.
7   See **2.68**.

PHOTOGRAPHS

2.21   As is well known, the police keep a 'rogues' gallery' of pictures of convicted criminals.[1] It is usual police practice to photograph a suspect at the same time as taking fingerprints.[2] The photograph of a person who has been arrested may be taken without consent, if:[3]

(1) he is arrested at the same time as other people, or at a time when it is likely that other people will be arrested, and a photograph is necessary to establish who was arrested, at what time and at what place;

(2) he has been charged with, or reported for a recordable offence[4] and has not yet been released or brought before a court;

(3) he is convicted of such an offence and his photograph is not already on record as a result of the above;[5] or

(4) an officer of at least the rank of superintendent authorises it, having reasonable grounds for suspecting the involvement of the person in a criminal offence and where there is identification evidence in relation to that offence.

Force may not be used to take a photograph and any photograph, negatives and all copies must be destroyed if the suspect is subsequently prosecuted and cleared of the offence (unless he has a previous conviction for a recordable offence) or is charged but not prosecuted (unless he admits the offence and is cautioned for it or has a previous conviction for a recordable offence).[6]

2.22   Thus, if a suspect has previous convictions for a recordable offence, the police may well be in possession of a photograph which may be used for identification purposes. Where a victim or other witness has given a description of a suspect, they may be shown a series of photographs, no fewer than 12 at a time, which are required to be, as far as possible, of a similar type.[7] As soon as a positive identification has been made from the photographs, unless the person identified is otherwise eliminated from enquiries, no other witnesses may be shown the photographs. At this stage, the suspect will become 'known', in that the police will have sufficient evidence to arrest him for the offence in question, and the victim and any witnesses will be asked to take part in a formal identification procedure if there is continuing dispute as to identity.[8]

---

1   Sprack *Emmins on Criminal Procedure* (Blackstone Press Ltd, London, 1997).
2   See **2.38**.
3   Code D para 4.2.
4   See **2.37**.
5   There is no power of arrest to take a photograph in pursuance of this provision which applies only where the person is in custody as a result of the exercise of another power (eg arrest for fingerprinting under s 27 of the Police and Criminal Evidence Act (PACE)).
6   Code D paras 4.3 and 4.4.
7   Code D Annex D para 3.
8   See further **2.68** to **2.73**.

GATHERING EVIDENCE FROM THE SUSPECT – SEARCHES, ARREST AND DETENTION[1]

2.23   In many cases, effective investigation of a sexual offence may require the police to search for evidence. Searches may involve bodily searches of the suspect, either to identify prohibited articles in his possession or to take items of clothing or bodily samples for forensic examination. Alternatively, searches may be made of premises occupied or controlled by the accused. Several powers to search will arise on the arrest of the accused, but searches may also be undertaken before an arrest has been effected.

Searching before arrest – applications for search warrants

2.24   Prior to the enactment of the Police and Criminal Evidence Act (PACE) 1984, the police had no general power to obtain a warrant to search for evidence. Section 8 of the PACE 1984 now empowers a justice of the peace to issue a warrant authorising an officer to enter and search premises if certain conditions are satisfied. On an application by a constable, the justice must be satisfied that there are reasonable grounds for believing:

(1)   that a serious arrestable offence[2] has been committed;
(2)   that there is material on the premises specified in the application which is likely to be of substantial value (whether by itself or together with other material) to the investigation of the offence;
(3)   that the material is likely to be relevant evidence;
(4)   that it does not consist of or include items subject to legal privilege, excluded material or special procedure material;[3] and
(5)   that any of the following conditions apply:
    (a)   that it is not practicable to communicate with any person entitled to grant entry to the premises,
    (b)   that it is practicable to communicate with a person entitled to grant entry to the premises, but it is not practicable to communicate with any person entitled to grant access to the evidence,
    (c)   that entry to the premises will not be granted unless a warrant is produced, and
    (d)   that the purpose of a search may be frustrated or seriously prejudiced unless a constable arriving at the premises can secure immediate entry to them.

Once a warrant has been issued, it must be executed in accordance with ss 15 and 16 of the PACE 1984.[4]

---

1   The following procedures are applicable to adult offenders.
2   See further **2.63**.
3   The PACE 1984 creates three categories of privileged material in respect of which the police cannot obtain an ordinary search warrant. Access to items subject to legal privilege cannot be obtained at all; for excluded and special procedure material, the police normally have to follow procedures set out in Sch 1 to the Act. See further, Stone *Entry, Search and Seizure: A Guide to Civil and Criminal Powers of Entry* (Sweet & Maxwell, London, 1997).
4   These provisions apply to all warrants to enter and search premises issued to a constable under any enactment.

2.25 In addition to the general power to issue search warrants contained in s 8 of the PACE 1984, there also exists a specific power relating to offences under the Protection of Children Act 1978. Where a justice of the peace is satisfied by information on oath that there are reasonable grounds for suspecting that, in any premises within his area, there is an indecent photograph or pseudo-photograph of a child, he may issue a warrant authorising an officer to search the premises, and seize and remove any articles which he reasonably believes to be, or to include, any such indecent photographs or pseudo-photographs.[1] In relation to pseudo-photographs, the power of seizure extends to copies and data stored on a computer disc or by any other electronic means.[2] The officer may require any information contained in a computer and accessible from the premises to be produced in a form in which it can be taken away and in which it is visible and legible.[3] The computer need not be situated in the premises entered, but must simply be accessible from those premises. Following the enactment of the Criminal Justice and Public Order Act 1994, offences under the 1978 Act are now classified as serious arrestable offences, which means that the police may also apply for a search warrant under the PACE 1984.[4] However, the conditions which must be satisfied and the level of proof required for the issue of a warrant under the 1978 Act appear to be less stringent that those required by the PACE 1984. The 1978 Act requires only 'reasonable grounds for suspicion', whereas the PACE 1984 requires 'reasonable grounds for believing'. Generally, reasonable grounds for believing requires a higher level of proof than reasonable grounds for suspicion. It has been suggested that:

> 'If ... there are ten steps from mere suspicion to a state of certainty ... then reasonable suspicion may be as low as step 2 or 3, whilst reasonable belief may be as high as step 9 or 10.'[5]

Police powers of arrest

'Arrestable offences'

2.26 Police powers of arrest are contained within the PACE 1984. The most important factor in determining an officer's power of arrest is the offence under consideration. Section 24(1) of the PACE 1984 provides a power of summary arrest in respect of arrestable offences defined in that section. (Summary in this context means done with despatch and without formalities.) Arrestable offences include offences for which a person, 21 years of age or over, may be sentenced to imprisonment for a term of 5 years[6] and also offences specifically listed.[7] These offences include offences under ss 22 and 23 of the Sexual Offences Act 1956

---

1   Protection of Children Act 1978, s 4(2).
2   Protection of Children Act 1978, s 7(9).
3   PACE 1984, s 20.
4   See further **2.24**.
5   Bevan and Lidstone *A Guide to the Police and Criminal Evidence Act 1984* (Butterworths, London, 1985) p 7.
6   PACE 1984, s 24(1)(b).
7   PACE 1984, s 24(2).

and offences under s 1 of the Protection of Children Act 1978.[1] Thus, the more serious offences will be arrestable offences within the meaning of the Act. Where a constable has reasonable grounds for suspecting that an arrestable offence has been committed, he may arrest without warrant anyone who he has reasonable grounds for suspecting to be guilty of the offence.[2] Thus, two tests of reasonable suspicion must be employed: there must be reasonable grounds to suspect that an arrestable offence has been committed and reasonable grounds to suspect that the person arrested is guilty of the offence. The fact that an arrestable offence has not actually been committed, or that the person arrested is not actually guilty of the offence does not render the arrest unlawful.

General arrest conditions

2.27   However, certain sexual offences do not fall within the definition of an arrestable offence – most notably offences under s 6 of the Sexual Offences Act 1956, s 160 of the Criminal Justice Act 1988 and s 54 of the Criminal Law Act 1977. This does not necessarily mean that no power of arrest exists in respect of these offences. Section 25 of the PACE 1984 provides that where a constable has reasonable grounds for suspecting that any offence which is not an arrestable offence has been committed, he may arrest the relevant person[3] if it appears to him that service of a summons is impracticable or inappropriate because any of the 'general arrest conditions' are satisfied. These conditions are:

(1) that the name of the relevant person is unknown to, and cannot be readily ascertained by, the constable;
(2) that the constable has reasonable grounds for doubting whether a name furnished by the relevant person is his real name;
(3) that:
    (a) the relevant person has failed to furnish a satisfactory address for service, or
    (b) the constable has reasonable grounds for doubting whether an address furnished by the relevant person is a satisfactory address for service;
(4) that the constable has reasonable grounds for believing that arrest is necessary to prevent the relevant person:
    (a) causing physical injury to himself or any other person,
    (b) suffering physical injury,
    (c) causing loss of or damage to property,
    (d) committing an offence against public decency, or
    (e) causing an unlawful obstruction of the highway; or
(5) that the constable has reasonable grounds for believing that arrest is necessary to protect a child or other vulnerable person from the relevant person.

---

1   The offence under the 1978 Act was only designated as an arrestable offence by the enactment of s 85 of the Criminal Justice and Public Order Act 1994.
2   PACE 1984, s 24(6).
3   Defined by s 25(2) to mean any person whom the constable has reasonable grounds to suspect of having committed or having attempted to commit the offence or of being in the course of committing or attempting to commit it.

'Reasonable grounds for suspicion'

2.28   The criteria of 'reasonable grounds for suspicion' is the legal threshold for the exercise of coercive police powers. However, a definition of what constitutes reasonable grounds for suspicion has proved elusive. Suspicion has been defined as 'a state of conjecture or surmise where proof is lacking (which arises) at or near the starting point of an investigation'.[1] It was made clear in the case that reasonable grounds to suspect is a lower standard than that required to establish a prima facie case, and, of course, arises much earlier in the sequence of events. In 1981 the Royal Commission on Criminal Procedure concluded that the criteria of reasonable suspicion could not be defined.[2] However, although the PACE 1984 contains no such definition, the Code of Practice issued under the Act does attempt to give some guidelines as to what constitutes reasonable grounds for suspicion.[3] These relate specifically to the powers of stop and search, but the annex makes it clear that the level of suspicion required is the same as the level that would justify arrest. Paragraph 1 states:

> 'Reasonable suspicion, in contrast to mere suspicion, must be founded on fact. There must be some concrete basis for the officer's suspicion, related to the individual concerned, which can be considered and evaluated by a third person. Mere suspicion, in contrast, is a hunch or instinct which cannot be explained or justified to an objective observer.'

2.29   The Divisional Court has suggested that the words 'has reasonable cause to suspect' import the requirement that the constable in fact suspects.[4] However, the officer's personal suspicion is not sufficient. The test as to whether or not reasonable grounds exist is an objective one, and if the exercise of the power is challenged on the basis that there were no reasonable grounds to suspect, the onus of establishing them lies with the officer. However, in practice, there has been a notable absence of reported cases where such challenges have been made. It would seem that as long as the police officer can show some grounds for suspicion, then that will suffice.

Action on arrest

2.30   As soon as a police officer has grounds to suspect that a person has committed an offence, he must caution the suspect before asking any questions for the purpose of obtaining evidence which may be given to a court in a prosecution.[5] Thus, a caution may be administered some time before an arrest is made, but if no caution has been given before arrest, it must be given as soon as the arrest is made (unless rendered impractical by the arrestee's behaviour).[6] The terms of the caution are set out in the Code of Practice:[7]

---

1   Lord Devlin in *Hussien v Chong Fook Kam* [1970] AC 942 at 948.
2   Report of the Royal Commission on Criminal Procedure (1981) Cmnd 8092 (HMSO, London).
3   Code A Annex B.
4   *Siddiqui v Swann* [1979] Crim LR 318.
5   Para 10.1 of Code C (Code of Practice for the Detention, Treatment and Questioning of Persons by Police Officers) (HMSO, London).
6   Ibid para 10.3.
7   Ibid para 10.4.

'You do not have to say anything. But it may harm your defence if you do not mention when questioned something which you later rely on in court. Anything you do say may be given in evidence.'

Once the arrest has been made, the suspect should be taken directly to the police station and no further interviews should be held until arrival at the police station.[1]

Searching the accused on arrest

2.31 Where the offence for which the suspect has been arrested involves physical contact with the victim, the investigating officers will be anxious to retain the clothing worn by the suspect at the time of the offence for forensic examination. Where the offence is one involving possession or distribution of prohibited material,[2] a search may be required in order to prove possession of the material and to retain it for evidential purposes. If an arrest is made within a reasonable time of the alleged offence, the suspect may still be wearing the clothing he wore at the time of the attack. An initial search of the suspect may be made by the arresting officer at the time of the arrest. An officer who arrests a suspect otherwise than at a police station may search him if he has reasonable grounds for believing that the arrested person may present a danger to himself or others.[3] The officer may also search the arrested person for anything which he might use to assist him to escape from lawful custody or which might be evidence relating to the offence.[4] This obviously includes prohibited material. However, the officer cannot require the arrested person to remove any of his clothing in public, other than an outer coat, jacket or gloves[5] and so, if the arrest has taken place in public, the arresting officer is not permitted to take articles of clothing at this stage.

Searching premises on arrest

2.32 If the arrest takes place some time later and the suspect is no longer wearing the clothing worn at the time of the offence, or does not have the prohibited material in his possession at the time of the arrest, alternative measures can be taken to recover the clothing or property at the time of arrest. The 1984 Act empowers an officer to enter and search the premises where the arrest occurred, or which the arrested person had left immediately before the arrest.[6] The purpose of this power is to allow the officer to search for evidence relating to the offence for which the person has been arrested and the officer must have reasonable grounds for believing that such evidence is on the

---

1   The reason for insisting that, in general, the suspect be taken straight to the police station is that the various procedures to protect suspects prescribed by the PACE 1984 and the Codes of Practice can only operate effectively at a police station. The prohibition of interviews outside the police station is relaxed only where the consequent delay is likely to lead to interference with evidence, harm to other persons, the alerting of other suspects or hindrance to the recovery of illegally obtained property.
2   For example, offences under the Protection of Children Act 1978.
3   PACE 1984, s 32(1).
4   PACE 1984, s 32(2)(a).
5   PACE 1984, s 32(4).
6   PACE 1984, s 32(2)(b).

premises.[1] Thus, if the officer has reasonable grounds for believing that the clothing the suspect wore at the time of the attack or the prohibited material is on the premises where the arrest occurred or which the arrested person had left immediately before the arrest, the officer may search those premises. The officer may seize and retain anything he finds (other than an item subject to legal privilege) if he has reasonable grounds for believing, inter alia, that it is evidence of an offence.[2]

Searching premises occupied or controlled by the accused

2.33   If the arrest occurs when the accused is away from his home, the police have further powers to search any premises occupied or controlled by a person who is under arrest for an arrestable offence,[3] if there are reasonable grounds for suspecting that there is on the premises evidence that relates to that offence, or to some other arrestable offence which is connected with or similar to that offence.[4] The officer may seize and retain anything for which he may search (other than an item subject to legal privilege).[5] However, unlike the power to search premises on arrest, these powers may only be exercised if an officer of the rank of inspector or above has authorised them in writing.[6]

Action on arrival at the police station

2.34   If the arrest occurs within a short time of the victim reporting the offence, care will need to taken if the suspect and victim are at the same police station. No contact must take place between the suspect and victim before any samples are taken for forensic examination, or the defence may allege that the evidence taken from the accused has been contaminated by contact with the victim. On arrival at the police station, the arresting officer must report with the suspect to the custody officer, who is an officer of at least the rank of sergeant who is not connected with the investigation. The role of the custody officer is to ensure that the suspect is treated in accordance with the provisions of the PACE 1984 and Codes of Practice issued under the Act during the period of detention.[7] The custody officer will inform the suspect of his rights, both orally and in writing: to consult privately with a solicitor; to have somebody named by him informed of his arrest; and to read the Codes of Practice.[8] A custody record will be opened – a standard format document that records the essential details of what happens to the suspect during his detention at the station.

---

1   PACE 1984, s 32(6).
2   PACE 1984, s 32(9).
3   See further **2.26**.
4   PACE 1984, s 18(1).
5   PACE 1984, s 18(2).
6   PACE 1984, s 18(4). No written authorisation is required if the search takes place before the arrested person has been taken to a police station, because his presence at a place other then the police station is necessary for the effective investigation of the offence. In such circumstances, the officer conducting the search must inform, as soon as practicable, an officer of the rank of inspector or above that he has made the search (s 18(5) and (6) of the PACE 1984).
7   PACE 1984, s 39(1).
8   Code C para 3.1.

Searching the suspect at the police station

2.35 The custody officer has a duty to ascertain and record on the custody record everything which an arrested person has with him.[1] If the custody officer considers it necessary, he may authorise a search of the person, which may not be an intimate search.[2] If the search involves the removal of more than outer clothing, it is classified as a 'strip search', which must be carried out by an officer of the same sex as the person searched, with nobody of the opposite sex (other than a doctor or a nurse) present.[3] Clothing and personal effects may be seized by the custody officer if he has reasonable grounds for believing that they may be evidence relating to an offence.[4] If it is necessary to remove a person's clothing for the purposes of investigation, replacement clothing of a reasonable standard of comfort and cleanliness must be provided and a person may not be interviewed unless adequate clothing has been offered to him.[5]

INTIMATE SEARCHES

2.36 An intimate search is defined as a search which consists of the physical examination of a person's body orifices other than the mouth.[6] Only an officer of the rank of superintendent or above can authorise such a search and he may only do so if he has reasonable grounds to believe that the person arrested may have concealed on him either anything which he could use to cause physical injury to himself or others and that he might so use it while in detention, or a class A drug[7] and that he was in possession of it with the appropriate criminal intent prior to his arrest.[8] Strict controls are imposed on the conduct of intimate searches. Those arrested for sexual offences will only be subjected to such a search if one of the two conditions is satisfied, neither of which directly relate to the commission of the offence or its investigation. Research has found that less than 1% of suspects are given an intimate search, such searches being connected to violent acquisitive crimes, such as aggravated burglary and robbery, or drug offences.[9]

Taking of samples – police powers

Recordable offences

2.37 The power to take fingerprints, non-intimate and intimate samples from the accused without consent only arises in certain circumstances where the accused has been involved in a 'recordable offence'. The category of recordable offences is defined in the National Police Records (Recordable Offences) Regulations 1985[10] and includes all offences punishable by imprisonment and a

---

1   PACE 1984, s 54(1) and (2).
2   See further **2.36**.
3   PACE 1984, s 54(7) and (9) and Code C Annex A.
4   PACE 1984, s 54(4)(b).
5   Code C para 8.5.
6   PACE 1984, s 65.
7   As defined by s 2(1)(b) of the Misuse of Drugs Act 1971.
8   PACE 1984, s 55(1).
9   Home Office Research Study 174 (1997).
10   SI 1985/1941.

limited number of other non-imprisonable offences. The vast majority of sexual offences are, therefore, recordable offences for the purpose of taking samples.

FINGERPRINTS

2.38   In many cases, the fingerprints (which includes palm prints) of a person suspected of a criminal offence will be taken with consent. If a suspect is detained at a police station, his fingerprints may be taken without consent if either of the following conditions are met:

(1) an officer of at least the rank of superintendent authorises them to be taken;[1] or
(2) the detained person has been charged with a recordable offence or informed that he will be reported for such an offence and he has not had his fingerprints taken in the course of the investigation of the offence by the police.[2]

Whether or not consent is given, the person must be told beforehand that the fingerprints may be the subject of a speculative search,[3] ie checked against other fingerprints contained in records held by or on behalf of the police or held in connection with or as a result of an investigation of an offence.[4]

FINGERPRINTS, ADVANCES IN TECHNOLOGY AND PROPOSALS FOR REFORM

2.39   In recent years, the availability of new technology has changed the way in which fingerprints can be taken and stored. In particular, using a technique called 'livescan', it is now possible for fingerprint impressions to be captured electronically and the images automatically down-loaded in digital form to local fingerprint bureaux to be processed and added to the national database. It is not clear whether the existing provisions of the PACE 1984 permit the taking of fingerprints electronically and the Home Office has put forward proposals to amend the PACE 1984 to put the issue beyond doubt.[5] The advances in technology also mean that fingerprints can be taken at any location, enabling police officers on patrol who suspect the involvement of an individual in an offence to verify the person's identity on the spot. However, the PACE 1984 currently only permits fingerprints to be taken without consent at a police station on the authorisation of a police superintendent. Therefore, the Home Office has proposed that the PACE 1984 should be amended to provide powers to take fingerprints without consent at any location on the authorisation of the officer of the rank of inspector or above.[6] It is also proposed that legislative provision

---

1   Authorisation may only be given where the officer has reasonable grounds for suspecting the involvement of the person concerned in a criminal offence and that the fingerprints will tend to confirm or disprove this (s 61(4) of the PACE 1984).
2   PACE 1984, s 61(3).
3   PACE 1984, s 61(7)(a).
4   PACE 1984, s 63A(1).
5   Home Office *Proposals for Revising Legislative Measures on Fingerprints, Footprints and DNA Samples* (July 1999) para 15.
6   Home Office *Proposals for Revising Legislative Measures on Fingerprints, Footprints and DNA Samples* (July 1999) paras 17–19. The increase in the range of officers permitted to give the authorisation required is proposed for purely practical reasons – police superintendents are not always readily available in the early hours of the morning.

should be made to take fingerprints without consent when a caution is issued if fingerprints have not been obtained at an earlier stage in the investigation,[1] and, in the case of young offenders, provision should be made to permit the taking of fingerprints in connection with warnings given for recordable offences.[2]

NON-INTIMATE SAMPLES

2.40 Non-intimate samples are defined to mean:[3]

(1) a sample of hair other than pubic hair;
(2) a sample taken from a nail or from under a nail;
(3) a swab taken from any part of a person's body including the mouth but not any other body orifice;
(4) saliva; and
(5) a footprint or a similar impression of any part of a person's body other than a part of his hand.

2.41 Such samples may be taken at any time with consent. They may only be taken without consent in three situations:

(1) where a person has been convicted of a recordable offence;[4]
(2) where a person has been charged with a recordable offence or informed that he will be reported for such an offence and, either he has not had such a sample taken from him in the course of the investigation of the offence by the police or he has had such a sample taken but either it was not suitable for the same means of analysis or, though so suitable, the sample proved insufficient;[5] and
(3) where a person is in police detention or is being held in custody by the police on the authority of a court and an officer of at least the rank of superintendent authorises it to be taken.[6]

As with fingerprints, whether or not consent is given, the person must be told beforehand that the sample may be the subject of a speculative search,[7] ie checked against other samples contained in records held by or on behalf of the police or held in connection with or as a result of an investigation of an offence.[8]

2.42 Prior to the enactment of the amendments contained in the Criminal Justice and Public Order Act 1994, saliva and swabs from the mouth were categorised as intimate samples and, thus, could not be taken without consent.[9] The change of status to non-intimate samples appears to have been motivated by

---

1   Home Office *Proposals for Revising Legislative Measures on Fingerprints, Footprints and DNA Samples* (July 1999) para 36.
2   Home Office *Proposals for Revising Legislative Measures on Fingerprints, Footprints and DNA Samples* (July 1999) para 38. See further **2.37**.
3   PACE 1984, s 65.
4   PACE 1984, s 63(3B).
5   PACE 1984, s 63(3A).
6   PACE 1984, s 63(3). Such authorisation will only be given where the officer has reasonable grounds for suspecting the involvement of the person in a recordable offence and that the sample will tend to confirm or disprove this (s 63(4) of the PACE 1984).
7   PACE 1984, s 63(8B).
8   PACE 1984, s 63A(1).
9   See **2.43**.

the fact that saliva can be used to obtain a DNA profile.[1] The samples can now be obtained without consent if the conditions outlined above are satisfied.

INTIMATE SAMPLES

2.43   Intimate samples are defined to mean:[2]

(1) a sample of blood, semen or any other tissue fluid, urine or pubic hair;

(2) a dental impression; or

(3) a swab taken from a person's body orifice other than the mouth.

Intimate samples may be taken from a person in police detention only if a police officer of at least the rank of superintendent authorises it to be taken and if the appropriate consent is given.[3] Following the enactment of the Criminal Justice and Public Order Act 1994, intimate samples may also be taken from a person who is not in police detention but from whom, in the course of the investigation of the offence, two or more non-intimate samples suitable for the same means of analysis have been taken which have proved to be insufficient, subject to the requirement of consent and authorisation of an officer of at least the rank of superintendent.[4] It has been pointed out that the addition of this new power removes any incentive that the police may have to request an intimate sample whilst the accused is in their detention in cases where a non-intimate sample may be just as likely to provide the necessary information and, thus, enables them to feel safe in the knowledge that an intimate sample can later be requested, even though the accused is no longer in police detention.[5]

2.44   Prior to the enactment of the Criminal Justice and Public Order Act 1994, authorisation to take both non-intimate and intimate samples could only be given where the officer had reasonable grounds for suspecting the person to be involved in a serious arrestable offence.[6] The extension of the provisions to include those suspected of involvement in a recordable offence has widened greatly the range of offenders from whom such samples may be taken – an extension which goes well beyond the recommendations of the Royal Commission on Criminal Justice, which had recommended that the category of serious arrestable offences be extended to include assault and burglary for these purposes.[7] The extension was thought necessary because of the development of DNA profiling,[8] which, as the Royal Commission pointed out, can be used to prove a suspect's innocence as well as guilt.[9]

---

1   Wasik and Taylor *Blackstone's Guide to the Criminal Justice and Public Order Act 1994* (Blackstone Press Ltd, London, 1995) p 74.

2   PACE 1984, s 65.

3   PACE 1984, s 62(1). Such authorisation will only be given where the officer has reasonable grounds for suspecting the involvement of the person in a recordable offence and that the sample will tend to confirm or disprove this (s 62(2) of the PACE 1984).

4   PACE 1984, s 62(1A).

5   Wasik and Taylor *Blackstone's Guide to the Criminal Justice and Public Order Act 1994* (Blackstone Press, London, 1995) p 73.

6   See **2.63**.

7   *Royal Commission on Criminal Justice* (1993) Cmnd 2263 (HMSO, London) chap 2 para 33.

8   See **2.50**.

9   *Royal Commission on Criminal Justice* (1993) Cmnd 2263 (HMSO, London) chap 2 para 32.

2.45   The sample, other than a sample of urine or dental impression, must be taken by a registered medical practitioner and a dental impression must be taken by a registered dentist.[1] As with fingerprints and non-intimate samples, the person must be told beforehand that the sample may be the subject of a speculative search,[2] ie checked against other samples contained in records held by or on behalf of the police or held in connection with or as a result of an investigation of an offence.[3]

2.46   There is no power to take intimate samples without consent. However, where consent is refused without good cause, in any subsequent trial the court or jury may draw such inferences from the refusal as appear proper.[4] The Code of Practice requires the person from whom the sample is to be taken to be warned of this, prior to the request being made and to be reminded of his entitlement to legal advice.[5]

Taking of samples – police practice

2.47   Guidance from the Home Office[6] and the Association of Chief Police Officers[7] advises that samples for the purposes of DNA sampling should only be taken from those suspected of offences against the person, sexual offences and burglary. Research conducted by the Home Office during 1995–96 found that non-intimate samples were taken from 7% of suspects in connection with a wide range of offences, including theft, criminal damage, drugs and public order.[8] Although this appears to suggest divergence from official guidance, it may well be that the police are seizing the opportunity to take 'intelligence-led' samples, ie taking samples from those suspected of crimes in the designated categories, even if they have been arrested on the occasion in question for another type of offence.[9] The largest proportion of samples (28%) were taken from those suspected of sexual offences, with 20% being taken from those suspected of violence against the person and 19% from those suspected of burglary.

2.48   The most common form of non-intimate samples taken were body or mouth swabs (74%), with hair being taken in 13% of cases, saliva in 6%, samples from under finger nails in 6% and body imprints in 1%. Custody officers interviewed stated that mouth swabs were the preferred method of taking a sample, despite hair, when plucked by the root, apparently being much better for DNA analysis. This preference hinged on only two mouth swabs being required for a non-intimate sample, compared to 10 separate hairs. The relative ease of taking a mouth swab and lack of pain meant that officers would normally

---

1   PACE 1984, s 62(9).
2   PACE 1984, s 63(8B).
3   PACE 1984, s 62(7A).
4   PACE 1984, s 62(10).
5   Code D para 5.2.
6   Home Office Circular 1995/16 National DNA Database.
7   Association of Chief Police Officers 'Memorandum of Understanding. DNA Database' (1995) unpublished.
8   Home Office Research Study 174 (1997).
9   Morgan et al 'Preliminary Study of the Use of DNA Evidence' Report to the Home Office Research and Statistics Directorate (1996) unpublished.

decide on this kind of sample in the first instance, only taking hair samples when a suspect's refusal made taking a swab difficult.[1]

2.49 The study found that intimate samples were taken in less than 1% of cases, usually connected with serious offences such as murder, rape and robbery. Blood was the most common intimate sample, taken in 70% of cases. Samples of pubic hair were taken in 16% of cases, swabs from body orifices were taken in 8% of cases and semen samples were taken in 2% of cases.

DNA profiling

2.50 One of the most significant advances in criminal investigation since the advent of fingerprint identification has been the use of DNA technology. DNA[2] is the genetic material contained in the nuclei of cells in the human body. DNA profiling is a technique which enables scientists to compare two biological samples and to determine the likelihood that theses samples originated from the same individual.[3] The technique was discovered in 1984,[4] and was first used in a criminal trial to convict a man of rape in 1987.[5] Since that date, the use of DNA technology in the criminal justice system has expanded rapidly. In cases involving the commission of a sexual offence where the identity of the perpetrator is in issue, DNA technology is likely to be of great importance, both in identifying the perpetrator and proving the innocence of other suspects. Sexual offences, by their very nature, normally involve the perpetrator depositing significant physical evidence from which DNA information can be extracted – hair, blood, saliva or, more usually, semen. Therefore, if a perpetrator leaves such evidence at the scene of an offence, or the evidence is collected from the victim at a later stage, and the perpetrator is subsequently detained on suspicion of having committed the offence, DNA technology can be used to link the suspect to the crime.

DNA databases

2.51 The potential use of DNA technology extends far beyond merely confirming the suspect's involvement in an offence. Just as the fingerprints of those convicted of offences can be recorded for future use, once a person has been convicted of an offence, any DNA profile obtained could be stored and used in any subsequent investigation. Prior to the enactment of the Criminal Justice and Public Order Act 1994, police powers to take samples from which a DNA profile could be obtained were limited. In order to make the most effective use of DNA technology, further measures were called for. In giving evidence to the Royal Commission on Criminal Justice, the police service pointed out that it is not uncommon for persons arrested for sexual offences to have previous convictions for other types of serious offences, for example burglary. In order to assist in the identification and conviction of such offenders, the police argued

---

1   Home Office Research Study 174 (1997) at 44.
2   Deoxyribonucleic Acid.
3   Steventon *The Ability to Challenge DNA Evidence* Research Study No 9 (Royal Commission on Criminal Justice, HMSO, London, 1993).
4   Jeffreys et al 'Hypervariable "mini satellite" regions in human DNA' (1985) *Nature* 314 at 67.
5   *R v Melias* (1987) *The Times*, 14 November.

that there should be a power to take non-intimate samples without consent for the purposes of DNA analysis from all those arrested for serious criminal offences, whether or not DNA evidence is relevant to the particular offence concerned.[1] It was argued that the relevant data of those who are then convicted should be retained so that, in any subsequent investigation where the identity of the perpetrator is unknown but DNA evidence comes to light, that evidence can be checked against the samples in a database. This recommendation was accepted by the Royal Commission and, as a result, the Criminal Justice and Public Order Act 1994 amended the PACE 1984 so that non-intimate samples may now be taken from a person without consent if:

(1) he has been charged with a recordable offence or informed that he will be reported for such an offence; and
(2) either he has not had a non-intimate sample taken from him in the course of the investigation by the police or he has had a non-intimate sample taken from him but either it was not suitable for the same means of analysis or, though so suitable, the sample proved insufficient.[2]

Alternatively, a non-intimate sample can be taken from a person if he has been convicted of a recordable offence.[3] In order to facilitate the taking of samples, the police have powers to require a person who is not in police detention but from whom they have power to take a non-intimate sample to attend a police station in order to have a sample taken.[4]

2.52   Further powers to take non-intimate samples without consent were introduced by the Criminal Evidence (Amendment) Act 1997, which extends the categories of persons from whom such samples may be taken. Samples may now be taken from a person convicted of offences listed in Sch 1 to the Act before 10 April 1995, if:

(1) he is still serving a sentence of imprisonment[5] on the date when the sample is taken; or
(2) he is detained under pt III of the Mental Health Act 1983 in pursuance of a Hospital Order or Interim Hospital Order following the conviction or a transfer direction given at a time when he was serving a sentence of imprisonment in respect of that offence.[6]

2.53   Samples may also be taken from persons detained following acquittal on the grounds of insanity or finding of unfitness to plead.[7] The offences listed in Sch 1 include various offences of violence and the following sexual offences:

---

1   *Royal Commission on Criminal Justice* (1993) Cmnd 2263 (HMSO, London) chap 2 para 34.
2   PACE 1984, s 63(3A).
3   PACE 1984, s 63(3B).
4   PACE 1984, s 63A(4).
5   Defined to include his being detained in any institution to which the Prison Act 1952 applies in pursuance of any other sentence or order for detention imposed by a court in criminal proceedings or to his being detained (otherwise than in any such institution) in pursuance of directions of the Secretary of State under s 53 of the Children and Young Persons Act 1933 (s 1(6) of the Criminal Evidence (Amendment) Act 1997).
6   Criminal Evidence (Amendment) Act 1997, s 1.
7   Criminal Evidence (Amendment) Act 1997, s 2.

(1) any offence under the Sexual Offences Act 1956, other than an offence under ss 30, 31 or 33–36 of that Act (ie excluding offences relating to living on the earnings of prostitution, exercising control over prostitutes and the keeping of brothels);

(2) any offence under s 128 of the Mental Health Act 1959 (intercourse with mentally handicapped person by hospital staff, etc);

(3) any offence under s 1 of the Indecency with Children Act 1960 (indecent conduct towards a young child);

(4) any offence under s 54 of the Criminal Law Act 1977 (incitement to commit incest); and

(5) any offence under s 1 of the Protection of Children Act 1978.

2.54 The Act came into force in March 1997 and, thus, only those detained for a period of two or more years following conviction (or, in some cases, acquittal on the grounds of insanity or unfitness to plead) will be caught by the provisions of the Act. Mouth swabs have been re-classified as non-intimate samples from April 1995 and so the police had an existing power to obtain non-consensual DNA samples after this date. The provisions of the 1997 Act are aimed at enabling DNA samples to be obtained from the more serious offenders, as judged by the sentence imposed by the court. Concerns have been expressed about the element of retroactivity involved, although it appears that challenges to the constitutionality of similar laws in the USA have been unsuccessful so far.[1]

2.55 The extended powers to take non-intimate samples are not aimed at obtaining evidence to be used against the suspect for the offence under investigation, as it only applies where the accused has already been charged or told that he will be reported for the offence, or where he has been convicted. Rather, they are aimed at allowing a database of samples to be built up for use on future occasions and for linking previously convicted persons with any future offences, in the same way as fingerprints are used. A national database was established in England and Wales in April 1995. By March 1998, the database contained profiles of more than 255,000 suspects and convicted persons, as well as 30,000 profiles developed from material found at crime scenes.[2]

DNA samples from persons not convicted – frequency databases

2.56 When a person from whom a sample has been taken is convicted of an offence, the information derived from the sample will be retained on the DNA database and may be used in the investigation of other offences, for example in a 'speculative search'. However, if a sample is taken during an investigation and a prosecution does not proceed or the suspect is subsequently acquitted of the offence in question, the sample and the information derived from it will not necessarily be destroyed. Giving evidence to the Royal Commission, the police argued that DNA databases should not be confined to samples from convicted persons but that other samples should be retained for the purposes of a frequency database.[3] The purpose of a frequency database is purely statistical. It

---

1   Redmayne 'The DNA Database: Civil Liberty and Evidentiary Issues' [1998] Crim LR 437 at 449 FN 44.

2   Redmayne 'The DNA Database: Civil Liberty and Evidentiary Issues' [1998] Crim LR 437.

3   *Royal Commission on Criminal Justice* (1993) Cmnd 2263 (HMSO, London) chap 2 para 36.

is not to match the samples taken from the suspect with a sample on the database, but to help demonstrate the statistical probability of another person having the same DNA profile. A similar database is not necessary for fingerprints, because it has long been accepted that each person's fingerprint is unique. The Royal Commission agreed that it would be desirable to have as many samples as possible entered on the frequency database, but emphasised the need for an independent body to oversee the functioning of the frequency database and for strong safeguards to exist in order to ensure that the samples on the frequency database could not be linked by the police or prosecution to the persons from whom they were taken.[1]

2.57 The PACE 1984 now provides that, if fingerprints or samples have been taken from a person in connection with an investigation and he is either no longer suspected of having committed the offence, has not been cautioned or prosecuted for the offence or has been cleared of the offence, then as a general rule, the fingerprints or samples must be destroyed.[2] Fingerprints must always be destroyed if the suspect is not convicted, but there are the following exceptions in the case of samples.

(1) The samples need not be destroyed if they were taken for the purpose of the same investigation of an offence of which a person from whom one was taken has been convicted. For example, if a sample is taken from several suspects in the investigation of any one offence, and one of the suspects is subsequently convicted of that offence, the sample taken from the remaining suspects need not be destroyed. However, the information derived from those samples (the DNA profiles) cannot be used in evidence against those who were not convicted of the offence, nor for the purposes of any investigation of an offence.[3]

(2) Even if the sample itself is destroyed, the information derived from the sample (the DNA profile) need not be destroyed, but cannot be used in evidence against the person from whom it was taken or for the purposes of any investigation of an offence,[4] ie it may form part of the frequency database.

2.58 The independent body and safeguards envisaged by the Royal Commission have not materialised and the database is currently managed by the Forensic Science Service. The Government has expressed the view that there is no need for independent supervision, as the DNA profiles are stored as computer codes and therefore are governed by the Data Protection Acts.[5]

DNA samples, volunteers and subsequent investigations

2.59 In serious cases, where the offender has not been identified, mass DNA screens may be carried out. For example, all males between specified ages living

---

1   *Royal Commission on Criminal Justice* (1993) Cmnd 2263 (HMSO, London) chap 2 paras 36 and 37.
2   PACE 1984, s 64(1)–(3).
3   PACE 1984, s 64(3A).
4   PACE 1984, s 64(3B).
5   Redmayne 'The DNA Database: Civil Liberty and Evidentiary Issues' [1998] Crim LR 437 at 439.

in a certain locality may be asked to provide samples for DNA analysis and in July 1999 it was estimated that 110 such mass DNA screens had been undertaken.[1] Once the sample has been taken, if the DNA profile of the volunteer is negative when checked against the specific crime scene profile, then the sample will be destroyed once the due legal process surrounding the specific offence in question is completed. The information derived from the sample (the DNA profile) may be kept, but cannot be used in connection with the investigation of another offence.[2]

2.60   However, police experience has shown that certain individuals will fit the profile of suspects in more than one investigation and, therefore, may be approached a number of times to act as volunteer donors in mass-screening exercises. There is said to be a concern that an increasing number of people will refuse to give further samples if they continue to be approached by the same or different police forces on different occasions for different offences. For this reason, the Home Office has proposed that the PACE 1984 should be amended to permit the retention and use of DNA samples and the information derived from them, with a volunteer's written consent.[3] Obviously, such a move would expand the national DNA database greatly, but would also be vehemently opposed by civil liberties pressure groups. The Home Office acknowledges that appropriate safeguards would be required to ensure, as a minimum, that samples were indeed being given and retained voluntarily and the right to withdraw consent at any time was available, but the proposal appears to be bringing a comprehensive national DNA database, including every citizen of the UK, one step closer.

Detention in police custody

2.61   The period between arrest and charge is often a vital one as far as the gathering of evidence is concerned, but it is also necessarily a short one in most circumstances. The PACE 1984 contains strict provisions on the detention of a suspect. When an arrested person is taken to a police station, the custody officer must decide whether there is sufficient evidence to charge him with the offence for which he was arrested.[4] If there is, the arrested person may be detained for such length of time as is necessary to enable the charge to be put to him, and then he may either be charged, or released without charge, either on bail or without bail. In the more usual case, where the custody officer does not have sufficient evidence before him to charge the arrested person, he must order his release unless he has reasonable grounds for believing that his detention before charge is necessary to secure or preserve evidence relating to the offence or to obtain such evidence by questioning him.[5] During the entire period of detention, the PACE 1984 requires regular reviews to be made to ensure that

1   Home Office *Proposals for Revising Legislative Measures on Fingerprints, Footprints and DNA Samples* (July 1999) para 50.
2   PACE 1984, s 64. See **2.57**.
3   Home Office *Proposals for Revising Legislative Measures on Fingerprints, Footprints and DNA Samples* (July 1999) para 51.
4   PACE 1984, s 37.
5   PACE 1984, s 37(2).

there are continuing grounds for detention without charge.[1] The review officer, who must be of at least the rank of inspector and who has not been directly involved in the investigation, must apply the same criteria as pertained to the custody officer when taking the initial decision to detain the person arrested.

Authorisation of continued detention by the police

2.62   As a general rule, the arrested person may only be detained without charge for a maximum of 24 hours.[2] However, the period of detention without charge may be extended to 36 hours if so authorised by an officer of the rank of superintendent or above who is responsible for the police station at which the person is detained, if the officer has reasonable grounds for believing that:

(1) the detention of that person without charge is necessary to secure or preserve evidence relating to an offence for which he is under arrest or to obtain such evidence by questioning him;

(2) the offence for which he is under arrest is a serious arrestable offence; and

(3) the investigation is being conducted diligently and expeditiously.[3]

'Serious arrestable offence'

2.63   The PACE 1984 categorises serious arrestable offences in two ways.[4] Certain offences are always classified as serious arrestable offences, others will only be so classified if the actual, intended or likely consequence of the offence comes within a defined range of outcomes. The following sexual offences will always be classified as serious arrestable offences:

(1) rape;

(2) incest with a girl under the age of 13;

(3) buggery with a person under the age of 16;

(4) indecent assault which constitutes an act of indecency;

(5) unlawful sexual intercourse with a girl under the age of 13; and

(6) offences under s 1 of the Protection of Children Act 1978.

2.64   Any other arrestable offence will be serious only if its commission has led, or is intended to lead to any of the following consequences:

(1) serious harm to the security of the State or to public order;

(2) serious interference with the administration of justice or with the investigation of offences or of a particular offence;

(3) the death of any person;

(4) serious injury to any person;[5]

(5) substantial financial gain to any person; or

(6) serious financial loss to any person.

---

1   PACE 1984, s 40.
2   PACE 1984, s 41(1). The 24 hours run from the time the detainee arrived at the police station or, if he initially attended at the police station voluntarily, from the time he was told he was no longer free to leave.
3   PACE 1984, s 42(1).
4   PACE 1984, s 116.
5   'Injury' includes any disease and any impairment of a person's physical or mental condition.

Authorisation of continued detention by the court

2.65   An arrested person may only be detained without charge for a period in excess of 36 hours if such detention is authorised by a magistrates' court. The court may issue a warrant of further detention if satisfied that:

(1) the detention of that person without charge is necessary to secure or preserve evidence relating to an offence for which he is under arrest or to obtain such evidence by questioning him;
(2) the offence for which he is under arrest is a serious arrestable offence; and
(3) the investigation is being conducted diligently and expeditiously.[1]

The warrant may authorise detention for a further 36 hours, but the magistrates may extend that period for a further 36 hours if the conditions above remain satisfied.[2] The maximum period that a detainee can be held without charge is therefore 96 hours. If, after that time, there is still insufficient evidence to charge him with an offence, he must be released.[3]

Rights of the arrested person during detention

2.66   The PACE 1984 affords the accused two fundamental rights whilst in police detention: the right not be held incommunicado[4] and the right to consult a solicitor.[5] However, the exercise of both of these rights may be delayed if the person is in detention for a serious arrestable offence and the delay is authorised by an officer of at least the rank of superintendent. The delay may only be authorised if the officer has reasonable grounds for believing that exercise of the right or rights:

(1) will lead to interference with or harm to evidence connected with a serious arrestable offence or interference with or physical injury to other persons; or
(2) will lead to the alerting of other persons suspected of having committed such an offence but not yet arrested for it; or
(3) will hinder the recovery of any property obtained as a result of such an offence.[6]

2.67   Such a delay is most likely to be authorised in cases where more than one person is suspected of being involved in the commission of the offence under investigation. This will be of particular relevance to the investigation of paedophile rings or networks. Prior to the enactment of the Criminal Justice and Public Order Act 1994, offences involving the possession and distribution of indecent photographs of children under the Protection of Children Act 1978 were not classified as serious arrestable offences, and so no authorisation could

---

1   PACE 1984, s 43(4).
2   PACE 1984, s 44.
3   If the police do not wish to release the suspect unconditionally, they may bail him to return to the police station at a later date when their enquiries are complete or they are in a position to take the matter further (s 47 of the PACE 1984). If the suspect does not return to the police station as requested, he can be arrested (s 46A).
4   PACE 1984, s 56.
5   PACE 1984, s 58.
6   PACE 1984, ss 56(5) and 58(8).

be given to delay exercise of the rights by the detained person. The re-classification of the offences as serious arrestable offences by the 1994 Act now means that, not only can the suspect be detained for longer periods before charge, but also that the suspect can be denied access to a solicitor and contact with persons outside the police station. Thus, if the police have arrested one member of a suspected paedophile ring, they can ensure that other members of the ring are not informed and so do not have the opportunity to destroy photographs and other evidence before the police have had time to act against them.[1]

Identification of suspects

2.68 In many cases of offences of sexual aggression, the perpetrator will not be previously known to the victim and, if the suspect denies any involvement in the offence, steps will need to be taken to confirm the identification of the suspect and his involvement in the offence. DNA evidence may well prove invaluable in linking the suspect to the offence,[2] but consideration may also be given to affording the victim the opportunity to identify the suspect as the person responsible for the offence. Similar identification evidence may be sought from any potential witnesses, who either witnessed the offence itself or saw the suspect in the vicinity at the time of the offence. Steps may well have been taken to identify the suspect at an earlier stage in the investigation,[3] but, where identity is in dispute, more formal identification methods may be used after a suspect has been arrested. Various modes of identification are available to the police, but it is clear, in the light of authority and the Codes of Practice[4] that there is a defined hierarchy of the procedures available.[5] A formal identification parade is the preferable form of identification evidence, followed by a group identification, then a video identification and finally identification by confrontation. Identification evidence is seen as being notoriously unreliable unless it takes place in tightly controlled circumstances and, at any eventual trial, juries are given severe warnings about convicting on identification evidence.[6] The key factor in all modes of identification will be the avoidance of contamination, achieved primarily by the appointment of an independent officer (the identification officer), who is not involved in the investigation and who is responsible for conducting the identification and ensuring that the evidence is not contaminated by contact between the witness and the suspect or other witnesses.

Identification parades

2.69 An identification parade can only be held with the consent of the suspect. The Code of Practice provides that, whenever a suspect disputes an

---

1   Wasik and Taylor *Blackstone's Guide to the Criminal Justice and Public Order Act 1994* (Blackstone Press Ltd, London, 1995) p 111.
2   See **2.18**.
3   See **2.19**.
4   Code D: Code of Practice for the Identification of Persons by Police Officers.
5   Letham *Police Detention: A Practical Guide to Advising the Suspect* (Sweet & Maxwell, London, 1998) p 179.
6   *R v Turnbull* [1976] 2 All ER 549.

identification, an identification parade shall be held if the suspect consents, unless:

(1) the identification officer considers that, whether by reason of the unusual appearance of the suspect or for some other reason, it would not be practicable to assemble sufficient people who resemble him to make a parade fair;
(2) the officer in charge of the investigation considers, whether because of fear on the part of the witness or for some other reason, that it is, in the circumstances, more satisfactory to hold a group identification; or
(3) the identification officer considers, whether because of the refusal of the suspect to take part in an identification parade or group identification or other reasons, that video film identification would in the circumstances be the most appropriate course of action.[1]

2.70   When the identifying witness is the victim of a sexual offence, it may be thought that fear on the part of the witness may include a desire to avoid a direct confrontation with the suspect[2] and, therefore, would justify the holding of a group identification rather than a formal identification parade. However, the parade may be held in a room equipped with a screen permitting witnesses to see members of the parade without being seen,[3] and thus direct confrontation is unnecessary. The parade must consist of at least eight people (in addition to the suspect) who so far as possible resemble the suspect in age, height, general appearance and position in life.[4] If there is more than one witness taking part, the witnesses should not speak to each other about the case, or see the suspect or any other parade members before inspecting the parade. Each witness who can make a positive identification does so by indicating the number of the person picked out. The witness may ask any parade member to speak or adopt a particular posture, but should first try to make an identification by appearance alone. If video films or photographs have been released to the media by the police for the purpose of recognising or tracing the suspect, the investigating officer must ask every witness after the parade whether they have seen any broadcast or published films or photographs relating to the offence and must record the replies.[5]

Group identification

2.71   A group identification takes place where the suspect is viewed by a witness amongst an informal group of people. The consent of the suspect should be sought but, if consent is refused, such identifications may take place covertly, without consent. The location of the identification is a matter for the identification officer and should be a place where other people are passing by, or waiting around informally, in groups such that the suspect is able to join them and be capable of being seen by the witness at the same time as others in the

---

1   Code D paras 2.3, 2.4, 2.7 and 2.10.
2   See **3.121** for procedures to avoid a direct confrontation in the court room setting.
3   Code D Annex A para 2.
4   Code D Annex A para 8.
5   Code D Annex A para 17A.

group.[1] If the suspect's consent is not forthcoming, the choice of locations will be limited by the places where the suspect can be found and the number of other people present at that time.[2] A witness may well find a group identification less traumatic than a formal identification parade, although such an identification will not carry as much weight in court as one resulting from a formal parade.

Video film identification

2.72 Identification by video film may well result in even less trauma for a witness, particularly if the witness is the victim of a sexual offence who has suffered considerable trauma as a result of the offence and has no wish to have any direct contract with the suspect, whether or not the contact takes place through a one-way screen, as in an identification parade, or at a distance, as in a group identification. The possibility of making an identification by video was introduced in the 1990 revision of the Code of Practice. Similar provisions apply as for an identification parade, in that the video must include at least eight persons, other than the suspect, who should all resemble the suspect in appearance.

Confrontation

2.73 Confrontation as a means of identifying the suspect is only used as a last resort. The weight attached to such an identification is limited and may well prove more traumatic for the witness than other modes of identification, although the confrontation may take place via a one-way screen,[3] thereby providing some measure of protection for a vulnerable witness.

WHEN POLICE INQUIRIES HAVE BEEN COMPLETED

2.74 Once the police have completed their inquiries, or once the time limits for detaining the suspect in custody without charge have expired, several options for further action are available. Dependant upon the nature of the offence, the age and record of the suspect and the evidence available, the police may:

(1) release the suspect unconditionally;
(2) bail the suspect to return to the police station at a later date;
(3) administer a caution to the suspect;
(4) report the suspect for summons;
(5) charge the suspect.

Unconditional release or bailing to return to the police station

2.75 If the police do not have sufficient evidence to charge the suspect,[4] but can no longer justify his continued detention, they must either release the suspect unconditionally or they may bail him to return to the police station at a

---

1   Code D Annex E para 3.
2   Code D Annex E para 4.
3   Code D Annex C para 4.
4   See **2.81**.

later date. If the suspect is released unconditionally but fresh evidence subsequently comes to the attention of the police, the suspect may be re-arrested for the same offence. If further inquiries are to be made which the police feel may result in sufficient evidence to proceed with a prosecution, for example if an identification parade is to be held or further witnesses are to be interviewed, they may grant the suspect bail and require him to return to the police station at a later date.[1] Conditions may be attached to the bail in the same manner as when bail is granted by the police after charging the suspect,[2] and the suspect is under the same duty to turn up at the police station as if it were a court.

Inconclusive inquiries and those suspected of sexual offences

2.76   If a suspect is unconditionally released following police inquiries, or if he is released on bail to return to the police station at a later date but this obligation is subsequently removed, unless the inquiry has completely exonerated the suspect, the police will retain information about the suspect and the inconclusive inquiry as part of their role in gathering criminal intelligence. In the past, such information has been restricted to use by the police in future investigative work. However, in future, the fact that a suspect has been arrested for a suspected offence could be passed onto a third party not responsible for criminal investigations. Following the recommendations contained in a White Paper in 1996,[3] Pt V of the Police Act 1997 creates a statutory framework regulating access to criminal records and criminal intelligence for employment purposes as well as for voluntary sector arrangements.[4] The primary aim of this part of the Act is to improve the speed and quality of police checks on people seeking jobs with direct access to children – a result of increasing public concern over the sexual abuse of children.[5] The Act enables the Secretary of State to issue certificates relating to a criminal-records check. Three types of certificate are provided for:

(1)   a criminal conviction certificate – available only to individual applicants, stating whether or not they have convictions recorded in central police records which are not spent under the Rehabilitation of Offenders Act 1974;

(2)   a criminal record certificate – available for occupations that are exempted from the provisions of the Rehabilitation of Offenders Act 1974, requiring a joint application by an individual and the organisation that is seeking the check; and

(3)   an enhanced criminal record certificate – restricted to, inter alia, those working on a regular, unsupervised basis with children or vulnerable adults.

---

1   PACE 1984, s 47(3).
2   See **2.99**.
3   *On the Record: Government's proposals for access to criminal records for employment and related purposes in England and Wales* Cmnd 3308 (Home Office, London, 1996).
4   See Emmerson and Friedman *A Guide to the Police Act 1997* (Butterworths, London, 1998).
5   See further chap 8.

Enhanced criminal record certificates

2.77   Criminal conviction and criminal record certificates will provide information only on convictions and cautions.[1] However, the enhanced criminal record certificate will provide for the disclosure to potential employers, voluntary organisations and licensing authorities of criminal intelligence extending beyond convictions and cautions. Such intelligence may include records of acquittals, the results of inconclusive or ongoing police investigations, and uncorroborated allegations from informants.[2] The availability of such certificates is confined to those seeking appointment to what are deemed to be sensitive positions (whether paid or unpaid). Such positions include:

(1)   positions involving regularly caring for, training, supervising or being in sole charge of persons aged under 18;[3]

(2)   positions involving regularly caring for, training, supervising or being in sole charge of persons aged 18 or over;[4]

(3)   judicial appointments;[5]

(4)   registration as a child minder or day carer under s 71 of the Children Act 1989;[6] and

(5)   the placing of children with foster parents.[7]

2.78   When these provisions are brought into force, any person applying for one of the above positions can be required to apply for an enhanced criminal record certificate.[8] The application must be accompanied by a statement from a registered person, ie a body corporate or unincorporate, a person appointed to a statutory office, or an individual who employs others in the course of a business who has been registered by the Secretary of State in a register maintained for the purposes of the 1997 Act,[9] that the certificate is required for the purposes of an exempted question[10] asked in relation to the appointment. Before issuing the certificate, the Secretary of State must request the chief officer of every relevant police force to provide any information which, in the chief officer's opinion, might be relevant to the applicant's appointment and ought to be included in the certificate.[11] The chief officer therefore has discretion as to what information he provides and there is no statutory restriction on the nature of the information, although the Secretary of State is obliged to issue a statutory code of practice regulating the use of information provided to registered persons.[12] If, in the opinion of the chief officer, the information should be withheld from the

---

1   See **2.82**.

2   Emmerson and Friedman *A Guide to the Police Act 1997* (Butterworths, London, 1998) p 100.

3   Police Act 1997, s 115(3).

4   Police Act 1997, s 115(4)(b).

5   Police Act 1997, s 116.

6   Police Act 1997, s 115(5)(e).

7   Police Act 1997, s 115(5)(f).

8   The Government has indicated that enhanced criminal record certificates should be available from Summer 2001 (Home Office Press Release 441/99).

9   Police Act 1997, s 120(1) and (4).

10   Namely, a question exempted from the general provisions of the Rehabilitation of Offenders Act 1974.

11   Police Act 1997, s 115(7).

12   Police Act 1997, s 122.

applicant in the interests of the prevention or detection of crime, but can, without harming those interests, be disclosed to the registered person, then the information will be provided directly to the registered person.[1]

Enhanced criminal record certificates and the European Convention on Human Rights

2.79   The overall effect of Pt V of the 1997 Act, if enacted, will be that any person who has ever been suspected of a sexual offence who subsequently applies for any position which involves contact with children or vulnerable adults may find that information about the suspicions can be passed onto a third party, on occasions without his knowledge, regardless of the outcome of any police investigation. This is clearly a radical step, presumably thought to be justified by the need to protect children and vulnerable adults from abuse, particularly sexual abuse. However, the measures are arguably an infringement of civil liberties. Article 8 of the European Convention on Human Rights provides that:

(1)   everyone has the right to respect for his private and family life, his home and his correspondence; and

(2)   there shall be no interference by a public authority with the exercise of this right except such as is in accordance with the law and is necessary in a democratic society in the interests of national security, public safety or the economic well-being of the country, for the prevention of disorder or crime, for the protection of health or morals, or for the protection of the rights and freedoms of others.

Disclosure of information other than convictions and cautions to third parties may be justified by art 8(2) as being a legitimate aim, ie necessary for the prevention of crime, the protection of health and rights of others. However, the interference must be proportionate to the legitimate aim and a blanket policy of disclosure without due consideration of the particular facts may give rise to a complaint under art 8.[2]

2.80   It could also be argued that disclosure of such information infringes the presumption of innocence contained in art 6(2). Care will need to be taken to ensure that the wording of the certificate is not open to the implication that the suspect was, in fact, guilty of the offence under investigation,[3] although the obvious reason for providing the information in the first place must be that it is relevant to the question of appointment.

Sufficient evidence to justify a prosecution

2.81   If, at any time during the investigation, an officer considers that there is sufficient evidence to prosecute a detained person, and that there is sufficient evidence for a prosecution to succeed, he must ask him if he has anything further to say and stop questioning him.[4] The detained person must then be brought

---

1   Police Act 1997, s 115(9).
2   Emmerson and Friedman *A Guide to the Police Act 1997* (Butterworths, London, 1998) p 91.
      See further chap 5.
3   Emmerson and Friedman *A Guide to the Police Act 1997* (Butterworths, London, 1998) p 92.
4   Code C para 16.1.

before the custody officer, who considers the evidence against the detained person and either supervises the making of a charge, or releases the detained person without charge. In determining whether or not there is sufficient evidence to justify a prosecution, the police will be influenced by the evidential sufficiency test contained in the Code of Practice for Crown Prosecutors,[1] ie whether there is a realistic prospect of conviction. Although it is the role of the police to decide if an offender should be charged, and if so with what offence, the police may call on the Crown Prosecution Service for advice in making this decision.

Sufficient evidence to prosecute – the use of cautions

2.82   One option available to the police when there is sufficient evidence to justify a prosecution is to caution the suspect. The practice of cautioning an offender as an alternative to prosecution was initially developed as a means of diverting juvenile offenders from the criminal justice system. Cautions are not, however, restricted to juvenile offenders and may also be administered to adult offenders, although the cautioning rate for juveniles remains very much higher than for adult offenders.[2] Current cautioning practice is dealt with by a Home Office Circular,[3] which incorporates National Standards for Cautioning. The main aim of the Circular is to discourage the use of cautions in appropriate cases (particularly indictable only offences), to increase consistency between forces and to promote better monitoring and recording of cautions. Following the publication of the Circular, the Association of Police Chief Officers (ACPO) issued more detailed and prescriptive guidance on cautioning which recommended the use of 'gravity factors' to improve objectivity and thereby improve consistency. The system suggested involved the allocation of a score according to the seriousness of the offence and a range of aggravating or mitigating factors. The final score would be a guide when deciding on a suitable disposal. Subsequent research undertaken on behalf of the Home Office found that 25 out of 42 police forces in England and Wales accepted gravity factors as a guide for cautioning decisions.[4]

Criteria for administering a caution

2.83   In order to administer a caution:

(1) there must be sufficient evidence to justify a prosecution, ie there must be sufficient evidence of the offender's guilt to offer a realistic prospect of conviction;
(2) the offender must admit the offence; and
(3) the offender (or, in the case of a juvenile, his parent or guardian) must understand the significance of the offence and give informed consent to the caution.

---

1   See **2.118**.
2   *Police Cautioning in the 1990s* Home Office Research Findings No 52 (Home Office, London, 1997).
3   Home Office Circular 18/1994.
4   *Police Cautioning in the 1990s* Home Office Research Findings No 52 (Home Office, London, 1997).

2.84 In deciding whether or not to administer a caution, the police must consider if it is in the public interest. The following factors should be considered.

(1) The police should take into account the public interest principles contained in the Code for Crown Prosecutors.[1]
(2) Commission of an indictable-only offence should lead to prosecution, regardless of the age or previous record of the offender, other than in the most exceptional circumstances. Home Office research found that the cautioning rate for indictable-only offences was 12% in 1994 and 11% in 1995 and that only six forces said that they would not, under any circumstances, caution for a serious indictable offence.[2]
(3) Triable-either-way offences may also be too serious for a caution. Consideration should be given to, inter alia, the harm resulting from the offence, whether the offence was racially motivated, whether the offence involved a breach of trust, and whether the offence was carried out in an organised way.
(4) The offender's attitude should be considered – in particular the wilfulness with which the offence was committed and the offender's subsequent attitude.
(5) The victim's view of the offence, and whether a caution is appropriate, should be sought and considered, although this is not conclusive. Concerns have been expressed that there is a danger of placing too much pressure upon some victims when they are at their most vulnerable,[3] and this concern may be seen as particularly pertinent in relation to sex offences where the victim is often severely traumatised by the offence itself.
(6) There should be a presumption in favour of cautioning rather than prosecuting certain categories of offender, such as the elderly and those who suffer from mental illness or impairment or a severe physical illness.
(7) An offender should only be cautioned for a second time if the subsequent offence is trivial or where there has been a sufficient lapse of time since the first caution to suggest that it had some effect.

The status of a police caution

2.85 There is no statutory basis for administering a caution,[4] however, the Home Office guidance on cautioning makes it clear that a caution is to be recorded by the police[5] and should be cited in court proceedings if they are relevant to the offence under consideration. However, it is noted in the guidance that, in presenting antecedents, care should be taken to distinguish between cautions and convictions, which should usually be listed on a separate sheet of paper. Cautions also form part of the criminal statistics collated by the Home

---

1   See **2.119**.
2   *Police Cautioning in the 1990s* Home Office Research Findings No 52 (Home Office, London, 1997).
3   May 'The Legal Effect of a Police Caution' [1997] Crim LR 491 at 492.
4   There was a statutory reference to the concept of a police caution in s 5(2) of the Children and Young Persons Act 1969, which required the police to consult with social services departments in cases concerning juveniles.
5   From November 1995, new police cautions for reportable offences have been stored on Phoenix, the computerised national criminal justice record service.

Office. The lack of a statutory basis for administering a caution has been a cause of concern and in 1993 the Royal Commission on Criminal Justice recommended that police cautioning should be governed by statute, under which national guidelines, drawn up in consultation with the CPS and police service among others, should be laid down in regulations. It was further recommended that these regulations should also govern the keeping of records of cautions so that information about whether a suspect has been cautioned previously can easily be transferred between police forces.[1] Following the enactment of the Police Act 1997, the creation of a Criminal Records Bureau within the Home Office and answerable to the Home Secretary, will bring all criminal record information under central control. In December 1998, the Home Office published plans for the Bureau to be based in Merseyside under the management of the UK Passport Agency, but estimated that it would take 2 years to establish the Bureau.[2] The Government subsequently revised this date and it is now estimated that the Bureau will start issuing certificates in July 2001.[3]

2.86   The precise status of a caution remains a matter of some dispute, particularly in relation to the good character of the offender.[4] On the one hand, it can be argued that a person who has received a caution has admitted a criminal offence and that therefore he should not be entitled to hold himself out as a person of good character. On the other hand, it can be argued that such a person has not been convicted of the offence and any admission was not made in judicial proceedings, therefore he cannot be said to have lost his good character. The inclusion of those cautioned for certain sexual offences in those who are subject to the notification requirements imposed by the Sex Offenders Act 1997[5] lends support to the former view – that a person who has been cautioned is not entitled to hold himself out as a person of good character. However, the Government's insistence that the notification requirements are an administrative device rather than punishment[6] may be seen to weaken this argument as, unlike punishment, administrative requirements are not only imposed on those who have lost their good character. Further status appears to have been accorded to cautions by the inclusion of police cautions in the information contained in a criminal record certificate and an enhanced criminal record certificate.[7] Although the subject of considerable debate and opposition during the passage of the Bill through Parliament,[8] the provisions mean that all existing and future cautions will be included in the category of information routinely supplied to employers and organisations who are entitled to ask questions concerning convictions which are spent under the Rehabilitation of Offenders Act 1974.

---

1   *Royal Commission on Criminal Justice* (1993) Cmnd 2263, chap 5 para 57.
2   Home Office Press Release 494/98.
3   Home Office Press Release 441/99.
4   May 'The Legal Effect of a Police Caution' [1997] Crim LR 491.
5   See further chap 6.
6   Cobley 'Keeping Track of Sex Offenders – Part 1 of the Sex Offenders Act 1997' [1997] 60 MLR 690 at 692.
7   Police Act 1997, ss 113, 115 and 116. See **2.77**.
8   HL Report col 524, 20 January 1997.

Cautioning sex offenders

2.87　　Criminal statistics show that in 1998, a caution was administered to 27% of all known sex offenders.[1] Known sex offenders are those found guilty or cautioned for indictable sexual offences and so do not include those found not guilty at trial. As would be expected from the criteria for cautioning, the percentage cautioned varied tremendously according to the offence charged. At one end of the spectrum, only 3.6% of offenders were cautioned for the most serious offence of rape, whereas at the other end of the spectrum, 56% of offenders were cautioned for unlawful sexual intercourse with a girl under the age of 16 and 50% were cautioned for indecency between males. Rather surprisingly, 29% of offenders were cautioned for having unlawful sexual intercourse with a girl under the age of 13 – an indictable-only offence the commission of which the Home Office guidance suggests should result in prosecution other than in the most exceptional circumstances. Admittedly, the numbers involved were small (of the 78 known offenders, 23 were cautioned) and no statistics are available on the age of offender and the circumstances in which the offence was committed, but the figures do indicate that the offence of having unlawful intercourse with a girl under the age of 13 is treated as being in a separate category to other indictable-only offences when deciding whether or not to administer a caution.

Trends in cautioning sex offenders

2.88　　Trends in the use of cautions can reflect not only policy shifts in official guidance, but also the public perception of certain types of offences. An examination of the number of cautions administered to sex offenders over the last 20 years, particularly developments in the last 5 years, reveal an interesting pattern which cannot be attributed to shifts in policy alone but arguably reflect the recent public and professionals concerns about sex offending. Research has shown that the cautioning rate for sexual offences has fallen dramatically since 1993, well beyond changes in rates for other offence categories.[2] During the 1980s there was a steady rise in the cautioning rate for all indictable offences[3] which reached a peak of 41% in 1992. The rate then remained constant for several years, but fell to 38% in 1997 and to 37% in 1998.[4] As the most recent guidance issued in 1994 was aimed at discouraging both multiple cautions and the use of cautions for serious offences, the halt in the overall growth in cautioning rates may be seen as attributable to this change in policy. However, the trend in the use of cautions for sex offenders shows a marked decrease in recent years. The cautioning rate for sex offenders in 1993 was 43%, but in recent years there has been a steady decline. In 1995 the cautioning rate for sex offenders had fallen to 32% and by 1998 it had fallen to 27%. This decline is significantly greater than the overall decline in the cautioning rate, leading to speculation that the police have taken the view that sexual offences are a special

1　　*Criminal Statistics for England and Wales 1998* (provided by the Home Office). 'Known sex offenders' are those found guilty or cautioned for indictable sexual offences.
2　　Soothill et al 'A Cautionary Tale: The Sex Offenders Act 1997, the Police and Cautions' [1997] Crim LR 482.
3　　Excluding motoring offences.
4　　Home Office Statistical Bulletin 21/99 *Cautions, Court Proceedings and Sentencing, England and Wales 1998*, table 6.

case – possibly influenced by the developing concerns about paedophilia and sex offending in general.[1]

Cautions, punishment and treatment – a lost opportunity?

2.89 The cautioning rate for sexual offences may well continue to decrease in future years. The inclusion of cautioned offenders in the registration provisions of the Sex Offenders Act 1997 has led to suggestions that that there will be at least two kinds of pressure to avoid using cautioning: accused sex offenders may want to exercise their right to a trial, as an acquittal may be the only way to avoid the registration requirements; and the police may want to avoid trouble which might follow from increased scrutiny of and challenge to their use of cautioning.[2] Furthermore, particularly in the case of offences of sexual aggression, the cautioning rate may decrease as a reflection of the increasingly punitive approach to sex offenders that is becoming evident in other areas, such as sentencing. Current cautioning rates are markedly higher for breaches of sexual taboo than they are for offences of sexual aggression. In 1998, 50% of known offenders were cautioned for indecency between males whereas the cautioning rate for indecent assault on a male was 22% and 24% for indecent assault on a female. This difference in cautioning rates is understandable, as a caution may be seen as a perfectly acceptable outcome in cases where the sexual activity is consensual and no harm is caused. When a caution has been administered, with the exception of the notification requirements imposed by the Sex Offenders Act 1997, no further obligations may be imposed on the offender. Yet there will undoubtedly be other cases where the offender has committed a comparatively minor offence of sexual aggression (perhaps an indecent assault which involved touching the victim on the outside of his or her clothes with no physical violence), which may be considered appropriate for a caution, but the offender would benefit from some assistance in controlling his sexual urges to prevent further, perhaps more serious, offences being committed. In 1993, the Royal Commission on Criminal Justice acknowledged the desirability, pressed on it by several witnesses including the CPS, of combining a caution with a requirement on the offender to co-operate with social work agencies or the Probation Service or to agree to consult a doctor or to attend a clinic.[3] However, neither the police nor the CPS felt that it should take the lead in administering such schemes, and the Royal Commission agreed that they may not in fact be the most appropriate services to take the overall responsibility, preferring the Probation Service. It appears that in at least one police area an informal system has been jointly developed between the police and the local Probation Service, and the Royal Commission felt that this may well provide a model for national development and recommended that the topic be looked at further. Given the increasing trend for agencies, particularly the police and Probation Service, to work together in protecting the public from any risk posed by sex offenders,[4] such schemes would no doubt fit in well with existing practices.

---

1   See **1.2**.
2   Soothill et al 'A Cautionary Tale: The Sex Offenders Act 1997, the Police and Cautions' [1997] Crim LR 482 at 489.
3   *Royal Commission on Criminal Justice* (1993) Cmnd 2263, chap 5 para 60.
4   See further chap 6.

The fact that currently an offender who has been cautioned cannot be obliged to seek treatment may well be seen as a lost opportunity.

Young offenders and the final warning scheme

2.90   The Crime and Disorder Act 1998 provides that the principal aim of the youth justice system is to prevent offending by children and young people.[1] Although cautions were initially developed as an means of diverting young offenders from the criminal justice system, the 1998 Act now provides for a new scheme of police reprimands and warnings, known as the final warning scheme, which will replace cautioning for young offenders.[2] The main objectives of the scheme are to end repeat cautioning and provide a speedy and progressive response to offending behaviour, to ensure appropriate and effective action when a young person starts to offend so as to help prevent re-offending, and to ensure that those who do re-offend after a final warning are dealt with quickly and effectively by the court system. Pilots of the final warning scheme began in October 1998 and the scheme will be brought into force nationally on 1 June 2000.[3] Under the scheme, instead of receiving a caution, young offenders may receive a reprimand, or in more serious cases, a warning. Offenders who have not previously been reprimanded, warned or charged, may be reprimanded, provided that the offence is not so serious as to require a warning. Offenders who have not previously been warned, or those whose previous warning was received more than 2 years previously, may receive a warning as long as the police officer considers the offence to be not so serious as to require a charge to be brought. The warning is a serious matter and any further offending behaviour will result in charges being brought in all but the most exceptional circumstances. In no circumstances can a young person receive more than two warnings.

2.91   The 1998 Act also places a duty on local authorities with social services and education responsibilities to establish one or more Youth Offending Teams for their area.[4] These teams will be responsible for coordinating the provision of youth justice services for those in the area who need them, and for carrying out the functions assigned to the teams in the Youth Justice Plan, which the local authority is required to formulate and implement annually.[5] The Youth Offending Teams are multi-agency and include probation officers, social workers, police officers and members nominated by the health authority and chief education officer for the area. When a warning is given to a young offender, the offender will be referred immediately to the local Youth Offending Team. The team is then under an obligation to assess the offender and arrange for him to participate in a rehabilitation programme, unless it is considered inappropriate to do so. Each rehabilitation programme is individual to the offender, but will always be targeted at achieving the overall aims of addressing offending behaviour and preventing re-offending. Thus the new final warning scheme for

---

1   Crime and Disorder Act 1998, s 37.
2   Crime and Disorder Act 1998, ss 65 and 66.
3   Home Office Press Release 032/2000.
4   Crime and Disorder Act 1998, s 39.
5   Crime and Disorder Act 1998, s 40.

young offenders may potentially achieve what the system of cautioning offenders cannot, namely the provision of treatment for young sex offenders without the need for a criminal conviction. However, although Home Office guidance on the establishment and operation of the rehabilitation programmes refers to the possibility of short-term counselling or group work to bring about behavioural change,[1] no specific mention is made of addressing the issue of treatment for sex offenders. It would be regrettable if this opportunity to encourage the treatment of young sex offenders at an early stage is not exploited fully.

Sufficient evidence to prosecute – proceeding by way of summons

2.92   If there is sufficient evidence to justify a prosecution, the police may proceed by way of reporting for summons, whereby the suspect is informed that the police intend to report him for possible summons in relation to the offence and he is then released unconditionally. An information is then laid before magistrates, containing a brief statement of the offence which the person named in it is suspected of having committed. If the information appears prima facie correct, the magistrate will issue a summons requiring the accused to appear before the magistrates' court to answer the allegation in the information. This method of commencing a prosecution will be of limited use in the case of sex offenders, except perhaps for the most trivial offences for which no power of arrest exists.

Sufficient evidence to prosecute – proceeding by way of charge

2.93   In the majority of cases where there is sufficient evidence to justify a prosecution, the police will proceed by way of charge. The detained person is cautioned,[2] the charge is written down on the charge sheet and read to him. Any reply he makes is recorded. The main advantage of proceeding by way of charge is that the police can continue to have a measure of control over the movements of the suspect, either by detaining him in custody for a further period after charge before making an application for a remand in custody to the court, or by imposing conditions of bail.

The presumption in favour of bail

2.94   Once a suspect has been charged, in most cases[3] there is a presumption in favour of bail and the custody officer must order his immediate release, either on bail or without bail, unless:

(1) if the person arrested is not an arrested juvenile:
  (a) his name or address cannot be ascertained or the custody officer has reasonable grounds for doubting whether a name or address furnished by him as his name or address is his real name or address,
  (b) the custody officer has reasonable grounds for believing that the person arrested will fail to appear in court to answer bail,

---

1   *The Establishment and Operation of the Rehabilitation (Change) Programmes under the Final Warning Scheme* (Home Office, London, January 1999).
2   See **2.30**.
3   See **2.95**.

    (c) in the case of a person arrested for an imprisonable offence, the custody officer has reasonable grounds for believing that the detention of the person arrested is necessary to prevent him committing an offence,

    (d) in the case of a person arrested for an offence which is not an imprisonable offence, the custody officer has reasonable grounds for believing that the detention of the person arrested is necessary to prevent him causing physical injury to any other person or from causing loss of or damage to property,

    (e) the custody officer has reasonable grounds for believing that the detention of the person arrested is necessary to prevent him from interfering with the administration of justice or with the investigation of offences or a particular offence, or

    (f) the custody officer has reasonable grounds for believing that the detention of the person arrested is necessary for his own protection; or

(2) if he is an arrested juvenile:

    (a) any of the requirements of paragraph (1) above is satisfied, or

    (b) the custody officer has reasonable grounds for believing that he ought to be detained in his own interests.[1]

Restrictions on the presumption in favour of bail for those charged with homicide or rape

2.95   Following concern about the level of offending committed by people who have been granted bail and the granting of bail to those accused of serious offences who had previous convictions for similar offences, the Criminal Justice and Public Order Act 1994 imposed a complete prohibition on the granting of bail, either by the police or the courts, in certain circumstances. The prohibition applied to any person charged with or convicted of one of the following offences:

(1) murder;
(2) attempted murder;
(3) manslaughter;
(4) rape; or
(5) attempted rape.[2]

2.96   The prohibition applied only if the person had a previous conviction in the UK for any of the above offences or culpable homicide and, in the case of manslaughter or culpable homicide, if he had been sentenced to imprisonment or, if he was then a child or young person, to long-term detention under any of the relevant enactments.[3] However, the Crime and Disorder Act 1998 relaxed the outright prohibition on the granting of bail by providing a rebuttable presumption that bail should be granted in these circumstances only if the court, or, as the case may be, the constable considering the grant of bail is satisfied that there are exceptional circumstances which justify it.[4] Although the prohibition

---

1   PACE 1984, s 38(1).
2   Criminal Justice and Public Order Act 1994, s 25(2).
3   Criminal Justice and Public Order Act 1994, s 25(3).
4   Crime and Disorder Act 1998, s 56.

has been removed, the general presumption in favour of bail, which applies in all other cases, is reversed in these circumstances and the onus is on the person charged to show that there are exceptional reasons why he should not be kept in custody. Home Office guidance suggests that, if the police decide to grant bail in such cases, the custody officer will wish to consult a more senior officer before authorising the release of the suspect on bail. Furthermore, it would also be advisable to consult the CPS before reaching a final decision to grant bail in exceptional circumstances and to make a record of the reasons for granting bail on the custody record.[1]

Restrictions on bail and human rights

2.97 Article 5 of the European Convention on Human Rights provides that those who are arrested shall be brought promptly before a judge or other officer authorised by law to exercise judicial power and shall be entitled to trial within a reasonable time or to release pending trial. The fundamental objective of art 5 is to prevent arbitrary detention. The requirement for 'trial within a reasonable period or release pending trial' is in fact two distinct and cumulative requirements – a detainee must be tried within a reasonable period and has a qualified right to release pending trial. The European Commission of Human Rights has held that the complete prohibition on the granting of bail to those with a relevant previous conviction charged with murder, manslaughter or rape which was contained in the original s 25 of the Criminal Justice and Public Order Act 1994 was a violation of art 5.[2] The Commission held that the defendant must be brought promptly before a judge who, having heard the defendant, must examine all the facts arguing for and against the existence of a genuine requirement of public interest justifying, with due regard to the presumption of innocence, a departure from the rule of respect for an individual's liberty.

2.98 The changes contained in the Crime and Disorder Act 1998, although originally introduced prior to the ruling of the European Commission, were made in an attempt to ensure that s 25 of the 1994 Act complied with art 5. However, doubts have continued to be raised over the compatibility of the provision, even in its amended form. It has been pointed out that there are alternative approaches to the proper construction and application of s 25 and that a court might conclude that where the section applies, it has no real discretion in the absence of some very unusual feature of the two relevant offences – that charged and that previously committed.[3] The Law Commission has expressed the view that it should be for Parliament to clearly spell out, within the context of the Convention, what weight should be given to different factors arguing for and against bail and has therefore proposed that s 25 be amended to ensure compliance with art 5. For the same reason, the Law Commission has also made recommendations for the reform of the provisions contained in Sch 1 to the Bail Act 1976 which permit a court to refuse bail if the offence charged is indictable and the defendant was on bail when he or she is alleged to have committed it, or if the defendant has already been granted bail and had been

---

1   Home Office Circular 34/98 para 20.
2   *CC v United Kingdom* [1999] Crim LR 228 European Commission of Human Rights.
3   Law Commission Consultation Paper No 157 'Bail and the Human Rights Act 1998' (1999).

arrested, for example for breach of a bail condition.[1] More generally, the Law Commission has proposed that magistrates and judges should be provided with appropriate guidance and training on making bail decisions in a way which is compliant with art 5.[2] There is no doubt that the Government will wish to give serious consideration to the responses to the proposals contained in the Law Commission Consultation Paper, with a view to implementing change to ensure compliance with the Human Rights Act 1998.

Police bail

2.99   Although the courts have long had the power to impose conditions on a grant of bail, before 1994, if there were no grounds to justify the continued detention of the suspect after charge, although the police could bail the defendant, thereby imposing the standard duty to surrender to custody, and could require the defendant to provide a surety or sureties, there was no power to attach any further conditions to the bail. This resulted in many defendants being brought before the courts to make applications for bail even though the police were quite willing to grant bail themselves, but were reluctant to do so in the absence of a power to impose conditions on the defendant. In 1993, the Royal Commission on Criminal Justice recommended that the police should have the additional power of releasing on bail subject to conditions[3] and this recommendation was implemented by the Criminal Justice and Public Order Act 1994. The police may now require the defendant to comply with such requirements as appear to the officer to be necessary for the purpose of preventing the defendant from:

(1)   failing to surrender to custody;
(2)   committing an offence whilst on bail; or
(3)   interfering with witnesses or otherwise obstructing the course of justice, whether in relation to himself or any other person.[4]

In addition to the power to impose conditions, the police, along with the courts, now also have the power to require the deposit of a security by the defendant or on his behalf, in any case where it is believed that the deposit of a security will increase the likelihood of a bailed defendant appearing in court when required.[5]

2.100   Research suggests that the police are now using bail with conditions for people who in the past would have been released unconditionally.[6] Police officers appear to be cautious about taking on the extra responsibility of granting bail in cases where there is a possibility of breach or reoffending, preferring to defer responsibility for bail to the magistrates, who may well be in possession of more accurate and detailed information about the offender's circumstances by the time their decision is made.[7]

---

1   Law Commission Consultation Paper No 157 para 1.28.
2   Law Commission Consultation Paper No 157 para 4.25.
3   *Royal Commission in Criminal Justice* (1993) Cmnd 2263 chap 5 para 22.
4   Bail Act 1976, ss 3 and 3A.
5   Crime and Disorder Act 1998, s 54(1). See further **2.104**.
6   Home Office Research Study 174 *In police custody: police powers and suspects' rights under the revised PACE Codes of Practice.*
7   See **2.106**.

Taking the defendant before the court

2.101   If the custody officer decides that bail should not be granted and it is intended that the proceedings shall be in the local magistrates' court, the person charged must be brought before the court as soon as is practicable, and in any event not later than the first sitting after he is charged with the offence.[1] If the proceedings are to be in a court other than the local magistrates' court, the person charged is to be removed to the relevant area as soon as is practicable, when similar time restrictions will take effect.[2] In practice, the broad effect of these provisions is that a person charged must be brought before a court on the day after he is charged (special Saturday sittings being arranged for those charged on a Friday), save that a person charged on a Saturday may be held over until the following Monday.[3]

Remands in custody by the courts

2.102   When a suspect is detained after charge and subsequently brought before a magistrates' court, the Bail Act 1976 provides what is commonly referred to as a 'right to bail'.[4] However, bail may be refused if the conditions set out in Sch 1 to the Act are satisfied. Part 1 of the schedule applies where the defendant has been charged or convicted of at least one offence punishable with imprisonment.[5] He need not be granted bail if:

(1) the court is satisfied that there are substantial grounds for believing that, if released on bail, the defendant would:
    (a) fail to surrender to custody,
    (b) commit an offence whilst on bail, or
    (c) interfere with witnesses or otherwise obstruct the course of justice, whether in relation to himself or some other person; or
(2) the offence with which he is charged is indictable only, or triable either way, and he was already on bail at the time of the charged offence;
(3) the court is satisfied that he should be kept in custody for his own protection, or, if he is a juvenile, for his own welfare;
(4) he is already serving a custodial sentence;
(5) the court is satisfied that lack of time since the commencement of the proceedings has made it impracticable to obtain the information needed to decide properly the questions raised in (1) to (3) above; or
(6) he has already been bailed during the course of the proceedings, and has been arrested under s 7 of the Act (absconding or breaking conditions of bail).

2.103   In deciding whether to withhold bail on the grounds that the defendant would abscond, commit further offences or interfere with witnesses,

---

1   PACE 1984, s 46(2).
2   PACE 1984, s 46(4).
3   Sprack *Emmins on Criminal Procedure* (Blackstone Press Ltd, London, 1997) p 16.
4   See, however, restrictions on the presumption in favour of bail (**2.95**).
5   If the defendant is charged with a non-imprisonable offence, the court may refuse bail only if it is satisfied that he should be refused bail for his own protection, if he is already serving a custodial sentence or if he has been bailed in the course of the proceedings and has been arrested under s 7 of the Act.

the court will have regard to such of the following conditions that appear to it to be relevant:[1]

(1) the nature and seriousness of the offence or default and the probable method of dealing with the defendant for it;
(2) the character, antecedents, associations and community ties of the defendant;
(3) the defendant's record in respect of the fulfilment of his obligations under previous grants of bail in criminal proceedings; and
(4) except in the case of a defendant whose case is adjourned for inquiries or report, the strength of the evidence of his having committed the offence, or having defaulted, as well as any others which appear to be relevant.

Custody time limits

2.104   If a defendant is remanded in custody, regulations prescribe the maximum period for which he may be held in custody pending trial:[2]

(1) 70 days between first appearance in the magistrates' court and committal proceedings;
(2) 70 days between first appearance and summary trial for an offence which is triable either way (reduced to 56 days if the decision for summary trial is taken within 56 days); and
(3) 112 days between committal for trial and arraignment.

2.105   The prosecution may make an application for an extension before the custody time limit expires, but such extension will only be granted if the court is satisfied that:

(1) there is good and sufficient cause for an extension; and
(2) the Crown has acted with all due expedition.

Should the time limit expire, the exceptions to the right to bail contained in Sch 1 to the Bail Act 1976 no longer apply and the defendant is effectively given a right to bail. However, the court can attach conditions to the bail[3] as long as they are conditions which must be complied with after the grant of bail, thereby allowing the court to restrict the movements of a defendant who is released pending trial.

Remands on bail by the court

2.106   If a defendant is granted unconditional bail, his only obligation is to surrender to custody at the appointed place and time, which will usually be a later court hearing. However, in many cases, the courts will take the view that, although a remand in custody is not justified, some further obligations should be imposed on the defendant, either in the form of requiring sureties or securities to ensure he does surrender to custody, or by imposing other conditions to prevent the commission of further offences or interference with witnesses.

---

1   Bail Act 1976, Sch 1, para 9.
2   Prosecution of Offences Act 1985, s 22.
3   See **2.108**.

Sureties and securities

2.107 A surety is a person who enters into a recognisance, ie an undertaking to pay the court a specified sum of money if the defendant fails to surrender to custody. The requirement to provide a surety or sureties is one of the most common requirements attached to a grant of bail. The specified sum only becomes payable if the defendant fails to surrender to custody, although the police or court responsible for granting bail must be satisfied that any person who stands as surety has the means to pay the specified sum if required. In contrast to a surety, the police and courts have a power to require a security to be given, either by the defendant himself or by someone on his behalf. A security requires the deposit of money or other property with the court which will be forfeited if the defendant fails to surrender to custody. Prior to 1998, a security could only be required where it appeared that the defendant was unlikely to remain in Great Britain. This restriction was removed by the Crime and Disorder Act 1998.[1]

Additional conditions of bail

2.108 The courts and, more recently, the police, have additional powers to require the defendant to comply with such other conditions as appear necessary to ensure that he does not abscond, commit further offences whilst on bail or interfere with witnesses or otherwise obstruct the course of justice whether in relation to himself or any other person.[2] This is a wide-ranging power, which is used extensively by the courts. The conditions imposed can restrict the movements of the defendant to a considerable degree. Conditions frequently imposed include the following:[3]

(1) a condition of residence, frequently expressed as a condition that the person is to live and sleep at a specified address;
(2) a condition that the person is to notify any changes of address to the police;
(3) a condition of reporting (whether daily, weekly or at other intervals) to a local police station;
(4) a curfew (ie that the person must be indoors between certain hours);
(5) a condition that a person is not to enter a certain area or building, or to go within a specified distance of a certain address;
(6) a condition that the person is not to contact (whether directly or indirectly) the victim of the alleged offence and/or any other probable witnesses; and
(7) a condition that the person's passport should be surrendered to the police.

2.109 In addition to such general conditions, which are available to both the courts and the police, the courts have further specific powers, which are not available to the police. A court can require a defendant to make himself available for the purposes of enabling inquiries or a report to be made to assist the court in dealing with him for the offence and can also require the defendant to reside at a bail hostel.[4] The courts may also require the defendant, as a condition of bail, to

---

1   Crime and Disorder Act 1998, s 54(1).
2   Bail Act 1976, s 3(6).
3   *Blackstone's Criminal Practice* D5.23.
4   Bail Act 1976, s 3(6)(d). See further chap 8.

attend an interview with a legal adviser before his next appearance in court.[1] The objective of this new provision is to try to ensure that a defendant receives legal advice and decides on the response to the allegation in the charge in advance of his court appearance so as to avoid a wasted hearing, although it does not remove the defendant's right to represent himself if he so chooses.[2]

Bail information reports

2.110 In order to improve the quality of the bail decision, the Probation Service provides the CPS with factual, verified information about an offender, including an assessment of any risk of harm the offender is thought to present to the public. The National Standards for the Supervision of Offenders in the Community contain guidance on the preparation of bail information reports. The reports should be objective, factual and impartial, should include details of relevant information such as accommodation and employment, be presented as a written report whenever possible or be made orally when a written report cannot be prepared in time, and then be written up as soon as possible thereafter, and, in cases where risk of serious harm to the public is apparent, the reports should be copied to the police, social services or health authority as appropriate.[3]

Breach of bail

2.111 If the defendant fails, without reasonable cause, to surrender to the custody of a court, he commits an offence and the court may issue a warrant for his arrest.[4] If the defendant has been bailed to return to the police station, but fails to do so, the police may arrest him without a warrant.[5] In order to prevent possible breaches of bail, where a defendant has been bailed by the court, a police officer may arrest the defendant without warrant:

(1) if he has reasonable grounds for believing that the defendant is not likely to surrender to custody;
(2) if he has reasonable grounds for believing that the defendant is likely to break, or has broken, any of the conditions of his bail; or
(3) in a case where the defendant was released on bail with one or more surety or sureties, if a surety notifies a constable in writing that the defendant is unlikely to surrender to custody and that for that reason the surety wishes to be relieved of his obligations.[6]

2.112 The defendant who has been arrested for actual or anticipated breach of bail must be brought before a magistrates' court as soon as practicable and in any event within 24 hours. If the court is of the opinion that the defendant is not likely to surrender to custody or has broken or is likely to break any condition of

---

1   Crime and Disorder Act 1998, s 54(2).
2   Home Office Circular 34/98 para 8.
3   *National Standards for the Supervision of Offenders in the Community* (Home Office, London, 2000) para B2.
4   Bail Act 1976, s 6(1).
5   PACE 1984, s 46A.
6   Bail Act 1976, s 7(3).

his bail, the defendant may be remanded in custody or may be granted bail subject to the same or different conditions.[1]

YOUNG OFFENDERS AND OTHER VULNERABLE OFFENDERS

2.113 The procedures for arrest and detention of suspects are generally applicable to all persons, regardless of age. However, it is acknowledged that some extra protection of the suspect may be necessary if he is a young person, or if he is considered particularly vulnerable.

2.114 The powers of arrest contained in the PACE 1984 apply irrespective of age. However, any person who arrests a young person[2] must take all reasonable steps to inform his parents of what has occurred.[3] When taken to the police station, the young person's continued detention there depends on the decision of the custody sergeant as to whether there is sufficient evidence to charge him or whether detention without charge is necessary to secure or preserve evidence relating to the offence or to obtain such evidence by questioning him.[4]

2.115 A young person should not usually be interviewed or asked to provide a statement unless an 'appropriate adult' is also present.[5] An appropriate adult is defined as either his parent or guardian, a social worker, or some other responsible adult unconnected with the police. The appropriate adult's role is not merely to act as an observer, but also to advise the young person and, if necessary, to facilitate communication with him. Following police investigations, if the young person is charged but not released, the custody officer usually must arrange for him to be taken into the care of the local authority and detained by them until he can be brought before the Youth Court.[6] In practice, young persons may often be released without charge to allow consultations with other agencies to determine whether a prosecution should proceed or

---

1   Bail Act 1976, s 7(5).
2   For these purposes, young persons are those under the age of 17 years. Those aged 17 or over are treated while in police detention as if they were adults. However, if a prosecution is commenced, those under the age of 18 will fall within the jurisdiction of the Youth Court. See **3.95**.
3   Children and Young Persons Act 1933, s 34.
4   See **2.61**.
5   Code C: Code of Practice for the Detention, Treatment and Questioning of Persons by Police Officers, paras 11.14–11.16. A juvenile may only be questioned without an appropriate adult being present if an officer of at least the rank of superintendent considers that delay will lead to physical harm to other people or harm to evidence connected with an offence, or alert other suspects not yet arrested for the offence, or hinder the recovery of property obtained from an offence – para 11.1 and Annex C to Code C.
6   PACE 1984, s 38(6). The juvenile can be kept in police custody if the custody officer certifies that it is impractical to make the necessary arrangements with the local authority, or if the juvenile is aged 15 or over, no secure accommodation is available, and the officer certifies that keeping him in such other local authority accommodation as is available would not be adequate to protect the public from serious harm from him.

whether a caution, or when in force nationally, a reprimand or warning, would be more appropriate.

2.116 Whilst, for these purposes, young persons include any person under the age of 17 years, it is also acknowledged that older persons may be vulnerable and need the additional protection of an appropriate adult if, for example, they are mentally ill or of low intelligence. The Codes of Practice thus make provision for an appropriate adult to be present when adults suffering from mental illness and those whose low intelligence make them incapable of understanding the significance of questions put to them by a police officer and/or the significance of their replies are being interviewed.

HANDING OVER TO THE CROWN PROSECUTION SERVICE

2.117 The CPS was created by the Prosecution of Offences Act 1985. The overall head of the service is the Director of Public Prosecutions, who is assisted by Chief Crown Prosecutors, each of whom is responsible to the Director for supervising the operation of the service in a particular area.[1] In many cases, the police may seek advice from the CPS at an early stage of an investigation, but once a suspect has been charged or informed he may be reported for summons, the entire conduct of the case is passed to the CPS and the evidence compiled by the police during their investigations is passed to the local office of the CPS. The case is then reviewed by a CPS lawyer. One of the major reasons for the creation of the service was to provide an independent check on whether police prosecutions were justified and, if not, to halt them at an early stage. For this reason, the CPS have a right to discontinue proceedings,[2] and thus the final decision as to whether a prosecution proceeds rests with the CPS, not the police. Guidance for the CPS in making this decision is contained in a Code for Crown Prosecutors issued by the DPP.[3] The police will already have considered many of the criteria laid down in the Code when making the initial decision to charge the suspect or report him for summons.[4] The code lays down two tests which must be satisfied before a prosecution can proceed: the evidential test and the public interest test.

The evidential test

2.118 Crown Prosecutors must be satisfied that there is enough evidence to provide a 'realistic prospect of conviction' against each defendant on each charge. This is an objective test, meaning that a jury or bench of magistrates, properly directed in accordance with the law, is more likely than not to convict the defendant on the charge alleged. In deciding this, Crown Prosecutors must consider the both the admissibility and reliability of the evidence in court. This will be particularly relevant in cases involving children as witnesses. Although attitudes towards the veracity and reliability of child witnesses have changed

---

1   Sprack *Emmins on Criminal Procedure* (Blackstone Press Ltd, London, 1997).
2   Prosecution of Offences Act 1985, s 23.
3   Prosecution of Offences Act 1985, s 10.
4   Home Office Circular 18/1994 para 3.

dramatically over the past two decades and the growing concern over the physical and sexual abuse of children has resulted in changes to the way in which children's evidence can be received by a court,[1] the decision to proceed with a prosecution in such cases will require careful consideration of the willingness and ability of the prosecution witnesses to give evidence in court. Other victims of sexual offences are also likely to be vulnerable as witnesses and similar considerations will apply.[2]

The public interest test

2.119   Once the evidential test has been satisfied, the Crown Prosecutor must then decide whether a prosecution is in the public interest. The Code states that, in cases of any seriousness, a prosecution will usually take place unless there are public interest factors tending against prosecution which clearly outweigh those tending in favour.[3] Given the increasing concern over sexual offending, it may be thought that sexual offences will always be viewed seriously and, if the police have already decided that a caution would not be appropriate, a prosecution will usually proceed. But the Code makes it clear that each case must be considered individually. A list of common public interest factors, both for and against prosecution, are provided, followed by a caveat that deciding on the public interest is not simply a matter of adding up the number of factors on each side and that Crown Prosecutors must always think very carefully about how important each factor is in the circumstances of each case and go on to make an overall assessment.

Some common public interest factors in favour of prosecution[4]

2.120   The more serious the offence, the more likely it is that a prosecution will be needed in the public interest. A prosecution is likely to be needed if:

(1)   a conviction is likely to result in a significant sentence;

(2)   a weapon was used or violence was threatened during the commission of the offence;

(3)   the offence was committed against a person serving the public (eg a police or prison officer, or a nurse);

(4)   the defendant was in a position of authority or trust;

(5)   the evidence shows that the defendant was a ringleader or an organiser of the offence;

(6)   there is evidence that the offence was premeditated;

(7)   there is evidence that the offence was carried out by a group;

(8)   the victim of the offence was vulnerable, has been in considerable fear, or suffered personal attack, damage or disturbance;

---

1   See further **3.125**.

2   See further chap 3 and the recommendations contained in *Speaking up for Justice: Report of the Interdepartmental Working Group on the Treatment of Vulnerable or Intimidated Witnesses in the Criminal Justice System* (Home Office, London, 1998).

3   Code of Practice for Crown Prosecutors para 6.2.

4   Code of Practice for Crown Prosecutors para 6.4.

(9)   the offence was motivated by any form of discrimination against the victim's ethnic or national origin, sex, religious beliefs, political views or sexual preference;

(10) there is a marked difference between the actual or mental ages of the defendant and the victim, or if there is an element of corruption;

(11) the defendant's previous convictions or cautions are relevant to the present offence;

(12) the defendant is alleged to have committed the offence whilst under an order of the court;

(13) there are grounds for believing that the offence is likely to be continued or repeated, for example, by a history of recurring conduct; or

(14) the offence, although not serious in itself, is widespread in the area where it was committed.

Some common public interest factors against prosecution[1]

2.121   A prosecution is less likely to be needed if:

(1)   the court is likely to impose a small or nominal penalty;

(2)   the offence was committed as a result of a genuine mistake or misunderstanding (these factors must be balanced against the seriousness of the offence);

(3)   the loss or harm can be described as minor and was the result of a single incident, particularly if it was caused by a misjudgement;

(4)   there has been a long delay between the offence taking place and the date of the trial, unless:
   (a) the offence is serious,
   (b) the delay was caused in part by the defendant,
   (c) the offence has only recently come to light, or
   (d) the complexity of the offence has meant that there has been a long investigation;

(5)   a prosecution is likely to have a very bad effect on the victim's physical or mental health, always bearing in mind the seriousness of the offence;

(6)   the defendant is elderly or is, or was at the time of the offence, suffering from significant mental or physical ill health, unless the offence is serious or there is a real possibility that it may be repeated (the CPS, where necessary, applies Home Office guidelines about how to deal with mentally disordered offenders; Crown Prosecutors must balance the desirability of diverting a defendant who is suffering from significant mental or physical ill health with the need to safeguard the general public);

(7)   the defendant has put right the loss or harm that was caused (but defendants must not avoid prosecution simply because they can pay compensation); or

(8)   details may be made public that could harm sources of information, international relations or national security.

---

1   Code of Practice for Crown Prosecutors para 6.5.

The public interest and young offenders

2.122   Specific reference is made in the Code of Practice to young offenders. Crown Prosecutors are required to consider the interests of a young person when deciding whether it is in the public interest to prosecute. The Code points out that the stigma of a conviction can cause very serious harm to the prospects of a young person and that young persons can sometimes be dealt with without going to court. However, it is also pointed out that Crown Prosecutors should not avoid prosecuting simply because of age and that the seriousness of the offence or past behaviour may make prosecution necessary.

Rape and CPS decision-making

2.123   The Home Office study of rape cases reported to the police in 1996 found that 50% of the cases crimed and detected by the police were submitted to the CPS for prosecution.[1] The CPS discontinued just over a quarter of these cases (28%), which was more than double the national discontinuance rate of 12% for 1996.[2] The majority of these cases were discontinued on evidential grounds. However, although it would rarely be in the public interest to discontinue a case of rape, 15% of the discontinued cases were dropped on this basis. These were non-stranger rapes where the complainant was unwilling to attend court and a witness summons to compel attendance was felt inappropriate.

2.124   The study also found that there was a significant association between the age of a complainant and whether a case was discontinued – those involving particularly young or particularly old complainants were most likely to be proceeded with. For example, no cases were discontinued when the complainant was over 45 years and only 14% were discontinued when the complainant was under 13 years. This compared to 34% of cases which were discontinued when the complainant was between 13 and 15 years, 33% of cases when the complainant was between 16 and 25 years and 29% of cases where the complainant was between 26 and 35 years. At first sight, it is difficult to see why the age of the complainant was such an important factor, particularly as most of the cases were discontinued on evidential grounds. Presumably, the credibility of the complainants was an important factor and complainants over 45 were all thought to be competent witnesses, whereas the 14% of cases discontinued where the complainant was under 13 involved very young children who were not thought to make credible witnesses.[3] However, this does not explain why so many cases were discontinued when the complainant was between these ages and presumably competent to give evidence, particularly when no significant association was found between other case circumstances, such as consensual contact, and the CPS decision to discontinue cases. However, other case circumstances were influential at an earlier stage as violence and age were found to predict no-criming decisions by the police and violence, age and consensual contact were found to predict the police taking no further action.

---

1   *A Question of Evidence? Investigating and Prosecuting Rape in the 1990s* Home Office Research Study 196 (Home Office, London, 1999).
2   About half of these were discontinued at or before the first court hearing, 16% before the second hearing and the remainder at or after the second court hearing.
3   See **3.17** to **3.21**.

Child victims and CPS decision-making

2.125   The decision to proceed with a prosecution in a case involving a child victim will inevitably focus initially on the credibility of the child. However, this will not be the only influential factor. A study conducted for the Home Office on the admissibility and sufficiency of evidence in child abuse prosecutions studied 94 cases of child abuse, involving 124 complainants.[1] The cases were secured in September and October 1996 and were obtained from three Child Protection Units (CPUs) and from the CPS in those areas. Sixty-seven of these cases (71%) involved sexual allegations. As the cases originated from CPUs, they were almost exclusively cases of intrafamilial abuse or cases where the complainant knew the alleged abuser and so, in many respects, can be seen as comparable with acquaintance and intimate rapes.

2.126   Of the 67 cases involving sexual allegations, six were discontinued by the police without reference to the CPS. Twenty-five cases were sent to the CPS for advice before charge, of which only four were prosecuted, together with 30 of the remaining 36 cases. Thus prosecutions were proceeded with in 34 of the 67 cases, ie 50%. The study found that the cases reviewed were often multi-faceted and that it was the interaction between several features that determined the prosecution decision. The following factors were found to be influential in the decision.

(1) **Assessing the complaint** – the complainant's account of the abuse was regarded as the most important piece of evidence, with prosecutors evaluating the strength of the complainant's evidence in terms of the account itself, and the demeanour of the child in telling it and looking primarily for clarity, coherence and the presence of details which indicated that the complainant had experienced abuse.

(2) **Assessing the child's demeanour** – videotaped interviews were generally thought to be an important innovation as they allowed prosecutors to form their own assessment of the child's evidence and of the child's strength as a witness.

(3) **Evidence to support the complainant's account** – some evidence other than the complainant's account was present in all of the 34 cases which the CPS considered suitable for prosecution. Such evidence included evidence of opportunity, recent complaint,[2] medical evidence, other witnesses, admissions by the suspect and similar fact evidence.[3] However, the strength of the evidence considered necessary was dependent upon the clarity and consistency of the complainant's account. Where the child was considered to have given a 'good account' of the abuse, evidence of opportunity, promptness of complaint, or minor medical signs could be viewed as satisfying the test of evidential sufficiency. In contrast, where the child's account was judged to be vague or unclear, cases were only prosecuted where there was other strong evidence to support the child's allegation.

---

1   Davis et al *An Assessment of the Admissibility and Sufficiency of Evidence in Child Abuse Prosecutions* Report for the Home Office (August 1999).
2   See **3.64**.
3   See **3.40**.

(4) **Evidence to undermine the complainant's account** – five main features were considered to undermine the child's account: previous complaints, failure to take earlier opportunities to complain, evidence of psychiatric problems, lack of parental support and hidden agendas, such as disputes within the family.

The effect of delay on prosecution

2.127   In recent years, an increasing number of victims of sexual offences have been coming forward to report the offence some time after the offence has been committed. This can probably be attributed to the general change in attitude to victims of such offences by the criminal justice system[1] and, in cases of child sexual abuse, the growing appreciation of the extent of the problem, resulting in a willingness to take reports of such offences seriously.[2] Although the Code mentions delay as a factor which could militate against a prosecution in certain circumstances, in the vast majority of cases where the offence is to be tried on indictment, there exists no specific time limit within which a criminal prosecution must be brought. The Crown Court has inherent power to prevent its process from abuse,[3] and if a long delay has made it impossible for the defendant to have a fair trial, the proceedings will be stayed. When considering an application to stay proceedings, the court will consider the reasons for the delay and whether there is a risk of serious prejudice to the defendant in meeting the stale allegations.[4] However, delay, even a very long delay, will not automatically result in serious prejudice to the defendant sufficient to justify staying the proceedings. In *R v Wilkinson*,[5] the defendant faced trial for indecent assault and incest against his two daughters and step-granddaughter some 28 years after the first incidence of abuse, and the Court of Appeal held that the trial judge had correctly decided that the prosecution was not an abuse of process. However, if such cases proceed to trial, the judge has a duty to confront the jury with the fact of delay and its potential impact on the formulation and conduct of the defence and on the prosecution's fulfilment of the burden of proof.[6]

Statutory time limits

2.128   Although there is no general time limit on the prosecution of offences, statutory provisions impose time limits in the following circumstances:

(1) s 127 of the Magistrates' Courts Act 1980 provides that information for a summary offence must be laid within 6 months;
(2) Sch 2, para 10, of the Sexual Offences Act 1956 provides that a prosecution for an offence under s 6 of the Act (unlawful sexual intercourse with a girl under the age of 16) must be commenced within 12 months from the commission of the offence; and

1   See **2.2**
2   See generally Cobley *Child Abuse and the Law* (Cavendish Publishing Ltd, London, 1995) chap 1.
3   *Connelly v DPP* [1964] AC 1254.
4   *R v Jenkins* [1998] Crim LR 411.
5   (1996) Cr App R 81.
6   *R v Percival* (1998) 142 SJLB 190 and *R v GY* [1999] Crim LR 825.

(3) s 7 of the Sexual Offences Act 1956 provides that a prosecution for offences of gross indecency between men and buggery where no assault is involved and the 'victim' is not under the age of 16 must be commenced within 12 months from the commission of the offence.

Consent of the Director of Public Prosecutions

2.129   The consent of the Director of Public Prosecutions is required before a prosecution can be brought for the following sexual offences:

(1)   homosexual offences where either or both of the parties are under 21;[1] and
(2)   offences of incest.[2]

The rationale of the requirement of consent appears to be that these are areas where a rigid application of the letter of the law is likely to be oppressive to the individual or offensive to public opinion[3] and the requirement does not prevent the police arresting and charging a suspect for the relevant offence. As consent can be given on the Director's behalf by a Crown Prosecutor and, as all prosecutions are now taken over by the CPS, which ultimately decides if the prosecution is to proceed, it would seem that a specific requirement of consent is effectively redundant. However, it will still be relevant if an individual commences a private prosecution.

---

1   Sexual Offences Act 1956, s 8. When the age of consent for homosexual activity was reduced to 18 years by the Criminal Justice and Public Order Act 1994, by an oversight no corresponding change was made to this requirement. If the age of consent for homosexual activity is reduced to 16 by the enactment of the Sexual Offences (Amendment) Bill, the DPP's consent will only be required when either or both parties are under 16 years of age. See further **1.24** to **1.28**.
2   Sexual Offences Act 1956, Sch 2.
3   Sprack *Emmins on Criminal Procedure* (Blackstone Press Ltd, London, 1997) p 74.

Chapter 3

THE CRIMINAL TRIAL

THE ADVERSARIAL SYSTEM OF TRIAL AND THE LAW OF EVIDENCE[1]

3.1   If an offender pleads guilty to the offence or offences with which he is charged, there will obviously be no need for a trial and the offender will appear in court to be sentenced.[2] However, where a criminal charge is disputed, a trial is necessary to determine guilt or innocence. In accordance with the common law traditions of open justice and the primacy of oral evidence, this trial takes the form of an adversarial contest between the prosecution and defence when both sides have the opportunity to present oral[3] evidence in one continual presentation. The substantive criminal law determines what facts need to be proved before an offender can be convicted,[4] but it is the law of evidence which determines who is responsible for proving those facts and also determines how those facts may be proved. The rules of evidence are thus crucial to the conduct of criminal trials in England and Wales.

The adversarial trial

3.2   In an adversarial trial, the function of the court is to listen impartially to the evidence called by both sides, weigh it up and then, by reference to the burden and standard of proof, determine which side has won the contest. The magistrates, judges and juries play no part in investigating criminal offences and take no active steps to discover the truth, which is supposed to emerge from the clash of conflicting accounts. Rather like referees at a boxing contest, they see that the rules of the contest are kept and count the points. The adversarial system attaches a great deal of importance to the idea of a 'day in court' and assumes that the oral testimony of witnesses at the trial is superior to any other type of evidence.[5] The evidence of the witnesses is then tested by being subjected to cross examination by the opposing side and in some circumstances, the 'boxing contest' can have a devastating effect on the victim of a crime. This is thought to be particularly true in rape cases, where, despite reforms intended to protect vulnerable witnesses, it has recently been suggested that some judges still take

---

1   For a full exploration of the law of evidence see Keane *Evidence* (Blackstone Press Ltd, London, 1998).
2   See chap 4.
3   In some circumstances, written evidence in the form of witness statements may be allowed, see further **3.111**.
4   See chap 1.
5   In contrast to the adversarial system of trial, most continental countries adopt an inquisitorial system of trial where the court is viewed as a public agency which takes the initiative in gathering information and builds up a file on the matter (the dossier) by questioning all those who may have useful information to offer. The court then reviews the dossier, applies its reasoning powers and determines where the truth lies.

the view that 'you let the parties take off their gloves and see who is left dead on the floor at the end of the trial'.[1]

3.3　　The underlying rationale for many of the rules of evidence can be found in the historical development of the adversarial system of trial, which has its roots in trial by ordeal. A court would decree that an accused should undergo some form of ordeal and the extent of any resulting injuries would be examined. The rationale of this was to enable God to show guilt or innocence – the judgment was deemed to be that of God, not the court. At the beginning of the 13th century, the Church withdrew its support for trial by ordeal, causing trial procedures to be reviewed throughout Europe. In Britain, the traditional adversarial contest remained, but the judgment of God was replaced by the judgment of a group of local people called upon to give their verdict on the matter. These neighbours were called upon to give a verdict, initially based on their local knowledge. Over the centuries, this group of local people developed into the jury – a group of independent assessors of fact who have no previous knowledge of a dispute, but who listen impartially to the evidence presented by each side and come to a verdict.

Evidence

3.4　　Evidence generally is something which would tend to prove or disprove any fact which has to be determined by the court. If a system of 'free proof' was adopted, then parties to a dispute would be entitled to call any evidence which tended to prove or disprove any fact which they were seeking to establish. However, as the jury developed into its present form, the judges adopted a paternalistic attitude towards the jury, as they were afraid that these 'lay'[2] people were not capable of discounting what was commonly considered to be unreliable evidence. Therefore, rules of evidence were developed in order to prevent certain evidence being admitted in the court room and, as a result, the current adversarial system of trial in England and Wales operates a system of 'controlled proof' whereby the way in which facts can be proved before a court is subject to controls, with many rules of exclusion. The next part of this chapter explains the nature of the evidence that is admissible at trial, and this is followed by a focus on the procedural aspects of the conduct of the trial.

CRIMINAL TRIALS AND ADMISSIBLE EVIDENCE

Roles of judge and jury

3.5　　If a trial takes place on indictment in the Crown Court,[3] the trial judge will supervise the conduct of the trial and will ensure that the rules of evidence are kept. The judge also decides any legal issues which arise during the trial, for example the admissibility of evidence, and sums up the evidence to the jury, summarising the main factual points covered and directing the jury on the law.

1　　Lord Justice Seddley (1999) *The Times*, 17 May.
2　　Namely, not trained or skilled in the law.
3　　See further **3.88** to **3.90**.

Following a guilty plea or a guilty verdict, the judge is responsible for passing sentence on the offender.[1] Once evidence has been ruled admissible by the judge, the weight to be given to the evidence and the credibility of any witnesses are solely matters for the tribunal of fact. The jury is responsible for determining all questions of fact and ultimately it decides on the guilt or innocence of an offender.[2] In a summary trial in the magistrates' court,[3] the magistrates fulfil a dual purpose, determining both questions of law and fact.

Inadmissible evidence – the rule against hearsay[4]

3.6   One of the major rules of exclusion relates to the admission of hearsay evidence, which is prima facie inadmissible in a court of law. Hearsay evidence is any out-of-court statement (ie a statement other than one made by a witness in the course of giving evidence in the proceedings in question) made by any person which is offered as evidence of the truth of its contents. Thus, there are two elements to hearsay evidence. First, it must be an out-of-court statement – something said or done outside the witness box. For example, a police officer repeating in court a statement made to him by the victim of an offence during the criminal investigation would be repeating an out-of-court statement. However, such evidence would only be hearsay evidence if the second element is satisfied – it must be repeated in order to prove the truth of the statement. There may well be other reasons for repeating an out-of-court statement, for example to show a child's use of age-inappropriate language, and this would not infringe the rule against hearsay. The rule against hearsay is a classic example of the judiciary's desire to prevent evidence thought to be unreliable being presented to the jury.[5] The admission of hearsay evidence is thought to be dangerous for two reasons. First, repetition of any statement involves the inherent danger of error or distortion, which increases in proportion to the number of repetitions and the complexity of the statement – one only has to consider the childhood game of 'Chinese whispers' to appreciate the danger of distortion. Secondly, it is said to be virtually impossible to engage in effective cross examination of a witness who is testifying about a hearsay statement, because the witness did not perceive the events in question.

3.7   Although there exist many common law and statutory exceptions to the rule against hearsay, the practical effect of the rule is that victims and witnesses are required to attend court on the day of the offender's trial, give their evidence about the offence in open court and then face cross examination by the offender or his counsel. This has no doubt been a major disincentive to report offences, particularly for victims of sexual offences who may have been severely traumatised by the offence itself. It is thought that many such victims and witnesses to the offence fail to report initially or withdraw the complaint before

---

1   See chap 4.
2   The trial judge can never direct the jury to convict, but may direct the jury to acquit the defendant.
3   See **3.88**.
4   See generally Choo *Hearsay and Confrontation in Criminal Trials* (Clarendon Press, Oxford, 1996).
5   Murphy *A Practical Approach to Evidence* (Blackstone Press Ltd, London, 1992).

the trial because they can not face the prospect of giving evidence in this way.[1] These are issues which are currently being addressed by reforms to the criminal justice system which aim to reduce the stress experienced by vulnerable witnesses who are required to give evidence in court.[2]

Judicial discretion

3.8 The court has no discretion to admit inadmissible evidence, no matter how cogent the evidence may be. Therefore, if hearsay evidence does not come within one of the recognised exceptions, it will not be admitted, despite any potential injustice. For example, in the case of *Sparks v R*[3] a man was charged with indecent assault on a young girl. The girl had told her mother that her assailant was a 'coloured boy', whereas the man charged was white. The girl was not called to give evidence, presumably because of her age,[4] and it was held that her description of the assailant was hearsay and therefore inadmissible. Although the resulting conviction was quashed on appeal for other reasons, the Privy Council agreed that the evidence was inadmissible, despite the fact that the jury had been left throughout the whole trial with the impression that the girl could not give any clue as to the identity of her assailant.

The discretion to exclude evidence

3.9 Although there exists no discretion to include inadmissible evidence, the court does have a discretion to exclude otherwise admissible evidence if it would affect the fairness of the trial. A limited discretion existed at common law,[5] but the Police and Criminal Evidence Act (PACE) 1984 now provides that in any proceedings the court may refuse to allow evidence on which the prosecution proposes to rely to be given if it appears to the court that, having regard to all the circumstances (including the circumstances in which the evidence was obtained), the admission of the evidence would have such an adverse effect on the fairness of the proceedings that the court ought not to admit it.[6] The discretion may be exercised in relation to a variety of evidence, including similar fact evidence,[7] identification evidence[8] and evidence of the offender's bad character.[9]

The burden of proof

3.10 The term 'burden of proof' may at first appear to be self-explanatory, but there exist several different kinds of burdens and unfortunately no

---

1   The Home Office has estimated that between 13,000 and 20,000 victims and witnesses may be affected. Home Office Youth Justice and Criminal Evidence Bill Part 2 – Questions and Answers (1998).
2   See **3.115** to **3.152**.
3   [1964] AC 964.
4   See **3.17** to **3.21**.
5   *R v Sang* [1980] AC 402.
6   PACE 1984, s 78.
7   See **3.40**.
8   See **3.68** to **3.70**.
9   See **3.42** to **3.47**.

consistent terminology has been adopted by the judiciary or academic commentators. The most significant burden – commonly called the 'legal burden' – is the obligation to persuade the tribunal of fact to the required standard of proof. A second burden – commonly called the 'evidential burden' – is the obligation to persuade the tribunal of law that there is sufficient evidence to make a decision by the tribunal of fact a reasonable possibility. In criminal trials, as a general rule, the prosecution bears the legal burden of proving every element of the crime charged in order to establish the defendant's guilt[1] and the prosecution will also usually bear the evidential burden.[2] Thus, if the trial takes place on indictment in the Crown Court, the prosecution will first have to discharge the evidential burden, by persuading the judge that there is sufficient evidence to justify the case being left to the jury, ie the prosecution must establish a prima facie case.[3] The prosecution must then discharge the legal burden, by persuading the jury to the required standard of proof of the guilt of the defendant. In the vast majority of trials for sexual offences, the defence will bear no burden of proof. For example, at a trial for rape, the prosecution must prove not only that the defendant had sexual intercourse with the complainant, but also that the complainant did not consent and that at the time of the intercourse the defendant either knew that the complainant was not consenting or was reckless as to the fact. In theory, this means that the defence does not need to offer any evidence. The defence will have the opportunity to cross examine prosecution witnesses,[4] including the complainant, and contested issues (such as identity of the offender or consent of the complainant) will no doubt be raised at this stage. However, in practice, to call no further evidence after the prosecution case could be a dangerous tactic. Once the prosecution have discharged the evidential burden and produced sufficient evidence on which the jury, properly directed, could find all the elements of the charge proved, there is a real danger of conviction and the defence would be well advised to call evidence to rebut the prosecution case.

3.11 The defendant may wish to raise an affirmative defence which is not simply a denial of the essential elements of the offence itself. For example, if the defendant is charged with having possession of an indecent photograph of a child,[5] he may claim he had a legitimate reason for having the photograph in his possession. In these circumstances, the legal burden of proving the defence rests on the offender, not the prosecution.[6]

The standard of proof

3.12 When the legal burden is placed on the prosecution, the required standard of proof is whether the facts in question have been proved beyond all

---

1   *Woolmington v DPP* [1935] AC 462. The legal burden of proving facts in issue will only rest on the defence if the defendant pleads not guilty by reason of insanity, or when a statute expressly or impliedly places a legal burden of proving a particular issue on the defence.
2   In exceptional cases, the legal and evidential burdens may be split. If the defendant wishes to rely on a defence such as provocation, self defence, duress or non-insane automatism, he will bear the evidential burden. Once this is discharged, the prosecution will bear the legal burden of disproving the defence.
3   For this reason, the evidential burden is sometimes called the 'duty of passing the judge'.
4   See **3.137**.
5   Criminal Justice Act 1998, s 160(1) – see app 1.
6   Criminal Justice Act 1998, s 160(2).

reasonable doubt.[1] In exceptional cases where the legal burden is placed on the defence, the required standard of proof is on the balance of probabilities, ie more probable than not.[2]

WITNESSES

3.13 One of the basic assumptions underlying the criminal justice system in England and Wales is that the oral testimony of witnesses in open court is superior to any other type of evidence. Thus, the oral testimony of witnesses often forms an essential part of a criminal trial. The procedure to be adopted when witnesses give evidence has been the subject of considerable debate in recent years, particularly when the witness is a child or is considered vulnerable in some way, and changes to traditional procedures have been made in an effort to reduce the stress traditionally associated with giving evidence in open court.[3]

Competence

3.14 The general rule of English law is that all witnesses are both competent and compellable, a rule said to be justified by the need to make available to the court, as far as possible, all relevant and admissible evidence which may assist it in the determination of the issues.[4] Several exceptions to the general rule of competence were developed at common law, but, following somewhat piece-meal reform over the last century, the Youth Justice and Criminal Evidence Act 1999, when in force,[5] will simplify the situation. The Act provides that at every stage in criminal proceedings all persons are (whatever their age) competent to give evidence.[6] This is subject to two qualifications:

(1) a person is not competent to give evidence in criminal proceedings if it appears to the court that he is not able to:
   (a) understand questions put to him as a witness, and
   (b) give answers to them which can be understood;[7] and
(2) a person charged in criminal proceedings is not competent to give evidence in the proceedings for the prosecution (whether he is the only person, or is one of two or more persons, charged in the proceedings).[8]

3.15 The latter exception to the general rule, relating to the evidence of the defendant, was enacted to reverse the unintended effects of s 80 of the

1   *Walters v The Queen* [1969] 2 AC 69.
2   *R v Carr-Briant* [1943] KB 607.
3   See further **3.115** to **3.152**.
4   Murphy *A Practical Approach to Evidence* (Blackstone Press Ltd, London, 1992).
5   Sections 53 to 57 of the 1999 Act, which reform the law about who is to be considered competent to give evidence in criminal proceedings and about when evidence may be given unsworn, are expected to be implemented by the end of 2000. *Action for Justice* (Home Office, London, 1999).
6   Youth Justice and Criminal Evidence Act 1999, s 53(1).
7   Youth Justice and Criminal Evidence Act 1999, s 53(3).
8   Youth Justice and Criminal Evidence Act 1999, s 53(4). The reference to a person charged in criminal proceedings does not include a person who is not, or is no longer liable to be convicted of any offence in the proceedings (whether as a result of pleading guilty or for any other reason) – s 53(3).

PACE 1984, which appeared to provide that, where a husband and wife were co-defendants in a case, but they were charged with different offences, each was a competent witness for the prosecution in respect of any other offences with which he or she was not charged.[1] It is now clear that co-defendants are not competent witnesses for the prosecution.

3.16 The general presumption of competence in all other cases is of more interest and has its roots, as least in part, in the growing recognition of the fact that many children are the victims of sexual offences, coupled with an acknowledgement that even very young children can make reliable witnesses. The procedural measures adopted to encourage the reception of evidence from children are now being extended to other vulnerable witnesses.[2] As a result, adult witnesses with physical or learning disabilities who in the past may have been deemed to be incompetent witnesses, may now, with help, be able to understand questions put to them, and give intelligible answers, and the provisions of the 1999 Act reflect this.

Children, competence and the oath[3]

3.17 Traditionally, children were not thought to be competent, trustworthy witnesses, therefore, it was argued, why waste the court's valuable time listening to a child's evidence?[4] However, in recent years, traditionally held beliefs about the competence of children have been challenged, causing society's attitude towards children as witnesses to change dramatically. There is no doubt that one of the major factors instrumental in bringing about such a change has been the increase in societal awareness of the existence of child abuse, both physical and sexual. In many cases of child abuse, the victim will be the only witness. If the child is not to be believed or not permitted to give evidence in court, the offender cannot be punished. The younger the child, the more acute the problem. This unsatisfactory state of affairs, combined with psychological research on the credibility of children, has led in recent years to a review of the role of a child as a witness in a criminal trial.

3.18 In accordance with traditional beliefs about the reliability of children as witnesses, for many years a child was deemed to be an incompetent witness merely by virtue of age. In early canon law a child below the age of puberty was barred from giving evidence in the ecclesiastical courts.[5] The common law originally would not allow a child under the age of 7 years to give evidence, but by 1779 it was acknowledged that there was no precise or fixed rule within which infants were excluded from giving evidence.[6] Thus, age itself ceased to be a bar to

---

1   This contrasted with co-defendants who were not married who would not be competent witnesses for the prosecution in respect of offences with which they were not charged.
2   See **3.115**.
3   By virtue of s 5 of the Oaths Act 1978, any witness who objects to be sworn is now permitted to make a solemn affirmation instead of taking the oath and such affirmation has the same force and effect as an oath. References to sworn evidence thus include both evidence given on oath and evidence given by a witness who has taken an affirmation.
4   See Cobley 'Child Victims of Sexual Abuse and the Criminal Justice System in England and Wales' (1991) 5 *Journal of Social Welfare and Family Law* 362.
5   Hedderman *Children's Evidence: The Need for Corroboration* (Home Office, London, 1987).
6   *R v Brasier* (1779) 1 Leach 199.

competence, but at the same time it was made clear that the judge always had a duty to determine a child's competence by questions to ensure the child understood the 'danger and impiety of falsehood'. At this time a witness was only permitted to give evidence on oath, and it was a commonly held belief that to lie on oath meant that the perjurer was sure to go to hell. Therefore, questioning witnesses to determine competence involved the witnesses asserting that they would 'go to hell fire' if they lied. This in turn was said to lead to a crash course of religious instruction before a child was questioned by the judge to ensure the child was fully conversant with the dangers of lying on oath and the attendant consequences of hell fire if he did so. It is, perhaps, reassuring to know that witnesses no longer need to be terrified of the devil and hell fire before being allowed to give evidence in court. In more recent times, the Court of Appeal has made it clear that a witness does not need to show an appreciation of the religious sanction of an oath, but merely to appreciate the particular importance of telling the truth in court.[1]

3.19   The Children and Young Persons Act 1933[2] allowed a child of tender years to give unsworn evidence provided that, in the opinion of the court, the child was possessed of sufficient intelligence to justify the reception of the evidence and understand the duty of speaking the truth.[3] It was the responsibility of the trial judge to examine a potential witness in court to ascertain whether he or she had the necessary understanding of the oath or of the concepts of truth and duty, and the burden of proving this rested with the party who had chosen to call the witness. Although, in theory, the 1933 Act allowed more children to be heard in court, it proved to be a bar in many cases because, although young children may be perfectly reliable witnesses, they were not always able to explain abstract concepts such as 'duty' and 'truth'. Furthermore, the judiciary were themselves reluctant to admit the evidence of young children. In 1958 the Lord Chief Justice commented that it was 'ridiculous' to suppose that any value could be attached to the evidence of a 5-year-old child.[4]

3.20   In 1989, the Report of the Advisory Group on Video Evidence criticised this approach, which was said to lead to the abandonment of prosecutions for a large number of serious violent and sexual offences against children.[5] As the Group commented, it seemed logical to suppose that a child who was not able to explain what the oath signified, or what concepts such as truth and duty meant, was rather less likely to be sophisticated enough to invent and consistently and successfully sustain falsehoods than other witnesses.[6] The Group recommended that the competence requirement for child witnesses should be dispensed with and not be replaced. Instead, it was proposed that if, once any witness had begun to testify, it became apparent that they could not communicate in a way which

---

1   *R v Bellamy* (1985) 82 Cr App R 222.
2   Children and Young Persons Act 1933, s 38(1).
3   As a general rule, the jury would attach less weight to unsworn evidence, and prior to 1988, it was not possible to convict on the uncorroborated unsworn evidence of a child witness. See further **3.31**.
4   *R v Wallwork* (1958) 42 Cr App R 153.
5   *Report of the Advisory Group on Video Evidence* (Home Office, London, 1989) para 5.8.
6   *Report of the Advisory Group on Video Evidence* (Home Office, London, 1989) para 5.11.

made sense, the judge should rely on his existing power to rule the witness incompetent.[1]

3.21 As a result of the growing pressure for change, the Criminal Justice Act 1991 provided that all children under the age of 14 years must give unsworn evidence, those over 14 years being required to give sworn evidence.[2] The 1991 Act was clearly intended to implement the proposals of the Advisory Group and create a presumption that all children were competent witnesses. However, the wording of the Act was open to the interpretation that, contrary to Parliament's intention, it in fact created a new competence requirement for children under 14 years of age. To clarify the situation, the Criminal Justice and Public Order Act 1994 made the presumption of competence explicit by providing that a child's[3] evidence shall be received unless it appears to the court that the child is incapable of giving intelligible testimony.[4] These provisions will be replaced by the Youth Justice and Criminal Evidence Act 1999, which re-enacts the presumption of competence and the requirement that children under 14 years of age must give evidence without taking the oath.[5] However, the Act makes a clear distinction between competence to give evidence and competence to take the oath. For the first time, witnesses over 14 years of age may now give unsworn evidence if they are not competent to take the oath.[6]

Adults with disabilities[7] and illnesses

3.22 Concern over child victims and their role as witnesses has tended to dominate debates on reform of the criminal justice system over the last two decades. However, attention is now being focused on other vulnerable victims and witnesses, including all victims of sexual offences.[8] As part of this movement, concern has been expressed over the position of adults with disabilities and illnesses. Such people are thought to be vulnerable in two ways: first, they may be vulnerable to crime as victims; and, secondly, as it is widely agreed that a person's physical and mental health and abilities may influence their experience as a witness, they may be vulnerable as witnesses.[9] As far as the first point is concerned, the precise extent of the groups' vulnerability to crime is not known. However, the following points have been made:[10]

---

1 *Report of the Advisory Group on Video Evidence* (Home Office, London, 1989) para 5.13.
2 Criminal Justice Act 1988, s 33A (inserted by the Criminal Justice Act 1991).
3 A child being a person under 14 years of age.
4 Criminal Justice Act 1988, s 33A(2A) (inserted by the Criminal Justice and Public Order Act 1994).
5 Youth Justice and Criminal Evidence Act 1999, s 55(2).
6 See **3.26**.
7 The term 'disabilities' includes both intellectual and physical disabilities.
8 See **3.115** to **3.152**.
9 *'Speaking up for Justice' Report of the Interdepartmental Working Group on the Treatment of Vulnerable or Intimidated Witnesses in the Criminal Justice System* (Home Office, London, 1998), Annex A, Section 3: Disabilities and Illnesses.
10 See Temkin 'Disability, Child Abuse and Criminal Justice' (1994) 57 *Modern Law Review* 402; *'Speaking up for Justice' Report of the Interdepartmental Working Group on the Treatment of Vulnerable or Intimidated Witnesses in the Criminal Justice System* (Home Office, London, 1998), s 3 and Sayce 'Response to Violence: A Framework for Fair Treatment' in Crichton (ed) *Psychiatric Patient Violence: Risk and Response* (Duckworth, London, 1995).

(1) physical disabilities may make it difficult for victims to run away and make them easier to overpower, thereby making them easier targets than the able bodied;

(2) large numbers of disabled and ill people require care, whether from their family or in a residential home, which increases the risk of abuse;

(3) disabilities and illnesses may make people more dependent on others, creating 'learned helplessness', which makes it more difficult to resist psychologically;

(4) people with disabilities may not be fully informed about sexual matters and may not understand the nature of abuse; those with physical disabilities who are dependent on others may have little or no concept of bodily integrity;

(5) communication difficulties may make it difficult to complain, and other disabilities may prevent the victim from finding an appropriate person who is prepared to take action;

(6) carers and police may not be prepared to recognise the abuse as such, and those with mental illness may have their allegations explained away as delusions; and

(7) in the past, there has undoubtedly been a tendency for society to treat disabled people and psychiatric patients as second-class citizens, thereby making them soft targets and reducing the likelihood of an appropriate response in the event of abuse being reported.

3.23   Prior to the reforms contained in the Youth Justice and Criminal Evidence Act 1999, witnesses over the age of 14 years were only permitted to give evidence if they were considered competent to take the oath. In practice, many adults with disabilities were placed in the same position as younger children. Whereas they may be able to understand questions put to them and give intelligible answers in return, they may not be able to show sufficient appreciation of the nature of the proceedings and the particular importance of telling the truth to be able to take the oath. The absence of a provision allowing a witness over the age of 14 years to give unsworn evidence meant that such adults were not permitted to give evidence at all. Admittedly, in practice, very few adults are actually declared incompetent in court, but it has been pointed out that it seems likely that those cases where the competency of a witness is in doubt are filtered out of the system long before the trial stage, either by the investigating officer or a later stage by the Crown Prosecution Service (CPS).[1]

3.24   As noted above, following the enactment of the Youth Justice and Criminal Evidence Act 1999, witnesses over the age of 14 years will be permitted to give evidence without taking the oath, thereby opening the way for more vulnerable victims to be heard in court.

Determining competence to give evidence

3.25   A witness is not competent to give evidence if it appears to the court that he is not able give intelligible testimony, ie he is not able to understand questions

---

1   *'Speaking up for Justice' Report of the Interdepartmental Working Group on the Treatment of Vulnerable or Intimidated Witnesses in the Criminal Justice System* (Home Office, London, 1998), chap 11.

put to him as a witness and give answers to them which can be understood.[1] The competence of any witness can be raised by either the prosecution, the defence or by the court itself, but the final determination of the matter rests with the judge as a matter of law. The burden of proving competence rests on the party calling the witness. Although the standard of proof required of the prosecution in criminal trials is generally beyond all reasonable doubt,[2] in determining the issue of competence, the required standard is on the balance of probabilities, regardless of which party bears the burden of proof.[3] The witness must be treated as having the benefit of any special measures that will be made available to the witness when giving evidence.[4] Thus, if the competence of a rape victim is raised and the court has given a direction that special measures, such as the use of screens or videolinks, will apply to evidence given by her, the judge must determine whether she is competent to give evidence with the assistance of such measures.[5] In the past, if a judge questioned a potential witness in order to determine competence, the generally accepted view was that the questioning should be done in the presence of the jury, the rationale being that this would assist the jury in deciding what weight should be accorded to the evidence if the witness was ruled competent.[6] However, more recently, the Court of Appeal has criticised this approach[7] and the 1999 Act specifically provides that any proceedings held for the determination of the question of competence shall take place in the absence of the jury (if there is one),[8] although any questioning of the witness must be conducted by the court in the presence of the parties.[9]

Sworn or unsworn evidence?

3.26   As previously noted, all witnesses under 14 years of age must give evidence without taking the oath. Witnesses over 14 years of age may only give sworn evidence if they have sufficient appreciation of the solemnity of the occasion and of the particular responsibility to tell the truth which is involved in taking an oath.[10] Witnesses who are able to give intelligible testimony are presumed to have a sufficient appreciation of these matters if no evidence tending to show the contrary is adduced (by any party),[11] ie witnesses who are competent to give evidence are presumed to be eligible to take the oath in the absence of evidence to the contrary. If such evidence is adduced, the same rules apply to determining whether the witness should take the oath as apply to the determination of competence. The party seeking to have the witness sworn must satisfy the court on the balance of probabilities that the witness is eligible to be sworn,[12] any proceedings to determine the issue must take place in the

---

1   Youth Justice and Criminal Evidence Act 1999, s 53.
2   See **3.12**.
3   Youth Justice and Criminal Evidence Act 1999, s 54(2).
4   Youth Justice and Criminal Evidence Act 1999, s 54(3).
5   See further **3.115** to **3.152**.
6   *R v Reynolds* [1950] 1 KB 606.
7   *R v Hampshire* [1995] 3 WLR 260.
8   Youth Justice and Criminal Evidence Act 1999, s 54(4).
9   Youth Justice and Criminal Evidence Act 1999, s 54(6).
10   Youth Justice and Criminal Evidence Act 1999, s 55(2)(b).
11   Youth Justice and Criminal Evidence Act 1999, s 55(3).
12   Youth Justice and Criminal Evidence Act 1999, s 55(4).

absence of the jury,[1] but any questioning of the witness must be conducted by the court in the presence of the parties.[2] If the witness gives unsworn evidence, the evidence will be received by the court and it will be for the jury to decide how much weight to attach to the evidence. If the offender is convicted, an appeal against conviction solely on the ground that a witness gave evidence unsworn when it appears to the Court of Appeal that the evidence should have been given oath will not be successful.[3]

Competence and the role of the expert witness

3.27   If an issue which the judge or jury has to determine requires special knowledge which they could not reasonably be expected to possess, it has long been accepted that an expert witness can be called to give evidence to assist the determination of the issue.[4] Expert witnesses occupy a privileged position in that they are entitled to express their opinion, whereas other witnesses are generally restricted to testifying about facts which happened in their presence or in their hearing.[5] Although the competence of a witness is generally an issue which the judge can determine without the assistance of an expert, in some situations the assistance of an expert may well be required. For example, it has been held that expert evidence would be admissible on the issue of whether a witness is suffering from a mental disability which might render him incapable of giving reliable evidence.[6] The Youth Justice and Criminal Evidence Act 1999 will make it clear that expert evidence may be received, both in determining the competence of a witness and in deciding whether the witness should take the oath.[7]

False evidence

3.28   It is obviously in the interests of justice that witnesses should tell the truth when giving evidence and it has long been recognised that that there is a need for a sanction for those who give false evidence. The sanction against false evidence on oath is prosecution for perjury. By s 1 of the Perjury Act 1911, perjury in judicial proceedings is committed if any person lawfully sworn as a witness wilfully makes a statement material in that proceeding, which he knows to be false or does not believe to be true. When provision was first made for the reception of unsworn evidence in the Children and Young Persons Act 1933, a new offence akin to perjury was created.[8] A similar offence is now to be found in the Youth Justice and Criminal Evidence Act 1999, which provides for a summary offence when a witness wilfully gives false unsworn evidence in such

---

1   Youth Justice and Criminal Evidence Act 1999, s 55(5).
2   Youth Justice and Criminal Evidence Act 1999, s 55(7).
3   Youth Justice and Criminal Evidence Act 1999, s 56(5).
4   *Buckley v Rice Thomas* (1554) Plowd 118.
5   There is a necessary exception on the question of identity.
6   *Toohey v Metropolitan Police Commissioner* [1965] AC 595. However, it should be noted that expert evidence will not be admitted on the question whether a witness is actlly giving reliable evidence, which is always a matter for the jury.
7   Youth Justice and Criminal Evidence Act 1999, ss 54(5) and 55(6).
8   Children and Young Persons Act 1933, s 38(2).

circumstances that, had the evidence been given on oath, he would have been guilty of perjury.[1]

Compellability

3.29   As a general rule, all competent witnesses are also compellable, ie they are obliged by law to give evidence and may be imprisoned for contempt of court if they refuse to do so. However, there are important restrictions on the compatibility of the spouse of an offender as a witness for the prosecution. Such restrictions were initially developed at common law, but are now to be found in the PACE 1984. As a matter of policy, the law has long been reluctant to force one party to a marriage to give evidence against the other party.[2] However, balanced against this reluctance was the realisation that, if the offence charged involved violence against the spouse, the victim of the offence may be the only available witness and without the victim's evidence, the offender could not be punished. Similar policy reasoning obviously also applies to offences committed against children of the family. As a compromise, the PACE 1984 provides that in any proceedings the accused's spouse is compellable[3] as a witness for the prosecution or on behalf of any person jointly charged with the accused if and only if:

(1)   the offence charged involves an assault on, or injury or threat of injury to, the wife or husband of the accused or a person who was at the material time under the age of 16;
(2)   the offence charged is a sexual offence alleged to have been committed in respect of a person who was at the material time under that age; or
(3)   the offence charged consists of attempting or conspiring to commit, or of aiding, abetting, counselling, procuring or inciting the commission of, an offence falling within (1) or (2) above.[4]

Corroboration

3.30   Corroboration is evidence which tends to support or confirm other evidence. As a matter of common sense, the evidence presented by one side to a dispute will inevitably be stronger if it is corroborated by other evidence and, in practice in criminal trials both prosecution and defence will look for corroborating evidence to support the evidence of any witnesses they call. Despite the fact that corroborating evidence is desirable in practice, as a general rule, courts in England and Wales may convict an offender on the uncorroborated evidence of one witness. However, in the past there have been exceptions to the general rule, most notably in relation to the evidence of child witnesses and the evidence of victims of sexual offences. In such exceptional cases where corroboration is required as a matter of law, the corroborating evidence must come from a source

---

1   Youth Justice and Criminal Evidence Act 1999, s 57.
2   See, for example, the dissenting judgment of Lord Edmund-Davies in *Hoskyn v Commissioner of Police for the Metropolis* [1979] AC 474 at 501.
3   The provision does not apply where a husband and wife are jointly charged with the offence unless that spouse is not, or is no longer liable to be convicted of that offence (s 80(4)).
4   PACE 1984, s 80(3).

independent of the evidence requiring to be corroborated and must implicate the offender.[1]

Child witnesses and corroboration

3.31   The belief that children do not make reliable witnesses has been traditionally reinforced by a mandatory requirement of corroboration. Prior to 1988, a person could not be convicted on the uncorroborated evidence of a young child who gave unsworn evidence.[2] If a child gave sworn evidence, a conviction without corroboration was possible, but only after the judge had warned the jury that it would be 'dangerous' to convict on the child's evidence without corroboration.[3] Once the warning had been given, the jury was free to convict without corroboration. In 1987, Home Office research concluded that a general legal requirement that children's evidence be corroborated did not appear to be necessary.[4] As a result, the Criminal Justice Act 1988 removed the corroboration requirement for both the sworn and the unsworn evidence of children.[5] Thus, there is no longer any legal requirement to corroborate the evidence of a child witness. However, there remains a danger that such evidence will continue to be treated with suspicion, both by judges and juries. At common law, in cases which do not, strictly speaking, require the jury to be warned of the danger of convicting on uncorroborated evidence, the judge has always had a discretion to emphasise to the jury that evidence from a particular source has, in previous cases, been shown to be unreliable. For many years, judges have treated the evidence of children with suspicion. It is commonly acknowledged that 'old habits die hard' and such suspicion may well be passed on to juries, who may also harbour their own doubts about the credibility of child witnesses. Thus, convicting on the uncorroborated evidence of a child witness may prove to be problematical and a practical requirement of corroboration arguably remains, despite the removal of a legal requirement.

Sexual offences and corroboration

3.32   Prior to 1994, there existed two distinct requirements of corroboration in relation to sexual offences. First, corroboration was a prerequisite to a conviction for the following offences under the Sexual Offences Act 1956:

(1)   s 2 – procurement of a woman by threats;
(2)   s 3 – procurement of a woman by false pretences;
(3)   s 4 – administering drugs to obtain or facilitate intercourse;
(4)   s 22 – causing prostitution of a woman; and
(5)   s 23 – procuration of a girl under 21.

These offences were said to belong to a class of charges which are easy to make and difficult to rebut. It has been suggested that the requirement of corroboration in relation to procuration offences may be justified on the grounds of

---

1   *R v Baskerville* [1916] 2 KB 658.
2   Children and Young Persons Act 1933, s 38. See *DPP v Hester* [1973] AC 296.
3   *R v Cleal* [1942] 1 All ER 203 and *R v Buck* [1981] Crim LR 108.
4   Hedderman *Children's Evidence: The Need for Corroboration* (Home Office, London, 1987).
5   Criminal Justice Act 1988, s 34.

public policy as the main prosecution witness is usually the female procured who, it is alleged, cannot be numbered among the most reliable accusers.[1]

3.33   Secondly, the judge had to warn the jury of the danger of convicting on the uncorroborated evidence of the victim of a sexual offence.[2] As with the warning previously required for child witnesses, once the jury had been so warned, it was free to convict without corroboration if it was satisfied that the witness was telling the truth. The rationale for requiring a corroboration warning was that sexual offences were said to be capable of being feigned more plausibly than other crimes and that the jury could not be expected to know about the psychological motives for so doing without special instruction. For many years, the general consensus of opinion was that the requirement should be retained,[3] although research with mock juries in the early 1970s suggested that the jury was more likely to convict if a corroboration warning was given, arguably because the warning served to emphasise the evidence required to be corroborated by repeating it and reminding the jury of it.[4] In recent times, attitudes towards victims of sexual offences have changed dramatically. Although the warning was required regardless of whether the complainant or defendant was male or female and whether or not consent was an ingredient of the offence, in practice defendants are more likely to be male and complainants female and, thus, the requirement was perceived to be an insult to women as it was based on a fundamental mistrust of the credibility of their evidence. This, combined with the growing awareness of the impact of the requirement on the prosecution of child sex abusers, led to calls for its abolition.[5] By virtue of the Criminal Justice and Public Order Act 1994, any requirement to give a warning about convicting on the uncorroborated evidence of the victim of a sexual offence has been abrogated[6] and the statutory provisions requiring corroboration for specific offences under the Sexual Offences Act 1956 have been repealed.[7]

EVIDENCE OF CHARACTER

3.34   Evidence of character can obviously be of importance in a criminal trial. Such evidence may perform two distinct functions. First, evidence of bad character may be adduced in order to challenge the credibility of any witness in the proceedings, whether the witness is giving evidence for the prosecution or defence, or indeed whether it is the offender himself who is giving evidence. Secondly, evidence of character may be adduced as proof of the defendant's guilt or innocence. In theory, the law of evidence makes a clear distinction between these two functions. For example, if evidence of bad character is

---

1   Cross *Cross on Evidence* (Butterworths, London, 1985) p 211.
2   *R v Jones* (1925) Cr App R 40, *R v Freebody* (1935) 25 Cr App R 69 and *R v Winfield* [1939] 4 All ER 164.
3   See, for example, the recommendations of the Criminal Law Revision Committee Eleventh Report.
4   [1973] Crim LR 208.
5   Law Commission Working Paper No 115 (1990) and Law Commission No 202 (1991) Cmnd 1620.
6   Criminal Justice and Public Order Act 1994, s 32.
7   Criminal Justice and Public Order Act 1994, s 33.

introduced during cross examination to challenge the credibility of a witness, the cross examiner must accept as final answers given in response to the questions and cannot seek to contradict the answer by calling further evidence in rebuttal on his own behalf. This is known as the finality rule or collateral evidence rule – the evidence adduced does not go to an issue in the case, it is merely collateral and thus a protracted enquiry into the credibility of witnesses is avoided.

3.35   Despite this distinction, in practice there is always a danger that a jury will fail to separate the two functions and evidence admitted solely in relation to credibility will in fact be taken into account as evidence of guilt or innocence. As a general rule, a witness can be cross examined about his previous conduct in an effort to discredit him as a witness, but the trial judge has a discretion to disallow cross examination as to credit and it has been held that he should exercise that discretion if questioning relates to matters so remote as to have negligible impact on the credibility of the witness.[1] It has been suggested that the grounds for exercising the discretion should not be so restricted and the rules on admissibility of evidence of the character of a witness should be tightened up.[2] There exist two distinct arguments in support of this. First, it is said that much of the character evidence currently admitted in evidence is of little value, but may be given undue weight by juries. Secondly, many witnesses find cross examination as to credit extremely traumatic, some claiming it makes them feel as if they themselves were on trial.[3] The problem can be particularly acute for the victims of offences, especially sexual offences, and some concessions have been made in relation to the cross examination of rape victims about their previous sexual history.[4]

3.36   In contrast to other witnesses, a defendant is generally entitled to assert his own good character, but is protected from having evidence of his bad character adduced, either as evidence of his guilt or to discredit him as a witness. There are, however, exceptions to this general rule.

Character of the defendant

Good character

3.37   If a defendant is of good character and has an unblemished record, he will obviously be anxious to adduce this record in court. As a matter of fairness to the defendant, evidence of his good character will be admissible at his trial.[5] It may be adduced either during the examination in chief of the defendant or any witnesses for the defence, or by cross examination of prosecution witnesses. According to the case of *R v Rowton*,[6] in which a school master was charged with an indecent assault on a boy of 14, such evidence must be confined to evidence of the defendant's reputation in the community and should not include evidence

---

1   *Hobbs v CT Tinling & Co Ltd* [1929] 2 KB 1.
2   Pattenden 'The Character of Victims and Third Parties in Criminal Proceedings Other than Rape Trials' [1986] Crim LR 367.
3   Rock *The Social World of the English Crown Court* (Clarendon Press, Oxford, 1993).
4   See **3.49**.
5   *R v Bryant* [1979] QB 108.
6   (1865) Lee & Ca 520.

of specific acts of the defendant, nor a witness's own opinion of the defendant. Although *Rowton* has never been overruled, it seems that in practice, it is not strictly adhered to[1] and witnesses will generally be allowed to state their opinion of the defendant's character. However, the restriction on admitting evidence of previous specific acts of the defendant remains.[2]

3.38   Where evidence of good character is adduced, the evidential value of the evidence has been a matter of some controversy in the past. However, guidance has now been given in the case of *R v Vye*,[3] where the Court of Appeal made it clear that evidence of good character serves two purposes. It supports the defendant's credibility (if that is in issue) and it is evidence of propensity which is inconsistent with guilt, on the basis that a person with good character is less likely to have committed the offence than a person with bad character. The Court of Appeal laid down the following three principles.

(1) If the defendant gives evidence, the judge should direct the jury as to the first purpose. If the defendant does not give evidence at trial, but relies on pre-trial answers or statements,[4] the judge should direct the jury to have regard to the defendant's good character when considering the credibility of those statements. If the defendant does not give evidence and has given no pre-trial answers or statements, no issue as to his credibility arises and a direction as to credit is not required.

(2) The jury should be directed as to the second purpose in every case in which there is evidence of the defendant's good character. It is for the judge in each case to decide how he tailors the direction to the particular circumstances, but he will probably wish to indicate that good character cannot amount to a defence.

(3) A full direction is required, even if a defendant of good character is tried jointly with a co-defendant of bad character.

Bad character

3.39   In sharp contract to the admissibility of evidence of the defendant's good character, evidence of his bad character is generally excluded at his trial. As is commonly said: 'You cannot give a dog a bad name and hang it.' Thus, evidence of the defendant's bad character cannot generally be admitted either as a challenge to his credibility or as evidence of his guilt. For example, a defendant facing a charge of rape who has several previous convictions for rape, is generally protected from having his past record brought to the attention of the jury during the trial,[5] despite the fact that such evidence could undoubtedly be very relevant to the jury in determining the question of guilt or innocence, both in that it may reflect badly on his credibility and also in that it shows a propensity

---

1   Keane *The Modern Law of Evidence* (Butterworths, London, 1996) p 386.
2   *R v Redgrave* (1981) 74 Cr App R 10.
3   [1993] 1 WLR 471.
4   The House of Lords in *R v Aziz* [1995] 3 All ER 149 made it clear that pre-trial answers of statements only includes mixed statements that are partly exculpatory and partly inculpatory which are tendered as proof of the facts they contain.
5   The court will be informed of any previous convictions if the offender is found guilty, and such evidence can be taken into account in determining the appropriate sentence. See further **4.26**.

to commit sexual offences. However, a defendant does not have an absolute right not to hide his previous bad conduct from the court and there are exceptions to the general rule of exclusion.[1] In certain, albeit limited, circumstances, evidence of bad character can be introduced by the prosecution as evidence of the defendant's guilt. In other circumstances, evidence of bad character may be elicited during cross examination of the defendant, but such evidence will be admissible only to challenge the credibility of the defendant.

BAD CHARACTER AS EVIDENCE OF GUILT

3.40 Although evidence of previous convictions and disposition of a defendant is not generally admissible to prove guilt because of the potentially highly prejudicial nature of such evidence, in certain circumstances its admission may be justified if its probative value outweighs its prejudicial effect.[2] This may be the case where there is a 'striking similarity' between previous misconduct and the offence charged. A useful illustration of the degree of similarity required was referred to by Lord Hailsham in *DPP v Boardman*,[3] when he said that in a sex case, while a repeated homosexual act by itself might be quite insufficient to admit the evidence, the fact that it was alleged to have been performed wearing the ceremonial headress of a Red Indian chief or other eccentric garb might well in appropriate circumstances suffice. However, although striking similarity will be the only basis on which evidence of bad character will be admissible to prove guilt where the identity of the offender is in issue, in other cases it may include evidence of crimes of preparation, or crimes which are effectively part of the same transaction as the offence charged.[4]

SIMILAR FACT EVIDENCE AND SEX OFFENDERS

3.41 Although such similar fact evidence is actually rarely admitted at criminal trials, there does appear to be a preponderance of cases involving sexual offences where the issue arises, particularly where an offender has allegedly committed offences against more than one victim. In the past, it has been suggested that sex offenders, particularly homosexual offenders, have a particular propensity to commit offences which distinguishes them from other offenders and justifies the admission of evidence of previous misconduct in circumstances where it would not otherwise be admitted. In the early part of the 20th century, it was suggested that homosexual offenders:

> '. . . seek the habitual gratification of a particular perverted lust, which not only takes them out of the class of ordinary men gone wrong, but stamps them with a hallmark of a specialised and extraordinary class as much as if they carried on their bodies some physical peculiarity.'[5]

More recently, the House of Lords has expressly stated that there is no special rule for sexual offences and that the basic test of admissibility remains the same whatever the offence charged.[6] Despite this, there remains a discernible

---

1 For a full account of the exceptions, see Keane *The Modern Law of Evidence* (Butterworths, London, 1996) chaps 15 and 16.
2 *DPP v P* [1991] 2 AC 447.
3 [1975] AC 421.
4 See dicta of Lord Mackay LC in *DPP v P* [1991] 2 AC 447.
5 *Thompson v R* [1918] AC 221.
6 *DPP v Boardman* [1975] AC 421.

tendency to treat sexual offences as a distinct category. For example, the Privy Council has held that breaches of indecency are not 'commonplace' and suggested that the fact that an offender has a perverted interest in young boys and commits homosexual offences against them is not commonplace, however unremarkable the method by which he commits those offences.[1] As each case must be determined on its own facts, it is difficult to draw any firm conclusions about when evidence of bad character will be admitted to prove guilt, but it would appear that a sex offender who has what could be described as a 'trademark' in the way in which he commits offences runs the distinct risk of having his previous conduct admitted as part of the prosecution case as evidence of his guilt of the offence charged.

BAD CHARACTER CHALLENGING CREDIT

3.42   As a general rule, witnesses can be cross examined on their bad character in order to challenge their credit as a witness, although such questions are only proper when the allegation they convey would, if substantiated, seriously impair the witness's credibility.[2] The defendant was made a competent witness for the first time by virtue of the Criminal Evidence Act 1898. However, the Act recognised that, unless specific provision was made, any defendant who testified could be cross examined on his past record. At common law, evidence of the defendant's bad character was generally inadmissible to prove guilt[3] and it was considered unfair to allow the defendant's past record to be adduced in order to challenge his credit in the same way as such evidence was admissible in relation to other witnesses. Therefore, the 1898 Act provided the defendant with a 'shield' to protect him from revelations about his bad character, but also provided that the shield could be lost in certain circumstances. Section 1(f) of the Act provides:

'A person charged and called as a witness in pursuance of this Act shall not be asked, and if asked shall not be required to answer, any question tending to show that he has committed or been convicted of or been charged with any offence other than that wherewith he is then charged, or is of bad character, unless –

(i)   the proof that he has committed or been convicted of such other offence is admissible evidence to show that he is guilty of the offence wherewith he is then charged; or

(ii)   he has personally or by his advocate asked questions of the witnesses for the prosecution with a view to establish his own good character, or has given evidence of his own good character, or the nature or conduct of the defence is such as to involve imputations on the character of the prosecutor or witnesses for the prosecution; or the deceased victim of the alleged crime;[4] or

(iii)   he has given evidence against any person charged in the same proceedings.'

3.43   The shield therefore protects a defendant from being cross examined about his previous bad character, which includes references to previous offences committed by him, whether or not they resulted in conviction. However, the protection can be lost in a number of ways. The provision contained in s 1(f)(i) allows cross examination of the offender on evidence which is admissible to

---

1   *Reza v GMC* [1991] 2 All ER 796.
2   *Hobbs v CT Tinling & Co Ltd* [1929] 2 KB 1 and *R v Edwards* [1991] 1 WLR 207.
3   See **3.40**.
4   The reference to the deceased victim of the alleged crime was introduced by s 31 of the Criminal Justice and Public Order Act 1994.

prove his guilt and has been considered above.[1] The remaining two subparagraphs require further elaboration.

Section 1(f)(ii) – putting the defendant's good character in issue
3.44   As previously noted, a defendant is entitled to adduce evidence of his good character, both in order to support his credibility and as evidence of propensity which is inconsistent with guilt.[2] However, a defendant who puts his own good character in issue inevitably runs the risk of the prosecution calling evidence in rebuttal, either by cross examining the offender personally or by calling witnesses to demonstrate the defendant's true character.

Section 1(f)(ii) – casting imputations
3.45   Whereas a defendant will normally have a choice as to whether or not to put his good character in issue, the same will not always apply to the second limb of the subsection, whereby the shield may be lost if the 'nature or conduct of the defence is such as to involve imputations on the character of the prosecutor or the witnesses for the prosecution or the deceased victim of the alleged crime'. It is clear that a mere assertion of innocence of the offence charged will not amount to an imputation on the character of the prosecutor or prosecution witnesses and, thus, a denial of liability, even if couched in strong terms, will not result in the loss of the shield[3] – to hold otherwise would obviously be to frustrate proper administration of justice. However, if an assertion goes beyond what is necessary for a denial of guilt, even if it is an essential part of the defence case, this will be capable of being regarded as involving imputations and the shield may be lost. For example, in *R v Bishop*,[4] a defendant charged with burglary, an essential element of which involves entering property as a trespasser, adduced evidence that he had had a homosexual relationship with the occupier of the property. The evidence was adduced, not to attack the character of the occupier, but merely to show that the defendant had permission to enter the property and, therefore, was not a trespasser. This was held to amount to an imputation on the character of the occupier, a prosecution witness, and thus the defendant lost the protection of the shield.

Casting imputations – alleging consent
3.46   The potential implications of the second limb of s 1(f)(ii) for a defendant facing a charge of rape who wishes to contend that the complainant consented to the intercourse are obvious – the defendant could be seen as making an imputation on the character of the complainant and would thereby lose the protection of the shield. However, it is clear that such a defendant will not lose the protection of the shield merely by alleging consent.[5] Two distinct justifications have been suggested for this. First, it can be argued that an allegation of consent is no more than a denial of guilt, and hence would come within the general exception in that it is nothing more than a denial by the

---

1   See **3.40** to **3.41**.
2   See **3.37** to **3.38**.
3   *Selvey v DPP* [1970] AC 304.
4   [1975] QB 274.
5   *Selvey v DPP* [1970] AC 304.

defence that the prosecution has established an essential ingredient of the offence charged.[1] Alternatively, it has been suggested that cases of rape are *sui generis*.[2] The former justification at least has the benefit of avoiding artificial distinctions, but makes it rather more difficult to justify decisions such as that in *R v Turner*,[3] where it was held that the allegation that the complainant not only consented but had also been guilty of gross indecency as a preliminary to the sexual intercourse, did not result in the loss of the shield.

Section 1(f)(iii) – giving evidence against a co-accused

3.47 The provision contained in s 1(f)(iii) allows cross examination of a defendant about his bad character if he has given evidence 'against any person charged in the same proceedings'. Thus, one defendant will be entitled to cross examine a co-accused on the co-accused's bad character. Although many sex offenders tend commit offences in isolation, in circumstances where the victim is the only witness, and will thus be facing trial alone, there has been increasing concern in recent years about the existence of paedophile rings. Prosecutions in such cases will invariably result in several offenders facing trial together. It is clear that the defendants need not be tried for the same offence, as long as they are charged in the same proceedings. The reference to giving evidence 'against' a co-accused has been explained by the House of Lords as meaning evidence which supports the prosecution case in a material respect or which undermines the defence of a co-accused.[4] It is not difficult to envisage a situation in which one defendant will be held to have given evidence against a co-accused and, thereby, find himself open to cross examination about his bad character.

Character of the complainant

3.48 As previously noted, it is generally possible to cross examine a witness, including the complainant, as to character in order to challenge the witness's credit and this will often exacerbate the ordeal experienced by the witness, whatever his or her role in the proceedings but particularly if she or he is the victim of the crime. Concerns have been raised about the manner in which cross examination of complainants is conducted, with particular attention being focused on complainants of sexual offences and procedural reforms to address this problem are dealt with below.[5] As far as the content of evidence adduced in cross examination as to character is concerned, judicial authority has focused traditionally on cross examination of the victim of rape. The evidence of the complainant in such cases tends to be critical for a number of reasons.[6] In the majority of criminal offences, the state of mind of the 'victim' is irrelevant. Rape is unusual in that an essential element of the offence is an absence of consent on the part of the complainant and, therefore, that person's disposition may be relevant as to the existence of consent, or at least as to the defendant's belief in the existence of consent. Furthermore independent evidence of the offence is

1   See Humphreys J in *R v Turner* [1944] KB 463.
2   See Devlin J in *R v Cook* [1959] 2 QB 340.
3   *R v Turner* [1944] KB 463.
4   *Murdoch v Taylor* [1965] AC 574.
5   See **3.141** to **3.152**.
6   See generally Keane *Evidence* (Blackstone Press Ltd, London, 1998).

often unavailable, particularly in cases where no physical violence is used. If the offence is reported quickly enough, medical evidence may be available to show that intercourse has taken place, but this will often be admitted and the disputed issue will often be consent. In the absence of other witnesses, available evidence will effectively be limited to that of the defendant and complainant, making the credibility of each crucial and in some cases effectively rendering the distinction between evidence going to credit and evidence going to guilt redundant.[1]

Cross examination of rape victims as to previous sexual history

3.49 Evidence of previous voluntary acts of sexual intercourse between the defendant and victim have traditionally been admissible if relevant to the issue of consent, which is itself in issue in the particular case. However, the admission of evidence of the victim's sexual experience with partners other than the defendant is more controversial. At common law, a rape victim could be cross examined about her promiscuity in general, but not about particular acts of intercourse with named men.[2] Yet it has long been recognised that it can be unfair to the complainant to introduce such evidence simply in order to show that she consented to intercourse with the defendant, particularly when evidence of the defendant's previous behaviour would not be admitted for fear of prejudicing the jury. Pressure for reform grew in the 1960s as the traditional censure of sexual relationships outside marriage relaxed. In 1975, the Advisory Group, which was set up to consider the law of rape following the decision of the House of Lords in *DPP v Morgan*,[3] noted that sexual relationships outside marriage, both steady and of a more casual character, were by then fairly widespread and commented that it seemed to be agreed that a woman's sexual experiences with partners of her own choice were neither indicative of untruthfulness nor of a general willingness to consent.[4] However, the Advisory Group did not go so far as to say that evidence of the complainant's previous sexual history with partners other than the defendant should never be admitted. There may well be circumstances in which such evidence could be highly probative and so, as a compromise the Advisory Group recommended that, as a general rule, evidence of previous sexual history should only be admitted when it involved the defendant. The only exception would be where the previous conduct with another person bore a striking resemblance to that alleged to have taken place with the defendant.

3.50 This recommendation led to the enactment of s 2 of the Sexual Offences (Amendment) Act 1976, which provided as follows.

---

1   See Seabrooke 'The Vanishing Trick – Blurring the Line between Credit and Issue' [1999] Crim LR 387, who argues that the difference between credit and guilt never reaches vanishing point, but what may properly be said to vanish in such cases is the *significance* of the difference.
2   Cross and Tapper *Cross on Evidence* (Butterworths, London, 1985) p 296.
3   [1976] AC 182.
4   Cmnd 6352, para 131.

(1) If at a trial any person is for the time being charged with a rape offence[1] to which he pleads not guilty, then, except with the leave of the judge, no evidence and no question in cross examination shall be adduced or asked at the trial, by or on behalf of any defendant at the trial, about any sexual experience of a complainant with a person other than the defendant.

(2) The judge shall not give leave in pursuance of the preceding subsection for any evidence or question except on an application made to him in the absence of the jury by or on behalf of a defendant; and on such an application the judge shall give leave if and only if he is satisfied that it would be unfair to that defendant to refuse to allow the evidence to be adduced or the question to be asked.

3.51   Although there was a clear expectation that the circumstances which justify cross examination on previous sexual history would be rare and s 2 of the 1976 Act was intended to enact the specific recommendations of the Advisory Group, the wording of the provision was vague. The courts interpreted it to mean that evidence should be admitted if it was unfair to the defendant not to admit it – the appropriate test was said to be whether it was more likely than not that the evidence sought to be adduced might reasonably lead the jury, properly directing in the summing up, to take a different view of the victim's evidence.[2] An illustrative example of the operation of s 2 is to be found in the case of *R v Viola*.[3] It was alleged by the prosecution that the defendant had raped the complainant in her flat at about midnight on a Tuesday, but the initial complaint of rape was not made until the following Friday. The only issue at the trial was whether the complainant had consented. The defendant applied to cross examine the complainant on the following allegations:

(1)   shortly before the alleged rape, the complainant was said to have made overt sexual advances to two men who visited her flat;

(2)   early on the Wednesday morning immediately following the alleged rape, a naked man (who was not the defendant) was seen allegedly in the complainant flat; and

(3)   on the Wednesday afternoon the complainant allegedly had consensual sexual intercourse with her boyfriend.

The trial judge refused to allow cross examination on any of these allegations, but the Court of Appeal held that leave should have been given to cross examine on the first two allegations, which were thought by the Court to be relevant to the issue of consent and circumstantially inconsistent with rape, thereby potentially leading the jury to take a different view of the complainant's evidence. The third allegation had no relevance to the issue of consent.

3.52   The wording of the 1976 Act and its interpretation by the courts has been subjected to considerable criticism. It has been suggested that, in practice,

---

1   Rape offence is defined by s 7(2) as meaning rape, attempted rape, aiding, abetting, counselling and procuring rape or attempted rape, incitement to rape, conspiracy to rape and burglary with intent to rape. The Court of Appeal has held that the provisions of the 1976 Act may also be taken into account to restrict cross-examination in cases other than rape where sexual intercourse is alleged – *R v Funderbunk* [1990] 2 All ER 482.

2   *R v Lawrence* [1977] Crim LR 492 and *R v Mills* (1978) Cr App R 327.

3   [1982] 1 WLR 1138.

evidence of the complainant's previous sexual history is frequently allowed, even where this appears to be in contradiction to the spirit of the legislation, if not the actual wording.[1] Research has shown that, out of 50 rape trials at the Old Bailey during one year,[2] applications for the admission of evidence of previous sexual history were made in 40% of the trials and 75% of these applications were successful.[3] This is supported by a further study which found that over half of all female acquaintance rape victims involved in the study had been questioned about their previous sexual history with men other than the offender, in some cases without even requesting the leave of the judge.[4]

3.53   Unsuccessful attempts were made to amend the law during the passage of the Criminal Procedure and Investigations Act 1996[5] and the Crime and Disorder Act 1998[6] through Parliament. In 1998, the Interdepartmental Working Group on the treatment of vulnerable and intimidated witnesses concluded that there was overwhelming evidence that the existing practice of the courts was unsatisfactory and that the law was not achieving its purpose.[7] The Group recommended that the law should be amended to provide a more structured approach to decision-taking and to set out more clearly when evidence of previous sexual history can be admitted[8] and the Youth Justice and Criminal Evidence Act 1999 now sets out the restrictions on the admissibility of evidence or cross examination about the complainant's sexual history in certain cases.[9]

3.54   The relevant provisions of the 1999 Act are of wider application than the 1976 Act in two respects. First, whereas the provisions of the 1976 Act applied only to a 'rape offence',[10] the provisions of the 1999 Act apply where a person is being tried for a 'sexual offence', defined to mean:[11]

(1)   rape or burglary with intent to rape;
(2)   an offence under any of ss 2–12 and 14–17 of the Sexual Offences Act 1956 (unlawful intercourse, indecent assault, forcible abduction, etc);
(3)   an offence under s 128 of the Mental Health Act 1959 (unlawful intercourse with a person receiving treatment for mental disorder by member of hospital staff, etc);
(4)   an offence under s 1 of the Indecency with Children Act 1960 (indecent conduct towards a child under 14 years of age);
(5)   an offence under s 54 of the Criminal Law Act 1977 (incitement of a child under 16 years of age to commit incest); and

---

1   *'Speaking Up for Justice' Report of the Interdepartmental Working Group on the Treatment of Vulnerable or Intimidated Witnesses in the Criminal Justice System* (Home Office, London, 1998) p 174.
2   This figure represented 85% of all rape trials at the Court during the same period.
3   Adler *Rape on Trial* (Routledge and Kegan Paul, London, 1987).
4   Lees *Carnal Knowledge: Rape on Trial* (Penguin, London, 1996), quoted in *Speaking Up for Justice* (above) p 174.
5   See *Speaking Up for Justice* (above) Chap 9, App C.
6   HL Deb Vol 598 cols 854–862, 19 March 1998.
7   *Speaking Up for Justice* (above) para 9.64.
8   *Speaking Up for Justice* (above) paras 9.70 and 9.72.
9   Implementation of ss 41 to 43 of the 1999 Act is expected by April 2000. *Action for Justice* (Home Office, London, 1999).
10   See **3.50**.
11   Youth Justice and Criminal Evidence Act 1999, s 62.

(6) offences of attempting or conspiring to commit, or of aiding abetting, counselling, procuring or inciting the commission of, any of the above.

3.55 Secondly, whereas the 1976 Act restricted the cross examination about any sexual experience of the complainant with a person other than the defendant, the provisions of the 1999 Act apply to evidence of any sexual behaviour or other sexual experience of the complainant (whether or not involving any accused or other person) other than anything alleged to have taken place as part of the event which is the subject-matter of the charge against the accused.[1] As the legislation does not limit the meaning of evidence in this context, it is to be understood as including secondary evidence of sexual behaviour, such as abortion.[2]

3.56 If the defence wishes to introduce evidence or ask questions about the complainant's sexual behaviour, it must make an application to the court. The application must be heard in private and in the absence of the complainant and the court must state in open court (but in the absence of the jury, if there is one) its reasons for giving, or refusing, leave.[3] The court may only grant leave if it is satisfied that one of the following criteria is met.

3.57 (1) The evidence or questioning relates to a relevant issue in the case and the issue is not an issue of consent.[4] This allows sufficiently relevant sexual history evidence to be adduced if it relates to, for example, whether the act alleged actually took place, or whether it was committed by the defendant or some other person. 'Issue of consent' is defined to include only issues as to whether the complainant in fact consented, and not issues as to whether the defendant honestly believed that the complainant consented.[5] Thus, a distinction is drawn between consent and a genuine but mistaken belief in consent and the defendant's honest but mistaken belief in consent therefore falls into the category of a relevant issue in the case other than consent.

3.58 (2) The issue that is being argued in the case is whether the complainant consented and the evidence or questioning relates to behaviour that took place as part of the alleged offence, or at or about the same time.[6] The original Bill referred to behaviour within 24 hours of the alleged offence, but following considerable opposition to a fixed time-scale, which is necessarily arbitrary, the reference to a fixed time was removed. Nevertheless, it is expected that 'at or about the same time' will generally be interpreted no more widely than 24 hours before or after the offence.[7]

3.59 (3) The issue is whether the complainant consented and the evidence or questioning relates to behaviour that is so similar to the defence's version of the complainant's behaviour at the time of the alleged offence (whether as part

---

1   Youth Justice and Criminal Evidence Act 1999, s 42(1).
2   *Youth Justice and Criminal Evidence Act 1999 Explanatory Notes*, para 145.
3   Youth Justice and Criminal Evidence Act 1999, s 43. If it gives leave, the court must also state the extent to which evidence may be adduced or questions asked in pursuance of the leave.
4   Youth Justice and Criminal Evidence Act 1999, s 41(3)(a).
5   Youth Justice and Criminal Evidence Act 1999, s 42(1)(b).
6   Youth Justice and Criminal Evidence Act 1999, s 41(1)(b).
7   *Youth Justice and Criminal Evidence Act 1999 Explanatory Notes*, para 148.

of the alleged offence or at or about the same time) that it cannot reasonably be explained as coincidence.[1] This provision was added as the result of a Government amendment on the Report. The following scenario was suggested as an example where it would be unreasonable to exclude such evidence:[2]

> 'A prosecution is mounted against the defendant, the allegation being that he has met the complainant at a party, followed her to her home, climbed in through an upstairs balcony and raped her. The defendant says that at the party where he agrees they met, she invited him to re-enact the balcony scene from Romeo and Juliet. He says that he indeed followed her home, climbed in and consensual sex took place between them. Subsequently, but prior to the trial, evidence comes into the possession of the defence that the week before, and again the week after but outside the 24 hour period, the same lady met another young man at a party, on each occasion inviting him back to her house in identical circumstances, where consensual sex had taken place with each young man on each occasion. The evidence goes to the issue of consent, not to whether the defendant thought that she consented because he was wholly unaware of either of those incidents at the time of the act in relation to which he is charged.'

It was suggested that most right-thinking people would consider that the evidence would put a very different light on the events which would be highly relevant to the jury's verdict and the Bill was amended accordingly.

3.60   In any of the three situations above, the evidence will be disallowed if it appears to the court to be reasonable to assume that the purpose (or main purpose) for which it would be adduced is to establish or elicit material for impugning the credibility of the complainant as a witness.[3]

3.61   (4) The evidence or questioning that the defence wishes to introduce is intended to dispute or explain evidence that the prosecution has introduced about the complainant's sexual behaviour, whether it was alleged by the prosecution to have taken place as part of the alleged offence or at some earlier or later date.[4] In some circumstances, the prosecution might wish to bring evidence that, for instance, the complainant has no sexual experience at all, or none of a specific nature. This provision allows the defence to rebut any such proposition, but the evidence adduced must go no further than to directly contradict or explain claims made by or on behalf of the complainant.

3.62   In addition to being satisfied that one of these four criteria has been met, before granting leave, the court must also be satisfied that a refusal of leave might have the result of rendering unsafe a conclusion of the jury or (as the case may be) the court on any relevant issue in the case.[5]

3.63   Although the provisions of the 1999 Act are more restrictive than those in the 1976 Act, it has been suggested that they actually go no further than the current practice of the courts.[6] Much will depend on the courts' interpretation of the new provisions in practice, but it is to be hoped that victims of sexual

---

1   Youth Justice and Criminal Evidence Act 1999, s 41(1)(c).
2   HL Deb vol 597 cols 45–46, 8 February 1999.
3   Youth Justice and Criminal Evidence Act 1999, s 41(4).
4   Youth Justice and Criminal Evidence Act 1999, s 41(5).
5   Youth Justice and Criminal Evidence Act 1999, s 41(2)(b).
6   Lord Thomas of Gresford, HL Deb col 1299, 15 December 1998.

offences who are required to give evidence in court henceforth will be better protected from unmeritorious attempts by the defence to impugn their character by focusing on their previous sexual history.

Previous consistent statements and recent complaints in sexual offences

3.64   As a general rule, when giving evidence, witnesses are not allowed to adduce evidence of the fact that they have previously made a statement consistent with their testimony. Evidence of such a statement would obviously infringe the rule against hearsay evidence if it were to be admitted as proof of what was said. Yet, the rule against previous consistent statements goes further than the rule against hearsay and prevents the fact that the statement was made being used as evidence of the witness's consistency. The reason for the rule is said to be that if the witness is available to give testimony, then no useful purpose is served by allowing the witness to relate a previous statement to the same effect – a witness's story is not enhanced by the fact it has been rehearsed out of court. However, there are several exceptions to the rule. One exception relates to the admissibility of evidence of previous identification.[1] A second exception relates to previous statements which are admissible to rebut allegations of recent fabrication. If it is alleged by the defence that a prosecution witness has recently made up an allegation, evidence of previous statements made by the witness which are consistent with the allegation may be admitted to prove the witness's consistency. This may be of particular relevance if it is alleged that the victim of a sexual offence has fabricated an allegation due to a vindictive desire for revenge on the alleged offender. For example, in *R v Tyndale*[2] an 11-year-old child complained that her mother's former boyfriend had sexually assaulted her on a number of occasions. There was strong animosity between the child's mother and the defendant, and the child was aware of this and shared her mother's feelings of ill-will towards the defendant. At the trial, the defence alleged that the allegations of sexual abuse were part of a campaign by the child and her family against the defendant, but the child claimed that she had complained on at least two occasions to her brother and sister that she had been sexually assaulted, such complaints having been made well before the relationship between the defendant and the child's mother broke down. It was held that evidence of the child's previous consistent statements was admissible to prove her consistency.

3.65   A third exception relates to a recent complaint in sexual cases, whereby evidence of a complaint may be given by the complainant and by any person to whom the complaint was made. The rationale underlying the exception to the general rule of exclusion is far from clear. In previous times, it seems that a woman was expected to complain within a short time of an outrage done to her, and her evidence should be treated with suspicion if she failed to do so. Accordingly, the exception has been described as 'a perverted survival of the ancient requirement that a woman should make a hue and cry as a preliminary to an appeal of rape',[3] although it is now clear that it is also applicable to male

---

1   See **3.69**.
2   [1999] Crim LR 320.
3   Oliver Wendall Holmes J in *Commonwealth v Cleary* (1898) 172 Mass 175.

victims of sexual offences.[1] The continued survival of the exception to the general rule has been described as an illogical anachronism,[2] but, despite a recommendation of abolition from the Criminal Law Revision Committee,[3] evidence of recent complaint in sexual cases continues to be admissible as an exception to the rule against previous consistent statements.

3.66   To be admissible, the complaint must have been made voluntarily and at the first opportunity reasonably afforded.[4] The complaint may be voluntary for these purposes if it was made in response to questioning, as long as the questioning was of a non-leading nature, and was not effectively putting words in the complainant's mouth. For example, questions designed to inquire about the complainant's distressed state will not generally offend against the rule. What amounts to a 'recent' complaint for these purposes is a question of fact and degree in each individual case and a complaint made a week after an alleged offence has been admitted.[5]

3.67   The complaint will be admitted for either of two purposes – to confirm the evidence of the complainant relating to the offence, or to rebut or disprove the complainant's consent, if consent is in issue.[6] Despite earlier decisions to the contrary, full facts of the complaint can be proved,[7] although the complaint is not admissible as evidence of the facts asserted in it (which would infringe the hearsay rule), but merely as original evidence supporting the complainant's consistency and negativing consent. Therefore, if the complainant does not give evidence and consent is not in issue, evidence of a recent complaint will be inadmissible.[8] If evidence of the complaint is admitted, the jury must be directed that they are not entitled to regard it as evidence of the truth of the matters stated in the complaint, although it has to be questioned whether or not a jury would understand the distinction or, even if they did, whether they would abide by terms of such an instruction.

IDENTIFICATION EVIDENCE

3.68   Although in many cases the central issue will be one of consent, cases inevitably arise where the central issue is the actual identity of the offender. Identification evidence may take one of several forms. Perhaps the most obvious (certainly the oldest) is eye witness identification, which has always been regarded as problematic, mainly due to the possibility of error. Advances in technology now mean that offenders can also be identified by evidence which is acquired scientifically, for example by fingerprints and, more recently, by DNA profiles. The advent of DNA profiling has been a great step forward in the

---

1   *R v Camelleri* [1992] 2 KB 122.
2   Cross and Tapper *Cross on Evidence* (Butterworths, London, 1985).
3   Cmnd 4991 para 232.
4   *R v Osborne* [1905] 1 KB 551.
5   *R v Hedges* (1909) 3 Cr App R 262.
6   *R v Lillyman* [1896] 2 QB 167.
7   *R v Lillyman* [1896] 2 QB 167.
8   *R v Wallwork* (1958) 42 Cr App R 153.

identification of unknown sex offenders,[1] but such scientific identification inevitably raises evidential problems which the courts are currently struggling to resolve.

Eye witness identification evidence

3.69 Eye witness identification may take one of two forms: either informal identification prior to the arrest of the offender or more formal methods during the police investigation (such as identification parades, group identification, video identification or confrontation).[2] Although witnesses are generally prevented from repeating out-of-court statements which are consistent with their testimony in court, evidence of previous identification is an exception to this general rule and a witness's out of court identification is admissible to prove the witness's consistency.[3] As long as the witness is able to confirm the identification in court, evidence of the previous identification may be given either by the identifying witness or by a third party, typically a police officer who was present at the previous identification. However, the courts have long been aware of the dangers of misidentification. Although advances in technology and extended police powers now result in scientific identification evidence being available in many cases of sexual offending, this will not always be the case and, thus, eye witness identification, frequently by the victim who may well be the only witness, becomes crucial to the prosecution's case. In response to concerns over the accuracy of eye witness identification,[4] in 1977 a five-judge Court of Appeal laid down guidelines to be observed by trial judges whenever the case against an defendant depends wholly or substantially on the correctness of one or more identifications of the defendant.[5]

The guidelines in *R v Turnbull*

3.70 In summary, the guidelines require the judge to warn the jury of 'the special need for caution' before convicting the defendant, instructing the jury of the reason for the need for such a warning. The judge should direct the jury to examine closely the circumstances in which each identification was made, taking into account, inter alia, the length of time he was under observation, the distance involved and the lighting at the time, whether he was known to the witness and what length of time had elapsed between the original identification and the subsequent identification to the police. The jury should also be directed to consider whether there was any material discrepancy between the description given by the witness to the police and the actual appearance of the defendant, thus the initial description given to the police may be crucial. If, in the judgment of the trial judge, the quality of the identifying evidence is poor, he should withdraw the case from the jury and direct an acquittal, unless there is other evidence which goes to support the correctness of the identification. The Court

---

of Appeal gave examples as to what may be considered poor-quality evidence, which included identification which depends on a fleeting glance or on a longer observation made in difficult conditions. As far as the victim of an offence is concerned, the former is more likely to be applicable to offences such as theft or robbery, whereas sexual offences will typically involve closer contact over a longer period of time. 'Difficult conditions' arguably extend beyond the physical circumstances in which the identification was made, such as rape carried out in the dark, and include the trauma experienced by the victim. An hysterical victim is unlikely to be able to give a clear description of the offender shortly after the attack takes place and this will undoubtedly be highlighted by the defence at the trial. In the absence of other evidence to support the correctness of the identification, such as scientific evidence, this will often be fatal to the prosecution's case.

Scientific identification evidence

Fingerprints

3.71   No two people have the same fingerprints and so an offender may be identified by his fingerprints and convicted, even if there is no other identification evidence and his identity is disputed.[1] An expert witness[2] must give evidence that fingerprints found at the scene of the crime, or on some object with which the case is concerned, match those taken from the offender. Fingerprints can only be said to match if there is a match of 16 ridge characteristics on any one digit or where prints are uplifted from two digits, no fewer than 10 matching characteristics for each digit.[3] The same standards apply to other forms of print, including palm and foot prints.

Blood

3.72   Prior to the advent of DNA profiling, the prosecution occasionally sought to introduce evidence that blood found at the scene of a crime matched the blood group of the offender. However, it is not possible to make a positive identification of an offender in this way. Scientific evidence from a blood sample can only indicate the degree of probability that the sample emanated from a proportion of the population which includes or excludes the defendant and it would seem that evidence of mere probability alone is insufficient to justify a conviction.[4]

---

1   *R v Castleton* (1909) 3 Cr App R 74.

2   An expert for these purposes is someone who has completed a course at a training authority approved by the Home Office and who has been engaged in the examination and comparison for at least 5 years.

3   *Archbold 'Criminal Pleading, Evidence and Practice'* (Sweet & Maxwell, London, 1999) para 14–97. However, it seems that these criteria may be departed from and the accepted opinion of fingerprint experts is now that a 100% certain identification can be made from a minimum of eight ridge characteristics from a single digit, and such evidence has been received by the courts – *Archbold News*, issue 1, 5 February 1999.

4   *Archbold 'Criminal Pleading, Evidence and Practice'* (Sweet & Maxwell, London, 1999) para 14–101.

DNA evidence[1]

3.73   The advent of DNA profiling in the mid 1980s has been described as the forensic breakthrough of the century.[2] DNA evidence can certainly be of considerable assistance in the investigation of sex offences, both in identifying the offender and proving the innocence of other suspects. Furthermore, it can result in the apprehension and conviction of offenders many years after the commission of the offence.[3] However, despite the supposed cogency of DNA evidence, its reliability has come under considerable scrutiny, both in the USA and the UK, leading to what has been described as the 'DNA war'.[4] Unlike fingerprints, which are unique to an individual, a match of DNA profiles cannot prove identity. Although, with the exception of identical twins, the DNA of every individual is unique, because of the amount of DNA contained in every cell in the human body, comparison of all the DNA from one source with all of the DNA from another source is impractical. Therefore, DNA profiling was developed by taking samples of DNA and comparing them with similar samples taken from another source. As only a small amount of the DNA from the two sources is compared, it is possible, although highly unlikely, for a match to occur by coincidence.[5] This necessitates an expert witness not only giving evidence that a match has been found, but also instructing the court on the probability of a match having occurred by chance. Prima facie, this would appear to be a relatively straightforward task. In practice, this has proved not to be the case. Although the use of probabilities is not entirely new to the courts, an erroneous chain of reasoning has tended to be adopted by the courts in relation to DNA evidence. This chain of reasoning has been called the 'prosecutor's fallacy' as the error usually favours the prosecution.[6]

The prosecutor's fallacy

3.74   The match probability[7] is the probability that an innocent individual, unrelated to the offender and chosen randomly from an appropriate population will match the DNA profile taken from the crime sample.[8] The likelihood ratio is the ratio of the probability of a match, given that he is guilty, to the probability of a match, given that he is innocent. This is usually calculated as one divided

---

1   See **2.50**.

2   (1987) *The Times*, 14 November.

3   For example, in April 1999 as a result of DNA evidence, a rapist was sentenced to life imprisonment after being apprehended 8 years after his last attack. (1999) *The Times*, 15 April.

4   See, generally, Redmayne 'Doubts and Burdens: DNA Evidence, Probability and the Courts' [1995] Crim LR 464 and references therein.

5   For a more detailed account of DNA profiling, see Redmayne 'Doubts and Burdens: DNA Evidence, Probability and the Courts' [1995] Crim LR 464.

6   Balding and Donnelly 'The Prosecutor's Fallacy and DNA Evidence' [1994] Crim LR 711.

7   Or random occurrence ratio.

8   The 'crime sample' may either be bodily samples from which DNA can be extracted which have been left on the victim following bodily contact or from similar samples left at the scene of the crime.

by the match probability.[1] Thus, the match probability and likelihood ratio relate to the following different questions.

(1) What is the probability that an individual would match the DNA profile from the crime sample given that he is innocent?
(2) What is the probability that an individual is innocent, if he matches the DNA profile from the crime sample?

The first question assumes the innocence of the defendant and asks about the chances of getting a match. The second question assumes that the defendant's profile matches and asks about guilt or innocence. It is this second question which is of direct relevance to the court. The prosecutor's fallacy consists of giving the answer to the first question as the answer to the second.[2] This error may be made by the expert witness, typically by a careless choice of words, or, even if the wording is clear, the jury may make the error inadvertently. In an effort to ensure consistency and to avoid the prosecutor's fallacy, the Court of Appeal has given the following guidance.[3]

(1) The scientist should adduce the evidence of the DNA comparisons together with his calculations of the random occurrence ratio. Whenever such evidence is to be adduced, the Crown should serve upon the defence details as to how the calculations have been carried out which are sufficient for the defence to scrutinise the basis of the calculations . The Forensic Science Service should make available to a defence expert, if requested, the databases upon which the calculations have been based.
(2) In giving evidence, the scientist should not go into matters which were for the jury. He should explain the nature of the DNA match and give the random occurrence ratio; he may be able to say how many people with matching characteristics are likely to be found in the UK or in a more limited sub-group. This will be the limit of the evidence he can properly and usefully give. He should not be asked his opinion on the likelihood that it was the defendant who left the crime stain, nor when giving evidence should he use terminology which might lead the jury to believe that he was expressing an opinion.
(3) The judge, when summing up, should explain to the jury the relevance of the random occurrence ratio and draw their attention to other evidence which provides the context which gives the ratio its significance.

Further problems in the admission of DNA evidence

3.75   DNA evidence can be used to identify an offender in one of two ways. DNA profiles may be compiled from samples taken from a person suspected of the offence and matched with profiles taken from the crime sample. Alternatively, if details of the offender are stored on a DNA database,[4] profiles from the crime sample may be checked against the DNA database, thus resulting in the

---

1   See Balding and Donnelly 'The Prosecutor's Fallacy and DNA Evidence' [1994] Crim LR 711.
2   *R v Deen* (1994) *The Times,* 10 January and *R v Gordon* (1995) 1 Cr App R 290.
3   *R v Doheny and Adams* (1997) 1 Cr App R 369.
4   See **2.51**.

identification of the offender. In the former case, there must necessarily exist other evidence of the offender's guilt and the DNA evidence will serve to corroborate this. However, in the latter case, where the offender has been identified as a result of a search of a DNA database, further evidential issues arise.[1] One such issue is the question of what is termed 'negative effect' – whether the fact that an offender has been located through the search of a database weakens the DNA evidence as a means of identifying him as the perpetrator. The size of the DNA database is crucial to the argument, as a database which consisted of profiles of the whole population of the UK could have a positive effect by eliminating every individual other than the offender. The issue is a complex one and not without controversy,[2] but its potential impact on jury verdicts would appear to be reduced by the guidance given by the Court of Appeal in *R v Doheny and Adams*[3] to the effect that the size of the population of possible perpetrators should be drawn to the jury's attention.

3.76 Further evidential issues arise from the fact that, if the jury is told that the defendant was identified as a result of a database search, this is tantamount to them being told that the defendant has previously been in trouble with the police[4] and, therefore, amounts to evidence of his bad character.[5] Although, as a general rule, the prosecution should not inform the jury of how the defendant came to be identified,[6] in practice it will often be difficult to prevent the jury from surmising this information from the evidence, with the resulting danger of prejudice to the defendant.

DNA and other evidence

3.77 If DNA evidence is properly interpreted, a conviction can be based on this evidence alone.[7] Yet in many cases there may be other evidence and it is important that the jury does not ignore this. Difficulties may arise, however, in the correct approach to take in assessing the numerical evidence associated with DNA, together with other evidence which typically has no numerical value. There exists a standard mathematical formula, known as Bayes Theorem, which can be used to combine different probabilities. Attempts have been made to use Bayes Theorem in cases involving DNA and other evidence, by expressing non-DNA evidence in terms of mathematical probability, thus making it more readily comparable with the DNA evidence.

3.78 A good illustration of how Bayes Theorem could be used in this context is taken from the case of *R v Adams*.[8] Adams had been charged with rape. The sole

---

1 See Redmayne 'The DNA Database: Civil Liberty and Evidentiary Issues' [1998] Crim LR 437.
2 See Redmayne 'The DNA Database: Civil Liberty and Evidentiary Issues' [1998] Crim LR 437 at 446–452 for a full exploration of the issue.
3 *R v Doheny and Adams* (1997) 1 Cr App R 369.
4 The same issue arises with fingerprint evidence and identification through photographs.
5 See **3.39** to **3.47**.
6 *R v Lamb* (1980) 71 Cr App R 198.
7 *R v Adams* [1996] Crim LR 898.
8 Ibid.

issue was one of identity and the prosecution case rested entirely on DNA evidence, resulting from a vaginal swab taken from the victim. The victim, who saw the offender's face for only a matter of seconds, failed to pick out the offender (or anyone else) at an identification parade and at the committal proceedings she gave evidence that Adams did not look like the man who had attacked her. Adams relied on an alibi, and both he and his girlfriend gave evidence in support of it. The defence argued that the only logical way to approach the case was to use Bayes Theorem to attach numerical values to the defence evidence (ie the non-DNA evidence) in order to compare it with the prosecution's case (ie the DNA evidence). The application of Bayes Theorem to the non-DNA evidence worked as follows.

3.79   The culprit was assumed to be aged between 18 and 60. It was known from population data that there were about 150,000 men in this age group living within 15 km of where the crime took place. The jury were invited first to assess the probability that the culprit came from this area (as in fact Adams did). If this probability was assessed as, say 75%, this gave as a starting point a chance of 1 in 200,000 (ie 150,000 x 100/75) that Adams was the culprit. The jury were then invited to assess as a percentage the probability of the victim's failure to identify Adams on the alternative hypotheses (a) that Adams was guilty or (b) that he was innocent. Percentage (a) would be divided by percentage (b) to give another figure. Two more figures would be produced by repeating this exercise for the probability of Adams' own evidence and for the probability of his girlfriend's alibi evidence. By multiplying the starting point figure and these three further figures, the jury could arrive at an overall figure for the probability of guilt on the basis of all the non-DNA evidence, which could be directly compared with the corresponding figure produced by the DNA evidence.

3.80   The judge took the jury through this evidence in his summing up, but left it to the jury to decide whether or not to use the evidence. Adams was convicted of rape and appealed, contending, inter alia, the judge had dealt inadequately with Bayes Theorem in his summing up. The Court of Appeal had grave doubt as to whether the Bayes Theorem evidence was properly admissible, expressing the view that it trespassed on an area peculiarly and exclusively within the province of the jury, namely the way in which they evaluated the relationship between one piece of evidence and another. However, because the Crown had accepted that the Bayes Theorem evidence was admissible and there had been no argument to the effect that it was not, the Court felt unable to give an authoritative ruling on the issue. However, the conviction was quashed on the basis that the judge had not indicated to the jury the more common-sense and basic ways in which it was open to them to weigh up the evidence which meant that their verdict could not be regarded as safe, and a retrial was ordered. At the retrial, the defence once again introduced Bayes Theorem evidence, even providing the jury with questionnaires and calculators to enable them to make the appropriate calculations. Adams was convicted and appealed, once again on the grounds that the judge misdirected the jury in relation to the Bayesian approach. The appeal was dismissed, the Court of Appeal strongly endorsing the view expressed in previous cases that 'to introduce Bayes Theorem, or any other similar method, into a criminal trial plunges the jury into inappropriate and unnecessary realms of theory and complexity deflecting them from their proper task'.[1] Although it has been argued strongly that, in this context, Bayes Theorem seems to provide the only coherent method for combining the non-scientific evidence with the numerical evidence associated with DNA profiling,[2] it is now clear that, in the absence of special features, expert evidence should not be admitted to induce juries to attach mathematical values to probabilities arising from non-scientific evidence adduced at trial.

CRIMINAL TRIALS AND PROCEDURE

Regulating access to prosecution material in cases of sexual offences

3.81 The evidence on which the prosecution case is based often includes material of a sensitive nature. Statements made to the police by victims of sexual offences may contain graphic details of the offence and evidence obtained from any medical examination, whether in the form of a medical report or photographs taken to record the injuries sustained by the victim, may well contain sexually explicit material. Growing concern over the activities of sex offenders in recent years has led to an awareness that unrestricted access to such sensitive material was being abused by some offenders and that statements made by the victims of sexual offences were even being circulated amongst sex offenders themselves as a form of pornography. The advent of video-recorded interviews with child victims exacerbated these problems, as offenders then had access to a visual copy of the victim 'reliving' the circumstances of the offence.

3.82 The Sexual Offences (Protected Material) Act 1997 was enacted in order to address these concerns. Although the Act received Royal Assent on 21 March 1997, it has not yet been brought into force. The Act makes provision for regulating access by defendants and others to certain sensitive material in cases involving sexual offences. For the purposes of the Act, sexual offences are defined as:[3]

(1) any offence under ss 1–7, 9–12 and 14–16 of the Sexual Offences Act 1956;
(2) any offence under s 128 of the Mental Health Act 1958;
(3) any offence under s 1 of the Indecency with Children Act 1960;
(4) any offence under s 54 of the Criminal Law Act 1977;
(5) any offence under s 1 of the Protection of Children Act 1978 or s 160 of the Criminal Justice Act 1988; and
(6) any offence of inciting, conspiring or attempting to commit any of the above.

3.83 The material protected by the provisions of the Act in proceedings for a sexual offence is material which is given by the prosecutor to any person under the Act and which is:

---

1   *R v Adams* (1996) 2 Cr App R 467 at 482 and *R v Doheny and Adams* (1997) 1 Cr App R 369 at 374.
2   Balding and Donnelly 'The Prosecutor's Fallacy and DNA Evidence' [1994] Crim LR 711 at 717. See also the views of Cooke 'The DNA Database' [1999] Crim LR 175.
3   Sexual Offences (Protected Material) Act 1997, Schedule.

(1) any statement relating to that or any other sexual offence made by any victim to the offence (whether the statement is recorded in writing or in any other form);

(2) a photograph or pseudo-photograph of the physical condition of any such victim; or

(3) a report of a medical examination of the physical condition of any such victim.[1]

3.84   If a defendant is legally represented, the protected material will be given by the prosecutor to the defendant's legal representative, as long as the representative gives an undertaking to discharge the obligations imposed by the Act.[2] These obligations are set out in s 4 of the Act and include, inter alia, an obligation to take reasonable steps to ensure:

(1) that the protected material, or any copy of it, is only shown to the defendant in circumstances where it is possible to exercise adequate supervision to prevent the defendant retaining possession of the material or copy or making a copy of it; and

(2) that the protected material is not shown and no copy of it is given, and its contents are not otherwise revealed, to any person other than the defendant, except so far as appears to him necessary to show the material or give a copy of it to any such person:

  (a) in connection with any relevant proceedings, or

  (b) for the purposes of any assessment or treatment of the defendant (whether before or after conviction).[3]

3.85   If the defendant is not legally represented, the prosecutor will give the protected material to an 'appropriate person' in order for that person to show the material to the defendant.[4] If the defendant is in a prison, the appropriate person will be the governor of the prison or his nominee. In other cases, the appropriate person will be the officer in charge of a police station which is suitable to enable the defendant to have access to the material, or his nominee.[5] The prosecutor may also pass the material to some other person where it appears necessary to do so either in connection with any relevant proceedings, or for the purposes of any assessment or treatment of the defendant (whether before or after conviction).[6]

3.86   If material has been disclosed under the provisions of the Act, it is an offence for the defendant to have possession of the material otherwise than while inspecting it in accordance with the provisions of the Act, or to give the material, or otherwise reveal its contents, to any other person.[7] If the material has been passed by the prosecutor to a legal representative, or to some other person (other than the authorised person) for one of the reasons specified, the legal representative or other person also commits an offence if he or she gives a copy

1   Sexual Offences (Protected Material) Act 1997, s 1(1).
2   Sexual Offences (Protected Material) Act 1997, s 3(2).
3   Sexual Offences (Protected Material) Act 1997, s 4(2).
4   Sexual Offences (Protected Material) Act 1997, s 3(3).
5   Sexual Offences (Protected Material) Act 1997, s 5(2).
6   Sexual Offences (Protected Material) Act 1997, s 5(7) and (8).
7   Sexual Offences (Protected Material) Act 1997, s 8(1).

of the material or otherwise reveals its contents to any person other than the defendant or to the defendant himself otherwise than in the circumstances permitted by the Act. In all cases, the person committing the offence is liable to 2 years' imprisonment following conviction on indictment.[1]

3.87　　Thus, when enacted, the 1997 Act will regulate access to sensitive material in cases involving sexual offences, thereby providing some, albeit limited, assurance of privacy to the victims of such offences.

Summary and indictable trials[2]

3.88　　Statistically, most criminal cases are tried in the magistrates' court, where the magistrates[3] act as both the tribunal of law and the tribunal of fact. However, the more serious offences will be tried in the Crown Court, where a judge determines issues of law but issues of fact are determined by a jury.

Classification of offences and mode of trial

3.89　　Criminal offences are categorised for the purpose of determining the court in which they will be tried. An offence may classified as a summary offence, which means that it may only be tried at a summary trial in the magistrates' court, an indictable offence, which means that it may only be tried on indictment at the Crown Court, or as a 'triable-either-way' offence, which means that it may be tried either at the magistrates' court or at the Crown Court. The vast majority of criminal cases begin in the magistrates' court, where summary offences will be tried and indictable offences will be committed for trial at the Crown Court.[4] Determination of the mode of trial of either-way offences also takes place in the magistrates' court.[5] A defendant charged with such an offence has a right to elect trial by jury at the Crown Court, regardless of the view of the magistrates' court. Similarly, if the court considers the offence is more suitable for trial on indictment, it may send the case to the Crown Court for trial, regardless of the views of the defendant. In deciding this, the court is required to have regard to the following matters:[6]

(1)　the nature of the case;
(2)　whether the circumstances make the offence one of a serious character;
(3)　whether the punishment which a magistrates' court would have the power to inflict for it would be adequate;
(4)　any other circumstances which appear to the court to make it more suitable for the offence to be tried in one way rather than the other; and

---

1　Sexual Offences (Protected Material) Act 1997, s 8(4).
2　For a full explanation of trial procedure in both the magistrates' court and the Crown Court, see Spack *Emmins on Criminal Procedure* (Blackstone Press Ltd, London, 1997).
3　In a magistrates' court the bench will consist of either two or three lay magistrates, who have no legal qualifications, or a single, legally qualified stipendiary magistrate.
4　The only exceptions are where a 'voluntary bill of indictment' has been preferred, which essentially means that a High Court judge has ordered the case be tried on indictment (see further Spack *Emmins on Criminal Procedure* [Blackstone Press Ltd, London, 1997] or where a notice of transfer has been served [see **3.102**].
5　Magistrates' Courts Act 1980, ss 19–20.
6　Magistrates' Courts Act 1980, s 19.

(5) any representations made by the prosecution or the defence.

Thus, a triable-either-way offence will only be tried at the magistrates' court if both the magistrates and the offender agree.[1]

3.90   In the past, concern has been expressed about defendants 'working the system' and demanding trial on indictment for no good reason other than to delay proceedings. In 1998 there were 18,500 cases in which defendants exercised their right to trial by jury for a triable-either-way offence and, in many of these cases, the defendants changed their plea to guilty when they eventually appeared in court. Other defendants are thought to opt for jury trial because they believe that their chances of acquittal are greater, but a contested Crown Court case costs an average of £13,500, compared with £2,500 for a hearing before magistrates.[2] As a result of these concerns, in May 1999 the Government announced its intention to abolish the defendant's right to choose trial on indictment for offences triable either way, and to allow magistrates to make the final decision.[3] The response to the Government announcement was immediate and predictable. There was fierce opposition to the proposal, particularly from many members of the legal profession.[4] Despite this, the Government published the Criminal Justice (Mode of Trial) Bill in November 1999. The Bill contained provisions to amend the procedure for determining the mode of trial for offences triable either way by removing the defendant's ability to elect for trial at Crown Court. In determining where the case should be tried, the magistrates' court would be required to permit the prosecutor and the accused to make representations and to have regard to any such representations made and also to matters specified in the Bill, which included the nature of the case and the character of the offence, whether the punishment which a magistrates' court would have the power to impose for it would be adequate, whether the accused's livelihood would be substantially diminished as a result of conviction or as a result of likely punishment, whether the accused's reputation would be seriously damaged as a result of conviction or as a result of likely punishment, and any other circumstances which appeared to the court to be relevant.[5] When the Bill was introduced to the House of Lords, it was immediately defeated; however the Government has announced its intention to introduce a second Bill into the House of Commons as soon as possible.[6]

Sexual offences

3.91   The classification of an offence is an indication of the seriousness with which it is viewed. Obviously, a further indication of seriousness is the maximum penalty which may be imposed for an offence and so offences which carry a high maximum sentence will be triable on indictment only. Many sexual offences fall into this category,[7] for example rape, unlawful sexual intercourse with a girl

---

1   Before consenting to summary trial, the offender must be warned that the case may be
     committed to the Crown Court for sentence if he is convicted after summary trial.
2   (1999) *The Times*, 20 May.
3   Home Office Press Release 155/99.
4   (1999) *The Times*, 20 May.
5   Clause 1 of the Criminal Justice (Mode of Trial) Bill.
6   (2000) *The Times*, 21 January.
7   See App 1.

under the age of 13, buggery and incest are all triable only on indictment. The remaining sexual offences, such as indecent assault, unlawful sexual intercourse with a girl under 16 and indecent conduct towards a young child are triable either way, the only relevant summary offence being possession of an indecent photograph of a child.

3.92 The most important factor which the magistrates will consider in determining the mode of trial will be whether they could impose adequate punishment, if the defendant is convicted. The maximum penalties they can impose are 6 months' imprisonment and/or a fine of £5,000 for any one offence and, for two or more offences, an aggregate of 12 months' imprisonment and/or fines of £5,000 for each offence. Further guidance is given in the National Mode of Trial Guidelines 1995, issued by the Criminal Justice Consultative Council. The Guidelines set out general considerations and then suggest features which are relevant in forming a judgment on the seriousness of particular types of offences, including indecent assault and unlawful sexual intercourse with a girl under 16 years of age.

3.93 In relation to indecent assault, the suggested features are:

(1) substantial disparity in age between complainant and defendant, and the assault is more than trivial;
(2) violence or threats of violence;
(3) a relationship of trust or responsibility between the defendant and the complainant;
(4) several similar offences, and the assaults are more than trivial;
(5) the complainant is particularly vulnerable; and
(6) the serious nature of the assault.

3.94 Similar features are relevant to unlawful sexual intercourse:

(1) wide disparity of age;
(2) a breach of a position of trust; and
(3) the victim is particularly vulnerable.

In essence, these are all factors which potentially impact on the seriousness of the offence, which in turn will generally dictate the appropriate sentence to be imposed.[1]

Young offenders and the Youth Court

3.95 Whereas adult defendants will have their case heard in the magistrates' court or the Crown Court, the desirability of making special arrangements to cater for criminal cases involving young defendants has been recognised since 1908, when the first juvenile court was established.[2] Subsequent legislation firmly established the procedures whereby young defendants were separated from their older counterparts and dealt with in a way thought to be more appropriate to their age, needs and understanding.[3] More recently, the Criminal Justice Act

---

1   See chap 4.
2   The Children Act 1908.
3   See, for example, the Children and Young Persons Acts 1933, 1963 and 1969.

1991 established the Youth Court which exists today. The Youth Court is a magistrates' court specially constituted for the purpose of hearing charges against young persons under the age of 18 years. As a general rule, when a person below this age is charged with any offence (other than homicide), he must be tried summarily by a Youth Court, and not by the magistrates' court or the Crown Court. There are, however, a number of exceptions to this general rule. A young defendant can be dealt with by the magistrates' court in the following circumstances:[1]

(1) he is charged jointly with an adult;
(2) he appears before the magistrates together with an adult, and although he is not charged jointly with the adult if the prosecution have chosen to charge them separately, the charge against him is that he aided and abetted the commission of the offence alleged against the adult or vice versa;
(3) he appears before the magistrates together with an adult, and the charge against him arises out of circumstances the same as or connected with the circumstances giving rise to the charge against the adult; or
(4) the adult magistrates' court began to hear the proceedings against him in the erroneous belief that he was an adult.

3.96   If a young person is dealt with by the magistrates' court and he pleads guilty or is found guilty,[2] his case will be remitted to the Youth Court for sentence, unless the magistrates are satisfied that such a remittal would be undesirable and that the case can be dealt with by a discharge, a fine or binding over the parent or guardian.[3]

Young offenders and the Crown Court

3.97   Unlike adult defendants, young persons have no right to elect to be tried on indictment at the Crown Court. A young defendant must be tried summarily (either in the Youth Court or the adult magistrates' court) unless:[4]

(1) he is charged with an offence of homicide;
(2) he is charged jointly with an adult who is going to be tried on indictment, and the magistrates consider that it is in the interests of justice to commit them both for trial; or
(3) the magistrates consider that he could properly be sentenced under s 53(2) of the Children and Young Persons Act 1933,[5] and either:
   (a) he is charged with an offence carrying a maximum sentence of 14 years' imprisonment or more, or with indecent assault on a woman or a man, or
   (b) he is a young person (ie has attained the age of 14 years or more) and is charged with causing death by dangerous driving or causing death by careless driving while under the influence of drink or drugs.

---

1   Children and Young Persons Act 1933, s 46 and the Children and Young Persons Act 1963, s 18.
2   In the Youth Court, convictions are replaced by findings of guilt.
3   Children and Young Persons Act 1933, s 56.
4   Magistrates' Courts Act 1980, s 24(1).
5   Section 53(2) of the 1933 Act enables the Crown Court to order a longer period of detention than its normal maximum.

Young offenders and sexual offences

3.98   As sexual offences tend to be committed in isolation, in most cases a young offender who commits a sexual offence will have no connection with an adult offender and, thus, will be tried in the Youth Court. However, if the offence with which he is charged is a serious one, a decision will be made by the Youth Court before the case starts as to whether the matters should be committed to the Crown Court so that that court can consider the long-term detention provisions of the 1933 Act if he is found guilty. In making the decision, a balance must be struck between, on the one hand, the objectives of keeping young offenders out of long-term custody and, on the other, the need to impose sufficiently substantial sentences on people who have committed serious crimes so as to provide both appropriate punishment and a deterrent to protect the public. Thus, a young defendant charged with rape should always be tried in the Crown Court.[1] Most other 'grave crimes' which may be tried in the Crown Court carry a sentence of 14 years or more. However, since October 1992, the offence of indecent assault on a woman under s 14 of the Sexual Offences Act 1956 is also regarded as a qualifying offence, despite the fact that it carries a maximum sentence of 10 years' imprisonment.[2] The rationale behind this amendment is not clear and the fact that it did not originally include an offence of indecent assault on a man under s 5 of the Sexual Offences Act 1956 was clearly anomalous. This anomaly was rectified by the Crime (Sentences) Act 1997, which extended the provision to include the offence of indecent assualt on a man.[3]

Young offenders, trial procedures and human rights

3.99   Following a ruling of the European Court of Human Rights in December 1999,[4] trial procedures for young offenders charged with serious offences are to be changed. In 1993 Jon Venables and Robert Thompson were charged with the murder of two-year-old James Bulger. Both offenders were aged 10 at the time of the offence. Their trial took place over three weeks at Preston Crown Court, where modifications, such as raising the floor level of the dock and shortening sitting hours were made to the courtroom and trial, to take account of their youth. The boys were convicted and sentenced to be detained at Her Majesty's pleasure.[5] The boys took their case to the European Court of Human Rights, complaining, inter alia, that, in view of their young age, their trial in public in an adult Crown Court and the punitive nature of their sentence constituted violations of their rights not to be subjected to inhuman or degrading treatment or punishment as guaranteed by art 3 of the European Convention on Human Rights. They further complained that they were denied a fair trial in breach of art 6 of the Convention. The European Court of Human Rights acknowledged that, while the public nature of the proceedings might have exacerbated the feelings of guilt, distress, anguish and fear experienced by

---

1   *R v Billam* (1986) 82 Cr App R 347.
2   Criminal Justice Act 1991, s 64.
3   Crime (Sentences) Act 1997, s 44. The provision applies for offences committed on or after 1 October 1997.
4   *T v United Kingdom, V v United Kingdom* [1999] TLR 871, ECHR.
5   See **4.118**.

the applicants, it was not convinced that the particular features of the trial process caused, to a significant degree, suffering going beyond that which would inevitably have been engendered by any attempt by the authorities to deal with the applicants and therefore it did not find that the boys' trial gave rise to a violation of art 3. However, the Court found that, despite the special measures which were taken in view of the age of the boys, the formality and ritual of the Crown Court must at times have seemed incomprehensible and intimidating for a child aged 11. In the circumstances, the Court did not consider that it was sufficient for the purposes of art 6 that the boys were represented by skilled and experienced lawyers and therefore found that the boys had been denied a fair hearing in breach of art 6.

3.100   As a result of the ruling, reform to the way in which young persons are tried for serious crimes is inevitable. The most likely model to be adopted is expected to be a criminal court in which judges and lawyers remove wigs and gowns and an informal environment is created. To a certain extent, this would mirror reforms made in recent years to ease the stress experienced by young victims and witnesses and which are currently being extended to other vulnerable or intimidated witnesses.[1] The Home Secretary is said to be against trying young persons charged with serious offences in a Youth Court and will not countenance a lowering of the age of criminal responsibility, which at 10 years is one of the lowest in Europe.[2] Any reforms to trial procedures would apply not only to young persons charged with murder, as in the James Bulger case, but also, at the discretion of the magistrates, to those charged with rape and indecent assault.

Committal proceedings

3.101   Before a criminal case can be tried on indictment at the Crown Court, it must be committed for trial by the magistrates' court. Historically, committal proceedings were designed to act as a filter to prevent weak cases reaching the Crown Court. Prior to 1967, the magistrates would review the evidence presented by the prosecution in order to decide if there was a prima facie case to answer.[3] However, this was time-consuming for both the court and witnesses and was deemed to be unnecessary in cases where the defence conceded that there was a prima facie case. The Criminal Justice Act of 1967 therefore introduced an alternative procedure whereby the magistrates could commit the case for trial without consideration of the evidence, if the defence agreed.[4] Despite this, pressure for reform of the system continued.[5] It was argued that committal proceedings, whether with or without consideration of the evidence, were not an effective filter and that they were expensive, cumbersome and time-consuming.

---

1   See **3.115** to **3.152**.
2   (1999) *The Times*, 17 December.
3   Namely, whether there was sufficient evidence on which a reasonable jury could convict the offender.
4   Criminal Justice Act 1967, s 1, re-enacted as s 6(2) of the Magistrates' Courts Act 1980. In 1993, the *Royal Commission on Criminal Justice* (Cmnd 2263) estimated that about 93% of cases were committed for trial without consideration of the evidence.
5   *The James Committee* (1975) Cmnd 6323 and the *Royal Commission on Criminal Justice* (1981) Cmnd 8092.

Furthermore, concern was expressed that the right of the defence to insist on consideration of the evidence, and thereby ensure that prosecution witnesses were required to give evidence at the committal proceedings as well as at the trial, could be abused.

Child witnesses and notices of transfer[1]

3.102   Concern about the potential abuse of committal proceedings by the defence was particularly acute when one of the prosecution witnesses was a child. In 1989, the Advisory Group on Video Evidence concluded that, in cases which involve children, the existing committal proceedings were irredeemably flawed.[2] The Group made recommendations aimed at protecting children from being required to give evidence at committal proceedings and which would also reduce the time taken for the case to come to trial at the Crown Court, thereby ensuring the events were fresher in the child's mind and enabling any therapy the child needed to be commenced at an earlier stage. The recommendations were enacted by the Criminal Justice Act 1991.[3] In certain circumstances, the Director of Public Prosecutions may now issue a notice of transfer, which effectively allows the case to proceed directly to the Crown Court. In order to issue such a notice, the proceedings must relate to one of the following offences:

(1)   an offence which involves an assault on, or injury or a threat of injury to, a person;
(2)   an offence under s 1 of the Children and Young Persons Act 1933 (cruelty to persons under 16 years of age);
(3)   an offence under the Sexual Offences Act 1956, the Indecency with Children Act 1960, the Sexual Offences Act 1967, s 54 of the Criminal Law Act 1977 or the Protection of Children Act 1978; and
(4)   attempting or conspiring to commit, or aiding, abetting, counselling, procuring or inciting the commission of any of the above.

3.103   The Director of Public Prosecutions must be satisfied that:

(1)   the evidence of the offence would be sufficient for the accused to be committed for trial;
(2)   a child[4] who is alleged to be the victim or to have witnessed the commission of the offence, will be called as a witness at trial; and
(3)   for the purpose of avoiding any prejudice to the welfare of the child, the case should be taken over and proceeded with without delay by the Crown Court.

3.104   Provision exists for the defence to apply to the Crown Court for dismissal of the charges. The judge must dismiss any of the charges specified in the notice of transfer in respect of which it appears to him that the evidence against the applicant would not be sufficient for a jury properly to convict him.

---

1   A notice of transfer can also be served in cases involving serious and complex fraud – see the Criminal Justice Act 1987.
2   (Home Office, London, 1989) para 6.6.
3   Criminal Justice Act 1991, s 53.
4   A child is defined to mean a person under the age of 14 years if the offence is one of violence or cruelty and a person under the age of 17 years for sexual offences. Criminal Justice Act 1991, s 53(6).

Although the judge can give leave for oral evidence to be given at the application, oral evidence cannot be adduced from the child witness.

Further changes to committal proceedings

3.105   Following the reforms relating to child witnesses, there was continued pressure to reform committal proceedings for all witnesses.[1] The Criminal Justice and Public Order Act 1994[2] contained provisions to abolish committal proceedings and replace them with a system of transfer for trial. The proposed system, which was purely administrative rather than judicial, was perceived by practitioners as a 'bureaucratic nightmare'[3] and was never brought into force. Instead, a revised committal procedure was introduced by the Criminal Procedure and Investigations Act 1996.[4] The magistrates' court continues to act as a filter, deciding whether there is sufficient evidence to commit a case to the Crown Court. The committal may take place without consideration of the prosecution evidence if the defence agree. The crucial change is that, if the defence contends that there is not sufficient evidence to justify committal or the defendant is not legally represented, the prosecution evidence which the magistrates consider is restricted to written evidence.[5] Thus, no witness can now be required to give evidence on two occasions, thereby removing a potential source of additional stress. This may be of particular importance for vulnerable witnesses, such as the victims of sexual offences, who in the past have sometimes found that appearance in court has been a form of secondary abuse, the only difference being that the secondary abuse is iatrogenic, inflicted by the criminal justice system rather than the offender.

The trial[6]

Multiple charges

3.106   The charge or charges against a defendant will be listed in the indictment. A jury may only try one indictment at a time. Where more than one offence is charged, each charge may be set out in separate counts of the same indictment. Charges may be joined in the same indictment in this way if they are 'founded on the same facts, or form or are part of a series of offences of the same or a similar character'.[7] From the defendant's point of view, the joining of counts on an indictment is potentially detrimental to his defence, particularly if offences have been committed over a period of time. A jury presented with

---

1   See, for example, the recommendations of the *Royal Commission on Criminal Justice* (1993) Cmnd 2263 paras 20–32.
2   Criminal Justice and Public Order Act, s 44 and Sch 4.
3   Sprack *Emmins on Criminal Procedure* (Blackstone Press Ltd, London, 1997) p 177.
4   For full details, see Card and Ward *The Criminal Procedure and Investigations Act 1996* (Jordans, Bristol, 1996), chap 6.
5   Magistrates' Courts Act 1980, s 5A, as amended by the Criminal Procedure and Investigations Act 1996, Sch 1, para 3.
6   The procedures described here are applicable to trials on indictment at the Crown Court, where the more serious offences will be tried. Similar procedural rules apply to trials in the magistrates' court and the Youth Court unless specifically stated.
7   Indictment Rules 1971, SI 1971/1253, r 9.

evidence that the defendant committed five rapes on five different victims over a period of time will arguably be more inclined to convict than if five separate trials were held, with the jury in each case being unaware of the other four rape allegations. The courts have adopted a wide interpretation as to what constitutes a 'series of offences'. In the case of *R v Baird*,[1] the Court of Appeal held that a count of indecent assault against one young boy was properly joined with a count of indecent assault against another young boy 9 years later and in *R v C*[2] counts of rape and attempted rape of the offender's daughter were held to be correctly joined in the same indictment, despite an 11-year gap between the two offences. Thus, in criminal prosecutions resulting from investigations into child abuse in institutions, defendants may find themselves facing trial for numerous offences committed over a long period of time.

Severing the indictment

3.107   Where an indictment contains more than one count, the court has a discretion to order separate trials for all or some of the counts. The discretion to sever the indictment in this way may be exercised where, before the trial, or at any stage of the trial the court is of the opinion that a person accused may be prejudiced or embarrassed in his defence by reasons of being charged with more than one offence in the same indictment, or that for any other reason it is desirable to direct that a person should be tried separately for any one or more offences charged in an indictment.[3]

Severing the indictment and sexual offences

3.108   The question of whether charges should be tried together or separately has caused some controversy in relation to sexual offences. In the case of *DPP v Boardman*,[4] the House of Lords indicated, obiter dicta, that separate trials of counts for sexual offences should be ordered if they were allegedly committed against different victims and there was not sufficient striking similarity between the offences to justify admission of the evidence relating to one offence as evidence of the defendant's guilt of the other offence under the similar fact rule.[5] However, later cases make it clear that the rule on joining counts in an indictment is wider than the rule on the admission of similar fact evidence and that counts could be tried together, even if the evidence of one complainant was not such as to be admissible on the charges concerning other complainants. In *R v Cannon*[6] the Court of Appeal pointed out that, even in sexual cases, the trial judge had a discretion as to whether or not to order separate trials and expressed the view that the Court would not interfere with the exercise of that discretion unless it was shown that the judge had failed to exercise it on the usual and proper principles. This approach has subsequently been endorsed by the House of Lords in *R v Christou*,[7] when it was emphasised

---

1   (1993) Cr App R 308.
2   (1993) *The Times*, 4 February.
3   Indictments Act 1915, s 5(3).
4   [1975] AC 421.
5   See **3.40**.
6   (1990) 92 Cr App R 16.
7   [1996] 2 WLR 620.

that, in exercising his discretion, the judge should seek to achieve a fair trial if the counts were tried together. If the evidence of one complainant is not admissible on the charges concerning other complainants, the judge must tell the jury to treat the charges separately.[1]

3.109   Despite the fact that the view expressed in *DPP v Boardman* clearly does not constitute a rigid rule, concerns have been expressed about the practice of severing indictments containing sexual offences. In 1997, a review of the safeguards for children living away from home was conducted by Sir William Utting and recommended that, in cases of child abuse, severance of counts should only be allowed if requested by the prosecution.[2] The following year, the Working Group on the treatment of vulnerable or intimidated witnesses in the criminal justice system recognised that the rule on severing indictments applied to all offences, not just sexual ones, and recommended that the rule should be reviewed as a whole, but taking into account concerns about the effects of severing indictments in the case of multiple allegations of rape and sexual offences against children.[3] The rule on severing indictments is now under consideration by the Home Office and the Lord Chancellor's Department.[4]

The principle of open justice and the need for witnesses to appear in court

3.110   Article 6 of the European Convention on Human Rights provides that 'in the determination ... of any criminal charge against him, everyone is entitled to a fair and public hearing within a reasonable time by an independent and impartial tribunal established by law ... ' and that:

> '... everyone charged with a criminal offence has the following minimum rights: ... to examine or have examined witnesses against him and to obtain the attendance and examination of witnesses on his behalf under the same conditions as witnesses against him.'

An important assumption underlying the trial procedure in England and Wales is that the oral testimony of witnesses in open court is superior to any other type of evidence and, thus, the adversarial system of trial accords precedence to the oral testimony of witnesses. This, together with the rule against hearsay evidence,[5] ensures compliance with art 6 because witnesses are generally required to appear in court in person at the trial of a defendant, give their evidence orally in open court and face cross examination by the opposing party. This requirement is said to have three distinct advantages.[6] First, it ensures that witnesses give evidence under oath, thus impressing on them the seriousness of the matter and guarding against lies by the possibility of a penalty for perjury. Secondly, it forces witnesses to submit to cross examination, said to be the

---

1   *R v Musquera* [1999] Crim LR 857.
2   Utting *'People Like Us' The Report of the Review of the Safeguards For Children Living Away From Home* (Department of Health and the Welsh Office, London, 1997), chap 20.
3   *Speaking up for Justice* Recommendation 56.
4   *Action for Justice* (Home Office, London, 1999) p 9.
5   See **3.6**.
6   Haugaard and Reppucci *The Sexual Abuse of Children: A Comprehensive Guide to Current Knowledge and Intervention Strategies* (Jossey-Bass, San Fransisco, 1988) p 355.

'greatest legal engine ever invented for the discovery of the truth'. Finally, it permits the jury that is to decide the defendant's fate to observe the demeanour of the witnesses in giving evidence, thus aiding the jury in assessing their credibility.

The admission of written statements

3.111 Although the essence of the rule against hearsay is that witnesses are required to appear in court in person and give oral evidence, the rule is subject to numerous exceptions, both common law and statutory, and in some circumstances it may be possible for a witness to avoid appearing in court by having an written statement admitted in evidence. One of the major drawbacks of admitting evidence in this way is obviously that the witness will not be available to face cross examination, which has the potential to cause considerable injustice. If the opposing party does not object to the admission of a witness's written statement in place of the oral testimony of the witness, then, provided the statement is signed by the witness and contains a declaration that it is true to the best of his or her knowledge and belief, the statement can be admitted as an exception to the hearsay rule.[1] However, if the defendant pleads not guilty to the charges he is facing, this provision is unlikely to assist the victim of an offence, who will usually be a crucial prosecution witness. The exceptions to the hearsay rule contained in ss 23–26 of the Criminal Justice Act 1988 may be of more assistance. The Act provides that a statement made by a person in a document[2] shall be admissible in criminal proceedings as evidence of any fact of which direct oral evidence by him would be admissible if, inter alia:

(1) the person who made the statement is dead or by reason of his bodily or mental condition unfit to attend as a witness; or

(2) if the statement was made to a police officer or some other person charged with the duty of investigating offences or charging suspects, the person who made it does not give oral evidence through fear or because he is kept out of the way.[3]

3.112 Thus, the victim of a sexual offence who has been so severely traumatised by events that she is unfit to attend as a witness, may have a written statement admitted in place of oral testimony. In these circumstances, although the statement will usually have been made to the police during the initial investigation, this is not a pre-requisite to its admission. However, the court may refuse to admit the statement if it is of the opinion that in the interests of justice the statement ought not to be admitted.[4] In so deciding, the court must have regard to, inter alia, any risk, and in particular to whether it is likely to be possible to controvert the statement if the person making it does not attend to give oral evidence in the proceedings, that its admission or exclusion will result in unfairness to the accused, or, if there is more than one, to any of them.[5] The inability of the defence to cross examine a witness who is central to the

---

1   Criminal Justice Act 1967, s 9.
2   'Document' is widely defined to include maps, photographs, discs, tapes and films as well as written documents (1988 Act, Sch 2, para 5).
3   Criminal Justice Act 1988, s 23.
4   Criminal Justice Act 1988, s 25(1).
5   Criminal Justice Act 1988, s 25(2)(d).

prosecution case would undoubtedly result in unfairness and, therefore, it is unlikely that a prosecution could proceed without the oral evidence of the victim.

3.113   If the witness is not unfit, but merely in fear of giving oral evidence, then a statement made to the police may be admitted. 'Fear' has been widely interpreted. It is sufficient to prove that a witness is in fear as a consequence of the offence or of something said or done subsequently in relation to the offence and the possibility of giving evidence in relation to it.[1] Thus, a traumatised victim may come within this provision. However, further restrictions apply in these circumstances, in that the statement cannot be admitted without the leave of the court and the court can only give leave if it is of the opinion that the statement ought to be admitted in the interests of justice.[2] Once again, it is highly unlikely that the statement of a key prosecution witness will be admitted in place of oral testimony.

Written statements and Article 6 of the European Convention on Human Rights[3]

3.114   A further consideration would, of course, be a potential breach of art 6 of the European Convention on Human Rights. The admission of hearsay evidence by the prosecution does not automatically constitute a breach of art 6. The European Court of Human Rights has expressed the view that, in determining whether there has been a breach of art 6, its task is to ascertain whether the proceedings considered as a whole, including the way in which the evidence was taken, were unfair.[4] It would appear to be crucial that a defendant should not be convicted solely on the basis of hearsay evidence.[5] No doubt the courts will be only too aware of the requirements of art 6 and the need to prevent injustice when exercising their discretion to admit written statements in evidence. The right of a defendant to cross examine prosecution witnesses, or to have them cross examined on his behalf, will continue to be of fundamental importance, despite recent changes to the way in which certain witnesses may give evidence.

Vulnerable witnesses and special measures

3.115   It has long been recognised that the experience of giving evidence and facing cross examination in open court can be a traumatic for all witnesses, particularly for those who are young or vulnerable in some way. Furthermore, if the witness is the victim of an offence, the direct confrontation with the offender in open court can be a further source of trauma, in some cases meaning that the witness is unable or unwilling to give a coherent account of events. In order to enhance the quality of evidence and to relieve some of the trauma experienced

---

1   *R v Acton Justices, ex parte McMullen* (1990) 92 Cr App R 98.
2   Criminal Justice Act 1988, s 26.
3   See, generally, Osbourn 'Hearsay and the European Court of Human Rights' [1993] Crim LR 255.
4   *Asch v Austria*, series A no 203 (1991) para 26.
5   *Kostovski v Netherlands*, series A no 166 (1989) 12 EHRR 434 and *Doorson v Netherlands* (1996) 22 EHRR 330.

by witnesses giving evidence in open court, exceptions to the general rule have been created. The initial impetus for making it easier for witnesses to give evidence in court came from the growing acknowledgement of the existence of child abuse as a serious problem in society and the realisation that children, even at a very young age, could make reliable, competent witnesses.[1] However, traditional evidential and procedural requirements excluded many children from the court room. The Criminal Justice Acts of 1988 and 1991 introduced measures to facilitate the reception of children's evidence.[2] Throughout the 1990s, there was continued pressure to extend similar provisions to other vulnerable witnesses, in particular to the victims of sexual offences. Following the recommendations of the working group on the treatment of vulnerable or intimidated witnesses in the criminal justice system, the Youth Justice and Criminal Evidence Act 1999, when brought into force,[3] will make provision for the court[4] to make a special measures direction in relation to certain witnesses in order to improve the quality of their evidence. Such special measures may include allowing the evidence to be given in private, the removal of wigs and gowns in the courtroom, screening the witness from the defendant, allowing evidence to be given by live video link, the video recording of evidence, examination of the witness through an intermediary and allowing the use of communication aids. These measures are considered in more detail below.

ELIGIBLE WITNESSES

3.116 Witnesses other than the accused will be eligible for special measures if:[5]

(1) they are under 17;
(2) they suffer from a mental disorder, mental impairment or significant learning disability which the court considers likely to affect the quality of their evidence;
(3) they suffer from a physical disorder or disability which the court considers likely to affect the quality of their evidence; or
(4) the court is satisfied that the witnesses are likely, because of their own circumstances and the circumstances relating to the case, to suffer fear or distress in giving evidence to an extent that is expected to affect its quality.

3.117 Thus, witnesses under the age of 17 will always be considered eligible. In other cases, in deciding eligibility, the court must consider any views expressed by the witness. In determining whether the fear and stress of a witness is likely to affect the quality of the evidence given, the court must take into account in particular:[6]

---

1   See **3.17**.
2   See **3.123** and **3.127**.
3   The Government is aiming to implement ss 16 to 17 of the 1999 Act in the Crown Court by the end of 2000. Targets for implementation in the magistrates' court have not yet been set. *Action for Justice* (Home Office, London, 1999).
4   For the purposes of the Act, a court means a magistrates' court, the Crown Court or the Criminal Division of the Court of Appeal – Youth Justice and Criminal Evidence Act 1999, s 63.
5   Youth Justice and Criminal Evidence Act 1999, ss 16 and 17.
6   Youth Justice and Criminal Evidence Act 1999, s 17(2).

(1) the nature and alleged circumstances of the offence to which the proceedings relate;
(2) the age of the witness;
(3) where relevant, the social and cultural background and ethnic origins of the witness, the domestic and employment circumstances of the witness, and any religious beliefs or political opinions of the witness; and
(4) any behaviour towards the witness on the part of the accused, members of the family or associates of the accused, or any other person who is likely to be an accused or witness in the proceedings.

3.118 Where the witness is a complainant in respect of a sexual offence,[1] the witness is eligible for assistance unless the court is informed that the witness does not wish to be so eligible.[2] Thus, the majority of victims of sexual offences will now be able to benefit from the various special measures aimed at improving the quality of their evidence, but which, perhaps more importantly from the victim's point of view, will also reduce the stress associated with giving evidence in open court.

PROCEEDINGS IN CAMERA

3.119 The principle of open justice requires the proceedings to held in public. For prosecution witnesses, the presence of the defendant's supporters in the public gallery can be intimidating and the presence of the public and the press may inhibit the victim of a sexual offence who is expected to give evidence of an intimate nature in open court. Although trials are usually held in public, an offender cannot insist on a public trial as of right. Certain statutory powers[3] enable a court to sit in camera, without the public or press being present, and a court also has an inherent power to hold a trial wholly or partly in camera or to take such other measures as may be deemed necessary in the interests of justice.[4] However, traditionally, such derogations from the principle of open justice have been strictly limited. In 1998, the working group on the treatment of vulnerable and intimidated witnesses in the criminal justice system recommended that the courts should have the power on a statutory basis to clear the public gallery, inter alia, in cases where the victim is giving evidence in a trial for the offence of rape or a serious sexual offence.[5] The Youth Justice and Criminal Evidence Act 1999 provides[6] that, if the proceedings relate to a sexual offence or it appears to the court that there are reasonable grounds for believing that any person other than the accused has sought, or will seek to intimidate the witness

1   By virtue of s 62 of the 1999 Act, a sexual offence means rape or burglary with intent to rape; an offence under any of ss 2 to 12 and 14 to 17 of the Sexual Offences Act 1956; an offence under s 128 of the Mental Health Act 1959; an offence under s 1 of the Indecency with Children Act 1960; and an offence under s 54 of the Criminal Law Act 1977.
2   Youth Justice and Criminal Evidence Act 1999, s 17(4).
3   For example, s 8 of the Official Secrets Act 1920 and s 37 of the Children and Young Persons Act 1933.
4   *Attorney General v Leveller Magazine* [1979] AC 440.
5   *'Speaking up for Justice' Report of the Interdepartmental Working Group on the Treatment of Vulnerable or Intimidated Witnesses in the Criminal Justice System* (Home Office, London, 1998) Recommendation 57.
6   The implementation of this provision in the Crown Court is expected by the end of 2000. *Action for Justice* (Home Office, London, 1999).

in connection with testifying in the proceedings, a special measures direction may include a provision that certain people be excluded from the courtroom while the witness gives evidence.[1] The direction will describe individuals or groups of people who are to be excluded although, for obvious reasons, the accused, legal representatives and any interpreters may not be excluded. The court must also allow at least one member of the press to remain if one has been nominated by the press. The freedom of any member of the press who is excluded from the courtroom to report the case will be unaffected, unless a reporting restriction is imposed separately.[2]

REMOVAL OF WIGS AND GOWNS

3.120   If the trial takes place on indictment, the judge and counsel will usually be attired in wigs and gowns. Whilst many witnesses expect this, and indeed it may even make the court appearance more 'exciting' in that it reminds them of court room dramas portrayed on the television, the wigs and gowns can be intimidating for some witnesses. The court has always had a discretion to order the removal of wigs and gowns, and indeed has often done so in the case of child witnesses.[3] The discretion has now been placed on a statutory basis in that a special measures direction may provide for the wearing of wigs or gowns to be dispensed with during the giving of an eligible witness's evidence.[4]

ORAL EVIDENCE – AVOIDING DIRECT CONFRONTATION

3.121   At common law, a defendant at a criminal trial always had a right to confront his accuser – a right that is reflected in other jurisdictions and is contained in the Sixth Amendment of the US Constitution which gives a defendant the right 'to be confronted with witnesses against him'. However, precisely how far this right of confrontation extends has not always been clear. At the turn of this century, it was generally thought that it included a right to face-to-face confrontation with a witness, but in 1919 the Court of Appeal held that, if there is a fear that the witness may be intimidated, the witness can give evidence out of sight of the defendant. In *R v Smellie*,[5] the offender was required to sit on the stairs leading to the dock, where he could not be seen by the witness but could nevertheless hear the evidence being given.

THE USE OF SCREENS

3.122   An alternative method of achieving the same objective is to erect screens in the courtroom which shield the witness from the defendant, but allow the jury to see both the witness and the defendant. The Court of Appeal first gave formal approval for the use of screens in 1989, when the Lord Chief Justice pointed out that a trial judge has a duty to see that justice is done, which means that he has to see that the system operates fairly, not only to defendants but also to the prosecution and witnesses.[6] However, the 1989 judgment related specifically to young children as witnesses and 4 years later, the Court of Appeal

---

1   Youth Justice and Criminal Evidence Act 1999, s 25.
2   See **3.156** and **3.160**.
3   *Speaking up for Justice* (above) para 8.79.
4   Youth Justice and Criminal Evidence Act 1999, s 26. Implementation of this provision in the Crown Court is expected by the end of 2000. *Action for Justice* (Home Office, London, 1999).
5   (1919) 14 Cr App R 128.
6   *R v X, Y, Z* (1989) 91 Cr App R 36 at 40.

stressed that, whereas it was permissible to use screens in the case of adult witnesses if it was otherwise impossible to do justice, such a course should be adopted only in the most exceptional cases and certainly not for every prosecution for a sexual offence.[1] The discretion of the court to give leave for the use of screens has now been placed on a statutory basis. A special measures direction may provide for the witness, while giving testimony or being sworn in court, to be prevented by means of a screen or other arrangement from seeing the defendant.[2] However, the witness must be able to see, and be seen by, the persons judging the case (the judge, magistrates or jury) and by at least one legal representative of the prosecution and defence.

VIDEO LINKS

3.123   Advances in video technology in recent years have led to further reform. The Criminal Justice Act 1988 for the first time permitted certain witnesses, with the leave of the court, to give evidence by live television link.[3] The provision only extended to two categories of persons: those who are outside the UK and children[4] where the charge involved a violent or sexual offence.[5] Video link systems were set up in Crown Courts throughout the country so that child witnesses could sit in a separate room in the court building which was linked by closed circuit television to the court room. Although the child could be seen on screens in the courtroom, the child could only see the judge, prosecution and defence counsel on a monitor in the room as questions were being asked. An evaluation of the video link for child witnesses was conducted 2 years after its introduction and concluded that the link enjoyed widespread acceptance amongst all those with experience of its use.[6] The research found that the majority of child witnesses (76%) were able to give evidence without being reduced to tears at any point and only one child was visibly distressed at all stages of examination. Unfortunately, very little research had been carried out on children testifying under traditional procedures, so comparison was difficult, but it was generally accepted that video links reduced the stress experienced by the child witness and hence improved the quality of the evidence they were able to give.

3.124   The apparent success of video links resulted in pressure for the provision to be extended to other witnesses who may benefit. As a result, a special measures direction may now provide for an eligible witness to give evidence by

1   *R v Schaub and Cooper (Joey)* (1993) *The Times*, 3 December.
2   Youth Justice and Criminal Evidence Act 1999, s 23. Implementation of this provision in the Crown Court is expected by the end of 2000. *Action for Justice* (Home Office, London, 1999).
3   Criminal Justice Act 1988, s 32.
4   A child was originally defined as being under 14 years of age. In respect of sexual offences, the age limit was raised to 17 years of age by the Criminal Justice Act 1991.
5   Section 32(2) of the 1988 Act applies the provision to offences involving assault on, or injury or a threat of injury to, a person; offences under s 1 of the Children and Young Persons Act 1933 (cruelty to persons under the age of 16); offences under the Sexual Offences Act 1956, the Indecency with Children Act 1960, the Sexual Offences Act 1967, s 54 of the Criminal Law Act 1977 or the Protection of Children Act 1978; and attempting or conspiring to commit, or aiding, abetting, counselling, procuring or inciting the commission of any of these offences.
6   Davies and Noon *An Evaluation of the Live Link for Child Witnesses* Report to the Home Office (1991).

means of a live link.[1] As such, special measures may now also be used in the magistrates' court, and this greatly extends the potential use of video links. Whilst such a move is to be welcomed, in that it undoubtedly alleviates the stress associated with giving evidence in open court and, thus, hopefully improves the quality of the evidence given, concerns have been expressed about removing the witness from the courtroom. One objection is that by avoiding a direct confrontation with the defendant, whether by the use of screens or video links, this could indicate to the jury that the witness has good cause to fear that person, thereby indicating his guilt. This objection has now been partially addressed by the 1999 Act, which provides that, where on a trial on indictment, evidence has been given in accordance with a special measures direction, the judge must give the jury such warning (if any) as he considers necessary to ensure that the fact that the direction was given in relation to the witness does not prejudice the defendant.[2] Furthermore, it has been argued that allowing a witness to give evidence via a live link enhances the credibility of the witness.[3] It is argued that the media bestows prestige and enhances the authority of an individual by legitimising his status, and that such considerations are of particular importance in a trial when the demeanour and credibility of the witness are crucial. Conversely, it can be argued that the screen image of a witness lacks the power of the witness's own presence, the defendant being more real to the jury, as they see him throughout the trial.[4] On occasions, it seems that prosecution counsel, when faced with a particularly impressive and resilient witness, have quite deliberately opted for an in-court appearance on the grounds of its greater impact.[5] Whether or not such practices continue with the extended use of video links remains to be seen. The 1999 Act provides that, once a direction has been given for the witness to give evidence by means of a live link, the witness may not give evidence in any other way without the permission of the court.[6] This, combined with the fact that the court can make a special measures direction of its own motion[7] and must consider the views of the witness, should ensure the protection of eligible witnesses from such tactics.

Video recording evidence

The Pigot proposals

3.125   During the passage of the Criminal Justice Act 1988 through Parliament, an Advisory Group on Video Evidence was set up, chaired by Judge

---

1   Youth Justice and Criminal Evidence Act 1999, s 24. Implementation of this provision in the Crown Court is expected by the end of 2000. *Action for Justice* (Home Office, London, 1999).
2   Youth Justice and Criminal Evidence Act 1999, s 32.
3   *Hochiester v Superior Court* (1984) quoted in Haugaard and Reppucci *The Sexual Abuse of Children: A Comprehensive Guide to Current Knowledge and Intervention Strategies* (Jossey-Bass, San Fransisco, 1988).
4   McKewan 'Child Evidence: More Proposals for Reform' [1988] Crim LR 813 at 820.
5   Davies and Noon *An Evaluation of the Live Link for Child Witnesses* Report to the Home Office (1991).
6   Youth Justice and Criminal Evidence Act 1999, s 24(2).
7   Youth Justice and Criminal Evidence Act 1999, s 19(1)(b).

Thomas Pigot QC.[1] The Advisory Group reported in December 1989[2] and proposed that the law should be changed so that at trials on indictment for violent and sexual offences, video-recorded interviews with children should be admissible in criminal trials. A scheme was suggested whereby the child would not be involved in the actual trial of the offender.

3.126   The Advisory Group envisaged that an interview with the child would be video recorded and the trial judge would subsequently rule on the admissibility of the video in place of the child's evidence in chief at a pre-trial application. The defendant's right to cross examine the child should then be retained by holding a preliminary hearing which would be held in less formal, more comfortable surroundings than the courtroom, with only the judge, counsel for each side, the child and either a parent or supporter present. The offender would be able to hear and view the proceedings through closed circuit television or a one-way mirror and would be able to communicate with his counsel in order to direct him or her to put any required questions to the child. At the preliminary hearing, any video recordings which had been allowed in evidence would be shown to the child witness, who may be asked to expand on certain aspects of it. The child would then usually be cross examined by defence counsel. The Advisory Group emphasised that these proceedings should be as informal as possible, and that the judge should control cross examination with special care. The preliminary hearing would itself be video recorded. At the eventual trial, the initial video-recorded interview would be shown at the point at which the child traditionally would give evidence in chief and the video recording of the preliminary hearing would be shown at the time when cross examination would usually follow. The Advisory Group also expressed the opinion that, once the recommendations in relation to child witnesses had been implemented, a high priority should then attach to extending the new measures to vulnerable adult witnesses, such as the elderly, handicapped or badly traumatised. If this proved to be impossible within a reasonable time, the Group thought that priority should be given to victims of serious sexual offences, who were said to face special and generally recognised difficulties.[3]

Evidence in chief and the Criminal Justice Act 1991

3.127   The recommendations of the Advisory Group were generally greeted with hope and enthusiasm, but when the Criminal Justice Act 1991 was introduced, those who had anticipated full implementation of the proposals were disappointed. In specified proceedings,[4] the Act amended the Criminal Justice Act 1988 to allow a video recording of an interview conducted with a child witness and which related to any matter in the proceedings to be given in evidence with the leave of the court, as an exception to the hearsay rule.

---

1   House of Commons (20 June 1988).
2   *Report of the Advisory Group on Video Evidence* (Home Office, London, 1989).
3   *Report of the Advisory Group on Video Evidence* (Home Office, London, 1989), para 3.15.
4   The proceedings were detailed in s 32A of the Criminal Justice Act 1988 and included, inter alia, trials on indictment for those offences listed in s 32(2) of the Act (see **3.102**), appeals to the Court of Appeal in respect of those offences and proceedings in Youth Courts for any such offence and appeals to the Crown Court arising out of such proceedings.

However, the video recording could only be admitted at the actual trial, no provision was made for a preliminary hearing to be held. Furthermore, the video would only be admitted if the child was available for cross examination at the trial. The cross examination could, of course, be conducted via a live video link, but nevertheless the child was still required to be in court on the day of the trial – something which many reformers had hoped to avoid. In order to facilitate the interviewing of child witnesses, a memorandum of good practice was issued as guidance by the Home Office and Department of Health.

3.128 Research indicates that the main benefit of allowing video-recorded evidence in court was the reduced stress on child witnesses,[1] although concerns were expressed that its use means that the child is precipitated straight into court for cross examination – 'the nastiest bit of the court appearance'.[2] The 1991 Act prevented the child being examined in chief on any matter which in the opinion of the court had been dealt with in the recorded testimony,[3] which was interpreted by some judges to mean that the child could not be asked any friendly questions by prosecuting counsel as a 'warm-up' to cross examination. This problem was alleviated by the Criminal Justice and Public Order Act 1994, which amended the legislation so that a child could be questioned on any matter not *adequately* dealt with in the recorded testimony.[4] Following the 1991 Act, it seems that the practice of admitting video recordings was by no means universal. Between October 1992 and June 1994, 1,199 trials took place in England and Wales involving child witnesses. From these, there were 640 applications to admit video-recorded interviews, 470 applications were granted, but in only 202 cases was the video known to have been shown in court.[5] In January 1998 the Crown Prosecution Service Inspectorate published a report on its thematic review of cases involving child witnesses,[6] concluding that the quality of video evidence had steadily improved, both technically and in terms of interviewing skills. The same year, the Working Group on the treatment of vulnerable or intimidated witnesses in the criminal justice system, while recognising that there may be room for improvement in the way interviews are conducted, considered that video-recorded evidence in chief would be a useful measure to assist those adult vulnerable witnesses who would be particularly distressed by having to give evidence in the formal court setting and who may have memory difficulties or suffer from communication problems, such as those with learning disabilities.[7]

The Youth Justice and Criminal Evidence Act 1999

3.129 Following the recommendations of the Working Group, s 27 of the Youth Justice and Criminal Evidence Act 1999 provides that a special measures direction may provide for a video recording of an interview of the witness to be

---

1   Davies et al *Video Taping Children's Evidence: An Evaluation* (Home Office, London, 1995).
2   Spencer (1994) *The Guardian*, 17 August.
3   Criminal Justice Act 1988, s 32A(5).
4   Section 51 of the Criminal Justice and Public Order Act 1994, amending s 32A(5)(b) of the Criminal Justice Act 1988.
5   Davies et al *Video Taping Children's Evidence: An Evaluation* (Home Office, London, 1995).
6   *The Inspectorate's Report on Cases Involving Child Witnesses – Thematic Report* (Crown Prosecution Inpectorate, London, 1998).
7   *Speaking Up for Justice* (above) para 8.44.

admitted as evidence in chief of the witness, both at the trial and for the purposes of committal proceedings.[1] The recording can be edited or excluded if the interests of justice so require. If a direction is made for a recording to be shown to the court, the court can later exclude the recording if there is not enough information about how and where the recording was made or if the witness who made the recording is not available for further questioning (whether by video,[2] in court or by live link) and the parties have not agreed that this is unnecessary. The video recording forms the whole of a witness's evidence in chief, unless the witness is asked to give evidence about matters not covered in the recorded interview or the court gives permission for the witness to be asked further questions about matters not covered adequately in the recorded interview.

3.130 Thus, following the enactment of the 1999 Act, all eligible witnesses may have their evidence in chief replaced by a video-recorded interview, thereby enhancing the quality of their evidence and also reducing the stress traditionally associated with giving evidence in court. In order to address the problem of sworn evidence, when a video recording is made of an interview with a witness aged 14 years or over, then, in anticipation of the recording being admitted as evidence in chief, the witness should swear an oath at the beginning of the interview, if someone is available to administer the oath and they are capable of being sworn.[3] If an oath is not taken, the evidence admitted will be evidence given unsworn.[4]

Video recording and cross examination

3.131 The admissibility of video-recorded interviews in place of evidence in chief is a significant step forward in the movement to protect vulnerable witnesses. However, more controversial issues arise in relation to the cross examination of such witnesses. The permitted content of the cross examination, particularly in relation to the previous sexual history of the complainant in rape cases, has already been considered,[5] but further procedural issues arise concerning the conduct of cross examination. The right of the defence to cross examine prosecution witnesses is considered fundamental to a fair trial. Indeed, abolition of the right has potentially devastating implications for human rights, as art 6(3)(d) of the European Convention on Human Rights provides that everyone charged with a criminal offence has the right to examine or have examined witnesses against him and to obtain the attendance and examination of witnesses on his behalf under the same conditions as witnesses against him. In formulating proposals for reform, in 1989 the Advisory Group on Video Evidence acknowledged that the right of cross examination must be retained and the Group focused on how to retain the right whilst at the same time alleviating the stress caused to the witness. A decade after the Advisory Group's recommendations were first made, the proposals resurfaced in the Youth Justice and Criminal Evidence Act, s 28 of which provides that, where the court has

---

1   Section 27 of the 1999 Act is expected to be implemented in the Crown Court by the end of 2000. *Action for Justice* (Home Office, London, 1999).

2   See **3.131**.

3   *Youth Justice and Criminal Evidence Act 1999 Explanatory Notes* para 117.

4   See **3.26**.

5   See **3.49**.

already allowed a video recording to be admitted as the witness's evidence in chief, the witness may be cross examined before trial and the cross examination, and any subsequent re-examination recorded on video for use at trial.[1]

3.132   The cross examination will not be recorded in the physical presence of the defendant, although he will have to be able to see and hear the cross examination and be able to communicate with his legal representative.[2] The recording may, but need not, take place in the physical presence of the judge or magistrates and the defence and prosecution legal representatives, although all these individuals must be able to see and hear the witness being cross examined and communicate with anyone who is in the room with the witness, such as an intermediary.[3] Witnesses who have been cross examined on video may not be cross examined again, unless the court makes a direction permitting another video-recorded cross examination. The court will only do so if the subject of the proposed cross examination is relevant to the trial and something which the party seeking to cross examine did not know about at the time of the original cross examination and could not have reasonably found out about by then, or if it is otherwise in the interests if justice to do so.[4]

3.133   The video recording of cross examination as permitted by the 1999 Act attracted strong opposition during the passage of the legislation through Parliament. Although the provisions were welcomed by the NSPCC, which had been calling for the implementation of the remaining recommendations from the Advisory Group on Video Evidence for some years, the Law Society, the law reform pressure group, Justice, and the civil liberties pressure group, Liberty, all expressed concern.[5] Whilst the principle of cross examining vulnerable witnesses outside the court room was generally accepted, it was argued that this would only be feasible during the course of the trial itself. Liberty argued that effective cross examination of a witness was dependent on the evidence of other witnesses, which would only be put to proof and therefore fully available at the trial. To allow for cross examination of a witness prior to trial would arguably place that witness's evidence in a different position to that of other witnesses and would be in breach of art 6. Furthermore, both Liberty and Justice pointed out that provision for re-opening cross examination of the witness at a later date if necessary illustrated the practical difficulties which may occur if, as anticipated, there were many applications to do so. The Government's response to such arguments was pragmatic. Acknowledging that inevitably there would be cases where the defence would only be ready or willing to cross examine witnesses shortly before a trial begins, Lord Williams of Mostyn pointed out that 'unless we start, we shall get nowhere'.[6] Clearly, the provisions have the potential to benefit some cases. If there are genuine reasons why cross examination cannot take place before the trial without prejudicing the defence case, then little more can be done – vulnerable witnesses can at least have the benefit of other special

---

1   The Government is aiming to introduce this measure for Crown Court cases in Autumn 2001. *Action for Justice* (Home Office, London, 1999).
2   Section 28(2). See further **3.151**.
3   See **3.134** to **3.136**.
4   Youth Justice and Criminal Evidence Act 1999, s 28(5) and (6).
5   Research Paper 99/40 (1999) Home Affairs Section, House of Commons Library.
6   HL Deb vol 596, col 1376, 1 February 1999.

measures available at the trial. The real concern is that the defence will be tempted to use delaying tactics to defeat the objective of the legislation. The courts will need to be alive to this possibility and take active steps to ensure that such abuse of the system does not occur to the detriment of vulnerable witnesses.

Use of intermediaries and aids to communication

3.134   The provision of special measures, such as the use of screens or video-recorded testimony will undoubtedly enhance the quality of the evidence given by many witnesses, whilst at the same time making the whole experience less traumatic for them. Yet it is acknowledged that there will continue to be a small number of witnesses who, although competent to give evidence, nevertheless have difficulty communicating in the usual way. This may be because the witness is very young or suffers from a disability which affects his or her ability to communicate. In 1989, the Advisory Group on Video Evidence recommended that a trial judge should be able to make special arrangements for the examination of very young or very disturbed children, extending where necessary to allowing the relaying of questions from counsel through a paediatrician, child psychiatrist, social worker or person who enjoys the child's confidence.[1] The Advisory Group recognised that this would be a substantial change and that there would be unease at the prospect of interposing a third party between advocate and witness. The dissenting member of the Group believed that the intervention of a specialist interlocutor would hinder rather than assist counsel in conducting the case – inevitably some of the counsel's forensic skills, timing and intonation would be lost. The recommendation of the majority was not enacted in the Criminal Justice Act 1991, but the issue was returned to by the Working Group in 1998,[2] when it was pointed out that, in addition to the potential use of intermediaries in communicating with children, there may be adult vulnerable witnesses with language and comprehension difficulties who could also benefit from the assistance of an intermediary in relaying questions. However, the Group expressed reservations about the use of an intermediary in interpreting the witness's reply to the court.

3.135   The Youth Justice and Criminal Evidence Act 1999 when in force will provide that a special measures direction may provide for any examination of the witness (however and wherever conducted) to be conducted through an interpreter or intermediary,[3] and may provide for the witness to be provided with any aid to communication that the court considers appropriate.[4] An intermediary is someone whom the court approves to communicate to the witness the

---

1   *Advisory Group on Video Evidence* (Home Office, London, 1989) para 2.32.
2   *'Speaking up for Justice' Report of the Interdepartmental Working Group on the Treatment of Vulnerable or Intimidated Witnesses in the Criminal Justice System* (Home Office, London, 1998) Recommendation 47.
3   Youth Justice and Criminal Evidence Act 1999, s 29. The Government is aiming to introduce this measure in the Crown Court by Autumn 2000. *Action for Justice* (Home Office, London, 1999).
4   Youth Justice and Criminal Evidence Act 1999, s 30. This measure is expected to be implemented in the Crown Court by the end of 2000. *Action for Justice* (Home Office, London, 1999).

questions the court, the defence and the prosecution ask, and then communicate the answers that the witness gives in reply. The intermediary will be allowed to explain questions and answers if that is necessary to enable the witness and the court to communicate.[1] The aids to communication are intended to be aids to overcoming physical disabilities with understanding or answering questions, such as sign boards and communication aids – the provision is not intended to cover devices for disguising speech.[2]

3.136   However, intermediaries and aids to communication are only available to witnesses eligible for special measures due to their age, or because they suffer from a mental disorder, mental impairment, significant learning disability or physical disorder or disability which the court considers is likely to affect the quality of their evidence.[3] Thus, the measures may prove valuable for child victims of sexual offences, but adult victims are excluded unless they suffer from a relevant disability.

The conduct of cross examination

3.137   The Working Group on the treatment of vulnerable and intimidated witnesses in the criminal justice system identified two main concerns about cross examination in sexual offences: that victims of sexual offences are cross examined more severely than for other crimes and that cross examination by the offender in person can be severely traumatic for the victim.[4]

The severity of cross examination

3.138   With the exception of rules relating to the previous sexual history of the complainant in a rape case, the rules on cross examination of witnesses are theoretically the same for sexual offences as they are for other offences. However, the view has been expressed that victims of sexual offences tend to be subjected to longer, more aggressive cross examination than other witnesses, arguably due to the fact that most sexual offences take place in private and consent is often a central issue to the defence case. It is generally accepted that rape victims find the experience of cross examination traumatic. Indeed, the experience has been described by rape victims as 'patronising', 'humiliating', 'being made to feel as if they were on trial' and 'worse than rape'.[5] However, other victims and prosecution witnesses in general also have also been reported as finding the process of cross examination humiliating and frustrating.[6] A study conducted in Australia[7] compared the trial transcripts of 40 rape cases and 44 serious assault cases and concluded that, although on average it took twice as long to cross examine complainants in the rape cases as it did in the assault trials, there were also strong similarities in the strategies used in cross examination. In

---

1   *Youth Justice and Criminal Evidence Act 1999 Explanatory Notes* para 123.
2   *Youth Justice and Criminal Evidence Act 1999 Explanatory Notes* para 128.
3   Youth Justice and Criminal Evidence Act 1999, s 18(1).
4   *Speaking up for Justice* (above) p 175.
5   *Women, Rape and the Criminal Justice System* (Victim Support, London, 1996).
6   Rock *The Social World of the English Crown Court* (Clarendon Press, Oxford, 1993).
7   Brereton 'How Different are Rape Trials? A Comparison of the Cross Examination of Complainants in Rape and Assault Trials' (1997) 37 *British Journal of Criminology* 242.

particular, the study found that assault victims were just as likely to have their character and credibility attacked, that attempts were made to exploit inconsistencies in the complainants' statements in both cases and, if assault complainants did not behave as expected (for example, reporting soon after the offence), this was raised in cross examination, as happened in the rape cases. The study concluded that too much attention had been given to improving rape trials in particular, and that more attention should be given to the weaknesses of the trial process in generally. A similar view has been expressed in England and Wales, where it has been suggested that the treatment of rape complainants in court stems largely from the inadequate regulation of cross examination as to credit in criminal proceedings and the nature of cross examination itself.[1]

Controlling cross examination

3.139 In general, the defence may ask a prosecution witness any question in cross examination provided it is relevant, is not prohibited by statute and provided the answer will not involve inadmissible material, such as hearsay. In the majority of cases, the cross examination will be conducted by defence counsel[2] and its conduct is regulated, both by the Bar's Code of Conduct, with which barristers have a duty to comply, and by the trial judge, who has a common law duty to restrain unnecessary or improper or oppressive questions.[3] Admittedly, defending counsel can be placed in a difficult position. On the one hand, the Bar's Code of Conduct provides that counsel must at all times promote and protect fearlessly and by all proper means his lay client's best interests,[4] but the Code then states that he must not make statements or ask questions which are merely scandalous, or calculated only to vilify or annoy the witness or some other person.[5] In defending a client's interests 'fearlessly', it is perhaps inevitable that an overzealous counsel may occasionally overstep the mark.

3.140 Yet research suggests that, in practice, this occurs regularly, with the Code being breached routinely by defence counsel and no intervention being made by either prosecution counsel or the trial judge.[6] The answer to the problem does not lie solely in legislation. The Working Group on the treatment of vulnerable and intimidated witnesses in the criminal justice system took the view that witnesses are performing a public duty and should be treated with dignity and respect when giving evidence in court. The Group recommended that the Lord Chief Justice should be invited to consider issuing a Practice Direction giving guidance to barristers and judges on the need to disallow unnecessarily aggressive and/or inappropriate cross examination.[7] If defence counsel prove themselves to be incapable of abiding by their Code of Conduct, trial judges must take steps to censure them. One Court of Appeal judge has called on judges to submit formal reports on aggressive barristers. Lord Justice Sedley has pointed out that there is a duty on the Bar and the Law Society to

---

1   Ellison 'Cross Examination in Rape Trials' [1998] Crim LR 605.
2   See **3.141** to **3.152**.
3   *Speaking up for Justice* (above) para 8.51.
4   Annex H para 5.1.
5   Annex H para 5.10(e).
6   Lees *Carnal Knowledge: Rape on Trial* (Penguin Books, London, 1996).
7   *Speaking up for Justice* (above) Recommendation 43.

police their advocates and misconduct in adversarial proceedings should be brought to their attention.[1] The Victims' Charter[2] declares that victims deserve to be treated with both sympathy and respect and that any upset and hardship connected with the victim's involvement with the criminal justice system should be minimised. If the criminal justice system is to do more than pay lip service to such declarations, stricter control of the cross examination of all victims must be exercised. In civil proceedings judges are now expected to be more intervention-ist and to take control of the running of the case. A similar approach should be adopted in criminal cases, with judges setting clear limits as to what will be tolerated in the cross examination of witnesses.[3]

Cross examination by the defendant in person

CHILD WITNESSES

3.141   Defendants in criminal proceedings are generally entitled to rep-resent themselves and cross examine prosecution witnesses in person. In 1989 the Advisory Group on Video Evidence recommended that defendants should be prohibited specifically by statute from examining child witnesses in person or through a sound or video link, expressing the view that the limitation which this placed on the defence was far less significant than the damage which could be inflicted upon the child and the interests of justice.[4] The recommendation was enacted by the Criminal Justice Act 1991.[5] However, the legislation did not make clear what procedure was to be invoked if a defendant refused legal represen-tation and there appears to be little information as to how this problem has been addressed subsequently. By 1998, the Working Group had only identified two cases, in one of which the judge had put questions to the witness on behalf of the defendant and another when no cross examination took place as the defendant refused the judge's help.[6] The former case was appealed to the Court of Appeal,[7] where it was said that, when an unrepresented defendant was statutorily prohibited from cross examining a witness, it was generally desirable for a judge to test the reliability and accuracy of the witness's evidence, but the judge should not descend into the arena on behalf of the defence. Whereas it was open for a judge in these circumstances to ask a defendant whether there were matters which he would like the judge to put to the witness, it was a matter for the judge to decide how to put those questions. If the judge followed these general precepts, the Court said it would be slow to interfere. Clearly, then, the judge may put questions to a child witness, but it is far from clear what view the Court of Appeal would take if a judge declined to ask such questions, either of his own motion or as a conduit-pipe for the defence.[8]

---

1   (1999) *The Times*, 17 May.
2   *The Victim's Charter: A Statement of the Service Standards for Victims of Crime* (Home Office, London, 1996).
3   Lord Justice Sedley (1999) *The Times*, 17 May.
4   *Report of the Advisory Group on Video Evidence* (Home Office, London, 1989) para 2.30.
5   Criminal Justice Act 1988, s 34A, which was inserted by s 55(7) of the Criminal Justice Act 1991.
6   *Speaking up for Justice* (above) para 9.35.
7   *R v De Oliveira* [1997] Crim LR 600.
8   See commentary on *R v De Oliveira* [1997] Crim LR 600.

3.142　　To date, the problem does not appear to have arisen and in 1999 the Home Secretary commented that there was no known example of the use of the power in the 1991 Act leading to any allegation of a miscarriage of justice.[1] The prohibition on personal cross examination of child witnesses, although admittedly controversial, passed through Parliament as part of the package for reforms for child witnesses with little difficulty. One reason for this is undoubtedly the fact that children as a class are considered vulnerable. During the debate in the House of Lords on the Youth Justice and Criminal Evidence Act 1999, it was pointed out that children need special protection in court as they are without exception under a disability by reason of age, they are less able to give evidence and may require specialist cross examination to elicit the truth and, therefore, the courts rightly take special powers to ensure that justice is done.[2] More difficult problems have been encountered in extending the prohibition to vulnerable adult witnesses.

VULNERABLE ADULT WITNESSES

3.143　　Although evidence suggests that only a small number of defendants are unrepresented in the Crown Court,[3] in 1996 and 1997 there were two high-profile trials in which the defendants were charged with rape and subjected the alleged victims to prolonged cross examination, over a period of several days, which they carried out in person and in one case with the defendant wearing the clothes that he wore in the original attack.[4] The cases of *Ralston Edwards* in September 1996 and *Milton Brown* in November 1997 were widely reported in the media,[5] leading to fears that the publicity may well influence other defendants to seek to cross examine witnesses in person. Earlier cases had made it clear that the trial judge has a discretion to prevent any cross examination which he considers to be unnecessary or oppressive, but in exercising this inherent power to prevent its process being abused by an unrepresented defendant, the Court of Appeal had stressed that it was to be exercised exceedingly sparingly and only in an obvious case.[6] The trial judges in the *Edwards* and *Brown* cases were, perhaps understandably, cautious in restraining the defendants during cross examination, being only too aware of the possibility of creating grounds for an appeal. Yet the effect on the victims was devastating and the publicity can only have deterred other victims from coming forward to report similar offences.

GUIDANCE FROM THE COURT OF APPEAL

3.144　　Following the case *R v Brown (Milton)*[7] the Court of Appeal gave advice to judges on the conduct of trials in which defendants, particularly those accused of rape or other serious sexual offences, dispense with legal representatives and cross examined complainants themselves. The Lord Chief Justice emphasised the presumption of innocence and pointed out that a trial could not be

---

1　　Jack Straw HC Debate vol 329, col 391, 15 April 1999.
2　　Baroness Mallalieu HL Deb vol 596, col 1389, 1 February 1999.
3　　*Speaking up for Justice* (above) para 9.29. At present almost all defendants receive legal aid and only 4% are either privately represented or unrepresented. *Speaking up for Justice* p 176.
4　　HC Debate vol 329, col 410, 15 April 1999.
5　　See, for example (1996) *The Telegraph*, 23 August and (1997) *The Telegraph*, 6 December.
6　　*R v Morley* (1988) 87 Cr App R 218.
7　　(1998) 2 Cr App R 364.

conducted on the assumption that a defendant is a rapist and a complainant a victim, as the purpose of the proceeding was to establish whether that was so or not. However, judges were the masters of proceedings in their own courts and they were not obliged to give unrepresented defendants free reign to ask whatever questions, at whatever length, they wished. The court then indicated how judges should control questioning.[1]

(1) It would often be desirable for the judge to discuss the course of proceedings with the defendant in the absence of the jury before the cross-examination of the complainant. The judge could then elicit the general nature of the defence and identify the specific points in the complainant's evidence with which the defendant took issue, and any points he wanted to put to her. If the defendant intended to call witnesses in his own defence, then the substance of their evidence could be elicited so that the complainant's observations on it might, so far as relevant, be invited.

(2) It would almost always be desirable in the first instance to allow a defendant to put questions to a complainant. But it should be made clear in advance that the defendant would be required, having put a point, to move on, and if he failed to do so the judge should intervene and ensure that he does.

(3) If the defendant proved unwilling or unable to comply with the judge's instructions the judge should, if necessary in order to save the complainant from avoidable distress, stop further questioning by the defendant or take over the questioning of the complainant himself.

(4) If the defendant sought by his dress, bearing, manner or questions to dominate, intimidate or humiliate the complainant, or it was reasonably apprehended that he would seek to do so, the judge should not hesitate to order the erection of a screen in addition to controlling questioning in the way indicated above.

3.145 The Lord Chief Justice acknowledged that the exercise of these powers would always call for the exercise of a very careful judgment, as the judge must not only ensure that the defendant had a fair trial but also (which was not necessarily the same thing) that the jury felt he had had a fair trial. However, he stressed that if, exercising the best judgment they reasonably could in circumstances which were always difficult, judges intervened to ensure that witnesses were not subjected to inappropriate pressure, they should understand that the Court of Appeal would be very slow indeed, in the absence of clear evidence of injustice, to disturb any resulting conviction.

3.146 The extent to which this clear guidance to trial judges has succeeded in stamping out the abuse perpetrated by unrepresented defendants on their alleged victims in court is a matter of some debate. In the House of Lords in February 1999 the Lord Chief Justice commented that, since the guidance, there had been no further example of the abuse.[2] However, the Home Office minister, Lord Williams of Mostyn, dissented from this view, claiming that there was abundant material to show that there had been many other cases – not cases which had gone to the Court of Appeal, but cases of women who simply could not

---

1   *Defendants in Rape Trials Cross-questioning Witnesses: Court of Appeal Offers Trial Guidance to Trial Judges* (Lord Chancellors Department, 6 May 1998).

2   HL Deb vol 596, col 1400, 1 February 1999.

bear the prospect of being cross examined by their alleged criminal violator.[1] Whilst it cannot be proved conclusively that many more victims have been deterred from reporting sexual offences by the prospect of cross examination by the defendant in person, it would be naive to conclude that guidance from the Court of Appeal, as welcome as it may be, has finally solved a problem which, in reality, can only be solved by statutory intervention.

STATUTORY PROVISIONS
3.147   In 1998, the Working Group acknowledged that removal of the defendant's right to cross examine a witness in person raises some complex legal issues, including the potential conflict with the right to a fair trial contained in art 6. However, on this point it was noted that the removal by the Criminal Justice Act 1991 of the defendant's right to cross examine certain child witnesses had not been challenged under the European Convention. The Group favoured a mandatory ban on personal cross examination by a defendant, but concluded that, in recognition of the impact such a ban would have on the defendant's rights, it should be limited to cases which were the cause of most concern, namely cross examination of the complainant in cases of rape and sexual assault.[2] In the case of other witnesses and other offences, especially those where intimidation was a factor, the Group recommended that the court should have a discretion to impose a prohibition on the defendant's cross examination.[3] The Group was also concerned with the procedures to be adopted in relation to an unrepresented defendant and recommended that if such a defendant was prohibited from personal cross examination, he should be granted legal aid, without means testing, to obtain legal representation for cross examination purposes only.[4] This was clearly felt to be compatible with the European Convention, as the European Court of Human Rights has held that a requirement of German law that a defendant must be legally represented was compatible with Art 6.[5]

3.148   The recommendations of the Working Group are now contained in the Youth Justice and Criminal Evidence Act 1999. A defendant charged with a sexual offence[6] is prevented from personally cross examining the complainant in connection with that offence or any other offence (of whatever nature) with which the defendant is charged in the proceedings.[7] The provisions of the Criminal Justice Act 1988 which prohibited unrepresented defendants from personally cross examining child witnesses in cases of sex and violence are replaced and extended by the 1999 Act to also prevent the cross examination in person of a child who is either the complainant of, or a witness to the commission of, certain offences under the Child Abduction Act 1984.[8]

---

1   HL Deb vol 596, col 1405, 1 February 1999.
2   *Speaking up for Justice* (above) Recommendation 58.
3   *Speaking up for Justice* (above) Recommendation 59.
4   *Speaking up for Justice* (above) Recommendation 60.
5   *Croissant v Germany* 25 September 1992, series A no 237.
6   See **3.118**.
7   Youth Justice and Criminal Evidence Act 1999, s 34. This provision will be implemented by April 2000. *Action for Justice* (Home Office, London, 1999).
8   Youth Justice and Criminal Evidence Act 1999, s 35. The additional offences are those under ss 1 and 2 of the Child Abduction Act 1984 – kidnapping, false imprisonment and abduction.

3.149   The absolute prohibition on personal cross examination of complainants by defendants extends only to charges of sexual offences, but the 1999 Act also gives the court a discretionary power, either on an application by the prosecution or on its own motion, to issue directions prohibiting personal cross examination by defendants in other cases. The court may give such a direction if it is satisfied that the circumstances of the witnesses and the case merit a prohibition, and that it would not be contrary to the interests of justice.[1] In determining whether a prohibition would improve the quality of the evidence given by the witness on cross examination, the court must have regard, in particular, to:[2]

(1) any views expressed by the witness as to whether or not the witness is content to be cross examined by the accused in person;
(2) the nature of the questions likely to be asked, having regard to the issues in the proceedings and the defence case advanced so far (if any);
(3) any behaviour on the part of the accused at any stage of the proceedings, both generally and in relation to the witness;
(4) any relationship (of whatever nature) between the witness and the accused;
(5) whether any person (other than the accused) in the proceedings is, or has at any time been, subject to the mandatory prohibition on cross examining the witness in person; and
(6) any special measures direction which the court has given, or proposes to give, in relation to the witness.

3.150   Thus, the court has a discretion to prohibit personal cross examination by the defendant in cases such as those under the Protection from Harassment Act 1997, where the complainant may be equally as vulnerable as a victim of a sexual offence. Any such direction will be binding unless and until the court considers that the direction should be discharged in the interests of justice and the court must state in open court its reasons for making, refusing or discharging directions.[3]

3.151   When a defendant is prevented from cross examining a complainant in person, either as a result of the mandatory prohibition or as a result of a direction given by the court, if the defendant is not legally represented and does not take the opportunity to appoint a legal representative, the court must consider whether it is necessary, in the interests of justice, for the witness's evidence to be tested. If it decides that it is, the court will appoint a legal representative to carry out the cross examination of the witness in the interests of the defendant. However, a court-appointed representative will not have been instructed by the defendant and so cannot be responsible for him.[4]

3.152   As far as funding of defence representation is concerned, where a defendant is banned from personally cross examining, he is able to apply for legal aid for his representative on the same means-tested basis as other

---

1   Youth Justice and Criminal Evidence Act 1999, s 36.
2   Youth Justice and Criminal Evidence Act 1999, s 36(3).
3   Youth Justice and Criminal Evidence Act 1999, s 37.
4   Youth Justice and Criminal Evidence Act 1999, s 38.

defendants in criminal cases. Court-appointed legal representatives are to be paid from central funds rather than from legal aid.[1]

ANONYMITY AND REPORTS OF PROCEEDINGS

3.153   One aspect of the principle of open justice is that the media should not be impeded from reporting what has taken place publicly in court. However, it always been recognised that, in exceptional circumstances, restrictions may justifiably be placed on the freedom of the press to report proceedings in court if it is necessary for the administration of justice, although such restrictions have been severely limited in the past.

Contempt of court

3.154   As a general rule, any media reporting which creates a substantial risk of prejudice to the course of justice amounts to contempt of court. The fair and accurate reporting of legal proceedings held in public is not contempt, provided the report is published contemporaneously and in good faith,[2] but a court has power to order that publication of reports on all or part of its proceedings shall be postponed if it appears to be necessary for avoiding a substantial risk of prejudice to the administration of justice in the proceedings before the court or any other pending or imminent proceedings.[3] A court may also impose a permanent ban on the publication of material which it has validly ordered to be communicated privately.[4]

Children and Young Persons Act 1933

3.155   The Children and Young Persons Act 1933 prohibits the publication of details likely to identify any child or young person involved in the Youth Court, whether as a defendant or witness.[5] However, by virtue of the Crime (Sentences) Act 1997,[6] the court now has a discretion to dispense with these provisions if satisfied that it is in the public interest to do so in relation to a child or young person who has been convicted of an offence and the Home Secretary has expressed the view that he would like to see that power used more widely.[7] The 1933 Act also allows any court to prohibit the reporting of details identifying children and young persons who are involved in proceedings before it as defendants, complainants or witnesses.[8] These restrictions have been extended to prohibit the reporting of English and Welsh proceedings in Scotland,[9] but do

---

1   Youth Justice and Criminal Evidence Act 1999, s 40. Following the implementation of the Access to Justice Act 1999, representatives appointed under these provisions will be funded under the new arrangements for legal representation in criminal proceedings.
2   Contempt of Court Act 1981, ss 2 and 4.
3   Contempt of Court Act 1981, s 4(2).
4   Contempt of Court Act 1981, s 11.
5   Children and Young Persons Act 1933, s 49.
6   Crime (Sentences) Act 1997, s 45.
7   HC Deb vol 329, col 395, 15 April 1999.
8   Children and Young Persons Act 1933, s 39.
9   Children and Young Persons Act 1963, s 57.

not extend to reporting in Northern Ireland and only apply once the criminal process has been activated in a particular case.

Complainants in sexual offences cases

3.156   The Sexual Offences (Amendment) Acts of 1976 and 1992 provide anonymity for a complainant in cases of rape and serious sexual offences.[1] From the time the allegation of the offence is made, the press may not publish anything which is likely to lead the public to identify the alleged victim, even if the identity is revealed in open court. The trial judge may direct that the prohibition on publicity is lifted if either publicity is required by the defendant in order to induce persons who are likely to be needed as witnesses at the trial to come forward and the conduct of the defence at the trial is likely to be substantially prejudiced if the direction is not given, or if at the trial the judge is satisfied that the imposition of the prohibition would impose a substantial and unreasonable restriction on the reporting of the proceedings at the trial and that it is in the public interest to remove or relax the restriction.[2]

Reform measures

3.157   In 1998, the Working Group on the treatment of vulnerable or intimidated witnesses in the criminal justice system made various recommendations, designed to ensure consistency in the time when the restriction took effect and the geographical area covered. It also recommended that the court should have a power to order that the press and media should not report details likely to lead to the identification of a witness in cases where press reporting is likely to exacerbate witness intimidation.[3] The Youth Justice and Criminal Evidence Bill, as initially introduced into the House of Lords, contained a number of clauses designed to implement these recommendations and to make a number of other changes. These provisions caused considerable controversy during the passage of the legislation through Parliament, not least because they included a mandatory restriction on the reporting of information, once a criminal investigation has begun, enabling the identification of any person under 18 years of age who is suspected of having committed the offence or is the victim of or witness to the alleged offence. Strong representations were made by the print and broadcasting media, which argued that the proposed changes imposed an undue burden on them and their ability to report news effectively and, as a result, the Bill was amended substantially during the report stage and third reading in the House of Lords.[4]

---

1   The 1992 Act extended the protection afforded to complainants in rape cases to those in cases involving offences under ss 2–7, 9–12 and 14–16 of the Sexual Offences Act 1956; s 128 of the Mental Health Act 1959; s 1 of the Indecency with Children Act 1960; s 54 of the Criminal Law Act 1977 and attempts to commit any of these offences.
2   Sexual Offences (Amendment) Act 1992, s 3.
3   *Speaking up for Justice* Recommendations 39 and 40.
4   HL Deb vol 598, cols 53–74, 8 March 1999 and HL Deb vol 598, cols 1222–1234, 23 March 1999.

The Youth Justice and Criminal Evidence Act 1999

Young people under the age of 18 years

3.158   Sections 44 and 45 of the 1999 Act are concerned with protecting young people under the age of 18 and are based on the restrictions imposed by the Children and Young Persons Act 1933. Similar restrictions are imposed on the reporting of information likely to identify young people involved in court proceedings, and the restrictions are extended to the identification of young people during the pre-charge stage of criminal investigations. The young people covered by the restrictions are those who are alleged to have committed, been the victim of, or witnessed the commission of the offence that is under investigation. The Government has announced that the restrictions relating to the identity of young offenders will be implemented in June 2000. However, no target date has been set for the implementation of the restrictions on the reporting of the identities of young witnesses and victims of crime, the Government claiming that it will keep the case for the implementation of these provisions under regular review.[1]

3.159   If the provisions are implemented, those who breach the reporting restrictions by identifying young victims and witnesses are provided with statutory defences in certain circumstances which are not available to publishers in respect of the identification of alleged offenders.[2] For example, if the breach of the reporting restrictions is in relation to identifying young victims and witnesses of any offence other than a sexual offence as defined by the Sexual Offences (Amendment) Act 1992, s 50 of the Act provides a defence. The court must be satisfied that the public interest demanded publication of the information and, because of that, the reporting restriction was substantial and unreasonable. The presence of these defences turns the restriction from a ban against identifying young victims and witnesses into a presumption against publishing such information.[3]

Adult witnesses

3.160   Section 46 of the Act allows courts to impose restrictions on reporting information leading to identification of an adult witness involved in criminal proceedings, if the court considers that the measure is needed because the victim's fear of, or distress at, giving evidence or co-operating with the party calling him is linked strongly to the likelihood of publicity.[4] Such witnesses may well be eligible for a special measures direction under the Act, but this fact alone will not make them eligible for the protection of a reporting restriction. In determining whether a witness is eligible for protection, the court must take

---

1   *Action for Justice* (Home Office, London, 1999).
2   Youth Justice and Criminal Evidence Act 1999, s 50.
3   *Youth Justice and Criminal Evidence Act 1999 Explanatory Notes* para 162.
4   Implementation of this provision in the Crown Court is expected by the end of 2000. *Action for Justice* (Home Office, London, 1999).

account of any views expressed by the witness[1] and, in particular, must take into account:[2]

(1) the nature and alleged circumstances of the offence to which the proceedings relate;
(2) the age of the witness;
(3) such of the following matters as appear to the court to be relevant, namely:
  (a) the social and cultural background and ethnic origins of the witness,
  (b) the domestic and employment circumstances of the witness, and
  (c) any religious beliefs or political opinions of the witness; and
(4) any behaviour towards the witness on the part of:
  (a) the accused,
  (b) members of the family or associates of the accused, or
  (c) any other person who is likely to be an accused or a witness in the proceedings.

3.161 Complainants in sexual offences will continue to be protected by the provisions of the Sexual Offences (Amendment) Acts and Sch 2 to the 1999 Act makes several changes to the restrictions contained in those Acts to ensure that the provisions are similar to those in ss 44, 45 and 46 of the 1999 Act.

3.162 Section 47 of the 1999 Act prevents the reporting, until the end of the court proceedings, of matters relating to any special measures directions given by the court[3] or directions under s 36 prohibiting the defendant from cross examining in person any particular witness.[4] Such restrictions do not extend to any evidence given by the witness in the case, or to the witness's identity, but of course in the case of sexual offences, the identity of the witness will often be protected by other provisions. The court has a discretionary power to lift the restrictions imposed by s 47, but if the defendant makes representations against it doing so, the court will have to consider whether lifting the restriction would be in the interests of justice.[5]

Anonymity and defendants in sexual offences cases

3.163 Several of the existing provisions may well prevent the reporting of details leading to the identification of the victim of a sexual offence and, following the enactment of the Youth Justice and Criminal Evidence Act 1999, the protection may also extend to witnesses. The same protection is not afforded to defendants themselves, unless they are under the age of 18 years. When the Sexual Offences (Amendment) Act 1976 first gave protection to rape victims, it was argued that it was only fair that, if the victim was to be protected from unpleasant publicity, then so too should the alleged offender. The Act, therefore, entitled a person accused of rape to anonymity until such time as he may be convicted of the offence.[6] However, the ban on the identification of suspected rapists was said by police to hamper their investigations as it prevented

---

1   Youth Justice and Criminal Evidence Act 1999, s 46(5).
2   Youth Justice and Criminal Evidence Act 1999, s 46(4).
3   See **3.115** to **3.136**.
4   See **3.141** to **3.152**.
5   Youth Justice and Criminal Evidence Act 1999, s 47(4) and (5).
6   Sexual Offences (Amendment) Act 1976, s 6.

them from publishing details or pictures of any person they might want to interview. Furthermore, it was argued that, whereas a ban on the identification of rape victims by the media was necessary to encourage the victims to come forward and report the offence, a suspected rapist had no more claim to anonymity that those suspected of any other offences. As a result of growing pressure, the provision protecting suspected rapists from publicity was repealed in 1988.[1]

3.164   More recently, attempts have been made to re-introduce a measure of protection from publicity for certain categories of suspected sexual offenders. Particular concern has been voiced over the vulnerability of teachers to malicious accusations of abuse from disgruntled pupils.[2] Statistics compiled by one of the largest teaching unions – the National Association of Schoolmasters/ Union of Women Teachers (NAS/UWT) – show that since 1991 there have been 974 police investigations into abuse allegations made against union members. In 792 of these cases, no grounds were discovered for prosecution, but publicity in 80% of the cases was said to do serious injustice to innocent teachers. In extreme cases, the publicity was alleged to have been a significant factor in the teacher's suicide.[3] As a result of these concerns, in March 1999 a Private Member's Bill was introduced into the House of Commons. The Sexual Offences (Anonymity of Defendants) Bill[4] aimed to provide for the anonymity of teachers and others regularly involved in caring for, training, supervising or being in sole charge of persons under 16 at an educational institution, who are accused of a sexual offence[5] against a child under their care or supervision. Although the Bill was supported by the National Association of Headteachers, it did not have the support of the other major teacher's union – the National Union of Teachers – which claimed the Bill would protect the guilty as well as the innocent.[6] No date was given for the second reading at the end of the Parliamentary session and, therefore, the Bill was lost.

---

1   Criminal Justice Act 1988, s 158.
2   See, for example, 'Wrongful accusations – has the pendulum swung too far?' in Cobley *Child Abuse and the Law* (Cavendish Publishing Ltd, London, 1995) p 137.
3   HC Deb vol 328, col 871, 30 March 1999.
4   Bill 78 Presented to the House of Commons on 30 March 1999.
5   The sexual offences referred to in the Bill are those under the Sexual Offences Acts 1956 and 1976. Reference to the Sexual Offences (Amendment) Act 1999 is no longer applicable as that Bill was defeated in the House of Lords on 13 April 1999. No mention is made of the Indecency with Children Act 1960 or the Protection of Children Act 1978 – a rather curious omission given the underlying intention of the Bill.
6   HC Deb vol 328, col 873, 30 March 1999.

Chapter 4
SENTENCING SEX OFFENDERS

THE CONCEPT OF PUNISHMENT

4.1   The criminal law is not simply a series of moral commandments: 'Thou shalt not rape.' It is a series of legal commandments backed up by the threat of punishment: 'You must not rape, and if you do, you may be sent to prison for life.'

4.2   It is generally accepted that the purpose of the criminal law is to announce to society that certain forms of behaviour are unacceptable and to secure that fewer members of society behave in such a way.[1] Thus, labelling conduct as criminal firstly serves a utilitarian purpose. It informs people what they may not do, and thereby indirectly informs that what they *may* do. Secondly, labelling conduct as criminal should ensure that fewer members of society indulge in such unacceptable conduct. It has been suggested that merely to announce that a certain form of behaviour is forbidden will, to some extent, ensure that fewer people behave in such a way. For example, it has been argued that there is no *a priori* reason why we should not content ourselves with simply announcing that killing or rape is forbidden – the mere announcement of the fact would to some degree ensure that fewer people are killed or raped – so that crime without punishment, or at least the threat of punishment, may be impractical, but it is not illogical.[2]

4.3   Whilst many would agree that punishment, or the threat of punishment, is necessary in practice in order to achieve the desired result, the contrary view has been expressed by penal abolitionists:

> 'I cannot imagine a position where I should strive for an increase of man-inflicted pain on earth. Nor can I see any good reason to believe that the recent level of pain infliction is just the right or natural one . . . I see no other defensible position than to strive for pain-reduction.'[3]

Those supporting penal abolition face a two-fold task: first, they must engage in a 'politics of bad conscience', thereby making it as difficult as possible to justify punishment; and, secondly, they must show that there are other ways of dealing more rationally with crimes.[4] Abolitionists' arguments may appear morally attractive and many would agree that, as an ideal, people would volunteer to abide by the law without the threat of punishment. However, we do not live in an ideal world, and as has been pointed out 'this ideal did not work in the Garden of

---

1   Hart *Punishment and Responsibility: Essays in the Philosophy of Law* (Clarendon Press, Oxford, 1968) p 6.
2   Packer *The Limits of the Criminal Sanction* (Stanford University Press, California, 1968) p 19.
3   Christie *Limits to Pain* (Martin Robertson, Oxford, 1982).
4   De Haan 'The Necessity of Punishment in a Just Social Order: A Critical Appraisal' (1998) *International Journal of Sociology of Law* 16 at 433.

Eden – which is why we are here'.[1] Thus, the prohibition alone is generally considered insufficient, it must be accompanied by a sanction, namely the threat of punishment.

Rationales and justifications of punishment

4.4   There exists a considerable body of literature on the philosophy and rationale of punishment.[2] In brief, four main rationales can be identified: retribution, deterrence, rehabilitation and incapacitation.

Retribution

4.5   The term 'retribution' is itself problematic, because it may be used to denote one of several distinct justifications, ie revenge, denunciation, atonement or 'just deserts', that the law-breaker is 'getting what he justly deserves'. All of these rationales are retrospective in nature, they focus on the offender's past behaviour and see punishment as being justified as a response to that past behaviour, either to avenge the individual victim or society as a whole, to denounce emphatically the behaviour, to make the offender 'pay for' his crime or merely to give the offender what he justly deserves.

4.6   The classical, so called 'strong', theory of retribution sees the offender's 'just deserts' as being both a necessary and a sufficient condition for justified punishment – punishment is justified merely because of the offender's past behaviour, no other rationale or justification is required. Other forms of retributive theory, which have been labelled 'weak retributivisim', regard the offender's 'just deserts' as a necessary, but not a sufficient condition for punishment. Although the offender's wrong doing gives the State a right to punish and to inflict 'just deserts', this right in itself is insufficient; there should be a further justification in each individual case. This further justification may take the form of rehabilitation, deterrence or incapacitation, the important point being that although retribution forms the central justifying factor, this in itself is insufficient, and further justification must be found in each individual case.

Deterrence

4.7   Unlike retribution, which is essentially retrospective, deterrence is prospective in that it focuses on the consequences of punishment. Whereas retribution is guilt based and sees punishment as being justified in the name of justice, deterrent theories (in common with rehabilitation) regard punishment as being justified for the sake of utility, ie to modify the future behaviour of the offender or others. Deterrence can be said to operate at several different levels. First, the threat of punishment acts as a general deterrence, in that it deters people from committing crimes. At this level, the effect of punishment on the individual offender is irrelevant. The offender is used as a means of achieving a

---

1   Van den Haag *Punishing Criminals: Concerning a Very Old and Painful Question* (Basic Books, New York, 1975) p 20.

2   See Ashworth *Sentencing and Criminal Justice* (Butterworths, London, 1995) and the references therein.

social goal – deterring others from committing crime. Secondly, the threat of punishment may act as an individual or special deterrence. Individual offenders are deterred by their experience of punishment because of its unpleasant effects.[1] Finally, the threat of punishment is said to act as a form of education. Punishment is seen as a concrete expression of society's disapproval of an act which helps to form and to strengthen the public's moral code and thereby creates conscious and unconscious inhibitions against committing crime.[2]

4.8 The effectiveness of punishment as a deterrent has been questioned. At the end of the 19th century, it was claimed:

'... if the wrongdoer calculate at all, it is not upon the probable account of the punishment, but upon the chances of detection – from which it follows that ... severe and barbarous punishments are not more effectual than milder ones as deterrents to crime.'[3]

Therefore, it is said to be unrealistic to construct sentencing arrangements on the assumption that most offenders will weigh up the possibilities of being punished in advance and base their conduct on rational calculation. Often, it is claimed, they do not.[4] Yet, even if it is accepted that people *are* deterred from committing offences by the threat of punishment, such a threat will only have a deterrent effect if past threats of punishment have been carried out. If past threats were not carried out, present threats would not be believed and, therefore, would be ineffective in deterring anyone from crime. Therefore, it is argued, if society fails to inflict punishment as threatened, or inflicts a lower level of punishment, those inclined to break the law would realise that the law has been bluffing, thereby drastically reducing the deterrent effect of punishment. In 1975, it was suggested that:

'the present low rate of punishment may bring this about. So far it has not, because the law still has a great deal of credibility handed down from past generations. We may be consuming this stock of credibility, as we do other resources, at a perilous rate ...'[5]

However, more recent trends in sentencing practice suggest the reference to the 'present low rate of punishment' is no longer quite so justified. The last decade has seen an increase in the proportion of offenders sentenced to immediate custody. Of those convicted of indictable offences 22.81% received an immediate custodial sentence in 1998, compared with only 15% in the early 1990s, a rise of 8%. The trend is particularly evident when considering those convicted of sexual offences. In 1993, 8% of offenders over the age of 21 who were convicted of an indictable sexual offence in the magistrates' court were sentenced to

---

1   Fitzmaurice and Pease *The Psychology of Judicial Sentencing* (Manchester University Press, Manchester, 1986) p 48.
2   Andenaes 'General Prevention' (1952) 43 J Crim, C & PS.
3   Pamphlet published by the Humanitarian League in 1893, quoted in Ashworth 'Sentencing in the 80s and 90s: The Struggle for Power' The Eighth Eve Saville Memorial Lecture given on 21 May 1997 at King's College, London.
4   *Crime Justice and Protecting the Public* (1990) Cmnd 965 (HMSO, London) para 2.8.
5   Van den Haag *Punishing Criminals: Concerning a Very Old and Painful Question* (Basic Books, New York, 1975) p 15.

immediate custody, as were 73% of those convicted in the Crown Court. In 1998 these figures had risen to 16% and 77% respectively.[1]

Rehabilitation

4.9   In common with deterrent theories, rehabilitation is prospective, in that it concentrates on the consequences of punishment. However, unlike deterrence, which aims to secure conformity through fear of punishment, rehabilitation theories see punishment as justified because it aims to reform the offender so that he becomes adjusted to the social order. Whereas retribution focused on the past behaviour of the offender (the offence), rehabilitation focuses on the future conduct of the offender. Therefore, the punishment inflicted depends on the individual offender, not his past offence.

4.10   It has been suggested that the rehabilitative idea is open to abuse. The question has been asked:

> 'Are we really entitled to change people by punishment? ... the concept of rehabilitation seems dangerously general and manipulable. For it is always possible that an assessment of an offender's rehabilitation will depend on an official belief in a degree of socialisation far broader than a mere willingness to conform to the criminal law ...'[2]

Incapacitation

4.11   Incapacitation is generally regarded as a form of social control. Imprisonment is the primary form of incapacitation, although other punishment, such as the removal of a driving licence or the imposition of a curfew order, may result in partial incapacitation. The underlying rationale is that society is protected while the offender is incapacitated, but to some extent this necessarily acknowledges the practical limitations of other rationales of punishment. Retribution only justifies punishment for the offender's past behaviour. If deterrence and rehabilitation were truly effective, there would be no need to incapacitate offenders. Retribution, deterrence and rehabilitation may well all involve incapacitation, ie it may be what the offender deserves, it may be the only effective deterrent and it may be necessary in order to rehabilitate the offender. However, in certain circumstances, an offender may be incapacitated for a longer period than that justified on the grounds of retribution, deterrence or rehabilitation[3] – the sole rationale being the need incapacitate the offender in order to protect the public.

4.12   There is no one generally accepted rationale of punishment, but such a conclusion is hardly surprising. It has been suggested that what is needed is the realisation that different principles or rationales are relevant at different points in any morally acceptable account of punishment and that the pursuit of one aim may be qualified by or provide an opportunity, not to be missed, for the pursuit

1   Home Office Statistical Bulletin 21/99 *Cautions, Court Proceedings and Sentencing, England and Wales 1998*.
2   Lacey *State Punishment; Political Principles and Community Values* (Routledge, London, 1988) p 31
3   Criminal Justice Act 1991, s 2(2)(b) and **4.67**.

of others.[1] Indeed, it has been questioned whether the conventional distinctions between rationales of punishment are distinguishable at all in sentencing practice. It has been suggested that it is remarkably difficult to generate ideal types of sentencing practice based either on single principles or on a combination of sentencing principles which differ from each other, and that, in practice, it is virtually impossible to infer sentencing purpose from sentencing practice.[2]

PUNISHING SEX OFFENDERS

4.13   Although the punishment of sex offenders may be justified by one or more of the preceding rationales, there are certain characteristics of both the offender and the offences committed that render certain rationales more appropriate than others.

Sex offenders and retribution

4.14   Given the current tendency to treat sex offenders as the most feared, hated and despised group of offenders,[3] retribution may be a strong justification for imposing punishment as a form of revenge. However, there may be a conflict of views between society as a whole and the individual victim, particularly in cases of intrafamilial abuse where sexual offences are committed against a child. In most cases, the commission of a sexual offence against a child will engender a public outcry and calls for revenge. Indeed, if no punishment were seen to be inflicted, there may be a danger that society, or certain sections of society, would take the law 'into their own hands' and inflict punishment as they saw fit. However, this desire for revenge is not necessarily reflected in the feelings of the victim. For example, although a child victim of intrafamilial abuse may well want the abuse to stop, she may have no wish to see the family torn apart and punishment inflicted on the abuser. Retribution as denunciation may also provide a strong justification for punishing sex offenders. Society's feelings of revulsion and disgust will call for the offender's conduct to be condemned as forcefully as possible. Similar considerations will apply to retribution as atonement – the offender may be 'purified through suffering'. However, if retribution is regarded as imposing an offender's 'just deserts', problems can arise.

Sex offenders and 'just deserts'

4.15   The concept of 'just deserts' incorporates a notion of culpability. The offender's culpability depends on an individual's perception of the offending behaviour. In some cases, the offending behaviour may be viewed from a

---

1   Hart *Punishment and Responsibility: Essays in the Philosophy of Law* (Clarendon Press, Oxford, 1968) p 3.
2   Fitzmaurice and Pease *The Psychology of Judicial Sentencing* (Manchester University Press, Manchester, 1986) pp 49–51.
3   See **1.1**.

perspective which allows it to be sanctioned in various ways. In sanctioning the offending behaviour, the offender's 'just deserts', or culpability, is thereby reduced to a certain extent. Perhaps the most common way the offending behaviour is sanctioned is to transfer part of the responsibility, and therefore part of the blame, for the offence on to the victim.

4.16   It is commonly acknowledged that offenders themselves often attempt to transfer responsibility in this way – to claim that a rape victim 'asked for it' by acting in a provocative manner or by wearing provocative clothing. What is not so commonly acknowledged is that it is not only offenders themselves who attempt to transfer responsibility. Various professionals, including those participating in the criminal justice system, may tend to do the same thing. This tendency has been most notable in cases involving children as victims. The practice of attributing responsibility to the child victim was especially prevalent in the early part of this century. Freud contended that child victims merely fantasised about abuse and were not to be believed.[1] Even if the child were believed, there was a tendency to hold the child partly responsible for the abuse. In 1907 it was contended that:

> '... in a great number of cases, the trauma [of sexual abuse] was desired by the child unconsciously, and that we have to recognise it as a form of infantile sexual activity.'[2]

The tendency to blame the child victim of a sexual offence is abundantly clear in the following extract from a judgment delivered in 1923:

> 'This wretched girl was young in years but old in sin and shame. A number of callow youths, of otherwise blameless lives so far as this record shows, fell under her seductive influence ... she was a mere "cistern for foul toads to know and gender in". Why should the boys, misled by her, be sacrificed?'[3]

At first sight, it may well be thought that the tendency to blame the victim has disappeared in more recent times. It would certainly be unusual for a judge to echo such sentiments in a judgment today. Yet, although such open displays of victim-blaming are no longer common, there is a danger that the underlying sentiments remain unchanged and perhaps there is still a tendency to blame the victim, thus reducing the offender's 'just deserts' as perceived by the sentencer.

4.17   Blame may also be transferred to third parties, particularly in cases of intrafamilial abuse. It seems that, in recent years, the focus of the literature on incest has shifted from assigning responsibility to the victim to assigning responsibility to the family in general and the mother in particular.[4] The mother may be said to be culpable in a number of alternative ways. First, she may actively encourage the abuse, unconsciously giving the daughter permission to participate in the abuse by allowing the situation to develop in which it can take place.

---

1   Cobley *Child Abuse and the Law* (Cavendish Publishing Ltd, London, 1995) p 132.
2   Abraham 'The Experiencing of Sexual Trauma as a Form of Sexual Activity' in Salter (ed) *Treating Sex Offenders and Victims: A Practical Guide* (Sage Publications, California, 1988) pp 26–27.
3   Salter *Treating Sex Offenders and Victims: A Practical Guide* (Sage Publications, California, 1988) p 32.
4   Kelly *Surviving Sexual Violence* (Polity Press, Cambridge, 1988) p 57.

Alternatively, the mother may deny all knowledge of the abuse and fail to take steps to protect the child. Finally, the mother may be held indirectly responsible by denying her husband sexual relations. It has been claimed: 'If a woman denies her husband his conjugal rights [he] may turn to the nearest available source of gratification – a dependant child.'[1]

4.18   It may well be argued that the concept of transferring blame, either to the victim or the mother, should have no place in judicial sentencing practice. Yet the truth is, in practice, it sometimes does. In February 1989, a judge gave a suspended prison sentence to a man who raped his 12-year-old daughter. The judge justified his leniency on the grounds that the offender's wife was not satisfying his sexual needs.[2] Admittedly, the justification for the sentence attracted widespread media attention and was heavily criticised. However, this was only because the trial judge was brave enough (or foolish enough?) publicly to announce his reasoning. Although judicial sentencers are obliged, in certain circumstances, to give reasons for the sentences they impose, these obligations are aimed primarily at justifying the imposition of a custodial sentence[3] and, in particular, justifying the length of a custodial sentence.[4] Judicial sentencers are not expected to divulge their precise calculations. This means that it is difficult to estimate the extent to which they are influenced by such blame-transference. Nevertheless, it is clear that in some cases an offender's perceived 'just deserts' will be reduced substantially in the view of the sentencer and this will inevitably be reflected in the sentence imposed.

Incapacitation – a sufficient justification for punishing sex offenders?

4.19   Obviously, retribution may not be the only justification for punishment. Sentencing a sex offender may well also provide opportunities for deterrence, rehabilitation and incapacitation. To imprison a convicted offender may well satisfy society's need for revenge and denounce the behaviour, thereby ensuring the offender gets his 'just deserts'. Yet it will also serve to incapacitate the offender and so protect society – while he is imprisoned he will not be a danger to society. At the same time, it may provide an opportunity to rehabilitate the offender.[5] Therefore, by the time of his release, the abuser will have received his 'just deserts', society has denounced his behaviour and been avenged, society has also been protected during the period of his incarceration and, if the rehabilitation has been effective, the offender will present no further danger to society. Thus, the one sentence may achieve several different aims. Although protection of the public through incapacitation of the offender may be advanced as a general aim in conjunction with other aims, problems arise if incapacitation is offered as the sole justification for imposing punishment on an offender. The problem is most acute when the punishment imposed on an offender is more severe than can be justified by the seriousness of the offence

---

1   Search *The Last Taboo: Sexual Abuse of Children* (Penguin Books, London, 1988) p 88.
2   (1989) *The Guardian*, 8 February.
3   Criminal Justice Act 1991, s 1(4).
4   Criminal Justice Act 1991, s 2(3).
5   See **5.37** to **5.69**.

or offences committed, typically when an offender is imprisoned for a longer than normal period and the extended period is said to be justified on the grounds of incapacitation. Nevertheless, current sentencing practice does allow for such sentences to be passed on those convicted of violent or sexual offences who are deemed to pose a risk of serious harm to the public.[1]

Deterring sex offenders

4.20   An alternative rationale, that of deterrence, is one which may be of limited relevance to sex offenders. Punishment as a general deterrent assumes that offenders will be deterred from abusing by the mere fact that other offenders have been punished. As an individual deterrent, it assumes that individual offenders are deterred by their experience of punishment because of its unpleasant effects. Both assumptions presuppose that offenders acknowledge the risk of being caught. The threat of punishment can only be an effective deterrent if an offender believes he is likely to be subjected to that punishment. Given the 'dark figure' of unreported crime and the small percentage of recorded cases that result in conviction, many sex offenders surely feel secure in the knowledge that their offending behaviour is unlikely to be reported to the police and, and even if the offence is reported and investigated the chances of a criminal conviction resulting (and thus punishment being imposed) are slight. The problem is aggravated by the concept of 'offender denial' – many sex offenders self-rationalise their activities, believing that they are not doing anything wrong. If an offender believes that he is not doing anything wrong, he is unlikely to be deterred from his activities.

Treating sex offenders – the rehabilitative ideal

4.21   The traditional methods of punishment, in particular imprisonment, are said to have very little rehabilitative effect on sex offenders. Indeed, it has been argued that imprisonment has the opposite effect in that it makes the offender more likely to offend on his release as there is said to be increasing evidence to suggest that the necessary herding of sexual offenders together under r 43 offers reinforcement in the form of opportunities for further sexual excitement and sharing of their sexual experiences.[2]

4.22   It would seem that the primary justification for imposing conventional punishment on sex offenders must be retribution, deterrence or incapacitation. However, it is now recognised that many sex offenders need some form of treatment before they can be successfully rehabilitated. Indeed, it has be suggested that:

> '... unless we face the challenge ... we will achieve nothing more than our Victorian forbears 100 years ago who, as men of their times, could not have envisaged the possibility of rehabilitation beyond the vengeance of retribution and the illusion of deterrence.'[3]

1   See **4.67**.
2   Glaser and Spencer 'Sentencing, Children's Evidence and Trauma' (1990) CLR 371 at 380.
3   Scott, 'Legally Enforced Treatment of the Incestually Abusing Parent – Problems of Policy and Practice' (1989) *Journal of Social Welfare and Family Law* 217 at 228.

The criminal justice system is currently striving to take heed of this warning and to increase the opportunities for convicted sex offenders to receive treatment as part of their sentence.[1]

PROCEDURE FOLLOWING CONVICTION

Adjourning for inquiries

4.23   Before passing sentence, the court must ensure that it has before it all relevant information in order to determine the appropriate sentence. In order to gather such information, it may be necessary to adjourn the proceedings. The magistrates' court has a power to adjourn the proceedings after convicting the offender and before sentencing him or otherwise dealing with him for the purpose of enabling inquiries to be made.[2] Such inquiries will normally consist of calling for a pre-sentence report[3] or a medical or psychiatric report.[4] The adjournment must be for no more than 4 weeks if the offender is remanded on bail or no more than 3 weeks if the offender is remanded in custody. There is no corresponding statutory provision for the Crown Court, but the Court has jurisdiction at common law to postpone the passing of a sentence[5] and will usually do so if inquiries need to be made.

Facts of the offence

4.24   If the defendant has pleaded not guilty and a full trial has taken place, the sentencer will be usually be fully aware of the facts of the offence. In the magistrates' court no problems will arise as the magistrates are responsible for both convicting and sentencing the offender. Problems may, however, arise in trials on indictment when the jury bears the responsibility of determining the facts and convicting the offender, but the judge bears the responsibility of passing sentence. In doing so, the judge must always respect the verdict of the court so that, if an offender has been found guilty of a lesser offence than that charged, sentence can only be imposed for that lesser offence, even if the judge personally believes that the evidence justified convicting the offender of a more serious offence.[6] If the factual basis of the conviction is not clear, the Court of Appeal has held that it is for the judge to assess the evidence as led before the jury, and decide on the basis of that evidence what the facts of the offence were. He is not obliged to accept the least serious construction of the evidence consistent with the jury's verdict, but any benefit of doubt should be given to the offender.[7]

---

1   See **5.37** to **5.60** and **6.50** to **6.61**
2   Magistrates' Courts Act 1980, s 10(3).
3   See **4.30**
4   See **4.46**
5   *Archbold 'Criminal Pleading, Evidence and Practice'* (Sweet & Maxwell, London, 1999).
6   *R v Hazelwood* [1984] Crim LR 375.
7   *R v Stosiek* (1982) 4 Cr App R (S) 205.

4.25　　If the offender pleads guilty and no trial takes place, it is the duty of the prosecuting counsel to summarise the facts of the offence.[1] This will be done by reliance on witness statements made by prosecution witnesses, including the victim of the offence. Problems can arise if the defence contests the prosecution version of events at this stage. If the conflict between prosecution and defence is substantial and involves a sharp divergence on questions of fact, the judge, having heard submissions from counsel, should either accept the defence account of events, as far as that is possible, or hold what is commonly known as a *Newton*[2] hearing, ie give both parties the opportunity to call evidence about the disputed matters, and come to his own conclusion.[3]

Antecedents

4.26　　Responsibility for providing the court with details of the offender's antecedent history rests with the police. Antecedents should contain the following information:[4]

(1)　personal details and summary of convictions and cautions;
(2)　previous convictions; and
(3)　recorded cautions.

If the antecedents are provided to the Crown Court it should also contain:

(1)　circumstances of the last three similar convictions; and
(2)　where the current alleged offence is within the term of an existing Community Order, the circumstances of the offence leading to the Community Order.

In the magistrates' court five copies of the antecedent report will be prepared in respect of each defendant and provided to the Crown Prosecution Service (CPS), which will be responsible for distributing them to others at the court hearing. Normally, two copies will be provided to the court: one to the defence and one to the Probation Service where appropriate. In the Crown Court, seven copies will be prepared in respect of each defendant. Two copies are to be provided directly to the CPS, the remaining five are sent to the Court. The Court will send one copy to the defence and one to the Probation Service, the remaining copies being for the Court's use. In either court, if a custodial sentence is imposed following conviction, a copy of the antecedents will be attached to the order sent to the prison.[5]

Spent convictions

4.27　　The antecedents will include a complete record of the offender's criminal history, in some cases dating back many years. The Rehabilitation of Offenders Act 1974 introduced the concept of 'spent' convictions, the underly-

---

1　　*R v Tolera* [1998] Crim LR 425.
2　　As decided in *R v Newton* (1982) 77 Cr App R 13.
3　　For further details, see Sprack *Emmins on Criminal Procedure* (Blackstone Press Ltd, London, 1997) p 317.
4　　*Practice Direction (Crime: Antecedents) (No 2)* [1997] 1 WLR 1472.
5　　*Archbold 'Criminal Pleading, Evidence and Practice'* (Sweet & Maxwell, London, 1999) paras 5.31 and 5.32.

ing rationale being that offenders become rehabilitated over a period of time and that past convictions thus become spent after the lapse of a period of time, which varies according the length and nature of the sentence. Once the conviction is spent, for most purposes the individual is treated as a rehabilitated person who has never been charged or convicted of a criminal offence.[1] However, the provisions of the 1974 Act do not apply to criminal proceedings,[2] so there is no statutory restriction on the admissibility of previous convictions, regardless of whether or not they would be treated as spent convictions for other purposes. Despite the lack of a statutory restriction, the Court of Appeal has recommended that that both courts and counsel should give effect to the general rationale underlying the 1974 Act and should not refer to a spent conviction when that can reasonably be avoided.[3] Thus, spent convictions should be clearly marked as such in the antecedents supplied to the court.

4.28   The rehabilitation period depends on the sentence passed as follows:

(1) if the offender was sentenced to life imprisonment or for a term exceeding 30 months,[4] the conviction never becomes spent;

(2) if the offender was sentenced to imprisonment for more than 6 months but not more than 30 months, the conviction will be spent after 10 years;

(3) if the offender was sentenced to imprisonment for 6 months or less, the conviction will be spent after 7 years;[5]

(4) if the offender was sentenced to detention in a young offender institute for a term of 30 months or less, the conviction will be spent at the same time as it would for an equivalent term of imprisonment, but if the offender is under 18 years of age at the time of his conviction, the relevant period is halved;

(5) if the offender was sentenced to a fine, Community Service Order or Probation Order, the conviction will be spent after 5 years, but if the offender is a juvenile at the time of his conviction, the relevant period is halved;

(6) if the offender was conditionally discharged or bound over to keep the peace or be of good behaviour, the conviction will be spent after 1 year or at the end of the order, whichever is the longer period;

(7) if the offender was given an Attendance Centre Order or secure training order, the conviction will be spent 1 year after the order expires;

(8) if the offender was discharged absolutely, the conviction will be spent after 6 months; and

(9) if the offender was disqualified from driving, the conviction will be spent after the disqualification period has expired.

4.29   If an offender is convicted of a second offence, other than a summary offence, during the rehabilitation period of an earlier offence, the rehabilitation

---

1   Rehabilitation of Offenders Act 1974, s 4(1).
2   Rehabilitation of Offenders Act 1974, s 7(2).
3   *Practice Direction (Crime: Spent Convictions)* [1975] 1 WLR 1065.
4   Or to equivalent sentences of detention in a young offender institution or detained under s 53 of the Children and Young Persons Act 1933.
5   In any case, where the sentence is suspended, the period is the same as if it had been immediate.

period of the earlier offence will continue to run until the second conviction becomes spent.[1]

Pre-sentence reports

4.30		In many cases, before deciding on the appropriate sentence, the court will obtain a pre-sentence report on the offender. A pre-sentence report means a report in writing which:

(1)	with a view to assisting the court in determining the most suitable method of dealing with an offender, is made or submitted by a probation officer or by a social worker of a local authority social services department; and

(2)	contains information as to such matters, presented in such manner as may be prescribed by rules made by the Secretary of State.[2]

4.31		There is a mandatory requirement to obtain and consider such a report when the offender is under the age of 18 years, unless the offence is triable only on indictment or there is a pre-existing report and the court relies on that report, and, in either case, the court thinks that a report would be unnecessary.[3] Where the offender is over the age of 18, the court is under a duty to obtain and consider a pre-sentence report before forming an opinion that only a custodial sentence can be justified[4] or before making a Community Order,[5] unless it is of the opinion that such a report is unnecessary. Home Office research conducted between 1994 and 1996 found that, although it was rare for either the Crown Court or magistrates' court to make a community sentence without seeing a pre-sentence report, in both courts around 15% of cases which received a custodial sentence were sentenced without a report.[6] The findings in the case of magistrates' courts are surprising, as guidance issued by the Magistrates' Association suggests that few cases suitable for summary trial could be regarded as so serious that a custodial sentence would be the only conclusion drawn by the sentencer and, thus, a pre-sentence report may not be considered necessary. In the Crown Court, offenders convicted of violent and sexual offences were most likely to be sentenced to custody without a report. The study found that no report was obtained in respect of 25% of the sex offenders sentenced to custody by the Crown Court. Almost a third of offenders sentenced to more than three years in prison were sentenced without a report, compared to one in 10 of those with shorter sentences. The study concludes that these findings, taken together, may indicate that sentencers were most likely to dispense with a pre-sentence report in the most serious cases where custody was virtually inevitable.

Contents of pre-sentence reports

4.32		Pre-sentence reports are prepared by probation officers if the offender is an adult and by local authority social workers if the offender is under the age of 13. For intermediate ages, the work is shared between the Probation Service and

---

1	Rehabilitation of Offenders Act 1974, s 6(4).
2	Criminal Justice Act 1991, s 3(5).
3	Criminal Justice Act 1991, s 3(2A).
4	Criminal Justice Act 1991, s 3(1).
5	Criminal Justice Act 1991, s 7.
6	Research Findings No 47, Home Office Research and Statistics Directorate.

social workers, with social workers generally taking responsibility for the report if a teenage offender or his family are already known to the local authority. The preparation of pre-sentence reports is governed by national standards,[1] and in some probation areas these are supplemented and enhanced by local guidelines.[2] The current national standards, which were published in January 2000 and revise earlier standards published in 1995, state that a pre-sentence report should contain an analysis of the offence or offences before the court, an assessment of the offender, and an assessment of the risk of harm to the public and the likelihood of re-offending.[3] The conclusion of the report should make a clear and realistic proposal for sentence designed to protect the public and reduce re-offending, including a proposal for custody where this is necessary.[4] In order to reduce delays in sentencing, where a specific sentence is envisaged by the court, a specific sentence report may be provided, setting out, inter alia, the offender's suitability for a particular penalty as requested by the court.[5] The inclusion of an assessment of the risk posed by an offender will be vital in the case of those convicted of violent or sexual offences as this information may be used by the sentencer in the process of determining whether a longer than normal sentence can be justified on the grounds of protecting the public from serious harm.[6]

Pre-sentence reports and sex offenders

4.33　As part of a thematic inspection of the work of the Probation Service with sex offenders, which was undertaken in 1996–97 and reported in 1998,[7] 331 pre-sentence reports on sex offenders drawn from 10 probation areas were assessed by checking adherence to the national standard for pre-sentence reports and additionally examining a few issues specific to sex offenders. The vast majority of the offenders were male (there being only one female offender). Of the offenders, 59% had committed offences of indecent assault (44% on a child under 16 years of age and 15% on an adult victim), 9% had committed rape, 8% had committed offences of unlawful sexual intercourse (2% on a victim under 13 years of age and 6% on a victim under 16 years of age), 5% had committed offences of gross indecency with a child, 5% had committed offences of indecent exposure, 3% had committed buggery, 3% had committed offences involving obscene photographs of a child, 1% had committed incest and 8% had committed other offences not specified.

4.34　The overall quality of 82% of the total sample was assessed as satisfactory, including 34% deemed to be very good. In total, 18% was found to

---

1 　*National Standards for the Supervision of Offenders in the Community* (Home Office, London, 2000).

2 　Osler *Introduction to the Probation Service* (Waterside Press, Winchester, 1995).

3 　*National Standards for the Supervision of Offenders in the Community* (Home Office, London, 2000) paras B.5–B.8.

4 　*National Standards for the Supervision of Offenders in the Community* (Home Office, London, 2000) para B.9.

5 　*National Standards for the Supervision of Offenders in the Community* (Home Office, London, 2000) para B.10.

6 　See **4.67**.

7 　*Exercising Constant Vigilance: The Role of the Probation Service in Protecting the Public from Sex Offenders* (Home Office, London, 1998).

be not satisfactory, including 2% rated as very poor. It was pointed out in the report of the inspection that all pre-sentence reports need to be of a satisfactory standard to provide the maximum assistance to the court in determining the most appropriate sentence, but that it was particularly important with sex offenders, given the level of risk many present.[1] Surprisingly, although the practice guidance in a number of services emphasised the importance of conducting home visits when preparing reports on sex offenders (with due regard to safety issues for the staff concerned), home visits were not conducted in 90% of cases, despite the fact that 66% of the offenders in the sample were remanded on bail. As the report concludes, it is hard to envisage any circumstances which could justify a failure to conduct a home visit to a sex offender bailed to an address other than a probation hostel or provided by a partnership agency when a community disposal of any kind is being considered.[2] It may also be added that a home visit may be central to the initial decision as to whether a community disposal was appropriate, making the apparent reluctance to make home visits an even greater concern. There may well be practical constraints, particularly time,[3] which influence whether or not a home visit is made, but it is important that the court is provided with as much information as possible in order to determine the most appropriate sentence.

4.35   In some areas, service policy required that all pre-sentence reports on sex offenders should be prepared by specialist or semi-specialist probation officers. In others, it was an expectation that all sex offender cases would be referred to the specialist probation officer for an assessment prior to a proposal being made to the court in a report. Overall, the percentage of pre-sentence reports prepared with specialist or semi-specialist input varied between areas from 56% to 98%. In some cases, it was found that offenders were sentenced to supervision in the community without there being any input into the assessment process by specialist staff. As the report of the inspection points out, although competent non-specialist probation officers could undertake much of the work necessary to assess the offender, input from specialist or semi-specialist staff undoubtedly enhanced the quality and consistency of pre-sentence reports when assessing sexual offending.[4]

4.36   There was a single clear proposal for a non-custodial sentence in 65% of the reports sampled, no single clear proposal in 16% and custody was the only sentencing option considered in 19% of the reports. It is interesting to note that a custodial sentence was actually passed by the court in 55% of cases (in 42% of cases the custodial sentence was for longer than 12 months).[5] Unfortunately, it is not possible from the information provided to relate the sentence passed to the

---

1   *Exercising Constant Vigilance: The Role of the Probation Service in Protecting the Public from Sex Offenders* (Home Office, London, 1998) para 4.8.
2   *Exercising Constant Vigilance: The Role of the Probation Service in Protecting the Public from Sex Offenders* (Home Office, London, 1998) para 4.10.
3   The normal adjournment time to prepare a pre-sentence report on an offender remanded on bail is a maximum of 15 working days.
4   *Exercising Constant Vigilance: The Role of the Probation Service in Protecting the Public from Sex Offenders* (Home Office, London, 1998) para 4.22.
5   *Exercising Constant Vigilance: The Role of the Probation Service in Protecting the Public from Sex Offenders* (Home Office, London, 1998) para 4.19 and app 1.

proposal made in the pre-sentence report, but the statistics given at least demonstrate that that the courts are quite prepared to pass a custodial sentence even when a clear proposal has been made for a non-custodial sentence.

4.37 The report of the inspection expressed some concern about the lack of reference in the pre-sentence reports to the use of s 44 of the Criminal Justice Act 1991, which allowed the sentencing court to direct that serious sex offenders should be supervised to the very end of their sentence, rather than the three-quarter point as is usual for other offenders.[1] Of the 248 reports prepared on offenders sentenced at the Crown Court, only 95 (38%) included a reference to s 44. It appeared that, where staff were proposing a non-custodial sentence, there was a feeling that reference to extended post-release supervision somehow weakened the proposal and that such reference should only be made in cases where custody was inevitable. The report of the inspection concluded that such a feeling was ill-founded, as there were examples of excellent pre-sentence reports both making well-argued proposals for a Probation Order and covering the possibility of extended supervision should a custodial sentence be imposed. More consistent use of reference to s 44 was recommended, to draw the attention of judges to the issue and provide the opportunity for longer periods of supervision. No doubt, this will be of increasing importance in the future in view of the introduction in the Crime and Disorder Act 1998 of extended sentences for those convicted of violent or sexual offences.[2]

The prosecutor and the sentencing process

4.38 Although the sentence is determined by the court, the prosecutor is under a positive duty to assist the court at the sentencing stage. The Code of Conduct for the Bar Council states that prosecuting council should be in a position to assist the court if requested as to any statutory provisions relevant to the offence or to the offender and as to any relevant guidelines laid down by the Court of Appeal, and should bring such matters to the attention of the court if in the opinion of the prosecuting council the court has erred.[3] The Court of Appeal has encouraged prosecutors to be more pro-active in discharging this duty. In the *Attorney-General's Reference (No 7 of 1997)*[4] the Court of Appeal pointed out that the practice of reticence by prosecuting counsel began before the Attorney-General had the power to refer unduly lenient sentences to the Court of Appeal,[5] when sentencing provisions were less complex than they are today, and before sentencing decisions were as fully reported as they are now. The Court suggested that judges should not be slow to invite assistance from prosecuting counsel in these matters and that counsel should be ready to offer assistance if asked. Furthermore, the Court hoped that judges would not be affronted if prosecuting counsel did offer to give advice on the relevant provisions and appropriate authority.

---

1   See **4.82** to **4.87**.
2   See **4.84**.
3   Code of Conduct of the Bar Council Annex H, para 11.8.
4   *R v Fearon* [1997] Crim LR 908.
5   See further **4.135**.

4.39   In order to discharge this duty effectively, the prosecutor should be in possession of all relevant material in respect of sentence, including information about the offender. Prior to the enactment of the Crime (Sentences) Act 1997, copies of the pre-sentence report had to be given to the offender or his solicitor,[1] but there was no requirement that the report be disclosed to the prosecution. The 1997 Act now provides that a copy of the report shall be given to:

(1) the offender or his counsel or solicitor; and
(2) the prosecutor, that is to say, the person having the conduct of the proceedings in respect of the offence.[2]

The disclosure requirement is subject to two exceptions:

(1) if the offender is under the age of 17 and is not represented by counsel or a solicitor, a copy of the report need not be given to him but shall be given to his parent or guardian if present in court;[3] and
(2) if the prosecutor is not of a description prescribed by an order made by the Secretary of State, a copy of the report need not be given to the prosecutor if the court considers that it would be inappropriate for him to be given it.[4]

The use that the prosecutor can make of the information contained in the report is restricted, in that the prosecutor is prohibited from using or disclosing the information other than for the purpose of:

(1) determining whether representations as to matters contained in the report need to be made to the court; or
(2) making such representations to the court.[5]

4.40   Disclosure of pre-sentence reports to the prosecutor inevitably encourages the prosecutor to assist the court in the sentencing process, but it also raises some potentially controversial issues. It has been pointed out that the disclosure may be seen by the offender as a factor inhibiting full and frank disclosure of relevant facts to a report writer and that, although the use that the prosecutor can make of the information contained in the report is restricted, in practice there appears to be nothing to prevent the prosecutor from initiating further inquiries into certain matters, as long as the source of the information is not revealed.[6] However, if a prosecutor did cause further inquiries to be made, he would arguably be 'using' the information for an unauthorised purpose.

The victim and the sentencing process

4.41   Traditionally, the role of the victim in a criminal trial has been confined to appearing as a witness for the prosecution. On one view, this is the correct approach to adopt, as it has been suggested that the introduction of the victim into the equation can upset the delicate balance of rights and interests which has

---

1   Powers of Criminal Courts Act 1973, s 46.
2   Crime (Sentences) Act 1997, s 50(2).
3   Crime (Sentences) Act 1997, s 50(3).
4   Crime (Sentences) Act 1997, s 50(4). This allows the court to withhold the information from a private prosecutor.
5   Crime (Sentences) Act 1997, s 50(5).
6   Ward *Criminal Sentencing; The New Law* (Jordans, Bristol, 1997).

been built up between the offender and the State.[1] Yet the victim is not to be totally ignored. Since 1973, the courts have had a general power to order compensation to be paid to the victim of an offence for personal injury, loss or other damage caused by the offence. The compensation is paid to the victim by an offender on conviction as part of his sentence and is to be of an amount as the court considers appropriate, having regard to any evidence and to any representations that are made by or on behalf of the offender or the prosecutor.[2] Thus, the prosecutor will be able to allowed to call evidence relating to any injury suffered by the victim. The amount awarded is relatively small, in 1998 24% of all offenders convicted of sexual offences in the magistrates' court were ordered to pay compensation, the average payment being £159. However, in the Crown Court only 1% of those convicted of sexual offences were ordered to pay compensation, the average amount payment being £396.[3]

4.42 Whether the victim should have the right to play a more active role in the sentencing process is a matter of some debate. In recent years, there has been a growing movement towards according rights to victims of crime[4] and improvements have certainly been made in several areas of the criminal justice system for victims of sexual offences.[5] However there has been particular controversy over the involvement of victims of sexual offences in the sentencing process, especially in cases of intrafamilial child abuse where the offence and resulting sentence may have a considerable effect on the child's welfare. It has been argued that there are three areas which could conceivably permit victims to influence the sentencing decision: victim impact statements, victim forgiveness and the effect of the sentence on the victim.[6]

4.43 Victim impact statements may be used to provide the sentencer with information about the impact of the offence on the victim, without the need for a further court appearance. Many jurisdictions have made statutory provision for the admission of such statements, some of which require the court to consider such statements before passing sentence.[7] The underlying rationale is that the impact of the crime helps to illustrate the totality of the offence. Whether or not the relative resilience of the victim should be a factor affecting the punishment imposed is a matter of some debate, but the 'egg-shell skull' principle, whereby the offender must take his victim as he finds him, has been accepted in our jurisdiction for many years.[8] The issue is likely to be of specific relevance to sexual and violent offences, where the psychological impact on the victim may be particularly severe. When an offender has been convicted of rape, the Court of Appeal has made it clear that the offence should be treated as aggravated where

---

1 Duff 'The Victim Movement and Legal Reform' in Maguire and Pointing (eds) *Victims of Crime: A New Deal?* (Open University Press, Milton Keynes, 1988).
2 Powers of Criminal Courts Act 1973, s 35. See generally Cobley 'Financial Compensation for Victims of Child Abuse' (1998) *Journal of Social Welfare and Family Law* 20(3) 221 at 226.
3 *Criminal Statistics for England and Wales 1998* (provided by the Home Office).
4 See, for example, *Victim's Charter: A Statement of the Rights of Victims of Crime* (HMSO, London, 1990).
5 See **2.2** and **3.115**.
6 Gillespie 'Victims and Sentencing' [1998] NLJ 1263.
7 See Ashworth 'Victim Impact Statements and Sentencing' [1993] Crim LR 498.
8 *R v Blaue* [1975] 3 All ER 446.

the effect upon the victim, whether physical or mental, is of special seriousness.[1] More radical versions of victim impact statements admitted in other jurisdictions allow the victim to make 'penal demands' and to express an opinion as to the appropriate sentence to be passed. Whilst the Court of Appeal has made it clear that it is acceptable for a sentencer to consider a victim impact statement before passing sentence, this is to be done for the purpose of ascertaining factual evidence relevant to sentencing and does not extend to allowing the victim to make penal demands. In *Attorney-General's Reference (No 2 of 1995)*[2] the offender had been convicted of offences of indecency relating to his daughter. In imposing a Probation Order on the offender, the trial judge declined to look at a statement made by the daughter as to the impact of the offences on her, taking the view that it was inappropriate to receive evidence which sought to aggravate the impact which the offending had on the victim. On appeal by the Attorney-General, the Court of Appeal varied the sentence to 2 years' imprisonment and expressed the view that it was wholly appropriate that a judge should receive factual information as to the impact of the offending on a victim. Furthermore, the judge was said to be well equipped to know whether the statement put before him contained evidence of fact relevant to sentencing or whether an attempt had been made to try to 'hot up' the case against an offender.

4.44   In cases where there has been a close relationship between the offender and victim prior to the offence, the victim may well be prepared to forgive the offender. However, just as the views of the victim, as opposed to the impact of the offence on the victim, will not be allowed to increase the sentence passed, so too the views of the victim should not be allowed to mitigate the sentence. It has been suggested by the Court of Appeal that victim forgiveness can have an effect, albeit an indirect effect, upon the sentencer as the forgiveness may reduce the possibility of re-offending and it may reduce the public outrage which sometimes arises where a defendant has been released into the community early.[3] Yet, unless victim forgiveness is taken to reduce the seriousness of the offence, in the case of custodial sentences, these considerations could not effect a sentence imposed under s 2(2)(a) of the Criminal Justice Act 1991, which requires the sentence to be commensurate with the seriousness of the offence.[4] The reduced risk of offending could only effect the imposition of a longer than normal sentence under s 2(2)(b) of the 1991 Act.

4.45   The final factor that may influence a sentencer is the effect of the proposed sentence on the victim. In contrast to victim impact statements and taking account of victim forgiveness, whereby the sentencer may be influenced by the harm caused by the offender and by the subjective feelings of the victim, in considering the effect of the sentence on the victim the sentencer is influenced by the potential harm caused to the victim by the criminal justice system rather than the offender. Once again, this will be of particular relevance to cases of intrafamilial child abuse, where a custodial sentence imposed on an abusing

---

1   *R v Billam* (1986) 82 Cr App R 347.
2   (1996) 1 Cr App R (S) 274.
3   *R v Darvill* (1987) 9 Cr App R (S) 225 at 227 per Lord Lane CJ.
4   See **4.63**.

parent or carer may have an adverse effect on the child. One of the main principles enshrined in the Children Act 1989 is that children are best cared for by both parents wherever possible.[1] Whilst no-one would suggest leaving a child with an abusing parent, in some cases of intrafamilial abuse where the offence would ordinarily be sufficiently serious to justify a custodial sentence, a non-custodial sentence with the long-term aim of re-integrating the offender back into the family when he no longer poses a risk to the child would be the preferred outcome from the child's point of view. In such cases, it has been asked whether society is really willing to see a child harmed just so that they can see a parent placed in prison.[2] In many cases the answer inevitably will be 'yes'.

Medical reports

4.46   In some circumstances, the court will wish to obtain a medical report on the offender before passing sentence and has the power to remand the offender (on bail or in custody) in order for the report to be prepared.[3] The court also has the power to remand the offender to hospital for the preparation of reports on his mental condition.[4] The court is required to obtain medical and psychiatric reports on the offender before ordering the detention of the offender in a mental hospital[5] or making a Probation Order with a requirement that the offender receive treatment for a mental condition.[6] The court is also required to obtain and consider a medical report before passing a custodial sentence (other than for murder), if the offender is or appears to be mentally disordered, unless in the circumstances of the case the court is of the opinion that it is not necessary to do so.[7]

4.47   In practice, it is often difficult to obtain psychiatric reports through the court and it has been suggested that it may be necessary for defence solicitors to take the initiative and ask a consultant who has been treating their client for a mental condition to prepare a report on him.[8] If the resulting report is considered to be adverse to the offender's case, it may be withheld from the sentencer. However, the Court of Appeal has indicated that a psychiatrist commissioned by the defence to assess an offender, and who discovers that his evidence is not to be put before the sentencer, is free to make his evidence available through other channels without breaching his duty of confidence to the offender.[9]

Mitigation

4.48   The sentencer is required to have regard to both mitigating and aggravating factors which impinge upon offence seriousness in determining the

---

1   See Cobley *Child Abuse and the Law* (Cavendish Publishing Ltd, London, 1995) chap 3.
2   Gillespie 'Victims and Sentencing' [1998] NLJ 1263 at 1265.
3   See **4.23**.
4   Mental Health Act 1983, s 35. See further **4.106**.
5   Mental Health Act 1983, s 35.
6   Powers of Criminal Courts Act 1973, s 3.
7   Criminal Justice Act 1991, s 4(1) and (2).
8   Sprack *Emmins on Criminal Procedure* (Blackstone Press Ltd, London, 1997) p 326.
9   *R v Crozier* [1991] Crim LR 138.

length of any 'commensurate' custodial sentence to be imposed,[1] but the sentencer is also allowed to mitigate an offender's sentence by taking into account any other matters which, in the opinion of the court, are relevant.[2] Many such matters may already have been brought to the attention of the court in the antecedents and any reports considered by the court, but it is common practice for the defence counsel to present a mitigating speech on behalf of an offender before sentence is passed, highlighting mitigating factors already before the court and introducing any new mitigating factors which may exist. Character witnesses may also be called on behalf of the offender at this stage. Common mitigating factors include the following.

Guilty pleas

4.49   Traditionally, the courts have treated a guilty plea as a mitigating factor for sentencing purposes. In rape and serious sexual assaults, the Court of Appeal has acknowledged that the extra stress which giving evidence can cause to a victim means that a plea of guilty, perhaps more so than in other cases, should normally result in some reduction from what would otherwise be the appropriate sentence.[3] However, in 1993 the Royal Commission on Criminal Justice recommended that 'the present system of sentence discounts should be more clearly articulated, with earlier pleas attracting higher discounts'.[4] As a result, when determining what sentence to pass on an offender who has pleaded guilty, the court is now *required* to take into account the stage in the proceedings for the offence at which the offender indicated his plea of guilty and the circumstance in which this intention was given.[5] In every case where the court has, in the light of the offender's guilty plea, imposed a sentence less severe than it otherwise would have imposed, an explanatory statement must be made in open court.[6] Criminal statistics show a marked difference in sentencing according to the plea. In 1998, of all offenders sentenced for indictable offences at the Crown Court, 60% received an immediate custodial sentence following a guilty plea, whereas 70% received the same sentence after a contested trial. The average sentence length was 19.4 months for those who pleaded guilty, but 36.8 months for those who pleaded not guilty. Similarly, of those sentenced for sexual offences, 67% received an immediate custodial sentence following a guilty plea, but 86% received the same sentence following a contested trial. The average sentence length was 33.5 months for those who pleaded guilty, but 50.7 months for those who pleaded not guilty.[7]

---

1   Criminal Justice Act 1991, s 3(3)(a). See **4.63**.
2   Criminal Justice Act 1991, s 28(1).
3   *R v Billam* (1986) 82 Cr App R 347.
4   Cmnd 2263 (1993) Recommendation 156.
5   Criminal Justice and Public Order Act 1994, s 48(1).
6   Criminal Justice and Public Order Act 1994, s 48(2).
7   Home Office Statistical Bulletin 21/99 *Cautions, Court Proceedings and Sentencing, England and Wales 1998* table 13.

Age

4.50 Whereas the fact that the victim of an offence, particularly a sexual offence, is very old or very young may be treated as an aggravating factor,[1] the age of the offender may be treated as a mitigating factor. This is particularly so when the offender is under the age of 21.

Other matters

4.51 Various other factors may be brought to the attention of the sentencer in an attempt to mitigate the sentence, including the offender's good character. If no victim impact statement has been admitted, the mitigation speech may well make reference to the attitude of the victim, including elements of forgiveness and the effect of any potential sentence on the victim.[2]

Derogatory assertions

4.52 In contrast to emphasising any forgiveness displayed by the victim, the offender may attempt to make derogatory assertions about the victim in an effort reduce his perceived culpability and, thus, mitigate the sentence. The treatment of victims of sexual offences during a criminal trial has been the subject of considerable debate and certain safeguards now exist to protect such vulnerable victims, both in the manner in which they give evidence and in the questions that can be asked about their previous sexual history.[3] However, such safeguards are inapplicable to proceedings after a guilty a plea has been entered or a conviction obtained. In 1993, the Royal Commission on Criminal Justice received evidence that the victim of an offence may have slurs cast upon him during the defence speech in mitigation and that such assertions were privileged and could be reported with impunity by the press, with no opportunity for the victim to redress the balance.[4] Following recommendations made by the Royal Commission, the Criminal Procedure and Investigations Act 1996 now empowers a court to make an order prohibiting the publication of derogatory assertions made in the course of a speech in mitigation. A full order can be made after the court has made a determination with regard to sentencing,[5] whereas an interim order can be made at any time before such determination. The order may be revoked by the court at any time, but will automatically cease to have effect at the end of a 12-month period beginning on the day on which it is made. Breach of an order constitutes a summary offence.[6]

4.53 The effect of such an order is that, as long as the order is in force, the assertion must not:

(1) be published in Great Britain in a written publication available to the public; or

---

1   *R v Billam* (1986) 82 Cr App R 347.
2   See **4.41**.
3   See chap 3.
4   (1993) Cmnd 2263 (HMSO, London) para 47.
5   As defined by s 58(9).
6   Criminal Procedure and Investigations Act 1996, s 60.

(2) be included in a programme included in a programme service for reception in Great Britain.[1]

4.54 The court can make a full order[2] in relation to an assertion where there are substantial grounds for believing:

(1) that an assertion forming part of the speech or submission is derogatory to a person's character (for instance, because it suggests that his conduct is or has been criminal, immoral or improper); and
(2) that the assertion is false or that the facts asserted are irrelevant to the sentence.[3]

4.55 If a derogatory assertion is made about a victim during the defence speech in mitigation and the court chooses to make an order prohibiting the publication of the assertion, the victim is at least protected to the extent that the assertion cannot be published in the media. However, before making an order, the court must be satisfied that there are substantial grounds for believing that the assertion is false or that the facts asserted are irrelevant to sentence. Given the acknowledged tendency for sex offenders to attempt to transfer part of the blame for the offence to the victim or another third party, and the suspicion that some sentencers may still be influenced by such blame transference as reducing an offenders just deserts,[4] there remains a danger that derogatory assertions about the victim of a sex offence may not be seen as irrelevant to sentence and, thus, no order can be made. In any event, the making of an order does nothing to alleviate the potential stress caused to the victim by the assertion having been made in the first place.

THE SENTENCING STAGE

The principles of sentencing

The background

4.56 Sentencing law in England and Wales is derived from two principal sources: legislation and judicial decisions. Traditionally, the role of legislation has been restricted to providing the courts with powers and prescribing maximum sentences for individual offences. Acting within the framework set by legislation, the courts previously have had considerable discretion in deciding the appropriate sentence, although such discretion has long been supervised by the Court of Appeal. Prior to the 1990s, it was argued that the decision-making process could be divided into two distinct stages.[5] The sentencer would first make a primary decision between what was conveniently, if inelegantly, known as a tariff sentence and an individualised sentence based on the needs of the

---

1   Criminal Procedure and Investigations Act 1996, s 59(1) and (2).
2   An Interim Order can be made where it appears that there is a 'real possibility' that a full order will be made in relation to the assertion at the appropriate time (s 58(3)).
3   Criminal Procedure and Investigations Act 1996, s 58(4).
4   See **4.15** to **4.18**.
5   Thomas *Principles of Sentencing* (Heinemann, London, 1979).

offender as an individual. The objective of a tariff sentence was to reflect the offender's culpability, but the objective of an individualised sentence was to seek to influence the offender's future behaviour. Having made the primary decision, the sentencer would then make a second decision by applying the appropriate body of principle to determine the precise form of the sentence or measure to be adopted. If the sentencer decided to impose a tariff sentence, he would identify the normal range of sentences for crimes of that kind, place the particular offence at an appropriate level within that range and then make any allowance for mitigating factors by reducing the sentence. However, if the sentencer decided to impose an individualised sentence, he would simply impose the appropriate sentence which seemed to meet the needs of the individual offender. In the former case, attention was focused on the offence, with allowances made for mitigating factors. In the latter case, attention was focused on the perceived needs of the offender, the offence itself being relevant only in so far as it indicated those needs. Thus, there was clearly no consistent rationale for the imposition of punishment. Indeed, in one judgment given in 1974[1] the Court of Appeal advocated retribution, deterrence, prevention or incapacitation and rehabilitation as being the four aims of sentencing without providing any explanation as to how these aims could be reconciled or which was to prevail where there was conflict between them.

The growing impetus for change – the 1990 White Paper

4.57 The lack of a consistent framework of sentencing became a growing cause for concern during the 1980s. In a White Paper published in 1990, although the Government expressed its support and admiration for the way in which the Court of Appeal had developed sentencing principles, particularly through the formulation of guideline judgments,[2] it argued that there was still too much uncertainty and little guidance about the principles that should govern sentencing.[3] The remedy proposed was a partnership between legislature and judiciary – legislation would provide a framework of requirements for imposing both custodial and non-custodial sentences and the Court of Appeal would be expected to use its judgments to develop more detailed principles based on the statutory framework. The objective of the proposed statutory framework was to promote the principle of proportionality of sentencing as the general approach. The Government's stated aim was to ensure that convicted criminals were punished justly and suitably according to the seriousness of their offences, in other words that they got their 'just deserts'. However, it was accepted that the 'just deserts' policy may not be appropriate in certain exceptional circumstances and the Government was prepared to compromise just desert requirements by permitting the use of predictive confinement by sentencers in cases where offenders had committed offences of a violent or sexual nature if it was necessary in order to protect the public from serious harm. Such an approach is not new, as the law has long allowed certain offenders to be

---

1   *R v Sergeant* (1974) 60 Cr App R 74.
2   For example, *R v Roberts and Roberts* (1982) 4 Cr App R (S) 8 and *R v Billam* (1986) 8 Cr App R (S) 48 in relation to rape.
3   *Crime, Justice and Protecting the Public: The Government's Proposals for Legislation* (1990) Cmnd 965 (HMSO, London) para 1.4.

detained for longer than was justified by their immediate offence. The original notion of preventive detention was replaced in 1967 by the extended sentence, which allowed a court to impose an extended term of imprisonment on a persistent offender who had been convicted on indictment of an offence carrying a maximum prison sentence of at least 2 years.[1] The definition of a persistent offender was wide and extended sentences, although imposed infrequently, tended to be used to punish an offender for his previous record rather than as a way of protecting the public.[2] In proposing reform, the Government clearly wanted to restrict predictive confinement to offenders who were perceived to be dangerous, rather than merely recidivist.

4.58   The White Paper also reflected the Government's policy of 'bifurcation' or 'twin track' sentencing, ie long sentences for serious offenders but shorter and, where possible, community sentences for less serious offenders. Two years previously the Government had issued a Green Paper in which it had floated ideas for tougher non-custodial penalties, asking sentencers what changes would be needed if they were to be persuaded to make more use of non-custodial sentences. The White Paper thus proposed that custodial sentences must be confined to serious cases only and a wider range of community sentences be introduced.

4.59   A further concern that was evident at this time was the existing system of parole, whereby those serving sentences of imprisonment could be released on licence before the end of their sentence and subjected to a period of supervision in the community, during which time they would be liable to be recalled to prison in the event of misbehaviour. Following increasing criticism of the system in the 1980s, the Government appointed the Carlisle Committee to review the parole system. The Committee reported in 1988[3] and made several proposals for reforming the system and restoring meaning to prison sentences. Most of these recommendations were endorsed by the Government in the 1990 White Paper.

Legislative intervention

4.60   The legislation which followed the 1990 White Paper – the Criminal Justice Act 1991 – has been described as a 'watershed'.[4] Following the proposals made in the White Paper, the main aim of the Act was three-fold: to provide a statutory framework of sentencing, to introduce a wider range of community penalties and to reform the parole system. The Act was amended substantially by the Criminal Justice Act 1993 and further legislative intervention in the sentencing process has now been made by the Criminal Justice and Public Order Act 1994, the Crime (Sentences) Act 1997, the Sex Offenders Act 1997 and the Crime and Disorder Act 1998. The following provides an outline of the legislative framework of sentencing, with particular reference to the sentencing of sex offenders.

---

1   Criminal Justice Act 1967, s 37.
2   Padfield 'Bailing and Sentencing the Dangerous' in West (ed) *Dangerous People* (Blackstone Press Ltd, London, 1996).
3   *The Parole System in England and Wales* (1988) Cmnd 532 (HMSO, London).
4   Ashworth 'Sentencing in the 80s and 90s: The Struggle for Power' The Eighth Eve Saville Memorial Lecture given on 21 May 1997 at King's College, London.

Custodial sentences

Criteria for custody

4.61   Section 1 of the 1991 Act created a set of criteria to assist the courts in determining when the imposition of a custodial sentence is appropriate. Where a person is convicted of an offence punishable with a custodial sentence other than one fixed by law or falling to be imposed under s 2(2) of the Crime (Sentences) Act 1997, the court[1] cannot pass a custodial sentence on the offender, unless one of two conditions is satisfied:[2]

(1) the court is of the opinion that the offence, or combination of the offence and one or more offences associated with it, was so serious that only such a sentence can be justified for the offence;[3] or
(2) where the offence is a violent[4] or sexual offence,[5] the court is of the opinion that only such a sentence would be adequate to protect the public from serious harm from him.[6]

Length of custodial sentence

4.62   The Act also lays down specific criteria for the proper determination of the length of any custodial sentence imposed. These criteria generally reflect the principle of proportionality which now underlies the sentencing process, but also acknowledge the need for protective sentencing in certain circumstances. Section 2 of the Act provides that the custodial sentence shall be:

(a) for such term (not exceeding the permitted maximum) as in the opinion of the court is commensurate with the seriousness of the offence, or the combination of the offence and one or more offences associated[7] with it;[8] or
(b) where the offence is a violent or sexual offence, for such longer term (not exceeding that maximum) as in the opinion of the court is necessary to protect the public from serious harm from the offender.[9]

---

1   The provisions apply both to magistrates' courts and Crown Courts.
2   The only exception being when an offender has refused to give his consent to a community sentence which is proposed by the court and requires that consent (Criminal Justice Act 1991, s 1(3)).
3   Criminal Justice Act 1991, s 1(2)(a).
4   By virtue of s 31(1) of the Criminal Justice Act 1991, a violent offence means any offence which leads, or is intended or likely to lead, to a person's death or physical injury to a person, and includes an offence which is required to be charged as arson (whether or not it would otherwise fall within this definition).
5   See **4.69**.
6   Criminal Justice Act 1991, s 1(2)(b). See further **4.67** to **4.86**.
7   One offence is to be regarded as associated with another offence if the offender is convicted of offences in the same proceedings, is sentenced for the offences at the same time, or if the offender is convicted of one offence and asks to have another offence or offences taken into consideration in sentencing for that offence (Criminal Justice Act 1991, s 31(2)).
8   Criminal Justice Act 1991, s 2(2)(a).
9   Criminal Justice Act 1991, s 2(2)(b).

Commensurate sentences – the 'seriousness' ground

4.63   The criteria contained in ss 1(2)(a) and 2(2)(a) of the 1991 Act reflect the general principle of proportionality which underlies the sentencing process. The Act does not define the word 'serious', although several statutory provisions govern the way in which the seriousness of the offence is considered:

(1) the sentencer is required to have regard to mitigating and aggravating factors which impinge upon offence seriousness;[1]
(2) the sentencer is permitted to take account of any other mitigating factor;[2]
(3) the sentencer may take into account any previous convictions of the offender or any failure of his to respond to previous sentences;[3]
(4) the sentencer is required to treat offending while on bail as an aggravating feature;[4] and
(5) when an offender has pleaded guilty, the sentencer is required to take into account the stage in the proceedings for the offence at which the offender indicated his intention to plead guilty and the circumstances in which this indication was given.[5]

4.64   In the White Paper preceding the Act, the Government had expressed the hope that the Court of Appeal would give further guidance, building on the legislative framework.[6] Shortly after the enactment of the provisions, in two decisions[7] the Court of Appeal adopted a definition previously applied to a similar provision relating to young offenders in the Criminal Justice Act 1982,[8] which decided that a custodial sentence would be justified on this ground if the offence 'would make all right-thinking members of the public, knowing all the facts, feel that justice had not been done by the passing of any sentence other than a custodial one'.[9] Such a definition has been criticised as being vacuous in that the 'right-thinking members of the public' referred to are, in reality, the judges and magistrates themselves.[10]

4.65   Any court passing a custodial sentence must explain in open court that either or both of the grounds specified in s 1(2) apply to the case and to explain why it has formed that view,[11] and must also explain to the offender 'in open court and in ordinary language' why it is passing a custodial sentence.[12]

---

1   Criminal Justice Act 1991, s 3(3)(a).
2   Criminal Justice Act 1991, s 28(1).
3   Criminal Justice Act 1991, s 29(1).
4   Criminal Justice Act 1991, s 29(2).
5   Criminal Justice and Public Order Act 1994, s 48(1).
6   *Crime Justice and Protecting the Public* (1990) Cmnd 965 (Home Office, London) para 2.17.
7   *R v Baverstock* [1993] 1 WLR 202 and *R v Cox* [1993] 1 WLR 188.
8   Criminal Justice Act 1982, s 1(4A)(c).
9   Lawton J in *R v Bradbourn* (1985) 7 Cr App R (S) 180.
10   Ashworth 'Sentencing in the 80s and 90s: The Struggle for Power' The Eighth Eve Saville Memorial Lecture given on 21 May 1997 at King's College, London.
11   Criminal Justice Act 1991, s 1(4)(a).
12   Criminal Justice Act 1991, s 1(4)(b).

Length of sentence

4.66　　Once the sentencer has determined that the offence, or the combination of the offence and one or more offences associated with it, was so serious that only a custodial sentence can be justified, consideration must be given to the length of the sentence to be imposed. In determining this, the sentencer will be bound by the statutory provisions referred to above,[1] but within this statutory framework the sentencer will choose a particular sentence by considering the tariff for the offence or offences, as laid down in guideline judgments by the Court of Appeal, and by following his or her own instincts. Although the 1991 Act appeared to make it clear that proportionality was the central feature to this decision, the Court of Appeal has interpreted the phrase 'commensurate with the seriousness of the offence' in s 2(2)(a) to mean 'commensurate with the punishment and deterrence which the seriousness of the offence requires'.[2] Thus, deterrence continues to be a permissible factor in setting general sentence levels, although it does not justify a sentencer in going above those levels in particular cases in the hope of enhancing the general deterrent effect.[3] The continuing reliance by the courts on deterrence has been criticised, as it is said to draw the sentencer away into the realms of predicating social effects on a very shaky basis, instead of trying to do justice in the particular case.[4] However, deterrent reasoning clearly underlies more recent legislative intervention in the sentencing process. Part 1 of the Crime (Sentences) Act 1997 requires a sentencing court, subject to limited exceptions, to impose a minimum term of imprisonment of 7 years for a third Class A drug trafficking offence[5] and a minimum custodial sentence of 3 years on an offender who is convicted of a third domestic burglary.[6] The clear rationale underlying these provisions is that of deterrence – 'persistent burglars and dealers in hard drugs are a menace to society, and they must know that if they continue offending they will go to prison for a long time'.[7] The 1997 Act also provides for the imposition of an automatic life sentence on an offender convicted for a second time of a serious offence.[8] Although the justification for this provision was said to be a belief that it was wrong that, under pre-existing provisions relating to such offences, an offender had to be released at the conclusion of a determinate sentence irrespective of whether he posed a continuous danger to the community,[9] there is clearly an increased element of deterrence in such sentences.

1　　See **4.61**.
2　　Lord Taylor CJ in *R v Cunningham* (1993) 14 Cr App R (S) 444 at 447.
3　　Ashworth *Sentencing and Criminal Justice* (Butterworths, London, 1995) chap 3.
4　　Ashworth 'Sentencing in the 80s and 90s: The Struggle for Power' The Eighth Eve Saville Memorial Lecture given on 21 May 1997 at King's College, London.
5　　Crime (Sentences) Act 1997, s 3(2).
6　　Crime (Sentences) Act 1997, s 4(2).
7　　Baroness Blatch, Minister of State, Home Office, HL second reading, cols 969–970.
8　　Crime (Sentences) Act 1997, s 2(2). See further **4.92**.
9　　Ward *Criminal Sentencing; the New Law* (Jordans, Bristol, 1997).

'Dangerous'[1] offenders

4.67 Although the general principle underlying the sentencing process is that of proportionality, different criteria may be applied when sentencing those convicted of a violent or sexual offence. There is no requirement that the offence or offences are so serious that only a custodial sentence can be justified, it is enough if only a custodial sentence would be sufficient to protect the public from serious harm from the offender.[2] Furthermore, the length of the custodial sentence does not have to be commensurate with the seriousness of the offence, those convicted of violent or sexual offences can be imprisoned (subject to the permitted maximum sentence for the offence) for as long as the court thinks is necessary to protect the public from serious harm from him.[3]

Violent offences

4.68 A violent offence is defined to mean an offence which leads, or is intended or likely to lead, to a person's death or to physical injury to a person and includes an offence which is required to be charged as arson (whether or not it would otherwise fall within this definition).[4]

Sexual offences for the purposes of sentencing[5]

4.69 For the purposes of the 1991 Act and related sentencing legislation,[6] a sexual offence is defined as an offence under:[7]

(1) the Sexual Offences Act 1956 (other than an offence under ss 30, 31 or 33 to 36 of that Act);[8]
(2) s 128 of the Mental Health Act 1959;
(3) the Indecency with Children Act 1960;
(4) the Sexual Offences Act 1967;
(5) s 54 of the Criminal Law Act 1977;
(6) the Protection of Children Act 1978;
(7) an offence of burglary with intent to rape under s 9 of the Theft Act 1968; and
(8) conspiracy, attempts and incitements to commit any of the above.

Serious harm

4.70 The 1991 Act provides that references to protecting the public from serious harm from an offender are to be construed as references to protecting members of the public from death or serious personal injury, whether physical

---

1   The term 'dangerous offenders' is used to include those who have been convicted of a violent or sexual offence who pose a risk of serious harm to the public, as defined by the Criminal Justice Act 1991.
2   Criminal Justice Act 1991, s 1(2)(b).
3   Criminal Justice Act 1991, s 2(2)(b).
4   Criminal Justice Act 1991, s 31(1).
5   For the problems of defining a sex offender, see chap 1.
6   Crime (Sentences) Act 1997 and Crime and Disorder Act 1998.
7   Criminal Justice Act 1991, s 31(1) (as amended).
8   These exceptions are offences relating to living on the earnings of prostitution and offences relating to brothel keeping.

or psychological, occasioned by further such offences committed by him.[1] However, the Act makes no mention of the likelihood of risk which must be perceived by the sentencer before the provisions of s 1(2)(b) can be relied upon and does not require a court to consider psychiatric or psychological reports. It will be sufficient if an individual or a small group of people are at risk of serious harm[2] and, in determining whether the harm to the public will be serious, the sentencer can have regard to the vulnerability of particular potential victims, for example children who may be in need of protection from a paedophile.[3]

Dangerousness as a justification for a custodial sentence

4.71 Dangerousness as a criterion for imposing a custodial sentence under s 1(2)(b) of the 1991 Act has received comparatively little attention from the Court of Appeal. In the vast majority of circumstances, if a longer than commensurate sentence is passed under s 2(2)(b), the initial decision to impose a custodial sentence can be justified by the seriousness of the offence in accordance with s 1(2)(a). For this reason, detailed consideration of the dangerousness criteria is to be found in the decisions of the Court of Appeal relating to the provisions of s 2(2)(b).

Dangerousness and longer sentences

4.72 The Court of Appeal has made it clear that sentencers should not make use of the powers contained in s 2(2)(b) lightly. It has been suggested that three main factors explain this reluctance:[4]

(1) judges are aware of the unreliability of predictions of dangerousness, with the danger of significant over-predictions;
(2) preventive sentences are a departure from the 'just deserts' rationale of the 1991 Act and, inevitably, raise issues of human rights and civil liberties; and
(3) as there is no precise measure for the appropriate length of a commensurate sentence, it is much more difficult to fix the length of a longer than normal sentence.

Predicting the risk posed by the offender

4.73 Risk assessment is not limited to the sentencing stage in a criminal trial. Some form of risk assessment may have been made at an earlier stage in the proceedings when deciding whether to remand the offender in custody,[5] although the relevant risk at this stage is framed in far wider terms, presumably explicable on the basis that remands in pre-trial custody cover only relatively short lengths of time.[6] Risk assessment will also play a crucial role in the timing of

---

1   Criminal Justice Act 1991, s 31(3).
2   *R v Hashi* (1994) 16 Cr App R (S) 121.
3   *R v Bowler* (1994) 15 Cr App R (S) 78.
4   Padfield 'Bailing and Sentencing the Dangerous' in Walker (ed) *Dangerous People* (Blackstone Press Ltd, London, 1996).
5   See **2.93** to **2.100**.
6   See Padfield 'Bailing and Sentencing the Dangerous' in Walker (ed) *Dangerous People* (Blackstone Press Ltd, London, 1996) p 93.

the release of an offender at the end of a custodial sentence,[1] in determining the appropriate supervision of the offender in the community[2] and in deciding whether the public should be alerted to a risk posed by an offender.[3]

4.74   Precisely how these issues are to be determined raises difficult issues. In attempting to predict the risk posed by an offender for the purposes of sentencing, the sentencer must consider not only the risk that the offender will commit further offences, but also the risk that, if he does so, the public will suffer serious harm. Thus, the nature of the offending behaviour will be crucial. The court will have before it information as to the facts of the offence or offences, the antecedent history of the accused (including any previous convictions), any pre-sentence, medical or psychiatric reports obtained and any further evidence pleaded in mitigation by the defence[4] and it is from this information that the sentencer must determine whether the criteria contained in s 2(2)(b) of the 1991 Act are satisfied.[5] The difficulties of predicting dangerousness for these purposes have to be acknowledged. A survey of available studies suggests that no method of prediction has yet managed to do better than predicting one false positive for every true positive, ie a success rate of 50% in predicting dangerousness, and that actuarial methods of prediction, based on selective objective characteristics of the offender, are more reliable than clinical predictions, based on the judgment of experienced diagnosticians.[6]

4.75   It seems that the best indicator of future behaviour is past behaviour and one of the major factors influencing the decision will be the offender's past record.[7] However, this should not be taken to mean solely previous convictions of an offender,[8] as many offences may never result in a conviction. This is particularly relevant in the case of sex offenders, given the acknowledged 'dark figure' of unreported and unrecorded crime in this area and the low conviction rate of those who are prosecuted.[9] If the offender is convicted of a string of offences committed over a period of years, or at least admits a long history of offending, the criteria contained in s 2(2)(b) may justifiably be said to be satisfied on those grounds alone, although the sentencer will also be influenced by the offender's reaction to his offending, for example lack of remorse and unwillingness to accept medical treatment – information that will usually be made available to the sentencer either in a pre-sentence report or a medical report.[10] If the previous offending has been directed specifically at a narrow group of individuals, such as the offender's children, and the offender is not thought to pose a risk to a wider circle of children, then, if the past victims can be protected by other means, the criteria for a longer than normal sentence may

---

1   See **5.93**.
2   See **6.27**.
3   See **7.15**.
4   See **4.48**.
5   For a detailed exploration of the problems of determining 'dangerousness', see Floud and Young *Dangerousness and Criminal Justice* (Heinemann Ltd, London, 1981) app C.
6   Ashworth *Sentencing and Criminal Justice* (Butterworths, London, 1995) p 169, commenting on the finding of the Floud Report of 1981.
7   *R v L* (1993) 15 Cr App R (S) 501.
8   *R v S* [1994] Crim LR 868.
9   See **1.69**.
10   *R v Fawcett* (1995) Cr App R (S) 55.

not be satisfied. More difficulties will arise if an offender is *suspected* of having a long history of offending, but he has been convicted of, or admitted, only a limited number of offences. In such circumstances, it is difficult to determine what weight can justifiably be attached to those suspicions in predicting future risk. It is clear that, in determining a commensurate sentence under s 2(2)(a) of the 1991 Act, a sentencer cannot take account of offences not proved to have been committed by the accused.[1] The Court of Appeal has found support for this view in the requirement in s 2(2)(a) that the custodial term must be commensurate with the seriousness of a combination of the offence and one or more offences associated with it, which, it is claimed, restricts the sentencer's consideration to the offences for which the offender is convicted or asks to be taken into consideration.[2] However, no such restriction is to be found in s 2(2)(b). In many cases, the sentencer will simply be unaware of suspicions about an offender's past behaviour. In the past, the Court of Appeal discouraged the police and prosecution, when presenting antecedents, from making generalised allegations prejudicial to the offender which are incapable of strict proof or disproof.[3] However, the recent statutory provision for enhanced criminal record certificates to contain non-conviction information[4] suggests a change of approach which may be reflected in sentencing practice. It is always possible that a pre-sentence report may contain some indication of suspicions, for example, if the offender's behaviour resulted in him being dismissed from his employment, but no criminal investigation was undertaken. Bearing in mind the imprecise nature of the exercise involved in determining risk, there seems to be no reason why unproven suspicions may not be taken into account if the sentencer is aware of them, as long as the risk assessment is made from a totality of the evidence and not based solely on unproven suspicions.

Justifying longer than normal sentences

4.76 The justification for any departure from the 'just deserts' rationale in the case of dangerous offenders in order to protect the public depends, first and foremost, on the ability to identify such offenders correctly. If it could be proved conclusively that an offender will commit further offences, if released, which will result in serious harm to the public, then a longer than normal sentence may be justified purely on the grounds of protecting the public. However, given the acknowledged difficulties encountered in determining dangerousness and the comparatively low success rate,[5] if those who pose a risk cannot be identified with any degree of certainty, how can longer than normal sentences ever be justified?

4.77 One answer is that it is a matter of the just redistribution of risk.[6] In 1981, the Floud Committee recommended that a protective sentence[7] should not be imposed unless the court is satisfied that, by reason of the nature of the

---

1   *R v Huchison* (1972) 56 Cr App R 307.
2   *R v Clark* [1996] Crim LR 448.
3   *R v Van Pelz* (1942) 29 Cr App R 10.
4   See **2.77**.
5   See **4.73**.
6   Floud and Young *Dangerousness and Criminal Justice* (Heinemann Ltd, London, 1981).
7   Defined to mean a sentence of imprisonment which, in order to protect the public against a risk of future harm, is made longer than would be justified on other grounds alone.

offence and his character, conduct and antecedents, the offender is more likely to do further grave harm[1] than other grave offenders of similar age and sex, and that there is no other permissible way of dealing with him which offers the necessary degree of protection for the public. Generally, it was argued, everyone is presumed to be free of harmful intentions, but an offender forfeits the presumption of harmlessness by the commission of a serious crime. Once the presumption has been lost, it becomes justifiable to protect the potential victims, who are unlikely to have harmful intentions, by imposing a longer than normal sentence on the offender. Such reasoning has been criticised on several grounds.[2] It is argued that the right to be presumed to be free from harmful intentions should not be extinguished forever just because a person commits a serious offence – after all, an accused is presumed innocent at the beginning of each criminal trial, regardless of any previous convictions, so why should a different approach be taken in the case of this presumption? Furthermore, it is argued that the notion of just redistribution of risk ignores the moral claims of proportionality and that the idea of a balance between the rights of the offender and the rights of the potential victim are too crude. An alternative approach suggested would be to retain proportionate sentencing and to introduce a form of civil confinement for the 'dangerousness' after the expiry of the commensurate sentence.[3] In the case of some mentally disordered offenders, civil confinement at some stage of the sentence may be possible,[4] and provisions in the Crime and Disorder Act 1998 now provide for extended sentences for the purpose of supervision at the end of a custodial sentence.[5] Such measures add to, but do not change, the power to impose longer than normal custodial sentences under s 2(2)(b) of the 1991 Act. The political agenda is clear – those who pose a risk of serious harm to the public will continue to be liable to a custodial term exceeding that justified by the seriousness of the offence committed. Such incapacitation will no doubt remain an essential part of the sentencing process for the foreseeable future, regardless of the apparent lack of a convincing justification.

Longer than normal sentences and human rights

4.78   The imposition of a longer than normal sentence potentially raises a significant human rights issue. The European Convention on Human Rights contains no single article which provides a specific right for an individual to challenge a sentence imposed by a criminal court. Similarly, no such right is contained in the Human Rights Act 1998, which is intended to give further effect

---

1   Grave harm was interpreted more widely than the concept of serious harm currently found in the Criminal Justice Act 1991, to include death, serious bodily injury, serious sexual assaults, severe or prolonged pain or mental stress, loss of or damage to property which causes severe financial hardship, damage to the environment which has a severely adverse effect on public health or safety, or serious damage to the security of the State.
2   See Ashworth *Sentencing and Criminal Justice* (Butterworths, London, 1995) p 171.
3   Ashworth *Sentencing and Criminal Justice* (Butterworths, London, 1995) and Woods 'Dangerous Offenders and the Morality of Protective Sentencing' [1988] Crim LR 424.
4   See **4.121** to **4.131**.
5   See **4.82** to **4.87**.

to the rights and freedoms guaranteed under the European Convention.[1] However, a sentence imposed under s 2(2)(b) of the 1991 Act could arguably be challenged as constituting a breach of art 5 of the Convention. Article 5(1) provides the right to liberty and security, but also provides that no-one shall be deprived of his liberty save in the following cases and in accordance with a procedure prescribed by law. The first case is the lawful detention of a person after conviction by a competent court. Prima facie, this would appear to cover all custodial sentences imposed after conviction. However, art 5(4) provides that anyone who is deprived of his liberty shall be entitled to take proceedings by which the lawfulness of his detention shall be decided speedily by a court and his release ordered if the detention is not lawful. In the case of discretionary life sentences,[2] the European Court of Human Rights has held that, once the tariff period had expired, offenders are entitled to have their continued detention reviewed.[3] An attempt has been made to argue that the same reasoning should apply to sentences imposed under s 2(2)(b). In *Mansell v UK*,[4] an offender had received a sentence of 5 years' imprisonment for indecent assault. The sentencing judge stated that, although the usual sentence for the offence would be 2 years and 6 months' imprisonment, in view of the offender's past record, a 5-year sentence would be imposed in reliance on s 2(2)(b) as such a sentence was necessary to protect the public from serious harm. Mansell argued that, after he had served the first 2 years and 6 months of his sentence, the remaining period should be subject to the same levels of review as a discretionary life sentence after the tariff period had elapsed.

4.79 The European Commission on Human Rights declared the claim manifestly ill founded. On the facts, it found that the sentence imposed under s 2(2)(b) contained only punitive and deterrent elements, whereas the latter part of a discretionary life sentence was based on the nature of the individual and, therefore, was subject to change over time. It has been suggested that each case must be decided on its own merits and, thus, if a judge were to state in a judgment made under s 2(2)(b) that the sentence was being given only due to the dangerousness of the individual to the public, it would be possible that, after the expiry of the usual sentence, the latter part of the sentence would fall within the parameters of the protection afforded by art 5(4).[5]

4.80 The argument has also been made that a sentence imposed under s 2(2)(b) could be challenged as constituting a breach of art 6, which provides the right to a fair trial and has been held to extend to the sentencing decision in a trial. The jurisprudence of the European Court has tended to favour tests of proportionality when determining the existence of a breach, but tests utilised at a domestic level, both in imposing the sentence and in a possible appeal, have tended to concentrate on the issues of 'reasonableness' or 'seriousness' and do not always incorporate proportionality. The differences in terminology has led

---

1   See further Cheney et al *Criminal Justice and the Human Rights Act 1998* (Jordans, Bristol, 1999).
2   See **4.97**.
3   *Thynne, Wilson and Gunnell v UK* (1990) 13 EHRR 666.
4   (1997) EHRLR 666.
5   Cheney et al *Criminal Justice and the Human Rights Act 1998* (Jordans, Bristol, 1999) para 5.5.4.

to the suggestion that, with the advent of the domestic Human Rights Act 1998, judges may be forced to scrutinise their decisions to impose a longer than normal sentence more carefully.[1]

Calculating the length of the sentence[2]

4.81   The only statutory restriction placed on the length of a sentence imposed under s 2(2)(b) is that it must be within the statutory maximum for the offence. The court is required to explain in open court that it is of the opinion that s 2(2)(b) applies and why it is of that opinion, and it must explain to the offender in open court and in ordinary language why the sentence is for such a term.[3] It has been pointed out that a useful research project would monitor and analyse the reasons given by sentencers.[4] In the absence of such research, the decisions of the Court of Appeal provide some guidance on the correct approach to take to the calculation of the appropriate length of sentence, but this guidance has remained at a fairly general level.[5] The usual approach is first to calculate what the proportionate sentence would be, based on the seriousness of the offence, and then to add the period of detention deemed to be necessary for public protection. Inevitably, this latter calculation will be influenced greatly by the sentencer's prediction of the risk posed by the offender.[6] The Court of Appeal has made it clear that some element of proportionality should be retained,[7] and thus a sentence under s 2(2)(b) should not be out of all proportion to the sentence which would be imposed under s 2(2)(a), ie one commensurate with the seriousness of the offence. The Court of Appeal has indicated that factors which would normally mitigate the sentence should be given less weight when considering a sentence under s 2(2)(b) than when considering a sentence under s 2(2)(a).[8] However, in many cases, factors which mitigate the seriousness of the offence will also affect the risk posed by the individual offender and, thus, will have been taken into account, both in deciding whether a custodial sentence was justified in the first place and in determining whether a longer sentence is necessary for public protection.

Extended sentences for sex offenders

The case for supervision on release

4.82   It has long been acknowledged that offenders, particularly those convicted of serious offences, may benefit from a period of supervision in the community following release from a custodial sentence. The arrangements for the release of all prisoners given a custodial sentence of 12 months or more

---

1   Cheney et al *Criminal Justice and the Human Rights Act 1998* (Jordans, Bristol, 1999)
     para 5.6.1.
2   See further **4.66**.
3   Criminal Justice Act 1991, s 2(3).
4   Padfield 'Bailing and Sentencing the Dangerous' in Walker (ed) *Dangerous People*
     (Blackstone Press Ltd, London, 1996) p 82.
5   Ashworth *Sentencing and Criminal Justice* (Butterworths, London, 1995) chap 6.
6   See **4.73**.
7   *R v Mansell* (1994) 15 Cr App R (S) 844 and *R v Crowe and Pennington* [1994] Crim LR 958.
8   *R v Walsh* (1995) 16 Cr App R (S) 204.

include a period on licence, during which time they will be supervised by the Probation Service in order to help them to adjust to life in the community and address their offending behaviour.[1] Those sentenced to life imprisonment will remain on licence for the rest of their lives.[2] However, there are said to be several features of sex offending which mark sex offenders out as being particularly apt for supervision.[3] First, sex offending may begin at an early age. In contrast to other forms of adolescent offending, it is a form of behaviour that adolescents tend to grow into rather than out of. Secondly, sexual offences are rarely one-off incidents. Thirdly, sex offending tends to become entrenched over time and patterns of escalating seriousness are not unusual. Fourthly, significant numbers of sex offenders may have suffered abuse themselves; and, finally, sex offenders are often heavily defensive and in denial. The acknowledged significance of supervision for sex offenders was reflected in the provisions of the Criminal Justice Act 1991, which allowed the courts to direct that serious sex offenders should be supervised to the very end of their sentence, rather than to the three-quarter point as is usual for other offenders.[4] However, there were concerns that the periods of supervision were inadequate to accommodate worthwhile treatment programmes and that, when sex offenders reached the end of periods of supervision in the community, there was no way of monitoring or controlling their activities.

4.83 In 1996, the Government expressed the belief that there was a strong case for strengthening the arrangements for supervising sex offenders following their release from custody to provide greater protection for the public and to improve the opportunity for such offenders to deal with their offending behaviour.[5] A consultation paper was issued in the same year[6] and provision was made in the Crime (Sentences) Act 1997 for the imposition of an extended supervision period on sex offenders at the end of a custodial sentence.[7] The 1997 Act created a presumption that an extended period of supervision would be imposed, unless there were exceptional circumstances. Such an approach was difficult to justify and, inevitably, would have led to inflexibility. Research has shown that sex offenders of different types exhibit different re-offending behaviour and, thus, not all types of sex offender will require the same length or type of supervision.[8] The relevant provisions of the 1997 Act were never brought into force, the Government preferring to replace the presumption with a discretion, allowing but not requiring, the court to pass an extended sentence. The relevant provisions are now contained in the Crime and Disorder Act 1998.

---

1   See chap 6.
2   See **4.90** to **4.99**.
3   *Sentencing and Supervision of Sex Offenders: A Consultation Document* (HMSO, London, 1996).
4   Criminal Justice Act 1991, s 44.
5   *Protecting the Public* (1996) Cmnd 3190 (HMSO, London) para 8.2.
6   *Sentencing and Supervision of Sex Offenders: A Consultation Document* (HMSO, London, 1996).
7   Crime (Sentences) Act 1997, s 20.
8   Ackerley et al *When Do Sex Offenders Stop Offending?* Home Office Research Bulletin no 39 (Home Office, London).

Extended sentences under the Crime and Disorder Act 1998

4.84	Section 58 of the 1998 Act introduces a new form of extended sentence for those convicted of violent or sexual offences.[1] The extended sentence consists of two distinct components: the custodial term and the extension period. The custodial term may be either a commensurate sentence imposed under s 2(2)(a) of the Criminal Justice Act 1991 or a longer-than-commensurate sentence passed under s 2(2)(b) of the Act. The offender will be released at the end of the custodial term in the same way as other offenders,[2] but he will be subject to licence, and thus supervision, for the whole of the extension period and will be liable to be recalled to custody at any time up to the end of that period. An extended sentence may only be passed if the court is satisfied that the normal period of licence to which the offender would be subject under the Criminal Justice Act 1991 would not be adequate to prevent the commission of further offences by the offender or to secure his rehabilitation.

Length of the extension period

4.85	The length of the combined custodial term and extension period must not exceed the maximum term permitted for the offence. Subject to this, the extension period itself may not exceed 10 years in the case of a sexual offence and 5 years in the case of a violent offence. Extended sentences may not be passed on violent offenders if the custodial term imposed is less than 4 years. Common sense would dictate that, the more serious the offence, the longer the period of supervision should be. The fact that the combined term must not exceed the maximum permitted for the offence leads to the rather peculiar result that, the more serious the offence, the longer the custodial term and the shorter the period of supervision. Thus, for example, a serious indecent assault may attract a custodial term of 8 years, either as a commensurate sentence or one justified by the need to protect the public, leaving a maximum extension period of only 2 years. Admittedly, in practice, the anomaly would be lessened by the fact that actual time served in custody would be considerably less than the actual custodial term imposed,[3] but for a less serious indecent assault which attracted a custodial term of only 2 years, the maximum extension period would be 8 years. No such problems will arise where the maximum sentence is life imprisonment, the only restriction being the 10-year limit on the extension period.

4.86	It remains to be seen how effective these provisions will be in preventing re-offending and rehabilitating the offender. Long-term follow-ups of offenders are notoriously difficult and there are inherent problems in establishing recidivism rate for sex offenders, most notably the fact that many such offenders may continue to commit offences but escape detection. Bearing these problems in mind, attempts have been made to track the criminal careers of those convicted of sexual offences. Research conducted for the Home Office estimated the periods for which those convicted of sexual offences were at risk of reconviction.[4] The research found a wide disparity between offences, but taking

1	Violent and sexual offences have the same meanings as in Pt I of the Criminal Justice Act 1991. See **4.67** to **4.69**.
2	See chap 5.
3	See chap 5.
4	Ackerley et al *When Do Sex Offenders Stop Offending?* Home Office Research Bulletin no 39 (Home Office, London).

the offence of rape as an example, the study followed the criminal careers of 346 men convicted of rape in 1973. Taking account of the estimated time spent in custody for the initial offence, the following findings were made:

(1) 61.3% of the sample were reconvicted of any standard list offence within 20 years, 92% of whom were reconvicted within 10 years;

(2) 16.5% of the sample were reconvicted of a sexual offence[1] within 20 years, 84.2% of whom were reconvicted within 10 years;

(3) 10.2% of the sample were reconvicted of a serious sexual offence within 20 years, 85.3% of whom were reconvicted within 10 years; and

(4) 37.6% of the sample were reconvicted of any sexual or violent offence[2] within 20 years, 83.8% of whom were reconvicted within 10 years.

4.87   Although the reconviction rates varied between offences, similar patterns emerged in all categories and it is evident that the vast majority of those who were reconvicted within 20 years were actually reconvicted within 10 years of release. For example, on average only 5% of first reconvictions for a violent or sexual offence for the entire sample occurred after 10 years, leading to the conclusion that, for most sex offenders, the 10-year limit on the extension period will be sufficient.

Suspended sentences

4.88   If an offender over the age of 21 is sentenced to a term of imprisonment of not more than 2 years, the sentence can be suspended for not less than 1 year and not more than 2 years if the court is of the opinion that:

(1) the case is one in which a sentence of imprisonment would have been appropriate even without the power to suspend the sentence; and

(2) the exercise of that power can be justified by the exceptional circumstances of the case.[3]

The Court of Appeal has adopted a strict approach to the need for exceptional circumstances, stating that the instances in which a suspended sentence would be appropriate would be few and far between.[4] Sexual offences which are so serious that only a custodial sentence can be justified will rarely be appropriate cases for the exercise of such a power. However, in *R v W (Robert)*,[5] the Court of Appeal held that a suspended sentence was appropriate for convictions of indecent assaults on the offender's sister where the assaults had taken place

---

1   Sexual offences included the 'serious sexual offences' of buggery of a male under 16 years of age, a female or animal, or a male where no consent was given and assault with intent to commit buggery, indecent assault on a boy or girl under the age of 16 years, rape, unlawful sexual intercourse with a girl under 13 years of age, incest, gross indecency and 'other sexual offences' of indecency between males, unlawful sexual intercourse with a girl under 16 years of age, procuration, abduction, bigamy, solicitation by men, and other offences of buggery and indecent assault not already included, plus other offences connected with obscene publications and indecent exposure.

2   Offences involving violence against the person.

3   Powers of Criminal Courts Act 1973, s 22 (as amended).

4   *R v Robinson* (1993) 14 Cr App R (S) 559.

5   (1996) 2 Cr App R (S) 84.

many years previously under strained circumstances. In some cases, the Court of Appeal has been influenced by the effect of a custodial sentence on the family of the offender and this may be particularly relevant in cases of abuse within the family. For example, in *R v Cameron*,[1] the offender had been convicted of assaulting one of his children and the Court suspended a sentence of imprisonment to take account of the decision of the local authority that it was in the best interests of the family if the offender could be rehabilitated into the family under supervision. However, it is doubtful whether the same approach would be adopted if the offender had been convicted of sexually, as opposed to physically, abusing his child.

4.89   The suspended sentence may be activated, with or without variation, if the offender is convicted of another offence punishable with imprisonment committed during the operational period of the suspended sentence.[2]

Life imprisonment

Mandatory life imprisonment – murder and sentences fixed by law[3]

4.90   A sentence of life imprisonment is mandatory for those over the age of 21 years convicted of murder.[4] The sentence is one fixed by law and, although the trial judge may make a recommendation about the minimum term the offender should serve in prison before being released on parole, such a recommendation is not binding on the Home Secretary. Since 1983, the trial judge is expected to indicate the tariff period necessary to meet the requirement of retribution and deterrence. This indication is sent in a report to the Lord Chief Justice, who adds his view. The indication is then forwarded to the Home Secretary, who may set a higher or lower tariff than the judges. The tariff period is a crucial element in determining when an offender will be released from prison.[5]

4.91   In respect of offenders aged between 18 and 20 years, the appropriate order is one of custody for life[6] and in respect of those under 18 years at the time the murder was committed, the appropriate order is one of detention during Her Majesty's Pleasure (HMP).[7] In both cases, the tariff period has been set by the Home Secretary, after receiving recommendations from the trial judge and the Lord Chief Justice.[8] This is an issue which has caused some considerable controversy in the case of offenders under the age of 18 years. In *R v Secretary of State for the Home Department, ex parte Thompson and Venables*,[9] following the highly publicised trial, the two offenders who were barely over the age of criminal responsibility were convicted of the murder of a young child. The trial judge

---

1   [1993] Crim LR 721.
2   Powers of Criminal Courts Act 1973, s 23.
3   Sex offenders will only be subject to mandatory life imprisonment if they are convicted of murder in addition to any sexual offence.
4   Murder (Abolition of Death Penalty) Act 1965, s 1(1).
5   See further **5.114**.
6   Criminal Justice Act 1982, s 8(1).
7   Children and Young Persons Act 1933, s 53(1).
8   Crime (Sentences) Act 1997, s 28(4).
9   *R v Secretary of State for the Home Department, ex parte Thompson and Venables* [1997] 3 WLR 23.

recommeded a tariff period of 8 years and the Lord Chief Justice recommended a period of 10 years. Following an orchestrated campaign by the media and outcry from the public demanding whole life tariffs, which admittedly influenced the Home Secretary, he set a tariff period of 15 years. A majority of the House of Lords accepted that it was lawful for the Home Secretary to set the initial tariff period, provided that it was subject to review and downward revision in the light of HMP detainee's progress in custody. In fixing the tariff, the Home Secretary was said to be bound to take a very different course from that applicable to mandatory adult lifers, in that he must balance the requirements of retribution against the welfare of the young offender in accordance with s 44(1) of the Children and Young Persons Act 1933.[1] However, following the ruling of the House of Lords, the European Court of Human Rights ruled that the Home Secretary's involvement in setting the tariff, which was clearly part of the sentencing exercise, amounted to a breach of the rights contained in arts 5 and 6 of the European Convention on Human Rights.[2] The Government has accepted the findings of the European Court and henceforth the tariff in such cases will be decided by the courts and administered through the Parole Board.

Automatic life sentences

4.92   The 1997 Act now provides for the imposition of automatic sentences of life imprisonment on any offender over the age of 18 years who is convicted of a serious offence committed after the commencement of the Act, if he has previously been convicted of another serious offence. An automatic sentence imposed under s 2(2) of the 1997 Act is not to be regarded as a sentence fixed by law,[3] and therefore the procedures and powers applicable to discretionary life sentences apply.[4] For the purposes of the 1997 Act, a 'serious offence' is defined to mean:

(1) an attempt to commit murder, a conspiracy to commit murder or an incitement to murder;

(2) an offence under s 4 of the Offences Against the Person Act 1861 (soliciting murder);

(3) manslaughter;

(4) an offence under s 18 of the Offences Against the Person Act 1861 (wounding, or causing grievous bodily harm with intent);

(5) rape or an attempt to commit rape;

(6) an offence under s 5 of the Sexual Offences Act 1956 (intercourse with a girl under 13 years of age);

(7) an offence under s 16 (possession of a firearm with intent to injure), s 17 (use of a firearm to resists arrest) or s 18 (carrying a firearm with criminal intent) of the Firearms Act 1968; and

(8) robbery where, at some time during the commission of the offence, the offender had in his possession a firearm or imitation firearm within the meaning of that Act.[5]

---

1   See further **4.112**.
2   *T v United Kingdom, V v United Kingdom* [1999] TLR 871, ECHR.
3   Crime (Sentences) Act 1997, s 2(4).
4   See **5.118**.
5   Crime (Sentences) Act 1997, s 2(5).

4.93   The introduction of an automatic sentence of life imprisonment has been heavily criticised, not only in that the mandatory requirement removes any discretion from the judiciary but also in the way the provisions have been framed.[1] It is not necessary for the serious offences to be the same, all that is required is that the offender should have been convicted of the first serious offence before committing the second. Thus, a conviction for unlawful sexual intercourse with a girl under the age of 13, followed many years later by a conviction for robbery while in possession of an imitation firearm will activate the automatic life sentence.[2] However, a person who is convicted on the same occasion for a number of rapes committed over a period of time will not qualify for an automatic life sentence. Furthermore, the list of serious offences leads to some unexpected and inexplicable results. For example, if a man has unlawful sexual intercourse with a 12-year-old girl, he commits a serious offence for the purposes of the Act, if he commits buggery on her, he does not.

4.94   Although all of the offences classified as serious offences for the purposes of the 1997 Act already carry a maximum sentence of life imprisonment, the maximum term is rarely imposed. It was pointed out in the White Paper preceding the Act that in 1994, of the 434 offenders convicted of rape or attempted rape, only 12 were sentenced to life imprisonment, with an average sentence of 6.6 years' imprisonment. Similarly, in the same year, of the 65 offenders convicted of unlawful sexual intercourse with a girl under the age of 13, none received life sentences and the average sentence was only 3.4 years.[3] In the House of Lords, the reason for the introduction of the automatic life sentence was said be two-fold:[4] first, to ensure that offenders who are convicted of a serious violent or sexual offence are not released from prison if they continue to prove a real danger to the public; and, secondly, offenders who are released would remain under supervision and be subject to recall for the rest of their lives. These two safeguards were said to provide real protection for the public against some of the most dangerous criminals in our society. This view has been contested strongly, as it has been pointed out that the Act does not empower judges to pass sentences on dangerous offenders which were not previously available, but it forces judges to pass sentences, which they would in any event have had the power to pass, which they do not consider appropriate to the particular case.[5]

The proviso – reversing the presumption of dangerousness?

4.95   The Act does provide an exception to the duty to impose an automatic life sentence, as a court need not impose such a sentence if it is of the opinion that there are exceptional circumstances relating to either of the offences or to

---

1   See, for example, Thomas 'The Crime (Sentences) Act 1997' [1998] Crim LR 83.
2   Although attempts were made during the passage of the Bill through Parliament to prevent convictions which were spent under the Rehabilitation of Offenders Act 1974 applying to the provisions of the 1997 Act, the Government resisted the attempts and, thus, there is no time limit between the commission of the serious offences.
3   *Protecting the Public* (1996) Cmnd 3190 (HMSO, London), p 47.
4   Baroness Blatch, Minister of State, Home Office, HL second reading, cols 968–969, 27 January 1997.
5   Thomas 'The Crime (Sentences) Act 1997' [1998] Crim LR 83.

the offender which justify it not doing so.[1] It was generally assumed during discussions on the Bill that the expression 'exceptional circumstances' would be interpreted in the same manner as the expression in s 22(2) of the Powers of Criminal Courts Act 1973, in relation to suspended sentences. However, it has since been pointed out that this is not necessarily so as the meaning of a particular expression must depend on its context, and the context of the expression in the 1973 Act is quite different from the context of the expression in the 1997 Act.[2] It is clear that the expectation is that the expression will be given a narrow interpretation and that mitigating factors alone will not be sufficient to constitute exceptional circumstances, although they may be relevant to the tariff to be set by the trial judge under s 28 of the 1997 Act.[3] Undoubtedly, the most credible approach to take is to decide the meaning of 'exceptional circumstances' by reference to the object of the legislation.[4] The Act assumed that a person convicted of a second serious offence will normally be a person whom it is unsafe to release at the end of what would have been the commensurate determinate sentence. The exceptional circumstances, either relating to the offences or to the offender, must therefore be such that such an offender can be shown to the court not to be dangerous in this sense.

4.96 In the normal course of events, if the sentencer is to impose a sentence longer than one commensurate with the seriousness of the offence, the offender must be convicted of a violent or sexual offence and it must be proved that the offender is dangerous in that a longer sentence is necessary to protect the public from serious harm.[5] As the 1997 Act appears to reverse the presumption in the case of offenders convicted of a second serious offence, if the sentencer relies on the proviso, in that there are said to be exceptional circumstances which justify not imposing a life sentence, it seems that the only sentence that can be imposed is one commensurate with the seriousness of the second offence, ie the sentencer would not be entitled to pass a longer than normal sentence by relying on s 2(2)(b) of the 1991 Act.

Discretionary life sentences

4.97 In addition to murder, where the sentence is fixed by law, and imposition of automatic sentences of life imprisonment for those convicted of a second serious offence, offenders convicted of common law offences and certain serious statutory offences may also be sentenced to life imprisonment at the discretion of the sentencer. For example, the offences of rape and unlawful sexual intercourse with a girl under the age of 13 carry a maximum sentence of life imprisonment. In determining the appropriate sentence, the sentencer must comply with the provisions of the Criminal Justice Act 1991, in that a life sentence can only be imposed if it is justified either on the ground of the

---

1   Crime (Sentences) Act 1997, s 2(2).
2   *Archbold 'Criminal Pleading, Evidence and Practice'* (Sweet and Maxwell, London, 1999) paras 5–204a.
3   See **4.99**. See further Ward *Criminal Sentencing; the New Law* (Jordans, Bristol, 1997) para 2.29.
4   Thomas 'The Crime (Sentences) Act 1997' [1998] Crim LR 83 at 87.
5   Criminal Justice Act 1991, s 2(2)(b). See **4.67** et seq.

seriousness of the offence or to protect the public from serious harm. The Court of Appeal has stated that there are two pre-conditions for the imposition of a discretionary life sentence:

(1) the offence must be very serious; and
(2) there should be good grounds for believing that the offender might remain a serious danger to the public which could not be reliably estimated at the date of the sentence.[1]

Although in earlier cases the Court of Appeal suggested that a sentence of life imprisonment would only be justified if the offence itself was grave enough to justify a very long sentence,[2] the Court now appears to have relaxed this requirement and, as long as the criterion of dangerousness is satisfied, the fact that the offence itself is not grave enough to justify a long sentence of imprisonment will not prevent the imposition of a life sentence.[3]

4.98   In the past, the Court of Appeal had referred to the offender being a person of *unstable* character, likely to commit grave offences in the future.[4] Later cases had made it clear that this did not mean that the offender was suffering from mental illness or disorder within the Mental Health Act 1983, so that a persistent sex offender who repeatedly commits serious sexual offences may satisfy the dangerousness criterion, whether or not there is a diagnosis of mental disorder or instability. For example, in *R v Hatch*,[5] the offender, who had numerous previous convictions for offences against young boys, pleaded guilty to four counts of buggery of boys, two counts of gross indecency and two counts of indecent assault on a male. He was sentenced to life imprisonment and the Court of Appeal dismissed his appeal against the sentence. There was psychiatric evidence that he did not suffer from a mental illness or other condition within the scope of the Mental Health Act 1983, but the Court found that he was suffering from a serious personality disorder and that the evidence showed that his sexual orientation was towards boys, that he was likely to continue to offend in the same way in the future and there was no prospect of effective medical treatment. It is now clear that, although the grounds which found a belief that the offender might remain a serious danger to the public for an indeterminate time will often relate to the mental condition of the offender, this will not inevitably be the case. The crucial question is whether, on all the facts, it appeared that the offender was likely to represent such a danger.[6]

Fixing the tariff period

4.99   A discretionary life sentence falls into two parts: the tariff period, which consists of the period of detention necessary to meet the requirements of retribution and deterrence, taking into account the seriousness of the offence, and the remaining part of the sentence during which the offender's detention

1   *Attorney-General's Reference (No 32 of 1996) (R v Whittaker)* (1997) 1 Cr App R (S) 261.
2   *R v Hodgson* (1968) 52 Cr App R 113.
3   *R v Parker* (1997) 1 Cr App R (S) 259.
4   *R v Hodgson* (1968) 52 Cr App R 113.
5   *R v Hatch* [1996] Crim LR 679.
6   *Attorney-General's Reference (No 32 of 1996) (R v Whittaker)* (1997) 1 Cr App R (S) 261.

will be governed by considerations of risk to the public. The Criminal Justice Act 1991 empowered the trial judge when passing a sentence of discretionary life imprisonment to set the tariff period. The relevant provisions of the 1991 Act have now been repealed and replaced by s 28 of the Crime (Sentences) Act 1997, but the procedure to be adopted remains substantially the same. The trial judge may fix what would have been the appropriate determinate sentence had a life sentence not been imposed, and then specify a portion of the sentence being between one-half and two-thirds of that term. Under the 1997 Act, the sentencer should then deduct from the specified period an appropriate period to compensate the offender for the time spent in custody on remand.[1] Although the sentencer is not required to specify a period under the 1997 Act, it is difficult to see why a sentencer would choose to refrain from influencing later events, and the Court of Appeal has said that a period should be specified in all but the most exceptional cases, where the offence alone is considered to be so serious that detention for life is justified, irrespective of the risk to the public.[2] The scheme of the legislation is that the judiciary should specify a period appropriate to the punishment or retribution required to deter the offender and others from committing similar grave offences and that the Parole Board should then decide whether the offender still represented a danger to the public.

COMMUNITY SENTENCES

4.100   A community sentence consists of one or more of the following Community Orders:

(1) a Probation Order;
(2) a Drug Treatment and Testing Order;
(3) a Community Service Order;
(4) a Combination Order;
(5) a Curfew Order;
(6) a Supervision Order;
(7) an Attendance Centre Order, and
(8) an Action Plan Order.[3]

4.101   In the 1990 White Paper,[4] the Government criticised the perceived assumption that custody was the only 'real' punishment, an assumption which was said to be reinforced by referring to other penalties as 'alternatives to custody', and expressed the belief that more offenders should be punished in the community. To this end, the Criminal Justice Act 1991 made significant changes, both to the structure of community sentences and to the circumstances in which such sentences could be imposed. The Act created a threshold provision, similar to that created for the imposition of custodial sentences. A community sentence may only be imposed if the sentencer is of the opinion that

---

1   Under the provisions of the 1991 Act, this period would have been deducted from the period specified.
2   *Practice Direction (Crime: Life Sentences)* [1993] 1 WLR 223.
3   Criminal Justice Act 1991, s 6.
4   *Crime, Justice and Protecting the Public* (1990). See **4.57**.

that the offence, or the combination of the offence and one or more offences associated with it, was serious enough to warrant such a sentence.[1] Once the threshold criterion has been satisfied, the sentencer must choose the community order or orders which are thought to be most suitable for the offender, and must ensure that the restrictions on the liberty of the offender are commensurate with the seriousness of the offence or offences. In deciding whether a community sentence is justified and whether the restrictions on the liberty of the offender are commensurate with the seriousness of the offence, the sentencer *must* take into account all such information about the circumstances of the offence or offences as is available and, in deciding which order or orders are most suitable for the offender, the sentencer *may* take into account any information about the offender which is before the court.[2] Much of this information will be contained in the pre-sentence report, which will usually have been prepared[3] and be available to the court. The extent to which the 1991 Act succeeded in increasing the use made of community sentences is debatable. Admittedly, magistrates' courts' use of community sentences for indictable offences increased steadily between 1992 and 1996, from 21% to 29%, and remained at 29% in 1997 and 1998. However, at the Crown Court, the proportion increased from 28% in 1992 to 34% in 1993 but then fell back to 27% in 1996 before rising to 28% in 1997 where it remained in 1998.[4]

Community sentences and consent

4.102   Prior to the enactment of the Crime (Sentences) Act 1997, the willingness of an offender to undergo periods of supervision or to comply with requirements or conditions had been seen a key characteristic of community sentences. Hence, the consent of the offender was required before a Probation Order, Community Service Order, Combination Order or Curfew Order could be imposed and consent was also needed in relation to particular requirements or conditions attached to Supervision Orders. However, the 1997 Act marked a departure of principle from what had gone before, based on the philosophy that it was wrong that offenders should be able to dictate their sentence to the court.[5] There is no longer a requirement that the offender consent to the making of a Probation Order, Community Service Order, Combination Order or Curfew Order.[6] However, the consent of the offender is now required before a requirement can be included in a Probation Order that the offender receive treatment for a medical condition or for drug or alcohol dependency.[7] This is seen as being confirmation that such treatment can only be properly, and effectively, undertaken with consent.[8] In the case of a Supervision Order made

---

1   Criminal Justice Act 1991, s 6(1). A Community Service Order or a Curfew Order may now be made in the case of persistent petty offenders even if the threshold criterion has not been met (Crime (Sentences) Act 1997, s 37).
2   Criminal Justice Act 1991, s 7.
3   See **4.30**.
4   Home Office Statistical Bulletin 21/99 *Cautions, Court Proceedings and Sentencing, England and Wales 1998* table 11.
5   Ward *Criminal Sentencing; the New Law* (Jordans, Bristol, 1997) p 136.
6   Crime (Sentences) Act 1997, s 38(2).
7   Crime (Sentences) Act 1997, s 38(3) and (4).
8   Ward *Criminal Sentencing; the New Law* (Jordans, Bristol, 1997) p 137.

on a young offender,[1] there is no longer a requirement of consent from the offender or, if he is a child, from his parent or guardian for the imposition of certain requirements such as refraining from certain activities or remaining in a particular place, but before imposing such requirements on an offender under the age of 16, the sentencer must obtain and consider information about the offender's family circumstances and the likely effect of the requirements on those circumstances.[2]

Sex offenders and community sentences

4.103 Those convicted of serious sexual offences will usually receive an immediate custodial sentence and attention will be focused primarily on the length of the custodial term and arrangements for the supervision of the offender in the community on his release. If the offence is not sufficiently serious to justify a custodial sentence, the sentencer will then consider whether the criterion for the imposition of a community sentence is satisfied, or whether other sentencing options, such as a discharge or a fine, should be imposed. However, even if the offence is serious enough to justify the imposition of a custodial sentence, in some circumstances the sentencer may be of the opinion that it would be more appropriate to impose a community sentence. Community Service Orders and Combination Orders, which include an element of community service, are unlikely to be thought appropriate for many sex offenders as the court must be satisfied, in the light of a probation officer's or social worker's report, that the offender is a suitable person to do community service.[3] In 1998, approximately 100 offenders sentenced for indictable sexual offences were given a Community Service Order and a similar number received Combination Orders.[4] A thematic inspection of the work of probation services with sex offenders which was carried out in 1996–97 reported that there was a 'surprisingly high' number of Community Service Orders made on offenders convicted of sexual offences, although three-quarters involved the less serious offence of indecent exposure.[5] It concluded that, whilst probation staff were exercising great care about the nature of the placements undertaken, there was nonetheless a pressing issue about the suitability of a sentence which contained no provision to address sexual offending and yet left sex offenders in the community.

Sex offenders and Probation Orders

4.104 A Probation Order is said to be the cornerstone of community sentences with a tradition going back to the 19th century.[6] A court may now make a Probation Order on an offender aged 16 or over, if it is of the opinion that the supervision of the offender is desirable in the interests of:

---

1   See further **4.112**.
2   Crime (Sentences) Act 1997, s 38(1).
3   Powers of Criminal Courts Act 1973, s 14.
4   Home Office Statistical Bulletin 21/99 *Cautions, Court Proceedings and Sentencing, England and Wales 1998* table 8.
5   *Exercising Constant Vigilance: The Role of the Probation Service In Protecting the Public from Sex Offenders* (Home Office, London, 1998) para 1.11.
6   Osler *Introduction to the Probation Service* (Waterside Press, Winchester, 1995) p 67.

(1) securing the rehabilitation of the offender; or
(2) protecting the public from harm from him or preventing the commission by him of further offences.[1]

The order must last for not less than 6 months and not more than 3 years. If the offender is under 18 years of age, he will be placed under the supervision of a member of a Youth Offending Team established by the relevant local authority, in all other cases the supervision will be undertaken by a probation officer.[2] Clearly, the fact that an offender is thought to pose a risk to the public will not prevent the making of a Probation Order, as protection of the public is one of the stated aims of the order. However, if the risk posed is thought to be significant and the offence is sufficiently serious to justify a custodial sentence, in the absence of extenuating circumstances a custodial sentence will no doubt be imposed.

4.105   A Probation Order may include various additional requirements with which the offender must comply, including a requirement as to the residence of the offender[3] (which may include a requirement to reside at an approved hostel or other institution for a specified period[4]). The offender may also be required to present himself at a specified place to participate or refrain from participating in specified activities and to attend at a probation centre.[5] Such requirements can only be imposed on the majority of offenders for a total of not more than 60 days. However, there is no such time restriction on the requirements which may be imposed on those convicted of a sexual offence.[6] The removal of the time restriction for sex offenders was first implemented by the Criminal Justice Act 1991. The clear objective was to increase the control that could be exercised over sex offenders in the community and, thus, to encourage the use of community sentences for such offenders, where appropriate. Clearly, this objective has failed. In 1992, 900 offenders sentenced for indictable sexual offences received a Probation Order, which accounted for 18% of all such offenders.[7] By 1998, the figure had fallen to 800 offenders, 17% of the total.[8]

Sex offenders and treatment[9]

4.106   If there is medical evidence before the court that the mental condition of the offender is such as requires and may be susceptible to treatment, but is not such as to warrant the making of a Hospital Order or guardianship,[10] the Probation Order may include a requirement that the offender receive treatment

---

1   Powers of Criminal Courts Act 1973, s 2(1).
2   Powers of Criminal Courts Act 1973, s 2(2) and (2A), as amended by the Crime and Disorder Act 1998.
3   Powers of Criminal Courts Act 1973, Sch 1A, para 1.
4   See further **8.7** to **8.23**.
5   Powers of Criminal Courts Act 1973, Sch 1A, paras 2 and 3.
6   Powers of Criminal Courts Act 1973, Sch 1A, para 4. A sexual offence is as defined by Pt I of the Criminal Justice Act 1991. See **4.69**.
7   *Criminal Statistics for England and Wales 1992* (Home Office, London, 1993).
8   Home Office Statistical Bulletin 21/99 *Cautions, Court Proceedings and Sentencing, England and Wales 1998* table 8.
9   See further **6.50**.
10   Within the meaning of the Mental Health Act 1983.

by or under the direction of a registered medical practitioner and/or a chartered psychologist.[1]

Sex offenders, alcohol and drugs

4.107   If the court is satisfied that the offender is dependent on alcohol, that his dependency caused or contributed to the offence and that his dependency is such as requires and may be susceptible to treatment, a Probation Order may include a requirement that the offender undergo treatment for the dependency.[2] The extent to which alcohol affects sexual offending is not known, but it is common knowledge that consuming alcohol diminishes the drinker's powers of self control. Thus, if a sex offender is found to be dependent on drink and there is evidence that he only commits offences whilst drunk, a Probation Order may be made with a requirement that the offender receive treatment for the dependency. Prior to the enactment of the Crime and Disorder Act 1998, the requirement could also extend to treatment for dependency on drugs. It may now only do so if no provision has been made for implementing the new Drug Treatment and Testing Orders.[3] It seems that relatively few such requirements have been imposed on offenders. It has been suggested that the reasons for this include:[4]

(1)   the neutral policy position of both the Home Office and the Probation Service, with no clear guidance on the use of the disposal being issued to sentencers;
(2)   a reluctance on the part of probation officers to make proposals for the use of such powers in pre-sentence reports, based on the view that coerced treatment is unlikely to be effective;
(3)   the lack of information for sentencers on what is available, what treatment involves and how it fits in with harm-reduction strategies;
(4)   a perceived lack of enthusiasm on the part of treatment providers to operate mandatory programmes; and
(5)   difficulties in getting the cost of treatment programmes met by local authorities under existing community care arrangements and the lack of any specific probation budget.

4.108   Growing concern about drug abuse led to a new order being introduced by the Crime and Disorder Act 1998. If the court is satisfied that the offender is dependent on or has a propensity to misuse drugs, and that his dependency or propensity is such as requires or may be susceptible to treatment, a Drug Treatment and Testing Order may be made.[5] Whereas the requirement that the defendant undergo treatment for alcohol dependency may only be

---

1   Powers of Criminal Courts Act 1973, Sch 1A, para 5.
2   Powers of Criminal Courts Act 1973, Sch 1A, para 6.
3   See **4.108**.
4   Card and Ward *The Crime and Disorder Act 1998* (Jordans, Bristol, 1998) p 219.
5   Crime and Disorder Act 1998, s 61. The order may only be made where the court has been notified by the Secretary of State that arrangements for implementing such orders are available in the relevant area. If no such notification has been received, the court can attach a requirement to a Probation Order that the offender receive treatment for dependency on drugs, subject to the same conditions as apply to alcohol dependency.

added to a Probation Order if the dependency 'caused or contributed to the offence', no such causal link is specified for the Drug Treatment and Testing Order, which is an Community Order in its own right. The order has effect for a period specified in the order, of not less than 6 months or more than 3 years and the offender must consent to the making of the order.[1] The order includes a requirement that the offender must submit to treatment, which may include residential treatment, by or under the direction of a specified person with a view to the reduction or elimination of the offender's dependency on or propensity to misuse drugs. The order also includes a testing requirement which requires the offender to provide a specified minimum number of samples during the period of the order. Throughout the period of the order, the offender will be placed under the supervision of a probation officer whose role is to supervise the offender to the extent necessary to enable him to report on the offender's progress to the court, to report to the court any failure by the offender to comply with the requirements of the order, and matters relating to revocation or amendment of the order. The order cannot be made at the same time as a custodial sentence, but can be combined with other Community Orders, such as Probation Orders and Curfew Orders.

Curfew orders – keeping sex offenders at home

4.109　　　The Criminal Justice Act 1991 introduced the Curfew Order as a community sentence. The order requires the offender to remain at a particular place for between 2 and 12 hours on any days over a period which must not exceed 6 months from the date when the order was made.[2] The order may also include requirements for electronic monitoring in order to keep a check upon the offender's whereabouts during the curfew.[3] The aim of the order is not to keep offenders at home for most of the day, but to allow them to work, to attend probation centres, to carry out community service or to receive treatment for drug abuse.[4] The orders were initially only available in a limited number of trial areas, starting in July 1995. Take-up was slow for several months, but the trials were extended and in 1998 Home Office statistics showed that well over 1,000 orders had been made, with more than 80% of offenders successfully completing their sentence.[5] In December 1999, electronically monitored Curfew Orders were made available to courts throughout England and Wales.[6]

4.110　　　Curfew Orders were initially seen primarily as being potentially helpful in reducing crimes of disorder and those such as thefts of and from cars. Research conducted for the Home Office on the first 2 years of the trials of Curfew Orders found that the most common offences for which the orders were imposed were theft and handling stolen goods, burglary and driving whilst disqualified.[7] The research found that no Curfew Orders were imposed on those convicted of sexual offences. Given the fact that the majority of orders were

---

1　　　Crime and Disorder Act 1998, s 61(6).
2　　　Criminal Justice Act 1991, s 12.
3　　　Criminal Justice Act 1991, s 13.
4　　　*Crime Justice and Protecting the Public* (1990) Cmnd 965 (HMSO, London) para 4.20.
5　　　HOC 31/1998 app A.
6　　　Home Office Press Release 389/99.
7　　　HORS 177.

imposed by the magistrates' court on adult offenders, this is, perhaps, not surprising as many sex offenders will be dealt with by the Crown Court where more severe sentences may be considered appropriate. Further research published in 1999 found that sentencers and probation officers are of the opinion that electronically monitored Curfew Orders might be appropriate as a high-tariff sentence for serious offenders where custody is a possibility, or to disrupt 'pattern' offending, such as shop-lifting, night-time burglary or public order offences on a Friday or Saturday night, or where extra punishment is called for.[1] On the other hand, electronic monitoring is not felt to be suitable, inter alia, where there are risks to the family or to the public, or where there are child protection issues, which would suggest that Curfew Orders will rarely be considered appropriate for sex offenders. However, the Curfew Orders may usefully be imposed on sex offenders who are not thought to present a significant risk to the public, but who would benefit from the discipline imposed by the order, perhaps combined with a Probation Order. Some sex offenders may benefit from being kept away from areas of temptation, such as waiting outside school in the afternoons. It remains to be seen whether more use will be made of Curfew Orders for sex offenders in the future.

Sentencing and the sex offender register[2]

4.111 As part of the Government's overall stategy for protecting the public against sex offenders, in June 1996 the Home Office issued a consultation document on the sentencing and supervision of sex offenders,[3] which included a proposal that convicted sex offenders should be required to notify the police of any change of address. Following an enthusiastic response to the proposal, Pt I of the Sex Offenders Act 1997, which came into force on 1 September 1997, now requires specified sex offenders to notify to the police their name and home address, and any changes thereto, within 14 days of the conviction or change. The primary aim of these provisions is to ensure that the police have up-to-date information on the whereabouts of convicted sex offenders for use in the investigation and detection of crime.[4] In introducing the 1997 Act, the Government was anxious to point out that the notification requirements were not to be seen as an additional form of punishment, but merely as an administrative device to secure the protection of the public.[5] The Court of Appeal has now made it clear that the notification requirements imposed by the Sex Offenders Act 1997 are not to be regarded as a penalty within the provision of s 28 of the Criminal Justice Act 1991 and are not to be taken into account when determining the appropriate sentence.[6] Therefore, a sentencer cannot impose a shorter custodial term than would otherwise be appropriate for the offence, simply in order to reduce the period during which the offender will be subject to the notification requirements.

---

1   Home Office Research Findings No 105 'Making the Tag Fit: Further analysis from the first two years of the trials of Curfew Orders' (1999).
2   See **7.1** to **7.15**.
3   (1996) Cm 3304 (HMSO, London).
4   HC Deb vol 289, col 70, 27 January 1997.
5   HC Deb vol 291, col 34, 25 February 1997.
6   *Attorney-General's Reference (No 50 of 1997)* (1998) 2 Cr App R (S) 155.

SENTENCING YOUNG OFFENDERS[1]

4.112　　The underlying principles of sentencing of young offenders are the same as for adult offenders, although a wider range of orders is available in the Youth Court, which will generally hear cases involving offenders under the age of 18 years,[2] and there are restrictions and limitations on the use of some orders by the Youth Court. Thus, a sentence passed on an offender of any age must generally be commensurate with the seriousness of the offence, or offences associated with it, or, in the case of a custodial sentence imposed for a violent or sexual offence, only such a sentence would be adequate to protect the public from serious harm from the offender. However, a court is also required to have regard to the welfare of any child or young person brought before it, either as an offender or otherwise, and must in a proper case take steps to remove him from undesirable surroundings, and to secure that proper provision is made for his education and training.[3] There is no statutory guidance on the interaction of the often competing welfare and 'just deserts' considerations and so, when a court is dealing with an offender under the age of 18, it must decide itself what weight to apportion to each in a given case and deal with any resulting tensions.[4]

Young offenders and custodial sentences

4.113　　The basic criteria for custody for both young offenders and adults are the same, but there is a different scheme of custodial provision. The age of the young offender is crucial. An offender under the age of 21 years may not be sentenced to imprisonment, but there are alternative custodial sentences available, depending on the age of the offender, including detention in a young offender institution, a Secure Training Order, detention under s 53 of the Children and Young Persons Act 1933 and custody for life. For offenders under the age of 18 years, detention in a young offender institution and Secure Training Orders will be replaced by Detention and Training Orders on 1 April 2000 when ss 73–79 of the Crime and Disorder Act 1998 are brought into force.

Detention in a young offender institution

4.114　　If a custodial sentence is justified, offenders who are 15 years or over but under 21 years at the time of conviction, will be sentenced to detention in a young offender institution.[5] In the Youth Court, for offenders aged between 15 and 17 years, the minimum sentence is 2 months (designed to prevent very short sentences for young offenders and to ensure that the seriousness of the offence or the protection of the public justifies more than a nominal sentence) and the

---

1　The age of the young offender and the sentence imposed will determine whether or not he is treated as an adult for the purposes of sentencing. Offenders under the age of 21 years cannot be sentenced to imprisonment. Some community sentences can be imposed on offenders aged 16 years or over, while others can only be imposed on offenders under the age of 18 years.

2　See **3.95**.

3　Children and Young Persons Act 1933, s 44.

4　See Gordon, Cuddy and Black *Introduction to Youth Justice* (Waterside Press, Winchester, 1999) p 97.

5　Criminal Justice Act 1982, s 8.

maximum is 6 months, which may be increased to 12 months in aggregate when there are two or more indictable or triable-either-way offences for which the court is sentencing on the same occasion. The Crown Court, however, can sentence offenders aged between 15 and 17 years to up to 2 years' detention for a single offence. The minimum term for offenders aged between 18 and 20 years is 21 days' detention, but the only maximum term in the Crown Court for such offenders is that which can imposed for the offence itself.

Secure Training Orders

4.115   Custodial sentences are not usually thought to be appropriate for offenders below the age of 15 years. However, persistent young offenders who were at least 12 years old at the time of committing the offence and who are under 15 years of age at the time of conviction, may be sentenced to a Secure Training Order by either the Youth Court or the Crown Court if the following conditions are satisfied:[1]

(1) the offence must be an imprisonable offence in the case of an adult;
(2) the offender has been convicted of three or more offences which are imprisonable in the case of an adult; and
(3) the offender has, either on the present occasion or on an earlier occasion, been found to be in breach of a Supervision Order or been convicted of an imprisonable offence whilst subject to such an order.

The minimum length of sentence is 6 months and the maximum is 2 years. The first half of the order is served in detention at a secure training centre and the second half involves compulsory supervision in the community.

Detention and training orders

4.116   Provision exists within the Crime and Disorder Act 1998 for a single custodial sentence, a Detention and Training Order, which will replace the sentences of detention in a young offender institution and Secure Training Orders for offenders under the age of 18 years from 1 April 2000. The order can be made in respect of:

(1) 15–17 year olds for any imprisonable offence which is so serious as to justify a custodial sentence;
(2) 12–14 year olds who, in the opinion of the court, are persistent offenders for offences so serious as to justify a custodial sentence; and
(3) 10–11 year olds for persistent offenders, but only when the court considers that custody is the only method of protecting the public from further offending.[2]

4.117   The term of the order can be 4, 6, 8, 10, 12, 18 or 24 months, although the total length of the order must not exceed the maximum term of imprisonment that a Crown Court could impose on an adult offender.[3] The

---

1   Criminal Justice and Public Order Act 1994, s 1. The provision only applies to offences committed on or after 1 March 1998.
2   The Home Secretary will determine whether this section ever needs to be introduced in relation to 10 and 11 year olds.
3   Crime and Disorder Act 1998, s 73(6).

order will usually be divided equally between time spent in detention and training, on the one hand, and supervision on the other.[1]

Sentences of detention under s 53(2) of the Children and Young Persons Act 1933

4.118   Offenders aged between 10 and 17 years who have been convicted on indictment[2] may be sentenced to detention under the Children and Young Persons Act 1933. Before imposing such a sentence, the Crown Court must be of the opinion that no other method of dealing with the offender is appropriate. The term of the detention may be anything up to the maximum sentence imposable for the offence, and, while serving the sentence, the offender is held in accordance with the Home Secretary's directions. The Prison Service has announced the creation of three enhanced units within the prison estate for offenders detained under this provision to provide an appropriate regime and level of care for the more vulnerable detainees.[3]

Custody for life

4.119   Offenders aged between 18 and 20 years may be sentenced to custody for life if the offence of which they have been convicted carries life imprisonment[4] and the same principles apply to custody for life as apply to imprisonment. An offender sentenced to custody for life must be detained in a young offender institution unless the Home Secretary directs otherwise.

Young offenders and community sentences

4.120   Probation Orders, Drug Testing and Treatment Orders, Community Service Orders, Combination Orders and Curfew Orders are available for 16- and 17-year-old offenders in the same way as they are for adult offenders. Attendance Centre Orders are available for offenders under the age of 21, although in practice most orders are imposed on boys under the age of 17.[5] Supervision orders, which are comparable to Probation Orders, and Action Plan Orders, which were introduced by the Crime and Disorder Act 1998,[6] are only available for offenders under the age of 18.

---

1   Crime and Disorder Act 1998, s 75(2).
2   See **3.97**. This will only be possible for a limited range of offences, including those punishable in the case of an adult with at least 14 years' imprisonment and indecent assault.
3   *HM Prison Service Annual Report and Accounts April 1998–March 1999* (The Stationary Office, London, 1999).
4   Criminal Justice Act 1982, s 8(2), as amended by s 63(5) of the Criminal Justice Act 1991.
5   Sprack *Emmins on Criminal Procedure* (Blackstone Press Ltd, London, 1997) para 23.8.
6   Crime and Disorder Act 1998, s 69. Action Plan Orders, which require a young offender to comply with an action plan intended to address his offending behaviour, are being piloted for 18 months from September 1998, with a view to nationwide implantation in 2000–2001.

MENTALLY DISORDERED OFFENDERS

4.121   In many cases, offenders may well receive treatment aimed at addressing their offending behaviour as part of any sentence imposed by the court. For example, sex offenders sentenced to custody may have the opportunity to take part in treatment programmes whilst in prison, and the sentencing court may, with the offender's consent, attach a requirement of treatment to a Probation Order.[1] However, when dealing with an offender suffering from mental illness or mental disorder, prior to the enactment of pt III of the Crime (Sentences) Act 1997, if the court wished to ensure that the offender received treatment for the illness or disorder, a choice had to be made between punishment and treatment. The 1997 Act now provides for more flexibility in dealing with mentally disordered offenders with a view to ensuring that such offenders receive effective treatment within a framework that ensures the immediate and longer-term safety of the public.

Hospital Orders

4.122   A Hospital Order authorises the conveyance of an offender to hospital and his detention there for an initial period of six months. This period may subsequently be extended by the doctor in charge of the offender's treatment. In making the order, the court is foregoing any question of punishment and is placing the offender in the hands of the doctors, relinquishing any further control over him. A Hospital Order may be made if the court is dealing with an offender for an imprisonable offence and:

(1)   the court is satisfied on the evidence of two registered medical practitioners that the offender is suffering from mental illness, psychopathic disorder,[2] severe mental impairment[3] or mental impairment[4] and that either:
    (a)   the mental disorder from which the defendant is suffering is of a nature or degree that makes it appropriate for him to be detained in a hospital for medical treatment and, in the case of a psychopathic disorder or mental impairment, that such treatment is likely to alleviate or prevent a deterioration of his condition, or

---

1   See **4.106**.
2   Defined by s 1(2) of the Mental Health Act 1983 to mean a persistent disorder or disability of mind (whether or not including significant impairment of intelligence) which results in abnormally aggressive or seriously irresponsible conduct on the part of the person concerned.
3   Defined by s 1(2) of the Mental Health Act 1983 to mean a state of arrested or incomplete development of mind which includes severe impairment of intelligence and social functioning and is associated with abnormally aggressive or seriously irresponsible conduct on the part of the person concerned.
4   Defined by s 1(2) of the Mental Health Act 1983 to mean a state of arrested or incomplete development of mind (not amounting to severe mental impairment) which includes significant impairment of intelligence and social functioning and is associated with abnormally aggressive or seriously irresponsible conduct on the part of the person concerned.

(b) in the case of an offender who has attained the age of 16 years, the mental disorder is of a nature or degree which warrants his reception into guardianship under the 1983 Act;[1]

(2) the court is satisfied that arrangements have been made for the offender's admission to the hospital which it is proposed to name in the order; and

(3) the court is of the opinion, having regard to all the circumstances including the nature of the offence and the character and antecedents of the offender, and to the other available methods of dealing with him, that the most suitable method of disposing of the case is by means of a Hospital Order.[2]

In making the Hospital Order, the court is not concerned with the gravity of the offence or offences committed and the order may be made even though there is no causal connection between the offender's disorder and the offences he has committed.[3]

Discharge from hospital

4.123   Once a Hospital Order has been made, an offender is treated as any other compulsory patient and any decision on his eventual release rests with the doctor in charge of the his treatment or a Mental Health Review Tribunal. The doctor may discharge the offender from hospital at any time or may authorise his continued detention, initially for a further 6 months and thereafter at yearly intervals. The offender himself may apply to a Mental Health Tribunal,[4] which may direct his discharge after considering whether the offender is still suffering from a mental disorder and, if he is, whether his health or safety or the protection of others require that he should continue to receive treatment and whether he would be able to look after himself properly out of hospital.

Restriction Orders

4.124   Although a Hospital Order can be made without reference to the gravity of the offence or the risk posed by an offender, in cases where the offender is thought to present a significant risk to the public and further control over his discharge is thought to be desirable, the Crown Court[5] may add a Restriction Order to the Hospital Order.[6] The effect of the restriction is that the offender may only be discharged on the direction of the Secretary of State or a Mental Health Review Tribunal. A Restriction Order may be made if it appears to the Crown Court, having regard to the nature of the offence, the antecedents of the offender and the risk of his committing further offences if set at large, that it

---

1   The effect of Guardianship Order is that the offender is placed of a local social services authority or a person approved by the authority. The guardian may require the offender to reside at a certain address and to attend places for treatment, training or education.

2   Mental Health Act 1983, s 37(2).

3   *R v McBride* [1972] Crim LR 322.

4   The tribunal consists of a legally qualified chairman, a psychiatrist and a layperson.

5   Although a magistrates' court has no power to make a Restriction Order, if the offender is aged 14 years or over and has been convicted of an imprisonable offence, the magistrates may commit the offender to the Crown Court. Mental Health Act 1983, s 43.

6   Mental Health Act 1983, s 41.

is necessary for the protection of the public from serious harm. A Restriction Order may be for a fixed term or without a time limit, although the Court of Appeal has indicted that the safer course would be to make the order unlimited in time, unless the doctors are able to assert confidently that recovery will take place within a fixed period.[1]

4.125 In determining whether to make a Restriction Order, the sentencer has to choose between an order without restriction (which might lead to the offender being at large within a few months) and an order with restriction (which might lead to the offender being detained for a long time, possibly longer than he would spend in prison if sentenced to imprisonment).[2] The assessment of risk is clearly a matter for the court, and a similar approach to that taken in determining whether the criterion contained in s 2(2)(b) of the Criminal Justice Act 1991 will be taken.[3] The court is required to assess not the seriousness of the risk that the offender will re-offend, but the risk that, if he did so, the public might suffer serious harm.[4] Danger to the public may be sufficient justification for the continued detention of the offender under s 2(2)(b) of the Criminal Justice Act 1991, although this relates only to violent and sexual offences and even here the sentence should not be out of all proportion to a commensurate sentence.[5] However, the underlying rationale for detention in hospital is that the offender's mental disorder justifies the making of the order and danger to the public should not of itself be sufficient justification for continuing detention by means of a Restriction Order, where there are no similar preconditions that must be met. Indeed, it has been held to be contrary to art 5 of the European Convention on Human Rights to continue a Restriction Order if the offender's mental condition does not justify it.[6]

Hospital Orders, Restriction Orders and sex offenders

4.126 Home Office statistics[7] show that in 1997, 701 offenders were given unrestricted Hospital Orders by the courts. Of these, 233 (33%) had committed offences involving violence against the person, while only 42 (5.99%) had committed sexual offences. In comparison, the courts made Hospital Orders with Restriction Order in only 211 cases. Once again, the majority of offenders (112) had committed offences involving violence against the person, while only 14 (6.6%) had committed sexual offences. Thus, the proportion of sex offenders subjected to a Hospital Order each year, with or without restriction, appears to be similar, at between 6% and 7%.

4.127 A similar pattern emerges when the number of offenders transferred to hospital from a Prison service establishment, either after sentence or while

---

1 *R v Gardiner* [1967] 1 All ER 895.
2 *Archbold 'Criminal Pleading, Evidence and Practice'* (Sweet & Maxwell, London, 1999) para 5–558.
3 See **4.67** et seq.
4 *R v Birch* (1989) 90 Cr App R 78.
5 See **4.81**.
6 *X v UK* (1981) 4 EHRR 188.
7 Kershaw and Renshaw *Statistics of Mentally Disordered Offenders in England and Wales 1997* Issue 19/98 (Home Office, London).

unsentenced or untried, are taken into consideration.[1] In 1997, a total of 1070 offenders were admitted to hospital subject to Restriction Orders. Of these 92 (8.6%) had been convicted, or were awaiting trial or sentence, for a sexual offence, compared to 416 (38.8%) who had been convicted of offences involving violence to the person. Thus, it appears that between 6% and 9% of offenders admitted to hospital for treatment for mental disorders each year will be sex offenders and approximately 68% of these offenders will be subject to a Restriction Order.

Psychopaths and the case for change

4.128   Prior to 1997, the provisions of the Mental Health Act 1983 meant that the sentencing court had to make a choice between punishment and treatment. In 1996, it was acknowledged by the Government that, in some cases, an offender needed treatment in hospital but the circumstances of the offences also required a fixed period to be served in detention, maybe because the offender was found to bear some significant responsibility for the offence, notwithstanding his mental disorder, or because the link between the offending behaviour and the mental disorder was not clear at the time of sentencing.[2] The problem was seen as being particularly acute in the case of psychopaths, who are said to lie at the intersection between so-called 'mad' and 'bad' – between those who clearly warrant treatment (the seriously mentally ill or handicapped) and those who should properly receive punishment.[3] Following the recommendations of an inter-departmental committee chaired by Sir John Reed,[4] the Government proposed change in the form of a hybrid order which would enable the courts to pass a prison sentence on the offender and at the same time order his immediate admission to hospital for medical treatment. The changes were implemented the following year by the Crime (Sentences) Act 1997.

Hospital and limitation directions

4.129   The 1997 Act amends the Mental Health Act 1983, giving the Crown Court power, in cases where the sentence is not fixed by law, to impose a sentence of imprisonment, but to direct that the offender be sent to hospital (the hospital direction) and his discharge from hospital shall be subject to the restrictions imposed by a restriction order under s 41 of the 1983 Act (the limitation direction).[5] There does not appear to be scope for the making of a hospital direction without a limitation direction.[6] Once the offender has been discharged from hospital, he will be transferred to prison to serve the remainder

---

1   Provision exists in ss 47 and 48 of the Mental Health Act 1983 for the transfer to hospital, by order of the Secretary of State, of prisoners serving a sentence in a prison establishment and of unsentenced and untried defendants in criminal proceedings who are held in a Prison Service establishment.

2   *Protecting the Public* (1996) Cmnd 3190, para 8.14.

3   Eastman and Peay 'Sentencing Psychopaths: Is the Hospital and Limitation Direction an Ill-considered Hybrid?' [1998] Crim LR 93.

4   Reed *Report of the Department if Health and Home Office Working Group on Psychopathic Disorder* (Department of Health/Home Office, London, 1994).

5   Mental Health Act 1983, s 45A(3).

6   *Archbold 'Criminal Pleading, Evidence and Practice'* (Sweet & Maxwell, London, 1999) para 5-560.

of the custodial term. The direction can only be made if the court is satisfied, on the written or oral evidence of two registered medical practitioners:

(1) that the offender is suffering from a psychopathic disorder;
(2) that the mental disorder from which the offender is suffering is of a nature or degree which makes it appropriate for him to be detained in hospital for medical treatment; and
(3) that such treatment is likely to alleviate or prevent a deterioration of his condition.[1]

4.130   In its current form, the direction may only be made in relation to offenders suffering from psychopathic disorders, but the Secretary of State has the power to extend its availability to offenders suffering from other mental disorders.[2] Although the initial proposal for a hybrid order of this nature envisaged it being available for psychopaths thought to be of uncertain treatability, with a view to encouraging psychiatrists to 'have a therapeutic go',[3] the court is now only empowered to make the direction if the offender's disorder is thought to be treatable. Initially, the court must consider the making of a Hospital Order – a requirement said to be a key safeguard to prevent the new powers being used to justify the imposition of a term of imprisonment where treatment, not punishment, is appropriate.[4] Although the Government initially seemed to justify the introduction of a hospital and limitation direction by reference to the offender's partial responsibility for the offence committed, no such requirement appears in the legislation or accompanying Home Office circular.[5] Having decided that a sentence of imprisonment is appropriate, the court must consider the making of a hospital direction. The length of the sentence of imprisonment will need to be determined, although it has been pointed out that it is not clear whether the length of sentence should be fixed before or after the decision to make a hospital direction or whether the length of sentence should be moderated in any way by the presence of the hospital direction.[6] Similarly, it is not clear how the sentencer should determine the appropriate length of sentence, although if the offender has been convicted of a violent or sexual offence as defined by the Criminal Justice Act 1991, common sense dictates that the psychopath at risk of a hospital direction is also likely to satisfy the criterion in s 2(2)(b) of that Act and hence a longer than normal sentence will be justified.

More radical proposals

4.131   The power to impose a hospital and limitation direction now allows the courts to combine punishment and treatment for a relatively small[7] group of

---

1   Mental Health Act 1983, s 45A(2).
2   Mental Health Act 1983, s 45A(10).
3   Eastman and Peay 'Sentencing Psychopaths: Is the Hospital and Limitation Direction an Ill-considered Hybrid?' [1998] Crim LR 93 at 96.
4   Ward *Criminal Sentencing; the New Law* (Jordans, Bristol, 1997) p 123.
5   Home Office Circular 52/1997.
6   Eastman and Peay 'Sentencing Psychopaths: Is the Hospital and Limitation Direction an Ill-considered Hybrid?' [1998] Crim LR 93 at 100.
7   For example, of the total 2,293 criminal orders made for all mentally disordered offenders during the year ending 31 March 1996, only 87 patients had an exclusive classification of

mentally disordered offenders who have been convicted of a criminal offence. Treatment may also be imposed on individuals who have not been convicted of a criminal offence if they satisfy the criteria for compulsory detention under the mental health legislation, and such detention will only be justified if treatment is likely to alleviate or prevent a deterioration of their condition. The fact remains that there are dangerous mentally disordered individuals who present a significant risk to the public and who are not effectively restrained, either by the criminal law or by the provisions of mental health legislation. Therefore, the Government has proposed, subject to Parliamentary time, the introduction of new powers for the indeterminate but reviewable detention of dangerously personality disordered individuals, whether or not such individuals were before the courts for an offence.[1]

APPEALS AGAINST SENTENCE

4.132   An offender sentenced by the magistrates' court has the right to appeal against the sentence to the Crown Court,[2] which may vary the sentence imposed by the lower court.[3] The power to vary the sentence includes a power to increase the sentence, as long as the Crown Court sentence does not exceed that which the magistrates could have passed.[4]

4.133   An offender sentenced by the Crown Court, either following conviction on indictment[5] or following summary conviction and committal to the Crown Court for sentence,[6] may appeal to the Court of Appeal against sentence. Leave to appeal is always required, unless the judge who passed sentence grants a certificate that the case is fit for appeal.[7] Notice of application for leave to appeal must be given within 28 days of the sentence being imposed.[8] The Court of Appeal may quash any sentence or order passed by the Crown Court, and replace it with a sentence or order it considers appropriate, provided:

(1)   the sentence it passes or order it makes is one which the Crown Court could have passed or made; and
(2)   taking the case as a whole, the appellant is not more severely dealt with on appeal than he was by the Crown Court.[9]

Thus, an offender who appeals against a sentence imposed by the Crown Court cannot have his overall sentence increased.

---

psychopathic disorder. See Eastman and Peay 'Sentencing Psychopaths: Is the Hospital and Limitation Direction an Ill-considered Hybrid?' [1998] Crim LR 93 at 95.
1   HC Deb vol 325, col 602, 15 February 1999. See further **7.63** to **7.73**.
2   Magistrates' Courts Act 1980, s 108(1).
3   Supreme Court Act 1981, s 48.
4   Supreme Court Act 1981, s 48(4).
5   Criminal Appeal Act 1968, s 9.
6   Criminal Appeal Act 1968, s 10.
7   Criminal Appeal Act 1968, s 11(1).
8   Criminal Appeal Act 1968, s 18.
9   Criminal Appeal Act 1968, s 11(3).

Criminal Cases Review Commission

4.134   As a matter of last resort, when all other methods of appeal through
the courts have been exhausted, an offender may appeal to the Criminal Cases
Review Commission, established by the Criminal Appeal Act 1995. In the past,
the Home Secretary had the power to refer any case dealt with on indictment to
the Court of Appeal in relation to conviction or sentence or both.[1] This power
has now been transferred to the Commission, which also has power to refer cases
decided in the magistrates' court to the Crown Court. Cases which are referred
by the Commission are dealt with by the Crown Court or Court of Appeal as an
appeal. Offenders wishing to challenge their sentence must provide either a
legal argument or information about themselves or the offences which was not
raised during the court hearing or any appeal.[2] The Commission will only refer a
case to the Crown Court or the Court of Appeal if it is of the opinion that there is
a real possibility of success.[3]

Attorney-General's References

4.135   Provision now exists for the Attorney-General to refer certain sentences imposed by the Crown Court to the Court of Appeal for review if he
considers the sentence to be unduly lenient.[4] The Court of Appeal must itself
grant leave and the offender must have been sentenced in the Crown Court for
either:

(1) an offence triable only on indictment; or
(2) an offence triable either way which is amongst those specified in an order
     made by the Home Secretary by statutory instrument.[5]

The following triable-either-way offences are specified:

(1) indecent assault on a woman or a man (ss 14 and 15 of the Sexual Offences
     Act 1956);
(2) threats to kill (s 16 of the Offences Against the Person Act 1861);
(3) cruelty to a person under the age of 16 (s 1 of the Children and Young
     Persons Act 1933); and
(4) attempts or incitement to commit any of the above.[6]

On such a review, the Court of Appeal may quash the sentence and replace it
with the sentence it considers to be most appropriate, provided the substituted
sentence is one which the Crown Court had power to pass. In most cases, the
substituted sentence will be more severe than that imposed by the Crown Court,
but need not necessarily be so. The Court of Appeal has held that a sentence is
unduly lenient where it falls outside the range of sentences which the judge,
applying his mind to all the relevant factors, could reasonably consider
appropriate.[7] However, in the same case it was pointed out that sentencing is an

---

1   Criminal Appeal Act 1968, s 17.
2   Cheney et al *Criminal Justice and the Human Rights Act 1998* (Jordans, Bristol, 1999).
3   Criminal Appeal Act 1995, s 13.
4   Criminal Justice Act 1988, s 36.
5   Criminal Justice Act 1988, s 35.
6   Criminal Justice Act 1988 (Reviews of Sentencing) Order 1994, SI 1994 No 119.
7   *Attorney-General's Reference (No 4 of 1989)* [1990] 1 WLR 41 at 46.

art rather than a science, that the trial judge is well placed to assess the weight to be given to various competing considerations, and that leniency is not in itself a vice. It is clear that, in deciding whether or not to increase a sentence imposed by the trial court, the Court of Appeal will take account of the 'double jeopardy' factor – that the offender is being sentenced for the second time with the attendant stress and uncertainty. For example, in *Attorney-General's Reference (No 29 of 1996)*,[1] the Court of Appeal found that the original sentence of a total of 7 years and 6 months imposed by the trial court for one count of rape and three counts of indecent assault was unduly lenient and that the appropriate sentence would have been 10 years, but that an appropriate discount should be made for the principle of double jeopardy. The Court eventually concluded that the difference between the correct sentence, once it was discounted for double jeopardy, and the sentence which the trial court had imposed, was not so great as to cause the Court, in the exercise of its discretion, to interfere.

The role of the Court of Appeal in sentencing

4.136   Consistency in sentencing is obviously of considerable importance. Beginning in the 1970s, in an effort to address disparity in sentencing practice and to give advice to sentencers, the Court of Appeal, under the guidance of the Lord Chief Justice, has issued guidelines for the assistance of the lower courts. Reform of the sentencing process during the early 1990s was aimed at achieving a partnership between the legislature and the judiciary, with legislation providing a framework of requirements for imposing custodial and non-custodial sentences, leaving the Court of Appeal to develop more detailed principles based on the statutory framework.[2] The introduction of automatic and minimum sentences by the Crime (Sentences) Act 1997 was seen by many as a further erosion of the judicial discretion which had previously governed sentencing practice to a great extent.[3] However, the provision of guidance by the Court of Appeal remains an important element in the development of sentencing jurisprudence. Decisions of the Court of Appeal may be cited as precedents which sentencers in the lower courts may be invited to follow. However, the usefulness of such citation has been questioned. Lord Taylor CJ has commented that comparing the facts of one case with the facts of another is not usually a particularly helpful exercise as the facts of criminal cases, particularly sexual cases, vary so enormously.[4]

4.137   More significant use is made of the guideline judgments issued by the Court of Appeal. A guideline judgment is a single judgment which sets out general parameters for dealing with several variations of a certain type of offence, considering the main mitigating and aggravating factors, and suggesting an appropriate starting point or range of sentences.[5] Most of the guideline judgments issued by the Court of Appeal have tended to involve offences which usually attract a substantial sentence of imprisonment and there has been little

---

1   (1997) 1 Cr App R (S) 224.
2   See **4.57**.
3   See **4.56**.
4   *Attorney-General's Reference (No 19 of 1992)* (1993) 14 Cr App R (S) 330 at 334.
5   Ashworth *Sentencing and Criminal Justice* (Butterworths, London, 1995) chap 1.

appellate guidance available on community sentences. As a result of growing concern over the lack of consistent guidance from the Court of Appeal, the Crime and Disorder Act 1998 for the first time imposed a statutory duty on the Court of Appeal to consider whether to frame guidelines, or to revise existing guidelines, in respect of categories of indictable offences.[1] In framing or revising guidelines, the court is obliged to have regard to the following matters:[2]

(1) the need to promote consistency in sentencing;
(2) the sentences imposed by courts in England and Wales for offences of the relevant category;
(3) the cost of different sentences and their relative effectiveness in preventing re-offending;
(4) the need to promote public confidence in the criminal justice system; and
(5) the views communicated to the court by the Sentencing Advisory Panel.[3]

The guidelines must include criteria for determining the seriousness of offences, including the weight to be given to previous convictions or any failure of the offender to respond to previous sentences. The statutory duty imposed by the 1998 Act reflects existing practice to a great extent. There is nothing that prevents the Court of Appeal issuing guidance on matters which do not fall within the statutory duty, for example guidance on the use of particular sentencing option rather than guidance in respect of categories of offences. The duty will, however, certainly focus the attention of the Court of Appeal on the need to formulate or revise guidelines in appropriate cases and, hopefully, should result in more guidance emanating from the Court in due course.

Sentencing Advisory Panel

4.138   The statutory duty imposed on the Court of Appeal is supplemented by the creation of a new body, the Sentencing Advisory Panel, which began work on 1 July 1999. The membership of the Panel is determined by the Lord Chancellor after consultation with the Home Secretary and the Lord Chief Justice.[4] The Panel currently has 11 members, said to represent a 'good mix of high calibre and experienced people, selected after an exhaustive and open recruitment process'.[5] If the Court of Appeal decides to frame or revise guidelines, the Court is required to notify the Panel. The Panel may, on its own initiative, propose to the Court of Appeal that guidelines be framed for a particular category of offence and may be required to do so by the Secretary of State. In either case, the Panel is required to:

(1) obtain and consider the views on the matters in issue of such persons or bodies as may be determined, after consultation with the Secretary of State and the Lord Chief Justice, by the Lord Chancellor;
(2) formulate its own views on the matters and communicate them to the Court of Appeal; and

---

1   Crime and Disorder Act 1998, s 80. Commencement date, July 1999.
2   Crime and Disorder Act 1998, s 80(3).
3   See **4.138**.
4   Crime and Disorder Act 1998, s 81(1).
5   Home Office Press Release 193/99.

(3) furnish information to the Court as to the sentences imposed by the courts in England and Wales for offences of the relevant category and the cost of different sentences and their relative effectiveness in preventing re-offending.[1]

The Panel will clearly serve in an advisory capacity, providing the Court of Appeal with a wider range of informed opinion than was previously available to the Court.

Sentencing and public opinion

4.139   The role which public opinion has, or should have, in influencing sentencing practice is controversial. Although some would argue that, in the past, in theory, sentencing decisions were influenced only by officially approved considerations,[2] judgments from the Court of Appeal have been shown to indicate that sentencing judges are at the very least duty-bound to consider the relevance of public opinion and possibly even required to factor that consider-ation into any sentence which they pass.[3] In practice, most sentencers are said to admit to having some regard to what they believe to be public opinion.[4] Indeed, one Lord Chief Justice has expressed the view that any sentence imposed must take account of public opinion and aim to leave all concerned with a feeling that justice has been done.[5] The establishment of the Sentencing Advisory Panel could mean that public opinion may play a greater, albeit indirect, role in sentencing. The Panel is required to obtain and consider the views of specified persons or bodies, and it is anticipated that the Panel will 'almost certainly' wish to consult beyond those organisations and that other organisations will offer their views of their own accord.[6]

4.140   Such consultation has the potential to have a significant impact on sentencing sex offenders. Prima facie, sexual offences undoubtedly form a category of offence about which the public tend to hold very strong opinions, and such opinions tend to be punitive in nature. This would result in harsher sentences being imposed on sex offenders if public opinion is taken into account. Yet such an approach requires caution, as a clear distinction needs to be drawn between informed opinion and public opinion. The British Crime Survey of 1996 found that there was a crisis of confidence in sentencers, who are seen as being out of touch and imposing sentences that are far too soft.[7] However, such attitudes were found to be based on mistaken assumptions about the sentences actually imposed on offenders in practice. Large majorities of respondents to the survey significantly underestimated the severity of the sentences passed on offenders in general and rapists in particular. For example, in 1995, 97% of adult males convicted of rape were sent to prison, but only 18% of respondents

1   Crime and Disorder Act 1998, s 81(4).
2   Walker and Padfield *Sentencing, Theory, Law and Practice* (Butterworths, London, 1996) para 6.18.
3   Shute 'The Place of Public Opinion in Sentencing Law' [1998] CLR 465 at 475.
4   Walker and Padfield *Sentencing, Theory, Law and Practice* (Butterworths, London, 1996) para 6.18.
5   Lord Taylor CJ [1993] *Journal of the Law Society of Scotland* 129.
6   Home Office Press Release 193/99.
7   'Attitudes to Punishment: Findings from the British Crime Surveys' (1998) HORS 179.

estimated within 10% of the correct figure; 26% gave a lower estimate of between 10% and 30% of the correct figure; while the remaining respondents (over 50% of all respondents) made estimates which were much too low. The most likely reason suggested for this ingrained belief in lenient sentences is that people receive information about sentencing largely from the media, and media news values militate against balanced coverage – erratic court sentences make news and sensible ones do not. However, research on the public portrayal of rape sentencing found that there was no evidence of a disproportionate focus in the media on acquittals and that the focus on non-custodial sentences was somewhat more erratic.[1] However, there was found to be an extraordinary focus in recent years on cases where convicted rapists received a custodial sentence of over 7 years, which would suggest that the public are actually receiving more information about sentences passed at the top the scale, rather than unduly lenient sentences. Whatever the reason for the misguided beliefs, correcting public misconceptions about sentencing trends would promote greater confidence in judges and magistrates, but this is obviously no easy task. To date, it appears that very limited use has been made of the communication techniques of the late 20th century in letting the public know about current sentencing trends, but is has been suggested that a successful strategy for tackling public misconceptions will almost certainly have to resort to these techniques.[2] Such a strategy would have to identify key audiences, such as opinion-formers, victims, potential offenders and people at risk of offending, and convey appropriately to each audience an accurate portrayal of current sentencing practice. It is only when such efforts have been successful that public opinion will become informed opinion, which in turn may influence sentencing practice through the Sentencing Advisory Panel.

SENTENCING SEX OFFENDERS IN PRACTICE[3]

4.141 In 1998, 4,600 offenders were sentenced for indictable sexual offences.[4] Of these, approximately 2,700 (58%) received an immediate custodial sentence, 1,200 (26%) received a community sentence, 300 (8%) were fined and 200 (4%) received an absolute or conditional discharge.[5]

Rape

4.142 Rape has always been regarded as a serious offence and the Court of Appeal has commented on several occasions that, other than in wholly exceptional circumstances, it calls for an immediate custodial sentence.[6] In 1998, 98% of offenders aged 21 and over sentenced for rape received an

1 Soothill and Grover 'The Public Portrayal of Rape Sentencing: What the Public Learns from the Newspapers' [1998] Crim LR 455.
2 'Attitudes to Punishment: Findings from the British Crime Surveys' (1998) HORS 179.
3 See generally Thomas *Current Sentencing Practice* (Sweet & Maxwell, London, 1982–to date Part B4.
4 Home Office Statistical Bulletin 21/99 *Cautions, Court Proceedings and Sentencing, England and Wales 1998* table 8.
5 The remaining offenders were either given a fully suspended sentence or otherwise dealt with.
6 *R v Roberts and Roberts* (1982) 4 Cr App R (S) 8 and *R v Billam* (1986) 8 Cr App R (S) 48.

immediate custodial sentence. The average sentence length was 74 months on a guilty plea and 86.2 months on a not guilty plea.[1] In 1986 Lord Lane CJ delivered the judgment in *R v Billam*, giving guidance to trial judges on sentencing offenders convicted of rape. Although the variable factors in cases of rape are so numerous it was said to be difficult to lay down guidelines as to the proper length of sentence, decisions of the Court of Appeal do at least give an indication of what current practice ought to be.

R v Billam – the starting points

4.143   For rape committed by an adult without any aggravating or mitigating factors, a figure of 5 years should be taken as the starting point in a contested case. If any of the following aggravating factors are present, the starting point should be 8 years. If the rape is committed by:

(1) two or more men acting together;
(2) a man who has broken into or otherwise gained access to a place where the victim is living;
(3) a man who is in a position of responsibility towards the victim; or
(4) a man who abducts the victim and holds her captive.

4.144   If the rape is committed by a man who has carried out a campaign of rape, committing the crime upon a number of different women or girls, he is said to represent a more than ordinary danger and a sentence of 15 years or more may be appropriate.

4.145   Where the offender's behaviour has manifested perverted or psychiatric tendencies or gross personality disorder, and where he is likely, if at large, to remain a danger for an indefinite time, a life sentence will not be inappropriate.

Aggravating factors

4.146   If any one or more of the following aggravating factors are present, the sentence should be substantially higher than the figure suggested as the starting point:

(1) violence is used over and above the force necessary to commit rape;
(2) a weapon is used to frighten or wound the victim;
(3) the rape is repeated;
(4) the rape has been carefully planned;
(5) the offender has previous convictions for rape or other serious offences of a violent or sexual kind;
(6) the victim is subjected to further sexual indignities or perversion;
(7) the victim is either very old or very young; or
(8) the effect upon the victim, whether physical or mental, is of special seriousness.

---

1   *Criminal Statistics for England and Wales 1998* (provided by the Home Office).

Mitigation

GUILTY PLEAS

4.147   The Court acknowledged that the extra distress which giving evidence can cause to a victim means that a plea of guilty, perhaps more so than in other cases, should normally result in some reduction from what would otherwise be the appropriate sentence. The amount of such reduction will depend on all the circumstances, including the likelihood of a finding of not guilty had the matter been contested.

VICTIM'S BEHAVIOUR

4.148   The Court expressly stated that the fact that a victim may be considered to have exposed herself to a danger by acting imprudently (for instance by accepting a lift in a car from a stranger) is not a mitigating factor; and the victim's previous sexual experience is equally irrelevant. But if the victim has behaved in a manner which was calculated to lead the offender to believe that she would consent to sexual intercourse, then the Court was of the opinion that there should be some mitigation of the sentence. Previous good character of the offender was said to be of only minor relevance.

Attempted rape

4.149   The starting point for attempted rape should be less than for the completed offence, especially if it is desisted at a comparatively early stage. But the Court pointed out that attempted rape may be made by aggravating factors into an offence even more serious than some examples of the full offence.

Rape and non-custodial sentences

4.150   The Court of Appeal has made it clear that, whilst immediate custodial sentences will be appropriate in the vast majority of cases of rape, a non-custodial sentence may be appropriate if there are exceptional circumstances. The case of *R v D*[1] provides a useful illustration of what the Court deems to be 'exceptional circumstances'. The offender had pleaded guilty to rape, indecent assault and incest. He had committed a number of indecent assaults on his sister, who was 2 years younger than him. The assaults included sexual intercourse without consent and were committed over a period of 7 years, beginning when he was 12 years old. The assaults ended in 1992 and the victim confided in her parents the following year. The offender agreed to have counselling, but when the counselling arrangement broke down, the police were informed. The offender readily admitted the offences, but he was initially sentenced to 4 years' imprisonment. On appeal, new evidence was produced in the Court of Appeal which consisted of a letter from the victim, expressing her concern at the sentence and the fact that the offender was not receiving the treatment he was deemed to be in need of whilst he was in prison, which was having a detrimental effect on the victim's own mental state. The Court took the view that this was a case where it was unlikely that the prison sentence would be of assistance to the

---

1   [1996] 1 Cr App R (S) 196.

victim, or to the general public or to the offender himself. Noting in particular the fact that the prison sentence had a positively adverse effect on the victim, the Court felt able to take a 'more merciful' approach and quashed the original sentence, substituting it with a Probation Order for 2 years, with a condition that the offender joined an extended group work programme for sex offenders.

4.151   However, if aggravating factors are present, a custodial sentence will be virtually inevitable. In *Attorney-General's Reference (No 24 of 1999)*,[1] the offender had separated from his wife, but the two still lived together by agreement. One night, the offender attacked his wife, placed tape over her mouth and nose and tied her up with a rope he had placed in the room for that purpose. He then threatened to kill himself, and possibly his wife, before cutting her clothes off with a Stanley knife and raping her. The attack was reported to the police three weeks later. The offender pleaded guilty and psychiatric evidence at the trial suggested he was suffering from acute depression at the time of the attack. He was sentenced to a 3-year Probation Order, with a condition of residence at a rehabilitation centre for sex offenders. The Attorney-General referred the case to the Court of Appeal on the grounds that the sentence was unduly lenient. The Court of Appeal pointed out that, although the offender was of previous good character and had shown genuine remorse for what he had done, there were significant aggravating factors in the case, including the fact that the attack had been carefully planned and the offender had used tape and a Stanley knife to threaten the victim. The sentencing judge was said to have paid great attention to the offender's rehabilitation needs and too little attention to the victim's suffering together with a lack of consideration of public opinion on marital rape cases. In sentencing offenders in similar cases, the Court said it would be necessary to consider the route that would best serve the needs of the offender without neglecting the need to protect the victim, whilst at the same time providing a clear indication of Parliament's intention. In considering all the circumstances of the case, the Court felt that the appropriate sentence following the guilty plea should have been in the region of 6 years' imprisonment. Allowing for the offender's acute depression and the issue of double jeopardy, the Court quashed the Probation Order and substituted a sentence of 3 years and 6 months' imprisonment.

Buggery and gross indecency

4.152   Offences of non-consensual buggery, whether committed on a male or female, committed after 3 November 1994, will be charged as rape and offenders convicted of buggery arising out of offences committed after this date must be sentenced on the presumption the buggery was consensual.[2] The maximum sentence is now life imprisonment if the person buggered was under the age of 16, 5 years' imprisonment if the offender is over 21 years of age and the person buggered is under 18 years of age, and 2 years' imprisonment in other circumstances. Prior to the extension of the definition of rape by the Criminal

---

1   *Sub nom R v Toby Fuller*, 29 June 1999, Court of Appeal.
2   *R v Davies* (1998) 1 Cr App R (S) 380.

Justice and Public Order Act 1994, in sentencing for non-consensual buggery[1] the court would refer to the *Billam* guidelines and sentence accordingly.[2] In cases of consensual buggery, the sentencing court will be concerned with the age of the participants and the relationship between them. In *R v Bradley*[3] the offender, who was aged 24, pleaded guilty to buggery of a boy of 15 whom he had met at a club providing a meeting place for homosexuals. The Court of Appeal agreed with the trial judge that an appropriate sentence for homosexual sex in these circumstances was 30 months' imprisonment. Where the offence takes place between consenting adult males in a public place, a custodial sentence for a first offence will not usually be considered appropriate.[4] Similarly, a first conviction for an act of gross indecency will not usually attract a custodial sentence, as a fine or Probation Order will usually be appropriate.[5]

Incest

4.153   The maximum sentence for incest is life imprisonment if committed with a girl under the age of 13 and 7 years' imprisonment in all other cases.[6] In *Attorney-General's Reference (No 1 of 1989)*,[7] the Court of Appeal gave the following guidance as the appropriate sentence to be imposed.

(1) Where the girl is over 16 years of age. Generally speaking, a range from 3 years' imprisonment down to a nominal penalty will be appropriate depending in particular on the one hand whether force was used, and upon the degree of harm, if any to the girl, and on the other the desirability where it exists of keeping family disruption to a minimum. The older the girl, the greater the possibility that she may have been willing or even the instigating party to the liaison, a factor which will be reflected in the sentence. In other words, the lower the degree of corruption, the lower the penalty.
(2) Where the girl is aged between 13 and 16 years. Here a sentence between about 5 years and 3 years seems on the authorities to be appropriate. Much the same principles will apply as in the case of girl over 16 years of age, although the likelihood of corruption increases in inverse proportion to the age of the girl. Nearly all cases in this and in other categories have involved pleas of guilty and the sentences in this category seem to range from about 2 years and 4 years, credit having been given for the plea.
(3) Where the girl is under 13 years of age. It is here that the widest range of sentences is to be found. If one can properly describe any case of incest as the 'ordinary' type of case, it will be one where the sexual relationship between husband and wife has broken down; the father has probably resorted to excessive drinking and the eldest daughter is gradually, by way of

---

1   At this time, the maximum sentence was 10 years where the person buggered was a male and life imprisonment where female.
2   *Attorney-General's Reference (No 25 of 1994)* (1994) 16 Cr App R (S) 562.
3   (1998) 1 Cr App R (S) 432.
4   *R v Tosland* (1981) 3 Cr App R (S) 365 and *R v Bedborough* (1984) 6 Cr App R (S) 98.
5   *R v Morgan and Docherty*, 28 September 1978, CA and *R v Clayton and Restrepo* (1981) 3 Cr App R (S) 67.
6   The maximum sentence for attempted incest is 7 years' imprisonment if committed with a girl under the age of 13 and 2 years' imprisonment in all other cases.
7   (1989) 11 Cr App R (S) 409.

familiarities, indecent acts and suggestions, made the object of the father's frustrated sexual inclinations. If the girl is not far short of her thirteenth birthday and there are no particularly adverse or favourable features on a not guilty plea, a term of about 6 years' imprisonment on the authorities would seem to be appropriate. It scarcely needs to be stated that the younger the girl when the sexual approach is started, the more likely it will be that the girl's will was overborne and, accordingly, the more serious would be the crime.

4.154   Other aggravating factors, whatever the age of the girl may be include (inter alia):

(1) if there is evidence that the girl has suffered physically or psychologically from the incest;
(2) if the incest has continued at frequent intervals over a long period of time;
(3) if the girl was threatened or treated violently by or was terrified of the father;
(4) if the incest has been accompanied by perversions abhorrent to the girl, eg buggery or fellatio;
(5) if the girl becomes pregnant by reason of the father failing to take contraceptive measures; and
(6) if the defendant has committed similar offences against more than one girl.

4.155   Possible mitigating factors include (inter alia):

(1) a plea of guilty: it is seldom that such a plea is not entered, and it should be met by an appropriate discount, depending on the usual considerations, that is to say how promptly the defendant confessed and his degree of contrition and so on;
(2) it seems that there was a genuine affection on the part of the defendant rather than the intention to use the girl simply as an outlet for his sexual inclinations;
(3) where the girl has had previous sexual experience;
(4) where the girl has made deliberate attempts at seduction; and
(5) where, as very occasionally is the case, a shorter term of imprisonment for the father may be of benefit to the victim and the family.

Unlawful sexual intercourse

4.156   The maximum sentence for unlawful sexual intercourse is life imprisonment if the girl is under 13 years of age and 2 years' imprisonment if the girl is aged under 16 years of age. Thus, the age of the girl will be crucial. If she is aged between 13 and 16 and the offender is not in a position of trust or authority, in cases where there is a substantial difference in age between the offender and victim[1] and a custodial sentence is appropriate, on a guilty plea the sentence will

---

1   In many cases where there is little difference between in age between the offender and victim, even if the offence does come to light it will not be thought to be in the public interest to bring criminal proceedings.

be in region of 6–9 months' imprisonment.[1] If the offence involved a breach of a position of trust or authority, the appropriate sentence will range between 9 months'[2] and 18 months' imprisonment.[3] If the girl is under 13 years of age, the Court of Appeal has emphasised that unlawful sexual intercourse is an extremely serious offence and must remain so – even in the relaxed time in which we live.[4] The age of the girl and her relationship with the offender will often be the decisive factors in determining the appropriate sentence. In *R v Robertson*,[5] the offender, who had pleaded not guilty, was convicted of four counts of indecent assault and one of unlawful sexual intercourse arising out of conduct with his two stepdaughters on various occasions over a period of years. The Court of Appeal stated that the sentence of 10 years' imprisonment was not wrong in principle, neither was it excessive in the circumstances. At the opposite end of the spectrum, in *R v Brough*,[6] the 22-year-old offender was intellectually impaired and was initially sentenced to 2 years' imprisonment for having sexual intercourse with a girl under the age of 13 on three occasions. The Court of Appeal substituted a sentence of 15 months' imprisonment.

Indecent assault and indecency with children

4.157   The maximum sentence for indecent assault on a man or a woman is now 10 years' imprisonment. Prior to 16 September 1985, indecent assaults on a women attracted a maximum penalty of only 2 years' imprisonment.[7] If the offence charged is one of indecency with a child under the age of 14, for offences committed on or after 1 October 1997 the maximum sentence is also 10 years' imprisonment, but for offences committed before this date, the maximum sentence is 2 years' imprisonment. The Court of Appeal has been reluctant to set 'sentencing tariffs' for offences of indecency, which cover a wide range of behaviour, from a slap on the buttocks of a adult to sexual abuse of a young child falling just short of sexual intercourse. The Court has acknowledged this wide spectrum of behaviour, noting that in each case, although it would take due notice of decisions in similar cases, the circumstances of indecency vary infinitely in their different circumstances.[8] Furthermore, sentences in earlier cases must also be viewed against the statutory framework which was in force at the time when the offences were committed. The increased sentencing powers in recent years have led the Court of Appeal to comment that, in most cases, the personal circumstances of the offender will have to take second place behind the plain duty of the court to protect the victims of sexual attack and to reflect the clear intention of Parliament that offences of this kind are to meet with greater

---

1   *R v Carter* (1997) 1 Cr App R (S) 434.
2   *R v Wood* (1990) 12 Cr App R (S) 129.
3   *R v Forsyth* (1987) 9 Cr App R (S) 126.
4   *R v Bulmer* (1989) 11 Cr App R (S) 586.
5   (1988) 10 Cr App R (S) 183.
6   (1997) 1 Cr App R (S) 55.
7   Although if the victim was under 13 and her age was stated in the indictment, s 2(1)(b) of the Indecency with Children Act 1960 provided that the maximum sentence was 5 years' imprisonment.
8   *R v Henderson* (1991) 12 Cr App R (S) 589.

severity than may have been the case in former years when the position of the victim may not have been so clearly focused in the public eye.[1]

Indecency and custodial sentences

4.158   The Court of Appeal has accepted that, where an indecent assault is of some significance and the offender is of full adult capacity, a custodial sentence will 'almost certainly' be required.[2] In 1998, 68% of the males aged 21 or over sentenced for indecent assault on a woman at the Crown Court after a guilty plea received an immediate custodial sentence and 78% of those who were sentenced after a contested trial received an immediate custodial sentence. The average length of sentence was 25 months after a guilty plea and 25.6 months after a not guilty plea. Similar sentencing patterns emerge when considering males aged 21 or over sentenced at the Crown Court for indecent assault on a man – 69% of those who pleaded guilty and 85% of those who pleaded not guilty were given an immediate custodial sentence, the average sentence length being 35.9 months' imprisonment on a guilty plea and 30.6 months' imprisonment on a not guilty plea. Although a higher proportion of those who plead not guilty receive a custodial sentence, the average length of the sentence is similar following guilty and not guilty pleas and, in the case of indecent assault on a man, is lower following a not guilty plea. In the absence of further information about the offences involved, it is difficult to reconcile such statistics. One possibility is that a significant number of the guilty pleas arise from plea bargaining, whereby an offender may contest an allegation of rape or attempted rape, but agree to plead guilty to a lesser charge of indecent assault. Such cases would inevitably involve serious indecent assaults and, thus, attract a relatively heavy sentence.

4.159   When determining the appropriate sentence, the courts will take account of aggravating and mitigating factors in the same way as they do when sentencing for rape. For example, in *R v Kempster*,[3] the offender was a man of 47 years of age of previous good character who had pleaded guilty to two counts of indecent assault on a 9-year-old girl, who was the daughter of an acquaintance. The offences consisted of touching the child's vagina and masturbating in her presence. In reducing his sentence of 3 years' imprisonment to one of 2 years' imprisonment, the Court of Appeal noted several aggravating factors which made the case a serious one – the young age of the victim, the fact that the offender was in a position of trust and that the conduct continued over a relatively protracted period. However, the Court then noted a number of 'strongly mitigating' factors, namely the offender's age and previous good character, the circumstances in which he was living at home, his remorse, the fact that there had been no use of force or attempt at penetration and, the 'most important' mitigating factor, the guilty plea.

4.160   The use of violence is a strongly aggravating factor, particularly when combined with grossly indecent assaults, when the maximum sentence may be appropriate. In *R v Ragusa*,[4] the offender was convicted of indecent assault, false imprisonment and robbery. Having gained access to the home of the victim, he

---

1   *R v Lennon* (1999) 1 Cr App R (S) 19.
2   *Attorney-General's Reference (No 35 of 1994)* (1995) 16 Cr App R (S) 635.
3   (1986) 8 Cr App R (S) 74.
4   (1992) 14 Cr App R (S) 118.

threatened her with a knife, tied her up, removed her clothes and subjected her to various indecent assaults, including oral sex. The offender, who had a previous conviction for rape in comparable circumstances, was eventually convicted on the basis of DNA evidence and sentenced to 10 years' imprisonment for the indecent assault and 12 years concurrent for false imprisonment. In dismissing an appeal against sentence, the Court of Appeal noted that, whereas the 12-year sentence could be justified for the false imprisonment alone, there were also two separate gross indecent assaults, each of which carried a maximum of 10 years' imprisonment, and on the facts, the maximum sentence would be justified.

4.161 In *R v Wyne Sully*,[1] the offender pleaded guilty to two counts of indecent assault on a female and was sentenced to 7 years' imprisonment. He had previously been involved in an 8-year relationship with the victim of the assault, 6 years of which had included consensual sexual intercourse. Whilst working as a taxi driver, he drove the victim to an isolated place, threatened her with a knife, penetrated her vagina with an inanimate object and forced her to conduct oral sex on him. He had eight previous convictions, two of which were for violence but not of a sexual nature. In mitigation, it was suggested that the sentence was manifestly excessive in the circumstances, in that the victim was not a stranger to the offender. The Court of Appeal noted that the attack was prolonged and at knife point and considered that the fact that the offender had had a pre-existing relationship with the victim made no difference at all. In fact, the acts which were carried out by the offender were to be considered worse than if she had been raped. Overall, the sentence imposed was one which was entirely appropriate and the appeal was dismissed.

Indecency and non-custodial sentences

4.162 Where the indecency is not deemed to be significant, a non-custodial sentence may be appropriate. At one time, the Court of Appeal expressed the view that a sentence of imprisonment was wrong 'in principle' for an offender with no previous convictions for sexual offences who commits an indecent assault in a crowded public place, such as on a bus or train, by rubbing himself against the victim.[2] However, more recently, the Court indicated that it had been wrong to lay down such a principle and that it would be open to a sentencing court in its discretion to impose a custodial sentence for such an offence.[3] In *R v Williams*,[4] the offender approached a stewardess on a train as it was about to depart and squeezed her breast. The Court of Appeal concluded that, on the facts of the case, combined with the fact the offender was previously a man of good character and the offence had been a single incident of offensive behaviour, a custodial sentence was not called for. Instead, the sentencing court should have imposed a substantial fine, one which would hurt the offender's pocket and make him think twice about repeating such conduct.

---

1   28 April 1999, Court of Appeal.
2   *R v Neem* (1992) 14 Cr App R (S) 18 and *R v Chagan* (1994) 16 Cr App R (S) 15.
3   *R v Townsend* (1994) 16 Cr App R (S) 553 and *R v Tanyildiz* (1998) 1 Cr App R (S) 362.
4   (1992) 13 Cr App R (S) 671.

Chapter 5

SEX OFFENDERS IN PRISON

THE PRISON POPULATION

5.1   In recent years, the imposition of custodial sentences by the courts has increased steadily. Between 1992 and 1997, the Crown Courts increased the proportional use of custody from approximately 44% to 60%. During the same period, the average length of a custodial sentence imposed on an adult offender rose from 21 months to 24 months.[1] The overall effect of this has been a dramatic rise in the prison population. In 1901, the average prison population in England and Wales was 18,980. By 1946, this figure had dropped to 10,635, but 20 years later had risen to 33,086 in 1966. Since the 1966, the figure has continued to rise, except for a slight fall in 1991, and by 1998 stood at 65,298.[2] The number of male prisoners was greater in 1998 than at any time in the last 100 years, but the number of female prisoners was about the same as in 1901. The average prison population in 1998 included:[3]

(1) 41,620 sentenced adult male prisoners (7% increase on 1997);
(2) 8,170 sentenced male young offenders (8% increase on 1997);
(3) 12,570 remand prisoners of both sexes (4% increase on 1997); and
(4) 3,110 females (16% increase on 1997), including 700 on remand and 330 sentenced young offenders.

At the end of March 1999, the prison population had fallen to 64,200. This reduction is thought to be largely attributable to the introduction of the Home Detention Curfew at the end of January 1999.[4]

Sex offenders and the prison population

5.2   In 1998, sex offenders accounted for 10% of the adult prison population under sentence. The actual number of sex offenders in prison has increased steadily, from 2,692 in 1988 to 4,795 in 1998. The vast majority of these are males (there were 15 female sex offenders under sentence in 1988 and 16 in 1998). Between 1997 and 1998 there was a 14% increase in the number of male sex offenders under sentence – the greatest increase for any offence group.[5]

---

1   *HM Prison Service Annual Report and Accounts April 1997 to March 1998* (The Stationery Office, London, 1998).
2   *Prison Statistics* (1998) table 1(a).
3   *The Prison Population in 1998: A Statistical Review* Home Office Research Findings no 94 (Home Office, London, 1999).
4   *HM Prison Service Annual Report and Accounts April 1998 to March 1999* (The Stationery Office, London, 1999) p 22. See **5.67**.
5   *The Prison Population in 1998: A Statistical Review* (Home Office, London, 1999). In 1998 (but not in 1997) the number of sex offenders included prisoners held on breach of licence conditions following conditional or discretionary release. The estimated underlying rate of increase in the number of sex offenders held is 14%.

5.3   On 30 June 1998 there were 2,369 male offenders serving custodial sentences for rape and 2,410 serving custodial sentences for other sexual offences, giving a total of 4,779 male sex offenders under sentence. There were only four female offenders serving sentences for rape[1] and 12 serving sentences for other sexual offences.

THE CHALLENGES POSED BY SEX OFFENDERS

5.4   The Statement of Purpose of the Prison Service, adopted in 1988, states:

> 'Her Majesty's Prison Service serves the public by keeping in custody those committed by the courts. Our duty is to look after them with humanity and help them lead law-abiding and useful lives in custody and after release.'[2]

The steady increase in the prison population presents obvious challenges to the Prison Service. In 1997–98, 12.2% of the prison population was held in units of accommodation intended for fewer numbers.[3] By 1998–99, this figure had fallen to 10%.[4] Although these figures are below the target key performance indicator for the Prison Service of 13% and 12% respectively each year, overcrowding in prisons remains a serious cause for concern. The Prison Service has no control over the numbers it is required to accommodate and, assuming that trends in sentencing observed over the last 20 years continue, the projected prison population for the year 2000–01 is 72,600. Suitable accommodation will need to be provided for these prisoners and the Prison Service is currently struggling to increase the capacity of existing prisons and to find sites on which to build new prisons.[5]

5.5   Yet the numerical element of overcrowding is only one aspect of the problem. Prisoners cannot be locked in a cell for 24 hours a day, they need a constructive regime which includes opportunities for work, education and association, all of which require resources. The growth in the prison population is undoubtedly placing undue pressure on Prison Service staff, making their task of treating prisoners with humanity and helping them to lead law-abiding and useful lives increasingly difficult. The provision of adequate resources is, as ever, problematical. These factors led the Chief Inspector of Prisons in March 1998 to refer to a problem that was becoming out of control, saying that while the competing pressures of increasing numbers of prisoners versus decreasing

---

1   Although a female cannot commit rape as a principal, it is possible for a female to be convicted of rape as a secondary offender – for aiding, abetting, counselling or procuring the offence. See further Smith and Hogan *Criminal Law* (Butterworths, London, 1996) chap 7.
2   Statement of Purpose of Her Majesty's Prison Service.
3   *HM Prison Service Annual Reports and Accounts April 1997 to March 1998* (The Stationery Office, London, 1998) Key Performance Indicators.
4   *HM Prison Service Annual Reports and Accounts April 1998 to March 1999* (The Stationery Office, London, 1999) Key Performance Indicators.
5   *HM Prison Service Annual Reports and Accounts April 1997 to March 1998* (The Stationery Office, London, 1998) Section 2.

resources continued to apply, the Prison Service would remain locked into that spiral, not of its own making, the direction of which seemed ever downwards.[1]

5.6   Although sex offenders form a relatively small percentage of the overall prison population, they present a particular challenge over and above that presented by the general prison population. The challenge is two-fold. First, many sex offenders suffer hostility and aggression from other prisoners and steps have to be taken to ensure their safety. Secondly, it has been recognised in recent years that simply keeping sex offenders in custody does little to prevent them re-offending on release. If sex offenders are to lead law-abiding and useful lives on their release, work must be undertaken with them during their custodial term in an effort to change their attitudes and behaviour in order to minimise the chances of their re-offending on release.

'Looking after them with humanity' – protecting sex offenders inside prison

5.7   For many sex offenders, one of the worst aspects of being in prison is not so much the removal of their liberty, but the hostility and abuse they face from other prisoners. Sex offenders in the community face similar problems, as society tends to view them as the most hated and despised group of offenders. However, at least sex offenders in the community have control over their own movements to some extent and can take steps to avoid conflict, although not always successfully.[2] Sex offenders in prison have no such option – effectively, they are trapped. It has been suggested that in all prisons there is a 'pecking order' among the prisoners: murderers and bank robbers are at the top, the run-of-the-mill offenders are in the middle and sex offenders are at the bottom, with those who offend against children being at the lowest point.[3] Verbal abuse of sex offenders by other prisoner, taunts and humiliations are common place. More seriously, physical assaults are not uncommon, particularly on the paedophiles. Although the Home Office does not compile statistics of assaults on prisoners relating to the nature of the prisoner's offending behaviour, making it difficult to predict the extent of the problem accurately, there is sufficient evidence from the cases that do come to light and from the prisoners themselves to suggest that the problem is by no means insignificant. Certainly, when a riot erupts and the prisoners take control of a prison, their two immediate priorities are said to be to raid the pharmacy for drugs and to beat up the sex offenders.[4] The problem tends to be compounded by the fact that, on a personal level, many prison staff share the other prisoners' contempt for sex offenders and may be tempted to 'turn a blind eye' to abusive incidents. Furthermore, for practical reasons, some staff are thought to encourage the existence of the prison pecking-order in the belief that it makes prisoners easier to control and can give them a useful 'hold' over sex offenders, who are forced to rely on them for

---

1   *Report of Her Majesty's Chief Inspector of Prisons, April 1996–November 1997* (Home Office, London, 1998).

2   See **7.80** to **7.85**.

3   Sampson *Acts of Abuse: Sex Offenders and the Criminal Justice System* (Routledge, London, 1994) p 85.

4   See, for example, Woolf *The Inquiry into Prison Disturbances April 1990* (1991) Cmnd 1456.

protection.[1] Prison authorities owe a common law duty of care to prisoners to take reasonable care for their safety[2] and this duty extends to taking reasonable steps to prevent attacks by other prisoners. It is an acknowledged fact that known sex offenders are vulnerable in prison and the prison authorities must bear this in mind when dealing with such offenders. In *H v Home Office*[3] a prisoner was awarded damages after the negligent disclosure of his convictions for sexual offences led to him being assaulted by other prisoners, and in *Steele v Northern Ireland Office*[4] a prisoner accused of sexual offences recovered damages for an assault by other prisoners even though he had refused advice from the prison staff to be accommodated in a protective wing.

5.8   The traditional response of the prison authorities to these problems has been to segregate sex offenders from the main prison population, either by the use of the Prison Rules which allow for the removal of prisoners from association or, more recently, by placing the offenders in a Vulnerable Prisoners Unit (VPU).

Removal from association

5.9   Section 47 of the Prison Act 1952 empowers the Secretary of State to make rules for the regulation and management of prisons, and for the classification, treatment, employment, discipline and control of prisoners.[5] The Prison Rules, made pursuant to s 47 have, for many years, contained provision for the removal of certain prisoners from association. Between 1964 and 1999, the relevant provision was to be found in r 43, and it became common practice to refer to a prisoner who had been segregated from the general prison population as being 'on rule 43'. The provision is now to be found in r 45 of the most recent Prison Rules, which are effective from 1 April 1999.[6] The content of the first two subparagraphs of the rule are identical to the provisions of the old r 43. Rule 45 provides as follows.

(1) Where it appears desirable, for the maintenance of good order or discipline or in his own interests, that a prisoner should not associate with other prisoners, either generally or for particular purposes, the governor may arrange for the prisoner's removal from association accordingly.

(2) A prisoner shall not be removed under this rule for a period of more than 3 days without the authority of a member of the board of visitors or of the Secretary of State. An authority given under this paragraph shall be for a period not exceeding one month, but may be renewed from month to month except that, in the case of a person aged less than 21 years who is detained in prison such an authority shall be for a period not exceeding 14 days, but may be renewed from time to time for a like period.

---

1   Sampson *Acts of Abuse: Sex Offenders and the Criminal Justice System* (Routledge, London, 1994) p 87.
2   *Ellis v Home Office* [1953] All ER 149.
3   (1992) *The Independent,* 6 May.
4   (1988) 12 NIJB 1.
5   By virtue of s 52(1) of the Prison Act 1952, rules made pursuant to s 47 of the Act are made by statutory instrument and are subject to the negative resolution procedure.
6   Prison Rules 1999, SI 1999/728.

(3) The governor may arrange at his discretion for such a prisoner as aforesaid to resume association with other prisoners, and shall do so if in any case the medical officer or a medical practitioner such as is mentioned in r 20(3) so advises on medical grounds.

(4) This rule shall not apply to a prisoner the subject of a direction given under r 46(1).[1]

5.10 The principal criticism of the rule is that it can be used to deal with two very different situations: to segregate and control prisoners who are likely to have an adverse effect on good order and discipline and to protect prisoners who are vulnerable to attack and therefore need to be separated for their own protection. As the Report of the Inquiry into Prison Disturbances pointed out, what the prison establishment should be seeking to achieve in relation to the two categories is quite different. In the case of the prisoner separated for reasons of good order and discipline, the removal from association needs to be fairly strictly imposed if the object of the exercise is to be achieved. However, in the case of the vulnerable prisoner, it is accepted that any more separation than is necessary to protect the prisoner is undesirable and the object from the start should be to return the prisoner to association if this is possible.[2]

5.11 Conditions and regimes for all prisoners subject to the rule tend to be intolerably poor,[3] but the use of the rule to protect vulnerable prisoners such as sex offenders has attracted specific criticism. In 1989 a Report by the Prison Service on the Management of Vulnerable Prisoners[4] acknowledged that being 'on the rule' for their own protection was undesirable for prisoners, whether convicted or unconvicted. Being 'on the rule' deprived them of normal association, it could prevent access to facilities for work, recreation and education and it kept a prisoner's offence at the forefront of the minds of those whose had to make assessments of him. In short, being 'on the rule' had become a stigma and the only real benefit derived was the physical protection from assault or intimidation. Further concerns have been voiced about the potential effect of grouping sex offenders together under the rule, which is said to offer reinforcement in the form of opportunities for further sexual excitement and sharing of their sexual experiences.[5] This problem is thought to be particularly acute for those who offend against children. Paedophile information is freely exchanged in some prisons and being 'on the rule' is said to foster the development of rings of sexual abusers – rings which sometimes survive beyond

---

1 Rule 46(1) allows the Secretary of State to direct a prisoner's removal from association and his placement in a close supervision centre of a prison, where it appears necessary for the maintenance of good order or discipline or to ensure the safety of officers, prisoners or any other person. Close Supervision Centres are designed to contain persistently disruptive prisoners and secure their return to a settled and acceptable pattern of behaviour.

2 Woolf *The Inquiry into Prison Disturbances April 1990* (1991) Cmnd 1456, para 12.196.

3 See 'Life "on the Rule"' in Sampson *Acts of Abuse: Sex Offenders and the Criminal Justice System* (Routledge, London, 1994) pp 90 et seq.

4 *Report of the Working Party on the Management of Vulnerable Prisoners*, Home Office Internal Document (Home Office, London, 1989).

5 Glaser and Spencer 'Sentencing, Children's Evidence and Children's Trauma' [1990] Crim LR 371 at 380.

the prison landings.[1] In the past, court transcripts from sex abuse cases have been circulated in prison as pornography. In an attempt to address this particular problem, Parliament passed the Sexual Offences (Protected Material) Act 1997 which seeks to regulate access by defendants to certain categories of material in proceedings relating to sexual offences.[2] The Act is not yet in force, but, in any event there are obviously many other sources of pornographic material, access to which cannot be so easily regulated.

The demise of r 43 for sex offenders

5.12   In 1990 the Prison Reform Trust recommended that the Home Office should expand initiatives which encourage integration of sex offenders and non-sex offenders in a properly structured environment, with the ultimate aim being the eventual disappearance of the rule.[3] In giving evidence to the Inquiry into Prison Disturbances, the National Association of Probation Officers suggested that the existence of the rule may be institutionalising and perpetuating the persecution of sex offenders as it provides many prisoners with a legitimised target for venting their frustration and anger, and concluded that what was needed ultimately was the political will to abolish the rule.[4] The Report of the Inquiry recommended that the rule should be amended so that there was no longer reference to removal from association in the prisoner's own interests and proposed an additional rule to deal specifically with the position of vulnerable prisoners such as sex offenders. It was suggested that the new rule would seek to achieve three purposes:

(1) it would place an obligation upon the governor of an establishment to take such reasonable steps as he considers necessary for the protection of prisoners whom he considers are vulnerable to attack from other prisoners;
(2) it would authorise the governor to remove from association, only to the extent which is reasonable, a prisoner who needs protection; and
(3) it would make the exercise of the second purpose for which the rule is provided subject to the same safeguards as are now contained in r 45(2).

5.13   This recommendation has not been followed and r 45 of the 1999 Rules continues to make reference to removal from association in the prisoner's own interests. However, in recent years the number of sex offenders removed from association under the rule has decreased dramatically. In 1989, there were 2,438 prisoners on r 43 for their own protection. By 1995, although the prison population had increased significantly, the number of prisoners on the rule for their own protection had fallen to 905. Although the statistics do not specify how many of those on the rule were sex offenders, it is acknowledged to be a large proportion.[5] In 1996, although the relevant chapter heading in the index of the prison statistics continued to refer to the 'Segregated inmates', the actual chapter referred only to 'Restraints and special cells' and contained no

---

1   Sampson *Acts of Abuse: Sex Offenders and the Criminal Justice System* (Routledge, London, 1994) p 92.
2   See **3.81**.
3   *Sex Offenders in Prison* (Prison Reform Trust, London, 1990) p 23.
4   Woolf *The Inquiry into Prison Disturbances April 1990* (1991) Cmnd 1456, para 12.198.
5   Sampson *Acts of Abuse: Sex Offenders and the Criminal Justice System* (Routledge, London, 1994) p 88.

information on the number of prisoners on the rule. By 1997, all reference to segregated inmates had disappeared from the official statistics. However, this does not mean that sex offenders are no longer segregated from the general prison population. In the late 1980s, as the number of prisoners 'on the rule' for their own protection reached a peak, a concerted effort was made to reduce the number of prisoners seeking the protection of the rule. Following the recommendations of the Management of Vulnerable Prisoners Working Party in 1989, prison governors were encouraged to make greater use of their powers to refuse a prisoner's request for protection under the rule, and some prisons have had considerable success in integrating sex offenders into the prison population.[1] However, some care does need to be taken with such an approach. Inevitably, there will be some sex offenders who will continue to need protection and who will be unable to survive on normal location. Furthermore, in 1998 an evaluation of the Sex Offender Treatment Programme (SOTP)[2] found evidence that normal location encouraged rapists to maintain denial and avoid treatment. The study recommended that all rapists (except those with high psychopathy scores) should be placed in VPUs or their equivalent.

Vulnerable prisoner units

5.14   Among the concerns about the use of r 43 to protect prisoners were the restrictions placed on prisoners subject to the rule, who were often denied access to the facilities available to other prisoners. Although such restrictions may be justified for short periods, many sex offenders are medium- or long-term prisoners who may require segregation for the entire custodial period. The development of VPUs aimed to provide a protected environment for these prisoners, without the need for the controls and resulting restrictions provided by the rule and where prisoners can have a regime comparable with that available to other prisoners. In 1994 nearly 2,000 prisoners were held in VPUs. This number had more than doubled by the following year, when over 4,000 prisoners were held in VPUs. Of course, whilst the development of VPUs at least removed the controls and restraints on ordinary prison life which were imposed by r 43, it did nothing to tackle the problem of grouping sex offenders together with the associated risk of increasing the likelihood of re-offending on release. The development of VPUs is closely connected with moves in recent years to meet the second challenge faced by the Prison Service: helping prisoners to lead law-abiding and useful lives.

'Helping them to lead law abiding and useful lives'

5.15   Whereas the responsibility for meeting the challenge of protecting of sex offenders in prison rests solely with the Prison Service, the Service has been assisted in meeting the second challenge by the increasingly close working relationship that has been developed with the Probation Service. Probation officers now play a central role in many aspects of the care of offenders whilst in custody, including input into sentence planning, the running of treatment

---

1   Circular Instruction 26/90. See Sampson *Acts of Abuse: Sex Offenders and the Criminal Justice System* (Routledge, London, 1994) p 95.

2   See **5.37**.

programmes for specific groups of offenders, such as sex offenders, and making a major contribution to the exercise of risk assessment that is crucial to the determination of when an offender will be released into the community.

The concept of 'throughcare' and the role of the Probation Service

5.16   The Probation Service is the major organisation in England and Wales for dealing with offenders in conditions of freedom[1] and for the first half of the 20th century the Service was reluctant to become involved with the custody-based activities with offenders, which were seen as being the responsibility of the Prison Service. It was not until the 1960s that the concept of 'throughcare' first came to be taken seriously and the work of the Prison Service and the Probation Service began to be integrated.[2] As the name suggests, 'throughcare' is based on the idea of continuity between work done with offenders inside prison to prepare them for release and the work done with them by probation officers after release. In an effort to secure effective throughcare procedures, probation officers began to be seconded to prisons to perform a welfare role and to prepare offenders for release. The introduction of parole in 1968[3] resulted in probation officers taking a major role in the preparation of reports for the Parole Board as well as supervising in the community the offenders released on parole. Although the concept of throughcare became more prominent in the 1970s, it saw a decline in the 1980s. However, the 1990s saw increasing emphasis being placed on throughcare and the role of probation officers within prisons once again assumed importance.

The introduction of sentence planning and moves towards a closer working relationship

5.17   The new sentencing and parole arrangements introduced by the Criminal Justice Act 1991 incorporated both custodial and community-based elements, and 'sentence planning' became a central feature of work with prisoners. Sentence planning has its origins in the practice of allocating training and work activities to life sentence prisoners according to individual need. The underlying idea is to provide clear guidance on the programmes and activities most suitable to a prisoner's needs. It provides opportunities to review the prisoner's progress throughout the sentence and it is also the mechanism for co-ordinating work done in prison with work done with prisoners following release.[4] In 1989 a formal system of sentence planning was introduced for young offenders and, by 1993, the system had been extended for all prisoners sentenced to 12 months' imprisonment or more.

5.18   The introduction of sentence planning called for even greater co-operation between the Prison Service and Probation Service than had previously existed and, in 1993, the Home Office issued the National Framework for the

---

1   Worrall *Punishment in the Community: The Future of Criminal Justice* (Longman, London, 1997) p 63 and see further chap 6.
2   *Automatic Conditional Release: The First Two Years* Home Office Research Study 156 (1996) p 3.
3   See **5.62**.
4   *Prison Service Annual Report for 1992/93*.

Throughcare of Offenders in Custody to the Completion of Supervision in the Community. At the end of 1995, there were 659 probation officers seconded to work in prisons, representing 8.4% of all probation officers, although by the end of 1996 these figures had fallen to 561 and 7.2%, despite the rising workload.[1] In April 1999, for the first time, a prison officer commenced a 2-year secondment with the West Midlands Probation Service as Assistant Chief Probation Officer,[2] thus making secondment a two-way process. However, the relationship between the two services has not been without its problems. In 1995, a joint report by the Prison Service and the Probation Service found that, although the theory behind sentence planning was a sound one, there were major structural problems with the way it had been implemented. In particular, it was said that a great deal still needed to be done to achieve the effective working relationship between the Prison and Probation Services on which sentence planning depends.[3] Similar problems became apparent in a thematic inspection by HM Inspectorate of Probation in 1998, when it was found that, in a sample of approximately 180 cases, there was no sentence plan on file for 28% of those offenders. The supervising probation officer had actively contributed to the plan in 24% of cases, had been consulted in 6% and apparently had not been consulted in 14%, and it was unclear what had happened in the remaining 28%.[4] In an effort to improve these working relationships, in 1997 the Home Secretary announced a ministerial review to look at ways in which the better integration of the two services could improve their efficiency and performance.

THE PRISONS–PROBATION REVIEW
5.19   The terms of reference of the Review were:

(1)   to identify and assess options for closer and more integrated work between the Prison Service and the Probation Service of England and Wales, including any implications for the structure, organisation, management, working practices, human resources, funding and legislation governing the functions of those services;
(2)   to examine international models reflecting good practice and to identify any lessons concerning the effectiveness, efficiency, organisation and management structures exhibited by those models; and
(3)   to provide a preliminary analysis of the options identified, including the estimated costs and benefits, as a basis for consultation.

5.20   In considering options for change, the Review decided that the options should seek to reduce re-offending, improve public protection, increase public confidence in community punishments imposed on offenders, whether as part of a prison sentence or as a community sentence, and increase the cost-effectiveness of programmes and their management. The Review identified four groups of options. The first – the 'zero plus' option – identified a change programme which involved a package of improvements to joint working of the two services and which could be implemented without structural change.

---

1   *Prisons/Probation Review: Final Report* (Home Office, London, 1998) para 3.3.
2   *Prison Service News* 12 April 1999.
3   Flynn *Introduction to Prisons and Imprisonment* (Waterside Press, Winchester, 1998) p 119.
4   *Exercising Constant Vigilance: The Role of the Probation Service in Protecting the Public from Sex Offenders* (HM Inspectorate of Probation, Home Office, 1998) para 4.36.

The remaining three options involved structural changes aimed at increasing the likely effectiveness of the change programme and organisational efficiency in the use of resources, either by aligning the services' boundaries with police force areas, or by restructuring on a regional or national basis. Overall, the Review concluded that the two services should remain separate, but that their structures should be harmonised, particularly in terms of boundaries and accountability. It was recommended that the zero plus option should be acted upon without delay, as progress did not depend on structural change. The proposals for structural change would require further consultation, but the Review concluded that a consultation document could be published in time to enable decisions to be taken to inform the 1999–2000 legislative programme.

NON-STRUCTURAL CHANGE – THE 'ZERO PLUS' OPTION
5.21   The essential components of the recommended package of improvements to the joint working of the two services without the need for structural change are as follows.

A national policy framework
5.22   The establishment of a national 'corrections' policy framework would set out the Government's main priorities, high and consistent national standards of delivery, and a timetables change agenda to achieve these.

Shared aims and objectives
5.23   A joint statement of shared aims and objectives by the senior management of both services, agreed with the Government, must be the starting point from which new planning arrangements involving both services will flow.

Names, language and terminology
5.24   It is important that the names, language and terminology used by the services should give accurate and accessible messages about the nature and aims of their work. On the probation side, some of the terms used have been criticised as being associated with tolerance of crime ('probation'), capable of being misunderstood ('community service'), and being too esoteric to be understood outside the two services ('throughcare'). Alternative names for the Probation Service include use of the terms 'corrections', 'protection', 'enforcement' and/or 'offender risk management' service or agency. A public consultation process should be used to test attitudes to these options.[1]

Joint strategic planning, linked training and job exchanges
5.25   Integrated planning and delivery in some, though not all, aspects of both services' work is required. The relevant areas are likely to include:

(1) matching offender behaviour and treatment programmes, common policy on selection, content, quality, training of staff and with refresher programmes continuing after release;

---

1   The Government subsequently announced its intention to change the name of the Probation Service to the Community Punishment and Rehabilitation Service. See **6.10**.

(2) an agreed offender resettlement programme, with common policy, standards etc;

(3) common training for both services, possibly jointly delivered, possibly joint standards audit and inspection in some areas, staff interchanges; and

(4) collaboration in resettlement, possibly along the lines of 'half-way houses', possibly involving other services in the independent sector as well.

Planning forums
5.26 A forum should be established in which the Home Office, including the Prison Service and Probation Service:

(1) meet, identify and agree what elements of the services they need to plan together;

(2) agree representation at national levels;

(3) develop plans and performance targets and standards;

(4) agree what respective resource contributions are necessary;

(5) resolve timing issues with regard to the planning cycle; and

(6) agree means of performance management (ie monitoring delivery and responding effectively to non-performance as it becomes evident).

National standards for joint work
5.27 Coverage of joint work with offenders by the Prison and Probation Services during their period in custody is minimal. A set of common national standards must be developed, covering areas of joint working, particularly sentence planning and pre-release resettlement work.

Joint inspection arrangements
5.28 The responsibilities of the Prisons and Probation Inspectorates differ fundamentally and, although there would be advantages to amalgamating the two to create a joint inspectorate, these advantages could to some extent also be achieved by closer integration of the two inspectorates and greater use of jointly planned inspections. The two inspectorates should develop further the arrangements for shared/joint inspection already established, by developing a joint approach to inspecting resettlement programmes/sentence management/risk and offender programmes, whether delivered in the prison or on release. Joint inspections should be arranged systematically as part of an annual programme.

Effective management of offender programmes
5.29 This should include:

(1) common approaches to accreditation of offender programmes, which need not necessarily be identical, but should be based on the same fundamental principles;

(2) common approaches and techniques for risk assessment and risk management based on agreed principles – a major step forward would be the adoption by all Probation Services and the Prison Service of a single assessment tool for assessing the risk of re-offending, and the training of staff in the use of this tool;[1] and

---

1   See **6.30**.

(3)	the maintenance of a positive and open attitude to information sharing which views public and staff protection as an over-riding priority and, where needed, the establishment of well-defined protocols for information sharing.[1]

Better information sharing and use of information technology

5.30	Efficient and effective data exchange is vital to a more integrated approach to joint working. The Case Records Administration and Management System used by the QUANTUM systems of the Probation Service and the Prison Service must be compatible with the police PHOENIX system, and the technical and business requirements relating to links between all three systems need to be established as quickly as possible.

Prisons and probation – towards a national 'corrections' service?

5.31	Adoption of the zero plus recommendations would continue the trend in recent years for the Prison Service and the Probation Service to work together closely. It also reflects the changing role of the Probation Service over the last few decades as the use and status of the Probation Order has undergone a radical transformation alongside the emergence of punishment in the community.[2] Arguably, the logical conclusion of this trend may be the amalgamation of the two services to form one national 'corrections' agency. The time has not yet come for such a giant step to be taken. The Prisons/Probation Review concluded that a full merger of the two services would require further study before it could be embarked upon with confidence, but that some separation at an operational level would continue to be necessary.[3] Although the area of joint interest between the two services is significant, and the needs of the two services overlap, they are not identical. Closer working relationships are to be encouraged as the extensive experience of the Probation Service in dealing with offenders in the community, accumulated over many decades, is of incalculable assistance to the Prison Service in 'helping prisoners to lead law-abiding and useful lives' and the Probation Service will continue to play a significant role in assisting the Prison Service in achieving this aim. However, it will, and indeed, should, remain an independent organisation for the foreseeable future.

The provision of treatment within prison

5.32	Whereas the need to protect sex offenders in prison has been acknowledged for many years, the desirability of providing some form of treatment for them whilst in prison has only been acknowledged recently. In fact, no Prison Service document mentioned issues relating to treatment prior to the publication in 1991 of the Report of the Inquiry into Prison Disturbances.[4] A number of different reasons have been advanced for the failure to address treatment issues in the 1980s. One major reason was thought to be the

---

1	See further **7.74**.
2	See further **6.9**.
3	*Prisons/Probation Review: Final Report* (Home Office, London, 1998) para 2.3.
4	Sampson *Acts of Abuse: Sex Offenders and the Criminal Justice System* (Routledge, London, 1994) p 100.

management structure of the Home Office, which was said to impede the development of a coherent policy on sex offenders. In 1990, the Prison Reform Trust noted that, according to one senior Home Office civil servant, a memorandum on the subject had to be circulated to 13 different people, none of whom had overall responsibility.[1] Another reason advanced was the structural problem underlying the British prison system. It has been argued that the increase in the prison population during the 1970s and 1980s, the crumbling buildings and degrading physical conditions, the grumbling industrial relations unrest and the series of riots and disturbances all made it almost impossible to effect the sort of strategic planning necessary to implement a coherent response to sex offending.[2]

5.33   However, perhaps the most important underlying reason was the demise of the rehabilitative ideal, which, until the late 1960s, had been the dominant principle of criminal justice. For many years, there have been claims and counter-claims concerning the overall purpose of imprisonment. During the 1960s, there had been increased reliance on rehabilitation, with the establishment of institutions with a 'therapeutic' ethos, such as Grendon Prison, which was opened in 1962. However, the 1970s brought disillusionment with the rehabilitative ideal. In 1974, research suggested that the rehabilitative efforts had had no appreciable effect on recidivism, leading to the conclusion that 'nothing works' in prison to influence offenders away from a life of crime.[3] Despite the fact that this research has now been discredited, at the time it was influential in supporting the trend away from reliance on rehabilitation.

5.34   In 1979, following a deterioration in industrial relations in prisons, a Committee of Inquiry into the UK Prison Services was convened.[4] The Committee concluded that prison staff had become disillusioned about the treatment objectives of imprisonment and argued that the rhetoric of teaching and training had had its day and should be replaced with 'positive custody', ie the principal purpose of work, education, physical exercise and other activities would no longer be to attempt to influence the behaviour of prisoners, but would simply be to keep them occupied and maintain their physical and mental well-being.

5.35   It was only towards the end of the 1980s that renewed interest was expressed in the rehabilitation of offenders and attention began to be focused on the desirability of providing therapeutic regimes for prisoners, particularly sex offenders. Research in the USA and Canada had begun to show that therapeutic work with sex offenders could produce positive changes in attitude, thereby reducing sexual recidivism.[5] In 1990, the Prison Reform Trust reported that similar results had been obtained from various initiatives inside the British

---

1   *Sex Offenders in Prison* (Prison Reform Trust, London, 1990) p 27.
2   Sampson *Acts of Abuse: Sex Offenders and the Criminal Justice System* (Routledge, London, 1994) p 100.
3   Martinson *What Works? Questions and Answers about Prison Reform* (1974) quoted in Flynn *Introduction to Prisons and Imprisonment* (Waterside Press, Winchester, 1998) p 108.
4   Committee of Inquiry into the United Kingdom Prison Service Cmnd 7673 (HMSO, London, 1979).
5   Barbaree et al *The Assessment and Treatment of the Adult Male Sex Offender – An Annotated Bibliography* (Ontario, 1988).

prison system.[1] However, these initiatives were being developed in a piecemeal fashion. A thematic inspection undertaken in 1990 by HM Inspectorate of Probation on the work of the Probation Service with sex offenders found that such opportunities as existed for work with sex offenders in prison had initially been instituted and developed as a result of individual interest and commitment rather than as a programme determined and promoted by management, and that there was concern from the staff involved about the limits of their knowledge and skill.[2] The Prison Reform Trust recommended that the Home Office should develop a coherent and integrated policy to meet the needs of sex offenders in prison, including the provision of suitable facilities to address their offending behaviour. The Trust pointed out that this was not to advocate that offenders should be sent to prison to be rehabilitated. Rather, it was said that to demand specialist facilities in prison was to recognise two things: first that their experiences in prison could and did have an effect on people (whether positive or negative); and, secondly, that there were techniques that may have some positive impact on people's attitudes or behaviour.[3] Following reorganis-ation of the Prison Service, a Director of Inmate Programmes was appointed, resulting in the responsibility for the treatment of sex offenders at last resting in a single department. A conference of prison staff working with sex offenders was organised in early 1991, when a call was made for increased coordination and co-operation between the various agencies involved in initiatives with sex offenders. [4] The issue of treatment was again referred to in the Report of the Inquiry into Prison Disturbances. The Report recognised that when sex offenders were subjected to assaults or worse, this made them feel, with justification, that they were the victims and focused their attention on their own condition and away from what they had done to *their* victims.[5] The Report stressed that sex offenders should be required to confront their criminal conduct and need to be assisted to avoid offending again. It concluded that, if the Prison Service was to be true to its Statement of Purpose, it had to place greater emphasis on the need to make therapy available.[6]

5.36   In response to these pressure, in June 1991, Kenneth Baker, the then Home Secretary, announced a new initiative for the treatment of sex offenders in prison – the SOTP.

THE SEX OFFENDER TREATMENT PROGRAMME[7]

Availability and eligibility
5.37   The programme is offered on a voluntary basis to all male prisoners convicted of a sexual offence or a violent offence with a sexual element, who are

---

1   *Sex Offenders in Prison* (Prison Reform Trust, London, 1990) p 26.
2   HM Inspectorate of Probation *The Work of the Probation Service with Sex Offenders* (Home Office, London, 1991) paras 6.11 and 6.15.
3   *Sex Offenders in Prison* (Prison Reform Trust, London, 1990) p 25.
4   See Sampson *Acts of Abuse: Sex Offenders and the Criminal Justice System* (Routledge, London, 1994) p 105.
5   Woolf *The Inquiry into Prison Disturbances April 1990* (1991) Cmnd 1456, para 12.215.
6   Woolf *The Inquiry into Prison Disturbances April 1990* (1991) Cmnd 1456, para 12.220.
7   The following details are taken from Beech et al *STEP 3: An Evaluation of the Prison Sex Offender Treatment Programme* (Home Office, London, 1999).

serving a long enough sentence to enable them to complete the programme. The initial strategy was based upon giving priority to prisoners serving 4 years or more. By 1992, it was evident that a lack of resources was placing considerable stress on the programme and priority was given to those serving from 7 years' imprisonment to life imprisonment, although it was hoped that a significant proportion of those serving over 4 years would have the opportunity to take part in the programme. Those serving less than 4 years were only to be admitted to the programme if they were a particularly high risk. However, by 1998, the advent of 'fast tracking' (running more sessions in a shorter period of time) made it possible to include more prisoners on shorter sentences, and men serving sentences of 2 or 3 years are now eligible if they have time to complete the programme. Where a prison has more eligible prisoners than treatment places available, priority is based on risk of re-offending, seriousness of offences, proximity to release and likely response to treatment. The Prison Service has sought to concentrate sex offenders in a limited number of prisons where resources can be built up and expertise developed. Originally, the SOTP was set up in 14 prisons, but by 1998 this had increased to 25 prisons, with approximately 600 offenders being treated each year as part of the programme. In 1998–99 the Key Performance Indicator target for prisoners completing the SOTP was 680. In 1997–98 nearly 700 programmes were completed, but this figure had fallen to 589 in 1998–99.[1] The target figure set for 2001–02 is 1,100. Clearly, more resources will be needed if this target is to be achieved. Prison establishments running the SOTP are subject to accreditation by an international panel of experts.

Cognitive-behavioural group therapy
5.38 The SOTP is based on structured group work, with some work with individual prisoners being undertaken where necessary. The treatment approach used is 'cognitive-behavioural'. The 'cognitive' aspect involves recognising the patterns of distorted thinking which allow the contemplation of illegal sexual acts and understanding the impact which sexually abusive behaviour has on its victims; and the 'behavioural' component involves reducing sexual arousal to inappropriate fantasies of forced sexual activity with children and adults. The treatment group works through a series of exercises defined by a detailed treatment manual.

Staffing
5.39 A treatment team of three members of staff, known as 'tutors', work with a group of eight offenders. Generally, two tutors run each session and the third acts as a back-up when needed. The treatment teams are made up of a mixture of staff, such as probation officers, teachers, psychologists, chaplains and prison officers, although prison officers form the largest group. All tutors are subject to a careful selection procedure which takes into account personality, attitude and ability to relate to and carry credibility with offenders. Potential tutors are assessed on a range of competencies, including understanding of cognitive-behavioural theory and concepts; application of cognitive-behavioural

---

1   *HM Prison Service Annual Report and Accounts April 1998 to March 1999* (The Stationery Office, London, 1999) p 9.

techniques; warmth and empathy; impartiality; clear use of language; flexibility of style; discussion-leading and presentation skills; team-working; agenda skills; skills for giving feedback; questioning skills; maintenance of boundaries; tenacity; professionalism; preparation; participation and open, coping style; and openness to feedback. Tutors must complete the national training course for the programme, which is a 2-week intensive residential course, and are also expected to attend additional update courses on specific topics.

Supervision

5.40 The treatment teams work under the supervision of a management team, which is comprised of a programme manager (responsible for the availability of staff, prisoners and facilities as well as associated practical issues), a treatment manager (responsible for assessment issues and for ensuring that the programme runs properly), and a throughcare manager (responsible for the interface between the programme and the Probation Service involved with the offenders in the group).

Components of the SOTP

5.41 The SOTP is made up of four components: the core programme, the extended programme, the booster programme and the thinking skills programme. The essential features of each component, as operated in November 1998, have been summarised as follows by the Sex Offender Treatment Evaluation Project Team.[1]

THE CORE PROGRAMME

5.42 The original programme comprised 35–40 2-hour sessions, but has been revised and expanded so that the programme now comprises a total of around 86 sessions and generally provides well over 160 treatment hours.[2] The revised programme began implementation in late 1994.

5.43 The primary purposes of the core programme are to increase the offender's motivation to avoid re-offending and to develop the self-management skills necessary to achieve this. Motivation is developed by undermining the excuses and rationalisations (cognitive distortions) that offenders use to justify their offending, increasing empathy with their victims by creating an emotional awareness of the victim's experience of the offence, and by examining the consequences of offending on their own lives. Self-management skills are increased by developing the offender's awareness of the behaviours, thoughts, feelings and situations that increase the likelihood of re-offending; and by teaching effective and realistic strategies to avoid or control these risk factors. This is generally known as 'relapse prevention'.

5.44 The programme is divided into 20 blocks, which cover each of the target areas in detail. The key areas are as follows.

---

1   Beech et al *STEP 3: An Evaluation of the Prison Sex Offender Treatment Programme* (Home Office, London, 1999) para 1.2.

2   Apart from treatment length, the key differences between the original and revised programmes were the inclusion of victim empathy work and the improvement of relapse prevention in the revised programme.

(1) Minimisation: given the tendency for sex offenders to deny or minimise aspects of their offending, it is important to encourage the offender to take responsibility for his behaviour, to recognise the harm caused to his victim and to get him to recognise that he is making excuses to justify his offending.

(2) Distortions: the distorted thinking used by the offender to justify and excuse the offence behaviour is identified and challenged, so that the individual can recognise and acknowledge the distortions for what they are.

(3) Victim empathy: an important deficit in sex offenders is their inability to empathise with their victim(s). Developing victim empathy is a central component of the cognitive-behavioural treatment programmes, the basic tenet being that if offenders have empathy with their victims, this will have an inhibitory effect upon their motivation to offend.

(4) Risk factor awareness: although offenders may become strongly motivated not to re-offend, this alone is probably insufficient to prevent further offending. The individual needs to become aware of the factors such as mood, thoughts, feelings and situations that led to previous offending.

(5) Coping strategies: having developed an awareness of the factors associated with re-offending, the individual then needs to develop strategies that will enable him to cope effectively with these 'risk factors'. It is important that these strategies are developed and practised in advance, so that the offender can employ them in stressful situations where he may be most vulnerable to relapse.

(6) Coping skills: the effectiveness of coping strategies may rely on the various skills of the offender. Therefore, treatment must focus on developing and strengthening such skills that are relevant to the relapse-prevention strategies.

(7) Maintenance: it is recognised that maintaining treatment progress is vital and is best achieved by having some form of maintenance programme once the main treatment programme is completed. Further treatment, support meetings and reviews of the relapse-prevention plan are suggested as being possible methods of maintenance according to the needs of the offender. Following completion of the core programme, individuals who remain in prison may participate in other treatment programmes and may obtain some form of support by keeping in contact with tutors. Those serving long sentences may attend the booster programme in the year prior to their release. Once in the community, maintenance depends on whether or not they are on parole and have a suitable programme to attend.[1]

5.45 In addition to the key treatment areas covered by the modules, the act of attending a group has an impact upon the individual due to the effect of the group processes that occur. Groups offer a forum for support and sharing problems which may be a completely new experience for many offenders, who are generally isolated individuals, often with interpersonal deficits and feelings of inadequacy. Having the experience of being valued, being able to help others, practising social skills and getting to know others in detail can improve greatly an individual's self-esteem and interpersonal functioning. Given that feelings of

---

1   See further **6.60** to **6.61**.

inadequacy and lack of appropriate relationships may be important vulnerability factors for many sex offenders, improvement in these areas may be significant in reducing the risk of re-offending.

THE EXTENDED PROGRAMME
5.46 This was always intended for offenders who had completed the core programme, but who still required further work in other areas. Originally, it was planned to involve four modules: anger management, relationship skills, fantasy modification, and further work on victim empathy and relapse prevention. The relationship skills module was produced and run by a few prisons, and other prisons have undertaken fantasy modification with individual prisons when needed. However, more recently, it was decided to convert all these modules into one full-length treatment programme.

THE BOOSTER PROGRAMME
5.47 This is intended for individuals serving long sentences who may already have completed the core programme and who will benefit from the programme being reinforced shortly before their release. Generally, it involves 60 hours of treatment, but varies according to the needs of the individuals. Its main function is to develop a realistic release and relapse-prevention plan.

THE THINKING SKILLS PROGRAMME
5.48 This programme is designed to address repeated failures in coping with the problems of everyday life which may be an important factor in producing the low-mood states which are frequently an important precursor to offending. In particular, it aims to improve the range of skills needed for effective problem-solving and decision-making (encouraging offenders to think through the consequences of their actions, to look for and consider possible alternative strategies, and to anticipate the reaction of others), and also teaches the productive ways of coping when their attempts at problem-solving do not succeed. Completion of the programme enables offenders to benefit more from subsequent treatment. The programme involves about 50 hours of treatment time.

An evaluation of the Sex Offender Treatment Programme
5.49 In 1991, the Home Office commissioned a group of forensic clinical psychologists as part of a Sex Offender Treatment Evaluation Project (STEP). Following an evaluation of community-based programmes,[1] in 1994 the STEP team commenced an evaluation of the prison SOTP and reported its findings in November 1998.

5.50 The study examined 12 treatment groups, two in each of six prisons. Comprehensive psychometric data were gathered on approximately 100 men prior to treatment. Eighty-two of these men were child abusers and so most of the analyses in the report focus specifically on this group of offenders. (The evaluation report noted that previous research had shown that a greater number of imprisoned rapists, as opposed to child abusers, are in denial, and are

---

1   Beckett et al *Community-based Treatment for Sex Offenders: An Evaluation of Seven Treatment Programmes* (Home Office, London, 1994).

probably less inclined to elect for treatment – engaging rapists in treatment is an issue which merits further attention.[1]) Seventy-seven of the 82 child abusers were seen at the end of the treatment programme, when further psychometric data was gathered and interviews were conducted with the men. The study also included a 9-month follow-up, with further psychometric testing and interviewing of 56 of the original sample. Approximately 40% of the men had left prison by the time of the follow-up, allowing comparisons to be made between those still in prison and those released into the community.

PSYCHOMETRIC TESTING

5.51 The psychometric tests administered before and after treatment were designed to measure change in four main areas.[2]

(1) Denial/admittance of deviant sexual interests and level of offending behaviours: scales here measured the offender's readiness to admit sexual fantasising and manipulations of his victim (sex deviance admittance); level of claimed normal sex drives and interests (social sexual desirability); readiness to deny his offending behaviours and the harm done to the victim (sex offence admittance); and level of denial of deviant sexual interests (lie scale) and sexual obsessions (obsessions).

(2) Pro-offending attitudes: scales here measured distorted thoughts about sexual contact with children and their sexuality (cognitive distortions); level of denial of the impact which sexual abuse has on the offender's own victim (victim distortions); and justifications used to excuse the offender's sexual deviance (justifications).

(3) Predisposing personality factors: scales here measured a number of personality dimensions which might predispose a person to offending, such as low self-esteem and under-assertiveness; inability to be intimate with other people (emotional loneliness); failure to accept accountability for his own behaviour (accountability), and limited extent to which the offender sees himself in control of his own life (locus of control).

(4) Relapse prevention skills: measuring the offender's ability to recognise situations where there is a risk of re-offending; generate effective strategies to get out of such potential risk situations; and recognise that he is still a potential offender even after treatment.

The impact of treatment

5.52 Two approaches were used to evaluate the impact of treatment. The first approach examined the extent to which treated child abusers showed statistically significant changes in the four main areas outlined above. The second, more sophisticated analysis, considered to what extent the child abusers had, by the end of treatment, a 'treated' profile.

STATISTICALLY SIGNIFICANT CHANGES

5.53 The study found that the offenders showed improvements in all four areas:[3]

---

1   Beech et al *STEP 3: An Evaluation of the Prison Sex Offender Treatment Programme* (Home Office, London, 1999) para 5.6.
2   Research Findings No 79 (Home Office, London, 1999) table 1.
3   See Research Findings No 79 (Home Office, London, 1999) table 2.

(1) Significant improvements were found in nearly all of the measures used to assess level of denial/admittance in terms of the offenders being more honest about their offending behaviour, ie less denial or more admission.

(2) All of the pro-offending attitude measures showed significant improvements in the right direction, ie decreased. Striking improvements were seen in the scales used to measure cognitive and victim distortions, but the offenders were rather less successful in tackling the self-justifications for their behaviour.

(3) All but one of the scales used to measure the predisposing personality factors showed significant improvement. Emotional loneliness was the only factor which did not show a significant change.

(4) Relapse prevention skills all showed significant improvement, although the recognition of risk situations and generation of strategies showed more improvement than the offender's recognition of himself as a potential future offender.

'TREATED' PROFILES – MEASURING OVERALL TREATMENT CHANGE

5.54   In order to qualify as having a 'treated' profile, an offender had to show changes across both pro-offending attitude measures and predisposing personality factor measures, which were sufficient (by the end of treatment) to make him largely indistinguishable from the profile of a non-sexual offender – an overall treatment change. Change was also looked at just in terms of pro-offending attitudes. [1] Using these rigorous criteria to judge treatment effectiveness, the study found that, of the 77 child abusers who completed the post-treatment questionnaires in the prison sample, 53 were successfully treated with regard to a reduction in pro-offending attitudes, and 26 showed changes on both measures, ie an overall treatment change. The remaining 24 showed no change at all. These results suggest that it is much more difficult to affect an offender's predisposing personality than his pro-offending attitudes. [2]

CHILD ABUSER PROFILES

5.55   An analysis, which made use of data from the evaluation study itself as well as data from previous studies, identified four main groups of offenders who could be distinguished in terms of their pre-treatment level of pro-offending attitudes and social inadequacy (their level of 'deviance'), and their level of admittance/denial (their level of 'denial'). The four groups were: low deviance/low denial; low deviance/high denial; high deviance/low denial; and high deviance/high denial. Analyses were then carried out, looking at the impact of treatment on the different deviancy/denial categories. As a result of the relatively small number of high deviancy cases in the prison sample, the two categories were collapsed into one. It was found that in:

(1) low deviancy/low denial men treatment was particularly effective; 59% showing an overall treatment effect; and 84% showing a significant reduction in pro-offending attitudes;

---

1   Beech et al *STEP 3: An Evaluation of the Prison Sex Offender Treatment Programme* (Home Office, London, 1999) p 6.

2   Research Findings No 79 (Home Office, London, 1999) p 3.

(2) low deviancy/high denial men treatment was less successful: 17% showing an overall treatment change; and 71% showing a significant reduction in pro-offending attitudes; and

(3) high deviancy men treatment was the least successful of these groups: 14% showing an overall treatment effect; and 43% showing a significant reduction in pro-offending attitudes.

5.56 The future classification of offenders according to their levels of deviancy and denial may well be a useful tool in assessing treatment needs. The extent to which the men denied their problems at the beginning of treatment was found to influence strongly whether they benefited from treatment. Therefore, if problems of denial can be addressed specifically by a specialised module before the offenders in high denial categories commence the core programme, the chances of a positive outcome following treatment will be enhanced greatly. The evaluation report noted that some prisons are already piloting 'Deniers Groups', which could be used as the basis of such a module.[1]

5.57 The relatively poor outcome for offenders in the high deviancy categories, although perhaps not surprising, is a matter of some concern. The study found that most of the high deviancy sample were still relatively socially incompetent by the end of treatment, ie they continued to exhibit low self-esteem, high levels of under-assertiveness and emotional loneliness, and still had high levels of emotional identification with children. This raises two issues. First, if social incompetence is linked to the risk of re-offending, then the core programme should itself address social incompetence – an area which is not currently included. This led the STEP team to recommend that a reconviction study be undertaken to establish whether or not there is a link between social incompetence and reconvictions.[2] Secondly, while the core programme does not address social incompetence, offenders in the high deviancy group should be given priority for admission into the extended programme component of the SOTP, which itself should be evaluated with regard to its impact on social skills, with additional treatment modules being developed, if necessary, to target specifically self-esteem, social skills and assertiveness.[3]

5.58 Overall, the findings of the evaluation of the SOTP and the effect of treatment in prison show cause for some optimism. In total, 76% of the men who had been released and agreed to be seen at the 9-month follow-up said they had found the core programme 'very helpful' and a further 20% said it had helped 'quite a lot'. Furthermore, probation officers working in the community appeared to have a high level of confidence and satisfaction in the quality of the core programme. However, two further points can be made.

5.59 The first relates to the importance of continued treatment and support. If treatment in prison can be effective in changing a sex offender's attitudes, efforts must be made to ensure that those positive changes are sustained

---

1   Beech et al *STEP 3: An Evaluation of the Prison Sex Offender Treatment Programme* (Home Office, London, 1999) Recommendation 2.

2   Beech et al *STEP 3: An Evaluation of the Prison Sex Offender Treatment Programme* (Home Office, London, 1999) Recommendation 6.

3   Beech et al *STEP 3: An Evaluation of the Prison Sex Offender Treatment Programme* (Home Office, London, 1999) Recommendations 4 and 5.

following the offender's release into the community. It has been pointed out that the SOTP attempts to change offenders' attitudes towards women and children in an environment in which women and children are largely absent and resolutions made by offenders in prison may not easily survive the transition into the world outside without considerable support.[1] The STEP team found that 55% of offenders who completed the programme with apparently treated profiles, were offered places on group treatment programmes in the community. Yet, 50% of offenders without treated profiles appeared not to have been offered any treatment at all. This is particularly important as the men whose pro-offending attitudes had not changed through treatment were found to lose any relapse-prevention skills acquired in treatment quickly. The team recommended that SOTP summary documents, which are sent to Probation Services, contain details of the impact of the programme on the offender, together with a recommendation as to what further treatment is required. For offenders with treated profiles, this might be a place on a maintenance programme, as opposed to further offence-specific treatment.[2] Ensuring continuity of treatment and supervision is of crucial importance to the effective management of sex offenders in the community. The provision of information in documents should go some way towards achieving continuity, but the emphasis should also be placed on personal contact between the professionals involved, in this case particularly between the seconded probation officer and prison staff responsible for the SOTP and the probation officer responsible for supervising the offender on his release. In a thematic inspection conducted by HM Inspectorate of Probation in 1998, it was found that in a sample of approximately 180 cases, although 57 of the offenders had attended a prison-based sex offender programme, supervising probation officers had attended a post-course meeting with the staff responsible for the SOTP to summarise and hand over the work in only 15 cases. In a further two cases it was clear that the probation officer had been invited to such a meeting, but had not attended. In some cases, the probation officer had not been invited or given sufficient notice of the meeting and in the remainder it was not possible to tell from the file why a meeting had not taken place. It was noted in the inspection report that Probation Service Guidelines often made no reference to the importance of liaising with the staff responsible for the SOTP or attending the post-course meeting to hand over the work, which the inspection found to be the subject of much adverse comment by seconded probation and other staff involved in the SOTP. Therefore, the report recommended that chief probation officers should issue guidance to staff about the importance of appropriate liaison with prison-based staff involved in the SOTP and the priority to be given to attending the post-course meeting.[3]

5.60   Secondly, the SOTP may well have an positive impact on offenders whilst in prison, but, as noted by the STEP team, the ultimate effectiveness of the core programme is the extent to which it reduces further sexual offending. The

---

1   Sampson *Acts of Abuse: Sex Offenders and the Criminal Justice System* (Routledge, London, 1994) p 118.

2   Beech et al *STEP 3: An Evaluation of the Prison Sex Offender Treatment Programme* (Home Office, London, 1999) Recommendation 20.

3   *Exercising Constant Vigilance: The Role of the Probation Service in Protecting the Public from Sex Offenders* (HM Inspectorate of Probation, Home Office, London, 1998) Recommendation 6.

team recommended that recidivism studies take place at 2-, 5- and 10-year intervals. However, given the inadequacy of reconviction data, it was strongly recommended that such studies should not only look at the official rates of reconviction (as gathered from criminal statistics), but also gather information from charges not proceeded with by the Crown Prosecution Service; findings of fact (of sexual abuse) as determined in the civil courts; and information from social services records which contain suspicions or allegations of sexual abuse.[1] Such research is vital and must form part of a long-term programme of research into the efficacy of treatment for sex offenders, whether delivered in prison or in the community.

RELEASE FROM PRISON

Fixed-term prisoners

The concept of early release

5.61   One of the fundamental concerns of all prisoners is when they will be regain their liberty. It is a well-known fact that offenders do not generally spend the entirety of their sentence in custody. A system of early release of prisoners has been used as an incentive to good behaviour for many years. Originally based on the 'ticket of leave' given to transported criminals as a reward for good behaviour after serving a proportion of their sentence, a general system of remission was in place towards the end of the last century when male convicts were eligible for one-quarter remission of their sentence and female convicts were eligible for one-third remission[2] – hardly a system which could be justified today! In 1940, all prisoners became entitled to one-third remission, although this appears to have been due to the pressure on prison places brought about by detention under wartime regulations, rather than because of any concern over discrimination.[3]

Discretionary release – the introduction of parole

5.62   More recently, in 1968 a system of parole was introduced.[4] Parole differed from remission in that it was discretionary, rather than an entitlement. The rationale underlying its introduction was that prisoners who showed promise or determination to reform should be able to earn a further period of freedom on parole, over and above the period of remission already allowed.[5] Prisoners became eligible for release on licence after serving one-third of their sentence, or at least 12 months, whichever was longer. This latter period was later reduced to 6 months.[6] The licence lasted until the day the prisoner would ordinarily have been released, that is after serving two-thirds of the sentence. The offender would then be at risk of being returned to prison if he committed

1   Beech et al *STEP 3: An Evaluation of the Prison Sex Offender Treatment Programme* (Home Office, London, 1999) Recommendation 25.
2   Livingstone and Owen *Prison Law* (Oxford University Press, Oxford, 1999) para 12.05.
3   Livingstone and Owen *Prison Law* (Oxford University Press, Oxford, 1999) para 12.06.
4   Criminal Justice Act 1967.
5   *The Adult Offender* Cmnd 2852 (HMSO, London, 1965).
6   Eligibility for Release on Licence Order 1983, SI 1983/1959.

another offence before the end of the sentence. The legislation provided for the appointment by the Home Secretary of a Parole Board, whose duty was to advise the Home Secretary about the release on licence of determinate and life prisoners, the conditions to be attached to such licences and the recall to prison of prisoners whose cases had been referred to the Board for consideration. The Board was assisted by Local Review Committees, which commenced the process of reviewing the suitability for release on parole of every prisoner who had become eligible for it. The ultimate decision on release rested with the Home Secretary.[1] Following growing public concern over the use of parole, particularly for serious offenders, in 1983 the then Home Secretary, Leon Briton, stated that, as a matter of policy, offenders sentenced to more than 5 years' imprisonment for sexual offences, or those involving drug trafficking, arson or violence, would only be granted parole when release under supervision for a few months before the end of a sentence was likely to reduce the long-term risk to the public, or in circumstances which were genuinely exceptional.[2] This, together with the reduction of the minimum period to be served in prison before eligibility for release on parole from 12 to 6 months and the later increase in remission to one-half for those serving 12 months or less,[3] had the effect of reducing the correlation between lengths of time actually served and the lengths of sentences passed by judges to an extent which many regarded as unacceptable. Further-more, the prospects of early release for offenders serving relatively short sentences contrasted sharply with the prospects of long-term prisoners, especially those subject to the policy adopted by the Home Secretary for sex offenders and others sentenced to 5 years' imprisonment or more.

The Criminal Justice Act 1991

5.63   During the 1980s, as penal policy moved increasingly towards a philosophy of 'just deserts' (ie punishment should be commensurate with the seriousness of offence as judged by the sentencing court, rather than tailored to the needs of personal circumstances of the individual offender[4]), it became increasingly difficult to justify a system of parole based on the selection by the Home Secretary of certain prisoners for early release. Pressure for reform of the system grew and in 1987 the Government set up a Review Committee under Lord Carlisle QC:

> '… to examine the operation of the parole scheme in England and Wales, its relationship with the current arrangements for remission, time spent in custody on remand, and partly and fully suspended sentences and their effect on the time which offenders sentenced to imprisonment spend in custody.'[5]

The Committee made various recommendations, the majority of which were accepted by the Government 2 years later in the White Paper[6] which preceded

---

1   The one exception was in the case of a prisoner recalled to prison following revocation of his licence. If the Board recommended the prisoner's immediate release, the Home Secretary was obliged to give effect to that recommendation.

2   Livingstone and Owen *Prison Law* (Oxford University Press, Oxford, 1999) para 12.13.

3   Effective in July 1987.

4   See **4.57**.

5   *The Parole System in England and Wales* (1988) Cmnd 532.

6   *Crime, Justice and Protecting the Public* (1996) Cmnd 965.

the Criminal Justice Act 1991. Part II of the 1991 Act created a new regime of early release which essentially remains in force to date, although various amendments have been by subsequent legislation. Remission has now been abolished and, except for adults sentenced to less than 1 year's imprisonment, all prisoners serve part of their sentence in the community.

The Crime (Sentences) Act 1997 and the Crime and Disorder Act 1998

5.64 Following a White Paper in 1996[1] and a call from the Conservative Government for greater transparency in the sentencing process, the Crime (Sentences) Act 1997 provided for the repeal of pt II of the 1991 Act and the imposition of a radically different scheme, under which offenders would serve a period of time more closely approximating to the sentence imposed by the court.[2] However, the following Labour Government viewed the proposed scheme as excessively complex and unsatisfactory, and the Crime and Disorder Act 1998 subsequently repealed the majority of the provisions of the 1997 Act which related to early release.[3] The 1998 Act presupposes the continued existence of the regime for early release established by the Criminal Justice Act 1991, although various amendments to the 1991 Act are made and a new system of home detention curfew is introduced.

The early release regime

5.65 For the purposes of early release, offenders are classified as either 'short-term' or 'long-term' prisoners. Short-term prisoners are those serving a sentence of imprisonment of less than 4 years, whereas those serving sentences of 4 years or more are classified as long-term prisoners.[4] If an offender has received two or more sentences, whether consecutive or wholly or partly concurrent, the sentences are to be treated as a single term if either the sentences were passed on the same occasion or, where they were passed on different occasions, the offender has not been released under pt II of the 1991 Act at any time during the period beginning with the first and ending with the last of these occasions, ie the offender has not been released on licence between the passing of the sentences.[5]

SHORT-TERM PRISONERS
5.66
(1) Short-term prisoners sentenced to a term of imprisonment of less than 12 months are released unconditionally after serving one-half of their sentence.[6]

---

1   *Protecting the Public – the Government's Strategy on Crime in England and Wales* (1996) Cmnd 3190.
2   Crime (Sentences) Act 1997, ss 10–28.
3   Crime and Disorder Act 1998, s 107 and Sch 10. The only provision of the 1997 Act not repealed is s 9, which deals with credit for periods spent on remand.
4   Criminal Justice Act 1991, s 33.
5   Criminal Justice Act 1991, s 51(2), as inserted by s 101 of the Crime and Disorder Act 1998.
6   Criminal Justice Act 1991, s 33(1)(a).

(2) Short-term prisoners sentenced to a term of imprisonment of at least 12 months but less than 4 years are released automatically on licence after serving one-half of their sentence (automatic conditional release).[1]

(3) The licence of a short-term prisoner remains in force until the date on which he would (but for his release) have served three-quarters of his sentence.[2]

(4) A short-term prisoner may be returned to prison if he commits any offence punishable with imprisonment before the date on which he would (but for his release) have served his sentence in full. A court may order that he be returned to prison for the whole or any part of the period from the date of the offence to the sentence expiry date.[3]

(5) Where a short-term prisoner has been returned to prison due to the commission of a further offence, if the sentence for the further offence is for a term of 12 months or less, he shall be released on licence after one-half of that sentence and the licence remains in force for a period of 3 months. Breach of the licence conditions render the prisoner liable to summary conviction.[4]

(6) The licence of a short-term prisoner may be revoked by the Home Secretary on the recommendation of the Parole Board and the prisoner recalled to prison.[5]

(7) Where a short-term prisoner has been recalled to prison, the period of licence is extended to the whole of the sentence.[6]

(8) A short-term prisoner may be released at any time by the Home Secretary on compassionate grounds, without consultation with the Parole Board.[7]

Short-term prisoners and the home detention curfew scheme
5.67　　In November 1997, the Home Secretary announced to Parliament his plans to tag electronically short-term prisoners nearing the end of their sentences as part of a disciplined return to the community. It was argued that, effectively, offenders in prison were placed in a straitjacket, in that they had no choice but to abide by prison rules. Removal of that straitjacket on release from custody often returned offenders to a disorderly lifestyle. The home detention curfew (HDC) scheme was designed to place strict controls on offenders in their home environment, helping them to learn self-discipline as opposed to acquiescence in prison discipline. Offenders should then carry this self-discipline into the period following the curfew, thus reducing their propensity to offend. The fact that the scheme will also have the benefit of reducing the prison population at a time of overstretched prison resources cannot be disregarded, although the Government claimed that this was not the

---

1　　Criminal Justice Act 1991, s 33(1)(b).
2　　Criminal Justice Act 1991, s 37(1).
3　　Criminal Justice Act 1991, s 40.
4　　Criminal Justice Act 1991, s 40(A), inserted by s 105 of the Crime and Disorder Act 1998.
5　　Criminal Justice Act 1991, s 39. Prior to the Crime and Disorder Act, a short-term prisoner who failed to comply with the conditions of his licence was guilty of an offence (s 38 of the 1991 Act). Section 103 of the 1998 Act repealed this provision and extended the provision in s 39 of the 1991 Act (which previously applied to long-term prisoners only) to short-term prisoners.
6　　Criminal Justice Act 1991, s 37(1A), inserted by s 104 of the Crime and Disorder Act 1998.
7　　Criminal Justice Act 1991, s 36.

underlying reason for introducing the scheme.[1] The scheme was introduced by ss 99 and 100 of the Crime and Disorder Act, which amend the Criminal Justice Act 1991.

Eligible offenders
5.68   Short-term prisoners serving sentences of 3 months or more who are over the age of 18 and who do not fall within the list of statutory exclusions are eligible to be considered for early release under the scheme. The list of statutory exclusions[2] includes violent and sexual offenders serving an extended sentence,[3] those subject to orders under the Mental Health Act 1983 and those who have been recalled or returned to prison. Initial projections estimate that 60,000 prisoners a year will be considered under the scheme, and there may be a total of 30,000 prisoners a year suitable for HDC, although this may vary, depending on future sentencing patterns. The governor of the prison in which the prisoner is being held is responsible for deciding suitability for the scheme, on the basis of a risk assessment. It is estimated that 5,000 risk assessments will be made each month. Assuming a 50% acceptance rate, it was estimated in 1998 that there will be about 2,500 prisoners placed on HDC each month and 4,000 on HDC at any one point in time.[4] By 28 April 1999, 4,274 offenders had been placed on the scheme and, of these, 184 (4%) had had their licences revoked.[5]

THE SCHEME
5.69   The Prison Service must carry out a risk assessment on all eligible prisoners who wish to participate in the HDC scheme, unless they are sex offenders,[6] Category A prisoners[7] or the prison governor responsible for authorising release on HDC judges that the time remaining until the half-way point of the sentence (when the prisoner would be automatically released) is insufficient to enable a risk assessment to be undertaken and a curfew of at least 14 days imposed. The risk assessment aims to balance any risk to the public presented by the bringing forward of the release date against the potential benefits of incorporating a period of HDC within the prisoner's sentence. In all cases, the first stage of the procedure is a standard suitability assessment, normally undertaken by a member of the probation team, involving consideration of the prisoner's paperwork and input from prison and home Probation Service staff. An enhanced assessment, undertaken by a board which includes a prison governor, may then be undertaken on prisoners who are thought to require further consideration. Following the risk assessment, a prisoner may only be refused release for one of five reasons:

(1)   an unacceptable risk to the victim or to members of the public;

---

1   See Card and Ward *The Crime and Disorder Act 1998* (Jordans, Bristol, 1998) para 7.85.
2   Criminal Justice Act 1991, s 34A(2).
3   See **4.82**.
4   *Home Detention Curfew: The Role of the Probation Service* (1998) Probation Circular 44.
5   HC Deb col 253, 12 May 1999.
6   See **5.73**.
7   All prisoners are classified in one of four security categories. Category A prisoners are those whose escape would be highly dangerous to the public or the police or the security of the State.

(2) a pattern of offending which indicates a likelihood of re-offending during the HDC period;
(3) a likelihood of failure to comply with the conditions of the curfew;
(4) a lack of suitable accommodation for HDC; or
(5) shortness of the curfew period.[1]

5.70 Eligible prisoners who are assessed as suitable will be released on licence after the 'requisite period', which varies according to the sentence imposed:[2]

(1) in respect of a prisoner serving a term of 3 months or more, but less than 4 months, a period of 30 days;
(2) in respect of a prisoner serving a term of 4 months or more, but less than 8 months, a period equal to one-quarter of the term; and
(3) in respect of a prisoner serving a term of 8 months or more, a period that is 60 days less than one-half of the term.

5.71 The licence must include a curfew condition which:[3]

(1) requires the released person to remain, for periods for the time being specified in the condition, at a place for the time being so specified (which may be an approved probation hostel); and
(2) includes requirements for the electronic monitoring of his whereabouts during the periods for the time being so specified.

5.72 The maximum period of the curfew condition is 2 months and the minimum is usually 14 days. The condition must remain in force until the date when the released person would (but for his release) have served one-half of his sentence. The condition may specify different periods of curfew for different days, but must specify at least 9 hours in any one day.[4] The conditions will be set by the prison governor and guidance suggests that in most cases, the curfew conditions will be for 12 hours a day, lasting from early evening to early morning.[5] If an offender breaks the curfew condition, or his whereabouts can no longer be monitored electronically, or it is thought necessary in order to protect the public from serious harm from him, the Home Secretary may revoke the licence and recall the offender to prison.[6]

SEX OFFENDERS AND HOME DETENTION CURFEW

5.73 Sex offenders serving an extended sentence are not eligible for early release under the HDC scheme.[7] Other sex offenders, although technically eligible under the scheme, are subject to restrictions. Offenders who will be subject to the requirements of Pt I of the Sex Offender Act 1997 on release[8] are said to present a particular type of risk to the public and Home Office

1 *Prison Service Order: Home Detention Curfew* (1998) chap 5.
2 Criminal Justice Act 1991, s 34A(4).
3 Criminal Justice Act 1991, s 37A.
4 Criminal Justice Act 1991, s 37A(2) (although the first and last days of the curfew period are excluded from this requirement).
5 *Prison Service Order: Home Detention Curfew* (1998) chap 6.
6 Criminal Justice Act 1991, s 38A.
7 Criminal Justice Act 1991, s 34A(2)(a).
8 See **7.1** to **7.15**.

documentation on risk assessment for HDC stresses that prison establishments must not commence a risk assessment on such prisoners unless there are exceptional circumstances which indicate that the individual's release might be appropriate.[1] No sex offender subject to the 1997 Act can be released without careful scrutiny and clear evidence of either minimal or no risk to the public at large and of a clear potential benefit to the chances of successful resettlement, treatment or supervision. As an example, the Home Office documentation suggests that if release into a treatment centre is judged central to the release plan of a prisoner who, whilst under supervision, is likely to present no significant risk to the public at large and if the curfew was considered to support the likely completion of treatment (by requiring the offender to remain in residency), this might qualify the case exceptionally as suitable for consideration.[2] If the case exceptionally appears to warrant assessment, in addition to consultation with the Probation Service, the police force for the area to which the offender is being considered for curfew should be approached for factual information relating to the offender's criminal antecedents (where this is not held by the prison) or criminal intelligence which is directly relevant to the curfew decision, and for any views on the suitability of the particular address, particularly in relation to victim issues.

5.74   Whereas most short-term prisoners will be released under the HDC scheme unless there are substantive reasons for refusal, there is a strong presumption that sex offenders will not be released under the scheme. Indeed, the risk posed by a sex offender will not even be assessed unless there are 'exceptional circumstances' and, even if a risk assessment is carried out, given the stringent conditions imposed and acknowledged difficulty of finding suitable accommodation for sex offenders on release from custody,[3] it seems likely that very few will be considered for release. It has been pointed out that care will need to be taken to avoid accusations of different standards being applied for different types of prisoner thus creating a potential for judicial review.[4] Admittedly, the same presumption applies to category A prisoners, but these prisoners will already have been assessed as presenting a serious risk to the public. There is no doubt that the Government wishes to be seen to be doing everything possible to protect the public from sex offenders. Given society's reaction to these 'modern folk-devils',[5] the early release of sex offenders clearly would be contrary to this aim. However, whether or not the HDC scheme operates in such a way as to be unduly discriminatory against sex offenders remains to be seen.

Long-term prisoners

5.75

(1) A long-term prisoner sentenced after 1 October 1992 must be released on licence after he has served two-thirds of his sentence.[6]

---

1   *Prison Service Order: Home Detention Curfew* (1998).
2   *Prison Service Order: Home Detention Curfew* (1998) para 2.7.
3   See **8.3**.
4   Card and Ward *The Crime and Disorder Act 1998* (Jordans, Bristol, 1998) para 7.92.
5   See **1.1**.
6   Criminal Justice Act 1991, s 33(2).

(2) A long-term prisoner serving between 4 and 15 years shall, if sentenced after 1 October 1992 and if recommended by the Parole Board, be released on licence when he has served one-half of his sentence. Any conditions attached to or inserted in the licence must be in accordance with the recommendation(s) of the Parole Board.[1]

(3) A long-term prisoner sentenced after 1 October 1992 to more than 15 years' imprisonment may be released on licence by the Home Secretary, if so recommended by the Parole Board, after serving one-half of his sentence.[2]

(4) A long-term prisoner sentenced before 1 October 1992 continues to be governed by the system in place prior to the 1991 Act. He becomes eligible to be considered for release on parole after serving one-third of his sentence and is entitled to be released after serving two-thirds of his sentence.

(5) Any long-term prisoner released on licence remains subject to the conditions of the licence until the date on which he would (but for the release) have served three-quarters of his sentence.[3]

(6) A long-term prisoner may be returned to prison if he commits an offence punishable with imprisonment before the date on which he would (but for his release) have served his sentence in full. A court may order that he be returned to prison for the whole or any part of the period from the date of the offence to the sentence expiry date.[4]

(7) Where a long-term prisoner has been returned to prison due to the commission of a further offence, if the sentence for the further offence is for a term of 12 months or less, he shall be released on licence after one-half of that sentence and the licence remains in force for a period of 3 months. Breach of the licence conditions renders the prisoner liable to summary conviction.[5]

(8) The licence of a long-term prisoner serving 15 years or more may be revoked by the Home Secretary and the prisoner recalled to prison, either on the recommendation of the Parole Board or without its recommendation if it appears to the Home Secretary to be expedient in the public interest to recall the prisoner before such a recommendation is practicable.[6]

(9) The licence of a long-term prisoner serving between 4 and 15 years may only be recalled to prison by the Home Secretary if the Parole Board so recommends.[7]

(10) Where a long-term prisoner has been recalled to prison, he must be released unconditionally after he has served three-quarters of his sentence (but for his release),[8] unless he is serving an extended sentence, in which case he may require the Home Secretary to refer his case to the Parole

---

1   Criminal Justice Act, ss 35(1), 37(5), 50(2) and 50(3) and Parole Board (Transfer of Functions) Order 1998, SI 1998/3218. The 1998 Order revoked SI 1992/1829, which made similar provision in relation to a long-term prisoner serving a sentence of imprisonment of less than 7 years.
2   Criminal Justice Act 1991, s 35(1).
3   Criminal Justice Act 1991, s 37(1).
4   Criminal Justice Act 1991, s 40.
5   Criminal Justice Act 1991, s 40A.
6   Criminal Justice Act 1991, s 39.
7   Criminal Justice Act 1991, ss 39(1) and 50(4) and Parole Board (Transfer of Functions) Order 1998, SI 1998/3218.
8   Criminal Justice Act 1991, s 33(3).

Board, which must direct his release only if satisfied that his confinement is no longer necessary for the protection of the public.[1]

(11) A long-term prisoner may be released at any time by the Home Secretary on compassionate grounds after consultation with the Parole Board.[2]

Extended sentences

Calculating the length of extended sentences[3]

5.76   Extended sentences consist of two distinct components: the custodial term (which is the normal period of imprisonment and supervision which would apply under the Criminal Justice Act 1991) and the extension period (a further period for which the offender is to be subject to licence).[4] In the absence of any return or recall to prison, the length of the custodial term determines whether the offender is a short-term or long-term prisoner for the purposes of determining release dates.[5] The release date in respect of the custodial term is calculated in the normal way, as though the custodial term were a normal sentence. The extension period is then added to these dates to produce the licence and sentence expiry dates for the extended sentence in the following way.

(1)   If the custodial term is less than 12 months, the extension period is added to the full sentence. Whereas the offender would otherwise have been released unconditionally after having served one-half of the sentence, he will be released at this half-way point on licence and the licence will remain in force until the end of the extension period.[6] For example, an offender sentenced to an extended sentence of 2 years, the custodial term of which is 1 year, will be released on licence after 6 months and remain on licence for a further 18 months. Total period from sentence to expiration of licence: 2 years.

(2)   If the custodial term is at least 12 months, but less than 4 years, the prisoner will be released on licence in the usual way after serving one-half of the custodial term. The extension period begins on the date which he would (but for his release) have served three-quarters of his custodial term, ie the extension period runs from the time the licence would expire if no extended sentence had been imposed.[7] For example, an offender sentenced to an extended sentence of 4 years, the custodial term of which is 2 years, will be released on licence after 1 year. This licence would normally expire 6 months after release, at which point the extension period will begin, extending the licence for a further 2 years. Total period from sentence to expiration of licence: 3 years and 6 months.

(3)   If the custodial term is for 4 years or more, the prisoner may be released on licence, on the recommendation of the Parole Board, after serving one-half of the sentence and must be released on licence after serving two-thirds of

1   Criminal Justice Act 1991, s 44A.
2   Criminal Justice Act 1991, s 36.
3   HOC 44/1998.
4   See **4.82**.
5   Criminal Justice Act 1991, s 44(2).
6   Criminal Justice Act 1991, s 44(5)(b).
7   Criminal Justice Act 1991, s 44(5)(a).

the sentence. In either case, the extension period begins on the date when he would (but for his release) have served three-quarters of his custodial term, ie the extension period runs from the time the licence would expire if no extended sentence had been imposed.[1] For example, an offender sentenced to an extended sentence of 9 years, the custodial term of which is 6 years, may be released, on the recommendation of the Parole Board, after 3 years, in which case the licence would normally expire one year and 6 months after release. If not released after 3 years, the offender must be released after 4 years, in which case the licence would expire 6 months after release. In either case, the extension period will begin when the licence would usually expire. Total period from sentence to expiration of licence: 7 years and 6 months.

Extended sentences, return and recall to prison

5.77		Extended sentence prisoners are liable to be returned to prison if they commit a further offence punishable with imprisonment in the same way as other prisoners,[2] but the sentence expiry date for these purposes includes the extension period.[3] Similarly, prisoners serving extended sentences are liable to be recalled to prison in the same way as other offenders, but for recall purposes the length of the extended sentence, rather than the custodial term of the sentence, determines whether the offender is regarded as a short-term or long-term prisoner.[4] Long-term extended prisoners recalled to prison following release on licence, and who are not successful in applying for parole, will be released on licence at the end of the extension period. They will then be subject to licence until the sentence expiry date of the extended sentence. Short-term extended prisoners recalled to prison following release on licence will be re-released on licence at the end of the period of recall set down by the court. They will be subject to licence until the sentence expiry date of the extended sentence.

Discretionary release – who decides?

5.78		Whereas short-term prisoners are now eligible for automatic conditional release at the half-way point of their sentence, the release of long-term prisoners continues to involve an element of discretion in that they may be released on licence at the half-way point of their sentence. If not released at this stage, they will be released on licence after serving two-thirds of their sentence. The decision whether or not to release a prisoner on parole is taken either by the Parole Board, or by the Home Secretary, dependent upon the length of sentence initially imposed. In 1988, the Carlisle Committee recommended that the Home Secretary's responsibility for releasing determinative sentence prisoners should cease and that such decisions should be taken by the Parole Board alone.[5] When the new scheme of early release was introduced by the Criminal Justice Act 1991,

---

1		Criminal Justice Act 1991, s 44(5)(a).
2		Criminal Justice Act 1991, s 40.
3		Criminal Justice Act 1991, s 44(2).
4		Criminal Justice Act 1991, s 44(7).
5		*The Parole System in England and Wales: Report of the Review Committee* (1988) Cmnd 532, Recommendation 53.

this recommendation was not acted upon and the Parole Board was delegated the power to make decisions only in relation to those prisoners sentenced after 1 October 1992 to 4 years' imprisonment or more, but less than 7 years. For prisoners serving 7 years or more, the Parole Board would make a recommendation to the Home Secretary,[1] who would then make the final decision following a recommendation for release, although there was no power to release a prisoner where the Parole Board had recommended against it.

5.79 In 1994, the Parole Board expressed the hope that, in time, sufficient trust in the system would be gained to allow the 7 years' threshold to be raised or abolished.[2] By 1998, it seemed that sufficient trust had been gained. During 1997–98, the Parole Board made 520 recommendations for release involving determinate sentence prisoners serving 7 years or more. Of these, all but two were approved by the Home Secretary. This led the Government to comment that increased delegation to the Parole Board would be a positive recognition of the quality of the Board's assessments in these cases and would reflect an outstanding track record of decision-making.[3] However, the quality of the Parole Board's work was not the only factor influencing change, as there were also admitted to be strong effectiveness and efficiency arguments supporting a move to increased delegation to the Parole Board.[4] It was estimated that overall savings in the order or £70,000–75,000 per annum could be made by reducing the duplication of decisions. Although not a vast sum, it was pointed out that this could be directly recycled within the Prison Service's much broader responsibility for developing constructive regimes.[5] As a result of these proposals, from December 1998, the Parole Board has had delegated power to decide applications for parole from all long-term prisoners serving sentences of less than 15 years' imprisonment.[6]

The Parole Board and the parole dossier

5.80 The Parole Board for England and Wales exists to carry out risk assessment to inform decisions on the early release of prisoners with the ultimate aim of protecting the public. The Board aims to be fair, open and consistent in all its decisions and to operate effective and efficient processes in order to consider cases in a timely manner.[7] The Board has over 80 members and is comprised of professional and lay people, including judges, psychiatrists, criminologists and probation officers. Three members of the Board are appointed as a panel to consider a prisoner's application for release. One of these three members must hold or have held judicial office and will act as the chairman of the panel. The panel is provided with a 'parole dossier' on the prisoner. The prisoner is given access to the various reports contained in the dossier and is also given an interview with a single member of the Parole Board

---

1   In reality, the decision was usually made by the Prison Service Parole Unit on behalf of the Home Secretary.
2   *Report of the Parole Board for 1993* (HMSO, London, 1994) p 2.
3   *Improving Parole Decision-making* Consultation Paper (Home Office, London, 1998) para 14.
4   *Improving Parole Decision-making* Consultation Paper (Home Office, London, 1998) para 15.
5   *Improving Parole Decision-making* Consultation Paper (Home Office, London, 1998) para 28.
6   Parole Board (Transfer of Functions) Order 1998 SI 1998/3218.
7   *Statement of Purpose: Report of the Parole Board 1997/98.*

some time before the panel meets. Following the interview, the prisoner is given an opportunity to make final, written representations to the Board, which are added to the dossier. The final dossier should the following information:[1]

(1) information about the offence for which the sentence was imposed, including summary of offence from police or pre-sentence reports and court transcript of sentencing remarks;
(2) the previous history of the prisoner, including previous convictions and any previous parole dossiers;
(3) reports on the prisoner during the imprisonment, including the prisoner's sentence plan and annual reviews, seconded probation officer's report and reports on offence related work, such as participation in the SOTP; and
(4) information relating to the application for release, including a report of an interview conducted with a member of the Parole Board, a home circumstances report, the prisoner's disclosure form and representations and a statistical risk indicator.

An oral hearing will then usually be held. The decision of the panel must be recorded in writing, with reasons, and communicated to the prisoner within seven days.[2]

Directions and training guidance to the Parole Board

5.81   Prior to the Criminal Justice Act 1991, the Parole Board made use of criteria in making parole decisions, but the status of these criteria were not always clear. Following the recommendations of the Carlisle Committee in 1988, s 32(6) of the 1991 Act gave the Home Secretary the discretion to give directions to the Parole Board as to matters to be taken into account in discharging any of its functions under the Act. The Home Secretary has now given directions and training guidance to the Board, which are published as an Appendix to the Report of the Board each year.

THE DIRECTIONS
5.82   In relation to the release of determinate sentence prisoners, the directions state that, in considering whether or not to recommend release on licence, the Parole Board shall consider *primarily* the risk to the public of a further offence being committed at a time when the prisoner would otherwise be in prison and whether any such risk is acceptable. This must be balanced against the benefit, both to the public and the offender, of early release back into the community under a degree of supervision which might help rehabilitation and so lessen the risk of re-offending in the future. The Board is directed to take into account that safeguarding the public may often outweigh the benefits to the offender of early release.

5.83   The directions also state that, before recommending early release on licence, the Parole Board shall consider whether:

(1) the safety of the public will be placed unacceptably at risk; in assessing such a risk, the Board shall take into account:

---

1   Prison Service Order 6000 and Appendix A Parole Board Rules 1997.
2   Appendix A of the Parole Board Rules 1997.

(a) the nature and circumstances of the original offence,
(b) whether the prisoner has shown by his attitude and behaviour to custody that he is willing to address his offending behaviour by understanding its causes and its consequences for the victims concerned, and has made positive effort and progress in doing so,
(c) in the case of a violent or sexual offender, whether the prisoner has committed other offences of a sexual or violent nature, in which case the risk to the public of release in licence may be unacceptable, and
(d) that a risk of violent or sexual offending is more serious than a risk of other types of offending;
(2) the longer period of supervision that parole would provide is likely to reduce the risk of further offences being committed;
(3) the prisoner is likely to comply with the conditions of his licence;
(4) the prisoner has failed to meet the requirements of licensed supervision, temporary release or bail on any previous occasion and, if so, whether this makes the risk of releasing him on licence unacceptable;
(5) the resettlement plan will help secure the offender's rehabilitation; and
(6) the supervising officer has prepared a programme of supervision and has recommended specific licence conditions.

TRAINING GUIDANCE

5.84   The directions are followed by training guidance,[1] which contains 12 factors to be taken into account by the Parole Board when making a recommendation about parole:

(1)   the offender's background, including any previous convictions and their pattern, and responses to any previous periods of supervision;
(2)   the nature and circumstances of the original offence;
(3)   where available, the sentencing judge's comments and probation and medical reports prepared for the court;
(4)   any risk to the victim or possibility of retaliation by the victim, victim's family or local community;
(5)   any risk to other persons, including persons outside the jurisdiction;
(6)   any available statistical indicators as to the likelihood of re-offending;
(7)   attitude and behaviour in custody, including offences against prison discipline;
(8)   attitude to other inmates and positive contributions to prison life;
(9)   remorse, insight into offending behaviour, attitude to the victim and steps taken, within available resources, to achieve any treatment or training objectives set out in the sentence plan;
(10)   the realism of the release plan and resettlement prospects, including home circumstances and the likelihood of co-operation with supervision, the relationship with the home probation officer, the attitude of the victim and local community, the extent to which the release plan continues rehabilitative work started in the prison, and the extent to which it lessens or removes the occurrence of circumstances which led to the original offence;
(11)   any medical or psychiatric considerations; and

---

1   The training guidance does not form part of the directions issued under s 32(6) of the Criminal Justice Act 1991.

(12) any other information, including representations by or on behalf of the
offender, which may have a bearing on risk assessment.

Statistical predictions

5.85   The decision whether or not to release a prisoner is essentially a
risk-assessment exercise. Prior to the system of early release introduced by the
Criminal Justice Act 1991, some, albeit limited, use was made of statistical
predictions of risk in determining whether a prisoner should be released on
parole. The reconviction predication score (RPS) assessed the likelihood of
reconviction within 2 years of a prisoner's release. The RPS for each male
prisoner was based on 16 predictive factors, such as age on first conviction, the
offence for which he was imprisoned and the time in his last job.[1] However, in
1988 the Carlisle Committee observed that many Parole Board members paid
little regard to the RPS in formulating their views on a case and, in view of the
move to the more risk-based system proposed in the report, the committee
expressed the view that the Parole Board should be under a duty to take into
account statistical predication techniques and, where appropriate, clinical
assessments, which would assist it in its work.[2]

5.86   Following the 1991 Act, the risk that is to be assessed is not simply
whether the prisoner will re-offend in the future, but whether he will re-offend *at
a time when he would otherwise be in prison*, ie from release to the two-thirds point of
sentence.[3] The RPS was clearly not designed for this purpose as it assessed the
likelihood of conviction within a fixed period. Furthermore, it was based on
reconvictions, rather than re-offending and, inevitably, delays in detecting the
offence and procedural delays within the criminal justice system meant that long
periods could elapse between commission of a further offence and reconviction,
thereby weakening the strength of the statistical prediction. An additional
disadvantage of the RPS was that it did not distinguish between different kinds of
reconvictions. In carrying out the risk-assessment exercise, a small risk of a
serious offence is thought to pose a greater threat to the public than a larger risk
of a less serious offence and, therefore, it was necessary to develop a prediction
tool that was able to distinguish between serious and non-serious re-offending.
With these points in mind, a new statistical prediction tool was developed: the
rate of reconviction score (RORS).

The rate of reconviction score[4]

5.87   The new score uses a statistical technique known as 'survival analysis',
which enables predictions to be made as to the probability of re-offending at any
point in time, ie the length of time a prisoner can 'survive' without re-offending.

---

1   Nuttall et al *Parole in England and Wales* Home Office Research Study 38 (HMSO, London,
     1977).
2   *The Parole System in England and Wales: Report of the Review Committee* (1988) Cmnd 532,
     para 330.
3   It must be remembered that long-term prisoners are entitled to be released when they have
     served two-thirds of their sentence and cannot be detained thereafter simply because there
     is thought to be a risk that they may re-offend at some time in the future.
4   Copas et al 'Development of a New Reconviciton Prediction Score' Home Office Research
     Bulletin No 36 (1994).

The score was developed from data collected from a sample of approximately 1,250 men and women[1] serving sentences of 4 years and over who had been discharged. The score is based on six items of information, all of which will have been available at the time the current sentence was imposed:

(1) age at conviction (the conviction for which the prospective parolee is currently serving his sentence);
(2) number of custodial sentences (including current sentence) while aged under 21 years;
(3) number of custodial sentences (including current sentence) as an adult aged 21 years or over;
(4) number of previous convictions;
(5) type of offence for which the prisoner is serving the current sentence, in six broad categories: offences of violence; sex offences; burglary; theft, fraud and forgery; drugs offences; and other offences; and
(6) whether male or female.

These six variables are then 'weighted' and result in a score from which the probability or risk of re-offending can be calculated, for lengths of parole varying from 1 to 24 months. The weighting of the variables differs for the risk of any re-offending (apart from minor summary offences, such as motoring offences) and for the risk of serious re-offending (which is taken as offending resulting in a further custodial sentence). For example, the weighting attached to a sexual offence is +1 for the risk of re-offending, but rises to +8 for the risk of serious re-offending, indicating that, if sex offenders re-offend, they are more likely to commit a serious offence which results in a custodial sentence and, therefore, present a greater risk to the public.

5.88 The sample of offenders on which the calculation of probability was based had all been sentenced prior to the October 1992. The current arrangements for supervision, whereby all long-term prisoners are on licence and supervised until the three-quarter point of their sentence, may well reduce the risk of re-offending during the supervision period, and thus the predictor will need to be revalidated on a sample of prisoners released under the current arrangements.

5.89 Each prisoner's RORS is now included in his parole dossier. The Parole Board is advised to treat the score as one piece of information along with all the other information in the dossier. In particular, as the RORS is based on information available at the time of sentence, importance should be attached to the prisoner's progress in prison, including participation in treatment programmes such as the SOTP. Although some concerns have been raised about the use of statistical predictions,[2] as long as the Parole Board does not place undue reliance on a prisoner's RORS, to the extent of allowing it to override other relevant information, it is a useful piece of information, and can make a valuable contribution to the overall exercise of risk assessment.

---

1   The sample contained too few women for a detailed calculation to made separately. An approximate prediction score has been calculated for women, but this provides only a rough guide to risk.
2   See, for example, Hirschmann 'Parole and the Dangerous Offender' in West (ed) *Dangerous People* (Blackstone Press Ltd, London, 1996).

Sex offenders and discretionary release

5.90   Statistics show that a smaller percentage of sex offenders are considered suitable for discretionary release than any other type of offender.[1] In 1997–98 the Parole Board considered early release in a total of 5,242 cases of determinate sentence prisoners. A decision to release (in the case of prisoners serving less than 7 years) or a recommendation for release (in the case of prisoners serving 7 years or more) was made in 2,008[2] of these cases (38.3%). Of these:

(1)   prisoners serving sentences for drug offences were most likely to be released – out of 1135 cases, 707 (62.3%) were released;
(2)   prisoners serving sentences for offences of violence were close to the overall average – out of 2,350 cases considered, 815 (34.7%) were released; and
(3)   prisoners serving sentences for sexual offences[3] were the least likely to be released – out of 705 cases considered by the Parole Board, only 122 (17.3%) were released.

5.91   As may be expected, those serving shorter sentences (between 4 and 7 years) were more likely to be released than those serving longer sentences (7 years or more). Of those sentenced after October 1992,[4] the Board considered a total of 3,466 prisoners serving shorter sentences, 1,486 (42.9%) of whom were released, and 1,352 prisoners serving longer sentences, 419 (31%) of who were released. The differential was more pronounced for sex offenders eligible for early release, 20.7% of those serving shorter sentences were released, but only 12.4% of those serving longer sentences were released. Thus, statistically, a sex offender sentenced to 7 years' imprisonment or more is less likely to be released under the early release scheme than any other offender.

5.92   The nature of the offence for which the prisoner is serving his current sentence will be taken into account in calculating his RORS and there exists an interesting correlation between the weight attributed to the type of current offence for the purpose of calculating the RORS and the number of prisoners released for each offence type. The weighting for drug offences is in negative figures (-8 for the risk of any re-offending and -11 for the risk of serious re-offending). For offences of violence, the weighting is neutral (-1 for the risk of any re-offending and +1 for the risk of serious re-offending). For sexual offences, however, there is a far heavier weighting (+1 for the risk of any re-offending and +8 for the risk of serious re-offending). Therefore, the higher the RORS, the less likely the prisoner is to be released.

Previous sexual offences, statistics and risk assessment

5.93   The Home Secretary's directions to the Parole Board specifically require the Board, in deciding whether the risk to the public if the prisoner were

---

1   *Report of the Parole Board 1997–98.*
2   Only two recommendations for release were not accepted by the Home Secretary.
3   Sexual offences for the purposes of the statistics are defined to include rape, indecent assault, unlawful sexual intercourse, incest, abduction, gross indecency/indecent assault on a child, buggery, indecency between males.
4   For these purposes, only those sentenced after October 1992 can be considered, as the vast majority of those sentenced to shorter sentences before this date had already been released.

to be released would be unacceptable, to take into account in the case of a violent or sexual offender, whether the prisoner has committed other offences of a sexual or violent nature (in which case, the risk to the public of release on licence may be unacceptable). The nature of any previous convictions is not taken into account in calculating a prisoner's RORS, which is based on the type of offence for which the prisoner is currently serving a sentence and the number (but not the type) of previous convictions and custodial sentences. This again illustrates that the RORS is only one of a number of pieces of information on which the Board should base its decision.

5.94 The directions are based on the assumption that previous sexual or violent offences increase the risk of further sexual or violent offences being committed in the future. A study of reconvictions of offenders sentenced or discharged from prison in 1994 found that in total 56% of all offenders discharged from prison were reconvicted of another offence within 2 years. However, of males discharged after custodial sentences for sexual offences, only 16% were reconvicted within 2 years and, among those reconvicted, only 14% were reconvicted for a sexual offence on first reconviction. In other words, less than 3% of those discharged for sexual offences were both reconvicted within 2 years and recorded a sexual offence at first reconviction.[1]

5.95 Prima facie, these statistics do little to support the assumption on which the directions are based. However, they are not thought to be representative of the true level of re-offending by imprisoned sexual offenders for the several reasons.[2] First, any estimate is based on relatively small numbers, which may be insufficient to give an accurate picture, as sex offenders are not a homogenous group – they include paedophiles, incest offenders, rapists and others who have very different characteristics and perhaps very different probabilities of re-offending. Secondly, a sex offender will be identified by referring to the offence recorded by the prison service. Some prisoners found guilty of sexual offences may only have been convicted of subsidiary offences – for example, an offender who rapes and kills his victim will be identified as a murderer, not a rapist. Even if a sexual offence is not actually committed, many offences may have a sexual motivation. It has been suggested that 15% of prisoners convicted of homicide or attempted homicide had a sexual motive for their offence.[3] Thirdly, the official reconviction statistics only refer to the first offence for which the prisoner is reconvicted. If a sex offender is first reconvicted of a non-sexual offence, any subsequent offence in the follow-up period will not be reported in the statistics. Finally, problems of reporting and recording sex offences,[4] combined with delays within the criminal justice system itself, mean that many sexual offences may be committed, but do not result in a conviction within the follow-up period of any study.

---

1 Kershaw *Reconvictions of Offenders Sentenced or Discharged from Prison in 1994, England and Wales* (Home Office, London, 1999) 5/99 para 3.4.

2 Marshall *Reconviction of Imprisoned Sexual Offenders* Home Office Research Study No 36 (Home Office, London, 1994).

3 Maden et al 'Sex Offenders Serving a Prison Sentence in England and Wales' (1993) unpublished paper quoted in Marshall *Reconviction of Imprisoned Sexual Offenders* Home Office Research Study No 36 (Home Office, London, 1994).

4 See **1.69**.

5.96 In order to overcome some of these problems, an analysis was undertaken of the reconvictions and criminal histories from a random sample of approximately 13,000 prisoners discharged in 1987 – about 20% of all those released from prison that year.[1] Of these 13,000 prisoners, 402 (3%) were found to been imprisoned for a sexual offence (even if it was not the main offence as recorded by the Prison Service). Of these, 48% had been convicted of indecent assault on a female, 20% had been convicted of gross indecency with a child and 15% had been convicted of rape, the remainder having been convicted on indecent assault on a male, buggery, attempted buggery, unlawful sexual intercourse and incest. Of the 402 sex offenders, 27% had previous convictions for sexual offences, compared to only 4% of the non sex offenders in the sample. In total, 7% of the sex offenders were reconvicted of a sexual offence within 4 years of their release from prison, compared to 1.3% of the non sex offenders. This illustrates that, statistically, sex offenders are more likely to have previous convictions for sexual offences and are more likely to be reconvicted of sexual offences than non sex offenders. However, it should be noted that, in numerical terms, a total of 28 sex offenders were reconvicted of a sexual offence, compared to 169 non sex offenders.

5.97 The study also found that sex offenders with previous convictions were more likely to be reconvicted of a sexual offence – 12% as compared to 5%. While the numbers involved were small, the difference is statistically significant and suggests that a history of sexual offending seems to indicate an increased risk of further sexual offending. Overall, the study found that those at greatest risk of reconviction for a sexual offence were those with current and previous such convictions (12% of the sample who met both these criteria were reconvicted of a sexual offence). The next most likely group to be reconvicted of a sexual offence were those with no current conviction for a sexual offence, but with at least one previous conviction for a sexual offence (6% of the sample who met both these criteria were reconvicted of a sexual offence). This group was closely followed by those serving a sentence for a sexual offence but with no previous convictions for such offences (5% of the sample who met both these criteria were reconvicted of a sexual offence). As would be expected, those with no history of sexual offending (either as a current offence or as previous convictions) were least likely to be reconvicted of a sexual offence (1% of the sample who met both these criteria were reconvicted of a sexual offence).

5.98 Unlike the general reconviction studies, these findings support the assumption on which the directions to the Parole Board are based. A history of sexual offending places a prisoner at greater risk of committing further sexual offences. The directions also require the Parole Board to take into account that a risk of violent or sexual offending is more serious than a risk of other types of offending. Clearly, a prisoner's criminal history will be of crucial importance to the release decision and, in the absence of any other evidence, a history of sexual offending will tend to militate against release.

---

1   Marshall *Reconviction of Imprisoned Sexual Offenders* Home Office Research Study No 36 (Home Office, London, 1994).

Other factors relevant to early release – the victim and local community

5.99   Additional factors which may militate against the release of a sex offender can be found in the training guidance, which includes reference to the possibility of retaliation by the victim, victim's family, or local community, and the realism of the release plan and resettlement prospects, including, inter alia, the attitude of the victim and the local community. The response of some communities to the release of sex offenders (particularly paedophiles), the problem of vigilante attacks and the difficulty of securing suitable accommodation for such offenders,[1] may well influence the decision of the Parole Board. Once these factors are added to the perceived risk posed by a sex offender, it is hardly surprising that such a small proportion of sex offenders are considered suitable for early release.

Other factors relevant to early release – admissions of guilt and participation on the Sex Offender Treatment Programme

5.100   On a more positive note, a prisoner's conduct during the custodial sentence may serve to counterbalance any factors militating against early release. The directions require the Parole Board to take into account whether the prisoner has shown by his attitude and behaviour in custody that he is willing to address his offending behaviour by understanding its causes and its consequences for the victims concerned, and has made a positive effort and progress in doing so. In addition, the training guidance requires the Board to take account of the prisoner's behaviour and attitude in custody, and any remorse, insight into offending behaviour, attitude to the victim and steps taken, within available resources, to achieve any treatment or training objectives set out in the sentence plan.

5.101   In relation to these factors, a prisoner's participation in the SOTP may well be crucial to the decision of the Board. Indeed, a prisoner's initial decision to participate in the programme may have been influenced by the prospect of a favourable decision by the Board. It has been suggested that, when the SOTP was first introduced, there was a deliberate, if unspoken, decision to use the possibility of a favourable parole decision as an incentive to prisoners to participate in the programme, or at least that was the perception of many prisoners.[2] However, a prisoner is faced with a dilemma. Participation in the SOTP requires the prisoners to admit their guilt, to face up to their offending behaviour, examine its causes and effects and to learn how to reduce the risk of re-offending and so a prisoner who denies his guilt is not eligible to join the programme.

5.102   The High Court has made it clear that the Parole Board must make its decision on the basis that a prisoner has committed the offences of which he has been convicted and that, where the pattern of offending behaviour is such that there is a significant risk of a further offence being committed, particularly an offence of a violent or sexual nature, and a prisoner has not demonstrated by his conduct in prison that such a risk has been reduced to an acceptable level, then a

---

1   See **8.6**.
2   Sampson *Acts of Abuse: Sex Offenders and the Criminal Justice System* (Routledge, London, 1994) p 116.

recommendation for parole is unlikely to be made.[1] Thus, a prisoner who has been convicted of a sexual offence but who maintains his innocence and who, therefore, has not taken part in the SOTP is unlikely to be released.

5.103   Even if a prisoner has admitted the offence for which he has been convicted and joins the SOTP, he may understandably be reluctant to admit any other, previously unknown, offending behaviour, as this would serve to increase the risk that he will re-offend in the future and militate against early release. If the SOTP is be effective, participants must be encouraged to be open and honest about their offending history. It can be argued that a prisoner who has been open and honest and who has made a genuine attempt to address his offending behaviour is less likely to re-offend than an prisoner who has admitted only his current offence and who participates in the programme but conceals many aspects of his offending in the belief that it will enhance his prospects of early release. Decisions of the Board should reflect this and prisoners made aware that genuine participation in the SOTP will enhance, not diminish, their prospects of early release.

Sex offenders and other statistical indicators

5.104   The sexual offending history of a prisoner obviously plays a significant part in the decision-making process of the Parole Board and it is generally accepted that this factor contributes most to the successful prediction of re-offending. However, this is not the sole factor on which statistical predictions can be based. A large meta-analysis,[2] described as 'the last word in respect of recidivism',[3] included nearly 29,000 sex offenders followed up on average for 4 or 5 years and found that over 20 variables contributed to the successful prediction of sexual recidivism, but for most of these the magnitude of the relationship was so small that it was of negligible practical use.[4] However, the analysis found that sexual recidivism was closely related to sexual deviance. It was suggested that sexual deviance could be inferred in a number of ways:

(1) from the presence of a lengthy history of sexual offending or an early onset of that offending;
(2) the commission of a variety of sex crimes;
(3) evidence of offences against boys or strangers; and
(4) penile plythsmography (the measurement of penile response to sexual stimuli).

Although a number of instruments have been developed in an attempt to organise some of these variables into risk-prediction tools, Grubin suggests that the validity of only two has been demonstrated to any extent: the Rapid Risk

---

1   *R v Secretary of State for the Home Department, ex parte Lillycrop and Others* (1996) *The Times*, 13 December, QBD.
2   A combination of data from a collection of studies.
3   Grubin *Sex Offending Against Children: Understanding the Risk* Police Research Series Paper No 99 (Home Office, London, 1998) p 32.
4   See Hanson and Bussiere 'Predicting Relapse: A Meta-analysis of Sexual Offender Recidivism Studies' (in press) *Journal of Consulting and Clinical Psychology* quoted in Grubin *Sex Offending Against Children: Understanding the Risk* Police Research Series Paper 99 (Home Office, London, 1998) p 34.

Assessment for Sex Offence Recidivism (RRASOR) and Structured Anchored Clinical Judgment (SACJ).[1]

RAPID RISK ASSESSMENT FOR SEX OFFENCE RECIDIVISM

5.105 The RRASOR was developed as a brief actuarial tool for screening purposes and was based on the finding of the large meta-analysis referred to above and data from a number of North American sex offender follow-up studies. The score is based on four variables (age, victim gender, relationship to victim and past sexual offences) and it is possible for an offender to score between 0 and 6 points. For the first three variables, 1 point is scored for each of the following: if the offender is aged less than 25; if any of the victims are male; and if any of the victims are not related to the offender. Additional weight is given to the fourth variable (past sexual offences, which include convictions and charges), 1 point is scored for one conviction or one to two charges; 2 points are scored for two to three convictions or three to five charges; and 3 points are scored for four or more convictions or six or more charges.

5.106 The score was tested on nearly 2,600 sex offenders released from prisons in England and Wales in 1979. Each offender's RRASOR score was calculated and reconviction[2] rates at 5 and 10 years determined.

(1) Of the 2,592 offenders, 13% had been reconvicted of a sexual offence within 5 years and 20% had been reconvicted of a sexual offence within 10 years.

(2) Of the sample, 20% had a RRASOR score of 0. Of this group, 4% had been reconvicted of a sexual offence within 5 years and 7% had been reconvicted of a sexual offence within 10 years.

(3) Of the sample, 31% had a RRASOR score of 1. Of this group, 8% had been reconvicted of a sexual offence within 5 years and 11% had been reconvicted of a sexual offence within 10 years.

(4) Of the sample, 29% had a RRASOR score of 2. Of this group, 14% had been reconvicted of a sexual offence within 5 years and 21% had been reconvicted of a sexual offence within 10 years.

(5) Of the sample, 13% had a RRASOR score of 3. Of this group, 25% had been reconvicted of a sexual offence within 5 years and 37% had been reconvicted of a sexual offence within 10 years.

(6) Of the sample, 5% had a RRASOR score of 4. Of this group, 33% had been reconvicted of a sexual offence within 5 years and 49% had been reconvicted of a sexual offence within 10 years.

(7) Of the sample, 2% had a RRASOR score of 5. Of this group, 50% had been reconvicted of a sexual offence within 5 years and 73% had been reconvicted of a sexual offence within 10 years.

STRUCTURED ANCHORED CLINICAL JUDGMENT

5.107 The SACJ system of classification was developed within the context of the SOTP.[3] The main distinguishing feature of the SACJ is that it is not

1 Grubin *Sex Offending Against Children: Understanding the Risk* Police Research Series Paper No 99 (Home Office, London, 1998) p 35.
2 Some of the data included charges as well as reconvictions.
3 See Grubin *Sex Offending Against Children: Understanding the Risk* Police Research Series Paper No 99 (Home Office, London, 1998) pp 36–38.

dependent solely on archival data about the offender, but is designed so that the assessment of risk can change over time as more information about the offender becomes available. The classification is a three-step process, with risk re-assessed at each step.

Step one
5.108   Step one is based solely on an offender's criminal history. One point is allocated for each of the following:

(1)   a current sexual offence;
(2)   a past conviction for a sexual offence;
(3)   a non-sexual violent offence in the current conviction;
(4)   a past conviction for non-sexual violence; and
(5)   more than three convictions of any sort.

Offenders who score 1 point are classified as low risk, those who score 2 points are classified as medium risk and those who score 3 or more points are classified as high risk.

Step two
5.109   Step two relates to aggravating factors. If two or more of the following are present, the individual is moved up one risk category level:

(1)   male victim, any sex offence;
(2)   stranger victim, any sex offence;
(3)   any non-contact sex offence;
(4)   substance abuse (not simply recreational);
(5)   ever been in care;
(6)   never married;
(7)   deviant sexual arousal; and
(8)   score of 25+ on the PCL-R.[1]

Step three
5.110   Step three is based on progress in prison. An offender's risk level can be increased or decreased according to his conduct. For example, successful completion of the SOTP would result in the offender being moved down a level – from high to medium or from medium to low risk, as the case may be. However, an offender who fails to complete the programme successfully will have his risk level increased.

5.111   Due to the relatively recent implementation of the SOTP and the provision of therapeutic regimes within prison, the SACJ system of classification has not been fully tested. However, a 'low information' version, based on information from step one and some from step two (victim gender, victim stranger, non-contact sex offences and marital status) was tested on 533 sex offenders released from prison in 1979 and followed up for 16 years:

(1)   30% of the sample were classified as low risk; of these, 9% had been reconvicted of a sexual offence within 16 years;

---

1   PCL-R is a psychopathy checklist, an instrument based on personality style and antisocial
      lifestyle. It has been shown to be a good predictor of violent (but not sexual) offending.

(2) 43% of the sample were classified as medium risk; of these, 23% had been reconvicted of a sexual offence within 16 years; and

(3) 26% of the sample were classified as high risk; of these, 46% had been reconvicted of a sexual offence within 16 years.

5.112   These results show that both the RRASOR and SACJ systems are useful tools for categorising offenders into risk groups. Such actuarial tools are clearly useful, not only in making decisions on release, but also for targeting high-risk offenders in order to make more efficient use of resources, both in relation to the provision of treatment and the supervision of offenders in the community.[1]

5.113   It has been pointed out that there remains the issue of the correspondence between reconviction and re-offending – if low reconviction groups are made of men who re-offend but are simply not caught, then the exercise achieves little. However, if this were the case, then the risk factors used in the scales would not be good predictors of re-offending, but of the ability to avoid detection, which is thought to be an unlikely conclusion.[2] Grubin argues that more work is needed in three areas. First, it is not clear whether either system is able to distinguish frequency of re-offending from severity, as the type of further offences committed are not specified in their results. Thus, it is not possible to see from the prediction tools whether the severity of offences committed by a sex offender is likely to increase over time. Secondly, both systems identify a significant middle group of offenders with a moderate conviction rate of between 20% and 25%. It remains to be seen whether either system can be refined to identify higher risk men in this group. Finally, neither instrument is likely to do well with respect to individuals who have committed their first sexual offence. On a wider level, it may also be added that no prediction tool can been devised to identify potential offenders before their first conviction. Although not relevant to discretionary release decisions, such an instrument would, if it could ever be devised, be of immeasurable assistance in protecting certain vulnerable groups of potential victims such as children.

LIFE SENTENCES

Mandatory and discretionary life sentences – two different regimes

5.114   Policy and practice in relation to the release of offenders sentenced to life imprisonment clearly show that those sentenced to a mandatory life sentence, where the sentence for the offence is fixed by law, are treated differently to those on whom a discretionary life sentence has been imposed. The distinction between mandatory and discretionary life prisoners was first referred to expressly in 1991 during the course of a Parliamentary debate on the Criminal Justice Bill when a Government minister explained that, in the case of a discretionary life sentence, the decision to release is based purely on whether the offender continues to be a risk to the public – the presumption is that once the

---

1   See chap 6.

2   Grubin *Sex Offending Against Children: Understanding the Risk* Police Research Series Paper No 99 (Home Office, London, 1998) p 39.

period that is appropriate to punishment has passed, the prisoner should be released if it is safe to do so.[1] However, the element of risk was said not to be a decisive factor in the imposition of a mandatory life sentence when, according to the judicial process, the offender has committed a crime of such gravity that he forfeits his liberty to the State for the rest of his life – the presumption is that he should remain in custody until the Home Secretary concludes that the public interest would be better served by his release than by his continued detention.[2] Such a distinction between the two forms of life sentences inevitably gives rise to concerns about procedural fairness, particularly as different regimes are applicable in relation to the release of the two categories of prisoners. The European Court of Human Rights has rejected the argument that those sentenced to a mandatory life sentence should be accorded the same rights to a review of their continued detention after the tariff phase of their sentence as are accorded to those sentenced to discretionary life sentences.[3] Thus, the two categories remain. Section 28 of the Crime (Sentences) Act 1997 widened the category of what had previously been referred to as 'discretionary lifers'. Section 29 of the Act replicates the relevant provisions of the Criminal Justice Act 1991 in relation to prisoners serving life sentences to whom s 28 does not apply – 'mandatory lifers'.

Mandatory lifers – s 29 of the Crime (Sentences) Act 1997

5.115　　As noted previously, the trial judge indicates his opinion of what the tariff period, ie the period necessary to meet the requirement of retribution and deterrence, should be.[4] The Lord Chief Justice then adds his view and the recommendations are communicated to the Home Secretary. The recommendations are also disclosed to the offender, who may make representations to the Home Secretary, who is responsible for setting the tariff period. The Home Secretary must give reasons for any departure from the judicial recommendations.

5.116　　The decision to release a mandatory lifer after the tariff period has been served rests ultimately with the Home Secretary, who may, if recommended to do so by the Parole Board and after consultation with the Lord Chief Justice together with the trial judge if available, order the offender's release on licence.[5] The Parole Board may not make such a recommendation unless the particular case, or class of case to which that case belongs, has been referred to it by the Home Secretary,[6] who will usually make the first referral to the Parole Board 3 years before the expiry of the tariff period and every 2 years thereafter. However, a ministerial review will be undertaken after 10 years' detention in order to consider whether there are any grounds for bringing forward the first review by the Parole Board and, thus, in cases where the tariff period exceeds 13

1　This was clearly also the rationale underlying the introduction of automatic life sentences under the Crime (Sentences) Act 1997, where the sentence is imposed on the basis of presumed dangerousness.
2　Angela Rumbold, HC, 16 July 1991, see Livingstone and Owen *Prison Law* (Oxford University Press, Oxford, 1999) p 374.
3　*Wynne v UK* (1994) 19 EHRR 333. See further **5.119**.
4　See **4.99**.
5　Crime (Sentences) Act 1997, s 29(1).
6　Crime (Sentences) Act 1997, s 29(2).

years, the date of the first review may be brought forward following such a ministerial review. In the exceptional case where the tariff period is set as being the offender's whole life, a ministerial review will be undertaken after 25 years in custody and will take into account not only whether anything has emerged to show that the crime was not as heinous as initially thought (and, therefore, whether the life tariff continues to be justified on the grounds of retribution and deterrence), but also whether the offender has made exceptional progress in custody (which would justify a referral to the Parole Board).

5.117 In reviewing the case, the Parole Board may make one of three possible recommendations: no further progress, a move to open conditions[1] or release. Directions to the Parole Board issued by the Home Secretary[2] require the Board to consider the risk of the offender committing further imprisonable offences after release. Until recently, it was thought that the continued detention of an offender after the tariff period would not be justified solely on the grounds that he may commit a further non-violent imprisonable offence on release, but the Court of Appeal has now made it clear that it is legitimate for the Home Secretary to prolong a mandatory lifer's detention on the grounds that he may commit a further imprisonable offence, albeit not a violent one.[3] The Directions make it clear that the Home Secretary, in taking the final decision on release, is concerned not only with the risk posed by the offender, but also with the wider political implications, including the effect on public confidence in the life sentence system which release may have, ie how the public would be likely to respond to the lifer being released at that juncture. In 1997–98, the Parole Board considered a total of 634 cases involving mandatory life sentences and recommended release in 112 cases (18%).[4]

Discretionary lifers – s 28 of the Crime (Sentences) Act 1997

5.118 The crucial distinction between mandatory lifers, governed by s 29 of the 1997 Act and discretionary lifers, governed by s 28 of the Act, is that the release of discretionary lifers is determined by the Parole Board, it is not at the discretion of the Home Secretary as is the case with mandatory lifers. The provisions of s 28 of the 1997 Act apply to offenders sentenced to life imprisonment who were under the age of 18 at the time of the commission of the offence for which the sentence was imposed (ie those detained during Her Majesty's Pleasure)[5] and those whose sentence was imposed for an offence the sentence for which is not fixed by law and the sentencing court has ordered that the section would apply to him as soon as he has served a part of his sentence specified in the order.[6] Thus, the sentencing court has a discretion to determine

---

1   The Home Secretary has made it clear that he considers a period in open conditions as essential for most life prisoners, as it allows the testing of areas of concern in conditions which are nearer to those in the community than can be found in closed prisons. Directions to the Parole Board under s 32(6) of the Criminal Justice Act 1991 – Transfer of Life Sentence Prisoners to Open Conditions.
2   Direction issued to the Parole Board under s 32(6) of the Criminal Justice Act 1991 – Release of Mandatory Life Sentence Prisoners.
3   *R v Secretary of State for the Home Department, ex parte Stafford* [1998] 1 WLR 503.
4   *Report of the Parole Board 1997–98* p 47.
5   Crime (Sentences) Act 1997, s 28(1)(b).
6   Crime (Sentences) Act 1997, s 28(2).

whether the offence is so serious as to call for lifelong punishment. If the court decides that the basis of the discretionary life sentence is exclusively punitive, it will not set the appropriate tariff period and the offender will fall to be dealt with under s 29 of the Act.[1] For these purposes, those sentenced to an automatic life sentence for a second serious offence are treated as discretionary lifers, unless, of course, the sentencing court decides otherwise.[2]

RELEASE OF DISCRETIONARY LIFERS
5.119 Prior to 1991, when a discretionary life sentence was passed, the trial judge would recommend the tariff period, ie the period that should be served to satisfy the requirements of retribution and deterrence, to the Home Secretary, who would then set the tariff period in accordance with the judicial recommendation. The date when the tariff period expired would determine the date when the prisoner's suitability for release would first be reviewed. Following a review by a Local Review Committee and the Parole Board, a recommendation would be made to the Home Secretary, who could release the prisoner if so recommended by the Parole Board, but was not bound to do so. In 1990, the European Court of Human Rights declared the Parole Board procedures to be insufficiently judicial to satisfy art 5(4) of the European Convention on Human Rights[3] and a new procedure for reviewing discretionary life sentences was enacted in the Criminal Justice Act 1991. Where the offender is aged 18 or over, the tariff period will now be set by the sentencing court, taking into account the seriousness of the offence, or the combination of the offence and other offences associated with it, and the credit which would have been given for periods of remand in custody if it had sentenced him to a term of imprisonment.[4] A discretionary lifer is entitled to have his case referred to the Parole Board as soon as he has served the tariff period and at 2-yearly intervals thereafter.[5] In practice, cases are referred to a Discretionary Lifer Panel of the Parole Board 6 months before the expiry of the tariff. The Panel consists of three Board members, including a judge and a psychiatrist. If the Panel is satisfied that the offender's continued detention is no longer necessary for the protection of the public,[6] it may direct the offender's release and, following such a direction, the Home Secretary is under a duty to release the offender on licence.[7] In 1997–98, Discretionary Lifer Panels considered a total of 278 cases and directed release in 39 cases (14%).[8]

Released prisoners and electronic monitoring

5.120 Advances in technology have already been utilised to facilitate the electronic monitoring of offenders in the community, either as part of the home

---

1   To date, there have been no known cases in which a full life tariff has been imposed in the case of a discretionary lifer.
2   Crime (Sentences) Act 1997, s 2(4).
3   *Thynne v UK* (1990) 13 EHRR 666.
4   Crime (Sentences) Act 1997, s 28(3).
5   Crime (Sentences) Act 1997, s 28(7).
6   Crime (Sentences) Act 1997, s 28(6).
7   Crime (Sentences) Act 1997, s 28(5).
8   *Report of the Parole Board 1997–98* p 46.

detention curfew scheme for those released from a custodial sentence[1] or as part of a Curfew Order imposed by the sentencing court.[2] The Government clearly intends to make further use of electronic monitoring, or 'tagging', and has announced plans to exend its use to thousands of offenders convicted of sexual or violent offences on their release from a custodial sentence. A Home Office minister has described the proposal as a public protection measure and has indicated that it could mean lengthy periods of tagging or indeed a lifetime tag.[3] The proposal is expected to form part of the Crime and Public Protection Bill which is anticipated in the near future.

---

1   See **5.67**.
2   See **4.109**.
3   (1999) *The Times*, 2 December.

Chapter 6

SEX OFFENDERS IN THE COMMUNITY: SUPERVISION AND THE ROLE OF THE PROBATION SERVICE

'VISIBLE' AND 'INVISIBLE' SEX OFFENDERS

6.1   It is impossible to know how many sex offenders are currently living in the community. Criminal statistics record how many offenders are convicted of sexual offences, how many receive custodial sentences and when they are released, and how many receive community sentences. These are the 'visible' sex offenders – offenders who have been convicted of a sexual offence, who are known to the authorities and may have restrictions placed on their lives in the community as a result of the conviction. Many of these 'visible' offenders will be supervised by the Probation Service for varying periods of time while living in the community, either as a result of being released on licence following a custodial sentence or as a result of a community sentence such as a Probation Order. The conditions of the licence or Community Order inevitably place some restrictions on offenders and enable a certain amount of control to be exercised over them. This control, combined with supervising officers' work towards rehabilitating the offender and, in some cases, participation in a treatment programme, aims to ensure that the public are protected. Even when the licence or community sentence comes to an end, it may be possible to exercise some control over these offenders, for example, the offender may be required to notify the police of any change to his name or address,[1] or he may be the subject of a Sex Offender Order.[2]

6.2   However, many sex offenders are 'invisible' in that they have never been convicted of a sexual offence. Some of these offenders may have aroused suspicion. They may have been the subject of an inconclusive police investigation or they may have been acquitted of a sexual offence. Even in the absence of a police investigation, they may simply have a reputation in the local community as being 'odd' or simply 'different', for example parents may warn their children to keep away from a man who lives alone and keeps himself to himself because 'you never know what he might do'. Yet these offenders can never be officially labelled as 'sex offenders' because they have never been convicted of a sexual offence. If their conduct gives sufficient cause for concern, some control over their movements may be possible, for example by an Anti-social Behaviour Order[3] or an injunction.[4] Alternatively, an individual may find his employment prospects curtailed through his inclusion on 'List 99' or

---

1   See **7.1**.
2   See **7.16**.
3   See **7.36**.
4   See **7.50**.

equivalent,[1] or, if offences against children are suspected and child protection is an issue, family life may be disrupted.[2] However, while such measures may be effective in protecting individual potential victims, there are inevitable limits as to what they can achieve for protection of the public as whole.

6.3   Perhaps most worryingly, there remains a core of sex offenders, living and moving freely in the community, who have never been the focus of a police investigation and who have never been suspected of committing sexual offences, even by those close to them. Protecting the public from the 'visible' sex offender is a formidable task. The last few years have seen a radical re-appraisal of the working practices of the professionals challenged with the task, accompanied by a dramatic increase in the number of legislative provisions on which these professionals can rely. Controlling the 'invisible' sex offender, however, is a far more difficult task and in many cases is simply not possible. One of the challenges currently faced by the criminal justice system is to ensure that more sex offenders become 'visible', and therefore subject to supervision and control while living in the community.

THE ROLE OF THE PROBATION SERVICE

The Probation Service

6.4   The Probation Service was officially established by the Probation of Offenders Act 1907 and is now the major organisation in England and Wales for dealing with offenders in conditions of freedom. The Probation Service is responsible for the enforcement of community sentences imposed by the courts and for the supervision and control of offenders released into the community following a custodial sentence. The Service also provides risk assessments of offenders to the courts, the Prison Service and the Parole Board.

6.5   In 1998, a total of 14,831 staff were employed in the Probation Service in England and Wales, of whom 7,171 were probation officers. This figure represented an 8% decrease on the peak level at the end of 1994. In 1998, the Service's main outputs per year were:[3]

(1)   over 227,000 pre-sentence reports produced for the criminal courts, which had risen from 208,000 since 1993;
(2)   the supervision in the community of over 140,000 offenders, which had risen from 113,000 in 1993–94;
(3)   additionally, the pre- and post-release supervision of over 70,000 prisoners and released prisoners, which had risen from 52,600 in 1993–94; and
(4)   the provision of 2,300 bed spaces in approved probation and bail hostels, of which 86% were normally occupied compared with 70% in 1993.

6.6   Projections in 1998 indicated a rise in the total number of persons requiring Probation Service supervision annually from 166,000 in 1993–94 to 223,000 by 2000–01.

---

1   See **8.144**.
2   See **8.65** to **8.144**.
3   *Joining Forces to Protect the Public* (Home Office, London, 1998) Appendix A.2.

The structure of the Probation Service

6.7 There are currently 54 separate, autonomous Probation Services throughout England and Wales. However, following the 1998 ministerial review of the work of the Prison Service and the Probation Service,[1] and the publication in August 1998 of a consultation document,[2] in April 1999 the Home Office announced plans for a new, unified Probation Service. Key proposed changes are:[3]

(1) a unified service led by a director with a full range of operational responsibilities appointed by the Home Secretary;
(2) 42 local areas to match police boundaries;
(3) chief probation officers to become civil servants, employed by the Home Office;
(4) a light regional arrangement which will reflect Governmental regional office boundaries;
(5) the services to be funded entirely by Central Government, ending current arrangements whereby 80% is paid centrally and 20% locally;
(6) the Home Secretary to take full responsibility for the performance of the Service and to be accountable to Parliament for it; and
(7) the Home Secretary to have greater powers to direct and require necessary outcomes and standards of Service delivery.

6.8 Some of these changes will require legislation, which the Government intends to introduce 'when Parliamentary time permits'. In the meantime, the 'zero plus' option put forward in the 1998 Review, and which is not dependent on structural change, will no doubt proceed.[4]

The changing role of the Probation Service[5]

6.9 The Probation Service has its roots in the work of the 19th-century police court missionaries, first employed by the Church of England Temperance Society in 1876 to 'reclaim' offenders charged with drunkenness or drink-related offences. In 1907, the Probation of Offenders Act gave magistrates' courts the right to appoint probation officers whose job was to 'advise, assist and befriend' offenders placed under their supervision.[6] Current legislation still directs probation officers to 'advise, assist and befriend' offenders, but it is now acknowledged that this is completely out of line not just with the expectations of the courts, but also with the reality of work which probation staff undertake day in and day out.[7] In addition to the increasingly close working relationship between the Prison Service and the Probation Service, the introduction of local partnerships to tackle crime problems in each area now requires much closer working between the Probation Service and other agencies such as the police,

1 *Prisons/Probation Review: Final Report* (Home Office, London, 1998). See **5.19**.
2 *Joining Forces to Protect the Public* (Home Office, London, 1998).
3 Home Office Press Release 123/99, 13 April 1999.
4 See **5.21**.
5 See generally Worrall *Punishment in the Community: The Future of Criminal Justice* (Longman, London, 1997), chap 5.
6 Worrall *Punishment in the Community: The Future of Criminal Justice* (Longman, London, 1997), p 66.
7 *Joining Forces to Protect the Public* (Home Office, London, 1998) para 2.1.

councils, social services and education and health authorities.[1] The work of the Probation Service is now more concerned with confronting offending behaviour, and controlling and monitoring offenders and, in 1998, the Government declared that 'the [Probation] Service now rightly recognises that its core function is public protection', adding that a great deal of important work in this area for the time being goes unsung.[2] Increasing emphasis is also now being placed on the effectiveness of the work of the Probation Service in supervising offenders in the community, as evidenced by the launch of an initiative on strategies for effective offender supervision.[3] The initiative acknowledges the need for thorough assessment of the risks presented by offenders and their offence-related needs, clearly articulated in supervision plans which detail the outcomes of planned interventions with offenders. Nowhere is this changing role more evident than in the work of the Probation Service in supervising sex offenders in the community, as will become evident in this chapter. However, the changing role, which has assumed increased significance over the last two decades, has not been accepted unequivocally by the Probation Service itself. A Home Office Research Study reported in 1997 that the move away from 'advising, assisting and befriending' and towards a more controlling approach to offenders had not been achieved without a good deal of agonising on the part of probation officers who have worried about 'the end of probation as we know it'.[4]

A new role, a new name?

6.10   The reference to 'end of probation' has assumed even more significance since 1997 as it is now proposed that the name of the Probation Service be changed in order to reflect the radical change in the nature of this work. In proposing the new unified national Probation Service, the government commented that it was important that the names, language and terminology used should give accurate and accessible messages about the nature and aims of the work of the Service, for example 'throughcare' could become 'resettlement'. Moreover, the very term 'probation' is set to disappear. Suggested alternative names for the service included:[5]

(1)   the Public Protection Service;
(2)   the Community Justice Enforcement Agency;
(3)   the Offender Risk Management Service;
(4)   the Community Sentence Enforcement Service;
(5)   the Justice Enforcement and Public Protection Service;
(6)   the Public Safety and Offender Management Service; or
(7)   the Community Protection and Justice Service.

In December 1999, the Home Office announced its intention to change the name of the Probation Service to the Community Punishment and Rehabilitation Service.[6] The new name is said to make clear the vital role played by the

---

1   See **7.74**.
2   *Joining Forces to Protect the Public* (Home Office, London, 1998) para 2.2.
3   '*Strategies for Effective Offender Supervision*' Report of the HMIP What Works Project (HM Inspectorate of Probation, 1998).
4   *Offenders on Probation* Home Office Research Study 167 (Home Office, London, 1997) p 1.
5   *Joining Forces to Protect the Public* (Home Office, London, 1998) para 2.14.
6   Home Office Press Release 390/99.

Service in protecting the public and also to send a clear message to offenders that being under supervision in the community is not a reprieve or a soft option.[1]

6.11   The nature of the work undertaken by the new unified Service will remain firmly focused on public protection and control. However, despite the increasing emphasis on the control and monitoring of offenders, particularly sex offenders, it would be wrong to conclude that the traditional role of the probation officer in 'advising, assisting and befriending' offenders has disappeared without trace. Rehabilitation of the offender remains one of the overall aims of both Probation Orders and the supervision of offenders after release from custody and, although provision of treatment for sex offenders in the community takes second place to control and monitoring, there remains at least a vestige of the traditional role of the probation officer.[2]

The supervision of offenders in the community

6.12   An offender may be supervised in the community by a probation officer, either as a result of a community sentence, most notably a Probation Order or a Combination Order, or following release from custody. All offenders sentenced after 1 October 1992 to 12 months' imprisonment or more will serve a period on licence following release. Short-term prisoners will be released automatically when they have served one-half of their sentence. Long-term prisoners may be released after serving one-half of their sentence and must be released after serving two-thirds of their sentence. Both short- and long-term prisoners will be on licence until the three-quarters point of their sentence. Provision was made in the Criminal Justice Act 1991 for sex offenders to be supervised to the end of their sentence[3] and, following the introduction of extended sentences by the Crime and Disorder Act 1998, offenders convicted of sexual or violent offences may now be on licence for up to 10 years following release.[4] Offenders sentenced to life imprisonment will remain on licence for the rest of their lives.[5]

The development of national standards

6.13   In the past, the Probation Service enjoyed relative autonomy to develop its own policies and practices, but over the last decade there has been a process of centralisation, culminating in the recent proposals for a national service. From 1989 to 1992, the Home Office complied a series of national standards directing practice in relation to all aspects of probation supervision and including detailed instructions about the administration of orders. Revised National Standards for the Treatment of Offenders in the Community were published in 1995[6] and

---

1   It is anticipated that the change of name will be contained in the forthcoming Crime and Protection Bill.
2   See **6.50**.
3   Criminal Justice Act 1991, s 44.
4   See **4.82** and **5.76**. The extension period begins when the offender would have served three-quarters of his sentence. If the offender is released prior to this date (as all short-term prisoners will be), the extension period could go beyond 10 years in some cases.
5   Crime (Sentences) Act 1997, s 31(1).
6   *National Standards for the Supervision of Offenders in the Community* (Home Office, London, 1995).

included standards on the preparation of pre-sentence reports, the requirements for the supervision of Probation Orders, Supervision Orders and
supervision before and after release from custody, the requirements of
Community Service Orders and Combination Orders, the management of
approved probation and bail hostels and bail information schemes. The
introduction of national standards severely limited the discretion of individual
probation officers and focused on the management of supervision rather than
on its content.[1]

6.14   Following the publication of the 1995 national standards, increasing
emphasis came to be placed on 'value for money' and the effectiveness of the
probation service in supervising offenders in the community. In 1996 a thematic
report of the work of the Probation Service in partnership with other agencies
pointed out weaknesses in offender assessment and supervision planning and
made recommendations to improve the outcome focus of assessment and
intervention.[2] In 1998 a report on effective offender supervision spelled out the
requirements on probation staff to assess offenders more accurately in terms of
offence related needs, relevant social circumstances and risk factors as key
elements in matching offenders to appropriate programmes.[3] Following this
report, a guide to effective practice was launched, which reinforced in a practical
manner the message from the main report and confirmed the need for good
offender assessment and supervision planning.[4]

6.15   In January 2000 the Home Office issued revised national standards,[5]
which reflect the intention that there should be more effective joint working
between the Prison Service and Probation Service. The revised national
standards refer to the Offender Assessment System (OAS), which will be based
on a new risk/needs assessment tool currently being developed for the Home
Office and which it is hoped will be available during 2000.

The revised national standards

6.16   The revised national standards provide that supervision in the community of either post-custodial licences or community orders shall:[6]

– address and reduce offending behaviour;
– challenge the offender to accept responsibility for the crimes committed
   and their consequences;
– contribute to the protection of the public;

---

1   Worrall *Punishment in the Community: The Future of Criminal Justice* (Longman, London,
     1997), p 73.
2   HM Inspectorate of Probation *Probation Services Working in Partnership: Increasing the Impact
     and Value for Money* (Home Office, London, 1996).
3   HM Inspectorate of Probation *Strategies for Effective Offender Supervision* (Home Office,
     London, 1998).
4   HM Inspectorate of Probation *A Guide to Effective Practice: Evidence Based Practice* (Home
     Office, London, 1998).
5   *National Standards for the Supervision of Offenders in the Community* (Home Office, London,
     2000).
6   *National Standards for the Supervision of Offenders in the Community* (Home Office, London,
     2000) para C8.

- motivate and assist the offender towards a greater sense of personal responsibility and discipline;
- aid reintegration as a law-abiding member of the community; and
- be arranged so as not to prevent the offender from being readily available to seek or take up employment, not conflict with an offender's entitlement to benefit, nor disrupt the working hours of an employed person, or the education of an offender in full time education and to take account of religious and cultural requirements.

Offender assessment[1]

6.17 The revised national standards place increased emphasis on the assessment of offenders, providing that all offenders supervised by the Probation Service must have a written assessment in relation to:

- the risks offenders present of causing serious harm to the victim or victims of the offence, to the public, to staff, or to themselves;
- the causes and patterns of the offending behaviour including the likelihood of reoffending;
- the offenders' offence related needs and circumstances; and
- the offenders' motivation to change their behaviour to address the risks they present and to resolve any offence related needs and circumstances.[2]

The supervision plan[3]

6.18 The national standards provide that, for offenders sentenced to Probation or Community Orders, or those released on licence following a custodial sentence, a written supervision plan must be completed within 15 working days of an order being made, or of the date of release. However, for offenders who present a risk of causing serious harm to the public, a plan which addresses how this will be managed must be available within 5 days of the order or release. The supervision plan must address the risk factors identified in the offender assessment and specify, where relevant:

(1) where an offender presents a risk of causing serious harm to the public, how this will be managed and, where possible, reduced. The level and intensity of supervision should be determined by the degree of risk and the likelihood of reoffending, indicated by the assessment. For example, this may require contact in excess of the minimum defined by the national standards and risk management panels/liaison with the police;[4]
(2) where there has been a direct victim, work on the offender's attitude to victims, including specific attention to racially motivated offending;

---

1 *National Standards for the Supervision of Offenders in the Community* (Home Office, London, 2000) para C9.
2 For offenders subject to a Community Service Order, the assessment must also relate to their health, skills, availability for work and any particular placement needs such as cultural or religious considerations. Offenders must not start a work placement until their risks have been assessed.
3 *National Standards for the Supervision of Offenders in the Community* (Home Office, London, 2000) para C10.
4 See further chap 7.

(3)   how the offender will be made aware of the impact of the offending;
(4)   how the likelihood of further offending is to be reduced;
(5)   how offending related needs and circumstances are to be addressed (eg employment, addictions, accommodation etc);
(6)   where the offence has been racially motivated, how the offender's racist attitudes and beliefs will be challenged and addressed;
(7)   the use to be made of relevant and accredited programmes of supervision;
(8)   where motivation to achieve the purposes of the order is poor, how this will be improved;
(9)   the liaison responsibilities of the managing officer eg with partnership agencies and/or other service staff;
(10)   in the case of Combination Orders, liaison arrangements between community service and probation supervision staff;
(11)   how other orders, such as concurrent Community Orders, will be supervised;
(12)   how and when any additional requirements will be enforced;
(13)   the exact nature and frequency of contact for the forthcoming period of supervision, and how compliance will be achieved; and
(14)   clear targets for progress which the offender understands.

Required levels of contact

6.19   The national standards set out the minimum required levels of contact, however it is pointed out that the minimum requirements are likely to be exceeded for offenders who pose risks of serious harm to the public, or a higher probability of reoffending, or for those who may be subject to additional order or licence requirements.[1] Thus sex offenders are likely to require more extensive contact, particularly in the early stages of supervision.

6.20   For offenders released on licence, the national standards require the Probation Service to ensure that the first appointment with the offender after release is arranged to occur on the day of release or, if not practicable, on the next working day. Arrangements must then be made for a further minimum of weekly contact during the first 4 weeks following release, making a total of 5 contacts in the first 4 weeks. One of these contacts must normally be a home visit, which should be arranged to take place within 10 working days of release. Contact must then be arranged to take place at least fortnightly for the second and third months following release, and thereafter, not less than monthly.[2]

6.21   For offenders subject to a Community Order, wherever possible the date of the first appointment should be given to the offender either by the Probation Service or by the court (acting on Probation Service advice) before the offender leaves court. This should be arranged to take place within 5 working days of the order being made.[3] Thereafter, at least 12 appointments should be made within the first 12 weeks of supervision, normally scheduled to take place

---

1   *National Standards for the Supervision of Offenders in the Community* (Home Office, London, 2000) para D2.
2   *National Standards for the Supervision of Offenders in the Community* (Home Office, London, 2000) para D11.
3   *National Standards for the Supervision of Offenders in the Community* (Home Office, London, 2000) para D7.

weekly. There should normally be a home visit made within the first 12 weeks of the order. Six appointments should be made within the second 12 weeks, after which appointments may reduce to monthly contact.[1]

6.22   The national standards require the Probation Service to ensure that for all offenders, at the first meeting the supervising officer:

(1) provides written information setting out what is expected of the offender during the period of supervision and what the offender can expect from the Probation Service;

(2) explains to the offender (and provides a copy of) instructions setting out the required standards of behaviour that apply during the period of supervision, which shall prohibit:

   (i)   further offending;
   (ii) violent or aggressive behaviour or threats of violence;
   (iii) other conduct or language that might reasonably give offence to probation staff, other persons on supervision or members of the public;
   (iv) other wilful or persistent non co-operation or behaviour designed to frustate the purpose of the offender's or other's supervision; and

(3) ensures that the offender signs the order or licence (where possible) and indicates that he or she understands its requirements.

THE EFFECTIVE SUPERVISION PLAN – QUEST FOR THE HOLY GRAIL?

6.23   The supervision plan can be regarded as the core of probation officers' work, setting out what the supervising officer will do and identifying why, when and how he will do it. However, devising an effective supervision plan for individual offenders has proved to be far from easy. As one senior manager of the Probation Service is quoted as saying:

> 'The history of the written and recorded cases assessment supervision plan and review system in this service has some parallels with the quest for the Holy Grail. No-one is absolutely sure what it looks like, but everyone is certain that when they find it they will know it. The problem is that the person who goes on to claim to have found it finds that no-one else agrees that it is it. The person then becomes a doubter themselves and search starts again.'[2]

6.24   As part of a thematic inspection undertaken in collaboration with 46 Probation Services in 1999, a total of 3,959 cases were scrutinised – 69% related to court orders and 31% to post-release supervision. The key findings were:[3]

(1) far too many supervision plans were either unsatisfactory or very poor and few addressed either comprehensively, or even partially, the requirements of the relevant national standard; similarly, supervision plan reviews were too often of an unsatisfactory or very poor quality;

(2) too often supervision plans did not draw explicitly on assessment processes or on previous assessments, such as those carried out for PSR and parole purposes;

---

1   *National Standards for the Supervision of Offenders in the Community* (Home Office, London, 2000) para D13.

2   *Offender Assessment and Supervision Planning: Helping to Achieve Effective Intervention with Offenders* (Home Office, London, 1999) para 4.46.

3   *Offender Assessment and Supervision Planning: Helping to Achieve Effective Intervention with Offenders* (Home Office, London, 1999) para 3.2.

(3) offenders signed 51% of supervision plans;
(4) the structure of supervision plans was very variable and, even when an area had a specific format, officers did not routinely adhere to it;
(5) few supervision plans conveyed an understanding by the officer of objective setting;
(6) there was generally little evidence of management guidance or oversight of offender assessment and supervision planning; and
(7) supervision plans were better when a structure was followed, when undertaken promptly and in more recent samples of work. Overall, they were better on offenders subject to community penalties than on those released from custody.

6.25 Based on these findings, the inspection report made the following six national recommendations.[1]

(1) There should be one national supervision plan format in place from April 2000, accompanied by clear guidance on content.
(2) Probation Services should ensure that all supervision plans are satisfactory by April 2001 and set appropriate local targets to ensure that this is achieved.
(3) Probation Services should identify those practitioners known to produce good quality supervision plans, identify the factors which make their offender assessment and supervision planning practices good, and use the information to spread good practice.
(4) Probation Services should ensure that there is better integration of assessment information into supervision plans.
(5) Probation Services should ensure that all supervision plan reviews are satisfactory by April 2001 and set appropriate local targets to ensure this is achieved.
(6) Her Majesty's Inspectorate of Probation should initiate and coordinate a series of regional seminars to disseminate the findings of this inspection and to consider future action, for those regions who wish to participate in such events.

6.26 In the past, far too many supervision plans failed to reach an acceptable standard. The revised national standards, with the increased emphasis on assessment of the offenders, combined with the guidance provided on effective practice,[2] will hopefully facilitate the preparation of effective supervision plans in the future.

Supervision and risk assessment in the community

6.27 As a result of the changing role of the Probation Service, with increasing emphasis being placed on control of the offender and protection of the public, assessment of the risk posed by an offender and the effective management of that risk have become a central feature of probation practice.[3] Risk assessments are essentially concerned with prediction: predicting the likelihood of an offender causing harm in the future, how serious the harm may be and to whom it may be

1 *Offender Assessment and Supervision Planning: Helping to Achieve Effective Intervention with Offenders* (Home Office, London, 1999) para 3.2.
2 HM Inspectorate of Probation *A Guide to Effective Practice: Evidence Based Practice* (Home Office, London, 1998).
3 See generally Kemshall *Risk in Probation Practice* (Ashgate, Aldershot, 1998).

caused. Risk assessment is obviously not restricted to the work of probation officers with offenders in the community – assessments may be made following arrest to inform decisions on bail or remands in custody, at the pre-sentence report stage to inform decisions on sentencing and throughout any custodial sentence to inform decisions on release and the imposition of licence conditions. However, risk assessment also now forms a crucial part of a probation officer's work in supervising offenders in the community.

Clinical v actuarial methods of predicting risk

6.28 Although the national standards refer to the need to assess the risk posed by an offender, they provide no further guidance on how such assessments are to be made. Clinical methods of predicting risk, which originate from the field of mental health, are essentially subjective in nature, based on observation of the offender, clinical assessment, knowledge, experience and professional training of the assessor. The use of clinical models is said to lead to cases being individualised, with assessors bringing their own theoretical perspectives, knowledge base and experience to the assessment process. Thus, the approach is open to bias and can be affected by the personal experience, values and beliefs of individual assessors.[1] In contrast, statistical or actuarial methods of prediction are objective and are based on predicting an individual's behaviour from how others have responded in similar circumstances, or from the individual's similarity to others who have proved to be risky in the past. Such objective methods of risk assessment have been shown to be more accurate than clinical methods, although actuarial methods tend to result in general predictions about groups of offenders rather than specific predictions about individual offenders.

The emergence of a 'new penology'

6.29 The recent years there has been increasing interest in actuarial methods of predicting risk in the criminal justice system. The reason for this lies partly in the penal policy of 'bifurcation' or 'twin track' sentencing which underlies the Criminal Justice Act 1991[2] and the increasing 'commercialisation of crime control'.[3] This has led to the emergence of what has been referred to as the 'new penology' or 'actuarial justice'.[4] Whereas the 'old penology' is said to be rooted in a concern for individuals and preoccupied with diagnosis, intervention and treatment of the individual offender, the 'new penology' is concerned with techniques for identifying, classifying and managing groups assorted by levels of dangerousness.[5] Although actuarial methods of predicting risk are increasingly being used to inform decisions on release from custody,[6] in the past the Probation Service has relied predominantly on clinical methods of prediction. It

---

1   Kemshall 'Offender Risk and Probation Practice' in Kemshall and Pritchard (eds) *Good Practice in Risk Assessment and Risk Management* (Jessica Kingsley Publishers, London, 1996).
2   See **4.58**.
3   Christie *Crime Control as Industry* (Routledge, London, 1993).
4   Feeley and Simon 'The New Penology: Notes on the Emerging Strategy of Corrections and its Implications' [1992] *Criminology* 30(4) at 449.
5   Feeley and Simon 'Actuarial Justice: the Emerging New Criminal Law' in Nelken (ed) *The Futures of Criminology* (Sage, London, 1994).
6   See **5.85**.

has been suggested that, with its roots in individualised therapeutic case work, the Service has found it easier to adopt the clinical method from the mental health arena than the actuarial model from criminological studies, but the warning has been given that, in its urgent need for predictive methods, the Probation Service is in danger of accepting uncritically the heritage of clinical inference without giving full consideration to the role actuarial studies of offender risk could make to assessment.[1]

Sex offenders and risk assessment in the community

6.30   In the past, there has been a tendency to use offence type as the main indicator of risk. Thus, sex offenders would all tend to be classified as high risk simply by virtue of the fact that they had committed a sexual offence in the past. In recent years, the increasing importance being attached to the supervision of sex offenders in the community and the need to prioritise resources, both practical and financial, within the Probation Service have resulted in the development of new risk assessment tools.

THE REVISED OFFENDER GROUP RECONVICTION SCALE

6.31   The Offender Group Reconviction Scale (OGRS) is a statistical risk score which provides an estimate of the probability that a convicted offender will be reconvicted at least once within two years of release from custody or from the start of a community sentence. The original OGRS, which was used by probation officers as an assessment tool when writing pre-sentence reports, predicted the probability of further convictions for any type of offence. This has now been revised to produce a model that predicts reconvictions for standard list sexual and violent offences within two years of the offender's release from prison or from the start of a community penalty and it is intended for the use of probation officers to assess the risk of sexual or violent offenders (defined by a previous or current conviction) being reconvicted for a further sexual or violent offence within two years.[2] The model is based on a sample of over 23,000 offenders sentenced to a community penalty or discharged from custody in 1995 with either a current and/or previous history of sexual or violent offending. The variables used are: gender; current offence group; age at current conviction; the Copas rate variable;[3] history of burglary; number of violent convictions; and number of sexual convictions. At first sight the inclusion of any history of burglary in the variables seems curious. However, the research found that sexual and violent offenders record on average twice as many convictions for burglary as all other types of offender.[4] It is suggested that this may be because some

---

1   Kemshall 'Offender Risk and Probation Practice' in Kemshall and Pritchard (eds) *Good Practice in Risk Assessment and Risk Management* (Jessica Kingsley Publishers, London, 1996) p 135.

2   Taylor *Predicting Reconvictions for Sexual and Violent Offences using the Revised Offender Group Reconviction Scale* Home Office Research Findings No 104 (Home Office, London, 1999).

3   The Copas rate is the rate at which offenders are convicted, ie an offender with five convictions within five years between first and current conviction will have a higher rate of conviction than an offender with five convictions within 10 years.

4   Taylor *Predicting Reconvictions for Sexual and Violent Offences using the Revised Offender Group Reconviction Scale* Home Office Research Findings No 104 (Home Office, London, 1999) table 3.

offenders set out intending to commit a burglary but also look for, or take advantage of, an opportunity to commit another crime such as rape.

6.32 The research on which the revised OGRS is based found that offenders who commit sexual and violent offences tend to be highly criminal individuals, recording an average number of convictions for all types of offence of 7.3, compared to an average of only 3.3 for all other offenders. Sexual and violent offenders also have a higher average number of reconvictions for sexual or violent offences than other offenders, 0.2 compared to 0.1 for other offenders, a finding which supports the view that a history of sexual offending increases the risk of further sexual offences being committed in the future. However, despite this, the actual number of reconvictions for sexual and violent offences is low,[1] and thus the average reconviction rate for sexual and violent offenders convicted of a further sexual or violent offence is only 20%. This low base rate of reconviction makes it difficult to interpret the difference between OGRS probability scores for offenders who pose low, average and high risks of reconviction. To address this problem, in the revised OGRS the scores for sexual and violent offending have been translated into risk bands, thus making it easier to interpret the level of risk. Thus offenders with a risk score of 0–10 present 'some risk', with an actual reconviction rate of 6%; those with a risk score of 11–16 present a 'moderate risk', with an actual reconviction rate of 15%; those with a risk score of 17–25 present a 'raised risk', with an actual reconviction rate of 21%; and those with a risk score of 25+ present a 'high risk', with an actual reconviction rate of 34%.

6.33 The OGRS for sexual and violent offenders therefore aims to identify four groups who represent differing levels of risk. But the model cannot identify which individuals within these groups will be reconvicted and it can therefore only be used as a screening tool, perhaps with a view to targeting further assessment at higher risk groups of offenders. Whilst the OGRS does have the advantage of being relatively cheap and easy to use,[2] it is argued that further assessment tools need to be developed which also take into account situational and behavioural factors.

6.34 Undoubtedly, there will be much attention focused on the formulation of guidance and risk-assessment models over the coming years. Although it must be recognised that no risk-assessment model is infallible and each case must be decided on its own merits, a comprehensive checklist has been suggested[3] which illustrates the number of factors involved and the balances that have to be achieved. The checklist combines the greater accuracy of actuarial methods with the clinical observation and personal knowledge of the assessor. It is designed to assist assessors in identifying 'hazards' which may lead to the 'danger' resulting. A hazard is defined as a condition which introduced the possibility that harm (ie loss, damage or diminution) will result from danger. The danger is the event

---

1   The low number of reconvictions can be attributed to, inter alia, low levels of reporting, low conviction rates and the length of court proceedings.

2   The OGRS is available as a Windows-based program. Probation staff enter the correct information and the OGRS will calculate the percentage probability of reconviction.

3   Kemshall 'Offender Risk and Probation Practice' in Kemshall and Pritchard (eds) *Good Practice in Risk Assessment and Risk Management* (Jessica Kingsley Publishers, London, 1996) p 140.

which, if it occurs, will cause the harm. Although the checklist can be used for risk assessment at any time, it seems particularly appropriate for use as part of the supervision plan and on-going process of risk assessment during the period of supervision. A summary of the checklist, together with its potential application to the assessment of the risk posed by a sex offender, is given below.

GENERAL PREDICTIVE HAZARDS
6.35   These are assessed objectively, employing actuarial methods based on information known to have relevance to the class of offence or offender, such as known reconviction rates, age and length of criminal career. If an offender has served a substantial custodial sentence, this information will already have been collated as the RORS, calculated as part of the parole dossier[1] and similar calculations can be made for other offenders. As noted previously, sex offenders are less likely to be released from custody under the early release scheme than other offenders and studies have shown that a history of sexual offending places an offender at a greater risk of committing further offences.[2] Therefore, employing actuarial methods is likely to result in sex offenders, particularly those with a previous conviction for sex offences, being assessed as posing a significant hazard and thereby a high risk to the public.

SPECIFIC HAZARDS
6.36   On the other hand, specific hazards are dependent upon clinical inference and include information specifically relevant to an individual offender, for example personal characteristics, attitudes and situational factors of the offender's immediate environment. Therefore, specific hazards are dependent on the offender himself, not the class to which he belongs. For example, a sex offender convicted of indecent assault on an adult but having admitted paedophiliac tendencies and living in a household with young children may present more of a hazard than other offenders convicted of the same offence.

STRENGTHS IN THE SITUATION, EITHER OF THE PERSON, OR OTHERS, OR OF THE ENVIRONMENT
6.37   Such strengths may serve to limit the hazards and, thus, reduce the danger. For example, a sex offender who participates in a treatment programme in the community may well reduce the hazard, and thus the danger, he presents. A paedophile who moves out of a household with young children while undergoing treatment would also diminish the hazard and accompanying danger he presents.

DANGER(S)
6.38   In most cases, the danger will be the risk of reoffending. The assessor has to weigh up the hazards against the strengths and decide upon the level of risk present. On a scale of 1–5 the assessor should estimate the risk of the danger occurring.

---

1   See **5.87**.
2   See **5.93**.

RISK OF WHAT AND TO WHOM? THE CONSEQUENCES OF THE RISK

6.39   These factors should all be taken into account, for example, a risk of rape may be viewed more seriously that a risk of indecent exposure, sex offenders may pose a risk to the public at large, to a specific group (eg children) or to an individual, and the consequences may differ, depending on the type of danger presented and the victim of the harm caused.

COSTS OF ACTING/NOT ACTING AND TO WHOM? THE CONSEQUENCES OF NO ACTION AND TO WHOM?

6.40   Part of the toleration calculation is an estimate of the costs of responding or not responding to the risk and the costs to all involved if the harmful event takes place – admittedly, some risks may not be worth the cost of intervention, but this is unlikely to be the case with sex offenders where any risk posed may well be deemed unacceptable.

ACTION REQUIRED TO MINIMISE THE HAZARDS AND/OR ENHANCE THE STRENGTHS

6.41   Action may be taken to reduce the hazards and/or enhance the strengths in any situation. Although general hazards cannot be addressed in this way, specific hazards can. Finding alternative accommodation for the sex offender with paedophiliac tendencies living in a household with a young child would reduce the hazard and providing opportunities for treatment would enhance the strengths. In more extreme situations, it may be necessary to consider recalling the offender to custody or taking action for breach of a community sentence.[1]

DATE FOR REVIEW

6.42   This will vary in individual cases. Risk assessment is an ongoing process, as risk changes over time. The effectiveness of any action taken to minimise the hazards or enhance the strengths must be assessed carefully. Changes in an offender's circumstances can affect the risk presented, either by diminishing it or increasing it, and it will be the responsibility of the supervising officer to monitor changes and assess risk throughout the period of supervision.

The effectiveness of supervision of sex offenders in the community

6.43   The findings of the developmental thematic inspection of offender assessment and supervision planning were disappointing and, prima facie, call the effectiveness of supervision in the community into question. However, the inspection focused on the format and content of the supervision plan itself, rather than its implementation in practice. In direct contrast with this, the thematic inspection of the work of Probation Services with sex offenders carried out in 1996–97 sampled a total of 343 cases, of which 158 were Probation and Combination Orders and 185 were throughcare licences.[2] This exercise focused

---

1   See **6.66** to **6.87**.
2   *Exercising Constant Vigilance: The Role of the Probation Service in Protecting the Public from Sex Offenders* (Home Office, London, 1998). For the sake of comparing the samples, identical questions were asked in each case.

on how sexual offending was addressed and risk assessed and managed rather than on adherence to every aspect of the national standard, although information was collected about frequency of contact and enforcement. Overall, it was assessed that 86% of the sample cases were supervised to satisfactory standards (40% were assessed as very good and 46% were assessed as satisfactory). Supervision was assessed as not satisfactory in 12% of cases and very poor in only 2%.[1] Other key findings included the following.[2]

Offending behaviour

6.44   This was tackled sufficiently in 83% of cases, with a higher percentage being achieved in the probation sample (89%) than the throughcare sample (78%). In 6% of cases there was no evidence that the offending behaviour had been tackled at all and in 11% the behaviour was tackled, but not sufficiently. There was a clear correlation in the throughcare cases between the length of licence and sufficient work being undertaken to address offending. Sufficient work was undertaken in:

(1)   65% of licences lasting less than 6 months;
(2)   86% of licences lasting between 6 and 11 months; and
(3)   80% or more of licences lasting longer than 11 months.

6.45   Probation staff undertook sufficient work to assist the offender in looking at his cycle of offending in 69% of cases (80% of probation cases and 60% of throughcare cases). In 10% of cases there was no evidence of any such work and in a further 11% there was some work taken, but it was not sufficient. In the remaining 10% of cases, the offender's continued denial of responsibility for or involvement in the offence precluded any possibility of such detailed discussion.

6.46   At the beginning of the supervision, 93% of offenders in the sample sought to justify or minimise their offences, eg by claiming that the victim initiated the assault or underestimating the extent of the harm caused. Such attitudes were challenged sufficiently in 72% of cases (82% of the probation cases and 62% of the throughcare cases). There was no evidence that the tendency to minimise the offences was challenged in 8% of cases and the tendency was challenged, but not sufficiently in 11 of cases. In 9% of cases, the extent of the offender's refusal to acknowledge responsibility for his offending was so great that it was not possible to begin work to increase acceptance of the harm he had caused.

Frequency of contact and home visits

6.47   The minimum level of contact required by the national standards throughout statutory supervision was monthly. This minimum was met in 93% of cases and in no area was the percentage less than 83%. For most sex offenders, a higher frequency of contact than that prescribed by the national standards was

---

1   *Exercising Constant Vigilance: The Role of the Probation Service in Protecting the Public from Sex Offenders* (Home Office, London, 1998) para 4.27.
2   *Exercising Constant Vigilance: The Role of the Probation Service in Protecting the Public from Sex Offenders* (Home Office, London, 1998) para 4.28.

required. In 88% of cases, sufficient appointments were judged to have been offered and in 5% an insufficient number. In the remaining 7% of cases, it was not possible to make a judgment on the information available.

6.48   Home visits were seen as making a particular contribution to risk assessment and management. Sufficient home visits for this purpose were judged to have been made in 53% of cases (65% of throughcare cases and 40% of probation cases). There was no evidence of any home visits being made in 24% of cases and an insufficient number made in 15% of cases. In the remaining 8% it was not possible to make a judgment on the information available.

6.49   Clearly, the overall findings of the inspection are positive, with over 80% of the work inspected being of a satisfactory standard and one-third of the total being assessed as very good. However, concern remains about the small proportion of cases where the standard of supervision was not found to be satisfactory. To address the practice issues raised by the cases sampled as part of the inspection, the inspection report recommended that:

> '... [the] Chief Probation Officers should improve the consistency and quality of work undertaken with sex offenders by issuing practice guidelines to staff about this work which should cover, inter alia, the content of work undertaken on an individual basis with sex offenders and, while paying due regard to staff safety, the importance of home visits when preparing reports on and supervising sex offenders.'[1]

TREATMENT PROGRAMMES FOR SEX OFFENDERS IN THE COMMUNITY

6.50   The majority of offenders supervised in the community will be required to confront their offending behaviour as part of their supervision plan. However, during the last decade there has been increased awareness of the desirability of providing specialist treatment for sex offenders in order to reduce the risk of re-offending. Since 1991, sex offenders sentenced to a custodial term may have had the opportunity to participate in the SOTP whilst in prison[2] and similar efforts have been made to ensure that sex offenders in the community also have access to specialised treatment programmes.

6.51   In 1993, research commissioned by the Home Office (the STEP project) found that all but 13 of the Probation Services in England and Wales were running some form of sex offender treatment programme.[3] Of the 63 probation-led sex offender treatment programmes in existence, only three had been running for more than 5 years, illustrating the rapid growth in the provision of community-based treatment in early 1990s. In common with the approach adopted by the SOTP, the main treatment approach found to be used in the community was cognitive-behavioural group therapy,[4] and there appeared

---

1   *Exercising Constant Vigilance: The Role of the Probation Service in Protecting the Public from Sex Offenders* (Home Office, London, 1998) para 4.29.
2   See **5.37**.
3   Baker and Morgan *Sex Offenders: A Framework for the Evaluation of Community-based Treatment* (Home Office, London, 1993).
4   See **5.38**.

to be three main models of treatment programme: full-time attendance for 1 or 2 weeks; 2 hours a week for 8 weeks to 6 months; or 2 hours a week for a year or more. This information was used to select six community-based treatment programmes for detailed evaluation in a later research study.

An evaluation of seven treatment programmes[1]

6.52   The six community-based programmes were chosen because they were well established and represented the range of sex offender treatment programmes offered by, or for, the Probation Service. In addition, the only residential private specialist centre for the treatment of child abusers in the UK was also evaluated. The programmes fell into the following categories:

(1) short-term intensive programmes: three programmes were looked at, offering, on average, 50 hours of group therapy over a 2-week period;

(2) short-term intensive group plus co-working programmes: one programme was seen which consisted of a full week of therapy followed by long-term co-working with the offender's probation officer and a programme leader;

(3) rolling long-term programmes: two open-ended programmes were evaluated, delivering 2 hours of therapy weekly or fortnightly.

(4) long-term residential programmes: offenders seen here were resident at the only private specialist centre for the treatment of child abusers in the UK. They had approximately 15 hours of group therapy per week (plus the equivalent time spent in individual, family work or time spent working on their own) for about, on average, a 31-week stay.

6.53   Detailed demographic data was collected on approximately seven offenders from each of the probation programmes and 20 offenders from the residential programme. Each offender was given a battery of standard and specially developed psychometric tests before they started therapy and again after a period of treatment. In total, 59 offenders completed pre- and post-testing. Of these, 88% had committed sexual offences against children. The rest of the sample had been convicted of adult rape, indecent exposure or making obscene telephone calls. As a result of the small numbers in these latter groups, all analyses were confined to the child abuser sample.

6.54   Following treatment, 54% of child abusers had profiles that were within the non-offending range on most of the psychological measures. Short-term treatment programmes were successful in reducing levels of denial, justifications for offending and levels of distorted thinking about children and sexuality in low deviancy men, but had little impact on highly deviant men. Long-term treatment was three times more successful than short-term treatment in producing change in highly deviant men and the long-term residential programme made more progress in changing offenders' attitudes than the other programmes. Overall, the probation-run programmes enabled offenders to understand their offending behaviour and its antecedents, but had little success in helping them develop strategies to minimise or even acknowledge future risk.

---

1   Becket, Beech, Fisher and Fordham *Community-based Treatment for Sex Offenders: An Evaluation of Seven Treatment Programmes* (Home Office, London, 1994).

Does treating sex offenders reduce re-offending?

6.55 Changing offenders' attitudes towards their offending behaviour is one way of assessing the impact of treatment, but the crucial question is whether or not treatment prevents further offences being committed. Examining the reconviction rates of offenders who have participated in treatment programmes is one obvious method of assessing this, but, because of problems of under-reporting of sexual offences and the difficulties in obtaining convictions, it is rather a crude measure. It has been recommended that recidivism studies should not only look at the official rates of reconviction, but should also gather other information such as finding of fact from the civil courts and information from social services records.

6.56 Whilst recognising the limits of reconviction studies, the third phase of the STEP project involves examining reconviction rates 2, 5 and 10 years after offenders have completed the programmes previously evaluated, to discover whether treated offenders were convicted of fewer or less serious offences. The 2-year follow-up study was completed in 1996.[1]

Which sex offenders are referred for treatment in the community?

6.57 The research identified 133 offenders who had been referred to one of the seven treatment programmes. Of these, 96 (72%) had been convicted of indecent assault as their main offence, 11 (8%) had been convicted of buggery or attempted buggery, eight (6%) had been convicted of rape or attempted rape, five (4%) had been convicted of incest, two (2%) had been convicted of gross indecency with a child, five (4%) had been convicted of unlawful sexual intercourse, three (2%) had been convicted of indecent exposure and three (2%) had been convicted of other, non-notifiable sexual offences. Additionally, 46 of the offenders had been convicted of a second sexual offence at the same time,[2] and 70 offenders had a previous conviction for a sexual offence.[3] The comparatively low percentage of offenders convicted of rape is explicable on the basis that most convicted rapists receive custodial sentences of sufficient length for them to participate in the SOTP in prison.[4]

Does going through treatment affect reconviction?

6.58 The majority of the 133 offenders referred for treatment had not been reconvicted of a further offence within 2 years. Only six (4.5%) offenders had been reconvicted of a further sexual offence within this period and five (4%) offenders were reconvicted of a non-sexual offence. Of those reconvicted of a further sexual offence, one had participated on a short-term programme, one on a rolling long-term programme and four on the long-term residential programme. The fact that the majority of those reconvicted of a further sexual

---

1 Hedderman and Sugg *Does Treating Sex Offenders Reduce Re-Offending?* Research Findings No 45 (Home Office, London, 1996).
2 Typically, gross indecency with a child (21 offenders) and indecent assault (16 offenders).
3 Typically, indecent assault (37 offenders), gross indecency with a child (12 offenders) and buggery or attempted buggery (10 offenders).
4 See **4.142**.

offence participated on the long-term residential programme should not be taken as a reflection on the quality of their treatment, but can be attributed to the fact that this programme targeted highly deviant offenders and, in fact, three of these offenders failed to complete treatment.

6.59   In order for a comparison to be made, the research identified 191 sex offenders who had been given Probation Orders in 1990, but who had not participated in a treatment programme. Of these, 17 (9%) were reconvicted of a further sexual offence in the 2-year period and 38 (20%) were reconvicted of a further non-sexual offence, ie the sex offenders in the probation sample were twice as likely to be reconvicted of a further sexual offence as those who had participated in a treatment programme and were five times more likely to be reconvicted of a further non-sexual offence.[1] The research also found that changes in deviancy do have some correspondence with changes in offending behaviour – for a 2-year period at least. Earlier research had identified that, following treatment, 54% of child abusers had profiles that were within the non-offending range on most of the psychological measures.[2] None of these offenders were reconvicted within 2 years.

The future of treatment in the community

6.60   Evaluating the effects of treatment is a difficult task – indeed, it has been pointed out that methodological perfection in this area is impossible.[3] However, the reconviction study concluded that, despite the small sample size and other limitations, the results are encouraging, a conclusion that has been echoed elsewhere.[4] In the past, the work of the Probation Service with sex offenders had developed unevenly, often depending on local initiative, without much support from central management. In recent years, there has been increasing interest focused on the treatment of sex offenders, both in prison and in the community. Obviously, there remains the ever-present problem of resources. In 1991, a survey of current practice of probation work with sex offenders concluded that cost was an important issue and one which, potentially, may override all other considerations. It was pointed out that any mismatch of treatment need and resource allocation will diminish the potency of practice and may prove counter-productive, in so far as the treatment of sex offenders is quintessentially an area in which the effects of inappropriate intervention may not be benign.[5]

---

1   In order to ensure that these results were not simply a reflection of differences between the samples, the predicted and actual reconviction rates were calculated for both groups using the Offender Group Reconviction Scale algorithm. This predicts the likelihood of an offender being reconvicted of any offence within 2 years, while controlling for differences in age, previous convictions and previous experience of youth custody. The actual rate of reconviction (9%) for the STEP sample was lower than the average predicted score (13%), whereas the actual rate for the general probation sample (29%) was higher than the predicted rate (23%).

2   Becket, Beech, Fisher and Fordham *Community-based Treatment for Sex Offenders: An Evaluation of Seven Treatment Programmes* (Home Office, London, 1994).

3   West 'Sexual Molesters' in Walker (ed) *Dangerous People* (Blackstone Press Ltd, London, 1996) p 64.

4   Marshall and Pithers 'A Reconsideration of Treatment Outcome with Sex Offenders' (1994) 21 *Criminal Justice and Behaviour* 10.

5   Warwick *Probation Work with Sex Offenders: A Survey of Current Practice* (Social Work Monographs, Norwich, 1991) p 42.

6.61   However, resources are not the only cause for concern. In 1996, a plea was made for legislation designed to increase penal controls on sex offenders to be used constructively to secure treatment rather than to produce more frequent and longer terms of imprisonment for all offenders.[1] In the same year, the Government expressed the view in a White Paper that there was a strong case for strengthening the arrangements for supervising convicted sex offenders following their release from custody to provide greater protection for the public and to improve the opportunity for such offenders to deal with their offending behaviour,[2] and a consultation document on the sentencing and supervision of sex offenders was published a short time later.[3] The proposals in the consultation paper were said to be directed at two specific aims: to improve the protection of the public and to enhance the opportunities for the treatment of such offenders. The proposals fall into five main categories. However, four of these categories, many of which have now been enacted,[4] relate solely to the first aim, namely the protection of the public. In fact, only one of the five categories – proposals to strengthen the arrangements for supervising offenders on their release from custody – relates to the second aim of enhancing the opportunities for sex offenders to receive treatment. The introduction of extended sentences in the Crime and Disorder Act 1998 goes some way towards meeting this aim, yet the legislation does nothing to ensure that effective treatment programmes will be available. This could have been foreseen from the stance of the consultation document in 1996. Disappointment was expressed at the time that the Government had not taken the opportunity to evidence firm support for the concept of treatment, as the second alleged aim of the proposals appeared to be little more than a cosmetic exercise intended, perhaps, to soften the rigid control measures proposed.[5] It seems that the plea for the effective use of penal controls to secure treatment rather than to produce more frequent and longer terms of imprisonment has not been fully heeded.

Alternative forms of treatment – castration as treatment

6.62   The cognitive-behavioural approach to treating sex offenders is generally regarded as perfectly acceptable method of treatment and, despite the difficulties encountered in assessing the effectiveness of such a treatment and the, as yet, unresolved problem of resources, such treatment programmes will no doubt continue to be developed throughout England and Wales. There also exists the possibility of rather more radical forms of treatment, based on medical intervention rather than psychological treatment.

---

1   West 'Sexual Molesters' in Walker (ed) *Dangerous People* (Blackstone Press Ltd, London, 1996) p 66.
2   *Protecting the Public* (1996) Cmnd 3190 (HMSO, London).
3   *Sentencing and Supervision of Sex Offenders: A Consultation Document* (HMSO, London, 1996).
4   For example, the Criminal Evidence (Amendment) Act 1997, which extends police powers to obtain DNA samples from offenders, the Sex Offenders Act 1997, which establishes the 'sex offender register' (see **7.1**), and the Sexual Offences (Protected Material) Act 1997, which, when in force, will regulate access to victim statements in sexual offences cases.
5   Cobley 'Sentencing and Supervision of Sex Offenders' (1997) *Journal of Social Welfare and Family Law* 19(1) 98 at 103.

Surgical intervention

6.63   Surgical intervention, whether by castration or dissection of the hypothalamus, is designed to cause disruption of male hormonal agents, thereby inhibiting arousal and controlling sexual aggression. However, side effects are numerous and permanent and, in practice, the use of surgical intervention is subject to considerable clinical and ethical controversy.[1] Although the possibility of introducing a voluntary castration Bill, which would allow surgical castration of a sex offender, with his consent, has been considered in the USA,[2] such a radical step is unlikely to be taken in England and Wales.

Chemical castration

6.64   A rather less radical treatment takes the form of pharmacological intervention, commonly referred to as 'chemical castration', which involves the offender taking anti-androgenal drugs in order to suppress the libido. Such drug treatment can only be administered to offenders with their consent and the effects are reversible, leading some to regard drug therapy as an unacceptable 'temporary' solution, as the offender might stop taking the necessary drugs at any time.[3] Issues of enforcement aside, the voluntary treatment of sex offenders with drugs clearly has potential. Indeed, it is by no means a recent idea. In the late 1970s at least one probation officer was working in collaboration with a GP to administer Cyproterone acetate (a libido suppressant drug) to sex offenders under his supervision.[4] Certainly, the available evidence of the impact of drug therapies on offending behaviour is impressive, with some studies claiming success rates of between 85% and 100%.[5]

6.65   More recently, hospital trials have been taking place with released offenders who have agreed to have monthly injections of a libido-suppressing drug. In 1998, it was reported that two offenders, described as 'self-admitted compulsive paedophiles', had abstained from re-offending over a 7-year period after being treated with the drug goserelin acetate, which lowers testosterone levels, and the Prison Service admitted that it was discussing the potential use of drugs as part of the overall sex offender treatment programme.[6] As the Government proposes to resort to yet more radical measures to protect the public from compulsive sex offenders,[7] there is every possibility that drug therapy will rapidly become more acceptable. Faced with the prospect of indeterminate detention, agreeing to receive an injection once a month as an alternative amounts to a negligible infringement of civil liberties. Even without the threat of such extreme measures, one consultant psychiatrist has commented '... most sex offenders I know are breaking their necks for this kind of

---

1   Warwick *Probation Work with Sex Offenders: A Survey of Current Practice* (Social Work Monographs, Norwich, 1991) p 13.
2   Loveland 'The Unkindest Cut?' (1996) *New Law Journal* 24 May at 744.
3   Ibid.
4   Warwick *Probation Work with Sex Offenders: A Survey of Current Practice* (Social Work Monographs, Norwich, 1991) p 27.
5   Warwick *Probation Work with Sex Offenders: A Survey of Current Practice* (Social Work Monographs, Norwich, 1991) p 13.
6   (1998) *The Independent*, 24 August.
7   See **7.64**.

treatment'.[1] Further research in this area, with controlled clinical trials, is essential.

SUPERVISION, CONTROL AND THE THREAT OF SANCTIONS

6.66   However effective the supervision of offenders in the community proves to be, it is crucial to ensure adequate procedures exist to enforce the conditions of the Probation Order or licence. In any case where an offender is being supervised in the community, the commission of a further offence will result in the imposition of a sanction. The consequences of failing to comply with the conditions of the Probation Order or licence differ according to the nature of the supervision.

Sanctions against re-offending – offenders on licence

6.67   All released prisoners who were sentenced after 1 October 1992 are liable to be returned to prison if they commit a further offence punishable with imprisonment before the date on which they would (but for their release) have served their sentence in full.[2] The court dealing with new offence, whether or not it passes any other sentence on the offender, may order the offender to be returned to prison for the whole or any part of the period which begins with the date of the order and is equal in length to the period between the date on which the new offence was committed and date on which the offender would (but for his release) have served his sentence in full. Following his return to prison, if the court passes a sentence of 12 months or less, the prisoner will be released on licence after serving one-half of the sentence and the licence will remain in force for a period of 3 months.[3] If the offender then breaches the conditions of the licence, he commits a summary offence punishable either by a fine or by imprisonment for the 'relevant period'. The 'relevant period' is the period equal in length to the period between the date on which the failure occurred or began and the date of the expiry of the licence. Following such a sentence, the offender will be released after serving one-half of the relevant period, subject to the licence if it is still subsisting.

6.68   For example, an offender who has been sentenced to 3 years' imprisonment for indecent assault is released on licence after serving 18 months. He commits a new offence of indecent assault 6 months after his release. The Crown Court orders his return to prison for 12 months and imposes a sentence of 6 months' imprisonment for the new offence, the sentences to run concurrently. The offender is released on licence after serving a further 6 months' imprisonment and the licence remains in force for 3 months. One month after release, the offender breaches the conditions of the licence, thereby committing a summary offence. The magistrates' court imposes a sentence of 2

---

1   Russell Reid, Consultant Psychiatrist at Hillingdon Hospital, West London, quoted in *The Independent*, 24 August 1998.
2   Criminal Justice Act 1991, s 40.
3   Criminal Justice Act 1991, s 40A (inserted by s 105 of the Crime and Disorder Act 1998).

months' imprisonment. The offender is released after 1 month and remains on licence for 1 month following release.

Sanctions against re-offending – revocation of community sentences

6.69 If a community order has been made by the magistrates' court and, on an application by the offender or supervising officer, if it appears to a magistrates' court that, having regard to the circumstances which have arisen since the order was made, it would be in the interests of justice, the court may:[1]

(1) revoke the order; or
(2) revoke the order and deal with the offender, for the offence in respect of which the order was made, in any manner in which it could deal with him if he had just been convicted by the court for the offence.[2]

The circumstances on which a Probation Order may be revoked include the offender's making good progress or his responding satisfactorily to supervision.[3] The commission of a further offence forms a factual basis for revocation, but it does not constitute a breach of the order. Therefore, if an offender is convicted of a new offence whilst subject to a Community Order, the court may revoke the order and deal with him for the original offence as well as for the new offence.

Re-offending – an effective sanction?

6.70 These sanctions against re-offending may have some deterrent effect on offenders, but their effectiveness as a control measure is probably limited. Certainly for those offenders released from custody on licence, the possibility of recall to prison, even in the absence of a new offence, is likely to be a far more effective means of controlling the offender's behaviour.

Control and release on licence

6.71 As part of the process of throughcare and sentence planning,[4] every offender is allocated a supervising officer following sentence. During the custodial part of the sentence the supervising officer is expected to maintain regular contact with the offender and with prison staff. This ensures that the prison is aware of relevant information about the offender's home circumstances, enables the supervising officer to contribute to sentence planning and lays the foundations for effective supervision in the community.

6.72 In the case of short-term prisoners, the supervising officer will complete a pre-discharge report which is sent to the prison establishment one month before the offender's release date. For long-term prisoners, the supervising officer will complete a parole assessment report, which is added to the parole dossier.[5]

---

1 Criminal Justice Act 1991, Sch 2, para 7(2).
2 As with actions for breach, if the original order was made by the Crown Court, the magistrates' court may commit the offender to the Crown Court, which has the same powers to deal with the offender, except that the sentencing powers are wider.
3 Criminal Justice Act 1991, Sch 2, paras 7(3) and 8(3).
4 See **5.16**.
5 See **5.80**.

CONDITIONS OF THE LICENCE

6.73   The conditions attached to the licence are determined by the prison governor, in the case of short-term prisoners, or by the Parole Board in the case of long-term prisoners. The conditions may vary, but all include a requirement to notify the supervising officer of any change of address, to attend when required and to arrive on time for an appointment and to comply with any reasonable directions of the supervisor. Additional licence conditions may be added. In completing the pre-discharge report or parole assessment report, the supervising officer will consider whether there is a need for additional licence conditions, taking account of risk assessment, child protection, victim concern or other relevant factors. The national standards published in 1995 suggested that a recommendation for extra conditions should normally only be taken from a specified list, although other conditions may be recommended if the supervising officer felt that they are justified by the circumstances of the case. Although the specified list does not form part of the revised national standards published in January 2000, it remains a useful illustration of the conditions that may be attached to the licence. The specified list provided that, while under supervision the offender may be required to:

(1)   attend upon such duly qualified psychiatrist/psychologist/medical practitioner for such care, supervision or treatment as that practitioner recommends;[1]
(2)   not engage in any work or other organised activity involving a person below a specified age, either on a professional or voluntary basis;
(3)   reside at a specified address (eg hostel)[2] and must not live elsewhere without obtaining the approval of the supervising officer; thereafter the offender must reside as directed by the supervising officer;
(4)   not reside in the same household as any child under a specified age;
(5)   not seek to approach or communicate with a wife/former wife/daughter/ son/child/grandchild/other named persons or members of their family without the prior approval of the supervising officer/and named social services department;
(6)   comply with any requirements reasonably imposed by the supervising officer for the purpose of ensuring that the offender addresses his alcohol/drug/sexual/gambling/solvent abuse/anger/debt/offender behaviour problems at a named course or centre.[3]

6.74   The imposition of such conditions potentially allows the supervising officer extensive control over an offender on licence, placing restrictions on where the offender lives, persons with whom he communicates, where he works and requiring him to undergo treatment or participate in rehabilitation programmes. Yet the conditions will only be effective if the offender complies with them.

---

1   A licence condition requiring the offender to attend upon a duly qualified practitioner for treatment will be added only when the practitioner has carried out an assessment prior to release.
2   See **8.7**.
3   *National Standards for the Supervision of Offenders in the Community* (Home Office, London, 1995) Supervision before and after custody, Annex A.

ENFORCEMENT OF THE LICENCE – BREACH ACTION AND RECALL TO PRISON

6.75   Prior to the implementation of the Crime and Disorder Act 1998, a short-term prisoner who failed to comply with the conditions of his licence committed a summary offence, punishable with a fine.[1] Although this offence was not sufficient to return the offender to prison under s 40 of the Criminal Justice Act 1991, the convicting court could suspend the licence and recall the offender to prison for a period not exceeding six months. However, the 1998 Act repealed this provision and amended the 1991 Act so that, from 1 January 1999, the circumstances in which prisoners released on licence may be recalled to prison are the same for short-term prisoners as for long-term prisoners.[2] The Home Secretary now has power to revoke the licence of any prisoner released on licence, whether or not there has been a technical breach of the licence conditions, and recall him to prison either on the recommendation of the Parole Board,[3] or without such recommendation where it appears expedient in the public interest to recall before it is practical to consult the board.[4] The Home Secretary has similar powers in relation to prisoners sentenced to life imprisonment.[5]

6.76   An offender's recall to prison will usually be initiated by the supervising officer. Throughout the period of the licence, the supervising officer will maintain contact with the offender, although the precise amount of contact will depend on the offender's progress, needs and an assessment of the risk he poses.[6] Short-term prisoners released prior to 1 January 1999 continue to be subject to recall only following breach of licence conditions. All prisoners released after this date will be subject to the same regime. National standards for the supervision of offenders in the community provide that any apparent failure to comply with the requirements of the licence should be followed up with the offender by an enquiry letter, interview, or telephone call to determine the reason for failure within two working days. The supervising officer must fully record every apparent failure within a further 5 working days, including whether or not any explanation was given by the offender, and if so what that explanation was and whether or not it was acceptable. If the explanation is not considered acceptable, or no explanation is given within the further 5 working days, the supervising officer should record the incident as an unacceptable failure to comply.[7]

6.77   Obviously, breach of the licence conditions may result in the supervising officer recommending the offender's recall to prison. The national standards provide that, where breach action is not taken after one failure to comply, the supervising officer must give the offender a formal written warning of the consequences of further failure. Where it is proposed not to take breach action after a second failure to comply, the supervising officer must arrange for

---

1   Criminal Justice Act 1991, s 38.
2   Crime and Disorder Act 1998, s 103.
3   Criminal Justice Act 1991, s 39(1).
4   Criminal Justice Act 1991, s 39(2).
5   Crime (Sentences) Act 1997, s 32.
6   See **6.22**.
7   *National Standards for the Supervision of Offenders in the Community* (Home Office, London, 2000) para D19.

an officer of at least Assistant Chief Officer level, or equivalent grade, to confirm this course of action and give the offender a formal written warning, which must be copied to the Parole Board. No more than two written warnings should be given within the total licence period and breach action must be commenced no later than the third failure to comply. If changed circumstances suggest an enhanced risk of serious harm to the public, and the offender is subject to licence, the supervising officer must inform the Parole Board.[1]

6.78   In considering whether to advise the recall of the offender, the Parole Board is guided by directions issued by the Home Secretary. In the case of determinate sentence prisoners, the Board is directed to consider whether the offender's continued liberty would represent an unacceptable risk to the public of further offences being committed. In considering this issue, the Board is directed to take into account, in particular, whether the offender is likely to commit further offences and whether the offender has failed to comply with one or more of his licence conditions or might be likely to do so in the future.[2] Directions are also issued in relation to the recall of offenders sentenced to life imprisonment.[3] These directions state that the offender may be recalled to prison 'if his behaviour gives cause for concern'. In deciding whether to recommend recall, the Board should consider whether the offender's continued liberty would present a risk to the safety of other persons or the offender is likely to commit further imprisonable offences, the extent to which the offender has failed to comply with the conditions of the licence or otherwise failed to co-operate with the supervising officer and whether the offender is likely to comply with the conditions of the licence and agree to supervision if allowed to remain in the community.

6.79   Offenders sentenced to life imprisonment remain on licence for the rest of their lives, and thus remain liable to be recalled over a period of many years. More detailed training guidance is provided for these offenders,[4] outlining factors which should be taken into account when considering recall. Although technically only applicable to the recall of those sentenced to life imprisonment, many of these factors are undoubtedly ones which will influence the decision to recall any offender on licence. The weight and relevance attached to each factor differs and may vary according to the circumstances of the case:

(1)   the offender's background, including any previous convictions and their pattern;

(2)   the nature and circumstances of the original offence and reasons for it;

(3)   the areas of concern arising from the original offence;

(4)   the extent to which the original areas of concern have reappeared or others have arisen while on life licence;

---

1   *National Standards for the Supervision of Offenders in the Community* (Home Office, London, 2000) para D23.

2   Secretary of State's Directions to the Parole Board – Recall of Determinate Sentence Prisoners issued under s 32(6) of the Criminal Justice Act 1991.

3   Secretary of State's Directions to the Parole Board – Recall of Mandatory Life Sentence Prisoners issued under s 32(6) of the Criminal Justice Act 1991.

4   The Training Guidance does not form part of the Directions to the Parole Board issued under s 32(6) of the Criminal Justice Act 1991.

(5)   general behaviour on life licence; including response to supervision, compliance with licence requirements and co-operation with the supervising officer;

(6)   the extent and seriousness of any further charges committed while on licence and/or charges which have been laid in connection with such offences;

(7)   home circumstances, including the offender's relationship with his family and friends and the suitability of his accommodation;

(8)   his work record including relationships with colleagues and employers;

(9)   where applicable, his performance during previous periods on licence;

(10)   the recommendation of the supervising authority; and

(11)   any other information (eg from police, social services or a psychiatrist) which may have a bearing on whether the offender should be permitted to remain on life licence.

RELEASE FOLLOWING RECALL TO PRISON

6.80   Where the licence of a short or long-term prisoner has been revoked, the prisoner must be released at the three-quarters point of his sentence, but will remain on licence, and thus liable to further recall, until the end of the sentence.[1]

Enforcement of community sentences

6.81   The requirements that the sentencing court may include in a Probation Order include requirements as to residence, activities and attendance at a probation centre as well as requirements as to treatment for mental conditions and drug or alcohol dependency.[2] The national standards provide that breach proceedings may be taken after one unacceptable failure to comply with the requirements of the order, where appropriate.[3] If breach action is not to be taken on the first unacceptable failure, the supervising officer must formally warn the offender, using a 'yellow card' warning letter. The national standards published in 1995 provided that a maximum of two warnings within any 12-month period of the order could be given before breach proceedings were instituted.[4] The revised guidelines published in January 2000 now provide that only one warning in any 12-month period of supervision can be given before commencing breach action.[5]

---

1   Criminal Justice Act 1991, s 33(3), as amended by s 104 of the Crime and Disorder Act 1998.

2   See **4.106**.

3   *National Standards for the Supervision of Offenders in the Community* (Home Office, London, 2000) para D20.

4   *National Standards for the Supervision of Offenders in the Community* (Home Office, London, 2000) para 23.

5   *National Standards for the Supervision of Offenders in the Community* (Home Office, London, 2000) para D21.

Breach proceedings[1]

6.82 Breach proceedings can be brought for a failure to comply with any of the requirements of an order, but not for the commission of a further offence during the currency of the order.[2] If the offender's conduct requires it, breach proceedings should be instituted within 10 working days. On an application (usually by the supervising officer), the magistrates' court may issue a summons requiring the offender to appear or issue a warrant for the offender's arrest. If it is then proved that the offender has failed, without reasonable excuse, to comply with the requirements of the order, the court may do one of the following:[3]

(1) impose a fine;
(2) make a Community Service Order of not more than 60 hours;[4]
(3) where the offender is in breach of a Probation Order and is under the age of 21, make an Attendance Centre Order; or
(4) where the original order was made by a magistrates' court, the court may revoke the order and deal with him, for the offence in respect of which the order was made, in any manner in which it could deal with him if he had just been convicted by the magistrates' court of the offence. If the court deals with the offender in this way, the court:
  (a) must take into account the extent to which the offender has complied with the requirements of the relevant order; and
  (b) in the case of an offender who has wilfully and persistently failed to comply with those requirements, may impose a custodial sentence notwithstanding the criteria for imposing a custodial sentence contained in s 1(2) of the Criminal Justice Act 1991.[5]

6.83 For example, an offender is convicted of an indecent assault and the magistrates' court imposes a Probation Order of 3 years' duration. The offender complies with the requirements of the order for 2 years, but then defaults on several occasions as the expiry date of the order approaches. Breach proceedings are brought 30 months after the order was made. The magistrates' court fines the offender, and the Probation Order continues. However, if the offender deliberately fails to comply with the requirements of the order from the beginning and breach proceedings are brought 3 months after the order was made, the magistrates' court would be entitled to revoke the Probation Order and impose a custodial sentence of up to 6 months' imprisonment for the original offence, even if the offence was not so serious that only a custodial sentence would have justified when the offender was convicted.

6.84 If the original order was made by the Crown Court, the magistrates' court may commit the offender to the Crown Court to be dealt with there. The powers of the Crown Court are identical to those of the magistrates' court, the

---

1 These proceedings relate to breach of Probation Orders, Community Service Orders, Curfew Orders and Combination Orders.
2 See **6.67**.
3 Criminal Justice Act 1991, Sch 2, para 3(1).
4 Where the offender is in breach of a Community Service Order, the total number of hours under both orders must not exceed 240 hours (Criminal Justice Act 1991, Sch 2, para 6(3) (b)).
5 Criminal Justice Act 1991, Sch 2, para 3(2), as amended by the Crime (Sentences) Act 1997.

only difference in practice being that the sentencing powers of the Crown Court are wider.[1] In the above example, if an offender had originally been sentenced at the Crown Court, the magistrates' court can commit the offender to the Crown Court, which could revoke the Probation Order and impose a custodial sentence of up to 10 years' imprisonment. Although the Court is not required to justify the imposition of custodial sentence in accordance with s 1(2) of the 1991 Act, it should have regard to the seriousness of the original offence in determining the length of the sentence.

Sex offenders and compliance with licence conditions and Community Orders

6.85   The thematic inspection of the work of Probation Services with sex offenders carried out in 1996–97 found that, generally, the offenders in the sample complied with the requirements of the order or licence, but in a small number of cases the order was not being enforced appropriately:[2]

(1) 34 offenders in the sample had missed three or more appointments in the previous 12 months (or during the course of supervision where this was less than 12 months);

(2) after the three absences, 13 were breached, five were given a formal written warning, seven were given verbal warnings[3] or some other action was taken and no action was taken in relation to the remaining nine;

(3) where breach action was not taken, there was no endorsement on the file of the line manager's agreement not to breach in 14 of the 21 cases; therefore, the offenders who were not breached without a manager endorsing this decision constituted 4% of the total sample;

(4) in seven cases, there were further failures to comply with the order, but in only one case was breach action subsequently taken; and

(5) in a total of 96 cases, the offender failed to comply with some other aspect of the order or licence; the failure was dealt with promptly in 79% of the cases, and in the remaining 20% action was either not taken or was inadequate.

6.86   The inspection report concluded that, given that it was essential that sex offenders were supervised to the highest standard and that breach was initiated in every case unless, in exceptional circumstances, there was written agreement at managerial level, there must be serious concern that the order was not being enforced appropriately in some cases. The revised national standards published in January 2000 now place increased emphasis on the rigorous enforcement of supervision.

Termination of statutory contact

6.87   The thematic inspection of the work of the Probation Services with sex offenders carried out in 1996–97 found that some sex offenders continued to be supervised on a voluntary basis after the statutory period of supervision, either

---

1   Criminal Justice Act 1991, Sch 2, para 4, as amended by the Crime (Sentences) Act 1997.

2   *Exercising Constant Vigilance: The Role of the Probation Service in Protecting the Public from Sex Offenders* (Home Office, London, 1998) para 4.28.

3   Two of the cases in which verbal warnings had been given involved an offender with mental health problems and one with learning difficulties.

on licence or as part of a community sentence.[1] The inspection report concluded that, whilst it was not always advisable to end supervision abruptly when the order or licence terminated, if the offender was willing to continue contact, the period of voluntary contact should be subject to a risk-management plan which included continued oversight from managers and plans for the withdrawal of the Probation Service and the final exchange of relevant information with the appropriate agencies. However, there are financial implications. Currently there is no specific provision in the cash limit formula for such continued supervision nor does it form part of the existing expectations on Probation Services. The inspection report urged the Home Office to give further consideration as to whether such continuing contact should be seen as an appropriate use of probation personnel.

THE PROBLEMS REGARDING THOSE SENTENCED BEFORE THE CRIMINAL JUSTICE ACT 1991

6.88 Offenders sentenced to a custodial term prior to the implementation of the Criminal Justice Act 1991 are entitled to be released when they have served two-thirds of their sentence and on release, they will be at liberty with no supervision or sanction against re-offending. In 1998 it was estimated that there were 150 offenders then in prison who would escape any control on their release.[2] Although the number of offenders to whom the pre-1991 Act provisions apply obviously decreases over the years, these release arrangements continue to apply to a number of offenders – by definition those who have received long custodial sentences – whose release without any control gives rise to inevitable concerns.

6.89 In 1992, 3 months before the Criminal Justice Act 1991 became law, Rhys Hughes was sentenced to 10 years' imprisonment for the rape and buggery of nine children. He refused any treatment for his offending behaviour whilst in prison and was released in September 1998 with no restrictions on his movements and no requirement of supervision. His decision to return to the Oxfordshire village where one of his victims still lived provoked anger and consternation in the village and made national headlines.[3] The release of sex offenders into a community where they are known inevitably gives rise to a danger of vigilante attacks. This is a problem that has become particularly acute for the police and Probation Service following the notification requirements imposed by the Sex Offenders Act 1997.[4] Fear of vigilante attacks has led some sex offenders sentenced before October 1992 to accept voluntary restrictions on their movements on release out of fear for their own safety.

6.90 The notorious paedophiles Sidney Cooke and Robert Oliver eventually requested secure accommodation from the authorities after their release. Oliver left prison in September 1997 and was chased from town to town by angry crowds

---

1   *Exercising Constant Vigilance: The Role of the Probation Service in Protecting the Public from Sex Offenders* (Home Office, London, 1998) para 4.74.
2   (1998) *The Times*, 27 March.
3   (1998) *The Independent*, 24 August.
4   See chap 7.

until he sought refuge in a Sussex police station. In April 1999, Oliver was said to be living in a medium secure psychiatric unit in Milton Keynes at a cost to taxpayers of a reported £5,000 a week.[1] Cooke was released in April 1998 after 11 years in prison. Before his release, plans were drawn up to place him under 24-hour surveillance on his release – an operation that would require 30 undercover officers working in shifts.[2] On his release, initially, Cooke was held voluntarily in police cells in London and then at an undisclosed location in Avon and Somerset, but even rumours of his presence were enough to trigger angry public demonstrations.[3]

6.91   In April 1999, it was announced that Lennie Smith, labelled 'one of Britain's most dangerous paedophiles', was to be released from prison, even though he was still considered to be a major danger to children.[4] Smith is suspected of being responsible for the murder of up to five children and has been diagnosed as HIV positive. He was sentenced to 10 years' imprisonment in 1992 for a series of sex attacks on a 6-year-old boy. Although the police and Probation Service hoped that Smith could be persuaded to go into protective custody, it was acknowledged that this could only be done on a voluntary basis. On his release in July 1999, Smith became one of the first offenders to participate in a pilot scheme at Nottingham prison, whereby released prisoners who require protection are allowed to live as free men in accommodation inside the prison.[5] Even if released sex offenders do agree to voluntary supervision and restrictions, there remains the question of funding such efforts. In August 1998, the cost to the public of protecting Robert Oliver since his release was estimated to have exceeded £100,000[6] and the annual cost of running the pilot scheme to accommodate released sex offenders within the prison at Nottingham has been estimated at a similar figure.[7]

6.92   Following the implementation of the Sex Offenders Act 1997 and the Crime and Disorder Act 1998, sex offenders sentenced before October 1992 may now be subject to some monitoring and control on their release.[8] However, the absence of a supervision requirement and the threat of enforcement of an order or licence continue to be a cause for concern.

---

1   (1999) *Daily Mail*, 7 April.
2   (1998) *The Times*, 27 March.
3   (1998) *The Independent*, 24 August p 3.
4   (1999) *Daily Mail*, 7 April.
5   (1999) *Daily Mail*, 20 July.
6   (1998) *The Independent*, 24 August p 3.
7   (1999) *Daily Mail*, 20 July.
8   See chap 7.

Chapter 7

SEX OFFENDERS IN THE COMMUNITY: SURVEILLANCE, CONTROL AND MULTI-AGENCY WORKING

KEEPING TRACK – THE SEX OFFENDER REGISTER[1]

7.1   One of the key factors in ensuring that the public are protected from any danger posed by a sex offender will be to keep track of the sex offender by monitoring his movements, at least to the extent of knowing where he lives. An offender who is under the supervision of a probation officer, either as a result of a community sentence or following release from custody, will be under an obligation to inform the probation officer of any change of address. During the period of supervision, the probation officer will be monitoring the risk posed by the offender, and failure by the offender to maintain contact may result in proceedings for breach of the order or, for those released on licence, revocation of the licence and return to custody.[2] However, with the exception of those released from custody following the imposition of a life sentence, such periods of supervision will usually be relatively short. Some attempt to address this problem in relation to sex offenders was made by the Criminal Justice Act 1991, which allowed the sentencing court to order that the offender be supervised to the end of his sentence, rather than to the usual three-quarter point[3] and following the Crime and Disorder Act 1998, the imposition of an extended sentence will result in a far longer period of supervision in the community.[4] However, some sex offenders are thought to present a continuing risk to the public and many of these offenders will be living in the community with no supervision. Although comprehensive, ongoing assessment of the risk posed by such offenders is not possible, in recent years the idea of 'tracking' such offenders – knowing where they are living in the community – has gained momentum and has culminated in the provisions of Pt I of the Sex Offenders Act 1997 and the creation of a sex offender 'register'.

7.2   The idea of compiling a list, or register, of sex offenders is not new. In fact, several national lists existed prior to the 1997 legislation, including the police national computer list, the national identification service list, the National Criminal Intelligence list, Scotland Yard's national paedophile index list, 'List 99' of the Department of Education and Employment and the Department of Health's Consultancy Service, as well as lists held by voluntary bodies such as the Scout Association and the National Society for the Prevention of Cruelty of Children.[5] Subsequent legislation has increased significantly the importance of

---

1   See Cobley 'Keeping Track of Sex Offenders – Part 1 of the Sex Offenders Act 1997' [1997] 60 MLR 691.
2   See chap 6.
3   Criminal Justice Act 1991, s 44.
4   Crime and Disorder Act 1998, s 58. See **4.82**.
5   HC Deb vol 289, col 49, January 1997.

'List 99' and the Department of Health's Consultancy Service Index for the purposes of child protection.[1] However, with the exception of offenders sentenced to life imprisonment, who may be required to report changes of address to their supervising officer or the police as a condition of their licence, offenders are not generally required to provide information about their whereabouts. Therefore, although the police national computer held details of many sex offenders, there was no provision for keeping the information up to date. During 1996, two attempts to introduce a national register by a private members' Bill failed,[2] but in June 1996, the Home Office issued a consultation document on the sentencing and supervision of sex offenders,[3] which included a proposal that convicted sex offenders should be required to notify the police of any change of address. The response was enthusiastic, with 87% of those responding supporting the proposal.[4] However, in October 1996 the then Home Secretary, Michael Howard, took the view that there was insufficient time to pass the required legislation prior to the next general election and the proposal did not appear in the Queen's speech.[5] There followed what has been described as 'one of the fastest U-turns in political history'[6] when, following a pledge of support from the Leader of the Opposition, the Prime Minister accepted the case for Government action. The Sex Offenders Act received Royal Assent on 21 March 1997 and was brought into force on 1 September 1997.[7]

The notification requirements and previous offences

7.3 The Act requires certain categories of sex offenders to notify the police of any change of name and address during a specified period. The notification requirements apply to all those convicted or cautioned in respect of an offence listed in Sch I to the Act,[8] and to those who are found not guilty of such an offence by reason of insanity, or found to be under a disability and to have done the act charged in respect of the offence, after the commencement of the Act.[9] The requirements also apply to those who were convicted before the commencement of the Act but had not been dealt with at the time of commencement of the Act,[10] and to those who had been convicted and, at the time of commencement of the Act, were serving sentences of imprisonment or detention, were subject to a Community Order or supervision following imprisonment, or were detained in hospital or subject to a Guardianship Order.[11] During the passage of the Bill through Parliament, there was considerable debate over whether the notification requirement should be retrospective and, thus, include all those convicted of sex offences in the past. The Home Office estimated that in England

1 Protection of Children Act 1999.
2 The Sexual Offences Against Children (Register of Offenders) Bill 27 February 1996 and Paedophiles (Registration and Miscellaneous Provisions) Bill 12 June 1996.
3 Cm 3304 (HMSO, London).
4 HC written answers 25 October 1996.
5 (1996) *The Times*, 22 October.
6 HC Deb vol 289, col 34, 27 January 1997.
7 Sex Offenders Act 1997 (Commencement) Order, SI 1997/1920.
8 See **7.80**.
9 Section 1(1).
10 Section 1(2).
11 Section 1(3).

and Wales there were 260,000 men who had been convicted of sex offences, including 110,000 convicted paedophiles.[1] Quite apart from the difficulty of finding previous offenders to inform them of the requirement, the enormity of the task was illustrated during the committee stage when it was estimated that, in its current form, the requirement would affect about 3,000 offenders per annum in England and Wales, with a further 1,000 people cautioned.[2] If the provisions were back-dated only 20 years, it was estimated that the requirement would affect nearly 100,000 people and the resulting burden placed on the police in attempting to assimilate such information would be considerable – as one Minister commented: 'We would have a dog's breakfast on our hands.'[3] The potential effect of making the notification requirements retrospective was shown by subsequent research,[4] which found that, if the requirements of the 1997 Act had always been in force, an estimated 125,000 men in the 1993 population had a conviction that would have required registration. Of these men, 100,000 had a conviction for an offence against a child. The decision to extend the provisions to those convicted before the commencement of the Act, but who were still in contact with the criminal justice system by virtue of their sentence, was clearly a practical compromise.

7.4　In introducing the Act, the Government was anxious to point out that the requirement to notify changes of address was not to be seen as an additional form of punishment, but was an administrative device to secure protection of the public.[5] The aim of the provisions was to ensure that the police would have up-to-date information on the whereabouts of convicted sex offenders and would be able to use the information for the investigation and prevention of crime.[6] It was accepted, however, that the requirement would also be a powerful deterrent and, therefore, presumably would fulfil one of the functions of punishment. In labelling the requirement an administrative device rather than punishment, problems of conflict with the principle of legality and possible breach of art 7 of the European Convention on Human Rights[7] have, prima facie, been avoided, although, in practice, the notification requirements will inevitably be seen as punitive to some degree. One of the first convicted offenders required to register under the Act alleged a violation of art 7. Ibbotson was convicted of various sexual offences in May 1996 and sentenced to 3 years and 6 months' imprisonment. He was released on licence on 20 August 1997, and, when the Sex Offenders Act 1997 came into force on 1 September 1997, he was required to register with the police and inform them of any change of name or address. The European Commission of Human Rights declared Ibbotson's application inadmissible.[8] Whether a measure amounted to a penalty within the

---

1　(1997) *The Times*, 20 February.
2　Standing Committee D col 6, 4 February 1997.
3　Minister of State for the Home Office, David Maclean, HC Deb vol 289, col 32, 27 January 1997.
4　Marshall *The Prevalence of Convictions for Sex Offending* Home Office Research Findings No 55 (Home Office, London, 1997).
5　HC Deb vol 291, col 238, 25 February 1997.
6　HC Deb vol 289, col 70, 27 January 1997.
7　Article 7 prohibits the imposition of a penalty heavier than the one applicable at the time the criminal offence was committed.
8　*Ibbotson v UK* [1999] Crim LR 153.

meaning of art 7 was said to depend on a number of factors, including whether it followed a criminal conviction, its nature and purpose, its characterisation in national law, the procedures involved in its implementation and its severity.[1] Bearing these factors in mind, the Commission expressed the view that the notification requirements contained in the 1997 Act are preventative rather than punitive, in the sense that inclusion on the register might help to dissuade an individual from re-offending.

What about suspicions?

7.5   The notification requirements are imposed only on a comparatively small number of offenders who have either been cautioned (which necessarily involves an admission of guilt) or against whom a formal finding that they committed the relevant act has been made by a criminal court. As the Children's Charities Consortium pointed out:

> 'The majority of children are not abused by convicted offenders and in the minority of cases where prosecution follows the disclosure of abuse, the rate of conviction remains disturbingly low.'[2]

Therefore, it is argued, the provisions merely target the tip of the iceberg. Attempts were made to widen the scope of the provisions by extending the notification requirements to those who have been found in a civil court, industrial tribunal or a disciplinary hearing, to have done anything which, in the opinion of a chief officer of police, would have constituted a relevant sexual offence if it had been tried in a criminal court.[3] Whilst there is undoubtedly merit in the argument that, where the protection of children is concerned, the appropriate standard by which to determine the extent of the notification requirements should be the civil standard of the balance of probabilities rather than the criminal standard of beyond all reasonable doubt, it was agreed that the proper forum for determining the matter must remain with the criminal courts. More radical proposals had been put forward by the charity Action on Child Exploitation, which recommended a register of all suspected paedophiles and child abusers, which would be supervised by a tribunal with the power to adjudicate on appeal.[4] Clearly, the Government was not prepared to go that far, arguing that there was enough to be done at that time in targeting convicted abusers.[5] Further legislative moves have now been made which enhance the opportunities for including suspected offenders on various official lists for the purpose of vetting those working with children,[6] but the provisions of the 1997 Act continue to extend only to those who have admitted a relevant offence, or against whom a formal finding of guilt has been made.

---

1   *Welch v United Kingdom* (1995) 20 EHRR 247.
2   HC Deb vol 289, col 36, 27 January 1997.
3   Standing Committee D col 16, 4 February 1997.
4   HL Deb vol 579, col 549, 14 March 1997.
5   HC Deb vol 289, col 37, 27 January 1997.
6   See **8.142** to **8.177**.

The Schedule 1 offences

7.6   During the passage of the Bill through Parliament, there was concern that the list of offenders should not include 'unnecessary' names where, for example, there were adult consensual acts or sexual offences of a comparatively minor nature. As a result, the notification requirements do not attach to offences under ss 10, 12, 13 and 16 of the 1956 Act (incest by a man, buggery, indecency with men, and assault with intent to commit buggery) if the victim or other party was aged 18 years or over.[1] In the case of indecent assault (ss 14 and 15 of the 1956 Act), if the victim is aged 18 years or over, the notification requirements will only apply if the offender is or has been sentenced to imprisonment for a term of 30 months or more, or is or has been admitted to hospital subject to a restriction order.[2]

7.7   The question of whether the notification requirements should be imposed on child offenders was also the subject of considerable debate. It was argued that, as the criminal justice system treats children differently from adults and the provisions were primarily concerned with the protection of children, child offenders should be treated separately from adult offenders. Attempts were made to remove children under the age of 16 from the ambit of the provisions completely, or alternatively to give the court a discretion to direct that the notification requirements should apply to those under 16 years of age.[3] Whilst there was clear agreement that young offenders could be distinguished, particularly in cases where the 'victim' was close in age to the offender, the Government was not prepared to accept the automatic exclusion of a young offender simply by virtue of age. The resulting compromise excludes from the notification requirements those under the age of 20 who commit offences under ss 6, 12 and 13 of the Sexual Offences Act 1956 (intercourse with a girl aged between 13 and 16, buggery and indecency between men).[4] However, this still means that the notification requirements may be imposed on very young offenders. In August 1999 a 10-year-old boy was found guilty of indecently assaulting an 8-year-old girl and was made the subject of a 3-year Supervision Order. He will also be subject to the notification requirements for 5 years from the date of his conviction.[5] Referring to the outcome as a 'legal quirk', the boy's solicitor pointed out that the boy would not have been subject to the notification requirements if he had assaulted an 18-year-old woman.

7.8   In summary, the notification provisions attach to the following offences:

(1)   s 1 of the Sexual Offences Act 1956 (rape);
(2)   s 5 of the Sexual Offences Act 1956 (intercourse with a girl under the age of 13);
(3)   s 6 of the Sexual Offences Act 1956 (intercourse with a girl aged between 13 and 16, except where the offender is under the age of 20);

---

1   Paragraph 2(b).
2   Paragraphs 2(b) and 3.
3   HC Deb vol 291, col 235, 25 February 1997.
4   Sex Offenders Act 1997, Sch 1, para 2(1).
5   (1999) *The Times*, 24 August.

(4)   s 10 of the Sexual Offences Act 1956 (incest by a man, except where the victim of or, as the case may be, the other party to the offence was aged 18 or over and the offender is not sentenced to imprisonment for a term of 30 months or more and is not admitted to a hospital subject to a Restriction Order);

(5)   ss 12 and 13 of the Sexual Offences Act 1956 (buggery and indecency between men, except where the offender is under the age of 20, or where the victim of or, as the case may be, the other party to the offence was aged 18 or over and the offender is not sentenced to imprisonment for a term of 30 months or more and is not admitted to a hospital subject to a Restriction Order);

(6)   ss 14, 15 and 16 of the Sexual Offences Act 1956 (indecent assault on a woman, indecent assault on a man and assault with intent to commit buggery, except where the victim of or, as the case may be, the other party to the offence was 18 or over and the offender is not sentenced to imprisonment for a term of 30 months or more and is not admitted to a hospital subject to a Restriction Order);

(7)   s 28 of the Sexual Offences Act 1956 (causing or encouraging prostitution of, intercourse with, or indecent assault on, a girl under the age of 16);

(8)   s 1(1) of the Indecency with Children Act 1960 (indecent conduct towards young child);

(9)   s 54 of the Criminal Law Act 1977 (inciting a girl under the age of 16 to have incestuous sexual intercourse);

(10) s 1 of the Protection of Children Act 1978 (indecent photographs of children);

(11) s 170 of the Customs and Excise Management Act 1979 (penalty for fraudulent evasion of duty, etc) in relation to goods prohibited to be imported under s 42 of the Customs Consolidation Act 1876 (prohibitions and restrictions, except where the prohibited goods did not include indecent photographs of persons who were, or appear to have been, under the age of 16); and

(12) s 160 of the Criminal Justice Act 1988 (possession of indecent photographs of children).

The international dimension

7.9   Given the increased mobility of offenders and a growing international concern about paedophile networks, the relationship between the notification requirements and offenders who either offend outside the UK and then return to the jurisdiction, or leave the jurisdiction having been convicted of a sexual offence was inevitably the subject of considerable debate. Part II of the 1997 Act created an offence in the UK for a British citizen or resident of the UK to commit, in a country or territory outside the UK, the offences listed in Sch 2, which include rape, buggery and indecent assault where the victim is under the age of 16, and possession of indecent photographs of children. The 'dual criminality' test is applicable, in that the conduct must amount to a criminal offence both in the UK jurisdiction and in the territory of the State in which it was committed.[1] It

---

1   See Mullan 'The Concept of Double Criminality in the Context of Extraterritorial Crimes' [1997] Crim LR 17.

is unlikely that many prosecutions will be brought in the UK under these provisions, as the view was expressed that the best place for prosecutions is the country in which the offences were committed.[1] Nevertheless, those that are successfully prosecuted in the UK will be subject to the notification requirements. The question then arises as to whether those who are convicted of the relevant offences abroad and subsequently return to the UK should also be subject to the requirements. Whilst there was considerable support from all sides of the House of Commons for such an extension,[2] the practical and bureaucratic difficulties that would be encountered in obtaining the necessary information and in recognising the judgments of foreign criminal courts were deemed to outweigh any potential benefit. Concern was also expressed that, having been convicted of a relevant offence in the UK, an offender could escape the notification requirements simply by leaving the jurisdiction, although if he returned within the prescribed period, he would once again become subject to the requirements. However, the inevitable problems of enforceability and of checking the reliability of information given concerning addresses abroad led to the rejection of calls to include foreign addresses within the notification requirements,[3] which at the present time extend only to those convicted and living within the UK. To many, the ultimate aim would be to construct a European register of paedophiles, a desire fuelled partly by the uncovering of the Belgian paedophile ring.[4] European co-operation is reportedly 'developing well',[5] and it is to be hoped that positive moves towards a European register will materialise in the future.

The notification requirements

7.10 Those subject to the provisions of the legislation are required to notify to the police their name and home address within 14 days of the conviction or the commencement of the Act.[6] Any subsequent changes of name or address must also be notified within 14 days, together with any address in the UK where the offender has stayed for a period or periods amounting to 14 days in any 12 months, which would, of course, cover any holiday in the UK in excess of 2 weeks.[7] 'Home address' refers to the offender's sole or main residence in the UK, or, where he has no such residence, premises in the UK which he regularly visits.[8] The irony of this is that if an offender is homeless, but regularly visits premises, perhaps for the purpose of indulging in paedophile activity, he is required to notify details of those premises to the police. However, an offender who has a home address, but visits the same premises, will not be under any obligation to notify the police of his visits, unless he stays at the premises for a total of 14 days during any 12-month period. The notification may be given orally or in writing in the police area in which the offender's home is situated and must

---

1   HC Deb vol 289, col 33, 27 January 1997.
2   HC Deb vol 289, col 29, 27 January 1997.
3   HC Deb vol 272, col 234, 25 February 1996.
4   HL Deb vol 579, col 558, 14 March 1997.
5   Standing Committee D col 34, 4 February 1997.
6   Section 2(1).
7   Section 2(2).
8   Section 2(7).

include the offender's date of birth. The NSPCC had suggested that the inclusion of a 'domestic profile' in the notification requirements would be of benefit.[1] It was argued that this would help combat registration of mere postal addresses and would obviously act as a useful trigger to warn the relevant authorities if there were vulnerable children in the household. Admittedly, domestic profiles may well change more rapidly than actual addresses, but if the measures are to be effective in protecting children, one would have thought that this is a fundamental piece of information that should be recorded and its omission is regrettable.

The registration period

7.11   The length of time the offender will be subject to the notification requirements is dependent upon the sentence imposed:[2]

(1)   an indefinite period is imposed on those sentenced to a term of imprisonment of 30 months or more and those admitted to a hospital subject to a Restriction Order;
(2)   sentences of more than 6 months' but less than 30 months' imprisonment attract a period of 10 years;
(3)   sentences of 6 months' imprisonment or less and admissions to hospital without a Restriction Order attract a period of 7 years; and
(4)   any other offenders are subjected to the requirements for a period of 5 years.

7.12   In practice, research suggests that about 20% of offenders subject to the notification requirements will remain subject to them for an indefinite period.[3] It had been argued that, given the deep-seated nature of paedophilia, an indefinite period should be imposed on all offenders or, alternatively, that the court be given a discretion to extend the period in the interests of justice.[4] In a similar vein, it was argued that the courts should have a discretion to vary the period so as to lift the notification requirements where there was evidence that the offender no longer presented a risk to the public. The Government resisted all attempts to introduce an element of flexibility, arguing that the set periods were proportionate to the seriousness of the offence, as it was established at the time of sentencing, and that it would be inappropriate to expect a court, perhaps years after the original trial, to re-assess the risk posed by the offender.[5] There can be little doubt that risk assessment will play a central role in the management of 'dangerous' offenders in the future and expertise in this area is developing.[6]

---

1   HC Deb vol 291, col 220, 25 February 1997.
2   Section 1(4).
3   Marshall *The Prevalence of Convictions for Sex Offending* Home Office Research Findings No 55 (Home Office, London, 1997). Of the 125,000 men in 1993 who would have been subject to the notification requirements, 25,000 would have been subject to them for life.
4   Standing Committee D col 19, 4 February 1997.
5   Standing Committee D cols 24–25, 4 February 1997.
6   See, for example, Association of Chief Officers of Probation *Position Statement: Guidance on Management of Risk and Public Protection* (1994) quoted in Hebenton and Thomas 'Sex Offenders in the Community: Reflections on Problems of Law, Community and Risk Management in the U.S.A., England and Wales' (1996) Int J Soc Law 24(4) at 427.

The refusal to build any form of discretion into the provisions is one that could lead to crazy bureaucratic requirements being imposed in certain circumstances.

Enforcement

7.13   The effective enforcement of the notification requirements obviously requires a sanction to be imposed on those who fail to comply. One option would have been to rely on the usual sanctions for breaching an order of the court, but it was decided to create a new criminal offence of failing, without reasonable excuse, to comply with the notification requirements and of providing information which the offender knows to be false.[1] The initial penalty proposed was a level 3 fine and/or 1 month's imprisonment.[2] However, in the light of strong representations from the police and child protection agencies, which were anxious to ensure compliance with the notification requirements, the penalty was subsequently raised to a level 5 fine and/or 6 months' imprisonment.[3]

7.14   Despite this sanction, ensuring compliance with the notification requirements is no easy task. Offenders who are cautioned or against whom a formal finding of guilt is made in relation to a relevant offence after the September 1997 will no doubt have their details recorded on the police national computer initially, but it remains to be seen whether subsequent changes to names or addresses are notified to the police. Certainly, those who were required to register due to a formal finding of guilt made prior to the commencement of the Act showed considerable reluctance to do so. Two weeks after the commencement of the Act, two-thirds of those required to register had failed to comply.[4] However, by the end of February 1999, 8,161 sex offenders were recorded on the police national computer as having notified the police of their details in accordance with the 1997 Act.[5]

Use of the information

7.15   If the notification requirements are complied with, the police are now able to keep track of all sex offenders convicted of the offences specified in the Act. Although popularly described as a 'register', the 1997 Act made no provision for the creation of a separate register and attempts during the passage of the Bill through Parliament to impose a duty on the Secretary of State to maintain such a register failed.[6] In practice, this is unlikely to be of any real significance as the information is stored on the Phoenix database of the police national computer and is accessible by all police forces in England and Wales and by the National Criminal Intelligence Service. The Government claims to have made it clear that the information must not just sit on the computer or gather dust on a file.[7] The police undoubtedly make use of the information for

---

1   Section 3(1).
2   *Sentencing and Supervision of Sex Offenders*, Cm 3304 para 57.
3   Standing Committee D col 59, 4 February 1997.
4   (1997) *The Independent*, 14 September.
5   HC written answers for 12 May 1999 (83586).
6   HC Deb vol 291, cols 214–230, 25 February 1997.
7   HC Deb vol 313, cols 304–305, 4 June 1998.

the investigation of crime, but far more controversial issues arise in the dissemination of the information to other agencies and, in some cases, to the community at large.[1]

CONTROLLING THE ACTIVITIES OF SEX OFFENDERS

Sex Offender Orders

7.16   In November 1997 the Government expressed the view that, despite the implementation of the Sex Offenders Act 1997 and the proposed introduction of extended sentences, communities still did not get adequate protection from the activities of sex offenders, particularly those who prey on children and other vulnerable people, and so it proposed the introduction of a Community Protection Order.[2] It had originally been intended that sex offenders would be caught by the proposed Community Safety Orders,[3] which were to be introduced in the Crime and Disorder Bill. However, the Government recognised that, in the case of sex offenders, the primary concern was to protect the public by putting measures in place which the offender would be expected to follow for a long time, whereas the proposed Community Safety Orders would be aimed at preventing further anti-social behaviour, probably over a far shorter period of time. Therefore, a new kind of order was proposed for sex offenders who posed a continued risk to the community. The resulting order – the Sex Offender Order – was introduced by s 2 of the Crime and Disorder Act 1998, which was implemented on 1 December 1998.

The nature of the order

7.17   A Sex Offender Order is an order in respect of a sex offender which prohibits him from doing any act specified in the order. It is a civil order, but breach of the order constitutes a criminal offence. Applications for the Sex Offender Order are made to the magistrates' court by the chief officer of police. As the order is a civil one, the magistrates' court will be acting in its civil capacity and so the civil standard of proof, ie on the balance of probabilities, applies.

The pre-conditions

7.18   In determining the grounds for making the Sex Offender Order, the Government expressed the view that a previous conviction or caution for a sexual offence should not itself be sufficient, but that a court would need evidence that the offender posed a current risk to the community.[4] The relevant provision is

---

1   See **7.80** to **7.88**.
2   *Community Protection Order: A Consultation Paper* (Home Office, London, November 1997).
      The proposed Community Protection Order was later to become the Sex Offender Order
      contained in the Crime and Disorder Act 1998.
3   The proposed Community Safety Order was later to become the Anti-social Behaviour
      Order in the Crime and Disorder Act 1998.
4   *Community Protection Order: A Consultation Paper* (Home Office, London, November 1997)
      para 5.

now contained in s 2(1) of the 1998 Act, which sets out two conditions which must be satisfied:

(1) that the person must be a sex offender; and
(2) that the person has acted, since the relevant date, in such a way as to give reasonable cause to believe that an order is necessary to protect the public from serious harm from him.

THE FIRST PRE-CONDITION – WHO IS A SEX OFFENDER?

7.19   Section 3 of the 1998 Act provides that a sex offender is a person who:

(1) has been convicted of a sexual offence to which Pt 1 of the Sex Offenders Act 1997 applies;
(2) has been found not guilty of such an offence by reason of insanity, or found to be under a disability and to have done the act charged against him in respect of such an offence;
(3) has been cautioned by a constable, in England and Wales or Northern Ireland, in respect of such an offence which, at the time the caution was given, he had admitted; or
(4) has been punished under the law in force in a country or territory outside the UK for an act which:
    (a) constituted an offence under that law, and
    (b) would have constituted a sexual offence to which Pt 1 of the Sex Offenders Act 1997 applies if it had been done in any part of the United Kingdom.

7.20   The definition of a sex offender for the purpose of making a Sex Offender Order is wider than that contained in the Sex Offenders Act 1997, as it includes those who have been committed the relevant offences abroad. Although there was considerable support from all parties in the House of Commons to extend the notification requirements in Pt 1 of the Sex Offenders Act 1997 to include offenders who commit offences abroad, the practical and bureaucratic difficulties that would be encountered in obtaining the necessary information and in recognising the judgments of foreign criminal courts were deemed to outweigh any potential benefit.[1] Presumably, the inclusion of such offenders within the remit of Sex Offender Orders can be explained on practical grounds. Whereas the number of sex offenders who commit offences abroad and return to the UK would cause practical and bureaucratic problems if all were automatically subject to the notification requirements, the potential number of such offenders who return to the UK and are thought to present a risk sufficient to justify the making of a Sex Offender Order will inevitably be small, thereby reducing the practical and bureaucratic problems to an acceptable level.

7.21   In an effort to avoid needless expenditure of time and effort proving offences committed abroad, the Act provides that the magistrates' court may assume that the offender has been punished abroad for a relevant offence, unless the offender serves a notice on the police:

(1) stating that, on the facts as alleged with respect to the act in question, the condition is not in his opinion satisfied;

---

1   See **7.9**.

(2) showing his grounds for that opinion; and

(3) requiring the police to show that it is satisfied.[1]

Once a sex offender, always a sex offender?

7.22   The timing of the commission of the previous offence has been a matter of some debate. The 1998 Act refers to those offences to which Pt 1 of the Sex Offenders Act 1997 applies. The notification requirements contained in the 1997 Act are generally only applicable to those who have been convicted or cautioned of a relevant offence after the commencement of the Act.[2] This led to the suggestion that the same restriction was applicable to the provisions of the 1998 Act, ie that offenders convicted or cautioned before the commencement of the 1997 Act were not sex offenders for the purpose of Sex Offender Orders.[3] If this were the case, it would clearly be a major restriction on the potential use of Sex Offender Orders. However, the offences to which Pt 1 of the 1997 Act applies are contained in Sch 1 to the Act, which makes no reference to the date of the conviction or caution. The restriction is imposed in relation to the notification requirements by s 1 of the 1997 Act, but this does not make the restriction applicable to the provisions of the 1998 Act. The Home Office clearly believes that offenders convicted of a relevant offence prior to the commencement of the 1997 Act are sex offenders for the purpose of s 2 of the 1998 Act. A press release to announce the implementation of Sex Offender Orders contained the following case example.[4]

> 'Mr X is cautioned for indecent conduct towards a young child in 1990. In January 1999 he begins hanging around outside primary school gates at the end of the school day, approaching departing children (not his own) offering them sweets and talking to them. This happens several times and staff and parents at the school are concerned and report the matter to the police. The police observe Mr X, check his previous records and consult other agencies involved in his case in 1990 or with subsequent involvement with Mr X. They decide there is no innocent explanation for his behaviour, and there is reasonable cause to believe his present behaviour, if it continues, could lead to serious harm whether psychological or possibly physical to the young children he appears to be targeting. The police apply for an order which is granted. In the order Mr X is prohibited from going within 200 metres of any school in a specified area between specified hours when children are likely to be entering or leaving (8am–10am, 12–2pm, 3–5pm). The names and addresses of the schools could be listed in the order.'

7.23   The issue is further clarified in guidance issued by the Home Office which contains the same case study and specifically states that eligibility is not limited to those required to register under the 1997 Act.[5] Therefore, a conviction for a relevant offence many years previously will be sufficient to satisfy the first pre-condition and the 1998 Act amends the Rehabilitation of Offenders Act 1974

---

1   Crime and Disorder Act 1998, s 3(6). Rules of court may set a time limit for such service of notice. The court may also permit the offender to require the police to show that the condition is satisfied without the prior service of a notice (s 3(7)).

2   The only exception being those who are still in contact with the criminal justice system by virtue of their sentence. See **7.3**.

3   See Card and Ward *The Crime and Disorder Act 1998* (Jordans, Bristol, 1999) para 5.60.

4   Home Office Press Release 472/98.

5   *Crime and Disorder Act 1998; Sex Offender Orders* Home Office Guidance Document (Home Office, London, December 1998) para 2.4.1 and Annex B.

to ensure that spent convictions can be relied on by the police in applying for Sex Offender Orders.[1] Given that the objective of a Sex Offender Order is preventative – to intervene at an early stage before further offences are committed – this is clearly both necessary and desirable.

THE SECOND PRE-CONDITION

7.24 Before a Sex Offender Order can be made, it must be proved that the offender has acted, since the relevant date, in such a way as to give reasonable cause to believe that an order is necessary to protect the public from serious harm from him. The relevant date is defined as being the latest date on which the offender has become a sex offender as defined by the 1998 Act or, if later, the date of commencement of s 2 of the 1998 Act.[2] Thus, whilst the previous offence may have been committed many years previously, the behaviour which gives rise to the current concern and which thus forms the basis of an application for a Sex Offender Order, must have taken place after 1 December 1998. For the purposes of this condition, the act does not have to amount to a criminal offence, nor does it have to lead to serious harm. All that is required is that the act gives rise to the necessary belief and an apparently innocent act such as offering sweets to a child may suffice, depending on the surrounding circumstances.

Serious harm

7.25 By virtue of s 18(2) of the 1998 Act, the expression 'serious harm' has the same meaning as in Pt 1 of the Criminal Justice Act 1991.[3] Section 31(3) of the 1991 Act provides that protecting the public from serious harm from an offender convicted of a violent or sexual offence means protecting the public from death or serious personal injury, whether physical or psychological, occasioned by such further offences committed by him. Home Office guidance points out that regard will have to be paid to the decisions of the High Court and the Court of Appeal when interpreting 'serious harm' in the light of the definition in s 31.[4] In the vast majority of applications for a Sex Offender Order, the concern will relate to the risk of serious harm caused by a further sexual offence. However, the legislation is not so limited. Reference in s 31 of the 1991 Act to 'such further offences' clearly relates to sexual or violent offences. Although it has been argued that Sex Offender Orders should not be used if an offender poses a risk of serious harm by a violent but non-sexual crime,[5] prima facie, there would appear to be no reason why this could not be done, as long as the offender was a sex offender for the purposes of the 1998 Act.

Assessment of present risk

7.26 The decision to apply for a Sex Offender Order lies with the police. However, an order will affect the management of the sex offender in the

1   Crime and Disorder Act 1998, Sch 8, para 36.
2   Crime and Disorder Act 1998, s 3(2).
3   See **4.70**.
4   *Crime and Disorder Act 1998; Sex Offender Orders* Home Office Guidance Document (Home Office, London, December 1998) Annex B.
5   See Card and Ward *The Crime and Disorder Act 1998* (Jordans, Bristol, 1999) para 5.68.

community for all the various agencies involved and so the police will usually consult with other organisations and professionals in making an assessment of the risk posed by the offender prior to an order being sought.[1] Home Office guidance suggests that, in making an assessment of the risk, a number of factors should be taken into account, including:[2]

(1) the risk that a further offence will be committed;
(2) the potential harm resulting from such an offence;
(3) the date, nature and circumstances of the previous conviction or convictions and any pattern which emerges;
(4) the current circumstances of an offender and how these might foreseeably change, such as work placements/environments; housing; family/relationships; stress/drink/drugs; proximity to schools/playgrounds, etc;
(5) the disclosure implications if an order is applied for and how the court process might affect the ability to manage the offender in the community – this is an important issue and will need very careful consideration, as a court process of this kind is necessarily an open one;
(6) an assessment of the accuracy and currency of the information about the individual (including an assessment of the status of those expressing concern and their reasons for doing so);
(7) the nature and pattern of the behaviour giving rise to concern and any predatory behaviour which may indicate a likelihood of re-offending;
(8) compliance, or otherwise, with previous sentences, court orders or supervisions arrangements; and
(9) compliance, or otherwise, with therapeutic help and its outcome.

The prohibitions

7.27　　In making an application for an order, the police are required to provide details of the offender's criminal history, in order to establish that he is a sex offender as defined by the Act, and details of the acts in respect of which the application is made. Before making an order, the magistrates need to be satisfied that the police have proved that it is more probable than not that the offender has acted in such a way as to give reasonable cause to believe that a Sex Offender Order is necessary to protect the public from serious harm from him. The order may prohibit the offender from doing anything described in it and the police are required to provide details of the prohibition or prohibitions sought,[3] although such recommendations obviously will not be binding on the court if it decides to make an order. The prohibitions that may be imposed are simply defined as those necessary for the purpose of protecting the public from serious harm from the offender.[4]

7.28　　By their nature, the prohibitions must be negative – there is no power to compel an offender to do anything, only not to take particular actions. In the

---

1　　See **7.74** to **7.79**.
2　　*Crime and Disorder Act 1998; Sex Offender Orders* Home Office Guidance Document (Home Office, London, December 1998) para 4.4.
3　　The Magistrates' Courts (Sex Offender and Anti-social Behaviour Orders) Rules 1998, SI 1998/2682, Sch 1.
4　　Crime and Disorder Act 1998, s 2(4).

consultation paper which preceded s 2 of the 1998 Act the view was expressed that a civil order of this kind could not impose positive obligations on an offender, such as a requirement to undergo supervision by the Probation Service, nor could it impose a curfew.[1] The reason for this was said to be that such obligations may well be regarded as imposing a penalty on the offender. Arguably, even negative prohibitions may be seen as imposing a penalty. Undoubtedly, this is true of positive obligations, such as a requirement to undergo supervision, but the distinction between a curfew and a negative prohibition is not so clear. It has been pointed out that in one sense, a curfew is a prohibition against doing certain acts (eg going outside during the terms of the curfew), but in another sense a curfew imposes positive obligations (eg to remain inside during the terms of the curfew).[2] In many cases, restricting an offender's movements in the vicinity of a school or playground will be deemed sufficient and more draconian measures, such as imposing a blanket curfew during specified times, will not be needed.

7.29   As breach of a Sex Offender Order constitutes a criminal offence,[3] certainty is essential. Whatever the prohibitions imposed, the order should be as specific as possible, so that it is readily apparent, both to the offender and to those enforcing the order what does and does not constitute a breach. The provisions of the 1998 Act are vague – the only criterion being that the prohibitions are necessary to protect the public from serious harm from the offender. Other jurisdictions appear to have been more specific in their legislation in this area.[4] For example, s 161 of the Canadian Criminal Code states that when a person is sentenced for an offence relating to a child, or when that person is discharged from a Probation Order, the court may make an order prohibiting the offender from:

(1) attending a public place or public swimming area where persons under the age of 14 are present or could reasonably be expected to be present; and
(2) seeking, obtaining or continuing any employment or voluntary position which involves children under the age of 14.[5]

7.30   Unlike the 1998 Act, the Canadian legislation does not require the offender to have acted in any particular way since the conviction, although presumably a court would only be minded to make such an order if the offender was thought to represent a continuing risk to children. In South Australia, a court may make a paedophile Restraining Order if the defendant has been loitering around children and has within the previous 5 years been convicted or released from imprisonment for a child sexual offence. The order restrains the offender from:

(1) loitering in the vicinity of a school, public toilet or place at which children are regularly present; and

---

1   *Community Protection Order: A Consultation Paper* (Home Office, London, November 1997), para 12.
2   Card and Ward *The Crime and Disorder Act 1998* (Jordans, Bristol, 1999) para 5.74.
3   See **7.32**.
4   See Gillespie 'Paedophiles and the Crime and Disorder Bill' (1998) 1 Web JCLI.
5   See **8.142** to **8.177** for way in which restrictions may be placed on the employment of sex offenders.

(2) children are present at that place at the time of loitering.[1]

Although it has been argued that the Canadian and Australian orders are more certain than the provisions of s 2 of the Crime and Disorder Act 1998,[2] this is not necessarily the case. Much will depend on how the magistrates' court, which, admittedly, has been given a great degree of flexibility, construct the prohibitions when making a Sex Offender Order. As long as the order relates to specific places and specific times, it has the potential to be more certain than its foreign counterparts.

Duration of the order and appeals

7.31   Once a Sex Offender Order has been made, it has effect for a minimum of 5 years and can only be discharged before this time with the consent of both parties.[3] The order itself may specify its duration, or it may continue until a further order.[4] After the 5-year period, either the police or the offender can apply to have the order varied or discharged.[5] While the order has effect, the offender is subject to the notification requirements of Pt 1 of the Sex Offenders Act 1997 and, thus, is required to notify the police of any change of name or address.[6] An offender may appeal to the Crown Court against the making of a Sex Offender Order.[7] On appeal, the Crown Court may make such orders as may be necessary to give effect to its determination of the appeal and may also make such incidental or consequential orders as appear to it to be just.[8]

Breach of the order

7.32   If, without reasonable excuse, a person does anything which he is prohibited from doing by a Sex Offender Order, he commits a criminal offence and is liable:

(1) on summary conviction, to imprisonment for a term not exceeding 6 months or to a fine not exceeding the statutory maximum, or to both; or
(2) on conviction on indictment, to imprisonment for a term not exceeding 5 years or to a fine, or to both.[9]

Therefore, breach of the order is an arrestable offence,[10] which gives the police power to intervene, potentially at a very early stage. The Police and Criminal Evidence Act 1984 provides that a police officer may arrest without a warrant anyone whom he has reasonable grounds for suspecting to be about to commit an arrestable offence.[11] Therefore, to return to the example used in the Home

---

1   Summary Procedure Act 1921, s 99AA.
2   Gillespie 'Paedophiles and the Crime and Disorder Bill' (1998) 1 Web JCLI.
3   Crime and Disorder Act 1998, s 2(7).
4   Crime and Disorder Act 1998, s 2(5).
5   Crime and Disorder Act 1998, s 2(6).
6   Crime and Disorder Act 1998, s 2(5).
7   Crime and Disorder Act 1998, s 4(1).
8   Crime and Disorder Act 1998, s 4(2).
9   Crime and Disorder Act 1998, s 2(8).
10   See **2.26**.
11   Police and Criminal Evidence Act 1984, s 24(7)(b).

Office guidance,[1] if Mr X was observed buying sweets and walking towards the local primary school at 3.30pm one day as the children were coming out of school, a police officer could arrest Mr X before he approached within 200 metres of the school. However, in practice, the police undoubtedly would wait until the prohibition had actually been breached before arresting Mr X, thereby obtaining evidence on which to base a conviction for breach of the order.

7.33 Breach of the accompanying requirement to notify changes of name and address to the police is not an arrestable offence as the maximum penalty is 6 months' imprisonment.[2] A power of arrest for breach of the notification requirements will therefore only arise if the general arrest conditions are satisfied.[3] Prosecutions for breach of Sex Offender Orders will be conducted in the usual way by the Crown Prosecution Service and the criminal standard of proof, ie beyond all reasonable doubt, will apply.

A useful order?

7.34 In November 1998, the Home Secretary stated that he hoped that Sex Offender Orders, together with other measures the Government would be taking against sex offenders, would be used as widely as possible to protect local communities and those most at risk.[4] Early indications suggest that the Home Secretary has been disappointed. In May 1999, approximately 5 months after the implementation of Sex Offender Orders, in response to a written question, a Home Office minister stated that the Home Office was aware of three Sex Offender Orders having been granted and that no information was held centrally to indicate the number of orders which had been applied for.[5] In response to media headlines referring to a 'failed pervert law', a Home Office spokesperson was quoted as saying: 'There is no crisis. Magistrates, police and lawyers need to be thinking about the orders as an option and that will take a little time.'[6] By October 1999, the Home Office was aware of 14 Sex Offender Orders having been granted.[7] It remains to be seen whether the number of orders granted continues to grow or whether it is indeed a 'failed pervert law'.

CONTROL IN THE ABSENCE OF A CONVICTION

7.35 As a conviction for a specified sexual offence is a pre-condition of the making of a Sex Offender Order, such orders can only be used to control 'visible' sex offenders and cannot be used to restrict the movement of 'invisible' sex offenders in the community, even if their conduct is sufficient to cause concern. However, in some circumstances, alternative control measures may be employed

---

1   See **7.22**.
2   Sex Offenders Act 1997, s 3.
3   See **2.27**.
4   *Crime and Disorder Act 1998; Sex Offender Orders* Home Office Guidance Document (Home Office, London, December 1998), preface.
5   HC written answers 11 May 1999 (83347).
6   (1999) *Daily Mail*, 24 May
7   HC written answers 25 October 1999 (94956).

which are not aimed specifically at sex offenders and, thus, do not have the commission of a sexual offence as a pre-requisite.

Anti-social Behaviour Orders

7.36   In September 1997, the Government expressed its intention to tackle the problem of anti-social behaviour which was said to cause distress and misery to innocent, law-abiding people and undermine the communities in which they live.[1] Although there already existed powers in the Housing Act 1996 and the Protection from Harassment Act 1997 to deal with certain kinds of anti-social behaviour and civil law injunctions could be obtained in some situations, it was felt that such powers did not provide a complete answer to the problem. Section 1 of the Crime and Disorder Act 1998 now provides for a new community-based order akin to an injunction – the Anti-social Behaviour Order. The nature of the order is similar to the nature of a Sex Offender Order, although there are significant differences between the two. Both are civil orders, made by a magistrates' court acting in its civil capacity. Whereas only the police can apply for a Sex Offender Order, either the police or the local authority can apply for an Anti-social Behaviour Order, although they must consult with each other before any application is made.[2] Both orders prohibit the person named in the order from doing anything described in it, although there are differences in the nature of the prohibitions that may be imposed in each case. Breach of either order is a criminal offence, subject to the same maximum penalty. The Anti-social Behaviour Order lasts for a minimum of 2 years, compared to a minimum of 5 years for a Sex Offender Order.

7.37   A magistrates' court may make an Anti-social Behaviour Order if it is satisfied that the following conditions are fulfilled with respect to any person aged 10 or over:[3]

(1)   that the person has acted, since the commencement date, in an anti-social manner, that is to say, in a manner that caused or was likely to cause harassment, alarm or distress to one or more persons not of the same household as himself; and

(2)   that such an order is necessary to protect persons in the local government area in which the harassment, alarm or distress was caused or was likely to be caused from further anti-social acts by him.

7.38   Although the order is referred to as an 'Anti-social *Behaviour* Order', s 1(1) of the 1998 Act requires that the person in relation to whom the order is sought has 'acted' in an anti-social manner. Whether or not the continuance of a state of affairs by failing to act is an 'act' for this purpose is not clear.[4] The behaviour must be such as to cause, or be likely to cause, harassment, alarm or distress to one or more persons not of the same household and the order must be necessary to protect persons in the area from further anti-social acts. The prohibitions that may be imposed by the order are those necessary for the

---

1   *Community Safety Order: A Consultation Paper* (Home Office, London, September 1997).
2   Crime and Disorder Act 1998, s 1(2).
3   Crime and Disorder Act 1998, s 1(1) and (4).
4   See Card and Ward *The Crime and Disorder Act 1998* (Jordans, Bristol, 1999) paras 5.16–5.17.

purpose of protecting from further anti-social acts persons in the local government area or adjoining area specified in the application.[1] The order lasts for a minimum of 2 years.

7.39 Home Office guidance gives examples of where the order might be appropriate, including:[2]

(1) where individuals intimidate neighbours and others through threats or violence or a mixture of unpleasant actions;
(2) where there is persistent unruly behaviour by a small group of individuals on a housing estate or other local area, who may dominate others and use minor damage to property and fear of retaliation, possibly at unsocial hours, as a means of intimidating other people;
(3) where there are families whose anti-social behaviour, when challenged, leads to verbal abuse, vandalism, threats and graffiti, sometimes using children as the vehicle for action against neighbouring families;
(4) where there is persistent abusive behaviour towards elderly people or towards mentally ill or disabled people causing them fear and distress;
(5) where there is serious and persistent bullying of children on an organised basis in public recreation grounds or on the way to school or within the school grounds, if normal school disciplinary procedures do not stop the behaviour;
(6) where there is persistent racial harassment or homophobic behaviour; and
(7) where there is persistent anti-social behaviour as a result of drugs or alcohol misuse.

7.40 The guidance makes it clear that this is not a definitive list, but is intended to illustrate the type of behaviour involved. The main test is said to be a pattern of behaviour which continues over a period of time but cannot be dealt with easily or adequately by prosecution of those concerned for a single 'snapshot' or criminal event.[3]

Sex offenders and Anti-social Behaviour Orders

7.41 Anti-social Behaviour Orders are clearly not intended primarily as a measure to control sex offenders. The deterrent of an Anti-social Behaviour Order is that, for most conduct, there is a higher penalty available for breach of the order than for the substantive act itself. The same is not true of a Sex Offender Order, as in many cases the maximum penalty for a sexual offence will be higher than the maximum of 5 years' imprisonment available for breach of the order. However, there may be situations in which no power to make a Sex Offender Order exists, but there does exist a power to make an Anti-social Behaviour Order. A person whose actions give rise to concern may not be a sex offender as required by s 2 of the 1998 Act, or there may not be reasonable cause to believe that an order is necessary to protect the public from serious harm from

---

1   Crime and Disorder Act 1998, s 1(6).
2   *The Crime and Disorder Act 1998: Anti-Social Behaviour Orders Guidance Document* (Home Office, London, 16 March 1999) para 3.9.
3   *The Crime and Disorder Act 1998: Anti-Social Behaviour Orders Guidance Document* (Home Office, London, 16 March 1999) para 3.10.

him, but the power to make an Anti-social Behaviour Order may nevertheless exist.

7.42   For example, Mr Y is known locally as a 'flasher' and enquiries reveal he has a previous conviction for indecent exposure. In recent months, several children have told their parents that he has been waiting outside their school and on several occasions has offered them sweets and invited them back to his house to play on his computer. Understandably, the parents are concerned, and they inform the police and the headteacher of the school. When the head-teacher approaches Mr Y and asks him not to loiter at the school gates because he is causing distress and alarm both to the pupils and their parents, Mr Y is abusive and continues to wait outside the school on a regular basis. There are no grounds to make an application for a Sex Offender Order, as indecent exposure is not a sexual offence as defined by Sch 1 to the Sex Offenders Act 1997. However, Mr Y's actions in waiting outside school and offering sweets to the children constitute anti-social behaviour in that they cause alarm and distress to the children and their parents, and an order is necessary to protect them from further anti-social acts by him. Therefore, a magistrates' court could make an order which prohibits Mr Y from going within a specified distance of the school during specified times.

'Stalking' and the Protection from Harassment Act 1997

7.43   Following several well-publicised cases, including two which involved members of the royal family as victims,[1] the 1990s saw an increased recognition of the problem of 'stalking'. There exists no legal definition of stalking, but it is generally taken to refer to a course of conduct which harasses, threatens, intimidates, molests or causes distress to an individual. Typically, it involves following the individual, waiting outside his or her home or workplace, making telephone calls, or sending faxes, emails and articles. On occasions, property may be damaged and physical assaults may occur. Although not directly related to sexual offending, the aim of the stalker is often to compel the victim to engage in, or re-engage in, a relationship with the stalker.[2] Thus, there may well exist a sexual motivation in many cases and, if not dealt with, the 'stalking' may escalate into the commission of a sexual offence.

7.44   Attempts to bring the activities of stalkers within the existing criminal law proved to be difficult in many cases, leading to what many regarded as an unacceptable and artificial stretching of the law of offences against the person.[3] In order to address the problem, the Protection from Harassment Act was passed in 1997. The Act creates two new criminal offences: a summary offence of

---

1   In January 1996, Bernard Quin, who had a reputation for being an 'infatuated stalker' of the Princess Royal, was found not guilty of behaviour likely to cause a breach of the peace when he attempted to break through a security cordon placed around the Princess. In March of the same year, Dr Klaus Wagner, a compulsive 'stalker' of both the Queen and Diana, Princess of Wales, was found not guilty of similar behaviour. See Lawson-Cruttenden and Addison *Blackstone's Guide to the Protection from Harassment Act 1997* (Blackstone Press Ltd, London, 1997) para 1.5.
2   Allen 'Look Who's Stalking: Seeking a Solution to the Problem of Stalking' (1996) 4 Web JCLI.
3   *R v Burstow, R v Ireland* [1998] AC 147.

criminal harassment[1] and an indictable offence of putting people in fear of violence.[2] Section 1 of the Act provides that a person must not pursue a course of conduct which amounts to the harassment of another and which he knows or ought to know amounts to harassment of the other.[3] The course of conduct, which includes speech, must involve conduct on at least two occasions, and although it contains no definition of harassment, the Act provides that reference to harassing a person include alarming the person or causing the person distress. The more serious indictable offence[4] is committed by a person whose course of conduct causes another to fear, on at least two occasions, that violence will be used against him, if the defendant knows or ought to know that his course of conduct will cause the other so to fear on each of those occasions. Thus, if a potential sex offender is following his victim, the criminal offences created by the 1997 Act may allow intervention at an early stage, before any sexual offence is actually committed. However, two other provisions of the Act may be of rather more relevance to the control of sex offenders in the community – the power of the criminal court to make a Restraining Order and the creation of a statutory tort of harassment.

Restraining Orders

7.45   Although the criminal law has long made provision to restrict the movements of offenders in the community pending their trial, initially by giving the court power to impose conditions of bail and more recently by the extension of the same power to the police,[5] until recently no such specific power existed to control the movements of an offender after conviction. This was an issue that the 1997 Act sought to address, albeit only in a limited number of situations. Section 5 of the Act allows a court, when sentencing an offender who has been convicted of an offence under s 2 or s 4 of the Act, to make a Restraining Order in addition to sentencing the offender or dealing with him in any other way. Such orders are to be made for the purpose of protecting the victim of the offence, or any other person mentioned in the order, from further conduct which amounts to harassment or will cause a fear of violence and may prohibit the offender from doing anything described in the order.[6] The offender who, without reasonable excuse, does anything prohibited by the order commits a criminal offence and is subject to a maximum penalty of 5 years' imprisonment.[7]

7.46   In many respects, Restraining Orders are similar to the Sex Offender and Anti-social Behaviour Orders that are now available by virtue of the Crime and Disorder Act 1998. All three orders can be used to restrict an offender's movements within the community with a view to protecting individuals or

---

1   Protection from Harassment Act 1997, s 2.
2   Protection from Harassment Act 1997, s 4.
3   The test is objective, ie a defendant ought to know that his course of conduct amounts to harassment of another if a reasonable person in possession of the same information would think the course of conduct amounted to harassment of another (s 1(2)). Various exceptions to the prohibition are contained in s 1(3).
4   Section 4(4) provides that the maximum penalty is 5 years' imprisonment.
5   See **2.99**.
6   Protection from Harassment Act 1997, s 5(2).
7   Protection from Harassment Act 1997, s 5(5).

members of the community, and all carry a similar penalty for breach. There are, however, several significant differences. Those deemed to be in need of protection will be specifically named in the Restraining Order and typically, the order will prohibit the offender from contacting his victim and will restrict his movements on the vicinity of the victim's home and place of work. In contrast, Sex Offender and Anti-social Behaviour Orders will not usually specify individuals in the order, but will specify the prohibited conduct in terms of locations and may refer to specific groups of individuals, such as children. Unlike the provisions of the 1998 Act, which specify a minimum period for the duration of Sex Offender and Anti-social Behaviour Orders, the 1997 Act makes no such limit, merely stating that a Restraining Order may have effect for a specified period or until further notice.[1]

7.47	Although no separate application to the court is necessary, as is required for Sex Offender and Anti-social Behaviour Orders, Restraining Orders can only be made when an offender has been convicted of an offence under the 1997 Act and, thus, the opportunities for making the orders will inevitably be limited. The explanatory memorandum to the Protection from Harassment Bill stated that it was anticipated that approximately 200 extra criminal cases a year would arise. However, doubts about such low expectations expressed a short time later have been proved justified.[2] The Act came into force on 16 June 1997. By the end of 1997, proceedings had been brought against 507 offenders under s 2 of the Act and 243 under s 4. Provisional figures for the period between January and September 1998 show that proceedings had been brought against a total of 3,011 offenders under s 2 of the Act and 1,094 under s 4.[3] Although the statistics do not reveal the number of Restraining Orders made, in 1997 proceedings were brought against 23 offenders for breach of a Restraining Order and this figure had risen to 234 between January and September 1998.

Extending the criteria for Restraining Orders

7.48	Clearly, more use is being made of the provisions of the 1997 Act than originally anticipated. However, the fact that such orders can only be made following conviction for an offence under s 2 or s 4 of the 1997 Act inevitably leads to anomalies. For example, an offender who persistently follows a victim, causing her alarm and distress, or even causing her to fear that violence will be used against her can be ordered not to contact the victim again, but someone who actually has physical contact with the victim and is convicted of indecent assault or even rape cannot be made the subject of a similar order. This has led to calls to extend Restraining Orders to other serious offences, so that a rapist could be prevented from contacting his victim or returning to the area in which the rape occurred on his release from prison. Such proposals for reform led to the introduction of a private members' Bill into the House of Commons in April 1999 – the Restraining and Protection Orders Bill.[4]

1	Protection from Harassment Act 1997, s 5(3).
2	Lawson-Cruttenden and Addison *Blackstone's Guide to the Protection from Harassment Act 1997* (Blackstone Press Ltd, London, 1997) para 1.7.
3	HC written answers for 21 May 1999 (84734).
4	HC Deb vol 330, 28 April 1999 (pt 21).

7.49 Based on the concept of the Restraining Order contained in s 5 of the 1997 Act, cl 1 of the Bill empowers the court to make an order when sentencing or otherwise dealing an offender for a specified offence. The specified offences are detailed in cl 1(5) and include any offence for which a person of 21 years of age or over (not previously convicted) may be sentenced to imprisonment for a term of 5 years[1] and various other offences involving public order and common assault. Thus, the more serious sexual offences will be specified offences for the purpose of the extended Restraint Orders.[2] The prohibitions that may be contained in the order are those that the court considers to be reasonably necessary to protect the victim or victims of the offence or offences for which the offender is being sentenced and to protect the public from further criminal acts by him. In determining what prohibitions are reasonably necessary, the court is to have regard both to the facts of the offence for which the offender is being sentenced and any previous criminal offences of which he has been convicted. The great advantage of the proposed order is that it could be imposed by the court at the time of sentencing and, if the provisions of the Bill were to be enacted, the range of measures currently available to control sex offenders in the community by restricting their movements would be greatly enhanced. However, no date was set for the second reading and the Bill was lost.

Civil law and the use of injunctions

7.50 The provisions of the Protection from Harassment Act 1997 and the Crime and Disorder Act 1998 which can be used to restrict the movement of sex offenders in the community require no action to be taken personally by victims or potential victims. Sex Offender Orders are made on application by the police, Anti-social Behaviour Orders are made on application by either the police or local authority, Restraining Orders under the 1997 Act may be made by the sentencing court and the proposed extended Restraint Order will be made either by the court of its own motion or on application by the prosecutor following conviction.[3] From a victim's point of view, it will usually be preferable to allow a third party, such as the police, local authority or court, to take the initiative in restraining the offender's movements. However, situations may arise in which the victim or potential victim, or someone acting on their behalf, may wish to take steps themselves to restrict the movements of an offender.

The Family Law Act 1996

7.51 One option would be to apply for an order under the Family Law Act 1996. The provisions of the Act are aimed primarily at domestic relationships and so, admittedly, their potential use to control sex offenders is limited. The Act widens the range of people who may be protected by a Non-molestation Order to include persons 'associated with the respondent' and relevant children.[4] An

---

1   Or might be so sentenced but for the restrictions imposed by s 33 of the Magistrates' Courts Act 1980.
2   See app 1.
3   There is no specific provision in the 1997 Act for the prosecutor to apply for a Restraining Order and the defence could well object if such an application is made. This apparent defect would have been remedied by the Restraining and Protection Orders Bill.
4   Family Law Act 1996, s 42.

'associated person' is a spouse or former spouse, a cohabitant or former cohabitant, a person who lives or has lived in the same household, a relative, persons who have agreed to marry one another, parties to the same family proceedings and, in relation to any child, persons who are parents of the child or who have or have had parental responsibility for the child.[1] However, although Non-molestation Orders may be expressed so as to refer to molestation in general, to particular acts of molestation or to both,[2] they cannot include a requirement that a person be excluded from a specified area and so cannot be used to restrict a sex offender's movements in the community.

7.52   An alternative approach may be to apply for an Occupation Order under the 1996 Act.[3] Occupation Orders may exclude the respondent from a defined area in which the dwelling-house which the applicant is entitled to occupy is included,[4] and so, arguably, could be used in certain circumstances to set up an exclusion zone around a particular house and prevent a sex offender coming within that zone. However, the relevant provisions of the 1996 Act are linked closely to property rights and, whilst they may be useful to restrict the movements of sex offender who has a close link with a family in the vicinity of the family home, they are unlikely to be of assistance in restricting the movement of sex offenders in general.

The inherent jurisdiction of the court[5]

7.53   The High Court has an inherent power to grant an injunction in all cases where it appears to be just and convenient to do so,[6] and this power can also be exercised by a county court.[7] However, there are limitations on the exercise of the inherent jurisdiction, in that it can only be used to support a legal right[8] and it cannot be exercised on a free-standing application, although on this latter point it is now clear that an applicant has only to show 'at least an arguable cause of action'.[9] In *Khorasandjian v Bush*,[10] the tort of nuisance was utilised to grant the plaintiff an injunction against the defendant who had previously been convicted of threatening and abusive behaviour. The court made it clear that the conduct to be restrained by the injunction need not in itself be tortious or otherwise unlawful, as long as the injunction is reasonably regarded as necessary for protection of a plaintiff's legitimate interests.[11] Further developments took place in 1996 when the Court of Appeal arguably created a common law tort of harassment for the first time.[12] More significantly, the Court affirmed the power of a court to include an 'exclusion zone order' in an injunction. In this case, the

1   Family Law Act 1996, s 62.
2   Family Law Act 1996, s 42(6).
3   Family Law Act 1996, s 33.
4   Family Law Act 1996, s 33(3)(g).
5   See, generally, Conway and Butler 'Not in my backyard – banishing paedophiles' (1997) New LJ 18 July at 1075.
6   Supreme Court Act 1981, s 37.
7   County Courts Act 1984, s 38(1).
8   *Richards v Richards* [1984] 1 AC 174.
9   *Burris v Azadani* [1995] 4 All ER 802 at 807.
10   [1993] QB 727.
11   [1993] QB 727 at 732.
12   *Burris v Azadani* [1995] 4 All ER 802.

Court affirmed that the plaintiff had a cause of action in nuisance and, in addition, under the tort of harassment, as the plaintiff had a legitimate interest in receiving protection from behaviour which might be highly stressful and disturbing.[1] The Court made an injunction which restrained the defendant, inter alia, from coming or remaining within 250 yards of the plaintiff's home address. However, the problem remained that there existed no power of arrest for breach of an injunction, which meant that the plaintiff would need to institute proceedings for contempt of court in the event of a breach.

The introduction of a statutory tort of harassment

7.54 In addition to creating the criminal offence of harassment, the Protection from Harassment Act 1997 also created a statutory tort of harassment which entitles the victim to a civil remedy, including damages for anxiety caused by the harassment and any financial loss resulting from the harassment.[2] More significantly, where the High Court or county court grants an injunction for the purpose of restraining the defendant from pursuing any conduct which amounts to harassment, if the defendant breaches the injunction without reasonable excuse, he is guilty of a criminal offence and is liable on conviction on indictment to a maximum of 5 years' imprisonment.[3] This penalty, of course, means that breach of the injunction is an arrestable offence for the purposes of the Police and Criminal Evidence Act 1984.[4] However, it has been pointed out that the police could find themselves in a difficult position and may be reluctant to become involved in enforcing injunctions taken out by individuals.[5] In addition to creating this criminal offence of breach of an injunction, the Act creates a new procedure, allowing the civil courts to issue an arrest warrant following a breach of the injunction on an application by the victim substantiated on oath.[6] Thus, victims could find themselves being advised by the police to use this provision if the police are reluctant to use their powers of arrest without warrant. Whichever route is chosen, statistics show that comparatively few proceedings are brought for breach of an injunction against harassment. Between the commencement of the Act in June 1997 and the end of December 1997, one person was cautioned and proceedings were taken against seven people, of whom only three (43%) were convicted. Provisional figures for January to September 1998 indicate that seven people were cautioned and proceedings were brought against 17, of whom eight (47%) were convicted.[7] Clearly, far more use has been made of the provisions in the 1997 Act creating criminal offences and allowing the sentencing court to make Restraining Orders.[8]

---

1 See Allen 'Look Who's Stalking: Seeking a Solution to the Problem of Stalking' (1996) 4 Web JCLI.
2 Protection from Harassment Act 1997, s 3.
3 Protection from Harassment Act 1997, s 3(6) and (9).
4 See **2.26**.
5 Lawson-Cruttenden and Addison *Blackstone's Guide to the Protection from Harassment Act 1997* (Blackstone Press Ltd, London, 1997) 6.4 and 6.9.
6 Protection from Harassment Act 1997, s 3(3) and (5).
7 HC written answers, 21 May 1999 (84734).
8 See **7.45**.

7.55   In theory, injunctions could obviously be relied upon to restrict the movements of a sex offender. Yet the use of injunctions is usually dependent upon an individual, or in the case of a child, someone acting on his or her behalf, bringing the necessary action. Admittedly, local councils do have power to apply for injunctions where they 'consider it expedient for the promotion or protection of the inhabitants of their area',[1] and the House of Lords has decided that this provision entitles local councils to apply for injunctions to prevent actual or anticipated criminal acts in their area.[2] However, the recent availability of alternative measures, such as Sex Offender Orders and Anti-social Behaviour Orders, suggests that there will be little need to resort to civil litigation in order to restrict a sex offender's movements within the community.

'THE LAST RESORT' – TAKING INDIVIDUALS OUT OF THE COMMUNITY

7.56   Despite all the control measures that may now be relied upon to protect the public from sex offenders, situations may still arise when an individual is thought to pose such a risk to the public that his continued presence in the community cannot be justified. Once the licence or Community Order (if any) has come to an end, in the absence of the commission of a further offence, the only way in which the offender can be detained against his will is by virtue of the compulsory detention provisions of the mental health legislation.

The Mental Health Act 1983

7.57   The Mental Health Act 1983, in addition to providing for Hospital Orders and Restriction Orders to be made in respect of offenders found to have committed criminal offences,[3] also makes various provisions for a person's compulsory admission to hospital in the absence of a criminal offence. There are three types of application for admission to hospital – known as 'sections' or 'orders'. In each case an order can only be made in respect of a person who is suffering from a mental disorder, which means mental illness, arrested or incomplete development of mind, psychopathic disorder and any other disorder or disability of mind.[4]

7.58   Section 2 authorises compulsory admission to hospital for assessment (or for assessment followed by treatment), and for detention for this purpose for up to 28 days. The application may be made by the patient's nearest relative or by an approved social worker[5] and must be supported by recommendations from two doctors, one of whom must be an approved specialist in mental disorder, that:

---

1   Local Government Act 1972, s 222.
2   *Stoke on Trent City Council v B&Q (Retail) Ltd* [1984] 2 All ER 323.
3   See **4.121** to **4.127**.
4   Mental Health Act 1983, s 1(2).
5   Mental Health Act 1983, s 11(1).

(1) the patient is suffering from mental disorder of a nature or degree which warrants the detention of the patient in a hospital for assessment (or for assessment followed by a medical treatment) for at least a limited period; and

(2) he ought to be so detained in the interests of his own health or safety or with a view to the protection of other persons.

Most forms of medical treatment may be given without the patient's consent during the period of detention.

7.59 Section 4 provides, in the case of urgent necessity, for the compulsory admission of a person to hospital for assessment for a period of up to 72 hours. The application need only be supported by one medical recommendation, which need not be made by an approved specialist. The grounds are the same as for an order under s 2, but both the applicant and the doctor must also state that it is of urgent necessity for the patient to be admitted under s 2 and that compliance with the provisions relating to that section would involve undesirable delay. There is no power to impose treatment without consent, but the admission may be converted into an ordinary s 2 order admission by the provision of a second medical recommendation within the 72-hour period.

7.60 Section 3 provides for the compulsory admission of a patient to hospital for treatment and for his subsequent detention for an initial period of up to six months. The application may be made by the patient's nearest relative or by an approved social worker,[1] however, if the nearest relative objects to the admission, the social worker must seek authority from a county court. The application must be supported by recommendations from two doctors, one of whom must be an approved specialist in mental disorders, to the effect that:

(1) the patient is suffering from mental illness, severe mental impairment,[2] psychopathic disorder[3] or mental impairment[4] and his mental disorder is of a nature or degree which makes it appropriate for him to receive medical treatment in a hospital;

(2) in the case of psychopathic disorder or mental impairment, such treatment is likely to alleviate or prevent a deterioration of his condition; and

(3) it is necessary for the health or safety of the patient or for the protection of other persons that he should receive such treatment and it cannot be provided unless he is detained under this section.

---

1   Mental Health Act 1983, s 11(1).
2   Defined by s 1(2) of the Mental Health Act 1983 to mean a state of arrested or incomplete development of mind which includes severe impairment of intelligence and social functioning and is associated with abnormally aggressive or seriously irresponsible conduct on the part of the person concerned.
3   Defined by s 1(2) of the Mental Health Act 1983 to mean a persistent disorder or disability of mind (whether or not including significant impairment of intelligence) which results in abnormally aggressive or seriously irresponsible conduct on the part of the person concerned.
4   Defined by s 1(2) of the Mental Health Act 1983 to mean a state of arrested or incomplete development of mind (not amounting to severe mental impairment) which includes significant impairment of intelligence and social functioning and is associated with abnormally aggressive or seriously irresponsible conduct on the part of the person concerned.

After the initial period, the detention may be renewed, on the advice of the responsible medical officer, for a second 6 months and, thereafter, for a year at a time. Most forms of treatment may be given without the patient's consent during the period of detention.

7.61   The mental health legislation also provides for the supervision of mentally disordered individuals in the community, either by virtue of a Guardianship Order, whereby the patient is placed under the supervision of the local authority,[1] or by supervision following release from hospital, whereby the patient is supervised by the health authority.[2] There is no requirement that treatment is likely to alleviate or prevent a deterioration of the patient's mental condition. However, in the case of a Guardianship Order, the order must be necessary in the interests of the welfare of the patient or for the protection of other persons, and, in the case of after-care supervision, it is necessary that that there would be a substantial risk of serious harm to the health or safety of the patient or the safety of other persons, or of the patient being seriously exploited, if he were not to receive the after-care services, and his being subject to after care under supervision is likely to help to secure that he receives those services. In either case, the guardian or supervisor can dictate where the patient lives, how he is to spend his time and who must be allowed to see him, but cannot insist that he accepts treatment for his disorder. Whilst such supervision obviously allows some control to be exercised over a mentally disordered person in the community, such control will inevitably be limited.

7.62   The overall effect of the mental health legislation is that, although a person whose mental condition causes concern in the community can be subject to compulsory detention for up to 28 days in the first instance, in the case of a person suffering from psychopathic disorder or impairment, continued detention after this time will only be possible if treatment is 'likely to alleviate or prevent a deterioration of the condition'. Therefore, psychopaths whose condition is not amenable to treatment cannot be detained against their will and this is seen increasingly as an unacceptable lacuna in the law. Cases such as that of Michael Stone, who was convicted of the brutal murder of Lynne and Megan Russell despite concerns being expressed, both by the authorities and by Stone himself, about the danger he presented, have been given a high profile in the media. Although attempts have been made in a private members' Bill to introduce a form of 'protection order',[3] there is general agreement that this is an issue which the Government itself should address and the Government has now acknowledged that the present situation is not acceptable.

The case for change – psychopaths and personality disorders

7.63   A psychopathic disorder is defined in the Mental Health Act 1983 as a persistent disorder or disability of mind (whether or not including significant impairment of intelligence) which results in abnormally aggressive or seriously

---

1   Mental Health Act 1983, s 7.
2   Mental Health Act 1983, s 25A, as introduced by the Mental Health (Patients in the Community) Act 1995.
3   Restraining and Protection Orders Bill, presented to the House of Commons on 28 April 1999. See **7.48**.

irresponsible conduct on the part of the person concerned.[1] The use of the term 'psychopath', although popular with the media, has been criticised as a damaging label involving much stigma[2] and in 1994 it was proposed that the term 'psychopathic disorder' in the mental health legislation should be replaced by the more generally understood and less stigmatising term 'personality disorder'.[3] Although this recommendation has yet to be acted upon, those who used to be labelled as psychopaths are being referred to increasingly as people with personality disorders. A personality disorder is said to be an inclusive term referring to a disorder of the development of personality. Although not a category of mental illness, it can potentially be regarded for legal purposes as a cause of 'unsound mind' and includes a range of mood, feeling and behavioural disorders including anti-social behaviour.[4]

DANGEROUS PEOPLE WITH SEVERE PERSONALITY DISORDERS

7.64   The increasing concern over the apparent lack of legislative powers to deal with the risk posed by some psychopaths, or those with a severe personality disorder, led to the publication of a consultation paper by the Home Office and the Department of Health in July 1999.[5] The paper acknowledged that, whereas personality disorders are common and the overwhelming majority of sufferers do not pose a risk to the public and live reasonably ordered, crime-free lives, there exists a small proportion of such people who suffer from the type of personality disorder that manifests itself in serious anti-social behaviour and that a minority of this sub-group pose a very high risk to society.[6] This small minority are referred to as dangerous severely personality disordered (DSPD) people – those who have an identifiable personality disorder to a severe degree, who pose a high risk to other people because of serious anti-social behaviour resulting from their disorder.

The size of the problem

7.65   In 1997, a study by the Office for National Statistics showed that there were about 1,400 men in prison who fell within the DSPD category. A further 400 male patients are detained on court orders under the legal category of psychopathic disorder in secure psychiatric hospitals, and there are estimated to be between 300 and 600 men in the community who are generally well known to local police, health and social services because of their dangerous and demanding behaviour and who might potentially fall into the DSPD group.[7] In total, therefore, it is estimated that 2,000 people over the age of 18 in England and Wales fall within the category of DSPD, over 98% of these are men and at any

---

1   Mental Health Act 1983, s 1(2).
2   DHSS *A Review of the Mental Health Act 1959* (HMSO, London, 1976).
3   Reed *Report of the Department of Health and Home Office Working Group on Psychopathic Disorder* (Department of Health and Home Office, London, 1994).
4   *Managing Dangerous People with Severe Personality Disorder – Proposals for Policy Development* (Home Office and Department of Health, London, 1999).
5   Ibid.
6   *Managing Dangerous People with Severe Personality Disorder – Proposals for Policy Development* (Home Office and Department of Health, London, 1999) pt 1, para 1.
7   *Managing Dangerous People with Severe Personality Disorder – Proposals for Policy Development* (Home Office and Department of Health, London, 1999) pt 2, paras 3 and 4

one time most are in prison or in secure hospitals. The overwhelming majority are thought to be people who have committed serious offences such as murder, manslaughter, arson, serious sexual offences or grievous bodily harm. At the present time, it is not known what percentage are actual or potential sex offenders, but further work has been commissioned to provide prospective data about the size of the DSPD group and, hopefully, this will shed more light on the nature of the risk posed by individuals within the group. In the meantime, although the number of DSPD sex offenders is very small when compared with the number of sex offenders overall, such offenders will invariably pose a serious risk to the public and existing provisions are clearly inadequate to meet this risk. The dilemma lies in providing adequate protection for the public while ensuring that the needs of DSPD individuals are met.

The way forward – a framework for the future

7.66   The Government has expressed its determination to protect the public and provide effective services for people in the DSPD group and proposes a new framework consisting of four essential elements:[1]

(1) the creation of powers for detention and continued supervision of DSPD individuals;
(2) the establishment of better means of identifying DSPD individuals and specialist assessment processes to inform decision-making at different points;
(3) the development of specialist approaches to the detention and management of those who have been detained; and
(4) the establishment of a comprehensive and continuing programme of research into the management of dangerous people with severe personality disorders to support development of policy and practice.

The way forward – options for change

7.67   If public safety is to be improved, changes in legislation are needed to provide authority for the detention, possibly indefinite, of DSPD people on the basis of the risk they present. There will also need to be changes in the way DSPD people are assessed and subsequently managed in detention. The Government is looking at a number of ways of achieving the necessary changes in the law and has outlined two possible packages of legislative and service changes.[2]

7.68   Option A maintains the current statutory framework and service structures and the location for management of DSPD individuals would be determined according to whether they were detained under criminal or civil legislation.

(1) Criminal justice legislation: A large majority of DSPD individuals are offenders and would continue to be held in prison. Moves would be made to facilitate greater use of the discretionary life sentence, for example, by

1   *Managing Dangerous People with Severe Personality Disorder – Proposals for Policy Development* (Home Office and Department of Health, London, 1999) pt 3, paras 3 and 4.
2   *Managing Dangerous People with Severe Personality Disorder – Proposals for Policy Development* (Home Office and Department of Health, London, 1999) pt 3, paras 7–34.

improving the quality of information available to the courts and extending its availability to a wider range of offences. At present, the courts give a discretionary life sentence in less than 2% of the cases where it is available, but it is thought that sentencing practice might change if changes in assessment and diagnostic procedures improved the quality of evidence available to the court about the risk of serious re-offending associated with presence of severe personality disorders. New powers would be provided to remand offenders for specialist assessment, so that courts would have all the information they need to decide on the appropriate sentencing disposal.

(2) Proceedings in civil legislation: DPSD individuals not subject to a current prison sentence would have to be managed in facilities run by the health service, whether or not they were likely to benefit from treatment in hospital. The existing requirement that treatment must be 'likely to alleviate or prevent a deterioration of his condition' before an individual can be detained would be removed in the case of DSPD individuals detained in civil proceedings and new powers for compulsory supervision and recall of DSPD individuals following discharge from detention would be introduced.

(3) Changes in the structure of prison and hospital services: As DSPD individuals would be detained in both prisons and health service facilities, it is acknowledged that it would be difficult to establish common standards for assessment and risk management. These problems could be partly overcome by central commissioning of DSPD services provided in prisons and health service facilities.

7.69 Option B creates a new legal framework for the detention of all DSPD individuals, based on the risk they present and their therapeutic needs, rather than whether they have been convicted of any offence. New powers would be introduced in both criminal and civil proceedings to provide for the indeterminate detention of DSPD individuals, with powers for supervision and recall following release from detention. Those subject to the new orders would be detained in services managed separately from mainstream prison and health service provision.

(1) Proceedings in criminal legislation: A DSPD disposal would be available on the basis of evidence that the offender was suffering from a severe personality disorder and, as a consequence of the disorder, presented a serious risk to the public. This would require a period of compulsory assessment in a specialist facility. A DSPD direction could be attached to any sentence passed by the higher courts, except mandatory life sentences which are fixed by law. The effect of the direction would be that the offender would be detained in a specialist facility until such time as he was no longer considered to present a serious risk on the grounds of his disorder. At that point, he would be released into the community or returned to prison to serve the remainder of his sentence. Release into the community would be subject to formal supervision and, as necessary, compliance with specified conditions, and the offender would be subject to recall for further assessment. Any sentenced prisoners, including one subject to mandatory life sentences, could be referred for consideration of making a DSPD Order in civil proceedings at any time during their term of

imprisonment. Such an order would result in transfer of the individual from prison to detention in specialist facilities.

(2) Proceedings in civil legislation: The DSPD Order would be made in civil proceedings on the basis of evidence that the individual was suffering from a severe personality disorder and as a consequence of the disorder presented a serious risk to the public. The order could only be made following a period of compulsory assessment in a specialist facility and the effect of the order would be that the individual would be detained in a specialist facility until such time as he was no longer considered to present a serious risk on the grounds of his disorder and could (subject to any necessary supervision) be released safely into the community. The individual would remain liable to recall for detention for further assessment.

(3) Changes in structure of services: Radical changes would need to be made to current organisational arrangements and a new specialist system would be set up for the management of DSPD individuals. The new service would be separate from, but with close links to, the Prison and Health Service.

7.70   Alongside these proposals for change, the Secretary of State for Health has also commissioned an expert group, under the chairmanship of Professor Genevra Richardson, to advise him on the scope for changes in the Mental Health Act 1983, and any legislative changes based on the proposals in the consultation paper will obviously need to take account of the recommendations of this group. Given the relatively small number of DSPD individuals, it can be questioned whether the radical changes required by option B can be justified. In particular, the proposal to extend the availability of discretionary life sentences to a wider range of offences may have implications far beyond the management of DSPD individuals. Whichever option, or combination of options, is chosen, some controversy is inevitable.

Indeterminate detention of DSPD individuals and human rights
7.71   The indeterminate detention of DSPD individuals on the basis of risk, regardless of whether or not they have committed a criminal offence, potentially raises issues of human rights. In the case of an offender convicted of a criminal offence, similar issues are raised by the imposition of a longer than normal sentence under s 2(2)(b) of the Criminal Justice Act 1991, as previously discussed.[1] However, even in the absence of a criminal conviction, art 5(1) of the European Convention on Human Rights also permits the lawful detention of '... persons of unsound mind'.[2] The detention must be prescribed by law and must not be arbitrary.[3] In the case of detention of persons of unsound mind, to meet an allegation of 'arbitrary' detention, three minimum conditions must be satisfied:[4]

(1) the individual concerned must be 'reliably shown' by 'objective medical expertise' to be of 'unsound mind';

---

1   See **4.78**.
2   European Convention on Human Rights, art 5(1)(e).
3   *Wintwerp v Netherlands Series* A/33 (1979–80) 2 EHRR 387.
4   *Managing Dangerous People with Severe Personality Disorder – Proposals for Policy Development* (Home Office and Department of Health, London, 1999) Annex B.

(2) the individual's mental disorder must be of a kind or degree warranting compulsory confinement; and

(3) the disorder must persist throughout the period of detention.

7.72   Both options for change proposed in the recent consultation paper meet these conditions. Indeterminate detention will be authorised only on the basis of evidence from an intensive specialist assessment, the procedures include a process of appeal and the authority to detain will be subject to regular independent review, thereby avoiding potential conflict with art 5(4).

7.73   Whilst there has been some considerable support for the proposal to detain convicted DSPD offenders at the end of their custodial sentence if they are assessed as presenting a continuing risk to the public, concern has been expressed at the idea of indeterminate detention in the absence of a conviction. Such detention has been opposed by the National Association for the Care and Resettlement of Offenders, which described the proposal as a 'bridge too far', and the pressure group Liberty, which claimed that detaining those who have committed no criminal offences, especially for long periods, is wrong.[1] The controversy over the proposed removal of the 'treatability' condition from the mental health legislation is fuelled by the fact that there is no universal diagnosis of 'personality disorder', which has been referred to a 'a dustbin diagnosis'.[2] There are fears that different psychiatrists may give a different diagnosis on the same person, which inevitably would lead to miscarriages of justice. Such fears can only be allayed by mental health professionals, who must produce convincing evidence of the accuracy and reliability of a diagnosis of personality disorder. Without such evidence, the proposed changes cannot be justified.

PROTECTING THE PUBLIC AND MULTI-AGENCY WORKING

Working together – the multi-agency approach

7.74   Whilst the Probation Service retains primary responsibility for the supervision and control of offenders in the community, the police also have a major role in controlling offenders by investigating and prosecuting offences. The creation of the sex offender register now ensures that the police are closely involved in monitoring the whereabouts of sex offenders in the community and enhances opportunities for working closely with the Probation Service. However, the Probation Service and the police are not the only agencies who may have a role to play in monitoring sex offenders in the community and, if the public is to be protected effectively, it is vital that all agencies co-operate and work together. Over the last few decades, the concept of interagency co-operation has been gaining ground in many areas. The concept has perhaps been most evident in cases of child abuse.[3] Although the primary responsibility

---

1   (1999) *Daily Mail*, 14 July.

2   Judi Clements of Mind (the mental health charity), quoted in (1999) *Daily Mail*, 14 July.

3   See Cobley *Child Abuse and the Law* (Cavendish Publishing Ltd, London, 1995) chap 4 'Working together – the practical framework of child protection'.

for protecting victims of child abuse rests with the local authority, it has long been recognised that the proper and effective investigation of child abuse and protection of children requires co-operation between all professions and agencies with staff who are in direct contact with children and their families, including the police, health authorities, family practitioner committees, local education authorities, the Probation Service and other voluntary agencies and there now exist well-established arrangements for inter-agency co-operation in cases of child abuse.

The development of crime and disorder partnerships

7.75   Inter-agency co-operation and multi-agency working have also been important elements in the management of the criminal justice process. For example, the Probation Service has long had a statutory duty to participate in arrangements concerned with the prevention of crime or with the relationship between offenders and their victims or the community at large.[1] In 1997, the Government published a consultation paper which acknowledged that there is a realisation generally that the police cannot be expected to fight crime alone and identified a wide range of partnership agreements operating in England and Wales, involving different agencies from the public and voluntary sectors at all levels.[2] The Crime and Disorder Act 1998 now places such co-operation on a statutory basis with the introduction of statutory crime and disorder partnerships. Local authorities and the police are now required to formulate and implement a strategy for the reduction of crime and disorder in their area[3] and obligations are placed on local authorities, the police, police authorities, health authorities and probation committees to co-operate in the development and implementation of the strategies.[4] Local authorities are also required to exercise their various functions with due regard to the need to do all that they reasonably can to prevent crime and disorder in their areas.[5]

Sharing information between the professions – the development of protocols

7.76   Effective multi-agency working relies on good relations, mutual trust and the exchange of all relevant information between the professions involved. In the past, conflicting professional ideologies and problems of confidentiality have posed sometimes insurmountable hurdles to effective inter-agency working.[6] However, significant advances have been made in recent years, with many agencies developing protocols governing joint working and the sharing of information. Such developments have been clearly evident in the work between the police and the Probation Service. In 1996–97, the thematic inspection of the role of the Probation Service in protecting the public from sex offenders found

---

1   Probation Rules 1984, SI 1984/647.
2   *Getting to Grips with Crime: A New Framework for Local Action* (Home Office, London, 1997).
3   Crime and Disorder Act 1998, ss 6 and 7.
4   Crime and Disorder Act 1998, s 5.
5   Crime and Disorder Act 1998, s 17.
6   See, for example, Cobley *Child Abuse and the Law* (Cavendish Publishing Ltd, London, 1995) chaps 4 and 5.

that there was extensive evidence of flexible and purposeful collaborative working between the Probation Services and other agencies and that, in particular, joint work with police officers was assuming an increasingly high priority and generally worked very well.[1] In February 1997, a survey of police forces in England and Wales on the disclosure of information about sex offenders was carried out on behalf of the Association of Chief Police Officers.[2] Out of the 36 forces who responded, 20 forces had developed some form of documented strategy, policy or protocol in the area of child protection. In addition, many forces were found to be running new schemes designed to increase the flow of information. In particular, some protocols were concerned with the exchange of information with the Probation Service in relation to recently released sex offenders and at least six forces had progressed to include action plans and monitoring devices for evaluating the success of new initiatives in this area. However, as the thematic inspection noted, these developments were all taking place in the absence of any centrally designed framework or guidance about such liaison.[3]

A statutory power to disclose

7.77 The introduction of statutory crime and disorder partnerships by the Crime and Disorder Act 1998 and associated obligations to co-operate in the development of crime and disorder strategies was accompanied by the provision of a statutory power to disclose information. Any person, who would not otherwise have the power to disclose information, can now lawfully disclose information where necessary or expedient for the purposes of any provision of the 1998 Act to a chief officer of police, a police authority, local authorities, the Probation Service or health authority, or to people acting on behalf of any of these bodies.[4] It is envisaged that the power to disclose will be used to reinforce the many existing and successful protocols for the sharing of information for crime and disorder purposes between, for example, the police and Probation Service.[5]

The common law duty of confidence

7.78 Although the 1998 Act now ensures that the various agencies have a *power* to disclose, the statute does not impose a *duty* to disclose and so all agencies must still decide the propriety of any particular disclosure for themselves. Any person proposing to disclose information not publicly available and obtained in circumstances giving rise to a duty of confidence will need to establish whether there is an overriding justification for doing so. The protection of the public will invariably amount to an overriding justification for disclosing the information to

---

1   *Exercising Constant Vigilance: The Role of the Probation Service in Protecting the Public from Sex Offenders* (Home Office, London, 1998) para 7.30.

2   *Disclosure of Information – Sex Offenders: Results of a Survey of Police Forces in England and Wales,* AJP Butler QPM, Chief Constable, Gloucester Constabulary on behalf of the Association of Chief Police Officers' Crime Committee.

3   *Exercising Constant Vigilance: The Role of the Probation Service in Protecting the Public from Sex Offenders* (Home Office, London, 1998) para 7.30.

4   Crime and Disorder Act 1998, s 115.

5   *Guidance on Statutory Crime and Disorder Partnerships* (Home Office, London, 1999) para 5.21.

other professionals, although wider disclosure to the community in general raises rather more difficult issues.[1] Even if a duty of confidence does not strictly arise, the courts have recognised that, resting on a fundamental rule of good public administration, there is a general presumption that information held by a public body should not be disclosed.[2] However, the presumption may be rebutted and the disclosure of information justified where is it judged to be desirable or necessary in the public interest.

Information-sharing agreements and data protection

7.79   It is inevitable that much of the information that needs to be exchanged between the various agencies will be held on a computer and, thus, will be subject to the provisions of the Data Protection Acts. The data protection regime is in place to ensure that data held about individuals are treated correctly, giving due regard to the privacy of individuals and requires that personal data are obtained and processed fairly and lawfully; are only disclosed in appropriate circumstances; are accurate, relevant and not held longer than necessary; and are kept securely. A checklist of issues to be addressed when setting up of information sharing arrangements has been drawn up by the Home Office and Data Protection Registrar as part of the guidance provided on the implementation of the Crime and Disorder Act 1998.[3] The main issues to be addressed include:

(1) consideration of the purpose of the information-sharing arrangement and whether parties have a legitimate basis for disclosing sensitive personal information as required by the Data Protection Act 1998 (this is unlikely to be a problem when sharing information with other agencies about a sex offender who is thought to pose a risk to the public);

(2) whether it will be necessary to share personal information in order to fulfil that purpose (de-personalised information is information presented in such a way that individuals cannot be identified and, therefore, it has no data-protection implications; however, it is unlikely that such de-personalised information will be sufficient when considering individual sex offenders);

(3) whether parties to the arrangement have the power to disclose personal information for the stated purpose;

(4) how much personal information will need to be shared in order to achieve the objectives of the arrangement;

(5) whether the consent of the individual should be sought before disclosure is made and what if the consent is not sought, or is sought but withheld (it will not always be the case that the prevention and detection of crime or public safety constitutes an overriding public interest for the exchange of personal information without consent, but if a sex offender is thought to pose a danger to the community disclosure to other agencies will usually be justified, although each case must be decided on its own merits); and

---

1   See **7.80** to **7.86**.

2   See Bingham LCJ in *R v Chief Constable for North Wales Police Area Authority and Others, ex parte AB and Another* [1997] 4 All ER 691.

3   *Guidance on Statutory Crime and Disorder Partnerships* (Home Office, London, 1999) para 5.23.

(6) whether the non-disclosure exemption applies. The Data Protection Acts 1984 and 1998 contain general 'non-disclosure' provisions, but allow a number of specific exemptions. There is an exemption which states that personal information may be disclosed for the purposes of the prevention and detection of crime, or the apprehension and prosecution of offenders, in cases where failure to disclose would be likely to prejudice these objectives. A party seeking to rely on this exemption will need to make a judgment as to whether, in the particular circumstances of an individual case, there would be a substantial chance that one or both of those objectives would be damaged noticeably if the personal information was withheld.

Disclosing information to the community and the 'outing' of sex offenders

7.80 The development of protocols and guidance on the exchange of information about sex offenders between professionals involved in the multi-agency risk-assessment process has removed many of the obstacles encountered previously and has enhanced the prospects of effective multi-agency working. The risk assessment itself will inform the more controversial decision as to whether information about a sex offender and the risk he is thought to pose should be disseminated more widely in the community.

7.81 Many would argue that the general public have a right to be told when a sex offender is living in their community and the proposed introduction of the sex offender register in 1996 led to calls for the public to have access to the information which would be held by the police.[1] Several states in the USA have a statutory system of community notification and the interest of the general public in England and Wales in the idea seems to have been sparked in particular by media attention to the US law, commonly referred to as 'Megan's Law',[2] which links federal anti-crime funding with a sex offender warning system. The statutory provisions vary between the different states, but the most extreme example of broad community notification is found in Louisiana, where the State Board of Parole requires a sex offender to notify the public by mail of his name, address and the offence for which he was convicted.[3] The requirements are very specific – people who live within one square mile in rural areas, or three square blocks in urban areas, of the proposed release address must be notified and offenders may also be required to conduct any other form of notification deemed necessary by the Board, for example car stickers, signs or flyers.

7.82 Although many of the US laws on community notification appear too extreme to be considered for adoption in England and Wales, the issue of community notification is nevertheless one which has been the subject of considerable debate this side of the Atlantic. Members of the public may claim that they have a right to be protected and, therefore, that they have a right to be

---

1 'Move to Alert Public about Sex Offenders' (1996) *Western Mail*, 18 October.
2 Hebenton and Thomas 'Sex Offenders in the Community: Reflections on Problems of Law, Community and Risk Management in the USA, England and Wales' (1996) 24(4) Int J Soc Law 427.
3 Nash *Police, Probation and Protecting the Public* (Blackstone Press Ltd, London, 1999) p 188.

told about sex offenders living in their community, but this must be balanced against the right of a sex offender to privacy. However, it has been suggested that, in practice, it is not so much a balancing of rights as a decision as to whose rights are the more important, on the basis that they compete with each other.[1] Yet the 'rights' issue is not the only consideration. It is argued that notification runs counter to the principles underlying the Rehabilitation of Offenders Act 1974 and, if offenders and their families are outcasts, normality will be an impossibility and the effect of any rehabilitation will be counteracted.[2] Certainly, if the members of the public are informed that a sex offender is living in their midst, there are the inevitable dangers of vigilante attacks, some of which may have tragic consequences, not only for sex offenders themselves but also for innocent parties. In one case in the North West an elderly man was beaten severely after being mistaken for a paedophile by vigilantes. The attack followed the publication of a photograph of the paedophile in the local paper, but the editor of the paper reportedly accepted no responsibility, claiming that the newspaper was reflecting public concern, a stance which was supported by 92% of those who took part in a telephone poll conducted by the newspaper.[3] In the West Midlands, a 14-year-old girl was killed in an arson attack intended for a sex offender.[4]

7.83   Fear of vigilante attacks may also have the effect of driving sex offenders 'underground' – encouraging them to move away from the area, sometimes disappearing without trace. In April 1998, the Association of Chief Officers of Probation published a dossier of 40 cases in which vigilante action had led to violence or caused offenders to move or to go underground.[5] The consequences of this are significant – not only does it make keeping track of such offenders far more difficult, but it can have a severely detrimental effect on any supervision arrangements, even bringing the supervision to an abrupt end if the offender disappears without trace. Such events can only increase the risk to the public.

7.84   The decision to notify a community, or sections of a community, about a sex offender living in the area is not an easy one to make. In some circumstances, the decision may be taken out of the hands of the responsible professionals because information about the sex offender becomes known in the community through informal channels. This may be because an offender is returning to an area where he is known, or the information may be 'leaked', typically through local newspapers, several of which have run campaigns to notify the public about sex offenders living in the locality.[6] Such informal notification frequently results in protests and threats of vigilante attacks, placing the police in what has been described as a 'no-win situation'.[7] Such problems can often be avoided by the controlled release of information to those in the community who are thought to be at risk or to those who can help reduce the risk. Although the problem of community notification has become increasingly

1   Nash *Police, Probation and Protecting the Public* (Blackstone Press Ltd, London, 1999) p 188.
2   'Law and the Lynch Mob' (1997) *The Guardian*, 19 February.
3   Nash *Police, Probation and Protecting the Public* (Blackstone Press Ltd, London, 1999) p 194.
4   'Law and the Lynch Mob' (1997) *The Guardian*, 19 February.
5   'Protecting the Public – and the Sex Offender' (1998) *The Times*, 29 September.
6   Nash *Police, Probation and Protecting the Public* (Blackstone Press Ltd, London, 1999) p 193.
7   'Feelings Erupt as Parents Storm Paedophile's Home' (1999) *Western Mail*, 16 June.

prominent with the advent of the sex offender register, it is one with which the police have been grappling for some time prior to 1997 and, as previously noted, resulted in the development of formal protocols for sharing information with other agencies in some areas. As far as notification to the wider community was concerned, the survey carried out on behalf of the Association of Chief Police Officers in February 1997 found that, of the 36 forces who responded, 14 had used a warning system of community notification on a very small number of occasions (usually to warn a school or schools of the threat posed by an individual who was perceived to be a significant danger to that group of children). On a few occasions, police had warned immediate neighbours with young children by identifying convicted offenders who had moved into nearby premises. On only one occasion had the police, via the media, alerted the general public to the potential danger of a particular man who was thought to be so dangerous that it would be negligent not to inform the local community. In all but three cases, the decision to disclose was taken with multi-agency agreement following lengthy risk assessment and consultation.

Legal challenges to disclosure

7.85   The practices adopted by the police forces which took part in the survey have effectively received judicial endorsement.[1] In 1997, two convicted paedophiles sought judicial review of the decision of the North Wales Police to disclose information about their background to the owner of a caravan site where they were living, arguing that the policy adopted by the police was unreasonable and that the police had, inter alia, harassed them,[2] breached a private law duty of confidentiality, committed the tort of misfeasance in public office and acted contrary to art 8 of the European Convention. The Queen's Bench Division of the High Court rejected these arguments. Bingham CJ held that there was a general presumption that public officials should not disclose information concerning offences. This presumption was said to be rooted in fundamental requirements of good public administration and arose from three considerations: first, the potentially serious effect that disclosure of information can have on the ability of offenders to lead normal lives on release from prison; secondly, the risk of violence being inflicted on offenders in the wake of disclosure; and, thirdly, the risk, following disclosure, that offenders may be driven into hiding. However, Bingham CJ pointed out that these considerations must be balanced against the need to afford protection against paedophiles who may re-offend and held that there is a strong public interest in ensuring that the police are able to disclose information about offenders where that is necessary for the prevention or the detection of crime, or for the protection of young or other vulnerable people. On the facts of the case, it was held that the policy operated by North Wales Police, which recognised the general presumption against disclosure and considered each case on its merits, was not unlawful. The court also considered that disclosure would not contravene art 8 of the European Convention on Human Rights (the right to respect for privacy and family life)

---

1   *R v Chief Constable for North Wales Police Area Authority and Others, ex parte AB and Another* [1997] 4 All ER 691, DC.
2   Contrary to s 3 of the Caravan Sites Act 1968.

where disclosure was made in good faith in the exercise of professional judgment and limited to what was reasonably necessary.

7.86   On appeal, the applicants argued that the police had reached the decision to disclose information about them in a procedurally unfair manner. The Court of Appeal concluded that any information that the applicants could have given to the police would not have prompted them to alter their decision on disclosure and, therefore, upheld the decision of the High Court.[1] It is clear that the police are expected to gather as much information as is reasonably practicable before deciding whether to disclose information and, as Lord Woolf pointed out, the subject of the possible disclosure will often be in the best position to provide information which will be valuable when assessing risks.

Disclosure and multi-disciplinary assessment of risk

7.87   The Sex Offenders Act 1997 makes no reference to the disclosure of the information notified. During the Parliamentary debates on the legislation, the Association of Chief Police Officers, whilst recognising the need for national guidance on some limited areas, expressed the firm view that, in order to maintain maximum flexibility in the arrangements for exchanging and using information, the most effective option would be a Home Office circular rather than a prescriptive code of practice.[2] This view was endorsed by the Association of Chief Officers of Probation.[3] Suggested amendments to the Bill to include provision for the Secretary of State, following consultations, to make regulations governing access to the information failed,[4] but shortly before the implementation of the Act, the Home Office issued guidance on managing information acquired under the provisions of the Act.[5] The guidance makes it clear that it is for the courts, not the Home Office, to give an authoritative statement on the law on disclosure of information, but does provide guidance which professes to be an 'extension of current good practice'. In line with previous practice, although the decision to disclose will remain a matter for the professional judgment of the police, a multi-disciplinary assessment of the risk posed by an individual will continue to be a central feature of the decision. The guidance makes it clear that the fact of a conviction is not the only factor to be considered in assessing risk, and suggests that assessment should also take account of:

(1)   the nature and pattern of previous offending;
(2)   compliance with previous sentences or court orders;
(3)   the probability that a further offence will be committed;
(4)   the harm that such behaviour would cause;
(5)   any predatory behaviour which may indicate a likelihood that he will re-offend;
(6)   the potential objects of the harm (and whether they are children or otherwise especially vulnerable);

---

1   *R v Chief Constable for North Wales Police Area Authority and Others, ex parte AB and Another* [1998] 3 All ER 310, CA.
2   HC Deb vol 291, col 229, 25 February 1997.
3   HL Deb vol 579, col 561, 14 March 1997.
4   HC Deb vol 291, cols 214–231, 25 February 1997.
5   HOC 39/1997, Appendix A.

(7) the potential consequences of disclosure to the offender and their family; and

(8) the potential consequences of disclosure in the wider context of law and order.

7.88   The nature of the information disclosed and the extent of its dissemination should be decided on a case-by-case basis, although it is anticipated that disclosure to a member of the general public will only occur in exceptional circumstances. The guidance identifies three specific areas of risk as examples of circumstances where disclosure may be justified: the workplace, schools and playgroups, and youth groups. In each case, disclosure should be made to a senior professional, headteacher or group leader, as appropriate. However, perhaps the crucial question is whether the information will then be disclosed further. The police are advised that, before making any disclosure, they should be prepared to give advice and guidance on what action is required to be taken by the person receiving the information. It is acknowledged that some responsibility will, inevitably, be transferred to the third party, but the police are required to take the lead in providing guidance on precisely how the third party should respond to the information to further the protection of a specific person or persons generally, and on restricting the use and preventing undesirable spreading of the information disclosed. Of course, once the information has been passed onto a third party, controlling any further disclosure of that information becomes very difficult – a fact which may well influence the decision to disclose in the first place.

Protecting the public – where do we go from here?

7.89   Owing to the nature of sex offending, protection of the public from sex offenders can never be absolutely guaranteed, but the key to providing the best possible protection lies in convicting the offender of a sexual offence. Without such a conviction, effective protection is simply not possible. There can be no custodial sentence, no compulsory supervision or treatment in the community and no Sex Offender Order can be made to restrict the offender's movements. Furthermore, keeping track of the offender will be difficult, as there will be no requirement for him to notify the police of any change of address. Control measures which do not have a conviction for a sexual offence as a pre-requisite, such as Anti-social Behaviour Orders, Restraining Orders and injunctions, will invariably be limited in the protection they can afford. The control measures and rehabilitative opportunities which are needed to ensure effective protection of the public, and which can only flow from a conviction for a sexual offence, have been strengthened considerably in recent years. More attention must now be focused on securing that crucial conviction.

Chapter 8

SEX OFFENDERS IN THE COMMUNITY: ACCOMMODATION, FAMILY LIFE AND EMPLOYMENT

'A ROOF OVER THEIR HEADS' – ACCOMMODATING SEX OFFENDERS

8.1   The provision of stable accommodation can be a key factor in the prevention of re-offending. In general, homelessness, with all its associated problems, tends to make offenders more vulnerable to the temptation of returning to a life of crime. Certainly, research has shown that among persistent petty offenders those who have homes, or reasonable security of accommodation, are proportionately less likely to re-offend than those who have no homes or are in insecure housing.[1] The absence of stable accommodation also makes the supervision of offenders in the community very much more difficult. For this reason, the provision of accommodation can be a critical factor in the effective management and control of sex offenders in the community. In recent years, increasing importance has been attached to the effective supervision and surveillance of sex offenders in the community, as evidenced by developments such as the provision of extended sentences in the Crime and Disorder Act 1998[2] and the notification requirements contained in the Sex Offenders Act 1997.[3] The Probation Service and the police, who bear the main responsibility for these tasks, face a difficult enough task without the additional problem of homelessness. Yet finding suitable accommodation for sex offenders may be one of the most difficult hurdles to be overcome.

Remaining in the community

8.2   Sex offenders who do not receive a custodial sentence and remain in the community will hopefully retain their existing accommodation, but this cannot be guaranteed, even if the offender's family are supportive. Such offenders may encounter accommodation problems for several reasons. First, if the offender is living in a household with children, the issue of child protection may arise.[4] If the offence consists of intrafamilial abuse, it is unlikely that the family will be able to remain in the same household in the immediate aftermath of the offence and this will often mean the offender finding alternative accommodation. Even if the offence is committed outside the family, there may still be child protection concerns which mean that the offender can no longer live at home. Secondly, even if the offender is not required to leave home in order to protect any

---

1   See Paylor *Homelessness and Ex-offenders: A Case for Reform* (Social Work Monographs, Norwich, 1992) p 3.
2   See **4.82** to **4.87**.
3   See **7.1** to **7.15**.
4   See **8.88** to **8.114**.

children, those living with the offender may not be prepared to tolerate his continued presence in the home. Inevitably, any relationship with a partner will be put under pressure when the offending behaviour becomes known, whether or not a criminal conviction results, and in many cases this will lead to the breakdown of the relationship with associated problems of accommodation. Other family members may well react in a similar manner, leading to the offender being excluded from his existing accommodation. Thirdly, even if the offender's family are supportive, the commission of a sexual offence, particularly if it results in a criminal conviction, may have ramifications for the offender's employment,[1] which in turn may result in a decline in the household income, necessitating a change of accommodation. Finally, sex offenders are not generally welcomed as residents in their local community. Vigilante attacks by neighbours, undertaken with a view to forcing the abuser to move out of the area, are not uncommon.[2] Even an offender with a supportive family and apparently stable accommodation may find himself the victim of such harassment to the extent that he and his family are forced to move to alternative accommodation – if it can be found.

Release from a custodial sentence

8.3　　Problems in securing and retaining suitable accommodation are not an inevitable consequence of the commission of a criminal offence. Indeed, many offenders who remain in the community will experience no such problems, although, as indicated in the previous section, sex offenders are arguably more likely to encounter problems due to the nature of their offending behaviour. However, a custodial sentence is likely to have far more serious implications for accommodation of all offenders. Research undertaken in 1990 suggests that the accommodation offenders go to on their release from a custodial sentence is nearly always worse, and less appropriate, than the accommodation they left prior to the period of imprisonment.[3] In total, 68 offenders from three prisons in Lancashire were interviewed shortly before they were due to be released and then again shortly after they had been released. Each offender was given an accommodation score: first, for the accommodation they had occupied prior to their arrest; and, secondly, for their accommodation at the time of the post-release interview. The score was calculated by allocating points based on certain criteria relating to the type and status of accommodation, and with whom the offender was living. For example, a house or flat was allocated 1 point, a hostel 5 points and sleeping out 8 points; a secure tenure was allocated 1 point, a lodger 4 points and sleeping out 6 points; and living with a partner and children was allocated 1 point, living with parents 6 points and sleeping out 10 points. Thus, an unattached offender sleeping rough would have the maximum accommodation score of 24 points. At the other end of the scale, an offender living with his partner and children in a house or flat with a secure tenure would have the minimum accommodation score of 3 points. Comparing the accommodation scores of the offenders before arrest and after release, it was found that:

(1)　35 (51.4%) experienced a negative change in their accommodation score;

1　　See **8.142** to **8.177**.
2　　See **7.82**.
3　　Paylor *Housing Needs of Ex-offenders* (Avebury, Aldershot, 1995).

(2) 28 (41.1%) experienced no change in their accommodation score; and

(3) 5 (7.3%) experienced a positive change in their accommodation score.

8.4   Earlier research of a similar nature carried out in the late 1970s found that, out of a sample of 100 men released into the Leeds area only 25% registered a negative change in their accommodation score, whereas 12% experienced a positive change in their score and 63% experienced no change in their score.[1] Although caution must be exercised in making direct comparisons between the two studies,[2] one clear point emerges from them: a very small percentage of offenders can expect a positive change in their accommodation score following a custodial sentence, and between one-quarter and one-half can expect a negative change. Unfortunately, the research gave no indication of the offences for which the custodial sentences were imposed or the length of the sentences themselves. Moreover, the research was carried out prior to the changes to the early release scheme brought about by the Criminal Justice Act 1991.[3] These changes may affect the outcome, particularly in the case of offenders sentenced to custodial terms of 4 years or more, who are unlikely to be recommended for release before serving two-thirds of their sentence, unless suitable accommodation is available for them on release.

8.5   Problems of retaining or finding suitable accommodation tend to be exacerbated for sex offenders who receive a custodial sentence. Just as those who remain in the community may face disruption to their family relationship, either through the intervention of the local authority social services to ensure the protection of any children or through the breakdown of their relationship with their partner or wider family, similar problems may be faced by those who receive a custodial sentence. Indeed, a custodial sentence arguably makes such problems more likely to occur. The very fact that a custodial sentence has been imposed indicates that the offence is serious.[4] Whereas a partner may be prepared to forgive what he or she sees as a minor indiscretion, a more serious offence may not be viewed in the same light. Even if a relationship survives the initial disclosure of the offence, the enforced separation during the custodial sentence will inevitably take its toll and sometimes leads to the breakdown of the relationship before the offender's release. Similarly, child protection may obviously be a concern on a sex offender's release from a custodial sentence. If the offender is employed and is an owner/occupier, a custodial sentence will invariably lead to the loss of his employment, which in turn may lead to the loss of his home if mortgage repayments cannot be maintained. Offenders living in accommodation provided by the local authority may find themselves classed as 'intentionally homeless' on their release and, thus, refused further assistance in finding alternative accommodation.[5] Finally, the danger of vigilante attacks may be more acute when a sex offender is released at the end of a custodial sentence, particularly if the offender seeks to return to the area where he committed the original offences.

---

1   Cordon, Kuipers and Wilson *After Prison* Papers in Community Studies No 21 (University of York, York, 1978).

2   Paylor *Housing Needs of Ex-offenders* (Avebury, Aldershot, 1995) p 171.

3   See chap 5.

4   Criminal Justice Act 1991, s 1(2).

5   See **8.61**.

Not in my backyard – what is suitable accommodation?

8.6 The availability of suitable accommodation for a sex offender may influence decision-making at several stages in the criminal justice system, for example when deciding whether or not to grant bail, when determining sentence and when exercising any discretion on the early release of the offender from a custodial sentence. However, inevitably, there will be situations in which the offender must be released into the community, despite the lack of any accommodation deemed to be suitable. Precisely what amounts to suitable accommodation may depend on many factors, including the offender's personal needs (either physical or mental) and the people with whom he wishes to live. Probably the most crucial factor will be the risk that the offender is thought to pose, either to the community in general or to vulnerable members of the community, such as children. For example, if the offender has committed sexual offences against children and is thought to pose a continuing risk to children, the primary concern may be to ensure that he does not live in the immediate vicinity of a school or playground. If the offender is thought to require a greater level of monitoring, accommodation with a concierge, caretaker or even CCTV may be thought desirable. In some cases, these factors may be taken into account if the offender is required to live in a controlled environment, such as a probation hostel, as a condition of his licence or Probation Order.[1] If the offender is not subject to any such conditions, if he is an owner/occupier or renting in the private sector, subject to any concerns about the protection of any children living in the property, there is little that can be done about the suitability of the accommodation, in terms of its structure and location. However, if a sex offender is to be allocated accommodation from the social sector, efforts can be made to ensure that the accommodation allocated is some distance from a school or playground, although, in practice, this often will not be possible to achieve.[2]

LIVING IN A CONTROLLED ENVIRONMENT

Approved probation and bail hostels

8.7 The idea of using hostels to provide a supportive environment with some element of control short of the restrictions imposed by a prison to accommodate offenders in the community dates back to the beginning of the 20th century.[3] By 1948, the arrangements were placed on a statutory footing when the Home Secretary was empowered to approve and regulate probation hostels.[4] Initially aimed at young offenders, from 1969 the hostels began admitting adult offenders. At this time, there was also a growing awareness of the need to provide a controlled environment in which to accommodate offenders on bail, who would otherwise be remanded in custody while awaiting trial. In 1971, the first hostel accommodating bailees opened as an experimental project and, within 3

---

1 See **8.7** to **8.23**.
2 See **8.46**.
3 The Criminal Justice Administration Act 1914 first established provisions for a residence requirement to be included in a Probation Order.
4 Criminal Justice Act 1948.

years, offenders on bail were also being accommodated in approved probation hostels. Hostels are now managed by Probation Services or voluntary management committees and are regulated by the Approved Probation and Bail Hostel Rules 1995.[1] Guidance on the running of hostels is provided by the *Hostels Handbook*, issued by the Home Office,[2] a guidance manual for assistant chief officers[3] and a guidance manual for voluntary committees, published by the National Association of Probation and Bail Hostels in conjunction with the Home Office.[4]

8.8   A thematic inspection of the work of approved bail and probation hostels reported that, in October 1997, there were 101 approved hostels in England and Wales, providing a total of 2,244 beds, of which 85% were then occupied.[5] Of the 101 hostels, 91 were generic, eight were 'bail only',[6] 60 were designated as 'men only', four as 'women only' and 35 accommodated both men and women. During the period of March 1997 to March 1998, between 62% and 64% of the residents were bailees, between 19% and 22% were subject to a condition in a Probation Order and between 10% and 13% were under statutory supervision following release from a custodial sentence.

The purpose of approved hostels

8.9   It is clear that hostels are not intended merely to meet the accommodation needs of an offender. The national standards state that the purpose of approved hostels is to provide an enhanced level of residential supervision with the aim of protecting the public by reducing the likelihood of offending. Approved hostels are for bailees, probationers and post-custody licensees, where their risk of causing serious harm to the public or other likelihood of reoffending means that no other form of accommodation in the community would be suitable.[7] Approved hostels are said to enhance supervision in that they:

(1) impose a supervised night-time curfew which can be extended to other times of the day (eg as required by a court order or licence condition);
(2) provide 24-hour staff oversight;
(3) undertake ongoing assessment of attitudes and behaviour;
(4) require compliance with clearly stated house rules which are vigorously enforced; and

---

1   SI 1995/302.
2   *Hostels Handbook* (Home Office, London, 1995).
3   *Approved Hostels: Guidance Manual for ACOs* (Home Office and Association of Chief Officers of Probation, 1996).
4   *Guidance Manual for Hostel Committees: Voluntary Managed Approved Probation and Bail Hostels* (National Association of Probation and Bail Hostels, 1997).
5   *Delivering an Enhanced Level of Community Supervision. Report of a Thematic Inspection on the Work of Approved Probation and Bail Hostels* (Home Office, London, 1998) para 3.21.
6   Although at the time of the inspection, two of these hostels were accommodating offenders who were there as a condition of an order.
7   *National Standards for the Supervision of Offenders in the Community* (Home Office, London, 2000) para E1.

(5) provide a programme of regular supervision, support and daily monitoring that tackles offending behaviour and reduces risks.[1]

8.10   The national standards published in 1995 required approved hostels to publish a statement of aims and objectives.[2] Despite this expectation, in 1998 the thematic inspection of approved hostels found that none of the 17 hostels inspected had published a statement which described comprehensively how residents would receive the 'enhanced level of supervision'.[3] However, on a more positive note, the inspection found that it was possible to identify practice, together with a range of programmes and facilities, via which an enhanced level of supervision was being provided. Aspects of enhanced supervision noted in the inspection report included:

(1) high contact levels between staff and residents as part of the on-going, daily routine of a 24-hour supervised regime;
(2) daily/weekly meetings for all residents which focused on the day-to-day operation of the hostel;
(3) offence-focused and needs-related programmes and facilities;
(4) regular key working, including formal and informal supervision sessions;
(5) constructive activities designed to promote socially acceptable behaviour;
(6) engagement with community resources, including education, training and employment initiatives, drug facilities, health/psychiatric services, etc;
(7) strict enforcement of hostel rules and court-imposed conditions;
(8) use of CCTV and other security measures; and
(9) regular liaison with appropriate statutory and voluntary organisations, including the police.

8.11   In addition to providing an enhanced level of supervision for offenders, hostels also provide a measure of control over the residents. Each hostel is required to operate within a set of local house rules detailing the requirements and restrictions on residents. National standards provide that these should include, inter alia, prohibitions on the use of alcohol, solvents and controlled drugs, and a requirement that residents be in the hostel between 11.00pm and 6.00am.[4] Each hostel is required to have a clear policy in respect of enforcement of the house rules. The national standards provide that minor infringements of the house rules may be dealt with by informal local warnings, which must be recorded. However, serious or repeated breaches will result in recall to prison, breach action or application for revocation of bail as appropriate.[5]

---

1   *National Standards for the Supervision of Offenders in the Community* (Home Office, London, 2000) para E2.
2   *National Standards for the Supervision of Offenders in the Community* (Home Office, London, 1995) para 8.7.
3   *Delivering an Enhanced Level of Community Supervision. Report of a Thematic Inspection on the Work of Approved Probation and Bail Hostels* (Home Office, London, 1998) para 6.2.
4   *National Standards for the Supervision of Offenders in the Community* (Home Office, London, 2000) para E4.
5   *National Standards for the Supervision of Offenders in the Community* (Home Office, London, 2000) para E12.

Sex offenders and approved hostels

8.12   There is no doubt that approved hostels have an important role to play, not merely in providing a roof over an offender's head, but, more importantly, in providing a supportive and controlled environment which may enable an offender to live in the community for a limited period without presenting an undue risk to others. During the period of residence, whether it be as a bailee, as a condition of a Probation Order or following release from a custodial sentence, work will ideally be undertaken with the offender to ensure his successful re-integration back into society at the end of his residency. Such an environment may be thought to be ideal for some sex offenders. Indeed, the thematic inspection of the role of the Probation Service in protecting the public from sex offenders reported in 1998 that approved probation and bail hostels had a valuable role to play in enhancing the supervision of sex offenders.[1] It was found that, in some areas, guidelines suggested that for higher risk offenders who were due for release on licence, approved hostels were the most appropriate location because they offered:[2]

(1) higher staffing levels;

(2) the requirement to stay in the hostel premises between 11.00 or 11.30pm and 6.00am (in some cases, an additional curfew had been required, for example so that the offender was in the hostel when children were going to and from school);

(3) the possibility of coupling residence at the hostel with a requirement to attend a sex offender programme;

(4) some specialist staff (in one case including forensic psychology staff) available for risk assessments and for providing support to hostel staff in working with the offenders;

(5) systems to ensure that important information was shared between all staff members daily; and

(6) the potential for close liaison with both social services and police services in relation to all sex offenders in the hostel whether convicted or on bail.

8.13   A more specific example was provided by information collated by Leicestershire, which showed that there had been 76 men charged with or convicted of sexual offences resident in its approved hostels in the course of 1995–96. Of these, 68% had completed their period of residence without re-offending or being subject to breach action for infringing the rules of the hostel, which was a significantly higher percentage than residents charged or convicted of other offences (45%).[3]

The profile of sex offenders in approved hostels

8.14   The thematic inspection of the work of approved probation and bail hostels found that, of the 1,943 residents about whom information was available,

---

1   *Exercising Constant Vigilance: The Role of the Probation Service in Protecting the Public from Sex Offenders* (Home Office, London, 1998) para 5.28.

2   *Exercising Constant Vigilance: The Role of the Probation Service in Protecting the Public from Sex Offenders* (Home Office, London, 1998) para 5.15.

3   *Exercising Constant Vigilance: The Role of the Probation Service in Protecting the Public from Sex Offenders* (Home Office, London, 1998) para 5.14.

430 (22%) were sex offenders. Of these, 233 (54%) were bailees, 63 (15%) were subject to a Probation Order with a condition of residence and 124 (29%) were released prisoners subject to parole or licence which required them to reside at a hostel as part of a planned strategy for their re-integration into the community.[1] Comparing these statistics with the overall profile of residents at approved hostels during the inspection period:

(1) sex offenders make up a smaller percentage of resident bailees than other offenders (54% compared with 62–64%);
(2) sex offenders make up a smaller percentage of residents subject to a Probation Order with a condition of residence than other offenders (15% compared with 19–22% residents overall); and
(3) sex offenders make up a significantly larger percentage of residents subject to post-release licence supervision and parole than other offenders (29% compared with 10–13%).

8.15   It would seem that the use of approved hostels is favoured for sex offenders being released at the end of a custodial sentence. Given the fact that over 50% of adult offenders convicted of an indictable sexual offence receive an immediate custodial sentence,[2] such a finding is hardly surprising.

Sex offenders and admissions policies

8.16   Whatever the perceived advantages of accommodating sex offenders in approved hostels, the nature of the offending behaviour and the reaction of the local communities can give rise to problems. One obvious problem relates to the admissions policies of the hostels themselves. The decision to make residence a condition as part of bail or a Probation Order is entirely the responsibility of the court and should be given effect on the basis that such a condition can only be rescinded by a further order of the court. The national standards now provide that hostel staff must respond to each referral as soon as possible and that admissions must be based on risk assessment procedures which do not automatically exclude any particular category of offence.[3] However, the previous national standards, published in 1995 made no specific reference to the automatic exclusion of certain categories of offenders, merely stating that each hostel was expected to have a policy setting out the category of residents who could safely and appropriately be accommodated there.[4]

8.17   Not all hostels are prepared to admit sex offenders – a few hostels adopt a policy of refusing to admit certain categories of offenders, including sex offenders, simply on the basis of their offence. The thematic inspection on the work of approved probation and bail hostels found that a few hostels were not admitting sex offenders as a result of a specific policy decision by the

1   *Delivering an Enhanced Level of Community Supervision. Report of a Thematic Inspection on the Work of Approved Probation and Bail Hostels* (Home Office, London, 1998) para 7.48. No information was available on the remaining 10 sex offender residents.
2   See **4.141**.
3   *National Standards for the Supervision of Offenders in the Community* (Home Office, London, 2000) para E5.
4   *National Standards for the Supervision of Offenders in the Community* (Home Office, London, 1995) para 8.11.

management committee based on local circumstances. Although the report does not elaborate on the 'local circumstances', they presumably relate to the location of the hostel, for example in the immediate vicinity of a school, and, perhaps more likely, to pressure exerted by local residents seeking an assurance that sex offenders would not be accommodated in the hostel. For the vast majority of hostels, no clear direction had been provided by the management committees on the admission of sex offenders, leaving hostel managers and their staff to determine an admissions strategy. As the inspection report comments, it is difficult to understand why the management committees were not providing guidance on this issue.[1] The residents' profile undertaken as part of the inspection found that 11 hostels at the time had no residents who were charged with or convicted of sexual offences and that approximately one-half of the hostels were accommodating on the nights in question between four and seven offenders charged with or convicted of sexual offences. It also found that a number of hostels accommodating sex offenders restricted the number in residence at any one time to retain a balanced cross-section of residents.[2]

8.18　　The refusal of some hostels to admit sex offenders has implications for the other hostels. The thematic inspection of the work of the Probation Service to protect the public from sex offenders found that when non-local sex offenders were resident in a hostel, they sometimes took up places in a sex offender programme which was resourced by the host area. Although there are strong arguments for some sex offenders to be removed from their home area and placed in a hostel at some distance from their victims, as the report of the inspection commented, it does seem unjust that some local communities had exerted pressure to exclude sex offenders with the result that there were in other local communities concentrations of sex offenders in hostels.[3]

Sex offenders and other residents

8.19　　Sex offenders are rarely welcomed as neighbours or living companions, and the potential problems of mixing sex offenders with other offenders may be no less acute in a hostel environment than when they are in prison.[4] There are two ways in which such problems can be addressed. The first requires the nature of the offending behaviour to be to be concealed from other residents, ie sex offenders are not identified as such to other residents. However, this approach will obviously make working with sex offenders more difficult, particularly work that requires them to confront their offending behaviour. It may also result in practical problems of supervision. The thematic inspection of the work of the Probation Service in protecting the public from sex offenders found that, in at least two services, sex offenders resident in approved hostels were sometimes located, fairly soon after arrival, in 'satellite' or 'cluster' accommodation which was run by the hostel and, although governed by the same rules about curfew,

---

1　*Delivering an Enhanced Level of Community Supervision. Report of a Thematic Inspection on the Work of Approved Probation and Bail Hostels* (Home Office, London, 1998) para 7.51.

2　*Delivering an Enhanced Level of Community Supervision. Report of a Thematic Inspection on the Work of Approved Probation and Bail Hostels* (Home Office, London, 1998) paras 7.49–7.51.

3　*Exercising Constant Vigilance: The Role of the Probation Service in Protecting the Public from Sex Offenders* (Home Office, London, 1998) para 5.20.

4　See **5.7** to **5.14**.

was in a separate location and normally without a permanent staff presence.[1] This form of accommodation, normally consisting of two-, three- or four-bedroomed houses rented from the local authority or the private sector, is used primarily as part of a move-on strategy for preparing residents, who have successfully completed a period of stay in the core hostel, for independent living. The transfer of sex offenders in the early stages of their period of residence was simply because these offenders may be at risk from other residents if their offence became known. The report of the inspection expressed concern over this practice because it was thought to be doubtful whether, except in the most exceptional cases authorised only by the hostel manager, locating residents in satellite or cluster units would meet the expectations of the courts of enhanced supervision of sex offenders, given that staff were not present permanently. This concern was echoed in the thematic inspection of the work of approved hostels, which recommended that the use of satellite or cluster units be discontinued for all offenders and further work undertaken to ensure the provision of adequate move-on accommodation.[2]

8.20   An alternative approach would be to provide specialist hostels, dealing exclusively with sex offenders. This would enable resources to be concentrated, making work with the offenders more efficient, and, at the same time, avoid problems of harassment by other residents. However, accommodating sex offenders together in this way arguably would not assist their re-integration back into the community. The thematic inspection of the work of approved hostels found that hostel staff were divided on the issue. The inspection found that there was no evidence that such a specialist hostel dealing exclusively with sex offenders was necessary and concluded that evaluation needed to be undertaken to determine whether it was more effective to concentrate sex offenders in a limited number of hostels, as opposed to distributing them more widely across the approved hostel network.[3]

Sex offenders, risk assessment and risk management

8.21   The national standards clearly envisage a risk assessment being undertaken prior to admission in order to determine whether the offender may be safely and appropriately accommodated there. Such a risk assessment may be seen as crucial, particularly in the case of a sex offender, but the thematic inspection into the role of the probation service in protecting the public from sex offenders found that there was a clear record that the risk of the offender causing serious harm whilst at the hostel had been sufficiently assessed prior to admission in only 53% of cases and no written risk assessment was on file in 28%

---

1   *Exercising Constant Vigilance: The Role of the Probation Service in Protecting the Public from Sex Offenders* (Home Office, London, 1998) para 5.19.
2   *Delivering an Enhanced Level of Community Supervision. Report of a Thematic Inspection on the Work of Approved Probation and Bail Hostels* (Home Office, London, 1998) para 10.22.
3   *Delivering an Enhanced Level of Community Supervision. Report of a Thematic Inspection on the Work of Approved Probation and Bail Hostels* (Home Office, London, 1998) para 7.56.

of the sample.[1] The findings were replicated in the thematic inspection on the work of approved probation and bail hostels.[2]

8.22   Both thematic inspections found that in many of these cases there was clear evidence that staff were vigilant in monitoring possible risk factors and liaising with other agencies to reduce risk as far as possible, even if this was not always evident on the written files. Such information that was recorded tended to be scattered across a number of recording systems which included the daily log, hostel diaries, registers, contact sheets as well as in individual resident case files, which could mean that, on occasions, important information was not easily accessible to a member of staff if urgently required.

8.23   Overall, it is fair to conclude that approved hostels are playing an important role in managing the risk presented by sex offenders.[3] In order to overcome any shortcomings in practice, it has been recommended that steps are taken to ensure that:[4]

(1)   a written risk assessment is undertaken prior to admission on all residents and this is reviewed regularly after admission;
(2)   a standard risk assessment schedule is introduced to enable the risk posed by offenders to be consistently assessed;
(3)   a written plan is prepared and reviewed regularly which sets out the action to be taken to address the risk posed by a resident following admission;
(4)   information about risk assessment and risk management currently held on hostel information systems is brought together into one file which is readily accessible to staff.

The revised national standards will no doubt assist in achieving these aims.

Who needs protecting? Flats in prison as an alternative use of a controlled environment

8.24   The underlying purpose of accommodating sex offenders in some form of controlled environment such as a hostel is to ensure the protection of the public, ie any control measures are imposed on the offenders with a view to protecting the public. However, a trial project introduced in July 1999 has a rather different underlying purpose, in that it uses a controlled environment to protect the offender from the public. Under the media headline of 'Paedophiles to live as free men in jail', in May 1999 the Government introduced a scheme designed to protect freed paedophiles from vigilante attacks by members of the public.[5] Under the scheme, which is piloted at Nottingham Prison, released sex offenders who are thought to be in danger of becoming the targets of vigilante attacks are to be offered accommodation in ground-floor flats at the prison,

---

1   *Exercising Constant Vigilance: The Role of the Probation Service in Protecting the Public from Sex Offenders* (Home Office, London, 1998) para 5.13.
2   *Delivering an Enhanced Level of Community Supervision. Report of a Thematic Inspection on the Work of Approved Probation and Bail Hostels* (Home Office, London, 1998) para 9.3.
3   *Exercising Constant Vigilance: The Role of the Probation Service in Protecting the Public from Sex Offenders* (Home Office, London, 1998) para 5.21.
4   *Delivering an Enhanced Level of Community Supervision. Report of a Thematic Inspection on the Work of Approved Probation and Bail Hostels* (Home Office, London, 1998) para 9.21.
5   (1999) *The Times*, 20 May.

which have been converted from offices and have television, radio, cooking facilities and a shared bathroom. Guards – or 'occupational support group officers' – are paid by the Home Office to protect the residents, who each have their own key to their rooms. The unit is separated from the rest of the prison and has been described as being 'like an embassy in a foreign country'.[1] To leave the unit, the residents must be let through several locked gates by the guards and, whilst outside the prison, the residents will be accompanied by police officers.

8.25 The scheme is clearly a measure of last resort, to be reserved for the most notorious offenders, such as Lennie Smith and Robert Oliver.[2] The obvious advantage is that the movements of such offenders can be constantly monitored, although the cost is high, both in terms of manpower and resources. The reaction of local residents, who were apparently not consulted about the scheme, has been predictable – Nottingham prison is in a residential area, with a school 150 yards away. The offenders living at the unit are amongst the most dangerous men in the country, yet they are 'free men' and some of them will not even be subject to compulsory post-release supervision as they were sentenced before the enactment of the Criminal Justice Act 1991. Residents living close to the prison claim that their homes have dropped in value by between £3,000 and £8,000 since surveyors allegedly began issuing warnings to potential buyers about the existence of the unit and the residents are reported to be considering legal action against the Home Office for compensation for the fall in property prices.[3] As the Home Office has pointed out, the offenders 'have to go somewhere and a prison is a secure environment for their safety and the public',[4] but who can blame the local residents for voicing the inevitable response: 'Yes, but not in our backyard.'

MOVING ON

8.26 Approved probation and bail hostels can only accommodate a limited number of offenders. For those offenders who do not require the enhanced level of supervision provided by the hostels and for those who may potentially benefit from such a controlled environment but for whom no place is available, alternative accommodation may be required if they are unable to return to the accommodation they occupied prior to their arrest. Even those offenders who are allocated a place in a hostel will find that their period of residence will necessarily be limited. At the end of this period, some offenders may be in a position to move back to their previous accommodation, although, as previously noted, sex offenders may be less likely than other offenders to be able to do so.[5]

---

1   (1999) *Daily Mail*, 20 July.
2   See **6.88** to **6.92**.
3   (1999) *Mail on Sunday*, 10 October.
4   (1999) *The Times*, 20 May.
5   See **8.2** to **8.5**.

8.27 For those offenders who are unable to return to return to their previous accommodation and are not in a position to buy their own property, a range of residential options may be available, including:[1]

(1) other hostels normally provided by the voluntary sector, but which do not afford the same level of enhanced supervision;

(2) social housing allocated by local authorities or registered social landlords; and

(3) accommodation in the private rented sector.

Hostels provided by the voluntary sector

8.28 The accommodation needs of offenders may be met by the voluntary sector, which has always been active in the hostel movement. Over the last 50 years, organisations such as the Langely House Trust and the Simon Community (later to become known as the National Cyrenians and then Homes for Homeless People) have sought to address the resettlement needs of offenders.[2] Whilst hostel accommodation tends to be unpopular with offenders themselves – most preferring self-contained accommodation, which gives them independence – hostels provided by the voluntary sector may at least provide a roof over an offender's head as well as offering a more structured environment than self-contained accommodation. Many hostels actually offer more than this by assisting the long-term resettlement of the offender in more permanent accommodation.

8.29 In the case of sex offenders, where hostel accommodation is necessary, the preferred option will inevitably be to allocate a place in an approved probation hostel, where the necessary supervision and control can be assured. Certainly for those convicted of serious sexual offences, this may be the only viable option and indeed may be a condition of any Probation Order or early release from a custodial sentence. Nevertheless, hostels provided by the voluntary sector may provide a suitable alternative for less serious sex offenders. Multi-agency working and effective communication between the professionals involved are essential in these circumstances. Those responsible for running the hostels must be made aware of the potential problems that may be encountered, for example the relationship between sex offenders and other residents, and should also be kept informed of the outcome of any risk assessment on the offender. A close working relationship with the Probation Service will be essential. Although there appears to have been no research directed specifically at sex offenders in this area, as long as the necessary support is available, there is arguably no reason why hostels provided by the voluntary sector cannot make a valuable contribution to the management and control of sex offenders in the community.

Social housing

8.30 The allocation of social housing to sex offenders has been the focus of much attention in recent years. It has been pointed out that a considerable

---

1   *Delivering an Enhanced Level of Community Supervision. Report of a Thematic Inspection on the Work of Approved Probation and Bail Hostels* (Home Office, London, 1998) para 10.20.

2   Paylor *Housing Needs of Ex-offenders* (Avebury, Aldershot, 1995) p 40.

proportion of known offenders probably find their own accommodation in the private sector,[1] but, short of action in the form of vigilante attacks seen in recent years in some areas of the country, little can be done to influence the availability of accommodation in the private sector. Individual landlords may be targeted in an effort to persuade them not to accept sex offenders as tenants, but the overall impact of such targeting is likely to be small. Furthermore, in many cases, sex offenders will not reveal their criminal history and so, unless the risk posed by an offender is thought to be sufficiently great to justify disclosure by the police,[2] the landlord will not know to whom he is renting property. Social housing is different because the allocation of accommodation is influenced to a certain extent by policy decisions on who should and who should not be allocated accommodation. In view of the tendency to view all sex offenders as 'modern folk devils',[3] it is hardly surprising that they may be seen as undesirable tenants and, therefore, be excluded from social housing. A policy of exclusion adopted by a local authority could have a potentially far greater impact than the decisions of individual landlords.

The legal framework

8.31   The legal framework for the allocation of social housing by local authorities in England and Wales is set out in the Housing Act 1996. Allocations from the waiting list or housing register are covered by Pt VI of the Act and the responsibilities of local authorities towards homeless people are contained in Pt VII. Local authorities are increasingly working strategically with other providers of social housing, such as registered social landlords (RSLs).[4] Indeed, in some areas where large-scale transfers of local authority housing have taken place, RSLs may be the main providers of social housing. Part VI of the 1996 Act covers most local authority nominations to RSLs as well as allocations of the authority's own stock. RSLs are also able to make allocations outside of local authority nomination arrangements. Such allocations are not covered by the 1996 Act, but are subject to guidance by regulators – the Housing Corporation in England and Tai Cymru in Wales. The 1996 Act has been described as making four important changes which may affect the rehousing of sex offenders by social landlords:[5]

(1) the requirement for local authorities to establish a housing register made up of qualifying persons from which all allocations are made (authorities may decide to exclude certain categories of people, including sex offenders, from the housing register);[6]
(2) a radical change to the duties owed by local authorities to a homeless applicant who is eligible for assistance, in priority need and not intentionally homeless[7] (previously, such applicants were eligible for a secure

1   Cowan et al 'Housing Sex Offenders: An Examination of Current Practice' (Chartered Institute of Housing, Coventry, 1999).
2   See **7.80**.
3   See **1.1**.
4   See Housing Act 1996, ss 1–7.
5   Cowan et al 'Housing Sex Offenders: An Examination of Current Practice' (Chartered Institute of Housing, Coventry, 1999).
6   See **8.33** to **8.41**.
7   See **8.52** to **8.63**.

tenancy, but now are only eligible for temporary accommodation for 2 years);[1]

(3) local authorities now have the power to set up introductory tenancy schemes for new tenants[2] (the tenancy is in reality a probationary period and offers limited security of tenure for 12 months, during which time Possession Orders[3] may be obtained in cases of anti-social behaviour, which may well include those convicted of sexual offences);

(4) the grounds on which a landlord may seek possession for anti-social behaviour have been extended and now include conduct by a tenant or visitor causing or likely to cause nuisance or annoyance to people in the locality, and conviction of using the accommodation or allowing it to be used for immoral or illegal purposes or an arrestable offence committed in, or in the locality of, the accommodation.[4]

8.32   Thus, the commission of a sexual offence can potentially result in an existing tenant losing his accommodation. However, a Possession Order will not necessarily be granted automatically where a partner or other family members are also tenants and local authorities are advised to consider all the options available to ensure that family members do not become homeless unnecessarily through no fault of their own.[5] In practice, the most controversial decisions relate to the initial allocation of accommodation to sex offenders, either from the housing register or because the offender is homeless.

Allocation of social housing

8.33   By virtue of Pt VI of the Housing Act 1996, local housing authorities are required to maintain a housing register of qualifying persons[6] and may only allocate accommodation to those who appear on the register.[7] Every authority is required to have an allocation scheme for determining priorities and the procedure to be followed in allocating accommodation.[8]

'QUALIFYING PERSONS'

8.34   The 1996 Act specifies certain categories of persons who are, or are not, qualifying persons. For example, persons who are subject to immigration control are not generally qualifying persons,[9] whereas some classes of homeless persons are always qualifying persons.[10] Subject to this, local housing authorities may decide what classes of persons are, or are not, qualifying persons.[11] This power is crucial as it allows a local housing authority to exclude certain classes of persons, such as sex offenders, from the housing register which, subject to any duty which

---

1   Housing Act 1996, ss 193–194.
2   Housing Act 1996, s 124.
3   Housing Act 1996, ss 127–130.
4   Housing Act 1996, s 144.
5   *Code of Guidance for Local Authorities on the Allocation of Accommodation and Homelessness* (Department of the Environment, Transport and the Regions, 1999) para 8.34.
6   Housing Act 1996, s 162.
7   Housing Act 1996, s 161.
8   Housing Act 1996, s 167.
9   Housing Act 1996, s 161(2); see also SI 1996/2753, SI 1997/631 and SI 1997/2046.
10   Housing Act 1996, s 161(3) and SI 1996/2753.
11   Housing Act 1996, s 161(4).

may arise under Pt VII of the 1996 Act,[1] effectively denies them accommodation in the social sector. The legislative provision only permits an authority to decide classes of persons who are, or are not, qualifying persons, and leaves no residual discretion to take account of individual circumstances where a person already falls within a class of qualifying or non-qualifying persons. Therefore, careful definition of the classes is essential. Guidance on the exercise of this power has been provided by the Department of the Environment, Transport and the Regions.[2]

8.35	In deciding which classes of persons are not qualifying persons, the first consideration should be the authority's role as a social landlord and broker of social housing, which is subsidised stock. Therefore, it is said to be incumbent on an authority to allocate tenancies primarily to meet housing need in their district, and to co-operate with other housing providers in so doing. One consequence of excluding a wide range of persons from the housing register might be to increase the pressure on other housing providers in the area (or, indeed, neighbouring local authorities). However, an authority does have responsibilities for the management and maintenance of their housing stock and they are entitled to decide on a rational basis whether granting a tenancy to a person is likely to result in disruption to the stability of the community or in serious breaches of the authority's standard tenancy conditions.[3]

8.36	Decisions as to which classes of persons are not qualifying persons must also be seen against the background of the relevant provisions in the Crime and Disorder Act 1998 relating to crime and disorder strategies.[4] Therefore, it is important that decisions to exclude classes of persons from the housing register on the grounds of the need to protect the community or reduce levels of crime on their estates are taken in consultation with relevant organisations in the criminal justice system, in particular the police and the Probation Service. As a general principle, authorities are advised to consult widely with other bodies, such as social services, health authorities, registered social landlords and relevant voluntary groups, when deciding classes of non-qualifying persons to ensure that vulnerable people are not excluded unnecessarily.[5]

Sex offenders as non-qualifying persons

8.37	The implementation of Pt VI of the Act in January 1997 led to speculation that local authorities would decide that sex offenders, as a class, were not qualifying persons.[6] Guidance from the Chartered Institute of Housing[7] urged authorities to consider very carefully before applying blanket bans on sex offenders and recommended that local authorities and RSLs should:

1	See **8.52**.
2	*Code of Guidance for Local Authorities on the Allocation of Accommodation and Homelessness* (Department of the Environment, Transport and the Regions, 1999).
3	*Code of Guidance for Local Authorities on the Allocation of Accommodation and Homelessness* (Department of the Environment, Transport and the Regions, 1999) para 3.10.
4	See **7.75**.
5	*Code of Guidance for Local Authorities on the Allocation of Accommodation and Homelessness* (Department of the Environment, Transport and the Regions, 1999) para 3.11.
6	(1997) *The Times*, 9 January.
7	*Rehousing Sex Offenders – A Summary of the Legal and Operational Issues* (Chartered Institute of Housing, Coventry, 1998).

(1) avoid introducing blanket bans for very broad classes of person;
(2) ensure that they do not attempt to assess the risk posed by offenders, as this is the role of specialist agencies such as the police and the Probation Service;
(3) work closely with other professionals engaged in the rehabilitation and reintegration of sex offenders;
(4) maintain a balance between the views of local authority councillors, RSL board members, a duty of care to existing tenants and staff and the needs and vulnerability of an individual applicant;
(5) ensure that they operate within the provisions of Pt VI of the Housing Act 1996 and the accompanying Code of Guidance;
(6) avoid excluding an individual in perpetuity on the basis of past behaviour (authorities and RSLs may wish to consider reserving the right to exclude an applicant on the basis of past behaviour for a fixed period of time); and
(7) RSLs should have regard to their constitutional objectives and regulator guidance.[1]

8.38   The guidance provided by the Housing Corporation and Tai Cymru require RSLs to avoid restrictions on access to their housing which are unnecessary or irrelevant to housing need, but acknowledge that RSLs may wish to consider excluding any applicants who would be non-qualifying persons in accordance with the policy adopted by the relevant local authority.[2]

8.39   In some circumstances, it seems that the commission of a sexual offence may even result in a non-qualifying person becoming a qualifying person. Local authorities are entitled to apply residential criteria for qualification purposes. For example, qualifying persons may include those who have resided in the district of the authority for a period of 6 months immediately prior to applying to be included on the housing register.

8.40   The Code of Guidance advises local authorities to consider whether certain groups of people should be included in the register, notwithstanding that they fail to meet a residence criterion.[3] The suggested groups include, inter alia, people leaving prison whose previous residence was in the area and, thus, a sex offender who has served a custodial sentence may be able to return to occupy social housing in his home area, despite not meeting the residency requirement. Obviously, this may not always be desirable, particularly if vulnerable victims are still living in the vicinity. An alternative approach would be to rehouse the offender away from the area, but obviously problems of residency requirements would then be encountered. To avoid such problems, the Code of Guidance suggests including in the list of qualifying persons an offender whose application has been supported by a probation officer on the ground that he should be relocated away from the area in which he committed a sexual offence.[4]

---

1   *Rehousing Sex Offenders – A Summary of the Legal and Operational Issues* (Chartered Institute of Housing, Coventry, 1998) para 2.1.
2   *Rehousing Sex Offenders – A Summary of the Legal and Operational Issues* (Chartered Institute of Housing, Coventry, 1998) para 2.2.
3   *Code of Guidance for Local Authorities on the Allocation of Accommodation and Homelessness* (Department of the Environment, Transport and the Regions, 1999) para 3.15.
4   *Code of Guidance for Local Authorities on the Allocation of Accommodation and Homelessness* (Department of the Environment, Transport and the Regions, 1999) Annex 2.

8.41   It seems that the feared blanket bans on sex offenders have not materialised and local authorities are not turning their backs on sex offenders when it comes to the allocation of social housing. Indeed, research on the practice of allocating social housing to sex offenders in a small number of local authorities found that, in spite of the housing legislation which leans towards exclusion of offenders and others, there was a strong feeling amongst most of the housing professionals contacted that sex offenders should be rehoused. Exclusion was only likely when an offender presented such a high risk that housing providers believed that the problems were beyond management within the community.[1]

Allocation, multi-agency working, risk assessment and risk management

8.42   Allocating social housing to sex offenders is not a task that can be undertaken in isolation and local housing authorities have had close working relationships with other agencies, particularly the police, Probation Service and social services, for many years. Even before the introduction of crime and disorder partnerships in the Crime and Disorder Act 1998, which place such co-operation on a statutory basis,[2] informal networks of communication between agencies had been established and, in many areas, multi-agency protocols for the exchange of information and the assessment and management of the risk posed by sex offenders and other dangerous offenders had been developed, which included input from housing providers. One advantage of the involvement of housing providers in such a forum and the sharing of information on offenders who pose a risk to the community at an early stage (eg prior to release from custody) is that an appropriate housing solution can be found more easily.[3] Research into the allocation of social housing to sex offenders has found that housing authorities and other agencies are supportive of the interagency approach, referring to improved relationships and the emergence of shared agendas, and also finding comfort in a shared sense of responsibility.[4]

8.43   Clearly, the involvement of housing professionals in multi-agency panels is seen as a positive development, and one which will no doubt continue to flourish with the advent of statutory crime and disorder partnerships. Yet the precise remit of the role of housing professionals in such partnerships is not fully defined. Research has found that in some cases local authority landlords come to the table in their traditional role of meeting housing need, whereas in others it is in the role of enabler of community safety.[5] Particular problems arise regarding risk assessment. Guidance issued by the Chartered Institute of Housing points out that risk assessment is a complex process and is the role of officers within

1   Cowan et al 'Housing Sex Offenders: An Examination of Current Practice' (Chartered Institute of Housing, Coventry, 1999).
2   See **7.75**.
3   *Rehousing Sex Offenders – A Summary of the Legal and Operational Issues* (Chartered Institute of Housing, Coventry, 1998) pt 5.
4   Cowan et al 'Housing Sex Offenders: An Examination of Current Practice' (Chartered Institute of Housing, Coventry, 1999).
5   Cowan et al 'Housing Sex Offenders: An Examination of Current Practice' (Chartered Institute of Housing, Coventry, 1999).

agencies such as the police, Probation Service and social services, which have specialist knowledge and training in this area. It emphatically states 'it is not the role of housing professionals'.[1] In practice, it seems that this guidance is ignored on occasions and that the role of housing professionals in multi-agency partnerships varies from being passed information considered sufficient for making an allocation of housing and assisting in managing the risk, to being involved in the actual assessment of risk.[2]

8.44 The provision of suitable accommodation is generally regarded as an important part of managing the risk posed by sex offenders. The study which examined the practice of allocating of social housing to sex offenders identified seven issues of risk management for housing professionals. In brief these are as follows.[3]

Lack of information

8.45 Decisions on the most suitable accommodation for sex offenders can only be made on the basis of sound information. In the past, housing professionals were often expected to make decisions without sufficient information. The increased willingness of agencies to develop protocols and share relevant information, together with the developments contained in the Sex Offenders Act 1997 and the Crime and Disorder Act 1998 will hopefully ensure that such problems diminish.

Suitable accommodation

8.46 This was described as the most difficult issue for many housing providers. Even if decisions can be made as to what amounts to 'suitable accommodation', in many cases it is simply not available. Of all the options, many professionals regard concierge and CCTV-controlled blocks as the best choice for risk-management purposes, but this means that those authorities that do have tower blocks, concierge- and warden-controlled properties are more likely to be called upon to provide accommodation for sex offenders. In turn, this leads to concerns over the 'bunching' of sex offenders. Placing offenders in temporary accommodation whilst more suitable accommodation is sought is also problematic, for example bed and breakfast accommodation is generally full of families and other vulnerable occupants.

Monitoring

8.47 The presence of CCTV, concierges or wardens in an accommodation block also has implications for the monitoring or surveillance of sex offenders. Although one authority commented that it would not place a convicted offender

---

1   *Rehousing Sex Offenders – A Summary of the Legal and Operational Issues* (Chartered Institute of Housing, Coventry, 1998) para 5.1.
2   Cowan et al 'Housing Sex Offenders: An Examination of Current Practice' (Chartered Institute of Housing, Coventry, 1999).
3   For a full exploration of the issues, see Cowan et al 'Housing Sex Offenders: An Examination of Current Practice' (Chartered Institute of Housing, Coventry, 1999).

in particular accommodation just because there was CCTV, in other areas, CCTV was considered to be an important part of the process because it was also believed that it would cause the occupants to modify their behaviour, at least in their accommodation. However, the ability to monitor a sex offender in his accommodation also raises the important question of who should be responsible for the monitoring. Although the ultimate responsibility remains with the police and the Probation Service, the role of housing officers is called into question. For example, should a warden be told that a tenant is in fact a convicted sex offender? Valuable opportunities to monitor the offender may be lost if a warden is unaware of the potential risk, yet the disclosure of information about the offender to third parties is not to be undertaken lightly.[1] The research concludes that there is a need for the roles of each partner institution to be defined, so that there is no gap in public protection and so that all agencies are comfortable and confident about the part they play.

Tenancy conditions

8.48   The insertion of specific conditions into tenancy agreements does not appear to be an option that is frequently utilised. The research study found only one example when a condition was inserted into the tenancy agreement with a sex offender that no children should enter the property. Three reasons are suggested for this: first, such conditions would be impossible to monitor; secondly, even if they were breached, it would be difficult to persuade a court to order eviction; and finally, it is not believed that such conditions would alter the offender's behaviour.

Short-term tenancies

8.49   The research study found that introductory tenancy schemes,[2] which offer limited security for 12 months, are seen by some housing providers as an appropriate risk-management method. Although not restricted to sex offenders, these short-term tenancies allow for a probationary period during which time a Possession Order can be obtained in cases of anti-social behaviour.

Bunching

8.50   The shortage of suitable accommodation inevitably leads to the risk of 'bunching', ie several sex offenders living in the same area or block. On the one hand, this could be regarded as facilitating surveillance, but it also raises concerns about increased opportunities for networking and the development of paedophile rings, and the potentially adverse effect of bunching on vulnerable residents. Indeed, it is not only those residents who may be deemed particularly vulnerable who may be concerned. If a general attitude of 'not in my backyard' prevails, and the community object to one sex offender living in their midst, the presence of several sex offenders in the neighbourhood can only exacerbate the problem. As the research study points out, the issue is perhaps one of

---

1   See **7.76**.
2   In the case of RSLs, starter tenancies have a similar effect.

perception, but if social housing is considered to be part of the solution, then it is damaging if it is perceived to be part of the problem.

Support

8.51   The decision to allocate social housing to a sex offender is only one stage in the process of risk management, which is the responsibility of all agencies. Housing providers need to be assured that support will be provided by the other agencies and that monitoring and support of the offender will be undertaken by other agencies whose role and expertise lies in these matters. This requires inter-agency co-operation and the planning of care packages which should generate a certain level of trust between the professionals. On occasions, the level of trust may be reduced, particularly in areas where there have been poor experiences of past community care initiatives. Yet previous failures are also viewed by some as a catalyst towards closer inter-agency working.

Homelessness

8.52   Whereas local authorities have the power to decide that certain categories of persons are not eligible for entry onto the housing register, no such blanket ban can be imposed under Pt VII of the 1996 Act, which sets out the duties owed by local authorities to the homeless or those threatened with homelessness.

8.53   A person is homeless if there is no accommodation in the UK or elsewhere which is available for his occupation, which he has a legal right to occupy and to which he can secure entry, which is reasonable for him to continue to occupy and which, if it is moveable, there is a place where he is entitled to place it and reside in it. A person is threatened with homelessness if it is likely that he will become homeless within 28 days.[1] Local authorities have a general duty to ensure that advice and information about homelessness and the prevention of homelessness is available free of charge to any person in their area.[2] Whenever someone approaches a local authority for housing or help in obtaining housing, if the authority has reason to believe that the applicant may be homeless or threatened with homelessness, the authority must make inquiries to satisfy itself of whether the applicant is eligible for assistance and what duty, if any, is owed to him under Pt VII of the Act.[3] A person is not eligible for assistance if he is a person who is ineligible for housing assistance, which generally includes persons who are subject to immigration control, unless they fall within a class of persons prescribed by regulations by the Secretary of State.[4]

8.54   While the inquiries are carried out, if the authority has reason to believe that the applicant may be eligible for assistance, homeless and in priority need, it has a duty to secure that accommodation is available pending the outcome of its inquiries and a decision on any further duty it may owe.[5]

---

1   Housing Act 1996, s 175.
2   Housing Act 1996, s 179.
3   Housing Act 1996, s 184.
4   Housing Act 1996, s 185. See also SI 1996/2753, SI 1996/2754, SI 1997/631 and SI 1997/2046.
5   Housing Act 1997, s 188.

'Priority need'

8.55   The main housing duties imposed by Pt VII of the 1996 Act only apply to a person who has a priority need for accommodation. The following have a priority need:[1]

(1) a person with whom dependent children reside or might reasonably be expected to reside;

(2) a pregnant woman or a person with whom she resides or might reasonably be expected to reside with;

(3) a person who is vulnerable as a result of old age, mental illness or handicap or physical disability or other special reason, or with whom such a person resides or might reasonably be expected to reside; or

(4) a person who is homeless or threatened with homelessness, as a result of an emergency such as fire, flood or other disaster.

Intentional homelessness

8.56   The nature of an authority's duties towards those who are homeless and have a priority need will depend upon whether they have become homeless, or threatened with homelessness, intentionally. The 1996 Act sets out three ways in which a person may become homeless, or threatened with homelessness, intentionally.[2] First, if the applicant deliberately does or fails to do anything, in consequence of which he ceases to occupy accommodation which is available for his occupation and which it would have been reasonable for him to continue to occupy.[3] Secondly, if the applicant colludes with another by entering into an arrangement under which he is required to cease to occupy accommodation which it would be reasonable for him to continue to occupy and the purpose of the arrangement is to enable him to become entitled to assistance under Pt VII of the Act and there is no other good reason why he is homeless.[4] Finally, an applicant who is given advice or assistance to secure accommodation under s 197 (which sets out the authority's duty where other suitable accommodation is available in the district) but fails to secure it when it could be reasonably expected that he would do so, will be treated as having become homeless intentionally if he makes a further homelessness application.[5] It is incumbent upon the authority to satisfy itself that an applicant is homeless or threatened with homelessness intentionally – no burden is placed on the applicant to prove he is not.

---

1   Housing Act 1996, s 189.
2   See further **8.61** to **8.63**.
3   Housing Act 1996, s 191(1). Similar provisions in s 196(1) apply to those threatened with homelessness.
4   Housing Act 1996, s 191(3). Similar provisions in s 196(3) apply to those threatened with homelessness.
5   Housing Act 1996, s 191(4). Similar provisions in s 196(4) apply to those threatened with homelessness.

A summary of duties owed under Pt VII[1]

8.57

(1) If an applicant is not eligible for assistance, or is eligible for assistance but is not homeless or threatened with homelessness, no duty is owed (apart from the general duty to secure that advice is available[2]).

(2) If an applicant is eligible for assistance, is homeless or is threatened with homelessness, but is not in priority need, there is a duty to give appropriate advice and assistance in any attempt by the applicant to secure his own accommodation[3] or to prevent the loss of his accommodation.[4]

(3) If an applicant is eligible for assistance, is homeless and is in priority need, but is homeless intentionally, there is a duty to secure that accommodation is available for a reasonable period to give the applicant an opportunity to find his own accommodation and to offer appropriate advice and assistance.[5]

(4) If an applicant is eligible for assistance, threatened with homelessness and in priority need, but is threatened with homelessness intentionally, there is a duty to give appropriate advice and assistance to prevent loss of accommodation.[6]

(5) If an applicant is eligible for assistance, is homeless, is in priority need and is not homeless intentionally, there is a duty to provide the applicant with advice and assistance to enable him to secure other suitable accommodation available in the area.[7] If no other suitable accommodation is available, there is a duty to secure accommodation for 2 years.[8]

8.58   A local authority may be assisted in carrying out its duties under Pt VII of the 1996 Act by, inter alia, other local housing authorities and registered social landlords who are required to co-operate 'as is reasonable in the circumstances'.[9]

Sex offenders and homelessness

8.59   The duties owed to those who are homeless are perhaps more likely to be of assistance to the family of a sex offender, rather than to the offender himself, particularly if there are dependent children in the family. If the commission of a sexual offence results in loss of the family home (because, in the absence of the main wage earner, mortgage repayments cannot be maintained or rent arrears accumulate) the remaining family members will be homeless and in priority need. There will be no question of intentionality and so the local

---

1   *Code of Guidance for Local Authorities on the Allocation of Accommodation and Homelessness* (Department of the Environment, Transport and the Regions, 1999) chap 10.
2   Housing Act 1996, s 197.
3   Housing Act 1996, s 192(2).
4   Housing Act 1996, s 195(5).
5   Housing Act 1996, s 190(2).
6   Housing Act 1996, s 195(5).
7   Housing Act 1996, s 197(2).
8   Housing Act 1996, s 193(2). In the case of an applicant in these circumstances being threatened with homelessness, as opposed to being homeless, a duty arises to take reasonable steps to secure that accommodation does not cease to become available (s 195(2)).
9   Housing Act 1996, s 213.

authority will have a duty to secure accommodation for the family for a minimum of 2 years. The family would also be eligible to be entered onto the housing register, so their long-term security of accommodation should be assured.

8.60   Rather more difficult issues arise if the offender himself is homeless because he is unable to return to his family. Assuming the offender is living alone, it is unlikely that he would be in priority need, unless he is considered vulnerable for a special reason. The 1996 Act does not permit local authorities to predetermine that some groups should never be considered vulnerable for a special reason. The Code of Guidance states that 'special reasons' may include a combination of circumstances which render the person less able than others to fend for himself in finding and keeping accommodation and points out that, where applicants have a real need for support, but have no family or friends on whom they can depend, they may be vulnerable for a special reason.[1]

8.61   Even if an offender is found to be in priority need, the more difficult question relates to whether or not he is homeless intentionally. Arguably, if the offender has become homeless as a result of a deliberate act (ie the criminal offence), he is homeless intentionally. However, such a general policy could have substantial implications for many offenders, not only sex offenders. The issue of offenders and intentional homelessness was considered by the High Court in the case of *R v Hounslow LBC, ex parte R*.[2] A 65-year-old applicant had a long history of sexual offences against children. When he was sentenced to 7 years' imprisonment for a number of indecent assaults on children, he terminated his tenancy as he could no longer afford to pay the rent of his accommodation. On his release, he applied to Hounslow LBC as a homeless person. The authority rejected his application on the grounds that the offences for which he had been imprisoned were deliberate acts in consequence of which he had ceased to occupy his original accommodation and, therefore, he was intentionally homeless.[3] The applicant applied for judicial review of the authority's decision. In the High Court, Stephen Richards, sitting as a deputy High Court judge, decided that the words 'in consequence of which' did not lay down a straightforward test of causation, but should be read as referring to the 'likely result' of the deliberate conduct. Therefore, in considering whether a person ceased to occupy accommodation in consequence of his deliberate conduct, the question to be asked was whether his ceasing to occupy the accommodation would reasonably have been regarded at the time as a likely consequence of the deliberate conduct. This objective test might be imputed to the fair-minded bystander in possession of all the relevant facts. On the facts of the case, the judge agreed with the authority that a fair-minded bystander, knowing of the applicant's long history of sexual offending against children and long periods in prison, would 'unhesitatingly conclude' that loss of accommodation was the likely result of committing further offences.

---

1   *Code of Guidance for Local Authorities on the Allocation of Accommodation and Homelessness* (Department of the Environment, Transport and the Regions, 1999) para 12.11.
2   (1997) 29 HLR 939.
3   The relevant definition of intentionality was at this time to be found in s 60(1) of the Housing Act 1985 which was identical to the definition now contained in s 191(1) of the Housing Act 1996.

8.62   The case caused considerable interest, but has not always been accurately portrayed. Although the media, in reporting the case, tended to portray that the idea that a 'jailed molester loses right to council house',[1] ie that it was the nature of the offences committed which led to the applicant being found to be intentionally homeless, this was not the basis of the decision. The nature of the offending was irrelevant. It was the overall picture, including the applicant's long history of offending, that made the loss of accommodation the likely result of committing further offences. Furthermore, guidance issued by the Chartered Institute of Housing suggests that, in future, an authority would need to demonstrate that in each case an applicant was involved in criminal activity *in the knowledge* that a conviction would result in a custodial sentence of long enough duration to cause loss of home.[2] However, this assumes a subjective test – that the offender himself was aware of the likely result of his actions. The correct test is objective and the crucial question is what would be foreseen as reasonably likely by a fair-minded bystander in possession of all the relevant facts.

8.63   The Code of Guidance makes it clear that decisions on intentionality must follow from the investigations carried out in each individual case and that general policies which seek to pre-define what is and what is not intentional homelessness must not be applied.[3] Therefore, the fact that a sex offender becomes homeless as a result of his offending will not be sufficient to conclude he is intentionally homeless. Yet any offender who commits a serious offence nevertheless runs the risk of being found intentionally homeless, particularly if he has a previous conviction. Any man who commits rape, where the 'starting point' for sentencing in a contested case will be 5 years' imprisonment,[4] will find it difficult to persuade an authority that a fair-minded bystander would not foresee a custodial sentence long enough to cause loss of his home as the likely result of a conviction.

Accommodation in the private rented sector

8.64   Whereas accommodating sex offenders in the social sector may afford opportunities for surveillance, keeping track of offenders who find accommodation in the private rented sector tends to be much more difficult. Furthermore, it is difficult to ensure that accommodation in the private sector is suitable. Prima facie there is nothing to prevent a sex offender renting a bedsit in a building next door to a primary school, although such a move may alert the authorities, if they are aware of it, to the need to seek alternative methods of control, such as a Sex Offender Order.[5] No statistics are available on the number of sex offenders currently being accommodated in the private rented sector. In many circumstances, private landlords will not be aware that a tenant is a sex offender. If an offender has recently been released from a custodial sentence

---

1   (1997) *The Times*, 20 February.
2   *Rehousing Sex Offenders – A Summary of the Legal and Operational Issues* (Chartered Institute of Housing, Coventry, 1998) para 2.3.
3   *Code of Guidance for Local Authorities on the Allocation of Accommodation and Homelessness* (Department of the Environment, Transport and the Regions, 1999) para 13.1.
4   See **4.143**.
5   See **7.16**.

and is under the supervision of the Probation Service, or if he is subject to the notification requirements imposed by the Sex Offenders Act 1997, a decision to disclose details of the offender's background to a landlord and/or neighbouring residents may be taken following a multi-disciplinary risk assessment.[1] However, offenders who are not subject to compulsory supervision or the requirements of the 1997 Act may well find it easy to escape surveillance and to 'disappear from view' by finding short-term accommodation in the private sector and moving regularly, perhaps to new areas. There is, therefore, a danger that many sex offenders may chose not to seek housing in the social sector for this reason – they know that they will remain visible in the social sector and prefer the element of choice and the comparative anonymity which the private sector can offer. Admittedly, the notification requirements of the 1997 Act will facilitate the tracking of many sex offenders in the years to come, whatever accommodation they are living in. However, 100% compliance with the requirements can never be guaranteed and the private sector may continue to attract those sex offenders who wish to become invisible.

FAMILY LIFE

8.65   Closely associated with issues of accommodation, the disclosure of the commission of a sexual offence may have serious repercussions for an offender's family life. Indeed, the offender may well find his family life torn apart when his sexual offending comes to light. His relationship with any spouse or partner may be placed under intolerable stress, regardless of the identity of the victim. In many cases, this will lead to the breakdown of the relationship, which in turn may result in accommodation problems. Although in many cases this will not involve State intervention, other than any criminal prosecution brought against the offender himself, in some cases the victim may apply to the courts for a Non-molestation Order in an effort to secure her safety or an Occupation Order, either simply to secure a right to occupy the family home or to exclude the offender from the home.[2] As disruptive to the offender and his immediate family as this may be, it is perhaps of comparatively little concern to others. The main concern will inevitably focus on any children living in the same household as the offender. In cases of intrafamilial sexual abuse, where the victim is a child living with the offender, immediate action will usually need to be taken to secure the child's safety, with due consideration then being given to long-term protection of the child.[3] In other cases, child protection concerns may also arise in relation to any children living in the same household, who may be thought to be at risk from the offender. Furthermore, the potential disruption to the offender's family life is not confined to the immediate aftermath of sexual offending. The commission of a sexual offence may have repercussions for the offender and his family for many years in the future, and the offender may well have restraints imposed on his access to children, not only in the field of employment, but also in any relationships he builds in his private life.

---

1   See **7.87**.
2   See **8.67** to **8.87**.
3   See **8.88** to **8.114**.

Sexual offences within the family – turning to the civil law for protection

8.66   As noted previously, the civil law may be used as a means of controlling sex offenders in the community in various ways, all of which may be used to protect members of an offender's family as well as the public in general.[1] However, when a sexual offence is committed against a member of the offender's family, or the behaviour of an individual is such as to give cause for concern that an offence may be committed in the future, further protective measures may be available to the victim or potential victim in the form of Non-molestation Orders and Occupation Orders. The orders can now be made under Pt IV of the Family Law Act 1996, which replaced the previous domestic violence legislation[2] and introduced a new uniform code applicable in all family courts.

Non-molestation Orders

WHAT IS MOLESTATION?
8.67   A Non-molestation Order is an order containing either or both of the following provisions:

(1) a provision prohibiting a person ('the respondent') from molesting another person who is associated with the respondent; and/or
(2) a provision prohibiting the respondent from molesting a relevant child.[3]

The order may be expressed so as to refer to molestation in general, to particular acts of molestation, or to both.[4] The term 'molestation' is not defined by the statute. The term was used in previous legislation and it has long been established by case law that violence is a form of molestation, but molestation may take place without the threat or use of violence and still be serious and inimical to mental and physical health.[5] Thus, Non-molestation Orders may be made to prevent the commission of sexual offences. Clearly, the commission of any offence of sexual aggression, where absence of consent by the victim is an essential component of the offence,[6] would amount to molestation. Breaches of sexual taboo may be more problematic. If the victim is an adult and gives consent, this is arguably not molestation, although the issue would presumably not arise as a consenting victim is unlikely to have applied for a Non-molestation Order in the first place. If the victim is a child, who the law deems to be incapable of giving consent, rather different considerations apply and a Non-molestation Order could be held to include such offences. However, once again, the issue is unlikely to arise, as, if a child is thought to be at risk from an offender, the local authority would be unwilling to rely on a Non-molestation Order to protect the child and undoubtedly would take more radical steps.[7]

---

1   See **7.50** to **7.55**.
2   For example, the Domestic Violence and Matrimonial Proceedings Act 1978, the Domestic Proceedings and Magistrates' Courts Act 1978 and the Matrimonial Homes Act 1983.
3   Family Law Act 1996, s 42.
4   Family Law Act 1996, s 42(6).
5   Per Viscount Dilhorne in *Davis v Johnson* [1979] AC 264 at 334.
6   See **1.5**.
7   See **8.88** to **8.114**.

WHO CAN A NON-MOLESTATION ORDER PROTECT?
8.68   In all cases, the person to be protected by the order must either be associated with the person against whom the order is made, or be a relevant child. The applicant and the respondent will be associated with each other if they:[1]

(1) are spouses or former spouses;

(2) are cohabitants or former cohabitants;

(3) 'live or have lived in the same household, otherwise than merely by reason of one of them being the other's employees, tenant, lodger or boarder';

(4) are relatives;[2]

(5) have agreed to marry one another (whether or not that agreement has been terminated);

(6) one is the parent of a child or someone who has or has had parental responsibility for the child, and the other is any other such person;[3]

(7) are parties to the same family proceedings (other than proceedings under Pt IV of the 1996 Act); or

(8) one is the natural parent or grandparent of an adopted child and the other is the child or the adoptive parent.[4]

8.69   A child will be a relevant child if he or she:[5]

(1) is living with or might reasonably be expected to live with either party to the proceedings;

(2) is a child whose welfare is in question in Children Act or Adoption Act proceedings; or

(3) is a child whose interests the court considers relevant.

WHEN CAN A NON-MOLESTATION ORDER BE MADE?
8.70   A Non-molestation Order may be made by the High Court, a county court or a magistrates' court. It may either be made on the application of an associated person, or on the court's own motion in any family proceedings.[6] In deciding whether to make an order, and if so in what manner, the court must have regard to all the circumstances, including the need to secure the health, safety and well-being of:[7]

(1) the applicant (or the person for whose benefit the court proposes to make an order of its own motion); and

---

1   Family Law Act 1996, s 62(3).
2   Defined by s 63(1) of the Family Law Act 1996 to mean the father, mother, stepfather, son daughter, stepson, stepdaughter, grandmother, grandfather, grandson or grand-daughter of the person or of the person's spouse, former spouse, cohabitant or former cohabitant or the brother, sister, uncle, aunt, niece or nephew (whether of the full blood or of the half blood or by affinity) of the person or of the person's spouse, former spouse, cohabitant or former cohabitant.
3   Family Law Act 1996, s 62(4).
4   Family Law Act 1996, s 62(5).
5   Family Law Act 1996, s 62(2).
6   Family Law Act 1996, s 42(2). The order can only be made of the court's own motion if the person against whom the order is made is a party to the proceedings and the court considers that the order should be made for the benefit of any other party to the proceedings (or any relevant child) even though no application has been made.
7   Family Law Act 1996, s 42(5).

(2) any relevant child.

The Non-molestation Order may be made for a specified period, or until further notice,[1] although an order which is made in other family proceedings ceases to have effect if those proceedings are withdrawn or dismissed.[2]

Occupation Orders

8.71   Whereas a Non-molestation Order may afford a victim or potential victim of a sexual offence a certain amount of protection, in some circumstances further measures, such as requiring the offender to leave the family home, may be desirable.

Entitled and non-entitled applicants

8.72   The Family Law Act 1996[3] makes a distinction between those who are entitled to occupy the family home by virtue of a legal or beneficial interest or a contractual or statutory right ('entitled applicants') and those who have no such entitlement ('non-entitled occupants'). Provision is made for two types of Occupation Order: a Declaratory Order, which declares, confirms or extends occupation rights in the family home; and a Regulatory Order, which controls the exercise of existing occupational rights; and the general scheme of the Act favours married couples and property owners by offering them a greater level of protection.

A SUMMARY OF THE MAIN PROVISIONS RELATING TO OCCUPATION ORDERS[4]

Section 33
8.73   If the applicant is entitled, whether or not the respondent is also entitled, the application is made under s 33 of the Act. The court has jurisdiction to grant an Occupation Order provided that the property is a dwelling-house[5] that either is, has been, or was at any time intended to be, the home of the applicant and any other person with whom the applicant is associated.[6] The order may contain any of the provisions listed in s 33(3)(a)–(g), which include a requirement that the respondent leave the property and a requirement that the respondent be excluded from a defined area in which the property is included. In deciding whether or not to make such an order, the court is required to have regard to all the circumstances, including the respective housing needs and housing resources of the parties and of any relevant child, the respective financial resources of the parties, the likely effect of any order, or of any decision

---

1   Family Law Act 1996, s 42(7).
2   Family Law Act 1996, s 42(8).
3   Family Law Act 1996, ss 33–40.
4   The scheme of the Act is complex. For a full explanation of the detailed provisions of the Act in relation to property rights and Occupation Orders, see Horton *Family Homes and Domestic Violence: The New Legislation* (FT Law and Tax, London, 1996).
5   Defined by s 63(1) as including any building or part of a building which is occupied as a dwelling and any caravan, house-boat or structure which is occupied as a dwelling, and any yard, garden, garage or outhouse belonging to it and occupied with it.
6   See **8.68**.

by the court not to make an order, on the health, safety and well-being of the parties and of any relevant child, and the conduct of the parties in relation to each other and otherwise.[1] The court is under a duty to make an order if it appears that the applicant or any relevant child is likely to suffer significant harm attributable to the conduct of the respondent if an order is not made, unless it appears that the respondent or any relevant child is likely to suffer as great or greater harm if the order is made.[2] If there is no risk of significant harm, there is no duty, but the court has a power to make an order, taking into account the factors mentioned above. Orders may be made under s 33 for a specified period, until the occurrence of a specified event or until a further order.[3]

Sections 35 and 36
8.74   If the applicant is not entitled, but the respondent is entitled, the application will be made under s 35 if the parties are former spouses,[4] and under s 36 if the parties are cohabitants or former cohabitants. As the applicant is not entitled, if the court makes an order under s 35 or s 36, it must include a provision dealing with occupation rights.[5] The order may also contain any of the provisions listed in ss 35(5) and 36(5), which include a requirement that the respondent leave the property and be excluded from the area. A similar checklist of factors must be considered as under s 33[6] and, if the parties are former spouses, a similar duty is imposed on the court to make an order if the significant harm test is satisfied.[7] In the case of cohabitants or former cohabitants, the court is merely requested to take relevant risk of significant harm into account in deciding whether or not to make an order.[8] Orders made under ss 35 and 36 must be made for a specified period not exceeding 6 months, but may be extended on one or more occasions for a further specified period not exceeding 6 months.[9]

Sections 37 and 38
8.75   If neither the applicant nor the respondent is entitled, the application will be made under s 37 if the parties are spouses or former spouses and under s 38 if the parties are cohabitants or former cohabitants. Applications under these sections will be comparatively rare, as in most cases at least one of the parties will be entitled to occupy the family home. No declaratory orders can be made, but regulatory orders, including requirements that the respondent leave the property and be excluded from the area, can be made in similar circumstances as under ss 35 and 36 respectively. The duration of an order made

---

1   Family Law Act 1996, s 33(6).
2   Family Law Act 1996, s 33(7).
3   Family Law Act 1996, s 33(10).
4   If the applicant is the spouse of an entitled respondent, the applicant will also be entitled and, thus, will apply under s 33.
5   Family Law Act 1996, ss 35(3) and (4) and 36(3) and (4).
6   Family Law Act 1996, ss 35(6) and (7) and 36(6) and (7).
7   Family Law Act 1996, s 35(8).
8   Family Law Act 1996, s 36(8).
9   Family Law Act 1996, ss 35(10) and 36(10).

under s 37 is subject to the same conditions as orders made under ss 35 and 36.[1] An order made under s 38 is subject to similar conditions, except that it may only be extended on one occasion.[2]

Ex parte Non-molestation and Occupation Orders

8.76   Although a respondent will normally be given notice of the proceedings and the order made inter partes, the court may make an ex parte[3] order in any case where it considers it just and convenient to do so. Before an order can be made ex parte, the court must have regard to all the circumstances and in particular to:[4]

(1) any risk of significant harm to the applicant or a relevant child, attributable to the conduct of the respondent, if the order is not made immediately;
(2) whether it is likely that the applicant will be deterred or prevented from pursuing the application if an order is not made immediately; and
(3) whether there is reason to believe that the respondent is aware of the proceedings but is deliberately evading service and that the applicant or a relevant child will be seriously prejudiced by the delay involved in effecting substituted service.[5]

Undertakings

8.77   If a court has the power to make a Non-molestation Order or an Occupation Order, it may accept an undertaking from any party, although this will usually be the respondent[6] and the undertaking is enforceable as if it were an order of the court.[7] However, no power of arrest may be attached to an undertaking[8] and the court is prevented from accepting an undertaking in circumstances when it would attach a power of arrest if an order was made.[9]

Enforcing Non-molestation and Occupation Orders

8.78   The court may attach a power of arrest to a Non-molestation Order or an Occupation Order if it appears to the court that the respondent has used or threatened violence against the applicant or a relevant child. If the order was made inter partes, there is a presumption that a power of arrest will be attached unless the court is satisfied that in all the circumstances the applicant or child will be protected adequately without one.[10] In the case of ex parte orders, the court has a discretion to attach a power of arrest if the violence criterion is satisfied and

---

1   Family Law Act 1996, s 37(5).
2   Family Law Act 1996, s 38(6).
3   Namely, one where the respondent has not been given the required notice of the proceedings.
4   Family Law Act 1996, s 45(2).
5   Or in a magistrates' court, by the delay involved in effecting service of proceedings.
6   Family Law Act 1996, s 46(1).
7   Family Law Act 1996, s 46(4).
8   Family Law Act 1996, s 46(2).
9   Family Law Act 1996, s 46(3).
10   Family Law Act 1996, s 47(2).

there is a risk of significant harm to the applicant or child, attributable to the respondent, if the power of arrest is not attached immediately.[1]

8.79 Where a power of arrest has been attached to an order, a police officer may arrest without warrant a person whom he has reasonable cause for suspecting to be in breach of any such provision.[2] If no power of arrest has been attached, an applicant who considers that the respondent has failed to comply with the order may apply to the relevant judicial authority[3] for a warrant for the arrest of the respondent.[4] A warrant will only be issued if the application is substantiated on oath and the court has reasonable grounds for believing that the respondent has failed to comply with the order.[5]

8.80 Following arrest, the respondent must be brought before the relevant judicial authority within 24 hours. The court may then either proceed to hear an application for the respondent's committal, remand the respondent in custody or on bail,[6] or merely adjourn the proceedings.

Sex offenders, Non-molestation Orders and Occupation Orders

8.81 In an ideal world, when a sexual offence has been committed, there would be no need for the offender's family to resort to the civil law for protection as the criminal law would ensure that the offender is removed from the community and is rehabilitated during the process of punishment. In reality, this cannot be guaranteed. Although, in serious cases the offender will be arrested and remanded in custody, the outcome of a criminal trial can never be guaranteed in the absence of a plea of guilty. Even if a convicted offender receives a custodial sentence, there inevitably will come a time when he will be released back into the community, albeit with certain controls imposed on him. At this stage, in common with alternative methods of ensuring the protection of the public,[7] civil law remedies should be seen as a matter of last resort for the protection of the offender's family. Perhaps the real advantage of Non-molestation or Occupation Orders is the fact that they can be used to intervene before any offence is committed and before any power of arrest arises in the criminal law. The following examples illustrate the potential use of Non-molestation Orders and Occupation Orders.

EXAMPLE 1
8.82 Mr and Mrs A have been married for 10 years. Mr A has no criminal convictions. They live in a house which is in registered in their joint names. They have no children and their relationship has been under considerable stress in recent years. Mrs A has been sleeping in a separate bedroom for the past 6

---

1 Family Act 1996, s 47(3).
2 Family Law Act 1996, s 47(6).
3 If the order was made by the High Court, the relevant judicial authority will be a judge of that court; if made by a county court it will be a judge or district judge of that or any other county court; and if made by a magistrates' court, it will be any magistrates' court – s 63(1) of the Family Law Act 1996.
4 Family Law Act 1996, s 47(8).
5 Family Law Act 1996, s 47(9).
6 See Family Law Act 1996, Sch 5, para 2(1).
7 See **7.50** to **7.55**.

months and Mr A is becoming increasingly frustrated with the situation. He constantly shouts abuse at Mrs A and 'demands his conjugal rights', threatening to teach her a lesson and force himself on her if she will not return to the matrimonial bed soon. Mrs A is frightened that he will carry out his threat and rape her one night.

8.83   In these circumstances, Mrs A could apply for a Non-molestation Order. The court must consider all the circumstances, including the need to secure the health, safety and well-being of Mrs A. In making the order, if the application is made inter partes, as Mr A has threatened violence against Mrs A, the court must attach a power of arrest unless it is satisfied that in all the circumstances Mrs A will be adequately protected without such a power of arrest.

8.84   Mrs A, as an entitled applicant, could also apply for an Occupation Order under s 33 of the 1996 Act. The court would have a discretion to make the order, having regard to factors such as housing needs and resources, financial resources and the health safety and well-being of Mr and Mrs A and their conduct in relation to one other and otherwise. If it appears that Mrs A is likely to suffer significant harm attributable to the conduct of Mr A if the order is not made, the court must make an Occupation Order, unless it appears that Mr A would suffer as great or greater harm than Mrs A if the order is made. The Occupation Order could require Mr A to leave the family home and exclude him from a defined area around the family home. As with the Non-molestation Order, a power of arrest must be attached unless the court is satisfied in all the circumstances that Mrs A will be adequately protected without such a power of arrest.

EXAMPLE 2

8.85   Ms B and Mr C had been cohabiting for 2 years when, following an argument, Mr C raped Ms B. He was convicted and was sentenced to 3 years' imprisonment. He was released after serving 18 months and made no effort to contact Ms B for a further 18 months. The day following his sentence expiry date, he called on Ms B, who had left the flat they shared and moved into a new flat rented from the local council. Ms B made it clear that she wanted nothing to do with him, but he pestered her continually in an attempt to rekindle the relationship, calling at her flat several times every day and phoning her in the middle of the night. Although he has not used or threatened violence, Ms B is frightened that he will assault her and may ultimately rape her again.

8.86   Although Mr C will be subject to the notification requirements under the Sex Offenders Act 1997, he will no longer be under the supervision of the Probation Service. As Mr C is a sex offender, the police may be willing to apply for a Sex Offender Order under the Crime and Disorder Act 1998, but would have to prove that Mr C has acted, since his conviction, in such a way as to give reasonable cause to believe that an order is necessary to protect the public from serious harm from him.[1] Alternatively, a prosecution may be brought under the Protection from Harassment Act 1997, with the possibility of a Restraining Order being made on conviction.[2] If these options were not followed, Ms B could apply

---

1   See **7.24**.
2   See **7.43** to **7.47**.

for a Non-molestation Order. As former cohabitants, Ms B is a person associated with Mr C and the court must consider all the circumstances, including the need to secure the health, safety and well-being of Ms B. No power of arrest could be attached as Mr C has not used or threatened violence against her.

8.87 Although on these facts, it may be thought that an Occupation Order that excludes Mr C from a defined area around Ms B's home would be most useful, no such application could be made, as her home has never been a joint home and has never been intended as such. If Ms B had remained in the home in which she and Mr C cohabited, if she was an entitled applicant she could apply for an Occupation Order under s 33 (as Mrs A in example 1, except that no power of arrest could be attached). If she had no entitlement to occupy the home, but Mr C was so entitled, she could apply for an Occupation Order under s 36. If an order is made under this section it must include a declaratory provision dealing with occupational rights. In deciding whether to make such a provision, the court must have regard to all the circumstances including, inter alia, the nature of the parties' relationship, the length of time which they lived together and the length of time which has elapsed since they ceased to live together. If the court decides not to make a provision giving Ms B occupational rights, no order can be made under the section. If the order is made, it may include a regulatory provision excluding Mr C from a defined area around the property. In so deciding, the court must have regard to whether Ms B is likely to suffer significant harm attributable to conduct of Mr C if the order is not made and balance this against the harm likely to be suffered by Mr C if the order is made.

Child protection and the Children Act 1989

8.88 Whereas an adult victim of a sexual offence may need to resort to taking action such as applying for a Non-molestation or Occupation Order, if the victim is a child or a child is thought to be at risk from a sex offender, responsibility for protecting the child will fall primarily on the local authority, which is under a statutory duty to safeguard and promote the welfare of children within its area who are in need.[1] The legal framework for the protection of children is contained in the Children Act 1989.[2] Prior to the implementation of the Act, the grounds for State intervention in a child's life were diverse. For example, a child could be taken into the care of the local authority by one of 17 routes and the conditions determining whether such compulsory measures could be taken varied according to the route by which the case proceeded. In order to address this problem, the 1989 Act introduced a uniform threshold criterion below which State intervention was not justified – that of 'significant harm'. 'Harm' is defined to mean ill-treatment or the impairment of health or development.[3] 'Health' means physical or mental health and 'development' means physical, intellectual, emotional, social or behavioural development. 'Ill-treatment' is not defined exhaustively, the Act merely stating that it includes sexual abuse and forms of ill-treatment which are not physical. The Act does not define

---

1   Children Act 1989, s 17. A child is taken to be in need if, inter alia, his health or development is likely to be significantly impaired, or further impaired, without the provision for him of services under Pt III of the 1989 Act.

2   See Cobley *Child Abuse and the Law* (Cavendish Publishing Ltd, London, 1995) chap 3.

3   Children Act 1989, ss 31(9) and 105.

'significant', but does provide that, where the question of whether the harm suffered by a child is significant depends of the child's health or development, his or her health or development is to be compared with that which could reasonably be expected of a similar child.[1] Thus, the child victim of a sexual offence undoubtedly suffers significant harm as defined by the 1989 Act. However, past harm is not sufficient – there must be reason to believe that the child is suffering, or is likely to suffer significant harm before State intervention in the child's life is justified. In many cases, where the child continues to live with the suspected offender, a finding of past harm will be sufficient to establish the risk of future harm. Any court proceedings initiated to protect a child will be civil proceedings and the relevant standard of proof will be on the balance of probabilities. This must be compared with criminal prosecutions, in which the offender's guilt must be established beyond all reasonable doubt.[2] Thus, a civil court may make a finding of fact that an offender has sexually abused a child, but a criminal trial based on the same facts may result in the acquittal of the offender.

The role of the local authority – the duty to investigate

8.89   Section 47 of the 1989 Act provides that, where a local authority is informed that a child who lives, or is found in, its area is the subject of an Emergency Protection Order or is in police protection, or it has reasonable cause to suspect that a child who lives, or is found, in its area is suffering or is likely to suffer significant harm, the authority shall make, or cause to be made, such enquiries as it considers necessary to enable it to decide whether it should take any action to safeguard or promote the child's welfare.[3] Alternatively, a court may direct a local authority to investigate a child's circumstances if a question arises with respect to the welfare of any child in any family proceedings and it appears to the court that it may be appropriate for a Care or Supervision Order to be made.[4]

8.90   Thus, when sexual offences come to light, if any children are living in the same household as the offender or are living in an environment where sex offenders are allowed unsupervised access, the local authority will be under a duty to investigate the circumstances of the case in order to determine whether any child is at risk and, if it is thought to be necessary, will then be responsible for instigating action to protect the child.

Intrafamilial abuse

8.91   If the victim of a sexual offence is a child living in the same household as the offender, the primary concern of the local authority will be to ensure that the victim and offender are separated. Removing a child from his or her home will inevitably be traumatic for the child and in many cases, if a non-abusing carer is

---

1   Children Act 1989, ss 31(10) and 105.
2   See **3.12**.
3   In making such enquires, if, for example, there are suspicions of sexual abuse and the local authority wants the child to be assessed but access to the child is denied by the carers, an application can be made for a Child Assessment Order under s 43 of the Children Act 1989.
4   Children Act 1989, s 37.

available to look after the child at home, the preferred option will be to remove the offender rather than the child. Only if this is not possible, will action have to be taken to remove the child.

Removing the offender

CRIMINAL LAW AS A MEANS OF CHILD PROTECTION[1]

8.92   Although police investigation of offences and the arrest of suspects are primarily aimed at the prosecution and punishment of an offender, the arrest of an offender and subsequent procedures within the criminal justice system may also act as a form of child protection. If a police officer has reasonable grounds for suspecting that an arrestable offence has been committed, he may arrest without warrant anyone who he has reasonable grounds for suspecting to be guilty of the offence.[2] In general, the offender may only be detained without charge for up to 24 hours.[3] If, at the end of this period, no charge has been made, the offender must be released and alternative forms of child protection considered. However, if at any time during this period the police believe that there is sufficient evidence to prosecute the offender, and that there is sufficient evidence for a prosecution to succeed, the offender will be charged.

8.93   Once charged, in most cases there is a presumption in favour of bail. If the offender is released on bail, either the police or the courts can impose any conditions that appear necessary to ensure that he does not abscond, commit further offences whilst on bail or interfere with witnesses or otherwise obstruct the course of justice, whether in relation to himself or any other person. Such conditions may include a requirement to live at a specified address, such as a bail hostel, not to go within a specified distance of a certain address or not to contact specified people, and may obviously be used to ensure a child's continued safety. In more serious cases, the offender will be remanded in custody by the court pending trial.[4] If the offender is convicted at the subsequent trial and a custodial sentence is imposed, the safety of the child can be assured during the currency of the sentence, although child protection may again become an issue when the offender is released.[5] If a custodial term is not imposed, or the offender is acquitted, alternative child protection measures may need to be considered by the local authority.

VOLUNTARY REMOVAL OF THE OFFENDER

8.94   In cases where the criminal law cannot be used to remove the offender from the home, because there is insufficient evidence for arrest or charge, but there are nevertheless continuing child protection concerns, informal pressure may be brought to bear on the offender. The offender, if faced with the stark choice of either leaving home himself or the child being removed by the local

---

1   See Cobley 'Child Abuse, Child Protection and the Criminal Law' (1992) 4(2) *Journal of Child Law* 78.
2   Police and Criminal Evidence Act 1984, s 24(6). See also **2.56**.
3   Police and Criminal Evidence Act 1984, s 41. See also **2.62**.
4   See **2.102**.
5   See **8.3**.

authority, may sometimes agree to leave voluntarily whilst the matter is investigated further. Indeed it has been said '. . . for [an abuser] to leave home following disclosure can be the most caring parental act possible under the circumstances'.[1] The 1989 Act recognises the potential benefit of this and local authorities are given specific power to facilitate such a move. Schedule 2 of the Act provides that where:

(1) it appears to a local authority that a child who is living on particular premises is suffering, or is likely to suffer, ill treatment at the hands of another person who is living on those premises; and
(2) that other person proposes to move from the premises;

the authority may assist that other person to obtain alternative accommodation. The assistance may be given as a cash payment.[2] However, bearing in mind the financial constraints imposed on local authorities, it seems doubtful whether this provision can be relied upon to any great extent in practice. In any event, it requires the co-operation of the offender, which may not always be forthcoming.

INVOLUNTARY REMOVAL OF THE OFFENDER
8.95   An Occupation Order applied for by a non-abusing partner may exclude the offender from the home and, thereby, protect any children living there, but in the absence of such an order, the removal of an offender from the family home without the intervention of the criminal law has, in the past, proved problematic. Although, during the passage of the 1989 Act through Parliament,[3] there had been considerable support for the inclusion of a power to oust a suspected offender from the family home, it was decided to await the outcome of the Law Commission's consultation on the issue. Thus, the Act, as originally passed, did not include provision to remove an offender.[4] Attempts by local authorities to overcome this omission failed. In *Nottingham County Council v P*,[5] a local authority attempted to oust a suspected offender by means of the private law provisions contained in Pt II of the Act.[6] The Court of Appeal made it clear that local authorities had a clear duty to initiate care or supervision proceedings and that, effectively, they were restricted to using the 'public law' route under Pt IV of the Act.[7] A partial solution to the problem was found in the use of the inherent jurisdiction of the High Court in relation to children, when it was decided that such jurisdiction could be relied upon to oust a suspected offender from the family home,[8] but the absence of a statutory power to oust a suspected offender continued to be a cause of concern.

8.96   This concern was addressed by the implementation of the Family Law Act 1996, which amended the 1989 Act to give a statutory power to oust a

---

1   Furniss *The Multi Professional Handbook of Child Sexual Abuse* (Routledge, London, 1991) p 234.
2   Children Act 1989, s 17 and Sch 2, para 5.
3   Standing Committee B, 25 May 1989, cols 325–329.
4   Hansard, 27 October 1989, HC Deb vol 158, cols 1314–1319.
5   [1993] 2 FLR 134.
6   See **8.114**.
7   Cobley and Lowe 'Ousting Abusers – Public or Private Law Solution?' [1994] 110 LQR 38.
8   *Devon County Council v S (Inherent Jurisdiction)* [1994] Fam 169 and *Re S (Minors) (Inherent Jurisdiction: Ouster)* [1994] 1 FLR 623.

suspected offender from the family home.[1] If a court makes an Emergency Protection Order[2] or an Interim Care Order in respect of a child,[3] it may now include in the order an exclusion requirement, which consists of one or more or the following provisions:

(1) a provision requiring the relevant person[4] to leave a dwelling house in which he is living with the child;

(2) a provision prohibiting the relevant person from entering a dwelling-house in which the child lives; and

(3) a provision excluding the relevant person from a defined area in which a dwelling-house in which the child lives is situated.[5]

8.97   The exclusion requirement may only be included if:

(1) there is reasonable cause to believe that, if a person ('the relevant person') is excluded from a dwelling-house in which the child lives:

 (a) the child will cease to suffer, or be likely to suffer, significant harm (in the case of an exclusion requirement to be included in an Interim Care Order),[6] and

 (b) the child will not be likely to suffer significant harm, even though he is not removed to accommodation provided by or on behalf of the applicant, or even though he does not remain in the place in which he is being accommodated (in the case of an exclusion requirement to be included in an Emergency Protection Order)[7]; and

(2) there is another person (whether a parent of the child or some other person) living in the dwelling-house from which the person is to be excluded who:

 (a) is able and willing to give to the child the care which it would be reasonable to expect a parent to give him, and

 (b) consents to the inclusion of the exclusion requirement.[8]

8.98   Where a court has the power to include an exclusion requirement in an order, it may accept an undertaking from the relevant person, which will be enforceable as if it were an order of the court.[9] This power may be useful in cases where there is a sufficient degree of co-operation, as it accords with one of the principles underlying the 1989 Act – that of working in partnership with families where possible. Where there is no such co-operation, in order to ensure that any exclusion requirement is complied with, the court may attach a power of arrest, which permits a police officer to arrest without warrant any person whom he has reasonable cause to believe to be in breach of the exclusion requirement.[10]

1   Family Law Act 1996, s 52 and Sch 6.
2   See **8.102**.
3   See **8.113**.
4   The 'relevant person' is the person whose exclusion will mean that the child will cease to suffer, or cease to be likely to suffer, significant harm.
5   Children Act 1989, ss 38A(3) and 44A(3).
6   Children Act 1989, s 38A(2)(a).
7   Children Act 1989, s 44A(2)(a)(i). Similar provisions apply in the case of frustrated access under s 44A(2)(a)(ii).
8   Children Act 1989, ss 38A(2)(b) and 44A(2)(b).
9   Children Act 1989, ss 38B and 44B, except that no power of arrest can be attached.
10   Children Act 1989, ss 38A(8) and 44A(8). Following arrest, ss 47(7), (11) and (12), 48 and Sch 5 to the Family Law Act 1996 apply.

8.99   Thus, if there are grounds for making an Emergency Protection Order or an Interim Care Order in respect of a child, and a non-abusing carer is living in the same house as the child and consents to the exclusion, the suspected offender can be excluded from the family home while the suspicions are investigated. The exclusion requirement is clearly intended as an alternative to removing the child and the requirement lapses if the applicant removes the child from the house to other accommodation for a continuous period of more than 24 hours.[1] This at least saves the child the trauma of being removed from home in the immediate aftermath of sexual offences coming to light, although the exclusion of the suspected offender will necessarily be short term, as it is restricted to the duration of the Emergency Protection Order or Interim Care Order. If, following investigations, the child is thought to be at risk from the suspected offender if he returns home and the criminal law cannot be relied upon to ensure his continued absence, the long-term protection of the child may only be assured by removing the child from the family home.

Removing the child

8.100   Although the preferred option will invariably be to remove the suspected offender rather than the child, this will only be possible if there is a non-abusing carer available to look after the child in the family home. In addition, unless an arrest has been made or the suspected offender agrees to move out voluntarily, the remaining carer must consent to any exclusion requirement. If these conditions are not fulfilled, alternative measures to protect the child will need to be considered.

PROTECTING THE CHILD IN AN EMERGENCY

8.101   It is generally acknowledged that the removal of a child from his or her home gives rise to public and professional concern, causes distress if not handled sensitively, and can be damaging both for the child and for the rest of the family. Official guidance therefore advises that, except where a child is in acute physical danger, planned emergency action will normally take place following consultation with all appropriate professionals.[2] Relatively few sex offenders who sexually abuse a child with whom they are living will pose a risk of 'acute physical danger' and any intervention should usually be planned in advance. One possible exception will be if there are suspicions of a 'paedophile ring' involving several children and adults in different households, in which case it will be important to prevent suspects from communicating with each other and destroying evidence. This may necessitate co-ordinated action at a time of day when the whole family is at home – typically referred to as 'dawn raids'.

EMERGENCY PROTECTION ORDERS[3]

8.102   Any person may apply for an Emergency Protection Order. The application is made to a family proceedings court, unless other proceedings in respect of the child have already commenced in the High Court or county court. The application can be made ex parte and for these purposes, a single justice can

---

1   Children Act 1989, ss 38A(1) and 44A(10).
2   *Working Together to Safeguard Children* (The Stationery Office, London, 1999).
3   Children Act 1989, s 44.

discharge the functions of the court, allowing orders to be obtained at short notice where necessary outside normal court hours. The court may make an order if, inter alia, it is satisfied that there is reasonable cause to believe that the child is likely to suffer significant harm if:

(1) he is not removed to accommodation provided by, or on behalf of, the applicant; or
(2) he does not remain in the place in which he is then being accommodated.[1]

8.103　　The order gives the applicant parental responsibility for the child, operates as a direction to any person who is in a position to do so to comply with any request to produce the child to the applicant and authorises the removal of the child at any time to accommodation provided by or on behalf of the applicant, or the prevention of the child's removal from any hospital in which he was being accommodated immediately before the making of the order.[2] The order may only be granted initially for a period not exceeding 8 days, although the local authority or NSPCC may apply to extend the order for up to a further 7 days.[3] Thus, if a suspected sex offender is living in the same house as a child and the child's safety can only be assured by removing the child from the home, an application can be made for an Emergency Protection Order which will at least provide short-term protection for the child while investigations are carried out.

POLICE PROTECTION[4]
8.104　　An Emergency Protection Order, although capable of being obtained at any time and at very short notice, nevertheless requires an application to be made to a court which necessarily results in some delay. In extreme emergencies, the delay could endanger a child and may even prove fatal. Police officers, however, have the power under the 1989 Act to take immediate action by removing or detaining a child without a court order where the officer has reasonable cause to believe that a child would otherwise be likely to suffer significant harm.[5] Although no specific powers of entry and search are conferred by the 1989 Act, police officers have a general power under the Police and Criminal Evidence Act 1984 to enter premises without a warrant for the purposes of saving life and limb.[6] A child may only be kept in police protection for up to 72 hours, but this period can at least provide a valuable 'breathing space' for the professionals involved and will allow time for the local authority to apply to the court for an Emergency Protection Order if necessary.

THE LONG-TERM PROTECTION OF THE CHILD
8.105　　Whether or not emergency action is necessary to protect a child, in many cases, especially in the absence of a criminal conviction, consideration will need to be given to the long-term protection of the child. If continued State intervention is necessary, this will usually be secured by a Care Order, or possibly

---

1　　Children Act 1989, s 44(1)(a). Orders may also be made where access to a child is being frustrated – see s 44(1)(b) and (c).
2　　Children Act 1989, s 44(4).
3　　Children Act 1989, s 45.
4　　Children Act 1989, s 46.
5　　Children Act 1989, s 46(1).
6　　Police and Criminal Evidence Act 1984, s 17(1)(e).

a Supervision Order. In other circumstances, the child's interests may be best served by use of the provisions contained in Pt II of the 1989 Act – commonly referred to as s 8 orders.

Care and Supervision Orders

8.106 By virtue of s 31 of the 1989 Act, only a local authority or other authorised person can apply for a Care or Supervision Order, and at the present time only the NSPCC has been so authorised by the Secretary of State. The court can only make an order if it is satisfied that:

(1) the child concerned is suffering, or is likely to suffer, significant harm; and
(2) the harm of likelihood of harm is attributable to:
  (a) the care being given to the child, or likely to be given to him if the order were not made, not being what is would be reasonable to expect a parent to give to him, or
  (b) the child being beyond the parental control.

THE THRESHOLD CRITERIA AND SEXUAL ABUSE

8.107 Before a Care Order can be made, two criteria must be satisfied. First, the court must be satisfied that the child is suffering or is likely to suffer significant harm. If it is alleged that the child 'is suffering' significant harm, it is now clear that the relevant time is not the time of the hearing itself, but the date at which the local authority initiated the procedure for protection under the Act.[1] Allegations that the child 'is likely to suffer' significant harm will usually be based on an allegation of past harm. In *Re H and R*,[2] the majority of the House of Lords made it clear that in such cases it is first necessary to establish the past harm as a fact. Thus, an allegation of past abuse will have to be proved on the balance of probabilities before it can be relied upon as the basis of the risk of future harm. However, where the allegation is a serious one, Lord Nicholls, who gave the only reasoned speech in the majority in *Re H and R*, stated that 'the more serious the allegation, the less likely it is that the event occurred, and hence the stronger should be the evidence before the court concludes that the allegation is established on the balance of probability'.[3] Whilst stating that he was applying the ordinary balance of probabilities test, Lord Nicholls went on to endorse the approach adopted to the standard of proof by the judge at first instance. Yet the judge at first instance had relied on an earlier decision of the Court of Appeal in *Re W*,[4] in which Bedlam J had expressed the view that allegations of sexual abuse made against a father involved grave imputations and that, although the father in the case had been acquitted of criminal charges arising out of the allegations, if they were found to be proved against him in civil proceedings, the stigma and disgrace would not be less than if he had been convicted. Bedlam J went on to state that the standard of proof required was commensurate with the serious nature of the allegations made, and so they must be proved beyond a mere balance of probability but not necessarily a standard as demanding as the criminal standard.

---

1   *Re M (A Minor) (Care Order: Significant Harm)* [1994] 3 All ER 298, HL.
2   *Re H and R (Child Sexual Abuse: Standard of Proof)* [1996] 1 FLR 80.
3   *Re H and R (Child Sexual Abuse: Standard of Proof)* [1996] 1 FLR 80 at 96.
4   *Re W (Minors) (Sexual Abuse: Standard of Proof)* [1994] 1 FLR 419.

8.108 The reasoning of both the Court of Appeal in *Re W* and the majority of the House of Lords in *Re H and R* has been criticised. Bedlam J's reference to the potential 'stigma and disgrace' faced by a father following a finding of fact in civil proceedings should surely not influence the outcome of child protection proceedings, where the paramount consideration must be the welfare of the child.[1] Furthermore, it has been submitted that *Re H and R* was decided wrongly and that the decision of the minority in the case, who favoured a one-stage test whereby all the available evidence was considered, is to be preferred.[2] However, allegations of abuse must now be established as a fact before they can be relied upon as the basis of a risk of future harm. Obviously, if the perpetrator of the abuse has been convicted of criminal offences arising out of the abuse, no problems will arise. However, in the absence of a criminal conviction, it seems that serious allegations, such as those involving sexual offences against a child, will, at the very least, require more convincing evidence to satisfy the court on the balance of probabilities than less serious allegations.

8.109 Secondly, the court must be satisfied that the harm or the likelihood of harm is attributable to, inter alia, the care being given to the child. In circumstances where it is found as a fact that a carer has abused the child and that the child is thus suffering or is likely to suffer significant harm, there will usually be little difficulty in establishing this causal link. If abuse by a third party is suspected, the causal link will only be satisfied if the carer has failed to do what it would be reasonable to expect a parent to do to prevent the harm. For example, if a carer persistently left a child in the sole custody of a person, knowing that that person was suspected of committing sexual offences against the child, the causal link would be satisfied.

8.110 Before making a Care Order, the court will approve a care plan drawn up by the local authority, setting out its plans for the care of the child, but once the order is made, it becomes the duty of the local authority designated by the order to receive the child into its care and to keep him in its care while the order remains in force.[3] The local authority acquires parental responsibility, which is shared with those who already have it in relation to the child. Once a Care Order is made, the court no longer has any role in monitoring the administrative arrangements for the child. Responsibility for the care of the child rests firmly with the local authority and the responsibilities of the court cease unless a substantive issue is brought back before the court. The care plan itself may provide for the permanent separation of the child from an abusive parent. In *Re S*,[4] a father with a history of sexual abuse of children, applied for leave to appeal against a Care Order. The care plan provided for the child's mother to take over care of the child from the local authority only once the mother had permanently separated from the father, with the local authority having the power to remove the child if the father returned to live in the family home. The

---

1   See Cobley *Child Abuse and the Law* (Cavendish Publishing Ltd, London, 1995) p 143.
2   Hemingway and Williams 'Re M and R: Re H and R' [1997] Fam Law 740.
3   Children Act 1989, s 33. A Care Order remains in force until the child reaches the age of 18
      – s 91(11). However, the child, the local authority or any other person with parental
      responsibility for the child may apply to the court for the order to be discharged before that
      time – s 39(1).
4   *Re S (A Minor: Care Orders: Child Abuse)* 23 July 1998 Court of Appeal (unreported).

Court of Appeal refused the application, holding that the court had a clear obligation to treat the welfare of the child as paramount and had to be child orientated and not parent orientated in its approach. The history of the father's offending and the expert evidence showed that, in making the Care Order, the judge had had no alternative but to conclude that the criteria in s 31 were satisfied and that the child would be at risk if the order had not been made.

8.111   Although there is a statutory presumption that the child who is the subject of a Care Order will be allowed reasonable contact with his parents, guardians and those with whom he was living before the order was made,[1] the court may make an order refusing contact on the application of the local authority or the child.[2] This will usually be a matter of last resort, to be relied upon only in extreme cases where there is thought to be no prospect of rehabilitation. The fact that a carer has committed a sexual offence against the child will not of itself necessarily result in contact being refused. In many situations, particularly if the offender admits responsibility for the offending behaviour and agrees to co-operate with the local authority and perhaps undergo treatment, the ultimate aim of the local authority will be the rehabilitation of the family and the child's return. Reasonable contact throughout the duration of the order will be an essential element of such rehabilitation, although no doubt in the early stages of the order any contact between the child and the offender will be supervised closely.

SUPERVISION ORDERS
8.112   A Supervision Order places the child under the supervision of the local authority or, if the local authority so requests, a probation officer.[3] The supervising officer has a duty to:

(1) advise, assist and befriend the supervised child;
(2) take such steps as are reasonably necessary to give effect to the order; and
(3) where the order is not complied with, or the supervisor considers that an order may no longer be necessary, to consider whether or not to comply to the court for its variation or discharge.

Unlike a Care Order, the local authority does not acquire parental responsibility. Although Supervision Orders may be useful in ensuring that the local authority has continuing contact with the family, their potential application in cases of sexual offending is limited. Admittedly, it is possible for the court to include a requirement that a responsible person (which could include an abusing carer) comply with any directions given by the supervisor[4] and the Court of Appeal in *Nottingham County Council v P*[5] considered that, with the abuser's consent, this provision could be used to ensure an offender's continued treatment at a specialist clinic at the local authority's expense. However, this will only be an effective route to ensuring that an offender receives treatment if the local

---

1   Children Act 1989, s 34(1). The local authority also has a duty to promote contact between the child and his parents, relatives, friends and others connected with him – Sch 3, para 15(1).
2   Children Act 1989, s 34(4).
3   Children Act 1989, s 35 and Sch 3.
4   Children Act 1989, Sch 3, paras 2 and 3.
5   [1993] 2 FLR 134.

authority is prepared to fund that treatment. Unlike treatment of the child, which the *court* has the power to order,[1] it is the *supervisor* who decides whether or not to give directions to a responsible person and, thus, the ultimate decision rests with the local authority, not the court.[2]

INTERIM ORDERS

8.113   There may well be circumstances where the court will not be in a position to make a final Care or Supervision Order, yet steps need to be taken to ensure the child is suitably protected while proceedings are progressing. Therefore, if the court adjourns proceedings on an application for a Care or Supervision Order, or the court gives a direction under s 37, and is satisfied that there are reasonable grounds for believing that the threshold criteria in s 31(2) are satisfied, the court may make an Interim Care or Supervision Order.[3] Such orders are limited for an initial maximum of 8 weeks, although may be extended for up to a further 4 weeks and the effect of the interim order is essentially the same as a full order.[4] Since the enactment of the Family Law Act 1996, the most significant potential of an Interim Care Order in cases of sexual offending undoubtedly lies in the ability of the court to oust the suspected offender from the home.[5]

'SECTION 8 ORDERS'

8.114   Although the protection of a child victim of intrafamilial abuse will usually be secured by the local authority applying for a Care Order, an alternative solution may be found in the orders available in s 8 of the 1989 Act. The section provides that, in any family proceedings under Pts I, II and IV of the 1989 Act (which includes applications for Care and Supervision Orders) subject to certain restrictions, the court has power to make any of the following orders:

(1) a Residence Order – an order settling the arrangements to be made as to with whom a child is to live;

(2) a Contact Order – an order requiring the person with whom a child lives, or is to live, to allow the child to visit or stay with the person named in the order, or for that person and the child otherwise to have contact;

(3) a Prohibited Steps Order – an order that no step, which could be taken by a parent in meeting his parental responsibility for a child, and which is of a kind specified in the order, shall be taken by any person without the consent of the court; and

(4) a Specific Issue Order – an order giving directions for determining a specific question which has arisen, or which may arise, in connection with any aspect of parental responsibility for a child.

Thus, for example, if a child is thought to be at risk from an offender living in the same house, but there is a grandmother who is prepared to offer a home to the child and the local authority is in agreement with the arrangements, a

---

1   Children Act 1989, Sch 3, paras 4 and 5.
2   See Cobley and Lowe 'Ousting Abusers – Public or Private Law Solution?' [1994] 110 LQR 38 at 42.
3   Children Act 1989, s 38.
4   Children Act 1989, s 38(4) and (5).
5   See **8.95** to **8.99**.

Residence Order could be made in favour of the grandmother, who would thereby acquire parental responsibility for the child. There are, however, several restrictions on the ability of the court to make s 8 orders, particularly in the case of local authorities who are not entitled to apply for a Residence Order or Contact Order and a court may not make such an order in their favour.[1] Furthermore, the court cannot make a Specific Issue Order or a Prohibited Steps Order with a view to achieving a result which could have been achieved by making a Residence or Contact Order.[2] These restrictions, combined with the Court of Appeal's insistence in *Nottinghamshire County Council v P*[3] that local authorities use the public law provisions contained in Pt IV of the Act to protect children, severely limit the potential use of s 8 orders in cases of intrafamilial abuse.

Protection of children outside the family

8.115　Whilst the provisions of the Children Act 1989 may be used to ensure that child victims of sexual abuse and other children living in the same household as the sex offender at the time of the offending are adequately protected once the offending comes to light, more difficult issues arise in relation to other children to whom the offender may be thought to pose a risk.

Criminal convictions and cautions – 'Schedule 1 offenders'

8.116　The most crucial factor which will determine the action that can be taken to protect children from sex offenders is a criminal conviction, which will often form the basis of controls and restraints placed on the offender to protect members of the public.[4] It has long been recognised that those who have been convicted or cautioned of certain offences may pose a risk to any children with whom they subsequently come into contact. Schedule 1 to the Children and Young Persons Act 1933 provides a list of specified offences against children and young persons, including offences of violence and sexual offences.[5] Those

---

1 Children Act 1989, s 9(2).
2 Children Act 1989, s 9(5).
3 [1993] 2 FLR 134.
4 See chaps 6 and 7.
5 Schedule 1 (as amended) contains the following offences when committed against a child or young person: murder; manslaughter; infanticide; any offence under ss 5 (manslaughter), 27 (abandoning a child), 42 (assault) and 43 (aggravated assault) of the Offences Against the Person Act 1861; s 2 (child stealing) of the Child Abduction Act 1984; ss 1 (cruelty to persons under the age of 16), 3 (allowing persons under the age of 16 to be in brothels), 4 (causing or allowing persons under the age of 16 to be used for begging), 11 (exposing children under the age of 12 to the risk of buggery) and 23 (prohibition against persons under the age of 16 taking part in performances endangering life or limb) of the Children and Young Persons Act 1933; ss 2 (procurement of a woman by threats), 3 (procurement of a woman by false pretences), 4 (administering drugs to facilitate intercourse), 5 (intercourse with a girl under the age of 13), 6 (intercourse with a girl under the age of 16), 7 (intercourse with a defective), 10 (incest by a man), 11 (incest by a woman), 14 (indecent assault on a woman), 15 (indecent assault on a man), 16 (assault with intent to commit buggery), 19 (abduction of an unmarried girl under the age of 18 from her parents or guardian), 20 (abduction of an unmarried girl under the age of 16 from her parents or guardian), 22 (causing the prostitution of a woman), 23 (procuration of a girl under the age of 21), 24 (detention of a woman in a brothel or other premises), 25 (permitting a girl under the age of 13 to use premises for intercourse), 26 (permitting a girl

convicted of such offences have commonly been referred to as 'Schedule 1 offenders', although there is now also a tendency to refer to those convicted of offences contained in Schedule 1 to the Sex Offenders Act 1997 and are thus subject to the notification requirements imposed by the Act as 'Schedule 1 offenders', so care should be taken to clarify which schedule is being referred to.

8.117   Although immediate child protection concerns will have been dealt with as soon as the offending came to light, Schedule 1 offenders may often pose a continuing threat to any children with whom they are allowed contact. In many cases, there is a justifiable fear that such offenders will deliberately seek opportunities to gain access to vulnerable children in the future. Provisions now exist to ensure that such opportunities cannot be gained during the course of employment,[1] but controls over an offender's personal life can be just as important. Following conviction for a Schedule 1 offence, the local authority will monitor carefully any contact the offender has with vulnerable members of his family and, if the offender intends to return to the family home following a custodial sentence, further child protection measures may be deemed necessary.

8.118   However, in many cases, the offender will not return to the family home, but will move on, possibly targeting other vulnerable children. The notification requirements contained in the Sex Offenders Act 1997 obviously facilitate keeping track of where offenders are living, but the information which must be notified under the Act does not include details of who the offender is living with, and the concern is that some offenders may deliberately build relationships with single mothers in order to gain a 'ready made' family and, thus, unrestricted access to children. During the passage of the 1997 Act through Parliament, it was suggested by the NSPCC that the notifiable information should include a 'domestic profile', as this would act as a useful trigger to warn of any vulnerable children in the household, but no such requirement was incorporated in the Act.[2]

8.119   The main responsibility for ensuring the protection of any children with whom the offender may be living rests with the relevant local authority, as part of its duty to safeguard the welfare of children in its area.[3] Clearly, if the local authority is aware that a Schedule 1 offender is living in its area, it is in a far stronger position to protect vulnerable children. Some local authorities have found it helpful for these purposes to maintain a list of all Schedule 1 offenders in their areas.[4] If a Schedule 1 offender is released at the end of a custodial sentence, the Prison Service, through the Probation Service, will notify the local

---

under the age of 16 to use premises for intercourse), 28 (causing or encouraging prostitution, or intercourse with or indecent assault on, a girl under the age of 16) of the Sexual Offences Act 1956 and any attempt to commit an offence under ss 2, 5, 6, 7, 10, 11, 12, 22 and 23 of that Act; any other offence involving bodily injury to a child or young person.

1   See **8.142** to **8.177**.
2   HC Deb vol 291, col 220, 25 February 1997. See further **7.10**.
3   Children Act 1989, s 17.
4   *Working Together under the Children Act 1989: A Guide to Arrangements for Interagency Co-operation for the Protection of Children from Abuse* (HMSO, London, 1991) para 6.52. The most recent guidance, *Working Together to Safeguard Children* (The Stationery Office, London, 1999), makes no specific reference to this practice.

authority that the offender has been discharged and is living in its area. The offender's living arrangements can then be monitored by the local authority and action taken to protect any children if necessary.

Child protection registers[1]

8.120   In each area a central child protection register is maintained which lists all the children in the area who are considered to be suffering or likely to suffer significant harm and for whom there is a child protection plan. When determining whether to register a child, a child protection conference should consider whether the child is at continuing risk of significant harm.[2] Clearly, many victims of intrafamilial abuse will be on the register, but its remit extends beyond this to other children who may be at risk. However, if an offender is convicted of a sexual offence against a child and subsequently moves into, or is a regular visitor to, a household in which a vulnerable child is living, following a child protection conference, the child's name may be added to the child protection register and details of the offender's criminal conviction recorded.

'New families' – fostering and adopting

8.121   It is obviously not realistic to expect local authorities to monitor the movements of Schedule 1 offenders constantly to ensure that no children are put at risk. Inevitably, there will be some offenders who will move constantly from one area to another simply in order to ensure that their movements are not being followed and such offenders are likely to be those who fail to comply with any requirements imposed by the Sex Offenders Act 1997. Whilst every effort will be made by the police and local authorities to ensure that offenders remain visible, this cannot be guaranteed. In recognition of the need to protect children from potential abusers, restrictions on those who seek work with children are now contained in the Protection of Children Act 1999.[3] In addition, further restrictions are now placed on those who are eligible to foster or adopt children. The Children (Protection from Offenders) (Miscellaneous Amendments) Regulations 1997[4] came into force on 17 October 1997. The main purpose of the regulations is to ensure that those with convictions for specified offences against children, and those who have been cautioned in relation to such offences do not adopt or foster children.

SPECIFIED OFFENCES
8.122   The offences which trigger the prohibitions on adoption and fostering are:

(1)   an offence under s 1 of the Sexual Offences Act 1956 (rape);
(2)   an offence specified in Schedule 1 to the Children and Young Persons Act 1933[5] except for:
    (a)   the offence of common assault or battery, or

---

1   See Cobley *Child Abuse and the Law* (Cavendish Publishing Ltd, London, 1995) p 88.
2   *Working Together to Safegaurd Children* (The Stationery Office, London, 1999) para 5.64.
3   See **8.156**.
4   SI 1997/2308.
5   See **8.116**.

(b) in the case where the offender was under the age of 20 at the time the offence was committed, an offence contrary to ss 6, 12 or 13 of the Sexual Offences Act 1956 (sexual intercourse with a girl between the ages of 13 and 16, buggery or indecency between men);

(3) an offence under s 1(1) of the Indecency with Children Act 1960 (indecent conduct towards young child);

(4) an offence under s 54 of the Criminal Law Act 1977 (inciting a girl under the age of 16 to have incestuous intercourse);

(5) an offence under s 1 of the Protection of Children Act 1978 (taking indecent photographs of children);

(6) an offence under s 160 of the Criminal Justice Act 1960 (the possession of indecent photographs of children); and

(7) an offence under s 170 of the Customs and Excise Management Act 1979 (prohibition and restriction on the importation of pornography) where the prohibited goods include indecent photographs of children under the age of 16.

THE PROHIBITIONS

8.123   Adoption agencies[1] are required by the regulations to obtain information about any criminal convictions and cautions when considering whether a person may be suitable to be an adoptive parent. A person is not to be regarded as suitable if he, or any member of his household over the age of 18, has been convicted or cautioned in respect of a specified offence.[2] The same prohibition applies to foster parents – local authorities are not to regard a person as suitable to act as a foster parent if he or any member of his household over the age of 18 has been convicted or cautioned of a specified offence.[3] The 1997 Regulations also amend the Schedule to the Disqualification for Caring for Children Regulations 1991[4] to include the specified offences except that, in this case, the exemptions for common assault and battery are omitted.[5] This means that a conviction or caution for a specified offence (which includes common assault or battery) disqualifies a person from fostering a child privately, being registered as a child minder or being involved in certain other activities involving children.

8.124   The Department of Health, which drew up the regulations, recognised that introducing an automatic ban on the approval to act as a foster carer or be a prospective adopter may, in exceptional cases, exclude people from being able to foster or adopt in an unjust way and could adversely effect the welfare of children if, as a consequence, an otherwise satisfactory placement were to be disrupted.[6] The Department has taken the view that the risk of this occurring is more likely where an adolescent has committed a 'one-off' minor infringement of the law, but as an adult is not considered to pose any risk to

---

1   The local authority must also carry out such checks when investigating an application for an adoption order in non-agency cases.
2   SI 1997/2308, reg 2.
3   SI 1997/2308, reg 3.
4   SI 1991/2094.
5   SI 1997/2308, reg 5(2).
6   Guidance to the Children (Protection from Offenders) (Miscellaneous Amendments) Regulations SI 1997/2308 LAC(97)17, para 5.

children in his care. It is for this reason that the regulations allow a discretion when considering whether to approve an applicant as a foster carer or prospective adopter where the criminal record checks disclose a conviction or caution for certain offences[1] committed when the offender was under the age of 20. However, guidance to local authorities makes it clear that, although the absolute prohibition would not apply in such cases, an applicant should only be approved in *exceptional* cases. Although the Department of Health initially thought that relaxing the absolute prohibition in such limited circumstances would be sufficient to avoid injustice, subsequent events proved this not to be the case.

8.125 The first challenge to the Regulations was made in 1998. Three children who were the subject of Interim Care Orders were placed by the local authority with foster parents (Mr and Mrs T) in 1996, with a view to their remaining with the foster parents permanently. However, in 1993 Mr T had been cautioned for assaulting a child in his care occasioning actual bodily harm, although he had later successfully adopted the child concerned. When the 1997 Regulations came into force, Mr T became a person disqualified from acting as a foster parent. Mr T initially challenged the application of the regulations to the placement of the children, arguing that, as any conviction or caution would be spent under the terms of the Rehabilitation of Offenders Act 1974, his caution could not be the basis for his disqualification from fostering. In February 1998, in the Family Division, Horowitz QC held that the 1997 Regulations were plainly within the contemplation of s 7 of the 1974 Act and provided a complete and enduring bar to a convicted person becoming a foster parent beyond any time limit which might otherwise apply under the 1974 Act, and he stated that there was no reason why a caution should be treated any differently from a conviction.[2]

8.126 Following the unsuccessful challenge, the local authority encouraged Mr T to intervene in the care proceedings to apply for Residence Orders in respect of the children under s 8 of the Children Act 1989. In February 1998, in the Family Division, Sir Stephen Brown P recognised that this was an attempt to bend the rules in a meritorious case. However, he held that the court could not accede to overriding the effect of the 1997 Regulations by making a Residence Order, but made a further Interim Care Order in the interests of the children, pending the determination of the substantive application.[3] The children were then made wards of court and the local authority appealed against the refusal of the lower court to make Residence Orders. In October 1998, the Court of Appeal agreed that it could not make orders to circumvent the intention of Parliament, but the applications for Residence Orders were not public law applications by the local authority but private law applications and, thus, the court was bound to have regard to all relevant factors, the welfare of the children being paramount. The public policy of protecting children had to be weighed against the other relevant considerations, and there was no reason why, in an exceptional case, the private law application should not succeed, provided an effective balancing exercise was undertaken.[4] At the substantive hearing in the Family Division,

---

1   Offences under ss 6, 12 and 13 of the Sexual Offences Act 1956.
2   *Lincolnshire County Council v RJ and Others* [1998] 1 WLR 1679.
3   *Re RJ (Foster Placement)* [1998] 2 FLR 110.
4   *Re RJ (Minors) (Foster Placement)* [1999] 1 WLR 581.

Cazalet J dismissed the care proceedings, but granted wardship with care and control of the children vested in Mr and Mrs T.[1]

8.127   Thus, the children remained with Mr T, despite the absolute prohibition on his becoming a foster parent. Obviously, the fact that such contortions had to be employed to achieve what everyone agreed was the desirable outcome for the children was a cause for concern and it quickly became apparent that Mr T was not an isolated case. A further challenge to the legality of the 1997 Regulations was made in the case of *R v Secretary of State for Health and Others, ex parte CB*.[2] Two children had been living with their paternal grandparents for 2 years. Care Orders were thought to be necessary to provide social services input and to support the grandparents against the manipulative attention of the parents and full Care Orders were made in July 1997. By this time, the local authority was aware that the grandfather had been convicted in 1962 an offence under s 6 of the Sexual Offences Act 1956. He had been 29 at the time and had been sentenced to 3 months' imprisonment. However, all the professionals involved took into account the period that had elapsed since then and felt that there was no risk to the children. The 1997 Regulations then came into force, disqualifying the grandfather from acting as a foster parent to the children. The grandfather challenged the legality of the regulations, claiming that they were ultra vires and contending that the effect of the regulations was very serious and meant that one child's future would, of necessity, have to be decided without regard to the welfare principle and indeed against the child's best interests. The judge was referred to 11 other cases where similar difficulties had arisen.

8.128   In the Queen's Bench Division, Scott Baker J held that the 1997 Regulations were not ultra vires and that the legislators were entitled to conclude as a matter of policy that the good of many should prevail over the detriment to the few. Although there was considerable sympathy for the local authority's position, it could not dictate the vires of the regulations which were intra vires and must be complied with, and the escape route of a Residence Order was the only realistic solution to this case if the regulations remained in their existing form.

8.129   The Department of Health has now recognised that the discretion preserved when the offender is under the age of 20 at the time of committing certain offences is insufficient and now takes the view that local authority discretion should be re-instated in a limited number of cases. For the time being, the courts will be forced to resort to escape routes such as Wardship or Residence Orders in some cases to ensure that a child's best interests are served.

Protecting children in the absence of a criminal conviction or caution

8.130   Whereas a criminal conviction or caution is often the key factor in protecting children outside the offender's immediate family, more complex

---

1   *Re RF (Wardship)* [1999] 1 FLR 618.
2   [1999] 1 FLR 505.

issues arise in the absence of such a conviction or caution, either because there has been no admission of guilt, there was insufficient evidence to justify a criminal prosecution or because any prosecution resulted in an acquittal. Problems may be encountered in two sets of circumstances. First, even though an offender has not been convicted of a criminal offence, a finding of fact may have been made in civil proceedings that he has abused a child. Alternatively, there may simply be a suspicion that an offender has abused a child, even though no finding of fact to that effect has been made in civil or criminal proceedings.

Findings of fact in civil proceedings

8.131   The different standards of proof required in criminal and civil trials may result in an offender being acquitted of criminal charges, yet on the same facts, civil child protection proceedings may find as a fact that abuse has taken place. However, information obtained in family proceedings is confidential and cannot be disclosed outside the proceedings without the leave of the court.[1] Furthermore, in the interests of frankness, a statement or admission in family proceedings is not admissible in evidence against the person making it or his spouse in criminal proceedings for an offence other than perjury.[2] Therefore, problems arise in deciding whether any information obtained in family proceedings may be disclosed to others.

8.132   In cases where the request for disclosure is made to assist further investigations, it is clear that the court in family proceedings is likely to disclose relevant information to the police or the defendant in criminal proceedings unless there are powerful reasons to the contrary[3] and disclosure has also been given to the General Medical Council, where a finding of sexual abuse had been made against a registered medical practitioner.[4] In *Re EC*,[5] the Court of Appeal indicated that the matters for the judge to consider in deciding whether to order disclosure were:

(1)   the welfare and interests of the child concerned and of other children generally;
(2)   the maintenance of confidentiality in cases involving children and the importance of encouraging frankness;
(3)   the public interest in the administration of justice and the prosecution of serious crime;
(4)   the gravity of the alleged offence and the relevance of the evidence to it;
(5)   the desirability of co-operation between the various agencies concerned with the welfare of children;
(6)   in cases where s 98(2) of the Children Act 1989 applied, fairness to the person who had incriminated himself and others affected by the incriminating statement; and

---

1   Administration of Justice Act 1960, s 12(1), and Family Proceedings Rules, SI 1991/1247, rr 4 and 10.
2   Children Act 1989, s 98(2).
3   See *Re L (Police Investigation: Privilege)* [1995] 1 FLR 999 and *Re EC (Disclosure of Material)* [1996] 2 FLR 725.
4   *A County Council v W (Disclosure)* [1997] 1 FLR 574.
5   *Re EC (Disclosure of Material)* [1996] 2 FLR 725.

(7) any other material disclosure which had already taken place.

8.133   Rather more difficult questions arise if there are no further investigations pending, but leave is sought to disclose findings of abuse in civil proceedings to others who are in a position to ensure the safety of any other children with whom the offender may come into contact. This issue arose in two unrelated cases which were considered by the Court of Appeal.[1] In the case of *Re L*, a father (L) had been acquitted at a criminal trial of charges of attempted rape and indecent assault on his stepdaughter and five other children. In care proceedings in respect of one child, it was found as a fact that L had sexually abused three children in his care, two of his children and the stepdaughter, and a Care Order was made in respect of the three youngest children. At the hearing, L, who had moved from the area to an undisclosed address, was given leave by the judge to write down his address. At the conclusion of the judgment, the local authority asked the judge to give leave for the address to be disclosed to it in order that it may alert the local authority of the area to which L had moved of his presence and the danger he might pose to children in the new area. The judge, who had found that L posed a considerable threat to the children of single female adults with whom he might cohabit but not to children generally, directed that L's address and the substance of the findings of sexual abuse be disclosed to the local authority in the area where L was then living, but that no disclosure should be made to the police or any other local authority without the leave of the court. L then appealed to the Court of Appeal against the granting of leave to disclose his address to the local authority.

8.134   At the same time as hearing L's appeal, the Court also heard an appeal in the case of *Re V*. The appellant, W, was a keen football player and coached junior football teams. In care proceedings, a judge made findings that W had perpetrated a relatively minor indecent assault on an 8-year-old boy some years previously and that W had a 'unusual and unhealthy' relationship with the 14-year-old boy who played at the local football club and was the subject of the care proceedings. The judge then gave leave for the local authority to send a letter to the league to which the football club was affiliated, informing them of the decision and a short summary of the behaviour found proved. W appealed against the order to send the letter to the league.

8.135   The Court of Appeal allowed the appeals, stating that as there were no pending investigations by the police or any other agency in respect of which the information sought to be disclosed might assist, the balance was clearly in favour of non-disclosure. In reaching the decision, Butler-Sloss LJ found that neither s 17 nor s 47 of the Children Act 1989 placed upon a local authority the general duty to inform other areas of the movement of those found guilty of sexual abuse in care or other family proceedings. Both local authorities had submitted that the findings of sexual abuse ought to be treated as analogous to specified convictions and cautions and that guidance from the Home Office, Department of Health and Department of Education, should be extended to abusers (so found) in family proceedings. Although, prima facie, this seemed to be an eminently sensible submission, Butler-Sloss LJ held that there was no ground

---

1   *Re L (Sexual Abuse: Disclosure); Re V (Minors) (Sexual Abuse: Disclosure)* [1999] 1 WLR 299.

upon which the court could, by analogy with existing legislation, give leave to disclose information about the appellants to outsiders – the matter was said to be one for Parliament and not for the courts.

8.136   The decision of the Court of Appeal has been described as 'a crushing blow to child protection'.[1] The decision was clearly influenced by the fact that the risk could not be related to a particular child or children and the Court was evidently uneasy at the prospect of authorising disclosure of information to a particular authority or body when the use that would need to be made of the information by the authority or body in the circumstances as they developed could not be anticipated. Butler-Sloss LJ referred to the case of *R v Chief Constable of North Wales Police, ex parte AB*,[2] and expressed the view that the caution urged by Lord Woolf MR that 'disclosure should only be made when there is a pressing need' was of general application and supported her conclusion as to non-disclosure. In the absence of an identifiable child or children who were at risk from the appellants, there could be no 'pressing need'. However, the inevitable consequence of the decision is that no-one would know if and when a pressing need arose. For example, if L moved in with a single mother and, thus, placed a child at risk, there presumably would then be a pressing need, but who would act on it? The local authority of the area in which L previously lived which knew about the findings of abuse would be the only one in a position to identify the risk, but it could hardly be expected to monitor the movements of L from afar in case the pressing need arose. At the same time, the local authority of the area in which L was then living would be blissfully unaware of the risk L posed to the child and, thus, no duty to investigate could arise under s 47 of the 1989 Act. Given the current climate of concern about the activities of sex offenders, particularly those who sexually abuse children, this appears to be a surprising and unacceptable lacuna in the law. There was no question in either of these cases that disclosure should be made to the general public – indeed, the disclosure initially authorised in L's case was arguably extremely limited. If a court has found as a fact that sexual abuse has occurred, albeit on the balance of probabilities rather than beyond all reasonable doubt, surely that information should be disclosed to those in a position to protect potential future victims of abuse, even if the victims cannot yet be identified. As the Court of Appeal is obviously not prepared to remedy the position, it is to be hoped that either the House of Lords or Parliament will be prepared to intervene at the earliest possible opportunity.

Protecting children against suspected offenders

8.137   Perhaps the most difficult issues arise when a person is suspected of having abused a child in the past, and is thus thought to present an unacceptable risk to any other children with whom he may subsequently live, but no criminal conviction has been obtained and no finding of fact made in civil proceedings. Before a decision can be taken to place a child's name on the child protection register together with details of the person suspected of abusing the child, the suspected offender must be given the opportunity to make representations,

---

1   Smith 'Passing on Child Abuse Findings – *Re V* and *Re L*' [1999] Fam Law 249.
2   [1998] 3 WLR 57. See **7.85**.

either in person or in writing.[1] However, if the suspected offender moves on and is thought to present a risk to other children, the question then arises as to whether the local authority is entitled to disclose its suspicions to third parties.

8.138   This question arose prior to the implementation of the Children Act 1989 in the case of *R v Devon County Council, ex parte L*.[2] The applicant, L, had been living with a woman and her two children. One of the children, a 4-year-old girl, made allegations of sexual abuse against L. The child was placed on the child protection register and L was arrested and interviewed by the police, but he denied the allegations. No criminal proceedings were instigated against him, although he was formally cautioned by the police at a later date. In the meantime, L moved into a series of households in which children were living. In order to protect these children, the local authority warned the mother in three of these households that L was suspected of sexually abusing a 4-year-old girl and indicated that if L continued to live in the household, child protection proceedings may be initiated to protect the children living there. In each case, L moved on, but eventually sought judicial review to stop the local authority passing on its suspicion that he had sexually abused the young girl. His application was dismissed because, on the facts, there was found to be no decision capable of review. However, Eastham J went on to say that, even if there had been a decision capable of review, there had been no denial of natural justice, the social workers concerned all having acted in good faith in approaching the mothers as they honestly believed on reasonable grounds that L was an abuser. On the facts, of course, L had been formally cautioned, which involved an admission of guilt, but it appears that L was illiterate and did not understand the implications of the caution. Hence, the decision of the court was clearly not based on the fact L had been cautioned. Although, as a result of the actions of the local authority, L had suffered prejudice, in the sense that he had had to leave where he was living on several occasions, Eastham J echoed the sentiment of Butler Sloss LJ in *R v Harrow LBC, ex parte D*[3] that, in balancing adequate protection for the child and fairness to the adult, the interest of an adult may have to be placed second to the needs of the child, and that all concerned in this difficult and delicate area should be allowed to perform their task without looking over their shoulders all the time for the possible intervention of the court.

8.139   Thus, the Devon County Council case seemed to establish that local authorities have the power to pass on information about suspected abusers in order to protect children, as long as they act in good faith. This power was recognised in the later case of *R v A Police Authority in the Midlands and A County Council in the Midlands, ex parte LM*,[4] but the court was at pains to point out that the power to disclose information about a person's intimate personal life was not free from restraint. In this case, the applicant, LM, applied for judicial review of the decisions of the police authority and local authority to divulge to a second local authority that allegations had been made in the past that he had sexually abused his 4-year-old daughter and an 11-year-old boy. No police action was

---

1   *R v Norfolk County Council, ex parte M* [1989] 2 FLR 120.
2   [1991] 2 FLR 541.
3   [1990] 1 FLR 79.
4   Queen's Bench Division, 6 September 1999 (unreported).

taken as a result of the allegations, although LM's daughter was placed on the child protection register. In 1995, some 6 years after the last allegation of abuse, LM established his own bus company which entered into a contract with the County Council's education department for the provision of school bus services. He gave permission for a police check to be made and, acting on information disclosed by the police and the social services department, the education department terminated the contract on the grounds that LM was unsuitable to be engaged in transporting vulnerable children and that there were significant grounds for concern regarding LM and his contact with children. In 1997 LM's company entered into a contract with another local authority to provide bus services for children. Fearing that that local authority would make enquiries, LM sought reassurances from the police authority and the local authority that they would not make disclosure of the allegations of sexual abuse. Both respondents refused to give the assurance sought. LM argued that disclosure would be in breach of art 8 of the European Convention for the Protection of Human Rights.

8.140   Following the decision of the Court of Appeal in *Re L; Re V*,[1] Dyson J in the Queen's Bench Division held that disclosure should only be made if there was a pressing need. In carrying out the balancing exercise between the need to protect children and the right of an individual to a private life, the court stated that the following factors should be considered:

(1) the belief of the person or the body making the disclosure as to the truth of the allegation;
(2) the interest of the third party in obtaining the information; and
(3) the degree of risk posed by the person if disclosure was not made.

On the facts of the case, it was decided that neither the police nor the local authority had demonstrated that there was a pressing need for disclosure and so the application was allowed and the decisions to disclose quashed.

8.141   The adoption in recent cases of the criterion of pressing need which must be established before disclosure can be justified is potentially a difficult hurdle for those concerned with child protection to overcome. Admittedly, the disclosure in the Devon County Council case could presumably be justified on the basis of pressing need if the facts occurred today, but the application of this criterion in the cases of *Re L; Re V* does little to engender confidence in the ability of local authorities to take adequate steps to protect children. In the absence of an identifiable potential victim, how is the pressing need to be established? Furthermore, if a local authority is not to be permitted to disclose to another local authority that a finding of fact has been made in civil proceedings that a man has sexually abused a child because there are no identifiable potential victims and, thus, no pressing need, how can a local authority justifiably disclose mere suspicions of abuse, which have not been tested in any legal proceedings, to third parties? In the interests of protecting vulnerable children, one can only refer back to the view expressed in previous cases that all those concerned in this difficult and delicate area should be allowed to perform their task without constantly looking over their shoulders for the possible intervention of the court,

---

1   See **8.133** to **8.135**.

and hope that clearer guidance will be soon forthcoming from either the House of Lords or Parliament.

Employment

'Vetting' – the background

8.142   It has long been acknowledged that individuals who are thought to present a risk to children and other vulnerable groups should not be allowed unrestricted access to such individuals through their employment, whether paid or voluntary. Sex offenders, especially those who offend against children, are seen as presenting a particular risk to children. In the past, an employer had three potential sources of information which could be consulted in order to check the background of an potential employee: a criminal record check, 'list 99' and the Department of Health's Consultancy Index.

CRIMINAL RECORD CHECKS

8.143   Under administrative arrangements between the Home Office and the Association of Chief Police Officers, criminal record checks could be made against those applying for work in the public sector which would give them substantial unsupervised access, on a sustained or regular basis, to children under the age of 16, or children under the age of 18 who have special needs. For residential staff, the checks could be carried out when such access would be to children under the age of 18 who are looked after by the local authority. Checks were not available to private organisations or to the majority of voluntary bodies, although certain national voluntary child care organisations (including Barnardo's and the NSPCC) had access to criminal record checks through their membership of the Voluntary Organisations Consultancy Service.[1]

'LIST 99'

8.144   Regulations made under s 218 of the Education Reform Act 1988 empower the Secretary of State for Education and Employment to direct an employer to suspend or terminate a person's employment as a teacher or as a worker who has regular contact with pupils or students under 19 years of age in schools, further education and the youth service, either on grounds of misconduct or on medical grounds.[2] The list containing details of those so barred or restricted is maintained by the Department of Education and Employment and is known as 'List 99'. In 1997, there were reported to be approximately 2,000 names on List 99.[3] Access to the list is strictly limited to individuals responsible for checking the suitability of those applying for relevant positions.

8.145   Those barred on the grounds of misconduct are listed separately from those barred on medical grounds, but no details of misconduct are given. Misconduct is not defined, but the regulations state that barring is automatic in

---

1   *Report of the Interdepartmental Working Group on Preventing Unsuitable People from Working with Children and Abuse of Trust* (Home Office, London, December 1998) Annex F, para A.

2   Education (Teachers) Regulations 1993, SI 1993/543, as amended.

3   Sir William Utting *People Like Us, Report of the Review of Safeguards for Children Living Away from Home* (The Stationery Office, London, 1997) chap 14, para 14.18.

the case of any person convicted of one of the following offences where the victim was a child under 16 years of age:[1]

(1) under the Sexual Offences Act 1956 – offences contrary to ss 1 (rape), 5 (sexual intercourse with a girl under the age of 13), 6 (sexual intercourse with a girl under the age of 16), 10 (incest by a man), 11 (incest by a woman), 12 (buggery), 13 (an act of gross indecency between men), 14 (indecent assault on a woman), 15 (indecent assault on a man) and 16 (assault with intent to commit buggery);

(2) under s 1 of the Indecency with Children Act 1960 (indecency with children under the age of 14);

(3) under s 54 of the Criminal Law Act 1977 (inciting a girl under the age of 16 to have incestuous sexual intercourse); and

(4) under s 1 of the Protection of Children Act 1978 (taking indecent photographs of children).

8.146   Approximately 80% of those on the list are barred automatically.[2] In other cases, the power is discretionary and is not limited to misconduct relating to children and young people. Examples of misconduct which are likely to lead to a bar or restriction include:[3]

(1) violent behaviour towards children or young people;

(2) a sexual, or otherwise inappropriate, relationship with a pupil (regardless of whether the pupil is over the legal age of consent);

(3) a sexual offence against someone over the age of 16;

(4) any offence involving serious violence;

(5) drug trafficking and other drug-related offences;

(6) stealing school property or monies;

(7) deception in relation to employment as a teacher or at a school, for example false claims about qualifications, or failure to disclose past convictions;

(8) any conduct which results in a sentence of more than 12 months' imprisonment; and

(9) repeated misconduct or multiple convictions, unless of a very minor nature.

8.147   Employers are required to report to the Secretary of State where a person has been dismissed from relevant employment on the grounds of misconduct, or where someone resigns in circumstances where he would have been dismissed or considered for dismissal on those grounds.[4] An individual can make representations where the Secretary of State is considering using his barring powers,[5] but there is no appeal process.[6]

---

1   SI 1993/543, as amended, reg 10(9) and Sch 4.

2   Sir William Utting *People Like Us, Report of the Review of Safeguards for Children Living Away from Home* (The Stationery Office, London, 1997) chap 14, para 14.18.

3   *Misconduct of Teachers and Workers with Children and Young Persons* DfEE Circular 11/95, para 9.

4   SI 1993/543, as amended, reg 11.

5   SI 1993/543, as amended, reg 10(4) and (5).

6   However, the Secretary of State has the power to withdraw or vary the terms of a direction, if he is satisfied that it would be appropriate to do so because new information is available or there is evidence of a material change in circumstances. SI 1993/543, as amended, reg 10(11).

DEPARTMENT OF HEALTH'S CONSULTANCY INDEX[1]

8.148 Unlike List 99, the Department of Health's Consultancy Index has no statutory basis. The Index operates on an advisory basis, whereby local authorities, private and voluntary organisations can check the suitability of those they propose to employ in a childcare post. Employers may refer a person for inclusion on the Index if that person has been dismissed, or has resigned or moved to a different post away from working with children, in circumstances where a child has been put at risk. Additionally, the police may also refer childcare workers or former child care workers who have received a caution or been convicted of a criminal offence. In 1997, there were approximately 750 names on the Index referred by employers and 4,800 referred by the police. In the same year, there were approximately 7,000 requests for checks against the Index made each month, and about six or seven of these were positive.[2] In 1998, the checks made were said to have doubled over the preceding 18 months and were then in the order of 140,000 a year.[3]

8.149 As it is advisory only, inclusion on the Index does not automatically prohibit the person from working with children. However, any person who has been cautioned or convicted of a sexual offence, particularly one involving a child victim, is highly unlikely to be considered suitable for employment in a childcare position. If a person on the Index has been referred by a former employer, the enquirer will then be responsible for seeking a reference from that employer, although, in practice, it is likely that the enquirer may decide not to pursue the person's application for employment any further.

Increasing awareness of the problem – the inter-departmental working group

8.150 In recent years, there has been an increasing awareness of the need to prevent sex offenders and others who are thought to pose a risk to children from seeking employment which will allow them unsupervised access to children. Whilst the availability of criminal record checks, List 99 and the Department of Health's Consultancy Index provided certain safeguards, concern was expressed that these safeguards were not fully integrated and that there was a need for a more streamlined approach to ensure that there were no loopholes. In 1997, the Report of the Review of Safeguards for Children Living Away from Home made a number of recommendations for improving recruitment and selection procedures in the childcare field.[4] In 1998, in an effort to address these concerns, the Government set up an interdepartmental working group of officials to consider additional safeguards to prevent those who are unsuitable from working with children, including the possibility of a central register backed up by a new criminal offence to prevent those on the register from applying for work

---

1   For a detailed account, see Sir William Utting *People Like Us, Report of the Review of Safeguards for Children Living Away from Home* (The Stationery Office, London, 1997) paras 14.21–14.35.
2   Sir William Utting *People Like Us, Report of the Review of Safeguards for Children Living Away from Home* (The Stationery Office, London, 1997) paras 14.22–14.23.
3   *The Government's Response to the Children's Safeguards Review* (1998) Cmnd 4105, November.
4   Sir William Utting *People Like Us, Report of the Review of Safeguards for Children Living Away from Home* (The Stationery Office, London, 1997), chap 13.

with children.[1] The group also addressed the issue of abuse of trust and, in an interim report published in November 1998,[2] made recommendations concerning the creation of the new criminal offence.[3]

Guidance for preventing the abuse of trust

8.151 In addition to the creation of a new criminal offence, the group recommended a major initiative to strengthen codes of conduct generally to protect young people from those in a position of authority over them. This recommendation has been acted upon by the Government, which has expressed the belief that all organisations involved with caring for young people and vulnerable adults should have Codes of Conduct to protect against sexual activity within relationships of trust. In September 1999, guidance was issued, setting out the main principles for such Codes.[4]

8.152 The guidance is intended to apply to those caring for young people[5] or vulnerable adults[6] in both paid and unpaid work, including volunteers, regardless of whether they are in the public, private, voluntary or volunteering sectors. Although it has no statutory force, the guidance contains principles of good practice and is intended to help organisations draw up their own Codes of Conduct on how to provide safeguards and prevent an abuse of trust involving some kind of sexual activity.[7] A relationship of trust is broadly defined as one in which one party is in a position of power or influence over the other by virtue of their work or the nature of their activity. The guidance is not to be interpreted as meaning that a genuine relationship cannot start between two people within a relationship of trust, but, given the inequality at the heart of a relationship of trust, the relationship of trust should be ended before any sexual relationship develops.

8.153 The guidance sets out model principles and suggests that Codes of Conduct on sexual activity within a relationship of trust should contain the following points:

---

1   HC Deb cols 304–305, 4 June 1998.
2   *Interim Report of the Interdepartmental Working Group on Preventing Unsuitable People from Working with Children and Abuse of Trust* (Home Office, London, 25 November 1998).
3   See **1.49** to **1.58**.
4   *Caring for Young People and the Vulnerable? Guidance for Preventing Abuse of Trust* (Home Office, Northern Ireland Office, the National Assembly for Wales, Department of Health and the Department for Education and Employment, 1999).
5   Namely, those under the age of 18.
6   No definition is given of a vulnerable adult, but services are identified where the relationship is so clearly one based on authority and trust and the potential for exploitation is so strong that any sexual relationship would be unacceptable while the relationship continues. The services include counselling services, all psychiatric services, residential care services, domiciliary care of various kinds, detention settings of all kinds, Probation Services and services specifically for those with learning disabilities. See Appendix B of the Guidance.
7   Sexual activity is defined objectively, ie that which would normally be recognised as sexual, in the circumstances, without knowledge of the intentions of the parties involved. Obvious examples are cited as sexual intercourse, oral sex and masturbation.

(1)   a clear policy statement on the paramount need to safeguard and promote
       the welfare of young people and vulnerable adults and protect them from
       sexual activity with those looking after them in a relationship of trust; it
       should be made clear that the purpose of the Code is two-fold in that it aims
       to protect both the young person or vulnerable adult being looked after
       from an unequal and potentially damaging relationship and also the
       person in a position of trust by preventing him or her from entering into
       such a relationship deliberately or accidentally by providing clear and
       enforceable guidance on what behaviour is acceptable;

(2)   an explanation of the relationship between the Code and policies and
       procedures for safeguarding young people and vulnerable adults more
       widely from other abuse;

(3)   an explanation of the circumstances in which a relationship of trust will
       arise and the responsibility that arises from the relationship;

(4)   a definition of those to be protected by the Code;

(5)   a clear statement that any behaviour which might allow a sexual
       relationship to develop between the person in a position of trust and the
       individual or individuals in his care should be avoided; and that any sexual
       relationship within a relationship of trust is unacceptable so long as the
       relationship of trust continues;

(6)   a clear supporting explanation of what behaviour is or is not acceptable
       within the particular organisation;

(7)   a clear statement that all those in the organisation have a duty to raise
       concerns about behaviour of staff, managers, volunteers or others which
       may be harmful to those in their care, without prejudice to their own
       position;

(8)   a clear statement that the principles apply irrespective of sexual
       orientation;

(9)   the detailed procedures to be put in place, including how to ensure abuse
       of trust is identified if it occurs; what to do if abuse of trust is reported or
       suspected; how to minimise the risk of situations where abuse of trust could
       occur or relationships that could lead to abuse of trust could develop; what
       an individual should do if he is concerned he is developing a relationship
       which could represent an abuse of trust or if he is concerned the other
       person is becoming attracted to him or if he is concerned that a colleague
       is becoming attracted to someone in his care or if he is concerned that his
       actions or words have been misunderstood; and

(10)   the sanctions for abuse of trust – the seriousness of the abuse of trust
       should be reflected in the sanction (this is an area which should always be
       taken very seriously with dismissal as a possible sanction).

8.154   Many organisations which work with young people or vulnerable
adults already have in place guidance or principles of good practice for the
protection of those in their care from sexual and other forms of abuse.[1] The
proposed Codes of Conduct to prevent abuse of trust go much further than this,

---

1   See, for example, *Safe from Harm* produced by the Home Office, *Safe and Alert* published by
     the National Centre for Volunteering and the codes issued by the General Medical Council,
     the United Kingdom Central Council for Nursing, Midwifery and Health Visiting, and the
     Council for Professions Allied to Medicine.

as they relate to conduct which may not be criminal, but is nevertheless unacceptable because of the relative positions of the parties concerned. The enactment of the proposed criminal offence of abuse of trust[1] will obviously extend the remit of the criminal law further in this direction, but will not include all forms of conduct covered by the guidance.

Legislative reform

8.155   The main report by the interdepartmental working group, published in January 1999, put forward four key recommendations:[2]

(1) to identify and ban unsuitable people from working with children;
(2) to create a new criminal offence which the 'unsuitable person' would commit if he worked with children;
(3) to provide a new definition of 'working with children'; and
(4) to create a 'one stop shop' – the Criminal Records Bureau – to provide access to information on people deemed unsuitable to work with children.

Some of these recommendations have now been enacted in the Protection of Children Act 1999, and further legislation to enact the remaining recommendations is expected shortly.

THE PROTECTION OF CHILDREN ACT 1999

8.156   When the Act is implemented, it will make four principal changes to the law with the objective of both creating a framework of a coherent cross-sector system to identify people unsuitable to work with children and to achieve a 'one stop shop' to compel or allow employers to access a single point for checking the names of people they propose to employ in a post involving the care of children.[3] The Act:

(1) places the Department of Health's Consultancy Index on a statutory basis, provides for the referral of names and creates a right of appeal to a new Tribunal;[4]
(2) amends the Education Reform Act 1988 to provide a power permitting inclusion on List 99 on the grounds that individuals are not considered fit and proper persons to work as teachers or in work involving regular contact with children, thus enabling a distinction to be drawn between those who are included on List 99 because they are unsuitable to work with children and those who are included on List 99 for other reasons (such as offences of dishonesty), and creates a right of appeal to the new tribunal;
(3) amends Pt V of the Police Act 1997 to enable the Criminal Records Bureau to disclose information about people who are included on either list along with their criminal records; and

---

1   See **1.54**.
2   *Report of the Interdepartmental Working Group on Preventing Unsuitable People from Working with Children and Abuse of Trust* (Home Office, London, 1999).
3   Protection of Children Act 1999, Explanatory Notes.
4   Details of the appointment, composition, tenure and management of the Tribunal are contained in the Schedule to the 1999 Act.

(4) requires childcare organisations proposing to employ someone in a childcare setting to ensure that individuals are checked through the bureau against the Department of Health List and the relevant category of List 99 and not to employ anyone identified on either list.

The Department of Health's list

8.157   Section 1 of the Act imposes a duty on the Secretary of State to establish a list of individuals who are considered unsuitable to work with children. The Act provides two ways onto the list, one through new procedures contained in s 2 of the Act and one by transfer from the Consultancy Index under s 3 of the Act. Section 4 provides a right of appeal against inclusion on the list.

8.158   Section 2(1) *requires* childcare organisations,[1] and *permits* any other organisation, to refer to the Secretary of State for possible inclusion on the list of certain individuals who are or have been employed in childcare positions,[2] if certain conditions are fulfilled. The first of the alternative conditions is that an individual has been dismissed, transferred or suspended on the grounds of misconduct (whether or not in the course of employment) which harmed a child or placed a child at risk of harm, or who would have been dismissed, or considered for dismissal, on such grounds had he not resigned or retired.[3] The second of the alternative conditions is that the organisation has dismissed the individual or he has resigned or retired or been transferred, and that information not available to the organisation at the time has since become available, so that the organisation subsequently forms the opinion that it would have dismissed, or considered dismissing, the individual on the grounds of misconduct (whether or not in the course of employment) which harmed a child or placed a child at risk of harm.[4]

8.159   When a reference is made, the Secretary of State may include the individual's name on the list provisionally. He must then invite observations from the individual and the employers and, after considering all the relevant information, must confirm an individual's inclusion on the list if he is of the opinion both that that the referring organisation reasonably considered the individual to be guilty of misconduct and that the individual is unsuitable to work with children.[5]

8.160   Section 3 of the Act provides for the transfer of names from the existing Consultancy Index to the new statutory list created by s 1 – essentially

---

1   A childcare organisation is one that is concerned with the provision of accommodation, social service or health care services to children, whose activities are by virtue of any prescribed enactment and which fulfils such other conditions as may be prescribed (s 12(1) of the Protection of Children Act 1999).

2   A childcare position is one that is concerned with the provision of accommodation, social services or health care services to children or the supervision of children, and is such as to enable the holder to have regular contact with children in the course of his duties, and is not a position in which employment of further employment may be prohibited or restricted by regulations made under s 218(6) of the Education Reform Act 1988 and is not in a position at an independent school which is a children's home for the purposes of Pt VIII of the Children Act 1989 (s 12(1) and (3) of the Protection of Children Act 1999).

3   Protection of Children Act 1999, s 2(2).

4   Protection of Children Act 1999, s 2(3).

5   Protection of Children Act 1999, s 2(4)–(8).

applying the effect of s 2 to persons listed on the Index. Section 4 provides for appeals against inclusion on the list to a new Tribunal established under s 9 of the Act. Those who have been provisionally included on the list for more than 9 months may, in certain circumstances, have the issue of their permanent inclusion determined by the Tribunal rather than by the Secretary of State. In all cases, the Tribunal must either allow appeals against inclusion on the list, or determine the matter in the individual's favour, if it is not satisfied that the individual is guilty of the misconduct as alleged, or that the individual is unsuitable to work with children. No finding of fact in a criminal court can be challenged before the Tribunal.

The Department of Education and Employment's list
8.161   Section 5 of the Act amends the Education Reform Act 1988 by substituting a new list of grounds for prohibiting or restricting employment by the Secretary of State, ie for inclusion on List 99. The present grounds are restated and two new grounds are added. The first is that the persons concerned are not 'fit and proper persons' to be employed as teachers or as workers who have regular contact with pupils or students under 19 years of age. The Act does not define persons who are not 'fit and proper'. The effect of this provision is to distinguish between those who are banned or restricted because they are not fit and proper persons to work with children, and those who are banned or restricted because of other misconduct. The latter would be banned or restricted from working as teachers or in other work with pupils and students under the age of 19, but would not be banned from working with children generally, as they have not been found to be a danger to children.

8.162   The second new ground is that the persons concerned are included (otherwise than provisionally) in the new statutory list under s 1 of the Act. Prior to the Act, the Secretary of State's powers did not extend to a person on the Consultancy Index. As a result of s 5, a person who is on the statutory list under s 1 (ie has been found to be unsuitable to work with children) will not be able to be employed as a teacher, or in other work with pupils and students under the age of 19. Section 6 establishes a statutory right of appeal against decisions of the Secretary of State to the newly established Tribunal.

The effect of inclusion in either list
8.163   Where a childcare organisation proposes to offer an individual employment in a childcare position, the organisation must ascertain whether the individual is included in the Department of Health's list, kept under s 1 of the Act, or List 99 and, if the individual is included in either list, the organisation must not offer him employment in such a position.[1] If the individual is being supplied by an employment agency or a nursing agency, the childcare organisation must satisfy itself that checks have been made and not offer the individual employment if he is included in either list.[2]

The 'one stop shop'
8.164   In order to establish the 'one stop shop' which the 1999 Act was designed to create and which enables or requires employers to access a single

---

1   Protection of Children Act 1999, s 7(1).
2   Protection of Children Act 1999, s 7(2).

point for checking the names of people they propose to employ in childcare posts, s 8 of the Act inserts two new sections in Pt V of the Police Act 1997. The amendments to s 113 of the 1997 Act (which deals with criminal record certificates) and s 115 of the 1997 Act (which deals with enhanced criminal record certificates) make the Department of Health list and List 99 available, via the Criminal Records Bureau, in any case where an application for either certificate is accompanied by a statement by the registered person that the certificate is required for the purpose of considering the applicant's suitability for a position (whether paid or unpaid) which is a childcare position or an educational post as a teacher, or which would otherwise bring the holder into regular contact with persons under the age of 19, or a position of such other description as may be prescribed.[1]

Reactions to the 1999 Act
8.165   Whilst there is general agreement that there is a need to tighten the procedures for vetting those applying for positions which involve unsupervised access to children, concerns have been expressed about certain aspects of the Act.[2] The NSPCC welcomed the introduction of the Bill into Parliament and urged MPs to support it, but expressed the view that the scope of the compulsory aspects of the legislation should be widened to include staff and volunteers in non-statutory organisations who would be working with children and also expressed concern that private individuals employing nannies are not within the remit of the legislation. On the other hand, concerns have been expressed relating to civil liberties. Liberty, the National Council for Civil Liberties, welcomed the overall aim of the legislation, but thought it could lead to an increased risk of employees being treated unjustly. In particular, concern was expressed that:

(1) the process for initial inclusion on the list is administrative rather than by a court;
(2) the threshold for an individual's initial inclusion is too low;
(3) the basis for inclusion is not confined to sexual or other intentional abuse;
(4) the onus is on individuals who are wrongly included to ensure that their names are removed from the list; and
(5) the provisions violate the right to privacy.

Whilst these concerns arguably have some merit, the rights of the individual must be balanced against the need to protect children. Once the new rights of appeal created by the Act are added into the equation, the balance is by no means unfairly weighted.

Sex offenders and the 1999 Act
8.166   In the current climate of concern, there can be little doubt that a criminal conviction for a sexual offence against a child will render the offender unsuitable to work with children – indeed, sexual offences against adults may

---

1   Police Act 1997, ss 113(3A) and 115(6A) as amended by s 8 of the Protection of Children Act 1999.
2   House of Commons Research Paper 99/21, February 1999.

well have the same effect. However, the provisions of the 1999 Act extend well beyond criminal convictions. A person may be included on the Department of Health's list on the grounds of misconduct (whether or not in the course of employment) which harmed a child or placed a child at risk which would be sufficient to dismiss, transfer or suspend an employee if the Secretary of State is of the opinion that the individual is unsuitable to work with children. Similarly, a person may be included on List 99 if he is not a 'fit and proper person' to be employed in an educational setting. Thus, any suspicions of behaviour amounting to sexual abuse of a child or young person may well be sufficient for inclusion on either list.

8.167   By requiring certain childcare organisations to refer individuals to the Secretary of State for inclusion on the Department of Health's list, the Act facilitates the supply of information necessary to ensure the adequate protection of children, although the definition of a childcare organisation is restricted to statutory agencies. Permitting other organisations to do so will also help to meet this objective, but every effort must be made to encourage these other organisations to make use of the referral process by publicising its existence. An organisation's willingness to refer an individual for inclusion on the list may well depend upon the nature of the misconduct, and, in this context, it is reasonable to speculate that the commission of sexual offence against a child will be one of the most forceful reasons for referring an individual.

8.168   Once an individual is included on either list, the final protective measure contained in the Act is to require all childcare organisations to ascertain whether an individual they are proposing to employ in a childcare position is included in either list and, if so, not to offer him employment in such a position. The requirement to check is an essential element of the process and the absolute prohibition on employment is also to be welcomed. However, even without the prohibition, in the past if an individual was included on the Consultancy Index because of sexual impropriety with a child, whether or not it resulted in a criminal conviction, this would usually have been sufficient to deter an employer from offering employment. Thus, the provisions of the Act should ensure that no known or suspected sex offenders, whether or not convicted, are given the opportunity to gain unsupervised access to children through their employment. Invisible sex offenders will, of course, continue to present a risk to children with whom they work.

FURTHER PROPOSALS FOR REFORM
8.169   Whereas, for several years, the Secretary of State has had statutory powers to ban unsuitable people from working in the field of education, and the Protection of Children Act 1999, when enacted, will also provide the Secretary of State with powers to ban unsuitable people from working with children in the health and social care fields, in July 1999 the interdepartmental working group published further proposals for reform.[1] It is proposed that all those convicted of serious criminal offences against children under the age of 18 should be banned from working with children, that a new criminal offence be created to support

---

1   *Report of the Interdepartmental Working Group on Preventing Unsuitable People from Working with Children and Abuse of Trust: Update* (Home Office, London, 1999).

the ban, whether the individual has been banned by the Secretary of State or a judge following conviction, and that the phrase 'working with children' should be re-defined. The Government has accepted these recommendations and intends to bring forward legislation in due course to implement them.[1]

Identification of those unsuitable
8.170   In addition to those identified as being unsuitable to work with children in a health and social care setting and in schools and educational institutions, the interdepartmental working group has now recommended that a third group of people should be identified as unsuitable to work with children.[2] These should be people who meet three criteria:

(1) are aged 18 or over;[3]
(2) are convicted of one of a list of criminal offences committed against children under the age of 18; and
(3) receive a prison sentence of 12 months or more.

8.171   It is envisaged that the ban would be imposed by the judge as part of the sentence and, as such, would be subject to appeal. There would be provision for the judge not to impose a ban if he considered there were exceptional reasons demonstrating the conviction did not indicate that the individual was a risk to children.

8.172   As a result of the severity of the proposed ban, which goes far beyond the provisions of the Protection of Children Act 1999, the working group further recommended that there should be a process for all those banned, by whatever method, for their bans to be reviewed by the new tribunal to be established under the 1999 Act. However, it is recommended that such a review should only be available 10 years after the imposition of the ban or release from prison, whichever is the later, and at 10-year intervals thereafter,[4] and only if the banned individual can demonstrate exceptional circumstances why the ban should be removed. Information on those banned would form part of the criminal and enhanced criminal record certificates from the Criminal Records Bureau when Pt V of the Police Act 1997 is enacted. The Government has announced that enhanced criminal record certificates should be available to people applying to work with children from the summer of 2001, and that by July 2002 the Criminal Records Bureau should also be issuing criminal record certificates and criminal conviction certificates.[5]

The ban on working with children
8.173   The idea of imposing a ban on those deemed unsuitable to work with children and imposing criminal liability on those who seek employment in contravention of the ban has been considered for some time. In 1996, the

---

1   Home Office Press Release 235/99, 29 July 1999.
2   *Report of the Interdepartmental Working Group on Preventing Unsuitable People from Working with Children and Abuse of Trust: Update* (Home Office, London, 1999) para 3.
3   It is recommended that there should be a discretion for a judge, in exceptional circumstances only, to apply the ban to someone under the age of 18.
4   For those exceptionally banned when under the age of 18, the relevant period before review would be 5 years.
5   Home Office Press Release 441/99.

Government issued a consultation document on the sentencing and supervision of sex offenders which proposed that those convicted of sexual offences against children should be banned from working with children and that a new criminal offence of seeking employment involving access to children be created.[1] It was thought to be unreasonable to require the prosecution to prove that an individual's *purpose* in seeking a particular job was to gain access to children, but at this time, no further consideration was given to the fault element that would be required.[2]

8.174   The interdepartmental working party has now proposed that an individual banned from working with children would be liable to criminal sanctions if he applied for, or accepted an offer of, or worked with children while banned. The offence would be an arrestable offence, subject to a maximum of 5 years' imprisonment, an unlimited fine, or both. It is suggested that there should be a defence if the individual did not know and could not reasonably have been expected to have known that the work in question constituted working with children and that there should also be a defence if the individual did not know, and could not reasonably be expected to have known, that he was banned from working with children. An employer or the equivalent who took a person he knew was banned from working with children for work he knew or could reasonably be expected to have known fell under the definition of working with children, would also be liable for an offence. Again, the offence would be an arrestable offence, subject to a maximum of 5 years' imprisonment, an unlimited fine, or both.

8.175   It is interesting to note that, under these proposals, the offence committed by the banned individual would appear to be one of strict liability, subject to a due diligence defence, ie that the individual will be convicted unless he can prove[3] that he neither knew, nor could reasonably have been expected to have known, either that he was banned from working with children or that the work in question constituted working with children. In contrast, in order to convict an employer who employs a banned individual, the prosecution must prove[4] that the employer knew that the individual was banned from working with children and that the employer either knew, or could reasonably have been expected to have known, that the work in question constituted working with children. Thus, it will be easier to convict the banned individual than the person who employs him.

'Working with children'
8.176   The interdepartmental working group has made detailed proposals as to what should constitute working with children for these purposes, recommending that any definition should go beyond the definitions for the specific health and social care and education bans covered by powers of the Secretary of State and should cover a wide range of work, including education,

---

1   *Sentencing and Supervision of Sex Offenders: A Consultation Document* (HMSO, London, 1996).
2   See further Cobley 'Sentencing and Supervision of Sex Offenders' (1997) *Journal of Social Welfare and Family Law* 19(1) 98.
3   The relevant standard of proof will be on the balance of probabilities. See **3.12**.
4   The relevant standard of proof will be beyond all reasonable doubt. See **3.12**.

health and social care, accommodation, leisure and sporting activities, religious activities and the criminal justice system. In particular, it is recommended that:

(1) the definition would apply regardless of the status of the work – it would apply to paid and unpaid work in the public, private, voluntary and volunteering sectors;

(2) it would be based on the concept of 'role' or 'position', not 'office' or 'employment';

(3) it should focus on key providers of services, not ancillary staff (except in particular settings such as schools and residential children's homes, where all staff would be covered);

(4) except in the specific settings, the contact between a child and an adult should be a normal part of the job, not incidental or one-off contact;

(5) immediate supervisors, managers and those in a position to take decisions to appoint or dismiss people working with children would themselves be classed as working with children; this would be limited to those with direct 'control' at 'one level up' from 'front line' child workers (in addition, some specified groups in the education and social services field, such as school governors, directors of social services and members of the local authority social services committees and charitable trusts in the area, are covered by the definition);

(6) 'children' would be defined as those aged under 18 years, except in the employment context where children should be defined as those under the age of 16 (those regularly training or supervising children under the age of 16 as part of the normal course of their duties, for example in the entertainment industry, should be covered by the definition; employers per se of children, even those aged under 16 years, should not be covered unless a system of licensing or registering such employers with local authorities were introduced);

(7) the same definition of working with children should form the basis for the scheme and for the definition within the new Rehabilitation of Offenders Act 1974 (Exceptions) Order.

Banning sex offenders from working with children
8.177   No recommendations have yet been made as to the list of criminal offences which would trigger the ban, but there can be no doubt that sexual offences will feature prominently in any such list. In a consultation exercise undertaken by the working party, the majority of respondents gave the definition of those unsuitable to work with children as being those that had been cautioned or convicted of a sexual or violent offence,[1] and there was general agreement that the ban should be automatic, in the absence of exceptional circumstances. However, those involved in fostering and adopting who have had experience of the difficulties caused by the Children (Protection from Offenders) (Miscellaneous Amendments) Regulations 1997,[2] tend to favour a more cautious approach. The National Foster Care Association expressed concern that a blanket definition may not be appropriate to all areas of work or situations, and

---

1   *Report of the Interdepartmental Working Group on Preventing Unsuitable People from Working with Children and Abuse of Trust: Update* (Home Office, London, 1999) Annex B.

2   SI 1997/2308.

argued that those fitting the criteria of unsuitability should not be banned immediately, without individual circumstances being considered. In support of this view, it provided an example of difficulties it had experienced in cases where people were unable to become foster parents due to offences they had committed in their youth and the Association did not feel that this should have any bearing on their adult suitability.[1] Many would argue that this is a valid point. Such problems may, of course, be overcome partly by the proposal to allow the tribunal established under the Protection of Children Act 1999 to review the ban after 10 years if there are exceptional circumstances. The dangers of hastily passed, ill-thought-out legislation have been only too apparent in recent years. It is to be hoped that lessons have been learnt from past mistakes.

---

1   See **8.121** to **8.129**.

Conclusion

SEX OFFENDERS – WHERE DO WE GO FROM HERE?

Much of this book has been devoted to the changes in policy, law and practice in relation to sex offenders which have taken place during the last decade of the 20th century. The impetus for many of these changes came from a growing public concern – some would even call it a panic or hysteria – about sexual offending, a concern which arguably has been fuelled by the media. Whilst particularly gruesome sex crimes have always featured prominently in the public eye, in recent years, sex offenders have been the focus of an unprecedented level of concern. Although there is nothing startlingly new about sexual offending, and there is no hard evidence to suggest that a growing number of members of society have suddenly become sexually depraved and are running amok throughout the land, leaving a string of sexually abused victims in their wake, sex offenders have been built into 'modern folk-devils' in the eyes of the public. As a result, sex offenders have been accorded a high priority on many social and political agendas, with an unprecedented level of political and legislative activity taking place in response.

However, responding to the demands created by such a rapid increase in public concern inevitably raises the danger of 'knee jerk' reactions, ie rapid responses which may be made without due thought and consideration. Whilst this may be understandable, particularly given the intensity of the public concern over sex offenders, care must be taken. As the rise in hysteria and panic levels out and the initial responses have been made, now is the time to take stock, to consider the effectiveness of recent reforms and to decide what, if any, further steps need to be taken – not only for the protection of society as a whole, but also in the interests of victims, and indeed sex offenders themselves. Looking to the future, two main issues emerge for further consideration. First, the increasing significance of a criminal conviction and the implications of a successful prosecution for the effective management of the risk posed by sex offenders. Secondly, the importance of risk assessment, both for the effective targeting of limited resources and for what is perhaps one of the most controversial areas in the eyes of the public – community notification.

CRIMINAL CONVICTIONS

The importance of a criminal conviction

Whilst the criminal justice system has always been a central feature of society's response to the problems posed by sex offenders, criminal convictions have now assumed an even greater significance. With increasing emphasis being placed on exercising strict control over sex offenders (see below), a criminal conviction is an essential pre-requisite to many of the control measures available. A criminal conviction and the resulting punishment may also serve to satisfy demands for retribution or revenge, thus helping to maintain law and order, and a conviction can also provide a route into treatment – an option which sex offenders may be unwilling to pursue of their own volition.

Control and criminal convictions as the 'crucial hook'

Issues of 'dangerousness' and the perceived need to protect the public from dangerous offenders (generally classified as violent or sexual offenders) have formed the basis of the Government's response to sex offenders. It is now clear that public protection is the paramount consideration and that this protection is ultimately to be achieved by exercising strict control over sex offenders by means of incapacitation, supervision and surveillance. Although the criminal justice system provides the opportunity for control to be exercised over all offenders, additional control measures are available for sex offenders. These include longer custodial sentences and extended periods of supervision on release (discussed in chapter 4) and the notification requirements imposed by the Sex Offenders Act 1997 and Sex Offender Orders available under the Crime and Disorder Act 1998 (discussed in chapter 7). Yet these measures can only be utilised once a criminal conviction has been obtained – the conviction effectively forms the 'crucial hook' on which the control measures can be hung.

Convictions, punishment and retribution

Public protection may well be the primary motivation underlying many of the control measures, but there also exists an ulterior, perhaps less transparent, motivation. Demands for increased public protection tend to be inextricably linked with demands for retribution and, in addition to providing the crucial hook on which control measures can be hung, a criminal conviction and the punishment which follows can also satisfy the demand for retribution. Indeed, in the absence of a criminal conviction, there is always a danger that sections of society may be tempted to 'take the law into their own hands' and dispense what they perceive to be their own form of justice in order to satisfy the demand for retribution. As discussed in chapter 4, given the current tendency to treat sex offenders as the most feared, hated and despised group of offenders, retribution may be a strong justification for imposing punishment on sex offenders. Demands for retribution are arguably a natural human response to the commission of sexual offences and, as such, they are to be expected. There is nothing intrinsically wrong in this, but the one caveat is that the demands must be recognised as such during the sentencing process. As a matter of principle, imposing custodial sentences commensurate with the seriousness of the offence can be justified on the grounds of retribution, deterrence or protection of the public, but the imposition of longer sentences can only be justified on the grounds that the public requires protection from the offender. There is a danger that, if demands for retribution are not recognised and caution exercised, longer sentences may be imposed as a form of revenge on a sex offender – something which cannot be justified, however great the demands for retribution.

Criminal convictions, rehabilitation and treatment

It is now clear that protection of the public from sex offenders is to be achieved through control measures, a pre-requisite of which is a criminal conviction. However, there exists an alternative route to protection – that of the rehabilitation of the offender. Admittedly, many of the control measures may provide an opportunity for the offenders to 'address their offending behaviour', but despite the development of programmes such as the Sex Offender Treatment Programme (discussed in chapter 5) and the excellent work undertaken by the Probation Service with sex offenders in the community in many areas (discussed in chapter 6), the rehabilitation of sex offenders has tended to take a back seat in policy discussions and legislative activity, with little more than lip service being paid to notions of rehabilitation and treatment. Perhaps this is understandable, as the Government is clearly influenced by public opinion and the associated demands for protection and retribution. However, the provision of treatment and the rehabilitation of offenders is one area in which the Government must be prepared to be more pro-active.

Although no firm assurances can be given that treatment can 'cure' sex offenders, it is clear that in many cases it will at least reduce the risk of further offending. This has important implications for protection of the public and the level of control that needs to be exercised over individual offenders (see below). It also reduces the number of potential future victims, which may be of great significance, not only to the potential victims themselves, but also to tackle what may become a cycle of sexual abuse. There is increasing evidence to suggest that young victims of sexual offences who were abused during their childhood may themselves become sex offenders in later life. Indeed, Sidney Cooke, one of the country's most notorious paedophiles, has blamed his actions on the abuse he suffered as a child. Whilst policy decisions obviously should not be made on the basis of such anecdotal evidence and further research is undoubtedly needed on the long-term effects of sexual abuse on children and on how the cycle of abuse can be broken, there is a strong argument for extending the provision of treatment for sex offenders.

This is not to suggest that treatment and rehabilitation should take priority and effectively replace more punitive measures based on protection of the public and retribution, not least because this would be viewed by many as an unacceptable 'soft option' for sex offenders. However, this should not prevent treatment being made available alongside traditional punitive measures. Punishment and treatment may well form an uneasy alliance, but they are not necessarily mutually exclusive and there is no reason why a criminal conviction should not afford opportunities for public protection, punishment *and* treatment.

Increasing the number of convictions for sexual offences

The increasing significance attached to criminal convictions suggests that the first priority must be to ensure that sex offenders are prosecuted and convicted. How can this be achieved?

Encouraging the reporting of sexual offences

Problems surrounding the 'dark figure' of unreported crime are particularly acute in relation to sexual offences and it would be unrealistic to aim for the complete elimination of that figure. Yet that is not to say that attempts cannot and should not be made to at least reduce it as the first step towards achieving more criminal convictions. The attitude of those in the front line of the criminal justice system, typically the police, is of fundamental importance to encouraging the reporting of sexual offences. Much has already been achieved in changing these attitudes (as discussed in chapter 2), but there is no room for complacency. Whilst some police officers will be specifically trained to interview victims, in many cases these officers may not be the victims' first point of contact with the criminal justice system and all police officers need to be aware of the importance of responding appropriately to the initial complaint and ensuring that the victim is supported in the early stages of the investigation. This support must then continue throughout the entire criminal justice process. Changes in the investigative procedure and the establishment of suites specifically designed for the examination and interviewing of victims are positive steps towards reducing the trauma experienced by victims, but efforts must now be made to address issues relating to the appointment and training of police surgeons, not only to ensure that the victim receives appropriate treatment and advice, but also because the medical evidence may well be of crucial importance at any subsequent trial.

Changes to the evidential requirements and trial processes, aimed at reducing the trauma traditionally experienced by vulnerable witnesses such as children and victims of sexual offences, should also ultimately encourage the reporting of sexual offences. The effect of these changes on the reporting of sexual offences will probably take some time to filter through the system, but as memories of well-publicised and highly traumatic rape trials fade and victims are assured that they will be supported throughout the entire criminal justice process, they may well be more prepared to come forward to report the offence in the first instance.

Effective investigation

Many sexual offences are committed by someone known to the victim. If the offence is one of sexual aggression, the most controversial issue is likely to be consent which, in the absence of physical violence, can often prove to be an insurmountable obstacle for the prosecution. The reality is that, unless radical changes are made in relation to the law of consent, such as placing the burden of proving consent on the defence, the issue of consent will continue to be controversial. All those involved in the investigative process are no doubt already aware of this, but continuing efforts must be made to ensure the most effective investigation and gathering of evidence.

Public concern tends to be greatest over predatory sex offenders, ie those who commit offences of sexual aggression against strangers. In such cases, identification will be the first essential step towards obtaining the crucial hook. The advent of DNA profiling has obviously been of considerable assistance in this respect, but the full potential of profiling can only be achieved by the establishment of a national DNA database. In the meantime, any further advances in forensic science must be exploited fully.

Evidence and court proceedings

Perhaps the most radical legislative reform has been the changes to the trial procedure contained in the Youth Justice and Criminal Evidence Act 1999 (discussed in chapter 3), which hopefully will go some way towards redressing the balance at a criminal trial in favour of the victim and thus improve the prospect of a conviction. Traditionally, the criminal trial process has centred around the rights of an offender. Whilst not suggesting that such rights are unimportant, it has been clear in the past that the balance was weighted firmly in favour of the offender and little or no allowance was made for any specific characteristics of the witnesses. Young or traumatised victims were often unable to give coherent evidence in court and this, combined with what many considered to be archaic rules of evidence in relation to sexual offences, resulted in the acquittal of many sex offenders.

Reforms introduced for children as witnesses by the Criminal Justice Acts of 1988 and 1991 paved the way for further reform later in the 1990s, culminating in the provisions of the 1999 Act. Although not directed solely at sexual offences, there can be little doubt that victims of sexual offences will be amongst the main beneficiaries of the reforms, which have the potential not only to make the whole experience of providing evidence to a criminal court less traumatic for victims of sexual offences of whatever age, but also ultimately to result in more criminal convictions, thereby providing more of the crucial hooks on which the control measures rely.

Sexual offences – reviewing the substantive criminal law

Whereas the reforms to the law of evidence and trial procedures have the potential to make a significant impact on the number of convictions for sexual offences, the impact of any reform to the substantive criminal law on the number of convictions is likely to be more limited. With many of the offences on the statute book dating back to the 19th century, reform to update the law and to remove anachronisms and inconsistencies within it is admittedly long overdue (as discussed in chapter 1). The narrowing of the remit of the criminal law by the reduction in the age of consent for homosexual activity will be counter-balanced by the new offence of abuse of trust. However, in the absence of radical reform to the offences of sexual aggression, the issue of consent will continue to pose a sometimes insurmountable barrier for the prosecution when the offender and victim are known to one another.

SEX OFFENDERS AND RISK ASSESSMENT

Sex offenders – a 'broad-brush' approach versus an individualised approach

All sex offenders may be subject to control measures once the crucial hook in the form of a criminal conviction is obtained. Some of the problems of defining sex offenders were considered in chapter 1, where it was seen that neither sex offenders nor sexual offences can be categorised as homogenous groups, but that a sex offender is generally defined as someone who commits a sexual offence, albeit the categories of sexual offence may differ according to the purpose for which the categorisation is made. In some areas, the law adopts what may be termed a 'broad-brush' approach, in that all those within the defined group will be subject to the same measures, irrespective of the risk posed by individual offenders. A classic example of this approach is to be found in the Sex Offenders Act 1997 (discussed in chapter 7), which requires all offenders cautioned for or convicted of an offence contained in Sch 1 to the Act to notify the police of any changes to their name or address.

By comparison, in other areas, the law adopts an individualised approach, whereby the control measures imposed are dependent on the individual offender, the circumstances of the offences committed and the risk he is thought to pose to other members of the community. For example, following the Criminal Justice Act 1991, a custodial sentence can only be imposed if either the court is of the opinion that the offence, or combination of the offence and one or more offences associated with it, was so serious that only such a sentence can be justified for the offence, or, if the offence is a violent or sexual offence, the court is of the opinion that only such a sentence would be adequate to protect the public from serious harm from him.

Whilst a broad-brush approach may be acceptable in relation to measures aimed at surveillance and control in the community, where the infringement of the offender's personal freedom is more limited and, on balance, may be justified by the perceived need to protect the public, it will arguably be unacceptable in relation to the imposition of a custodial sentence, where the greater infringement of the offender's liberty will require an individual approach to be taken. That being said, the Crime (Sentences) Act 1997 (considered in chapter 4), which imposes an automatic life sentence on those convicted of a second serious offence as defined by the Act, regardless of the risk posed by the offender or the circumstances surrounding the commission of either offence, clearly applies the broad-brush approach to custodial sentences and arguably cannot be justified as a result.

Risk assessment and the allocation of resources

Theoretical problems of justification aside, the adoption of a broad-brush approach has further practical implications. The resources available within the criminal justice system, both human and financial, inevitably are limited and every effort needs be made to target these resources where they will be most effective. This requires a degree of discretion which the broad-brush approach simply cannot provide. Imposing the notification requirements on all sex offenders may well prove to be an excessive burden on administrative resources and the impact of an automatic life sentence on those convicted of a second serious offence, although the numbers concerned are likely to be small, will in many cases prove to be an unnecessary burden on the Prison Service.

On the other hand, an individualised approach has far greater potential for the effective allocation of resources. As protection of the public from sex offenders is the paramount consideration, then in all cases an assessment of the risk posed by an individual offender must be carried out. Resources can then be allocated on the basis of need – the greater the risk posed by an offender, the more stringent the control measures that will need to be employed.

Risk assessment, protection of the public and community notification

The protection of the public from sex offenders can never be guaranteed. Even if all visible offenders were incarcerated for indefinite periods, which itself could never be justified, there would remain the problem of invisible offenders (as discussed in chapter 6). Instead, a compromise must be accepted. In the vast majority of cases, sex offenders will spend a considerable amount of their lives living in the community and control measures are imposed to ensure that the risk thereby posed to the public is reduced to the minimum level which is consistent with the rights of the offender and the resources available.

The effective management of sex offenders in the community now relies increasingly on interagency co-operation and multi-disciplinary assessment of risk (as discussed in chapter 7). Close working relationships have developed between the Prison Service, the Probation Service and the police. All of these professionals have a vital role to play in protecting the public, a crucial part of which is the assessment of the risk posed individual by offenders. Other professionals may also have an input into this process for specific purposes, such as ensuring that sex offenders living in the community are allocated appropriate housing where possible (as discussed in chapter 8). Inter-agency working is facilitated by the introduction of statutory crime and disorder partnerships, and the flow of information between the agencies is assisted by the development of protocols and guidance on the exchange of information (as discussed in chapter 7). Thus, a practical framework has been developed within which the various agencies work together towards the ultimate aim of protecting the public.

Although public confidence in the professional competence of these agencies may be high in many areas, where sex offenders are concerned it seems that the public panic or hysteria which led to the creation of sex offenders as modern folk devils remains all too evident. Whatever reassurances are given, and despite the cogent arguments advanced about fear of vigilante attacks and the potential of forcing sex offenders 'underground' and out of contact with the public protection agencies, certain sections of the public simply do not trust the professionals to protect them from the risk posed by sex offenders. Instead, it is claimed that members of the community have a right to know when a convicted sex offender is living in their midst so that they can take steps to ensure their own safety and that of their family. The problem lies in delineating precisely who should be provided with crucial information about the offender.

The controversy and the dilemmas it presents were illustrated vividly during an Adjournment Debate in the House of Commons on 10 November 1999. In line with Home Office policy, Mr Richard Shepherd, MP for Aldrige-Brownhills in the Midlands, had been informed by the Home Office that a convicted paedophile with a long history of abusing children was to be released at the end of a custodial sentence and accommodated in a bail hostel in his constituency. After advising senior police officers and probation officers of his intention, Mr Shepherd released the letter informing him of the offender's release to the public, as a result of which the offender was accommodated elsewhere. Justifying the decision to disclose, Mr Shepherd commented during the debate:

> 'It is intolerable that I should know of a situation and therefore be able quietly to make arrangements further to ensure my safety or that of those whom I love, while denying my friends and neighbours and those who elected me the same opportunity. Should anything go wrong with what experience has reluctantly led me to conclude is now a rather mechanistic and bureaucratic framework, and a child were abducted or a woman raped, when such a crime might have been avoided if children were accompanied and women warned, would I not be party to a great wrong?'

There can be little doubt that the issue of community notification will continue to be one of the most controversial, and certainly the most visible, of issues in the continuing debate over the most effective response to sex offenders in the community. What, then, can be done?

Risk assessment will inevitably play a central role as it has never been suggested that *all* convicted sex offenders should be identified as such to the community in which they live. Yet risk assessment alone, however accurate it may be, will not solve the problem. Equally important will be the effectiveness of the control measures put in place to address the risk.

Perhaps the key lies in increasing public confidence in the abilities of the professionals to provide adequate protection. One way to address this would be a more visible categorisation of 'risk' that could be readily understood by the public. For example, in New Jersey in the USA, sex offenders who reside in the community are classified in one of three 'tiers' based on the degree of risk they pose to the public. Neighbours are notified of tier 3 (high risk) offenders. Registered community organisations involved with children or with victims of sexual abuse, schools, day care centres and summer camps are notified of tier 3 and tier 2 (moderate risk) offenders. Law enforcement agencies are notified of the presence of all sex offenders, including tier 1 (low risk) offenders. Such a system has the advantage of a clear structure that would help engender confidence in the system. The adoption of a classification system in this country need not lead to radical changes in practice, in fact it would make little difference to the way in which risk is currently assessed. The provisions of the Sex Offenders Act 1997 ensures that the police are notified of the presence of all sex offenders. If an offender is thought to present an unacceptable risk and it is thought necessary to notify members of the community of his presence, the offender will simply be categorised as a tier 3 offender. The need for more limited disclosure would result in an offender being categorised as tier 2. Low risk offenders would be required to comply with the provisions of the 1997 Act, but no further disclosure of their whereabouts could be made. However, such a system arguably would have the effect of increasing public confidence, in that communities could be assured that they would be informed of the presence of any high-risk offenders living in their midst.

Yet this alone would not eliminate the problem. The public need to have confidence, not only in the ability of the professionals to assess and categorise the risk posed by an offenders, but also in the steps that are taken after a risk assessment has been made. As long as the protection system is perceived to be a 'rather mechanistic and bureaucratic framework', demands for the outing of sex offenders will continue unabated. Only when the public has sufficient faith and confidence in the criminal justice system and the practical application and effectiveness of the control measures it provides will it be content to abandon its professed 'right to know' and leave the responsibility for protecting the public with those professionals specifically charged with the task. That time has clearly not yet arrived.

Appendix

DEFINITIONS OF SEXUAL OFFENCES

RAPE OF WOMAN OR MAN

Section 1 of the Sexual Offences Act 1956

'(1) It is an offence for a man to rape a woman or another man

(2) A man commits rape if –

    (a) he has sexual intercourse with a person (whether vaginal or anal) who at the time of the intercourse does not consent to it; and

    b) at the time he knows that the person does not consent to the intercourse or he is reckless as to whether that person consents to it.

(3) A man also commits rape if he induces a married woman to have sexual intercourse with him by impersonating her husband.'

Mode of prosecution: On indictment
Maximum punishment: Life imprisonment

PROCUREMENT OF A WOMAN BY THREATS

Section 2 of the Sexual Offences Act 1956

'(1) It is an offence for a person to procure a woman, by threats or intimidation, to have sexual intercourse in any part of the world.'

Mode of prosecution: On indictment
Maximum punishment: Two years' imprisonment

PROCUREMENT OF A WOMAN BY FALSE PRETENCES

Section 3 of the Sexual Offences Act 1956

'(1) It is an offence for a person to procure a woman, by false pretences or false representations, to have sexual intercourse in any part of the world.'

Mode of prosecution: On indictment
Maximum punishment: Two years' imprisonment

ADMINISTERING DRUGS TO OBTAIN OR FACILITATE INTERCOURSE

Section 4 of the Sexual Offences Act 1956

'(1) It is an offence for a person to apply or administer to, or cause to be taken by, a woman any drug, matter or thing with intent to stupify or overpower her so as thereby to enable any man to have unlawful sexual intercourse with her.'

Mode of prosecution: On indictment
Maximum punishment: Two years' imprisonment

INTERCOURSE WITH A DEFECTIVE

Section 7 of the Sexual Offences Act 1956

'(1) It is an offence, subject to the exception mentioned in this section, for a man to have unlawful sexual intercourse with a woman who is a defective.
(2) A man is not guilty of an offence under this section because he has unlawful sexual intercourse with a woman if he does not know and has no reason to suspect her to be a defective.'

Mode of prosecution: On indictment
Maximum punishment: Two years' imprisonment

SEXUAL INTERCOURSE WITH PATIENTS

Section 128 of the Mental Health Act 1959

'(1) Without prejudice to section 7 of the Sexual Offences Act 1956, it shall be an offence, subject to the exception mentioned in this section, –
  (a) for a man who is an officer on the staff of or is otherwise employed in, or is one of the managers of, a hospital or mental nursing home to have unlawful sexual intercourse with a woman who is for the time being receiving treatment for mental disorder in that hospital or home, or to have such intercourse on the premises of which the hospital or home forms part with a woman who is for the time being receiving such treatment there as an out-patient;
  (b) for a man to have unlawful sexual intercourse with a woman who is a mentally disordered patient and who is subject to his guardianship under the Mental Health Act 1983 or is otherwise in his custody or care under the Mental Health Act 1983 or in pursuance of arrangements under Part III of the National Assistance Act 1948, or the National Health Service Act 1977 or as a resident in a residential care home within the meaning of Part I of the Registered Homes Act 1984.
(2) It shall not be an offence under this section for a man to have sexual intercourse with a woman if he does not know and has no reason to suspect her to be a mentally disordered patient.'

Mode of prosecution: On indictment
Maximum punishment: Two years' imprisonment

Section 1 of the Sexual Offences Act 1967

'(4) Section 128 of the Mental Health Act 1959 ... shall have effect as if any reference therein to having unlawful sexual intercourse with a woman included a reference to committing buggery or an act of gross indecency with another man.'

INTERCOURSE WITH A GIRL UNDER THE AGE OF 13

Section 5 of the Sexual Offences Act 1956

'It is a felony for a man to have unlawful sexual intercourse with a girl under the age of 13.'

Mode of prosecution: On indictment
Maximum punishment: Life imprisonment

INTERCOURSE WITH A GIRL UNDER THE AGE OF 16

Section 6 of the Sexual Offences Act 1956

'(1) It is an offence subject to the exceptions mentioned in this section, for a man to have unlawful sexual intercourse with a girl under the age of 16.
(2) Where a marriage is invalid under section 2 Marriage Act 1949, or section 1 Age of Marriage Act 1929 (the wife being a girl under the age of 16) the invalidity does not make the husband guilty of an offence under this section because he has sexual intercourse with her, if he believes her to be his wife and has reasonable cause for the belief.
(3) A man is not guilty of an offence under this section because he has unlawful sexual intercourse with a girl under the age of 16, if he is under the age of 24 years and has not previously been charged with a like offence, and he believes her to be of the age of 16 or over and has reasonable cause for the belief.'

Mode of prosecution: Triable either way (prosecution within 12 months of the offence charged)
Maximum punishment: Two years' imprisonment on indictment

INCEST BY A MAN

Section 10 of the Sexual Offences Act 1956

'(1) It is an offence for a man to have sexual intercourse with a woman he knows to be his granddaughter, daughter, sister or mother.
(2) In the foregoing subsection "sister" includes half sister, and for the purposes of that subsection any expression importing a relationship between two people shall be taken to apply notwithstanding that the relationship is not traced through lawful wedlock.'

Mode of prosecution: On indictment (consent of the DPP required)

Maximum punishment: Seven years' imprisonment or life imprisoment if with a
girl under 13 years of age

INCEST BY A WOMAN

Section 11 of the Sexual Offences Act 1956

'(1) It is an offence for a woman of the age of 16 or over to permit a man who she
knows to be her grandfather, father, brother or son to have sexual intercourse
with her by her consent.

(2) In the foregoing subsection "brother" includes half brother, and for the
purposes of that subsection any expression importing a relationship between
two people shall be taken to apply notwithstanding that the relationship is not
traced through lawful wedlock.'

Mode of prosecution: On indictment (consent of the DPP required)
Maximum punishment: Seven years' imprisonment

INCITING A GIRL UNDER 16 TO HAVE INCESTUOUS SEXUAL INTERCOURSE

Section 54 of the Criminal Law Act 1977

'(1) It is an offence for a man to incite to have sexual intercourse with him a girl
under the age of 16 whom he knows to be his granddaughter, daughter or
sister.

(2) In the preceding subsection "man" includes boy, "sister" includes half sister,
and for the purposes of that subsection any expression importing a relationship between two people shall be taken to apply notwithstanding that the
relationship is not traced through lawful wedlock.'

Mode of prosecution: Triable either way
Maximum punishment: Two years' imprisonment on indictment

BUGGERY

Section 12 of the Sexual Offences Act 1956

'(1)   It is felony for a person to commit buggery with another person otherwise
than in the circumstances described in subsection 1A below or with an animal.

(1A) The circumstances referred to in subsection (1) are that the act of buggery
takes place in private and both parties have attained the age of eighteen.

(1B) An act of buggery by one man with another shall not be treated as taking place
in private if it takes place –
(a) when more than two people take part or are present; or
(b) in a lavatory to which the public have or are permitted to have access,
whether on payment or otherwise.

(1C) In any proceedings against a person for buggery with another person it shall be for the prosecutor to prove that the act of buggery took place otherwise than in private or that one of the parties to it had not attained the age of eighteen.'

Mode of prosecution: On indictment

Maximum punishment: Life imprisonment if with a person under the age of 16 years or with an animal; 5 years' imprisonment if the defendant is aged 21 or over and the other person is aged under 18; 2 years' imprisonment in all other cases

ASSAULT WITH INTENT TO COMMIT BUGGERY

Section 16 of the Sexual Offences Act 1956

'It is an offence for a person to assault another person with intent to commit buggery.'

Mode of prosecution: On indictment

Maximum punishment: Ten years' imprisonment

GROSS INDECENCY BETWEEN MEN

Section 13 of the Sexual Offences Act 1956

'It is an offence for a man to commit an act of gross indecency with another man whether in public or private, or to be a party to the commission by a man of an act of gross indecency with another man, or to procure the commission by a man of an act of gross indecency with another man.'

Mode of prosecution: On indictment

Maximum punishment: Five years' imprisonment where the defendant is aged 21 or over and the other person is under 18; 2 years' imprisonment in all other cases

INDECENT ASSAULT ON A WOMAN

Section 14 of the Sexual Offences Act 1956

'(1) It is an offence, subject to the exception mentioned in subsection (3) of this section, for a person to make an indecent assault on a woman.

(2) A girl under the age of 16 cannot in law give any consent which would prevent an act being an assault for the purposes of this section.

(3) Where a marriage is invalid under section two of the Marriage Act 1949, or section 1 of the Age of Marriage Act 1929 (the wife being a girl under the age of sixteen), the invalidity does not make the husband guilty of any offence under this section by reason of her incapacity to consent while under that age, if he believes her to be his wife and he has reasonable cause for the belief.

(4)   A woman who is a defective cannot in law give any consent which would prevent an act being an assault for the purposes of this section, but a person is only to be treated as guilty of an indecent assault on a defective by reason of that incapacity to consent, if that person knew or had reason to suspect her to be a defective.'

Mode of prosecution: Triable either way
Maximum punishment: Ten years' imprisonment

INDECENT ASSAULT ON A MAN

Section 15 of the Sexual Offences Act 1956

'(1)   It is an offence for a person to make an indecent assault on a man.
(2)   A boy under the age of 16 cannot in law give any consent which would prevent an act being an assault for the purposes of this section.
(3)   A man who is a defective cannot in law give any consent which would prevent an act being an assault for the purposes of this section, but a person is only to be treated as guilty of an indecent assault on a defective by reason of that incapacity to consent, if that person knew or had reason to suspect him to be a defective.'

Mode of prosecution: Triable either way
Maximum punishment: Ten years' imprisonment

ABDUCTION OF A WOMAN BY FORCE OR FOR THE SAKE OF HER PROPERTY

Section 17 of the Sexual Offences Act 1956

'(1)   It is a felony for a person to take away or detain a woman against her will with the intention that she shall marry or have unlawful sexual intercourse with that or any other person, if she is so taken away or detained either by force or for the sake of her property or expectations of property.
(2)   In the foregoing subsection, the reference to a woman's expectations of property relates only to property of a person to whom she is next of kin or one of the next of kin, and "property" includes any interest in property.'

Mode of prosecution: On indictment
Maximum punishment: Fourteen years' imprisonment

ABDUCTION OF AN UNMARRIED GIRL UNDER THE AGE OF 18 FROM HER PARENT OR GUARDIAN

Section 19 of the Sexual Offences Act 1956

'(1)   It is an offence, subject to the exception mentioned in this section, for a person to take an unmarried girl under the age of eighteen out of the possession of her parent or guardian against his will, if she is so taken with the intention that she shall have unlawful sexual intercourse with men or with a particular man.

(2) A person is not guilty of an offence under this section if he takes such a girl out of the possession of her parent or guardian as mentioned above, if he believes her to be of the age of eighteen and had reasonable cause for the belief.

(3) In this section "guardian" means any person having parental responsibility for or care of the girl.'

Mode of prosecution: On indictment
Maximum punishment: Two years' imprisonment

ABDUCTION OF AN UNMARRIED GIRL UNDER THE AGE OF 16 FROM HER PARENT OR GUARDIAN

Section 20 of the Sexual Offences Act 1956

'(1) It is an offence for a person acting without lawful authority or excuse to take an unmarried girl under the age of sixteen out of the possession of her parent or guardian against his will.

(2) In the foregoing subsection "guardian" means any person having parental responsibility for or care of the girl.'

Mode of prosecution: On indictment
Maximum punishment: Two years' imprisonment

ABDUCTION OF A DEFECTIVE FROM HIS OR HER PARENT OR GUARDIAN

Section 21 of the Sexual Offences Act 1956

'(1) It is an offence, subject to the exception mentioned in this section, for a person to take a woman who is a defective out of the possession of her parent or guardian against his will, if she is so taken with the intention that she shall have unlawful sexual intercourse with men or with a particular man.

(2) A person is not guilty of an offence under this section because he takes such a woman out of the possession of her parent or guardian as mentioned above, if he does not know and has no reason to suspect her to be a defective.

(3) In this section "guardian" means any person having parental responsibility for or care of the girl.'

Mode of prosecution: On indictment
Maximum punishment: Two years' imprisonment

DETENTION OF A WOMAN IN A BROTHEL OR OTHER PREMISES

Section 24 of the Sexual Offences Act 1956

'(1) It is an offence for a person to detain a woman against her will on any premises with the intention that she shall have unlawful sexual intercourse with men or with a particular man, or to detain a woman against her will in a brothel.

(2) Where a woman is on any premises for the purpose of having unlawful sexual intercourse or is in a brothel, a person shall be deemed for the purpose of the foregoing subsection to detain her there if, with the intention of compelling or inducing her to remain there, he either withholds from her her clothes or any other property belonging to her or threatens her with legal proceedings in the event of her taking away clothes provided for her by him or on his directions.

(3) A woman shall not be liable for any legal proceedings, whether civil or criminal, for taking away or being found in possession of any clothes she needed to enable her to leave premises on which she was for the purpose of having unlawful sexual intercourse or to leave a brothel.'

Mode of prosecution: On indictment
Maximum punishment: Two years' imprisonment

PERMITTING A GIRL UNDER THE AGE OF 13 TO USE PREMISES FOR INTERCOURSE

Section 25 of the Sexual Offences Act 1956

'It is a felony for a person who is the owner or occupier of any premises, or who has, or acts or assists in, the management or control of any premises, to induce or knowingly suffer a girl under the age of thirteen to resort to or be on those premises for the purpose of having unlawful sexual intercourse with men or with a particular man.'

Mode of prosecution: On indictment
Maximum punishment: Life imprisonment

PERMITTING A GIRL UNDER THE AGE OF 16 TO USE PREMISES FOR INTERCOURSE

Section 26 of the Sexual Offences Act 1956

'It is a felony for a person who is the owner or occupier of any premises, or who has, or acts or assists in, the management or control of any premises, to induce or knowingly suffer a girl under the age of sixteen to resort to or be on those premises for the purpose of having unlawful sexual intercourse with men or with a particular man.'

Mode of prosecution: On indictment

Maximum punishment: Two years' imprisonment

PERMITING A DEFECTIVE TO USE PREMISES FOR INTERCOURSE

Section 27 of the Sexual Offences Act 1956

'(1) It is an offence, subject to the exception mentioned in this section, for a person who is the owner or occupier of any premises, or who has, or acts or assists in, the management or control of any premises, to induce or knowingly suffer a woman who is a defective to resort to or be on those premises for the purpose of having unlawful sexual intercourse with men or with a particular man.

(2) A person is not guilty of an offence under this section because he induces or knowingly suffers a defective to resort to or be on any premises for the purpose mentioned, if he does not know and has no reason to suspect her to be a defective.'

Mode of prosecution: On indictment
Maximum punishment: Two years' imprisonment

CAUSING OR ENCOURAGING PROSTITUTION OF, INTERCOURSE WITH, OR INDECENT ASSAULT ON, GIRL UNDER THE AGE OF 16

Section 28 of the Sexual Offences Act 1956

'(1) It is an offence for a person to cause or encourage the prostitution of, or the commission of unlawful sexual intercourse with, or the indecent assault on, a girl under the age of sixteen for whom he is responsible.

(2) Where a girl has become a prostitute , or has had unlawful sexual intercourse, or has been indecently asssaulted, a person shall be deemed for the purposes of this section to have caused or encourage it, if he knowingly allowed her to consort with, or to enter or continue in the employment of, any prostitute or person of known immoral character.'

Mode of prosecution: On indictment
Maximum punishment: Two years' imprisonment

PROCURING OTHERS TO COMMIT HOMOSEXUAL ACTS

Section 4 of the Sexual Offences Act 1967

'(1) A man who procures another man to commit with a third man an act of buggery which by reason of section 1 of this Act is not an offence shall be liable on conviction on indictment to imprisonment for a term not exceeding two years.'

Mode of prosecution: On indictment
Maximum punishment: Two years' imprisonment

INDECENT CONDUCT TOWARDS A YOUNG CHILD

Section 1 of the Indecency with Children Act 1960

'(1) Any person who commits an act of gross indecency with or towards a child under the age of 14, or who incites a child under that age to such an act with him or another shall be liable on conviction or indictment to imprisonment for a term not exceeding ten years or on summary conviction to imprisonment for a term not exceeding six months, to a fine not exceeding the statutory maximum, or to both.'

Mode of prosecution: Triable either way
Maximum punishment: Ten years' imprisonment

INDECENT PHOTOGRAPHS OF CHILDREN

Section 1 of the Protection of Children Act 1978

'(1) It is an offence for a person –
   (a)   to take or permit to be taken any indecent photograph or pseudo-photograph of a child; or
   (b)   to distribute or show such indecent photographs or pseudo-photographs; or
   (c)   to have in his possession such indecent photographs, or pseudo-photographs with a view to them being distributed or shown by himself or others; or
   (d)   to publish or cause to be published any advertisement likely to be understood as conveying that the advertiser distributes or shows such indecent photographs or pseudo-photographs, or intends to do so.
(2)   For the purposes of this Act, a person is to be regarded as distributing an indecent photograph or pseudo-photograph if he parts with possession of it, or exposes or offers it for acquisition by another person.
(3)   Proceedings for an offence under this Act shall not be instituted except by or with the consent of the Director of Public Prosecutions.
(4)   Where a person is charged with an offence under section 1 (b) or (c), it shall be a defence for him to prove –
   (a)   that he had a legitimate reason for distributing or showing the photographs or pseudo-photographs or (as the case may be) having them in his possession; or
   (b)   that he had not himself seen the photographs or pseudo-photographs and did not know, nor had any cause to suspect, them to be indecent.'

Section 7 of the Protection of Children Act 1978

'(1)   The following subsections apply for the interpretation of this Act.
(2)   Reference to an indecent photograph include an indecent film, a copy of an indecent photograph or film, and an indecent photograph comprised in a film.

(3) Photographs (including those comprised in a film) shall, if they show children and are indecent, be treated for all purposes of this Act as indecent photographs of children, and so as respects pseudo-photographs.

(4) References to a photograph include –
   (a) the negative as well as the positive version; and
   (b) data stored on a computer disc or by other electronic means which is capable of conversion into a photograph.

(5) "Film" includes any form of video-recording.

(6) "Child", subject to subsection 8, means a person under the age of 16.

(7) "Pseudo-photograph" means an image, whether made by computer graphics or otherwise howsoever, which appears to be a photograph.

(8) If the impression conveyed by a pseudo-photograph is that the person shown is a child, the pseudo-photograph shall be treated for all purposes of this Act as showing a child and so shall a pseudo-photograph where the predominant impression conveyed is that the person shown is a child notwithstanding that some of the physical characteristics shown are those of an adult.

(9) References to an indecent pseudo-photograph include –
   (a) a copy of an indecent pseudo-photograph; and
   (b) data stored on a computer disc or by other electronic means which is capable of conversion into a pseudo-photograph.'

Mode of prosecution: Triable either way
Maximum punishment: Three years' imprisonment

POSSESSION OF AN INDECENT PHOTOGRAPH OF A CHILD

Section 160 of the Criminal Justice Act 1988

'(1) It is an offence for a person to have any indecent photograph of a child (meaning in this section a person under the age of 16) in his possession.

(2) Where a person is charged with an offence under subsection (1) above, it shall be a defence for him to prove –
   (a) that he had a legitimate reason for having the photograph in his possession; or
   (b) that he had not himself seen the photograph and did not know, nor had any cause to suspect, it to be indecent; or
   (c) that the photograph was sent to him without any prior request made by him or on his behalf and that he did not keep it for an unreasonable time.

(3) A person shall be liable on summary conviction of an offence under this section to imprisonment for a term not exceeding six months or a fine not exceeding level 5 on the standard scale or both.

(4) Sections 1(3), 2(3), 3 and 7 of the Protection of Children Act 1978 shall have effect as if any reference in them to that Act included a reference to this section.'

Mode of prosecution: Summary trial
Maximum punishment: Six months' imprisonment

INDEX

References are to paragraph number and Appendix.

Conviction – *cont*
  previous, *see* Conviction, previous
  procedure after   4.23–4.55, *see also*
      Sentence
  protection of public/child achieved
      by   7.89, 8.116
  reconviction, risk of, *see* Risk
      assessment; Treatment
  'Schedule 1 offenders', notification
      requirements   8.116, 8.117
Conviction, previous
  see also Statistics
  antecedents   4.26–4.28
  certificate   2.76, 2.77
  evidence on   3.39, 3.42, 3.43
  information about
      criminal records   2.76–2.80, 2.86
      early release decision, for   5.93,
          5.94
      prior to sentencing   4.26
  sex offenders
      likelihood of reconviction   5.97,
          5.98, 5.104
      statistics   5.96
  spent   4.27, 4.28
Corroboration, *see* Evidence
County court
  injunction   7.53
Court
  defendant to be brought before, time
      for   2.101
Court of Appeal
  appeal to, on sentence
      Attorney-General's reference
          4.135
      Crown Court, from   4.133
      leave   4.133, 4.135
      reference from CCRC   4.134
  cross-examination by defendant in
      person, guidance   3.141–3.152
  expert evidence, guidance   3.74
  identification of offender by victim,
      guidelines   3.70
  incest, guidelines   4.153
  sentencing
      Advisory Panel   4.137, 4.138,
          4.140
      guideline judgments   4.137
      guidelines   4.57, 4.64, 4.136
      role   4.136, 4.137
      statutory duty as to guidelines
          4.137

Crime
  age of criminal responsibility, *see* Age of
      criminal responsibility
  classification, *see* Trial
  definitions   1.4, Appendix
  grave   3.98
Criminal Cases Review Commission
      4.134
Criminal Code, proposal for   1.43,
      1.44
Criminal Records Bureau   8.172
  see also Criminal records, access to
  disclosure extended to DoH
      Consultancy Index and List 99
      8.156, 8.164
Criminal records, access to   2.76–2.80,
      2.85, 2.86, 8.143
  criminal conviction certificate   2.76,
      2.77, 2.86
  criminal record certificate   2.76
  additional information on,
      proposal   8.172
  DEE (List 99) and DoH lists,
      availability of   8.164
  enhanced criminal record certificate,
      see Enhanced criminal record
      certificate
Cross-examination   3.137–3.152
  Code of Conduct   3.139, 3.140
  control of   3.139, 3.140, 3.144
  defendant in person, by   3.141–
      3.152
      adult witness   3.143–3.148
      child witness   3.141, 3.142, 3.148
      guidance (CA)   3.144–3.146
      removal of right, mandatory and
          discretionary   3.147–3.152,
          3.162
  legal aid where personal ban   3.152
  legal representative (court-appointed),
      by   3.151, 3.152
  problems   3.137, 3.138
  right   3.110, 3.112, 3.114
  video-recording of witness, and
      3.131–3.133
Crown Court   3.88, 3.89
  antecedents for sentencing   4.26
  appeal from, on sentence   4.133
  appeal to, on sentence, powers
      4.132
  committal to, *see* Committal
      proceedings
  community order   6.84